# COMPUTING
# TODAY

**Houghton Mifflin Company · Boston**

Dallas   Geneva, Illinois   Palo Alto   Princeton, New Jersey

# COMPUTING TODAY

## Microcomputer Concepts and Applications

### Second Edition

**David R. Sullivan**

**Theodore G. Lewis**

**Curtis R. Cook**

*Oregon State University*

CREDITS

**Cover photography by Gorchev and Gorchev.**
Part 1 Radio Shack
Chapter 1 Photo Researchers, Inc.
Figure 1.3 Courtesy of Amdahl Corporation
Figure 1.4 Courtesy of Commodore Electronics Ltd.
Figure 1.5 Courtesy of Hewlett-Packard Company
Figure 1.8 Courtesy of Apple Computer, Inc.
Figure 1.11 Photo from Xerox Corporation
Chapter 2 Courtesy of International Business Machines Corporation
Figure 2.2 Courtesy of Motorola, Inc.
Figure 2.4 Courtesy of Texas Instruments
Figure 2.6 Courtesy of Digi-Data Corporation
Figure 2.10b Maxtor Corporation
*(Credits continued on page C-1.)*

Printed in the U.S.A.

Library of Congress Catalog Card Number: 87-81410

ISBN: 0-395-42329-5

ABCDEFGHIJ-RM-9543210-898

# Brief Contents

*v*

# Contents

# *Preface*

## THE PURPOSE OF COMPUTING TODAY

This book teaches how to use computer systems effectively. To meet this objective, it explains computers from a user's perspective and teaches the concepts necessary to master practical applications. Thus, the basic motivation behind the current edition hasn't changed from the principles that guided the development of the highly successful first edition. The content and organization of *Computing Today* are well suited to a variety of introductory courses in computing. It can be used in a campus-wide computer literacy course for non-technical as well as technical students or in a first course on information processing.

The first edition of *Computing Today*, published in 1985, was the first introductory textbook to combine the concepts of personal computing into a unified and comprehensive treatment of the field. It was immediately put to use at hundreds of colleges.

*Computing Today* took a different approach from many of the books it inspired. For example, instead of emphasizing the keystroke-level differences of popular application programs such as how the commands for moving a paragraph differ between Multimate and WordPerfect, the first edition of *Computing Today* focused on underlying concepts that form a basis for using programs, comparing their overall value, and understanding computing in general.

The second edition of *Computing Today* is an extensive and up-to-date revision of the first edition.

### Approach

Whenever possible, personal computing has been used as a vehicle to introduce and explain general computing concepts. In the last ten years personal computing has grown from a hobbyist activity—a mere curiosity in the field of computing—to a discipline worthy of serious study. Personal computers today are small, affordable, powerful, and understandable. They make an ideal vehicle for presenting general data processing concepts that may otherwise seem obscure and intangible. By now, nearly all important information-processing activities have a counterpart in the field of personal computing. Thus we are able to use personal computers to explain how *all* computers work.

### Application Software

We continue to stress the underlying concepts that form a basis for using programs, rather than emphasize the keystroke-level differences of popular application programs. The need to know about practical application software has grown so quickly that many textbooks are unable to keep pace. Application software has changed the way professionals approach everyday tasks. Writers using word processing make many more drafts, which tends to smooth out the rough edges. Then desktop publishing takes the manuscript one step further and produces a typeset-looking final document. Planners and analysts using spreadsheet programs test out more hypothetical situations. Data management programs provide new ways to extract information from large amounts of data. One implication of these trends is that is has become more important to know how to use and select software than to understand in great detail how computers work or how programs are written. By teaching how to evaluate computer systems and computer-related products, this book addresses the needs of the ordinary computer user as well as computer specialists. Technical issues are not avoided, but they are presented in the context of how they affect the user.

There are thousands of programs available. Each has its own feature set, command structure, and user interface. It was a challenge to see beyond the superficial differences among programs and find the essence of word processors, spreadsheets and other application software. For example, moving a paragraph is conceptually identical in all word processors; organizing a file of data is conceptually similar in different data management systems. Knowing these concepts will serve you well no matter which computer or software package you select.

## NEW FEATURES

This edition of *Computing Today* retains the basic philosophy and writing style that contributed to the quality and success of the first edition, but many changes and improvements have been made.

- An entirely new chapter on desktop publishing describes how page composition programs help arrange text and graphics on a page such as the one you are reading. Even if you don't use desktop publishing methods today, the developments in this area are important to know about. Within a year or two, desktop publishing features are almost certain to be in new releases of many word processing programs.

- Improvements in operating systems and application software interfaces made it desirable to have separate chapters devoted to each topic.

- The coverage of local area networks has been upgraded to occupy a full chapter, reflecting their growing importance in an era of distributed computing. This chapter not only describes the technical details of network architecture and hardware, it also discusses the practical aspects of how local area networks affect the average user.

- A new chapter on expert systems explains how knowledge and judgment can be stored in intelligent application programs. This chapter shows how microcomputer-based expert system shells can provide an alternative to traditional procedural programming methods for the development of decision support systems.

- Throughout the text, topics of special interest and current trends are discussed in boxed inserts. Many of the boxed inserts come from recent articles in trade magazines such as *InfoWorld* and *ComputerWorld*.

- Seven color inserts or "windows" give an in-depth view of the hardware and software in common use. Each window is a series of carefully scripted photographs, selected by the author, that tell a story about a specific topic.

## ORGANIZATION OF THE BOOK

*Computing Today* is designed to accommodate a variety of course formats. Its six major parts have been kept as independent as possible. After completing Part One, the remaining parts can be studied in any order.

Part One describes the basics of computing. Chapter 1 surveys the relationships between hardware and software. Chapters 2 and 3 describe the inner workings of computers from their central processing engines to their input and output devices. Finally, Chapters 5 and 6 describe how to operate a computer by explaining the purpose and function of an operating system and by illustrating the use of visual and textual user interfaces.

Parts Two, Three, and Four deal with the concepts underlying word processing, spreadsheet analysis, and data management. Part Two fully describes the most pervasive use of computers: word processing. Chapter 6 covers elementary word processing techniques such as editing and printing, and Chapter 7 explains more advanced techniques for formatting, organizing, and writing. Chapter 8 extends these ideas to the realm of desktop publishing and explains how advances in printer, display, and software technology have blurred the boundaries between writing and publishing.

Part Three introduces spreadsheet analysis. Chapter 9 explains the concept of an electronic worksheet and the methods used to store numbers, text, and formulas. Chapter 10 covers the more advanced features of spreadsheet programs leading to the realm of modeling and the development of professional-quality spreadsheet templates.

Part Four concludes the presentation of the three most widely used application software areas by discussing data management. Chapter 11 describes file management programs, the simplest form of data management software. Chapter 12 extends the file management concepts to include the database management systems used on mainframes, minis, and micros. Database management is the engine that drives most data processing and business applications.

Part Five examines applications of computing in the burgeoning fields of graphics, communications, and local area networks. Chapter 13 shows how the graphical capability of computers can be used to make bar charts, line graphs, and other types of presentation graphics. It also discusses the powerful graphics systems used to design airplanes, computers, and buildings. Chapters 14 and 15 discuss how telecommunications and local area networks are helping establish a worldwide web of distributed computing.

Part Six touches on a variety of topics to broaden the student's perspectives about computing. Chapter 16 goes into depth about how an expert system is developed. Chapter 17 is a general overview of programming and compares features of different programming languages. Chapter 18 traces the computer revolution from its roots to contemporary society. It provides coverage of the generations of mainframe computers, includes a unique treatment of the development of personal computers, and concludes with some projections about the future. Finally, Chapter 19 discusses the thorny problems associated with protecting the intellectual property right of software developers.

## SUPPLEMENTARY MATERIALS

The following supplementary materials are available to accompany *Computing Today:*

- **Software Solution Series.** This series currently consists of seven inexpensive tutorial manuals explicitly designed to offer solutions to the problems encountered by countless numbers of educators who wish to include as a component of courses they teach, instruction on popular commercial application software programs. Educational versions of the actual program disks to accompany many of these manuals are available without charge to adopters.

- **A Test Bank.** The Test Bank contains more than 1700 true-false, matching, and multiple choice test questions. In addition, some student lab exercises and assignments are provided.
- **GPA.** Grade Performance Analyzer. A software program designed to aid users of the text in maintaining student test scores.
- **Microtest.** A disk containing questions from the Test Bank.

## CREDITS AND ACKNOWLEDGMENTS

Barry Shane of Oregon State University wrote the material for the Expert Systems chapter. He wrote a remarkably understandable explanation of what an expert system is and how one is developed. I feel lucky to have attracted him to the project.

I also want to thank the following reviewers:

Harvey Blessing, Essex Community College, Maryland
Larry Dold, San Joaquin Delta College, California
Terry Dorsett, Central Arizona College, Arizona
James Gips, Boston College, Massachusetts
David F. Harris, College of the Redwoods, California
Neil Snyder, Wright State University, Ohio
Laurence Krieg, Washtenaw Community College, Missouri
Gerald Meyer, The City University of New York, Fiorella H.
    LaGuardia Community College, New York
George L. Miller, North Seattle Community College, Washington
Marty Murray, Portland Community College, Oregon
Robert Stewart, Iowa State University, Iowa
Kenneth Thomason, Umpqua Community College, Oregon
Henry Weiman, Bronx Community College, New York
Charles F. Kirby, Louisiana State University, Louisiana
Karen Watterson, Shoreline Community College, Washington
Lawrence Campo, Macomb Community College, Missouri

Feel free to write to me with suggestions, questions, or comments. The address is: David Sullivan, College of Business, Oregon State University, Corvallis, Oregon, 97330.

*David Sullivan*

# *COMPUTING TODAY*

# Basic Concepts of Computing

Never before has a generation been privileged to witness such startling inventions as atomic power, space travel, personal computing, and genetic engineering. Incredibly, all these have been introduced within the last fifty years. Computing ranks with the most revolutionary inventions of our time and goes even beyond the others in one respect: It allows ordinary people to participate in an extraordinary discovery.

Steadily declining costs and improvements in performance have moved computers from data processing centers to homes, offices, shopping centers, and even cars. Now the average person has within reach a powerful agent for change. But what are people going to do with these easily available computers? Clearly, computers are pervasive, and they are capable of revolutionizing nearly every area of life.

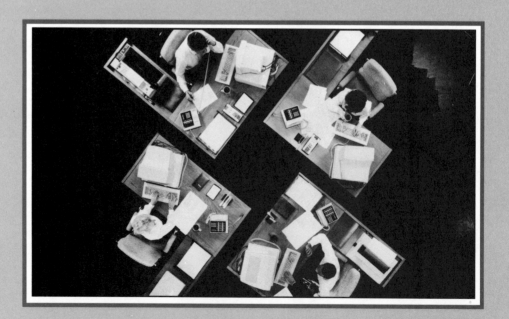

# Part One

The pervasiveness of computers presents a problem: How should you learn to evaluate and use them? By introducing you to some fundamental computing concepts, we hope to make it easy for you to gain a working knowledge of applications such as word processing, graphics, and communications. Mastering the concepts discussed in this first part of the book will ensure your being able to successfully use a computer in your own specialty. And knowing the basic principles and terminology will make it easier for you to stay abreast of issues and evaluate the ways in which society puts its computers to work.

Part I takes the first step in preparing you to understand and evaluate the computer world by teaching some basic computer concepts. In Chapter 1, we outline the anatomy of a computer system, define some common terms, and examine the steps in a typical computer session. In Chapter 2, we explain how the thinking part of a computer—the central processing unit—and storage devices work together to execute the series of instructions known as a program. In Chapter 3, we give details on how information enters and leaves computers. In Chapter 4, we examine the role of the operating system—the master control program—that manages the computer and supervises all other programs. Then in Chapter 5, we introduce you to application software—the programs that accomplish tasks for the user.

# Introduction to Computers

Computers accept information (input), manipulate information (processing), retain information over time (storage), and present the results of processing (output). At this level, every computer—from huge mainframes to hand-held models—works the same way. Once you understand the relationships among a computer's parts, the mystery of how computers work will diminish. Giving you an overall perspective of how a computer system's hardware and software fit together is a major goal of Chapter 1. Throughout the chapter, we define basic computer terms that every computer user is expected to know. We also compare the uses of large, medium, and small computers.

Just knowing what the parts are is not enough. You also need to understand how these parts interact to perform useful work. For this reason, we close the chapter with a computer session that illustrates the components of a computer system in action.

## BASIC CONCEPTS

A computer is actually a complete system, composed of many interacting parts. Computer systems are made of hardware and software. The **hardware** is the physi-

cal equipment you can see and touch, such as the disks and the monitor. The **software** is the intangible "control" that governs the computer and is the total of all the programs that can be run on the computer system. A **program** is a list of instructions that the computer hardware follows. Programs tell the hardware how to behave and thus give the computer system its "personality."

If a computer were a component stereo system, we might imagine the music to be the software and the record player to be the hardware. In a stereo system, information is recorded on the surface of a platter, entered into the stereo through a stylus, and sent to the speakers to be converted into sound. In a computer system, information is recorded on the surface of magnetic tape, magnetic disks, and other devices; it is entered through a keyboard or some other special equipment attached to the computer; and it is sent to a monitor or another device designed to accept electrical signals and convert them into human-readable form. A printer, for example, converts electrical signals into intelligible text. Figure 1.1 shows the similarity between a stereo and a computer system. Both systems receive some type of input, process it, and then produce some kind of output.

Despite these similarities, computer systems differ significantly from stereos or any other kind of mechanical system. Every time a particular record is played, the stereo system repeats exactly the same tune; it can play whatever is on the record but cannot create new music. A computer system, however, can produce different and possibly surprising results each time it is run. It is the computer system's software that provides the "intelligence" for a computer system to "play back" a different "tune." Thus software is the "mind" of a machine, whereas hardware is the "body." Without the mind, the body does not know what to do.

All computer systems are limited in what they can store. The computer is a **digital** device; that is, it is restricted to *discrete* values. The channel selector on a television set is a digital device because it restricts you to a discrete set of channels; you cannot, for example, select channel 3.14159. In contrast, **analog** devices have *continuous*

**Figure 1.1**
Stereo and computer systems are somewhat analogous.

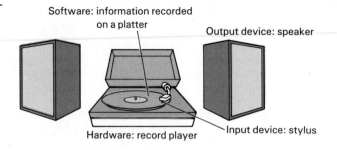

Software: information recorded on a platter

Output device: speaker

Hardware: record player

Input device: stylus

**(a) A stereo system**

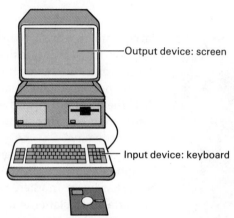

Output device: screen

Input device: keyboard

Software: information recorded on a disk

**(b) A computer system**

values. For example, a water faucet is an analog device because it allows you to adjust the flow of water in one smooth, continuous action.

Digital computers work with only two alternatives. Like a light switch, a computer can "remember" an "on" or "off" but nothing in between. To store numbers, letters, and graphical images, the computer must encode all information in switches that can have only one of two discrete values. For convenience, we assign a 0 or 1 to represent whether a switch is on or off.

Each 0 or 1 is one **bit** (**bi**nary digi**t**) of information. A bit does not store much information, so bits are grouped to form more useful units. The next larger unit contains eight bits and is called a **byte**.

A number containing only two kinds of digits—0 and 1—is a **binary number**. (This is why modern computers are often called binary computers.) Binary numbers are just like decimal numbers except for one important difference: They build numbers from the numerals 0 and 1 instead of the numerals 0 through 9. For example, 0100 is the binary number equivalent of the decimal number 4.

Everyone knows that computers can manipulate many kinds of data: text, numbers, and even pictures. But how is this possible if all the data must be stored as binary 1's and 0's? The answer lies in the use of binary codes.

Computers use many different codes to store information. For example, ASCII (American Standard Code for Information Interchange) stores text in small computers, and EBCDIC (Extended Binary Coded Decimal Interchange Code) and other codes store text in larger computers. **ASCII** associates a particular seven-bit pattern of 1's and 0's with each printable character on the keyboard. Thus the letters of the alphabet; the numerals 0 through 9; and special characters such as $, &, and % are each defined by a seven-bit ASCII pattern. For example, uppercase letters (A, B, C, and so on) are represented by seven-bit binary numbers that are equivalent to the decimal numbers from 65 to 91. Lowercase letters (a, b, c, and so on) range from the binary equivalents of 97 to 123. A question mark is stored as 0111111—the binary equivalent of 63. Even a blank space has a code: the binary number for 32.

In Appendix A, "How Computers Process Information," we cover binary numbers and coding schemes in more detail.

## HARDWARE COMPONENTS

Every computer system has hardware components that perform four basic functions: input, output, processing, and storage. As Figure 1.2 illustrates, even a small computer has

- An input device such as a keyboard

- An output device such as a monitor (and most likely a printer)

- A central processing unit (CPU) for processing data

- A short-term memory, called primary memory, to hold programs and data temporarily while they are being used

- A long-term memory, called external storage or secondary storage, to read and write permanently stored programs and data

- A peripheral device such as tape or disk drives or any I/O device

An **input device** senses events in the computer's environment (such as pressure on a key) and converts them into electrical signals that the CPU can process. Input devices perform much the same function as human sensory organs that receive information, convert it into a new form, and then send it to the brain. A keyboard, mouse, digital thermometer, and speech recognition unit are examples of input devices.

An **output device** accepts electrical signals from the CPU and converts them into a new form. For personal computers, the most common output devices are printers and monitors. Other output devices include the warhead on a cruise missile and the electronically adjustable air vents of a computer-controlled building.

Collectively, input and output devices are called **I/O devices**.

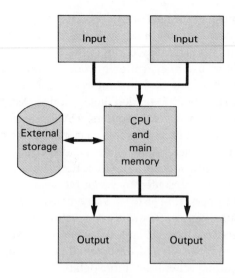

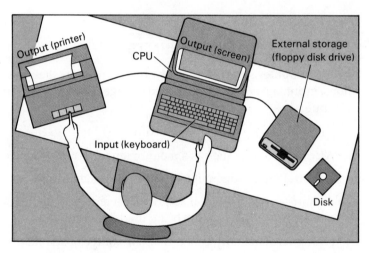

The **central processing unit (CPU)** contains electronic circuitry that performs arithmetic, logical comparisons (such as deciding which of two numbers is larger), and data-moving operations. The CPU also temporarily holds programs and the information to be processed in its memory while it is working. The memory in a CPU is often called **main memory**, **primary memory**, or **random-access memory (RAM),** which means that the content of any memory location can be read or modified independently of all other cells. Think of it as the computer's short-term memory that holds the data and programs currently being executed. The capacity of primary memory helps determine the "size" of the computer. A programmable calculator's primary memory might store only a few hundred numbers, whereas a mainframe computer's primary memory can store millions of numbers, letters, or picture elements.

Primary memory is *volatile*; that is, when the computer is turned off, the information is lost. Another form of memory is needed to provide permanent storage of

**Figure 1.3**
An Amdahl mainframe computer system consists of two central processing units and attachments for storage and communications. Many "simultaneous" users (not shown here) are supported by such machines.

programs and data. Called **external storage** or **secondary storage,** this memory is obtained by storing copies of both program and data *outside* the computer, usually on external magnetic media such as a tape or a disk like that shown in Figure 1.2. Magnetic storage devices generally have a larger capacity than primary memory but are slower and transfer information in larger blocks. Because magnetic media retain information even after the computer is shut off, they are not volatile. You can remove tapes or disks from the computer, store them for months, and then put them back into the tape or disk drive without having lost information.

A **peripheral** is a generic term for an auxiliary device that is attached to a computer. Tape and disk drives are peripherals, as are all I/O devices.

## Types of Computers

Computers come in all shapes and sizes, but they are usually classified into three broad categories: mainframes, minicomputers, and microcomputers.

**Mainframes** are the largest, fastest, and most expensive computers (see Figure 1.3). They are found in banks, insurance companies, large corporations, and government organizations. Mainframes usually serve many users and functions and are considered general-purpose machines. They are particularly good for problems requiring extensive mathematical calculations or for sharing large volumes of information among many people. Like a television network, they provide valuable and important services in bulk, but the users have little control over these services. Very

**Figure 1.4**
A Digital Equipment Corporation VAX minicomputer. Whether used for dedicated applications or as general-purpose computer systems, minicomputers offer economy of scale in the middle of the cost-performance range.

large mainframes, called *supercomputers,* are used primarily for the analysis of scientific and engineering problems.

**Minicomputers**, or **minis**, are a smaller version of mainframes (see Figure 1.4); they are slower and cheaper than mainframes. Often, minicomputers satisfy the general-purpose computing needs of a department or small business. Other minicomputers are dedicated to specific applications. For example, minicomputers may be used to control an assembly line in a factory, record data in a research laboratory, or help programmers develop programs for other computers.

Both mainframe and minicomputers are **timesharing systems**, which means they can divide their attention among many users. With a timesharing system, some users might be entering data while others are receiving output. The simplest way to implement timesharing in a computer is to allocate short periods of processing (known as *time slices*) to each user's program in a round-robin fashion. If the time slices are short enough, it may seem to each user as if the computer is responding instantly.

**Microcomputers**, or **micros**, are the smallest, least powerful computers (see Figure 1.5). They are even more specialized than minicomputers and are often *embedded* in other devices, for example, in cars, clock radios, burglar alarms, toys, microwave ovens, or space vehicles. They are also at the heart of all **personal computers**—computers designed to be used by one person. Microcomputers offer computer users advantages and disadvantages somewhat like those offered television watchers by a video tape recorder: Although you must buy the personal computer or video tape recorder and buy or rent disks or tapes, you have complete control over how you use the equipment.

# Computer Applications

*Computers are powerful tools that are rapidly changing the way we work and play. Once they were used only by highly trained specialists in expensive data processing centers. Now they are found sitting on desks, buried inside appliances, hidden under grocery store check-out counters, and sitting on laps. This photo essay takes an in-depth look at important computer applications in several fields, ranging from home computing to publishing, mechanical engineering, and the management of merchandise and material.*

**1.** Once hidden in temperature-controlled rooms, computers now practically litter the office landscape.

# HOME
# COMPUTERS

2. Most home computers (and many office computers) are occasionally used to play games. Because of their larger memory capacity, personal computers can play more sophisticated games than can video game machines. Many educational programs, such as Spelling Bee Games and SAT Word Attack Skills, are ''games'' with an educational theme.

3. A computer can help you set up a budget, record and track expenses, and manage investments. But some activities, such as balancing a checkbook, are so simple they may be more work to do on a computer than to do by hand.

4. Computers no larger than a briefcase can run on batteries in any location. Despite their small size, they can have memory capacities rivaling much larger computers.

6. Portable computers can provide instant price quotes for complicated sales. Financing alternatives can be compared without delay. Once an order for a sale has been taken, the portable computer can transmit the order over a normal telephone line to the corporation's main computer, and immediate confirmation of the order can be received.

5. Most transportable computers snap up into a suitcase-size unit. This computer includes a full-size detachable keyboard, a 9-inch display, a disk drive, two expansion slots that allow optional circuit boards to be plugged into the computer, a built-in printer, and 800 kilobytes of memory—all in a 25-pound package.

7. Portable computers that require an external power source and weigh 20 pounds or more are often called *transportable computers*. They can be used at both work and home.

# VERTICAL MARKET APPLICATIONS

*Vertical software addresses the needs of people in a specific discipline or occupation, such as those of architects or farmers, who have very different information-processing needs. Software firms have created tens of thousands of programs that solve problems in specific occupations. This page illustrates software for the health-care market.*

8. Shared Medical Systems (SMS) Corporation provides computer-based information systems to hospitals and physician groups. This photo shows SMS's Practice Management Services software, which allows physicians to spend more time practicing medicine, and less time worrying about administration and bill collection.

9. A constantly changing mass of federal and local regulations sets the legal requirements for record keeping in the medical field. Computerized medical systems can help hospital executives cope with these challenges.

10. The series of bars on the folder constitutes a code that can be read by a device called a *bar code reader.* This computerized coding system makes it easier to maintain accurate records regarding all aspects of a patient's stay.

# EDUCATION

11. Personal computers can be an invaluable aid in preparing reports, essays, and assignments.

12. Using a computer can be thought provoking. For many activities, computers are better information processors than people.

```
Now that your program is back in
memory, why don't you change line
30 (press RETURN for a hint if you
don't remember how to change a
line).


]LIST

10 PRINT "ROSES ARE RED"
20 PRINT "VIOLETS ARE BLUE"
30 PRINT "I LOVE MY APPLE"
40 PRINT "AND PROGRAMMING, TOO!"
50 END

]30 PRINT "I'm having fun..."*
```

13. This screen shows a tutorial program—that is, a program that guides a student through the basics of using computer programs. The best tutorial programs are highly interactive and encourage the student to experiment; the worst ones are little more than automated slide shows.

14. Education software can be fun as well as instructive. These simulation programs teach by emulating the responses of a system, such as the development of waves in an ocean.

# OFFICE AUTOMATION

15,16. In the past, commercial and production workers were the primary computer users in corporations. But now, office workers have abandoned paper and pencil methods and use computers for retrieving information, budgeting and forecasting, word processing, and so on.

17. The "knowledge workers" in modern offices often use terminals linked by a central mainframe computer that provides electronic mail, access to collections of data called databases, a variety of application programs, and shared access to peripheral devices such as printers.

18. Instead of using a central mainframe computer, an employer might provide a personal computer for each worker. This approach can allow each employee to use excellent software for word processing, financial analysis, and other tasks.

19. Most surveys of offices find that word processing is the most important computer application. Word processing software varies widely, from easy-to-use programs that are suitable for writing simple memos and reports to programs that are designed for professional typesetters.

20. Almost any computer can be used for word processing. This personal computer is used with a laser printer to produce typeset-quality documents.

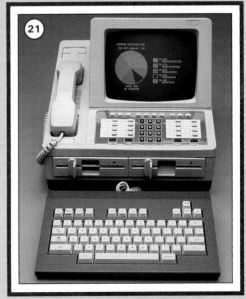

21. The fields of computing and communications are merging rapidly. This computer combines a personal computer compatible with an IBM PC, a telephone, and a variety of computing and communications services in one compact unit. It offers fast, easy access to remote computers and databases, convenient one-touch dialing of telephone numbers, and the ability to execute a wide range of personal productivity software.

# PUBLISHING

*Computers are involved in every aspect of publishing, from the creation of text through the generation of typeset artwork for the presses.*

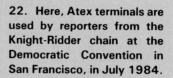

22. Here, Atex terminals are used by reporters from the Knight-Ridder chain at the Democratic Convention in San Francisco, in July 1984.

23. News reporters are never far from computer terminals.

24. The abundance of terminals at the Orlando (Florida) *Sentinel* is typical of newsrooms today.

25. Reporters translate their thoughts into text with the help of high-quality word processing systems.

26. Pagination systems allow editors to preview an entire page at once, with all text in place exactly as it will appear when printed.

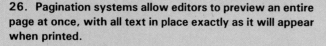

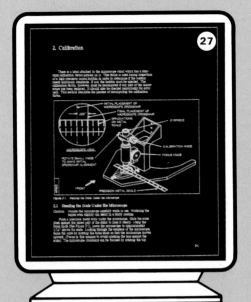

**27,28.** On state-of-the-art composition systems, both text and graphics can be merged on one page and previewed at a graphics workstation. These screens show pages from a maintenance manual and the Yellow Pages.

**30.** Here we see a scroll of typeset copy, ready for printing.

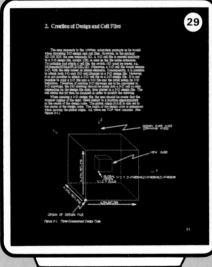

**29.** This screen image of a page from a user manual is ready to be typeset.

*window 1*

# MERCHANDISE AND MATERIAL MANAGEMENT

*Automated systems for the management of merchandise and material rely on having each inventory item labeled in a machine-readable manner.*

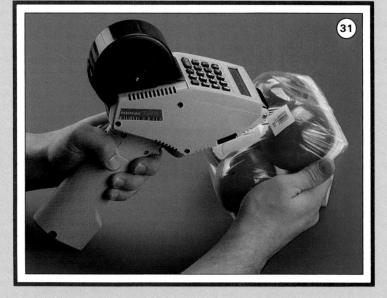

31. This hand-held printer prints and dispenses gummed labels. The labels can be printed with bar codes such as UPC (Universal Product Code), as well as several human-readable fonts. Information for the labels can be entered through the keypad on the printer, or the printer can be connected to a computer.

32. Many check-out counters use laser scanning systems to read UPC codes on merchandise. These systems not only speed up the check-out process but also help the store keep an accurate inventory.

33. At Ford Motor Company's largest transmission plant in Livonia, Michigan, ScopeScan units are used to track testing on the assembly line. Each ScopeScan unit is a laser bar code reader.

34. This GERBERmover computerized manufacturing system is used in the garment and allied industries to reduce handling and track inventory. All the operator has to do is touch a button, and the hangers are automatically moved by the computer. The system monitors the time, production count, operation number, and employee identification number.

35. Each of the hangers is numbered and bar-coded, enabling individual hangers to be tracked by computer. This hanger's bar code is on the back side.

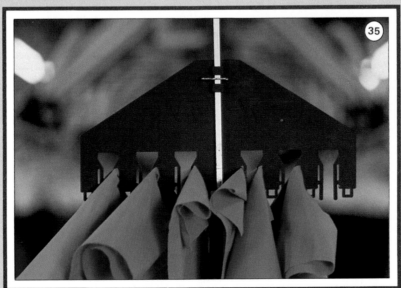

# COMPUTER-AIDED MECHANICAL ENGINEERING

Computers are routinely used in mechanical engineering for a full range of design tasks: modeling in two and three dimensions, analyzing the strength of parts, drafting, computing a part's center of gravity, and so forth. Although the hardware and software required for these tasks are specialized and expensive, the expense can be justified by improved designs and shorter product development cycles. These two pages describe just one mechanical engineering task: analyzing the structural properties of mechanical systems by using what is called finite element analysis software.

36. The first step in finite element analysis is to create an electronic model of the part or system to be analyzed. In this case the part to be studied is a spring that fits on one piece of an assembly and holds another piece in place.

37. The next step is to generate an electronic mesh that represents the part as a large number of tiny building blocks, or "elements." These elements, together with descriptions of their strengths and interrelationships, become the basis for a simulation of how the part will perform.

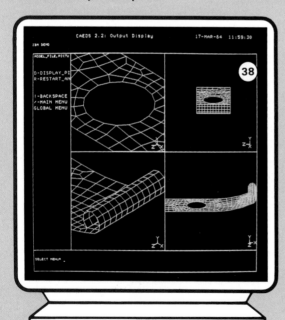

38. Once an electronic model has been created, it can be viewed from a variety of perspectives at once.

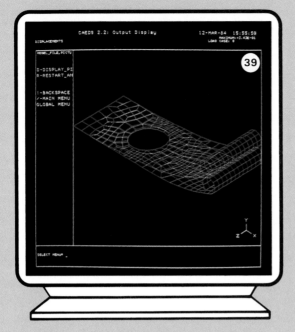

**39.** After the loads to be placed on the front of the spring are described, the finite element analysis software calculates how the spring will deform under stress. The blue drawing represents the undeformed shape: the deformed shape is in red.

**40.** The colored lines shown on this model of the spring are the stress contours. This is exactly the type of information an engineer needs to predict where, when, and how the spring will fail.

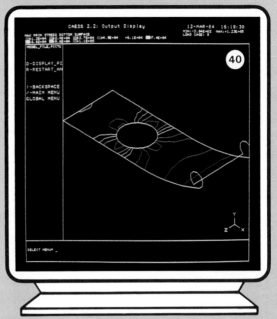

**41.** The model of the spring shown in earlier photographs is called a *shell model,* because in the model the spring had no thickness. Finite element analysis can also be applied to three-dimensional models, as in this model of a trip lever. The deformation of the trip lever has been exaggerated in this picture to make it visible; the actual deformation is very small.

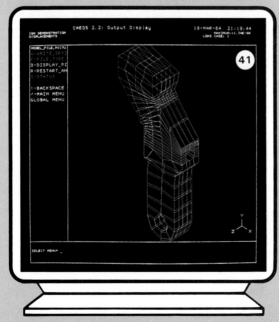

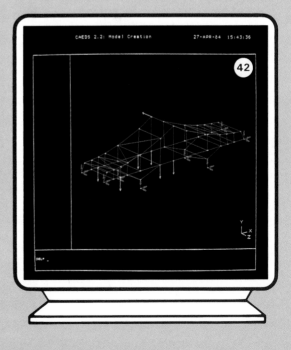

**42.** A model of an entire system, such as this bridge, can also be analyzed to look for structural or vibration problems.

*window 1*

# COMPUTER-AIDED MANUFACTURING

*Numerically controlled (NC) machines can cut, stamp, and grind nearly any material. For most manufacturing operations NC machines are faster and more accurate than people, but they are less adaptable to new tasks. Although there is a tremendous variety of NC machines, this page shows only NC machines that cut.*

44. This NC router cuts shoe patterns quickly and accurately. It can cut hard materials up to ¼-inch thick.

43. Shoe designs can be scaled from one size to another quickly when the designs are stored electronically.

45. Before an NC fabric cutter is used, the layout of the patterns must be determined.

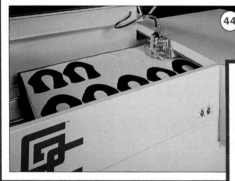

46. This NC cutting system is designed to cut limp materials for the apparel, aerospace, automotive, and related industries. It can cut through many plies of fabric at once.

47. This automated signmaking system can cut letters from adhesive-backed vinyl, draw text with ballpoint pens, and cut silkscreen masters from film. Commands can be entered on the keyboard, or the signmaker can be driven by a personal computer running graphics software.

# MILITARY APPLICATIONS

*Computers play a vital role in military command, control, and communications systems. Because military equipment is designed to be used in the hostile environment of war, military computers are frequently built to specifications that call for high standards of ruggedness, reliability, and performance.*

48. Computer-based simulation systems are frequently used when actual tests are impractical or expensive. This STAGS Dragon (Simulated Tank Anti-Armor Gunnery System) is being tested at Fort Benning, Georgia. It trains students without using live ammunition.

49. This stand-alone special-purpose computer uses high-speed processing to analyze telemetry data from a satellite.

50. This engineer is programming a path for an aircraft through a simulated battlefield on a Loral Electronic Environment Simulator.

51. Air control and tracking systems at the U.S. Navy's Virginia Capes site help controllers monitor 86,000 square miles. These systems feature exceptionally clear and large vector graphics displays.

*window 1*

# SMALL BUSINESS APPLICATIONS

*Small businesses can't afford to buy large computers or to develop software themselves. This explains why large corporations were the first to adopt computer technology. The development of personal computers and inexpensive packages of software for businesses has allowed small businesses to participate in the computer age.*

52. Off-the-shelf software packages provide instant solutions to most of the data processing problems encountered by businesses. For example, accounting packages can manage the payroll, accounts receivable, accounts payable, and general ledger. Business transactions and customer lists can be recorded, stored, and reported by what are called database management systems. Word processing programs help with business correspondence. The list of business application programs goes on and on.

53. With spreadsheet programs, business relationships can be entered into "electronic worksheets." Often spreadsheet programs are used to create financial projections and then to analyze alternative business scenarios.

**Figure 1.5**
A personal computer system with a detached keyboard, printer, monitor, and system unit (underneath the display) containing two microfloppy disk drives.

During the last fifteen years, the popularity of mainframe computers has declined steadily, and minicomputers and personal computers have captured growing shares of the market. In 1987, for the first time ever, data processing managers budgeted more for minicomputers than for mainframe computers, as Figure 1.6 shows. Personnel costs continue to take the largest bite out of data processing

**Figure 1.6**
The typical data processing budget in 1987. (Adapted from *Datamation*, April 1, 1987.)

## Typical Data Processing Budget
## (estimated for 1987)

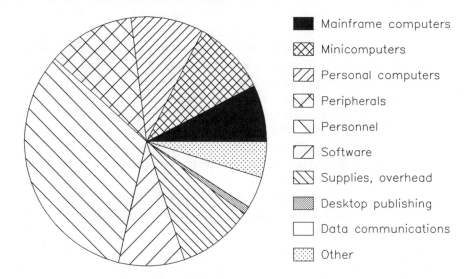

■ Mainframe computers

▨ Minicomputers

▥ Personal computers

▽ Peripherals

◸ Personnel

▱ Software

◺ Supplies, overhead

▦ Desktop publishing

□ Data communications

▨ Other

budgets, roughly a third of each dollar. Other important categories include peripherals (primarily printers and storage devices), supplies (such as paper, disks, and ribbons), various types of software, and data communications devices that permit computers to communicate among one another. The software category in Figure 1.6 is understated because much of the personnel expense in a typical data processing department is devoted to writing software.

## Personal Computer Hardware

A personal computer is a small computer that uses a **microprocessor,** a single integrated circuit, as the basis for its central processing unit. Usually, a personal computer costs less than $5,000, uses disk drives for secondary storage, accepts data from a keyboard, and displays output on a **monitor**.

Figure 1.7 illustrates the organization of a typical personal computer system. The parts of a personal computer are tied together by a set of parallel conductors called a **bus** (shown as colored lines in the center of the figure). The bus performs the same role as an intercom: It allows any device to broadcast messages to all other devices. Just as with an intercom system, rules govern who gets to talk when, and there are ways to interrupt normal messages with high-priority messages. The activity on the bus is moderated by the *bus interface unit*, a part of the microprocessor.

The microprocessor contains three other parts. The **arithmetic/logic unit (ALU)** contains all the electronics necessary to calculate (add, multiply, and so on) and perform logical operations (compare numbers and make decisions). The **control unit** retrieves instructions from memory in the proper sequence, interprets the instructions one at a time, and provides the arithmetic/logic unit and other parts of the computer with the proper control signals to implement the instructions. The **registers** are memory cells on the microprocessor itself and act as a high-speed scratch pad for the microprocessor to use while performing computations.

Primary memory consists of integrated circuit memory chips. It holds the programs and data being actively used by the computer system. Part of primary memory is called the *display memory*, which holds a coded representation of the information to appear on the screen. The *video driver's* job is to read the display memory, decode its data into a visual image, and send the image to the monitor.

Information can enter the system from a keyboard, mouse, disk drive, modem, or any other input device. For example, pressing a key on the keyboard generates a unique coded signal that can be stored in memory, processed by the microprocessor, or displayed by the video driver.

A **disk drive** enables the computer system to read or write information on a magnetic disk. The analogy with a video tape recorder is especially apt here. To play and record a television show or a movie on a video tape, you need a video tape recorder. Similarly, a computer needs a disk drive to read and write programs and data on a disk.

A **modem** (short for *mo*dulator-*dem*odulator) is an input-output device for sending and receiving coded messages from other computers through the telephone system.

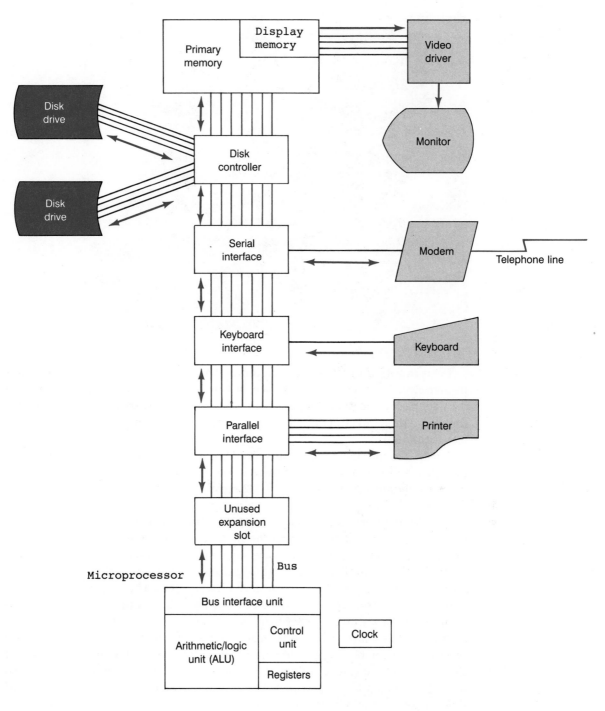

**Figure 1.7**
The organization of a typical personal computer system.

**Figure 1.8**
Video disk players combined with personal computers are being used increasingly in education and training.

Every input, output, and external storage device in a computer system must have its own electrical circuitry, or **interface**, linking it to the bus. The interface may conform to the specifications for a *standard interface*, or it may be a *custom interface* like the one required to support a special-purpose device such as a video disk player (see Figure 1.8).

A standard interface, often called an **I/O port**, makes it easy and reliable to connect pieces of equipment that adhere to the standard (see Figure 1.9). The best-known standard interface is the **RS-232 serial port,** which defines the timing and other electrical properties to connect a computer to modems, mice, printers, and other serial devices. A *serial device* is any I/O device that communicates by sending or receiving a string of bits one after the other through one data line. A *parallel device*, in contrast, sends or receives information in packets all at once over many (usually eight) data lines. Parallel interfaces can send and receive data faster than serial interfaces because they send more bits in each time segment. The industry standard for parallel interfaces is the **Centronix parallel interface.** Both the RS-232 and the Centronix interfaces work faster than most printers or modems.

An **expansion slot** is a connector inside your computer where a custom interface or *adapter card* can be plugged into your system. Expansion slots are used to extend the hardware by adding extra primary memory, more disk drives, modems, and so forth. (See Photos 16, 17, and 18 of Window 2.) An **adapter card** is a circuit board that contains special I/O interface circuits; for example, a display adapter or a disk controller card. A *combination card* integrates many functions on a single card. One combination card might include extra RAM and serial and parallel ports; another might include extra RAM and a disk controller.

**Figure 1.9**
Devices can be con-
nected to standard
I/O ports by plug-
ging cables into the
back of your per-
sonal computer.

## SOFTWARE COMPONENTS

We have seen that the organization of a computer includes input and output devices, external storage units, and a central processor with its associated memory. This structure is simple, even trivial, but how does it work? In this section, we explore how software controls the hardware.

First, we examine a concept that lies behind all computer programs: the idea of storing instructions inside the same machine that executes the instructions. Then, we explore the events that occur in a typical computer session, from turning on the machine to loading programs, processing data, and ending the computer session.

### Stored Program Concept

The most profound concept in all computing goes back to the dawn of modern science. In the mid-1800s—when Darwin was formulating the theory of evolution, electromagnetism was being discovered, and the Industrial Revolution was in full swing—Charles Babbage was attempting to build the first stored-program computer. A **stored-program computer** is a machine controlled by software stored within the hardware. The controlling software is called a *stored program* because the machine holds the program in its memory while the program is guiding the actions of the hardware.

One hundred years passed before Babbage's idea was rejuvenated and used in modern stored-program computer systems. (For a brief history of computing, see Chapter 18.) Today, the operation of all computers depends on a memory that contains instructions in the form of a program and facts in the form of data. Stored programs are essential to modern computing because they are held within the computer machinery itself, making a computer self-contained and automatic. Thus unlike other kinds of calculating machines such as pocket calculators, stored-program machines can operate under their own control by executing instructions stored in their memory.

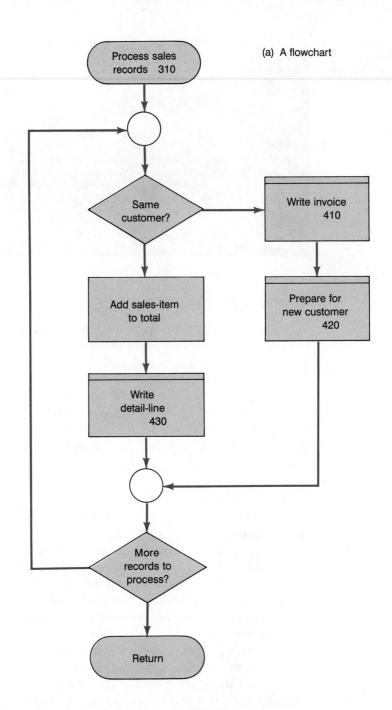

**Figure 1.10a**
Software controls a computer system. The flowchart **(a)** describes one part of an accounts receivable system. It acts as a blueprint from which the program fragment **(b)** is developed.

(a) A flowchart

Process sales records 310

Same customer?

Write invoice 410

Add sales-item to total

Prepare for new customer 420

Write detail-line 430

More records to process?

Return

A CPU's circuits can execute a limited number of different instructions. Each instruction is assigned a pattern of binary bits. One pattern might instruct the processor to compare two numbers and store the location of the larger number in a particular register. Another pattern might tell the processor to multiply the number in one register by the number in another. Thus a modern computer executes programs constructed of long sequences of 1's and 0's.

**Figure 1.10b**

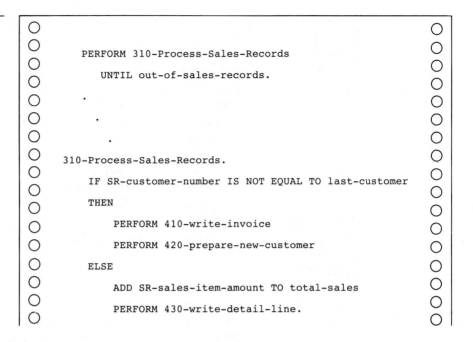

```
      PERFORM 310-Process-Sales-Records

         UNTIL out-of-sales-records.

              .

                 .

                    .

   310-Process-Sales-Records.

      IF SR-customer-number IS NOT EQUAL TO last-customer

      THEN

          PERFORM 410-write-invoice

          PERFORM 420-prepare-new-customer

      ELSE

          ADD SR-sales-item-amount TO total-sales

          PERFORM 430-write-detail-line.
```

(b) A program fragment

Although computers understand only binary instructions, programmers try to avoid writing in binary code because it is tedious and error prone. Instead, programmers express their logic in more understandable ways. They usually begin by creating an outline of their ideas or by drawing a flowchart similar to the one shown in Figure 1.10(a). This helps organize their thoughts before writing instructions in a **programming language,** such as the COBOL instructions shown in Figure 1.10(b). **COBOL** is the most widely used business programming language. It allows the programmer to use English-like statements to describe processing instructions to the computer.

But how does the computer execute a program written in COBOL? Clearly, the circuits of the computer cannot execute a COBOL program directly because COBOL statements are not written in the computer's binary instruction code. The COBOL program must be translated into binary instructions. This is done with the help of a *compiler* or an *interpreter*, two broad classes of programs that translate other programs into binary instructions.

## Events in a Computer Session

On the surface, the events in a personal computer session might seem straightforward. You start the computer by turning on the power and placing a disk in the disk drive. The CPU transfers a program from the disk to the primary memory, where the program takes control of the CPU. Acting under the program's control, the CPU shifts data back and forth between primary memory and the disk to process it. Data cannot be directly processed while it is on disk; it must be brought into primary memory to be totaled, compared, displayed, printed, and so forth. The program allows you to control its operation by typing commands on a keyboard or by using another input device. Eventually, the program gives up control of the computer and ceases to operate. When this happens, you must tell the computer what to do next. No matter what directions you give the computer, however, the same pattern is followed: A program is transferred to memory, where it takes over control; it processes data; and finally it terminates. This three-part process is called *program execution*.

After a bit of thought, however, the events in a computer session may not seem so clear. For example, when the CPU wants information from a magnetic disk, it must first read the information from the disk into primary memory. Only information stored in primary memory is directly accessible to the CPU. But the CPU can do nothing without the intelligence of software. If the software is not permanently stored in the primary memory, how does the computer hardware know how to get information when it is turned on?

This knowledge comes from two features. First, a small amount of nonvolatile memory, called **read-only memory (ROM),** is built into the computer. This retains information even when the computer is off. Second, the program in ROM instructs the CPU to read another program from a disk, thus performing a self-helping start-up when the computer is first turned on. This is called **booting** the computer (a reference to "pulling yourself up by your bootstraps").

Including software inside the computer to help run other software is basic to all computer systems. The special software that controls the running of other software is called the operating system. An **operating system** is a program that controls the operation of the computer itself. Through the CPU, the operating system controls all I/O devices—the keyboard, monitor, printer, disk drives, and every other device connected to the computer. The operating system also makes it easy for people to operate the computer.

There are many different kinds of operating systems; some are for mainframe computers, some are for minis, and still others are for personal computers. Mainframe and minicomputer systems typically use a timesharing operating system, whereas personal computer systems typically use a single-user operating system. A timesharing operating system controls several programs that run along side one another. This allows several users to use the computer system simultaneously; to each user, it seems as if no one else is using the computer. In contrast, a single-user operating system is simpler because it needs to manage only one program at a time and does not need to monitor computer usage for billing purposes.

Application programs are also supervised by the operating system program. The operating system is like an air traffic controller at a busy airport, and the application programs are like airplanes. The controller determines what each airplane is allowed to do and when it is permitted to do it. Similarly, the operating system tells when each application program is allowed to run on the CPU.

**Application programs** perform useful tasks for people. Programs that solve mathematical equations, manage payrolls, process words, display graphs, manage data, and play games are all examples of application software. Application software

**Figure 1.11**
Visual interfaces simulate a real desktop with sheets of paper, icons, and menus.

temporarily converts a general-purpose computer into a special-purpose machine that does exactly what you want done. A general-purpose microcomputer, for example, becomes a video arcade machine when it runs a game program, a planning tool for the designer when running an architectural layout program, and a testing tool when running a simulation program.

We can classify application software into two broad categories: vertical software and horizontal software. **Vertical software** is designed to serve a narrow group of specialists. Examples of vertical programs are medical billing systems, project estimation systems for building contractors, and information storage for thoroughbred horses. **Horizontal software** is designed to serve a wide group of users who, in turn, must tailor the programs to their own needs. Examples of horizontal programs are word processors, spreadsheet programs, and programs to set up and manage *databases*, which are collections of logically related data. We concern ourselves largely with horizontal programs, because of their general applicability to a wide variety of users. Horizontal software, however, may be cumbersome and inefficient compared with vertical software specifically designed for special needs.

To use any program, you must operate it through a keyboard, mouse, or some other kind of input device. To guide its users, every program employs a **user interface**—a protocol for communicating between the computer and the user. A friendly user interface is easily understood and does not intimidate users, but since computers are sophisticated machines, nearly everyone is intimidated by a user interface at some time. Once you understand the logic and underlying model of the interface, using a computer can be as easy and comfortable as driving a car.

There are two main types of interfaces: text-oriented and visual. A *text-oriented interface* requires typed commands and displays messages on the screen in words; a *visual interface* employs pictures called **icons** and menu systems for making selections. Figure 1.11 shows a visual interface; our examples in the next section illustrate a text-oriented interface.

# A BRIEF COMPUTER SESSION

We now illustrate the interaction between software and hardware in a computer system by walking through a typical session with a personal computer. Using a personal computer is much like using a large timeshared computer via a terminal; the principal difference is that on a mainframe, you must **log on**, that is, identify yourself, by typing an identification number and a password.

## Booting The Computer

If the computer is turned off, you must first insert a copy of the operating system disk into the disk drive. Then flip the power switch on to boot the operating system into primary memory. Recall that a permanent bootstrap program is read from ROM; it instructs the computer to read the operating system program from the disk into primary memory, thus bringing the computer to life.

Some disks contain both a copy of the operating system and an application program. These disks may also contain instructions that cause them to load the operating system into memory and immediately proceed to load the application program into another part of memory. This can be convenient because the computer will immediately begin to run an application program, such as a word processing program or a game. For example, nearly all program disks for Apple II computers are configured this way.

With most computers, the first message shown on the display screen comes from the operating system. This message varies depending on the make and model of computer. The message may be the computer's operating system prompt. In computer jargon a **prompt** is any message that tells you that the computer is waiting for you to enter an answer, supply it with needed information, or respond to an alert message. Here are some likely prompt lines:

```
Ok?
A>
 :
```

These cryptic messages tell you the computer is waiting for you to give it a command. A **command** is an instruction you enter that tells the computer what you want it to do next.

## Loading a Program

Suppose we want to use the computer to run a word processing program to enter and print a short letter. (For more details on word processing, see Chapter 6). Before you can run a program, you must load it into the computer. To load a program, enter either its name or an abbreviation as a command to the operating system. For example, suppose you respond to the prompt A> by typing the command WRITE (your response is shown in color):

A>WRITE

Typing WRITE and then pressing [Return] or [Enter] causes the program to be copied from the disk into primary memory and executed. The CPU *executes* a program by performing each instruction, one at a time.

Next, the word processing program will prompt you for input. For example, its first prompt may request a name.

Enter the name of the document to type or edit: MYLETTER

Typing MYLETTER and pressing [Return] or [Enter] causes the word processing program to fetch the text previously stored on the disk under the name MYLETTER if it already exists, or if no text by that name exists, it may create a new document called MYLETTER.

If MYLETTER is new, the word processor clears the display screen and waits for you to type text just as if the computer were a typewriter. For example, you might enter the following letter:

February 12, 1848
Mr. Wilkins Micawber
Care of Mr. Namby's
Coleman Street

Dear Mr. Micawber,

   I regret that I am forced to write you in the matter of a loan you have failed to repay when due. You and I have had more than one such business dealing.
   If the sum of 24 pounds, 7 shillings, 9 pence (principal, interest, and penalty) has not been received by this office before the close of business on Monday the 20th of this month, the matter will be turned over to my solicitors, Kenge and Carboy of Lincoln's Inn.

Ralph Nickleby

After the letter is entered, you can store it, print it, or correct it by editing the text displayed on the screen. These operations require you to give commands to your personal computer.

## Entering Commands

Terminals and personal computers have special keys on their keyboards that simplify many operations. One of the most important is the **control key**, labeled Ctrl on most computer keyboards. (Apple II keyboards have a key marked with a small apple.) To enter many commands, you press this key and hold it down while pressing another key. For example, suppose you want to save our sample letter. Saving a document means copying it from primary memory to the disk, thus making a permanent copy on the disk. The exact command for doing this varies from one word processing program to another, but with some programs, pressing [Ctrl] and [S] simultaneously directs the program to save a document.

The keyboard has other special keys to help you operate various programs and give commands easily. For example, a word processing program may also use keys marked Ins (for inserting material), Del (for deleting material), and PgDn (for moving down through the document). These keys are likely to take on other meanings when other programs are run on the computer.

## Quitting

Sometimes the most difficult command to discover is the one that causes a program to stop running. Usually, if you remember just a few commands, you can ask the program to tell you what the other commands are, including the command that will stop a program and return control to the operating system. Suppose pressing [Ctrl]-[L] causes a list of choices to appear on the screen such as

P = Set page parameters
G = Get another document
X = Exit this program

Pressing [X] at this point takes you out of the word processor program. The operating system takes control of the computer, displays its prompt, and waits for you to enter a command.

If you are running a mainframe or minicomputer, you must tell the operating system you are leaving. This is called **logging off**. Often logging off is as simple as typing

A>logoff

A personal computer, however, serves only one user at a time; so you need not log off. Simply remove the disk and turn the power off.

---

### Summary

Like other mechanical systems, a computer is a complete system composed of moving parts. Unlike other machinery, however, a computer can produce different results each time it is run. Software is the "mind" of the computer, that which tells the hardware (the "body") what to do.

A computer is digital device; that is, it can store only discrete values. A computer can "remember" on or off but nothing in between. Zeros and ones represent on and off to a computer. A number containing only two kinds of digits is a binary number, and modern computers are often called binary computers. Computers use binary codes to manipulate many kinds of data.

Computers come in three sizes: mainframe, mini, and micro. Each has its role in society. Mainframes are found predominantly in large organizations; minicomputers are used in more dedicated applications such as factory automation, universities, and medium-sized organizations; and micros are used in dedicated applications such as personal computers or household appliances.

Regardless of their size or cost, all computers have the same basic functional organization: Input devices capture information in a machine-processable format; the CPU processes information stored in primary memory; storage units provide long-term, low-cost storage of data; and output devices present the processed information in a usable format.

All computers also use software. Software is classified according to its purpose. Application software is designed to solve real-world problems such as found in the fields of accounting, engineering, or factory control. System software, on the other hand, is designed to control the computer itself, such as the various kinds of operating systems.

## Key Terms

adapter card

analog

application program

arithmetic/logic unit (ALU)

ASCII code

binary number

bit

booting

bus

byte

central processing unit (CPU)

Centronix parallel interface

COBOL

command

control key

control unit

digital

disk drive

expansion slot

hardware

horizontal software

icons

input device

interface

I/O device

I/O port

logging on, logging off

mainframe

main memory

micro, microcomputer

microprocessor

mini, minicomputer

modem

monitor

operating system

output device

peripheral

personal computer

primary memory

program

programming language

prompt

random access memory (RAM)

read-only memory (ROM)

registers

RS-232 serial port

software

stored-program computer

timesharing system

user interface

vertical software

vertical software

## Discussion Questions

1. What are the two main components of a computer system? Explain how they work together.

2. What are the differences among micro, mini, and mainframe computers? How are they alike?

3. When a computer is first turned on, what causes the CPU to transfer a program from disk to primary memory?

4. What are the two principal kinds of user interface? Which kind do you think is the easiest to learn? To use?

5. What is the difference between vertical and horizontal software? Is a medical billing program considered a vertical or a horizontal program? Is a tax preparation program? Are games like PacMan? What programs might lie on the border between the two types of software?

6. What is the relationship between application software and operating system software?

7. Suppose a movie projector, camera, and film are compared with a computer system. What is the computer's equivalent of film? Of the projector? Is this a good analogy?

8. Computers communicate with each other over the telephone. When, if ever, would a telephone be an I/O device?

9. What is the "mind" of a computer, and what is its "body"? Can computers think?

10. An RS-232 interface is used for serial communication, whereas a Centronix interface is used for parallel communication. Which does your computer use to communicate with your printer?

## Exercises

1. How does a computer determine whether the contents of a memory word is an instruction or data, such as a number or letter?

2. Suppose a memory location contains the binary equivalent of the decimal number 66. What could the 66 represent?

3. List your daily activities that could be computerized. Which would be accomplished better or faster with the help of a computer? Be realistic—would you save time by balancing a checkbook with a computer?

4. Examine the keyboard of your terminal or personal computer. Which keys are used to give commands and which are used to enter data into the computer? Can you tell the difference?

5. Cars are vehicles for moving people; computers are vehicles for moving information. Prepare a report on the kinds of information computers are capable of moving over communication lines.

6. Who makes computers? List all the computer manufacturers you can think of, then compare your list with the *Datamation 100*, a list of the top 100 computer companies given each year in a June issue of *Datamation*.

# The CPU and Storage

**The Central Processing Unit**
*Comparing Central Processing Units*
*Primary Memory*

**External Storage**
*Tapes*

*Disks and Disk Drives*
*File Storage Methods*

**Comparing Memory Systems**

In Chapter 1, we explain how information is coded in a computer's memory. Now, we examine how information is processed in a computer's central processing unit (CPU). Close interaction between the processor and primary memory, with its stored programs, is responsible for the "reasoning power" of computers. External memory is closely tied to the CPU, so we also examine the role of external memory in the overall computer system and the exchange of information between external and primary memory, which is called *file access*. Throughout this chapter, we compare the cost, speed, and reliability of the various memory technologies.

## THE CENTRAL PROCESSING UNIT

Figure 2.1 shows a useful way of thinking about the parts of a CPU. Primary (main) memory is shown divided into a great many storage cells; think of them as somewhat like the safety deposit boxes on a bank vault wall or as post office boxes. Each box or cell has its own unique electronic **address**—a number identifying its location—and can hold one *word* of information at a time. A **word** is a fixed-length packet of bits that is handled as a unit by the computer. Early personal computers worked on 1 byte of information at a time. Today, most computers work on 16-, 32-, or 64-bit words at a time. For example, an IBM mainframe word consists of 32 bits, or 4 bytes.

The *arithmetic/logic unit* (ALU) does all the computing; it can add, subtract, multiply, and divide numbers; it can compare two numbers to determine the larger; and it can move bits from one place to another. The ALU works exclusively on encoded binary numbers. It takes its orders from binary-encoded instructions stored like any other information in primary memory.

The *control unit* supervises the CPU; it fetches numbers from memory and interprets them as instructions. The control unit dissects each instruction and then directs the flow of information through the ALU, input/output devices, and primary memory.

## Comparing Central Processing Units

The physical appearance of CPUs differs more than their logical structure does. A mainframe's CPU fills a large box and requires many circuit boards or ceramic chip-carrying modules. In contrast, a personal computer's CPU is often mounted on a single plastic circuit board and can be hidden inside the keyboard or monitor. In every personal computer, the control unit and ALU are combined into a single circuit or chip (see Figure 2.2). Because this component is so small, it is called a microprocessor.

CPUs operate quickly, though the mainframe's CPU is faster than the personal computer's. The components of CPUs are designed to operate independently of one another; for example, the ALU might be multiplying two numbers while the control unit is looking ahead to read the next instruction. This technique, called **pipelining**, allows several instructions to work their way through the parts of the CPU and be in various stages of completion. Until the most recent generation of microprocessors was released, it was safe to say that mainframe computers make more use of pipelining than microcomputers. Now, there are single-chip microprocessors with hundreds of thousands of circuits and the ability to run several programs concurrently.

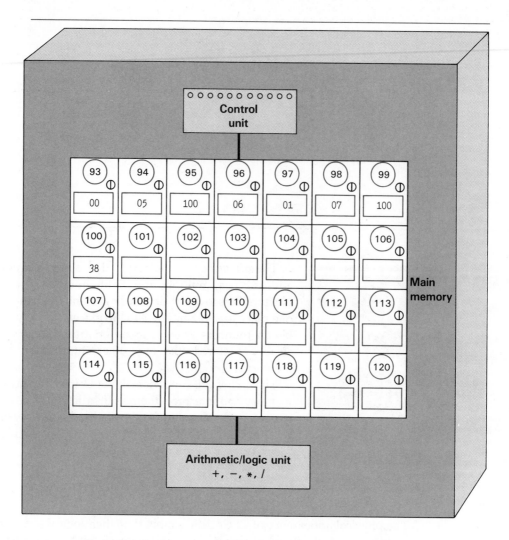

**Figure 2.1**
A simplified view of a central processing unit.

Although the gap between the performance of a mainframe's CPU and a micro-processor's has been shrinking steadily, important differences between small and large computers do exist. If the CPU of a Macintosh II microcomputer could carry out the same instructions as the CPU of an IBM 3090 mainframe at the same speed, IBM would lose a lot of business. Instead, the CPUs of different types of computers vary greatly in how fast they process instructions, in which instructions they can carry out, and in how many different instructions they can handle. These differences determine the power of a computer and whether it can execute a given program.

Because each instruction is extremely simple, completing a useful task takes hundreds, thousands, or even millions of primitive operations. Obviously, a CPU must work quickly to be useful. Most computers operate at speeds measured in

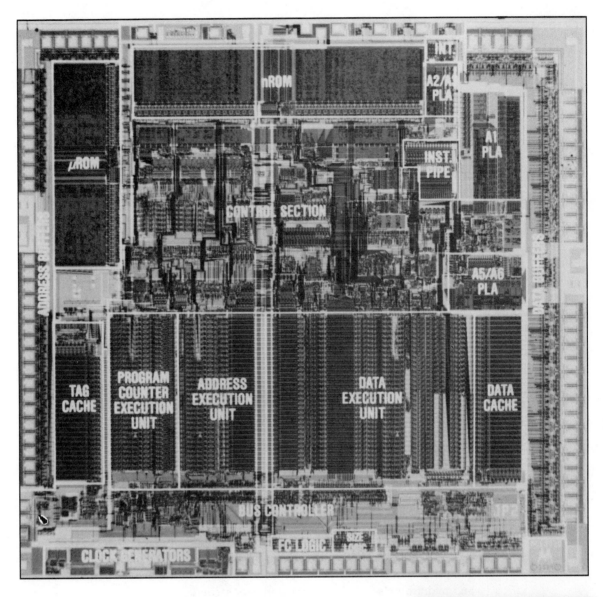

- μROM
- nROM
- INT.
- A2/A4 PLA
- A1 PLA
- INST. PIPE
- CONTROL SECTION
- A5/A6 PLA
- ADDRESS BUFFER
- DATA BUFFER
- TAG CACHE
- PROGRAM COUNTER EXECUTION UNIT
- ADDRESS EXECUTION UNIT
- DATA EXECUTION UNIT
- DATA CACHE
- BUS CONTROLLER
- FC LOGIC
- CLOCK GENERATORS

**Figure 2.2**
The Motorola 68020 microprocessor that lies at the heart of a Macintosh II. **(a)** A view that labels the various portions of the chip. **(b)** The completed chip, packaged in a ceramic housing and ready to be soldered on a circuit board.

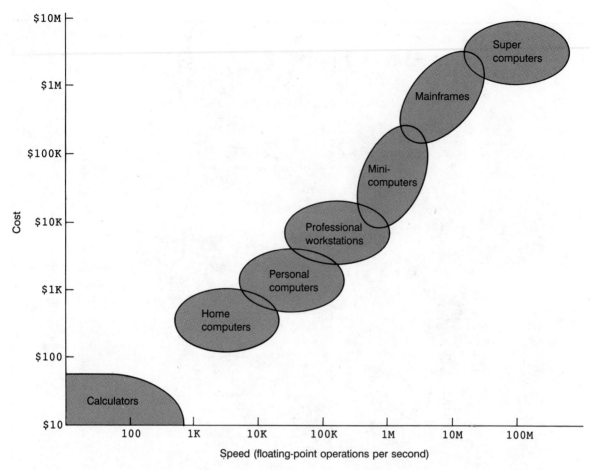

**Figure 2.3**
A comparison of the cost and performance of current computers

fractions of a second. A **nanosecond** is one billionth of a second; there are 1 million **microseconds**, or 1,000 **milliseconds**, in a second. The operating time of a microcomputer's CPU is measured in microseconds, whereas that of a minicomputer's and mainframe's CPU is measured in nanoseconds.

The collection of instructions that a computer can perform is its **instruction set**. Large computers have large instruction sets, and small computers have smaller instruction sets. Besides the number of instructions in a computer's instruction set, the capability of each instruction is important. A mainframe computer has very powerful instructions, and a personal computer has simple instructions. For example, a mainframe computer might have a single instruction for multiplying two 64-bit numbers, but it might take a personal computer thirty instructions to compute the same numbers. Clearly, the power of a computer's instruction set influences how fast the computer can process data.

Because computers differ in both the size of the instruction set and the power of the instructions, comparing one computer with another is difficult. A general

**Figure 2.4**
A packaged memory chip sits on top of a wafer of similar memory chips.

measure of performance is the **MFLOP** (million floating-point operations per second). A 1-MFLOP computer can perform 1 million floating-point operations a second. A **floating-point number** is any number with a decimal point, such as 3.14159. Figure 2.3 compares the cost and performance of various types of computer systems. As a rule of thumb, smaller computers provide more computing power per dollar. For example, according to a recent *Sceintific American* article, "In 1987 the approximate relative cost of executing one million instructions per second on a mainframe computer is 100 units; on a minicomputer it is 40 units, on a personal computer it is three units, and on an embedded computer (if one were powerful enough) it would be .15 unit." [1]

As the size of a car's engine is not important for in-town driving, so a computer's processing power is not important for some applications. Having a system in which the software makes full use of a processor with limited capabilities is much better than having a system in which poor software runs on a potentially powerful processor.

## Primary Memory

The primary memory of a computer is composed of *integrated circuits (ICs)*. These high-speed electronic circuits are capable of quickly saving and retrieving information. In today's technology, ICs are printed on small chips cut from thin slices (or wafers) of large silicon crystals (see Figure 2.4). Hence the circuits are called **memory chips**.

It is easiest to build and use memory chips that have a round number of storage cells in binary arithmetic, which in decimal numbers, means 2, 4, 8, and so on. Today's memory chips tend to have between $2^{18}$ and $2^{20}$ cells; this is 262,144 to 1,048,576 bits of storage. A more convenient unit of measure for memory uses the symbol K. In the metric system, K is the symbol for 1,000; however, when memory is being measured, K is the symbol for $2^{10}$, or 1,024. Thus a memory chip with 16,384

---

1. Abraham Peled, "The Next Computer Revolution," *Scientific American*, October 1987, p. 58.

*One of the hottest subjects in personal computers is the relative capabilities of microprocessors. The newest microprocessors promise vast improvements in speed and the ability to work with much larger amounts of memory.*

The secret to designing a successful microprocessor is to make it compatible with an existing microprocessor—that way it inherits the ability to run existing programs. Thus microprocessors are designed in families. Each new member operates faster, provides new features, and is given a higher model number. For example, IBM PCs use Intel's family of microprocessors, which includes the 8080, 8088, 8086, 80286, and 80386. Apple Macintoshes use Motorola's 68000 or its more capable 68020.

A program written for one microprocessor family will not run on microprocessors in another family unless it is rewritten or translated from one instruction set to the other. Similarly, a program that takes advantage of the new features of a microprocessor will not run on earlier microprocessors in the same family.

Depending on how a program was written, translating it can be as much work as writing it from scratch.

Five factors have a major influence on a microprocessor's power.

First, how many bits of data are processed in one operation? (An analogy is the size of the scoop on a steam shovel.) For example, you might look at the number of bits transferred between the microprocessor and primary memory at once—8 bits with the 8088, 16 bits with a 80286 or 68000, and 32 bits with a 80386 or 68020. Alternatively, you might compare the number of bits processed internally in each operation. The Mostek 6502 in an Apple II processes 8 bits in each operation; an 8088 processes 16 bits; and the 80286, 80386, 68000, and 68020 microprocessors can manipulate 32 bits.

Second, how many instructions are in the instruction set, and how powerful are they? (analogy: the number of useful attachments for a tractor).

Third, how long does it take to complete an instruction? (analogy: the time it takes a steam

binary storage cells is called a 16K-bit chip. Similarly, **kilobit** means 1,024 bits of memory, and **kilobyte (KB)** means 1,024 bytes.

To designate the memory capacities of modern computers, we need even larger units. A **megabyte (MB)** is 1,024KB, or $2^{20}$ bytes, which is roughly a million characters of storage. Primary memory of 64MB or more is common in large computer installations, but 4MB is considered a lot of memory in a personal computer. A **gigabyte (GB)** is 1,024MB, roughly a billion characters. Large mainframe disk drives hold 5 to 10GB of information, but personal computers are more likely to have hard disk drives that hold 20 to 40MB or to use even smaller floppy disk drives.

The amount of memory the computer has is important in determining what the computer can do. A computer with less than 64KB of memory is limited to trivial applications because it can execute only tiny programs. A machine like this might be able to play video games and balance a checkbook, but it will not be able to run a full-featured word processing or spreadsheet program. For most professional or business applications, a computer must have at least 256KB of memory.

shovel to dump each scoop). This is influenced by the **clock rate**, which paces all the operations in the CPU. Clock rates are measured in **megahertz (MHz)**, or millions of cycles per second. For example, an IBM PC has a 4.77 MHz clock rate, which means there are 4,770,000 ticks (called **clocks**) of the CPU's clock each second. Another factor to consider is the number of clocks it takes to complete an instruction. It takes an IBM PC four clocks to transfer 1 byte from primary memory to the microprocessor, and it can take more than a hundred clocks to multiply two 16-bit numbers.

Fourth, how many operations can be going on at the same time? (analogy: the number of workers on an assembly line). For example, while a 80386 is processing one instruction in its arithmetic/logic unit, it is decoding a second in its control unit, and fetching a third from memory with its bus interface unit.

Fifth, how much primary memory can the processor manage? The maximum amount of primary memory is limited by the length of each memory address. (As an analogy, consider how many telephones can be dialed with a seven-digit telephone number.) This factor can be quite important because it determines the largest program the processor can load into memory at once and execute.

A microprocessor will use either a 16-, a 20-, a 24-, or a 32-bit memory address. The 6502 uses a 16-bit memory address, which limits it to $2^{16}$, or roughly 65,000 locations for primary memory. The 8088 uses a 20-bit address for a maximum of slightly more than 1 million addresses. The 68000 uses a 24-bit address for a maximum of about 16 million addresses. The newest microprocessors use 32-bit addresses, so the maximum amount of memory they can manage is effectively unlimited.

Most computers do not have as much physical memory as their processor can address, which makes it possible to add memory to the computer later. If a program asks the processor to retrieve information from a nonexistent memory location, a processing error is likely to occur. This is similar to dialing a nonexistent telephone number.

## Memory Management Techniques

When you buy software for a personal computer, you must match the software's requirement for primary memory with your computer's amount of memory. A 512KB program cannot run on a 256KB personal computer. Mainframe computers (and a few of the newer personal computers), however, are equipped with **virtual memory**—a feature that allows them to accommodate programs larger than the primary memory. In a computer with virtual memory, the hardware simulates a very large memory by automatically moving parts of a running program from primary to external (disk) memory as the program runs. Thus a 1MB memory might appear to be 100MB in size when running a large program.

Personal computers are sometimes programmed to approximate the virtual memory of their larger cousins by using **program overlays**. This technique partitions a large program into many shorter segments. Each segment is *swapped* from disk into primary memory as needed and removed from primary memory when not needed. In this way, a small computer can act like a big computer, though it is at the expense of processing speed.

## A Word About . . . The Evolution of the IBM PC

*Every three years IBM has announced a new generation of personal computers with vastly different capabilities.*

When IBM announced the original IBM Personal Computer (PC) on August 12, 1981, it clearly didn't understand how the computers would be used. IBM took out full-page ads in *The Wall Street Journal* aimed at encouraging fathers to buy a PC for their kids. It offered models equipped with only 16KB of memory and no disk drives—models suitable only for playing games or experimenting with how a computer worked. But the home market was not a significant factor in the success of the PC. Instead, PCs were snapped up by businesses and professionals who wanted a reliable personal computer with the backing and support of a major computer vendor.

Essential to the success of the IBM PC was its open hardware architecture and expansion slots. Other companies began offering circuit boards with extra memory, more I/O ports, modems, clocks, and a host of other features. Disk manufacturers offered disks larger and cheaper than could be bought from IBM. These products corrected many of the deficiencies of the original PC. Scores of companies copied the entire PC; their products become known as *PC clones.*

In 1984, a new member—the IBM PC AT—was added to the "IBM Personal Computer family." Although the AT boasted a faster processor and more memory, it could run all the same software as the original PC. The AT never became as popular as the PC, partly because of its higher price. What is more, few application programs took advantage of the microprocessor's more advanced features, such as the ability to manage several megabytes of primary memory. This, in turn, was due to the limitations of the machine's operating system.

In 1987, IBM effectively replaced the entire Personal Computer family by announcing a new family of IBM Personal System/2 computers. These computers use microfloppy disks, boast better display systems, and incorporate a new type of expansion slot. Although these changes make the hardware of the Personal System/2 computers incompatible with the hardware of the PC family, the new computers can run all the previous software.

### Table 2.1
### The Evolution of the IBM PC

|  | IBM PC (Personal Computer) | IBM AT (Advanced Technology) | IBM PS/2 (Personal System/2 Model 80) |
|---|---|---|---|
| Announcement Date | August 1981 | August 1984 | April 1987 |
| Microprocessor | Intel 8088 | Intel 80286 | Intel 80386 |
| Clock Speed | 4.77 MHz | 8.0 MHz | 16 MHz |
| Transistors in Microprocessor | 5,500 | 134,000 | 275,000 |
| Bus Width | 8 bits | 16 bits | 32 bits |
| Amount of Standard Memory | 48 KB | 256 KB | 1 MB |
| Announced Memory Capacity | 256 KB | 3 MB | 16 MB |
| Size of Floppy Disk | 160 KB | 1.2 MB | 1.44 MB |
| Size of Hard Disk | — | 20 MB | 44 MB |
| Price | $2,235 | $5,795 | $6995 |

Program overlays have another disadvantage. They require that the programmer break the program into segments and write instructions specifying when each segment is to be swapped in or out. In contrast, virtual memory is **transparent** because it is built into the hardware and operates without requiring the programmer's attention.

Virtual memory and overlays were invented to compensate for the high cost of primary memory, but over the last twenty years, manufacturing techniques have lowered the cost of memory chips. A reliable rule of thumb has been that every three years the number of bits per chip quadruples, whereas the cost per chip stays constant. As a result, the price of memory has been dropping about 30 percent each year for two decades. Perhaps the next generation of computers will have sufficiently large primary memories so that virtual and physical memory sizes will be the same.

## ROM and RAM

The two major types of primary memory are ROM and RAM. **Read-only memory (ROM)** is memory manufactured to permanently store a fixed set of information. This book is similar to ROM because its information can be read but cannot be changed. **Random-access memory (RAM)** implies that any piece of information can be read with equal difficulty and delay. In fact, the name *RAM* is misleading because ROM is also a random-access memory.

The real difference between ROM and RAM is that information stored in RAM can be changed, whereas information in ROM cannot. You can write new information into RAM. RAM allows the computer to store information quickly for later reference. In most computers, RAM holds

- The active parts of the operating system, the program that manages the operation of the computer

- The application program being executed (for example, a word processing program)

- Part or all of the data used by the application program (for example, a letter being written with the word processing program)

- A representation of the data being shown on the video display

- Anything else likely to change frequently (for example, the time of day in the computer's clock or information about the disk in external storage)

Most RAM is *volatile*—that is, when even a short interruption in the computer's power supply occurs, the contents of RAM are erased. Obviously, storing your only copy of work in RAM is unwise. ROM, however, is *nonvolatile*—that is, when the computer is turned off, the contents of ROM are not lost.

Because ROM is slightly cheaper than RAM as well as nonvolatile, manufacturers use ROM for permanently storing often used programs in the primary memory of the computer. The ROM chips containing these programs are in the computer when you buy it. For example, in all personal computers, ROM stores the instructions that tell the computer what to do when the power is turned on. A simple version of the

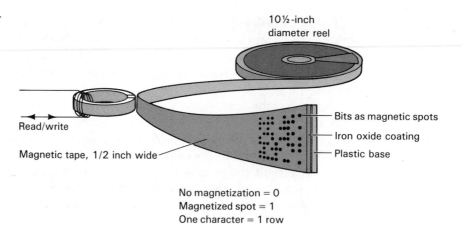

**Figure 2.5**
When the tape containing magnetic spots moves through an electrical field, a 1 or 0 is sensed by the read/write head. A 1 or 0 is written on the tape by energizing the electromagnetic field to induce a charge (1) or not (0).

10½-inch
diameter reel

Read/write

Magnetic tape, 1/2 inch wide

Bits as magnetic spots
Iron oxide coating
Plastic base

No magnetization = 0
Magnetized spot = 1
One character = 1 row

BASIC programming language is often also included in a personal computer's ROM.

Portable computers can compensate for their limited (or nonexistent) external storage by using ROM to store application programs. The microcomputers in cars, microwave ovens, calculators, and video games are instructed to perform their special-purpose, fixed functions by a program stored in ROM.

## EXTERNAL STORAGE

External storage is where programs and data are stored when the power is turned off. External storage devices such as tapes and disks store information as magnetic spots on magnetic oxide surfaces. A tape drive or disk drive reads and writes on tapes or disks by moving them past a read/write head (see Figure 2.5). The head reads their magnetized surfaces, converting the information into electrical impulses that it sends to the computer. On a given drive, a magnetic north pole might represent a binary 1, and a magnetic south pole, a binary 0. Hence magnetic storage devices use a binary encoding scheme similar to that used in primary memory.

External storage devices are used extensively in all computer systems because of the following three advantages:

1. Because magnetic spots do not need a constant supply of power to "refresh" themselves (as most RAM chips do), tapes and disks are *nonvolatile*. This means the tape or disk can be removed from the computer system, set aside, and used again later. As a result, tapes and disks are stored in libraries of information called *archives*. An **archival copy** is any information on tape or disk set aside for use later on. Word processor documents, large databases, and spreadsheet analyses are all candidates for archival storage.

2. For each unit of storage, external memory is *less expensive* than primary memory. A tape or removable disk can store about a million characters per dollar, whereas primary memory can store only about a thousand characters per

dollar. Thus magnetic storage devices are a thousand times less expensive than electronic memories per stored character.

3. Because of the nonvolatility and low cost of magnetic media, most external storage can be *replaced* by additional media. A full disk can be replaced by an empty disk, thus extending the computer's effective storage capacity. This capability makes personal computers especially useful in the modern office.

The three most common forms of magnetic media are magnetic tapes, floppy disks, and hard disks. All these can be erased and recorded again and again. As new information is entered, it automatically writes over whatever was there before. To avoid accidental erasure, both tapes and floppy disks can be **write-protected**. That is, they can be altered so that you can neither write nor change any information on them. This is usually done by removing a plastic ring or tab from the tape's reel or case or by covering a notch on the disk's jacket. Tape recorders and floppy disk drives will not write on write-protected media. Most hard disks cannot be write-protected.

## Tapes

Computer information is stored on tapes similar to the tapes that store stereo music, but information is stored on each differently. A stereo tape probably stores music as a continuous signal, much like the continuous stream of water from a kitchen tap. A computer tape stores *digitized* information; that is, each piece of information is a bit whose value is either a 0 or a 1.

Tape density is measured by the number of bits per inch (bpi) recorded on the tape. The bits on a tape typically are arranged in 9-bit bytes across the width of the tape. The ninth bit, a **parity bit,** is used to detect and correct single-bit errors. Mainframe tape drives store 6,250 or more characters per inch.

Tapes provide **sequential storage**; that is, information is recorded sequentially, one record behind another. Reading and writing from tapes is therefore slow. To read the last item on a tape, you must wind the tape past all the previous items. The time it takes to begin reading the desired information from a storage device is the device's **access time**.

Despite their slowness, tapes have several uses. Tape has been around since the earliest days of modern computing, so almost every mainframe and minicomputer can read 1/2-inch reel-to-reel tapes produced by any other computer. Hence tapes are used for exchanging and converting information.

In mainframe computer centers, the low cost of tape makes it a good medium for the long-term storage of large quantities of data. The social security files, income tax returns, and census data kept by the U.S. government are all stored on tape. The most frequent use of tape is for archival storage of infrequently used data.

Tapes are also useful if you are using a personal computer with a hard disk drive. A **streaming tape drive** can copy all the data from a hard disk onto a 1/4-inch cartridge tape in minutes. If the hard disk fails, thousands of records of information

**Figure 2.6**
A tape recorder that can store 2.5 gigabytes of data on a standard home video cassette.

can be lost, so backing-up the hard disk with streamer tapes can save you hours of anguish. Streaming tape drives for personal computers are usually the same size as floppy disk drives. Figure 2.6 illustrates another alternative: a streaming tape drive that consists of a modified video tape recorder and can store an incredible 2.5 gigabytes (2,500MB) on a standard video cassette tape.

## Disks and Disk Drives

A *disk drive* is a mechanical device for converting magnetic spots on the surface of a magnetic disk into electrical signals understandable to a computer. Magnetic fields must be in motion before they can be sensed by the drive; thus magnetic disks must rotate. The floppy disks in personal computers rotate at 300 rpm (revolutions per minute); hard disks typically rotate at 3,600 rpm. Disk drives are therefore subject to wear and tear. In fact, the most common failures in computer systems occur in mechanical devices such as keyboards, printers, and disk drives.

Figure 2.7 shows how information is organized on a magnetic disk. Think of each disk as a collection of short tapes, with each tape placed in a concentric arc around the disk. In Figure 2.7, a **track** is equivalent to one of the imaginary pieces of tape.

Each track is divided into pie-shaped wedges called **sectors** so that the disk drive can quickly access a piece of the track. When information is requested of the disk drive, the rotating disk first positions the requested sector under the read/write head; then the information from that sector is copied into primary memory. Thus the smallest amount of *accessible information* on a disk is the sector.

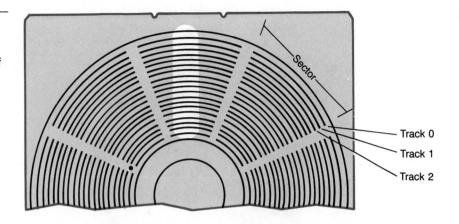

**Figure 2.7**
Organization of a disk. A *track* is one complete rotation of the disk. A *sector* is a piece of a track. Each sector stores a fixed number of bytes.

Sector

Track 0
Track 1
Track 2

Each sector contains a fixed number of bytes that are encoded in the binary number system just as if they were in primary memory. When converted into electrical signals, they represent a group of eight 0 or 1 bits.

### Floppy Disks

The most common external storage device for personal computers is the floppy disk drive. As Figure 2.8(a) shows, it reads magnetic spots from the surface of a **floppy disk**, a magnetic disk sealed inside a square cardboard jacket. It is called a floppy disk because it has a flexible base, made of Mylar (plastic). This base supports the

**Figure 2.8**
**(a)** Floppy disks are low-cost, low-density storage media for personal computers. **(b)** Reading and writing from a floppy disk is done by a drive. It holds the floppy in place, spins the disk inside the protective jacket, and either records or senses the magnetic spots on the surface of the disk.

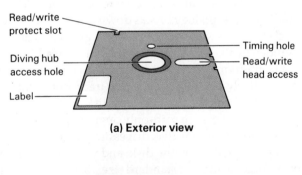

Read/write protect slot
Timing hole
Diving hub access hole
Read/write head access
Label

**(a) Exterior view**

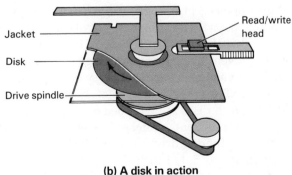

Jacket
Read/write head
Disk
Drive spindle

**(b) A disk in action**

**Figure 2.9**
A 5 1/4-inch minifloppy and a 3 1/2-inch microfloppy disk

magnetic oxide recording surface. Unless a floppy disk is encased in a hard plastic protective shell, it can be bent slightly without damage.

Unlike tape devices, floppy disk systems are random-access storage devices. (Recall that a random-access device is any storage device that can retrieve information, regardless of its location on the device, in roughly the same amount of time.) As the disk rotates, the read/write heads of floppy disk drives can move in and out to quickly access a sector of information on any part of the disk (Figure 2.8b). Because of this, disks are preferred to tapes even though they are more expensive.

In several ways, floppy disk drives are like stereo record players. In both systems, a mechanical arm rubs against the disk to sense the information recorded on the disk's surface. But the analogy breaks down quickly. Floppy disks store data in concentric tracks; records store songs in spiral grooves. The pickup arm of a record player is guided by the groove in a record, but the read/write head of a floppy disk drive must be positioned over a magnetic track on a smooth recording surface. The difficulty of actively locating a magnetic track rather than passively following a physical groove is the main reason floppy disk drives cost more than record players. Moreover, record players are read-only devices; you cannot use them to add information to a record. But floppy disk drives are true input/output devices; with them, you can write information on the disk, and you can read from it.

Floppy disks come in three standard sizes: 8 inch, 5 1/4 inch, and 3 1/2 inch. IBM developed the original 8-inch floppy disks to load test programs into their mainframe computers. Soon the disks became popular among small business owners because floppy disk drives cost less than hard disk drives. Today, the 8-inch size is rarely used. Improvements in manufacturing techniques led to the availability of 5 1/4-inch disks—sometimes called *minifloppy disks*—with almost the same storage capacity and reliability as 8-inch disks. Most disks in use today are 5 1/4 inch. Both 8-inch and 5 1/4-inch disks are wrapped in a stiff cardboard envelope to protect them from dirt, body oils, and scratches. An oval slot in the envelope exposes some of the disk, allowing the disk drive's read/write head to get to the recording surface.

Figure 2.9 compares 5 1/4-inch floppy disks with 3 1/2-inch disks—called *microfloppy disks* or *microdiskettes*. Each 3 1/2-inch disk is housed in a rigid plastic

**Figure 2.10**
Hard disks. The obsolete hard disk platter on the left is now used as a coffee table. On the right is a modern hard disk drive that is the same size as a full-height 5 1/4-inch floppy disk drive. It stores 760 megabytes of information—about 150 times the original capacity of the obsolete platter.

shell and can be carried safely in a shirt pocket. A sliding metal cover protects the read/write slot. The 3 1/2-inch disks are rapidly eating into the market for mini-floppy disks because they offer more storage, are more convenient and less easily damaged, and use smaller drive units.

Several "standards" for recording information on floppy disks are promoted by computer manufacturers. One personal computer might store 800 KB of data on a disk; another might store only 360 KB on the same disk. Of course, there is also a lack of standards for typing on paper. The number of lines of text per page, size of the type, and whether text is typed on both sides of the page depend on the typist and the typewriter, not on the paper. But whereas humans can easily read text in a wide variety of formats, personal computers are less flexible. Personal computers normally read and write disks in only their own format, but sometimes you can buy special programs that will translate between the formats used by different brands.

Floppy disks can be stored for later use. You can use as many floppy disks as it takes to store your information, but only one disk per disk drive can be **on-line**, that is, under the direct control of the computer.

### Hard Disks

**Hard disks** use rigid aluminum platters to support a highly polished, magnetic oxide recording surface. A bent hard disk is worse than useless because it will damage the hard disk drive's read/write heads. Like a floppy disk system, a hard disk system is a random-access storage device. Figure 2.10 compares an obsolete hard disk platter with a more recent hard disk drive.

Hard disks were invented before floppy disks. Since the 1960s, they have been the primary external storage device for large computers. During this time, their size has shrunk, their price has dropped, the density of data stored has grown, and their reliability has increased. Hard disk prices are constantly falling; in 1987, hard disks cost about one dollar for each 50,000 characters of storage. To put this in perspec-

*You need to follow some simple precautionary rules whenever you use tapes or disks. These rules stem from the fact that magnetic media are less reliable than paper-based storage. It is difficult to erase all the writing from a piece of paper, but a magnetic disk can be erased by any strong magnetic field.*

Your first line of defense against accidental erasure of magnetic media should be to take good care of tapes and disks. Treat them as you would treat yourself. Avoid extreme temperatures and dusty or dirty environments. Do not let anything come into contact with the recording surface, including your fingers, which deposit an oily film on everything they touch. Near electrical devices be especially cautious. Tapes can lose information if they are placed above the motors in a tape drive. The ringer in a telephone can create a magnetic field strong enough to erase data from floppy disks under the phone.

But the most important rule—one that should be followed religiously—is to keep two copies of any information you do not want to lose. Then if one of the copies turns out to be unusable, you still have a duplicate, a **backup** copy.

Backing-up a floppy disk is more convenient if you have two disk drives. You place the original disk in one drive, the backup disk in the other, and give a COPY command, which completes the process in one step. Backing-up a floppy disk on a single drive system is more complicated. You swap the original and backup disks in and out of the drive while the CPU copies portions of the original disk into RAM and then writes them on the backup disk. Eventually, the computer will tell you the copy has been made, but this might be after eight or ten swaps. The number of swaps depends primarily on the relative sizes of RAM and the disks.

Backing-up a hard disk is both more important and more difficult because of its larger storage capacity. The least expensive method is to copy the contents of the hard disk onto floppy disks. This is slow and uses many floppy disks. A 40MB hard disk, for example, holds the same amount of information as thirty-four 1.2MB floppies. One backup method is to buy two hard disk units. Another is to buy a streaming tape drive, a cartridge tape system especially designed to backup and restore the information on hard disks.

tive, ordinary typing paper costs about one dollar for each 250,000 characters of single-sided storage.

Modern hard disks for mainframes and minicomputers store much more information than floppy disks. Hard disks used by mainframe computers can store gigabytes; hard disks attached to personal computers can store between 10 and 500 megabytes. The principal reason hard disks can store more information than floppy disks is they are *denser*; that is, they pack more information per square inch. The aluminum platters used in hard disks are less sensitive than the Mylar used in floppy disks to variations in temperature, humidity, and mechanical stress, which allows the hard disk drive to have more tracks per radial inch and to write more bits per inch along each track.

Another method of packing more information into a hard disk system is to use more recording surfaces by stacking several platters on top of one another, as Figure

# The Computer Itself: The Central Processor and Storage

*Although a supercomputer has thousands of times the speed and storage of a personal computer, they both perform four basic functions: input, output, processing, and storage. This photo essay illustrates the processing and storage components of modern computer systems.*

1. Row after row of integrated circuits are visible in this view of three circuit boards that form a high-speed graphics processor. The brown connectors on the circuit boards are used to plug the graphics processor into a DEC VAX minicomputer. The graphics processor outperforms a VAX 780 by as much as 50 times for graphics tasks such as rotating a model or changing a perspective.

# INSIDE THE SYSTEM UNIT

*Personal computers are housed inside a system unit containing a CPU, primary memory, and—in most systems—disk storage.*

2.   Inside this Macintosh you can see the CRT in front of a circuit board containing analog electronics. The microfloppy disk drive is a metal box below the CRT. Both the CPU and primary memory are hidden on a digital circuit board below the floppy disk drive.

3.   This early IBM PC has two floppy disk drives. The power supply and fan are housed in the black box at right, and four optional circuit boards are standing at left.

4–5.   At the left is an IBM AT; on the right is a Compac 386. Both have the same basic organization: the disk drives are at the right-front; behind them are the power supply and fan; and on the left is room for optional circuit boards.

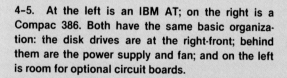

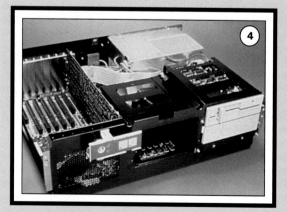

# THE SYSTEM BOARD

At the heart of most personal computers is a system board. *It is a large flat circuit board that lies across the bottom of the system unit.*

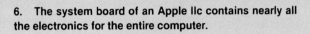
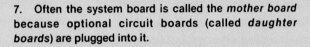

6. The system board of an Apple IIc contains nearly all the electronics for the entire computer.

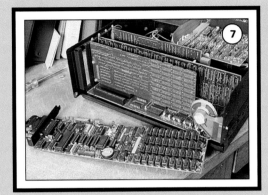

7. Often the system board is called the *mother board* because optional circuit boards (called *daughter boards*) are plugged into it.

8. The "brain" of many IBM and compatible personal computers is the Intel 80286 microprocessor, the large gray integrated circuit at the center of this photo. Depending on the speed of the computer's clock, its operations are paced at speeds of 6 to 12 million cycles per second. The microprocessor receives and sends data in 2-byte chunks. Theoretically, it can manage 16 megabytes of internal memory, but few machines have that much actual memory.

9. Also on the system board is memory. In this photo the author has removed a 256-kilobit memory chip from an IBM AT-clone. The larger chips to the left are ROM chips containing a portion of the MS-DOS operating system.

*window 2*

# EXTERNAL STORAGE

Long-term memory requires some form of external storage. The most common external storage devices are floppy and hard disk drives.

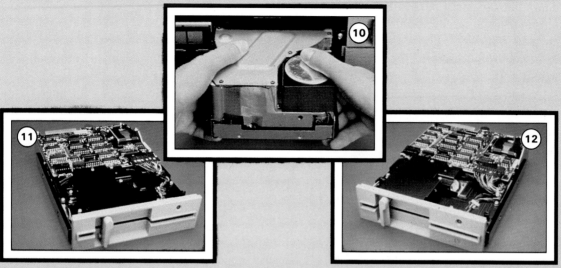

10–12. Here are three types of external storage. On the top is a 20MB (megabyte) hard disk; on the bottom are 1.2MB and 360KB floppy disk drives. Both floppy disk drives look identical from the front.

13. The blue ribbon cables of this IBM AT connect the disk drives to a disk-controller circuit board, which in turn plugs into the system board.

14. This shows the installation of a 40MB hard disk drive. It stores the equivalent of about 13,000 pages of single-spaced typed text.

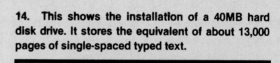

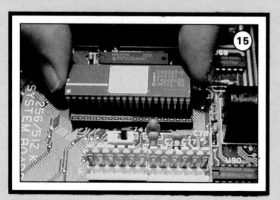

15. An optional math coprocessor is installed in an IBM AT by pushing it into an empty socket on the system board. For programs that perform extensive mathematical operations, this can increase the processor's speed by a factor of ten or more.

# ADDING OPTIONS

*The basic capabilities of a personal computer can often be expanded by adding chips or circuit boards.*

**16.** The yellow arrow points to a circuit board that provides two interfaces (or *ports*) for controlling peripheral devices such as printers, plotters, monitors, or mice.

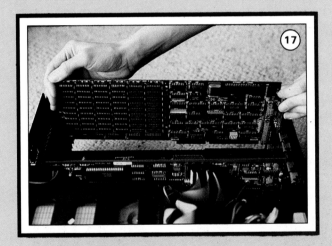

**17.** The capabilities of most computers can be increased by shoving optional circuit boards into *expansion slots*. This photo shows the addition of a multifunction board that provides an additional megabyte of memory and several interface ports.

**18.** This rear view of the IBM AT-clone shows eight expansion slots filled with four cards: a disk-controller card, an EGA (enhanced graphics adapter) display card, a multifunction card with memory and two interface ports, and a mouse-controller card. The three gray cables lead to a color display, a laser printer, and a mouse.

# DISK STORAGE

**Storage on disks provides fast and reliable access to large quantities of data.**

20. Even a tiny particle of dust can scratch the surface of a spinning hard disk, so manufacturing is done in "clean rooms" to reduce the number of airborne particles.

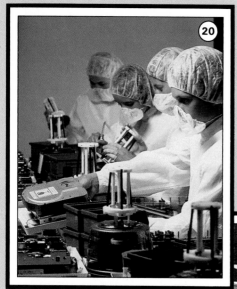

19. Hard disks store data on rapidly spinning metal platters that are coated with magnetic oxides. Each platter is polished to a mirror finish to provide a uniform surface for extremely dense storage of data.

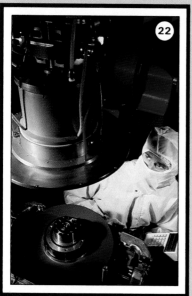

21. Large-capacity hard disks are created by stacking a number of disk platters into one disk drive assembly, called a disk pack. The read/write heads of the disk drive move in and out between the disk platters, storing data on both sides of most platters.

22. A disk drive assembly is loaded with contamination-free precision by a special-function industrial robot.

**23.**

**24.** In this photo an IBM 3380 disk drive is being assembled in Vimercate, Italy. Model 3380 disk drives are among the most powerful of IBM's disk drives. Each 3380 disk pack can store 2.5 gigabytes (a gigabyte is roughly one billion characters) and has a data transfer rate of 3MB per second.

**23.** These 5 1/4-inch hard disk drives fit in the same space as a standard 5 1/4-inch floppy disk drive and feature from 20 to 40MB of storage, a data transfer rate that exceeds 1/2MB per second, and an average access time of 40 milliseconds (less than 1/20th of a second).

**25.** A disk pack is inserted in a disk drive. Removable disk drives are slightly more expensive and are more likely to be damaged by dust particles than fixed disks. In a fixed disk the disk platters are permanently sealed inside a housing at the factory. The obvious advantage of a removable disk drive is that more than one disk pack can be purchased for each drive, enabling data to be stored inexpensively on off-line disk packs.

**26.** Optical disks hold the promise of providing very large amounts of storage. For example, this removable 12-inch disk can record 1.2 gigabytes (1,200 megabytes) per side. Over 140 of these cartridges can be mounted in a jukebox system, replacing roughly five million pages of data that would fill more than 500 4-drawer file cabinets.

*window 2*

# TAPE STORAGE

28. Increasingly, mainframe computer centers are switching to magnetic tape cartridges, which are easier to load and require less storage space.

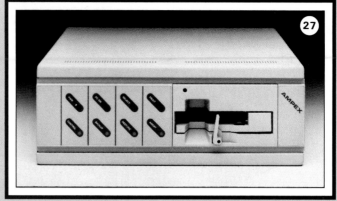

27. This small storage unit is designed for personal computer systems. It combines a 20MB fixed disk with a 25MB tape drive for backing-up the fixed disk. The tape drive accepts 1/4-inch tape cartridges and can find any file on the tape in 92 seconds.

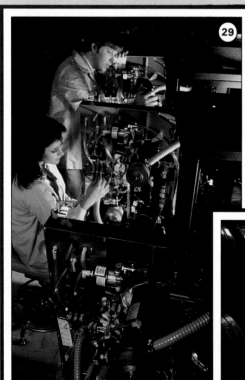

29. Large commercial tape drives use vacuum systems to start and stop loops of tape quickly without placing excessive stress on the tape. Here, data cables are being attached to tape drives made by Storage Technology Corporation.

30. Magnetic tape is an excellent medium for inexpensive, long-term data storage. Because tapes provide sequential data storage, they are rarely used when data is being processed. Instead, they are used to back-up hard disks and to store infrequently used data.

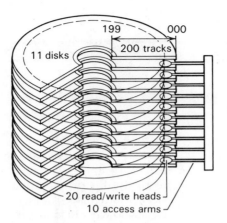

**Figure 2.11**
A multiple-platter hard disk contains many recording surfaces to increase recording capacity.

11 disks

199 · · 000
200 tracks

20 read/write heads
10 access arms

2.11 shows. Instead of reading from only one track at a time, a multiple-platter hard disk drive can simultaneously read from one track on each disk surface.

Hard disks have another advantage: They transfer data faster than floppy disks. Because they store data more compactly along each track, every revolution of the disk brings more data beneath the read/write heads. Moreover, hard disks spin faster than floppy disks. The standard speed for 5 1/4-inch floppy disks is 300 rpm. But a 5 1/4-inch hard disk is likely to rotate at least ten times faster, from 3,000 to 5,000 rpm; thus the transfer rates are faster for a hard disk.

The fast spinning of a hard disk makes the environment inside a hard disk drive very windy. The read/write heads are carefully shaped so that they float on a cushion of air a few thousandths of an inch above the disk. Maintaining this gap is important. At 3,000 rpm (approximately 200 mph at the edge), a read/write head that collides with the disk platter soon becomes hot and scorches itself and the platter. Although this doesn't happen often, after a **head crash**, all data on the disk is lost forever, and the disk drive must be sent back to the factory for repair.

Access times are also faster for hard disks than floppy disks. Whenever a computer is operating, its hard disk is spinning. This keeps the disk heads floating properly, and there is no waiting for the disk to come up to speed. Floppy disks cannot afford to turn constantly because their disk heads rub against the recording surface whenever the disk is turning. Floppy disks have roughly an 80-hour expected life of turning time. This is adequate as long as the disk is turning only while reading or writing, but it is not long enough to allow continual rotation. To bring a floppy disk to operating speed takes about half a second.

Some hard disk drives accept **removable disk** cartridges, or disk packs, that are similar to floppy disks. Changing hard disk cartridges takes longer than changing floppy disks because removable hard disk drives go through an air filtration cycle before beginning operation.

Other hard disks called **fixed disks** are built with the disk platter permanently mounted inside an air-tight, factory-sealed unit. Fixed disks do not need an air filtration system because dirty air cannot get in. But fixed disks also have a disadvantage.

## A Word About . . . *Optical Disks*

*Optical disks may eventually push hard disks into museums along with 78-rpm phonograph records and buggy whips. But it seems more likely that magnetic storage will continue to dominate, leaving optical storage with applications that require rapid access to large-scale databases made up of permanent or historical records.*

**Optical disks** store large amounts of information on rigid plastic disks that are removable like floppy disks. They use the same laser-based technology as audio *compact disk (CD)* players, which debuted in 1983 and already have higher sales than turntables. An incredible 550MB of information fits on one side of a CD. With the appropriate interface, any personal computer can read the digital signals on a CD. High-volume production techniques allow many copies of a master disk to be made for less than $5 a copy. This provides a low-cost solution to massive data storage needs, but its usefulness is restricted because the contents of a standard CD cannot be altered. For this reason, read-only optical disks are called **CD ROM disks**. The main advantage of CD ROM drives is they are inexpensive to build because of the vast market for audio CD players. CD ROM drives sell for less than $800, and their price is likely to fall rapidly.

One of the first general applications of CD ROM technology is Microsoft Bookshelf, a $295 disk containing a collection of ten reference works. The disk offers a potpourri of writers productivity tools, including complete copies of the *1987 World Almanac and Book of Facts*, the *Chicago Manual of Style*, *Bartlett's Familiar Quotations*, and the *U.S. Zip Code Directory*. Included with the CD ROM disk is software that allows the disk to work conveniently with a variety of word processing programs.

Some optical disk drives can write on the disk by burning small marks on its surface with a laser. Later, these marks can be sensed by another, lower-power laser. These disk drives are thus called *write-once, read-many* **(WORM) drives**. Although they are not yet practical for temporary storage of data that must be altered frequently, the drives provide a reliable way to backup hard disks. They also appeal to business users who want to maintain an audit trail of the activity in a computer system: It is not possible to erase information from a WORM drive.

A 5 1/4-inch optical disk can store from 200 to 800MB of information—about five hundred times the amount of information of a similarly sized floppy disk. Larger optical disks can hold up to 4GB (4,000MB). Like floppy disks, optical disks are removable and interchangeable. This makes it practical to distribute copies of large databases. A large firm might distribute optical disks containing the firm's parts catalog to branch offices. Each branch office would then have instant access to complete information about the firm's products and prices without having to search through reams of paper or peer at microfiche. In this application, the non-erasability of the media is an advantage.

A 5 1/4-inch optical disk drive. The WORM drive can store 800 megabytes on each disk.

Once a fixed disk becomes full of information, old data must be deleted before new data can be stored.

In short, hard disks offer several advantages over floppy disks. A 20MB hard disk can store hundreds of useful programs and still have enough room for the equivalent of several thousand pages of typed text. Every piece of information in the disk is instantly available; access times are less than a tenth of a second.

Hard disks also have several disadvantages. Hard disk drives are noisier than floppy disk drives because of their constant high-speed spinning. More important is their sensitivity. Head crashes can be caused by dust or cigarette smoke inside the drive or a good thump to the side of the drive. Because hard disks operate on extremely precise mechanical tolerances, they are more sensitive to shock than floppy disks. This has retarded their use in portable computers. Of course, bouncing any disk drive on a hard surface is a bad idea, but bouncing a hard disk drive can be disastrous.

## File Storage Methods

### Disk Storage

The amount of information stored on a disk depends on four factors:

1. The number of tracks (concentric circles) of data from the inside to the outside edge of the disk. Generally, between 40 and 80 tracks are on a floppy disk, and between 200 and 1,000 on a hard disk.

2. The number of sectors per track. Recall that a sector is the smallest unit of information sent between the disk drive and the CPU.

3. The number of bytes stored in each sector. Generally, floppy disks store between 128 and 512 bytes per sector; hard disks for large computers can store 8,000 bytes or more per sector.

4. Whether data is written on one or both sides of the disk, that is, whether storage is *single sided* or *double sided*. As we have seen, hard disks often use multiple platters to extend the capacity of a single drive.

For example, the Apple Macintosh records 80 tracks on a double-sided microfloppy (3 1/2-inch) disk. Each track has an average of 10 sectors, and each sector stores 512 bytes. This gives $80 \times 10 \times 512 \times 2 = 819,200$ bytes, or 800KB per disk.

It is easy to get carried away with the technical details of how information is stored on disks. Just as you do not have to know much about a record to play it, so you do not have to know much about a disk to store information on it. Your computer automatically handles the details of storing your information, determining which tracks and sectors to use. When the disk becomes full, the computer will not allow you to store new information until you delete some old information. You should know the storage capacity of each disk, but knowing how this figure relates to tracks and sectors is not so important. It is useful, however, to know how the information stored on a disk or tape is organized.

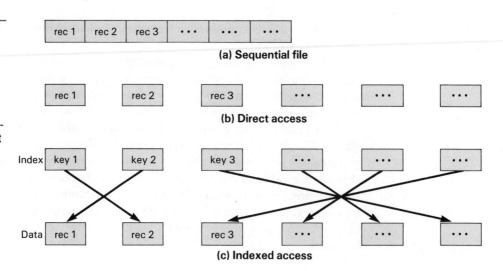

**Figure 2.12**
**(a)** With a sequential file access is slow because intermediate records must be read to access a certain record. **(b)** Direct-access files permit fast access because intermediate records can be skipped in order to get a certain record. **(c)** Indexed files provide flexible access because records can be retrieved in ascending order by first looking up field values in an index file.

**(a) Sequential file**

**(b) Direct access**

**(c) Indexed access**

## File Storage

How information is organized on a disk can affect how long it takes a computer to retrieve data and how much room it takes to store a file. In this section, we briefly introduce the terminology that describes file structure.

A **file** is a collection of information stored on a tape or disk. Think of a disk as a filing cabinet drawer full of manila folders (files), each of which can contain a different type of information. Some files hold text (as in a word processing document), and others hold numbers, pictures, or programs. A file that contains pure text is a *text file*. A file that contains a program is a *binary file* because programs contain binary information understandable to the hardware.

A disk or tape can store many files, so a special **directory** file is kept on each disk or tape to keep track of all other files. A directory is like a telephone book—it contains the name and number of every file on the disk. A *filename* is any string of characters assigned to the file, such as PAYROLL, CHAP.2, or MYPROG.BAS. The name uniquely identifies each file; it is used by an application program to locate, open, read or write, and close a file. The *file number* identifies the file's location on the disk; we can let the computer take care of the number and not be concerned with it.

Rather than a single directory, most computer systems use a **hierarchical directory**, a treelike structure containing many subdirectories. The **root directory** contains the names of files and other subdirectories, much as one file folder can be used to group other file folders. Each **subdirectory**, in turn, contains the names of files or more subdirectories. Subdirectories help group files logically so that you can find them easily. For example, you might use a different subdirectory to store files related to each of your classes. A hierarchical directory is particularly important if you use a hard disk because a hard disk can store thousands of files.

Files can also be categorized according to how their information is read (see Figure 2.12). A **sequential file** contains information that can be accessed only sequentially—as if it were on a tape. Most programs are stored on disk as sequential files because they are loaded all at once into primary memory. An entire sequential file can be quickly loaded into memory.

Some files contain data that need to be accessed out of order. A **record** is collection of related data items, such as a name and address in a mailing list. A **direct-access file** contains records that can be accessed directly without reading all intervening records in the file. Direct-access files must be stored on direct-access devices such as disks. Obviously, the main advantage of a direct-access file is the speed that any particular record can be found in. However, the main disadvantage of a direct-access file is that it cannot store variable-length records.

An **indexed file** is actually two or more direct-access files. One file contains the data, and one or more other files contain the indexes to the data file (see Figure 2.12). The indexes are used like an index in a book. Values called *access keys* are taken from the data file and placed in the indexes in ascending order. Data is retrieved by first consulting the appropriate index; then the "page number" from the index is used to find the desired record in the data file.

Indexed files are flexible. Records can be retrieved in a certain order without having to sort them. New information is entered, old information deleted, and information retrieved according to its content rather than its position within the data file. An indexed file requires more disk space (to store the indexes) and takes more processing steps to store data than a direct-access file.

Software developers agonize over selecting a file structure because of the trade-offs among speed, storage overhead, and flexibility. Sequential files are good for storing text to be sent to another computer by telephone, programs to be read into memory, or text created by a word processor. Direct-access files are good for storing frequently accessed and updated information such as that found in a database management system or business application. Indexed files are good for a variety of applications ranging from database management to accounting.

# COMPARING MEMORY SYSTEMS

No one would put up with the slow speed of external storage if primary memory were nonvolatile, removable, and cheap. But as Table 2.2 shows, each storage method has its merits. Most computer systems, particularly large ones, combine several storage methods in an attempt to blend the best features from each technology.

Table 2.2 reveals an extraordinary range of speeds and cost among storage methods. Access times and transfer rates vary by many powers of ten. For example, the difference in access time between a floppy disk drive and primary memory is greater than the difference in speed between a slug and a jet airplane.

Compare the cost of the access mechanisms with the cost of the removable recording media. The one-time cost of a removable hard disk drive may deter you from buying one even though each disk pack is relatively inexpensive per unit of storage. Floppy disk drives are ten times more expensive per byte of on-line storage than the disk drives used by mainframes, but a floppy drive serves the need for a low-cost, direct-access, removable-medium mechanism.

Storage methods are continually being developed to serve a special need or fill a niche in price and performance. For example, a **mass storage unit** combines

**Table 2.2**
**A Comparison of Memory Storage Methods**

| Storage Type | Access Mechanism | | |
| --- | --- | --- | --- |
| | *Type* | *Access Time* | *Cost of Drive ($)* |
| **Microcomputers** | | | |
| RAM/ROM chips | Random | 200 ns | 500/MB |
| 3 1/2-inch microfloppy | Direct | 0.2–.4 sec | 100–400 |
| 5 1/4-inch floppy | Direct | 0.2–.4 sec | 50–200 |
| Cartridge hard disk | Direct | 40–90 ms | 800–2,000 |
| Fixed disk | Direct | 20–90 ms | 200–5,000 |
| Streamer tape | Sequential | About 1 min | 500–2,000 |
| Optical disk (WORM) | Direct | 0.2 sec | 1,600–4,000 |
| Optical disk (CD-ROM) | Direct | 0.4 sec | 500–900 |
| **Minis and Mainframes** | | | |
| RAM/ROM chips | Random | 10–150 ns | 2,000–10,000/MB |
| Removable disk | Direct | 25 ms | 5,000–35,000 |
| Fixed disk | Direct | 25 ms | 15,000–40,000 |
| Mass storage unit | Combined | 1–6 sec | 500,000–1,000,000 |
| Tape | Sequential | About 1 min | 5,000–20,000 |

Notes:  KB = kilobyte       min = minutes
MB = megabyte     sec = seconds
GB = gigabyte      ms = millisecond (thousandth of a second)
ns = nanosecond (billionth of a second)

several tape cartridges, a jukeboxlike tape-loading mechanism, a hard disk drive, and an intelligent controller into a unit that can manage many gigabytes of on-line storage.

## Summary

All computers—from hand-held models to huge mainframes—have the same functional organization. The four functional units are the CPU with its primary memory, external storage, input units, and output units. We discussed the CPU, primary memory, and external storage in this chapter. We discuss the input and output units in the next chapter.

The CPU has a control unit that supervises the rest of the CPU, including the arithmetic/logic unit, which does all calculations and data manipulation. Instructions from a stored program are copied from primary memory to the control unit, where they guide the hardware's operations.

For personal computers, the CPU consists of a microprocessor, memory chips, and some timing and support chips, all of which are usually mounted on one circuit board. A microprocessor is a single chip containing both the control unit and the ALU. Personal computers can do the same things larger computers can do, but they are slower and store less information.

For accessing large amounts of information quickly, on-line external storage devices are needed. Direct-access storage devices, such as disk drives, provide fast

| | **Media** | | | |
|---|---|---|---|---|
| **Capacity** | **Transfer Rate/Second** | **Cost of Media ($)** | **Volatile?** | **Principal Use** |
| 64KB–4MB | 1MB–5MB | – | Yes | Main memory |
| 400KB–1.6MB | 30KB | 1–5 | No | On-line/archive |
| 400KB–2MB | 30KB | 1–3 | No | On-line/archive |
| 10MB–40MB | 0.4MB | 90 | No | On-line/archive |
| 10MB–300MB | 0.4MB–1MB | – | No | On-line |
| 20MB–500MB | 60KB | 20 | No | Back-up/archive |
| 200MB–800MB | 0.2MB | 50–100 | No | On-line/Archive |
| .5GB–4GB | 0.2MB | 20 | No | On-line ROM |
| 1MB–64MB | 4MB–64MB | – | Yes | Main memory |
| 100MB–500MB | 1MB–3MB | 0.5K–1K | No | On-line/archive |
| 0.5GB–5GB | 2MB–4MB | – | No | On-line |
| 0.5GB–5GB | 3MB | 10 | No | On-line/archive |
| 100MB–500MB | 0.05MB–1MB | 10 | No | Archive |

access to any data they contain. Long-term storage of archival information is achieved by low-cost, permanent media such as magnetic tape and optical disks.

## Key Terms

access time

address

archival copy

backup

CD ROM disks

clocks, clock rate

direct-access file

directory

file

fixed disk

floating-point number

floppy disk

gigabyte (GB)

hard disk

head crash

hierarchical directory

indexed file

instruction set

kilobit

kilobyte (KB)

mass storage unit

megabyte (MB)

megahertz (MHz)

memory chips

MFLOP

microsecond

| | |
|---|---|
| millisecond | sector |
| nanosecond | sequential file |
| on-line | sequential storage |
| optical disks | streaming tape drive |
| parity bit | subdirectory |
| pipelining | track |
| program overlay | transparent |
| random-access memory (RAM) | virtual memory |
| read-only memory (ROM) | word |
| record | WORM drive |
| removable disk | write-protected |
| root directory | |

## Discussion Questions

1. Each word of a personal computer's memory is of limited size—8, 16, or 32 bits, depending on the computer. How can a computer represent very large and very small numbers in such small words?

2. Would it make sense to have WOM, write-only memory?

3. Why are there so few kinds of microprocessors?

4. What determines the speed of a CPU? When can you say one CPU is faster than another?

5. In a truly random-access memory, each word of memory can be located in exactly the same length of time. Is this true for floppy disks and hard disks? For internal memory?

6. Why is a hard disk drive faster than a floppy disk drive, and why does a hard disk hold more information than a floppy disk?

7. What is the difference (if any) between a CPU and a microprocessor?

8. What is a head crash? What causes a head crash?

9. Compare a disk with a book. What part of a book is analogous to the disk's directory? To the disk's files?

10. What are the advantages of sequential file structures compared with direct-access file structures?

## Exercises

1. Look in a microprocessor's reference manual to find the relative speeds for the operations for arithmetic and data movement. How much faster is addition than division?

2. Look up the memory size of your personal computer (or any personal computer if you do not have one) and the memory requirements of some popular application programs.

3. A record player is a read-only device. List some other read-only or write-only devices in your home.

4. Find the number of tracks, the sector size, and the density for the floppy disks on your personal computer. How many bytes of data can be stored on each disk?

5. What is a cylinder? List the reasons why mainframe disks are faster and able to store more information than personal computer disks.

# Input and Output

| Input Devices | Output Devices |
|---|---|
| *Keyboards* | *Printers* |
| *Selection Devices* | *Displays* |
| *Other Input Devices* | *Plotters* |
| | *Other Output Devices* |

Input and output devices are the eyes, ears, arms, legs, and mouth of a computer. They allow the computer to communicate and interact with its environment. Without them, computers would be useless.

*Input devices* are conversion machines that translate events in the computer's environment into digital signals, a process called *digitizing*. Pressing a key on a keyboard is one frequently digitized event, but the arrival of radio waves at a satellite receiver and the vibration of air pressure at a microphone can also be digitized. In fact, anything that can be sensed electronically is a candidate for computer input. Some machines allow a computer to "hear" by converting spoken words into electrical signals; others allow a computer to "see" by converting printed text into electrical signals. Input devices are often as sophisticated and cleverly designed as the computer systems they serve.

*Output devices* are also conversion machines, but they convert digital signals into actions. For example, printers accept digital signals and convert them into the placement of ink on paper.

For automobiles, a steering wheel has been found to be the single best "input device," but computers use a diversity of input devices including keyboards, light pens, mice, character recognition devices, voice recognition devices, and the infrared sensor in the nose of a heat-seeking missile. Output devices range from printers, displays, plotters, telephones, and speech synthesizers to missile warheads. There are literally thousands of types of input and output devices, each with its own special use and niche in the marketplace.

In this chapter, we emphasize the input and output devices you are most likely to use. We also give you information about choosing the right I/O device for the task at hand and using it correctly.

## INPUT DEVICES

### Keyboards

By far the most common input device is the keyboard. It is standard equipment on virtually every personal computer. Except for specialized applications, such as drawing pictures or pointing at objects on the screen, the keyboard is the primary way of communicating with computers. In the future, keyboards will likely be replaced by microphones attached to speech recognition units, enabling you to talk to computers (see Figure 3.1). But today, if you want to use a computer effectively, you must have some ability to type.

The standard layout for typewriter keyboards was developed in the last century. Known as the *QWERTY keyboard* (after the first six alphabetic keys), it was deliberately designed to slow typing to prevent the hammers on early mechanical typewriters, from jamming on their way to the paper. With the invention of improved mechanical typewriters and then electric typewriters, this goal became irrelevant. It is of no concern whatsoever with computer keyboards. Still, the QWERTY layout is used on nearly all computer keyboards. Typists, accustomed to the layout, did not want to change.

A badly designed keyboard can make an otherwise reasonable computer hard to deal with. *Membrane keyboards,* which have pictures of key-tops drawn on a flat plastic membrane, rely on pressure to register each keystroke and are not suitable for extensive typing. Portable terminals and personal computers often have *compact keyboards,* which have less than full-size keys or reduced spacing between keys. Unless you have small hands, you may find it difficult to touch-type on a compact

**Figure 3.1**
This keyboard includes a voice recognition unit that is limited to a vocabulary with at most 160 words. The operator speaks into the microphone. A processor inside the keyboard analyzes the spoken sounds. Eventually each spoken word is converted into a keystroke or series of keystrokes.

keyboard. Even among full-size, full-stroke keyboards, a wide range of options and quality exist. Some keyboards feel mushy. They do not have a clear point at which the key seems to fall through to the bottom of the stroke. You may find it easier to type if an audible click accompanies each keystroke. But if the click is produced by mechanical key switches, you cannot adjust the volume. Other keyboards generate clicks through a speaker, permitting the sound to be adjusted up for work in a busy office or down for late-night typing at home.

The main thing to remember when using a computer keyboard is the keys do not have fixed meanings. On a typewriter, striking the [P] key will always print the letter *P* on the paper. But on a computer keyboard, striking the [P] key might display a letter *P* on the screen, or print a file, or pull an address out of a list of mailing labels. It all depends on how the program instructs the CPU to interpret the character.

Each keyboard has its own quirks. Most computer keyboards have **repeating keys.** Pressing one of these keys for more than a second generates a constant stream of characters. Clumsy typists find repeating keys a bother because of the need to delete extra characters.

A particularly useful feature is a **keyboard buffer,** which allows you to continue typing even though the CPU is busy doing other tasks. The buffer stores the characters you type until the CPU is ready to accept them. This feature, sometimes called *type-ahead*, makes slow programs more bearable. You can begin typing a new command or text while the CPU is still working on the last operation. Keyboard buffers have room for a limited number of characters, from two to twenty or more. Characters in the buffer do not appear on the screen until the CPU has accepted them for processing and echoed them to the screen. If the buffer becomes full, the keyboard is likely to beep in response to further typing.

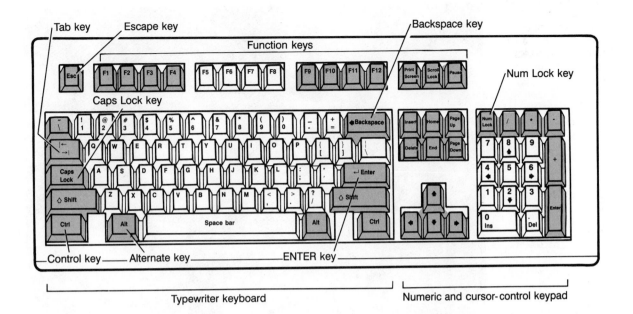

Tab key    Escape key                                    Backspace key
                         Function keys                                    Num Lock key

Caps Lock key

Control key ——— Alternate key ——————— ENTER key ——

Typewriter keyboard              Numeric and cursor-control keypad

**Figure 3.2**
The layout of an IBM PC keyboard

Computer keyboards usually have more keys than a typewriter keyboard. The
extra keys can help you give commands, point at objects, and enter numbers. Let
us look at some of the keys on a IBM PC keyboard (see Figure 3.2):

- *Function keys* are used to give commands. In some programs, the function keys
  are *user-programmable;* that is, you can give them whatever meaning you want
  while using that program. Other programs give the function keys preassigned
  meanings and often provide a plastic keyboard overlay or *template* to help you
  remember what each key does.

- Except for typing normal text, the most common typing operations on computers are entering numbers and moving the **cursor,** a highlight that indicates
  where things will happen next. The cursor often is a blinking rectangle or underline. On an IBM PC, entering numbers and moving the cursor are combined in a dual-purpose *numeric and cursor-control keypad.* The *Num-Lock key*
  determines which mode is active. Pressing Num-Lock once locks the keypad
  in numeric mode so that the 8/up-arrow key generates the number 8. Pressing
  Num-Lock again returns the keypad to it cursor-movement mode. In this
  mode, pressing the 8/up-arrow key is likely to move the cursor up the screen
  one line.

- The *control key* (labeled Ctrl) operates like the shift key, but instead of a capital
  letter, it generates a *control letter* that has a different character code. Control letters rarely appear on the screen; instead, they are used to give commands to

programs. To type a control letter, you press [Ctrl] while pressing another key. The effect will depend entirely on the program being run. For example, pressing [Ctrl] and the up-arrow key in a word processing program may move the cursor to the top of the screen. Some manuals use the caret symbol (^) to describe control letters, as in ^B.

- Like the control key, the *alternate key* (labeled Alt) is used in combination with other keys to give commands.

- The *Caps-Lock key* is a toggle key: One tap activates it, and the next deactivates it. When Caps Lock is "on," it raises all the alphabetic keys to uppercase. Unlike the Shift-Lock key on a typewriter keyboard, the Caps-Lock key affects neither the punctuation keys nor the symbol/number keys on the top row of the keyboard. To obtain characters on the upper half of the keys, such as the colon, you still need to use one of the Shift keys.

- The *Enter* or *Return key* is used to enter commands. For example, if you have highlighted an item on a menu, pressing Enter is the usual way to acknowledge that you want to select the highlighted item. When you are using a word processor, the Enter key is also used to create new paragraphs.

## Selection Devices

Many computer operations involve pointing, selecting, or moving items already on the screen. Often you can perform these tasks more quickly with a pointing device

**Figure 3.4**
A pen is used to point to an area on a tablet, as shown here, or directly on the display screen.

than with the cursor keys. In this section, we discuss several pointing devices: the touch screen, touch tablet, pen, mouse, and puck.

Most people would say their finger is the most natural pointing device. The **touch screen** in Figure 3.3 uses invisible sensors to tell where a finger or pencil touches the surface of the screen. The screen looks perfectly normal because the sensors are hidden in the slanted surface surrounding the screen. The accuracy of a touch screen is limited to the nearest character or, even worse, group of characters. But then fingers are far too blunt to point to tiny dots on the screen.

Touch screens work in a variety of ways. Perhaps the most common mechanism is the *infrared detector*. Infrared rays (heat) scan the surface of the screen. When your finger interferes with the scanning rays, sensors pick up the obstruction and transmit information about the location touched.

A **touch tablet** is an electronic blackboard that can sense a pencil or stylus on its surface. The touch-sensitive tablet transmits the location of the stylus to the computer whenever it is touched.

Figure 3.4 shows a related pointing device, the *digitizing pen*. One type of digitizing pen, the **light pen,** reads light from the display screen, thus allowing you to point to a spot on the screen. Another type, the **sonic pen,** uses reflected or emitted sound to determine the position of the pen. If you listen closely, you can hear a sonic pen crackle.

To use either a light pen or a sonic pen, you aim it at a region of a touch tablet or screen and then press a button on the pen. The pen reads the location of the region and sends this information to the computer. The computer uses the information to determine what was being pointed at when the button was pressed.

Figure 3.5 shows a **mouse,** a hand-operated pointing device. As you drag the mouse across a flat surface, it relays directional information to the computer. On

**Figure 3.5**
A mouse is used
mostly to point at
and select options
on the screen.

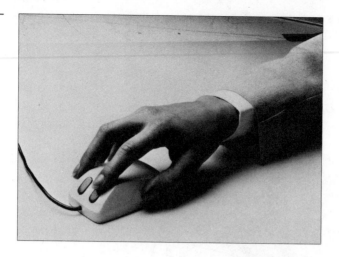

top of most mice are one or two buttons, which are pressed when you want the computer to take notice of the cursor's current position on the screen.

A **puck** is used much like a mouse, but it also has a small magnifying glass with cross hairs. It is especially good for entering pictorial data from architectural drawings, maps, aerial photographs, blueprints, and medical images.

Both the mouse and puck can register very small movements, permitting you to point to precise locations. Becoming accustomed to using either of these takes a very short time, although most people are skeptical until they have tried one. But if your desk looks like a rat's nest, working with a mouse will be difficult because you need clear desktop space to use it effectively. The major advantages of a mouse over other pointing devices are its accuracy and proven efficiency. Your arm is not likely to tire as quickly when using a mouse as when you use a pen or touch screen. Furthermore, a mouse is inexpensive and rugged.

## Other Input Devices

Input devices may be hand-held or as large as a 200-inch telescope. They may be on-line and used for interactive data entry, or they may be used to collect data in batches before processing. An amazing variety of input devices exists, and each provides a computer with a specific kind of tactile, visual, audible, or other input.

Some input devices go well beyond the abilities of our own senses. Magnetic resonance scanners allow computers to "see" inside our bodies. Temperature-sensing devices collect on-line data about the temperature and humidity of buildings so that a computer can adjust the climate of a warehouse, factory, or office building. Signals from video cameras in robots on an assembly line allow computers to control the actions of "seeing-eye" robots. Scientific labs use a variety of sensors to collect data from experiments; the data is entered automatically into the computer's memory for processing and graphical display. Obviously, to assume the sensory abilities of computer systems are inherently limited is groundless. This prejudice only discourages the innovative use of computers.

# OUTPUT DEVICES

The two output devices most familiar to people who use computer systems are printers and visual display units like screen monitors. Printers provide a permanent, printed record of information. Displays provide a quick and inexpensive way to view information.

## Printers

Typewriters combine a keyboard for input and paper for output in one device. Personal computers separate these functions into two units, a keyboard and a printer. Anything typed on a typewriter is printed automatically because the keyboard and print mechanism are mechanically (or electrically) coupled. A computer's keyboard is not connected directly to the printer. Instead, the keyboard and printer are each connected separately to the CPU. Characters typed on the keyboard are *not* automatically sent to the printer (or display screen) unless the program tells the CPU to do so.

Printers are classified in many ways. They can be classified according to whether they use an impact or a nonimpact method of placing ink on the page. Most printers used with personal computers today are **impact printers**. Like a typewriter, they form an image by bringing ribbon and paper into physical contact with each other. **Nonimpact printers** are quieter than impact printers because no print hammer or similar mechanism actually strikes the paper. Examples of nonimpact printers include thermal, ink-jet, and laser printers.

Another way to classify printers is on how much they print at a time. **Character printers** print only one character at a time by moving the print mechanism back and forth across the page. **Line** and **page printers** print an entire line or page of characters in one operation. Because they cannot slow down or pause during a print operation, these printers generally have a print buffer that lets them store a line or page of information before the printing starts. On page printers, these buffers can be quite large. For example, an 8 1/2-by-11-inch page filled with 300 dots per inch contains 8,415,000 dots, roughly a megabyte of memory.

Yet another way to classify printers is on whether they generate a pattern of dots or fully formed, raised images. **Dot matrix printers** create each character by printing dots in a pattern, but **daisy-wheel printers** create each character by striking an embossed image of a character against an inked ribbon and paper.

Dot matrix printers are so called because of how they produce each character. Instead of printing a solid letter, a matrix printer prints an array of dots in a pattern that only approximates the font of a typewriter (see Figure 3.6). Most inexpensive dot matrix printers use a *print head,* a mechanism that holds from nine to twenty-four short wires or pins. As the print head sweeps back and forth across the paper, the pins shoot forward into the ribbon to create dots on the paper.

The number and size of the dots determines the quality of the print. The best matrix printers use many small, overlapping dots to build each character. The least

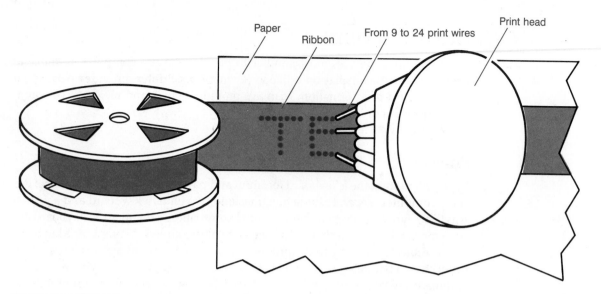

**Figure 3.6**
**(a)** As the print head of a dot matrix printer moves back and forth, tiny wires or pins strike an inked ribbon to form dots on the paper. **(b)** A sample from the Epson LQ-1500, a 24-pin matrix printer. It prints draft-quality letters at 200 cps and near-letter-quality letters at 67 cps.

Until now you had to make a decision, letters, or slow printing with a daisy

*Introducing the*

In draft mode, the LQ-1500 del CPS and in the letter quality mode 67 CPS. The LQ-1500 can print up to elite, proportional, *italic,* super control.

expensive ones generate crudely shaped characters clearly identifiable as computer output. For example, inexpensive 9-pin printers have a resolution of about 75 dots per inch, whereas high-quality 24-pin printers can have a resolution of better than 200 dots per inch. Most manufacturers claim their 24-pin printers produce *letter-quality* output, but this is arguable.

There are also nonimpact dot matrix printers, such as thermal printers and ink-jet printers. **Thermal printers** burn dark spots on heat-sensitive paper. The paper is usually expensive, has a shiny surface, and tends to fade over time. On the positive side, thermal printers are inexpensive and make only a whispering, crinkly noise as they singe the paper.

**Ink-jet printers** work by squirting tiny droplets of liquid ink at the paper. On some systems, magnetic fields deflect each drop to the proper position by acting on the drop's static electricity. The print head shown in Figure 3.7 fires droplets straight

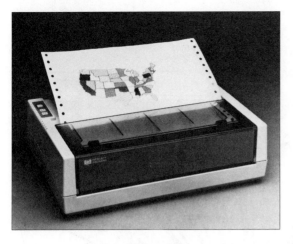

**Figure 3.7**
On the left is an inexpensive 150-cps ink-jet printer. On the right is a close-up view of the printer's disposable print head, which contains a rubber pouch of liquid ink.

at the paper from twelve microscopic nozzles arranged vertically along the print head. In this system, each droplet is ejected by instantly vaporizing a tiny amount of ink behind one of the nozzles, giving momentum to the ink in the nozzle.

If your output need not look as if it were just removed from an office typewriter, matrix printers have several attractive features:

- They are less costly than daisy-wheel printers. Roughly, they range from $200 to $1,000 instead of from $400 to $2,000.

- They are much faster than daisy-wheel printers. Slow matrix printers print 60 **characters per second (cps),** but 200 cps or more is not unusual.

- They usually are not limited to one size or style of character (see Figure 3.6). Because the characters are formed from dot patterns, they can be arranged in Greek, gothic, boldface, or italic fonts with equal ease.

- They can print graphical images as well as text. With the proper software, a matrix printer can print bar charts, line graphs, company logos, letterheads, your personal signature, and even coarse-grained photographs.

**Daisy-wheel printers** can generate output indistinguishable from that of a good typewriter. This means the edges of each printed character are smooth, or fully formed.

The *daisy wheel* is a flat plastic or metal circle with ninety-six or more spokes radiating from its center (see Figure 3.8). On the tip of each spoke is an embossed image of a character. The wheel rotates continuously. As the required spoke moves in front of the print hammer, the spoke is struck onto the ribbon and paper, causing one character to be printed.

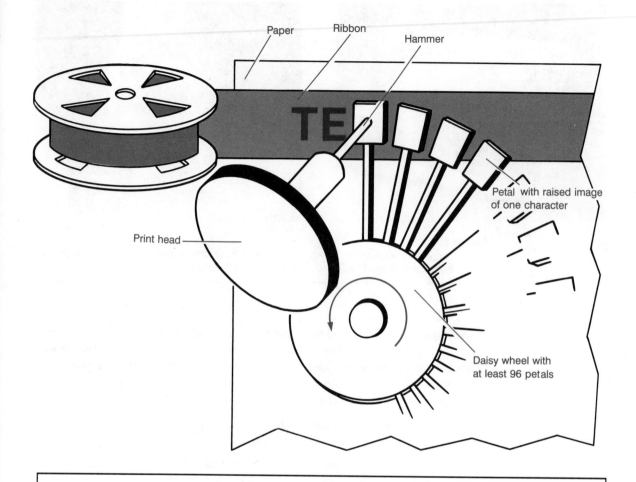

Paper    Ribbon    Hammer

Print head

Petal with raised image
of one character

Daisy wheel with
at least 96 petals

**Bold letters** are printed twice, shifted slightly for the second printing.

Super scripts and Sub scripts require the paper to be advanced and retracted.

**Double-striking** is not visible with a quality ribbon, but works with faded cloth ribbons.

<u>Underlining</u> <u>text</u> is used more than ~~striking out passages~~.

Overprinting prints two characters in the same position, as in Ø.

Changing the **pitch** (the number of characters printed per inch) c a n   s t r e t c h   a   l i n e   o u t or squeeze it together.

**Figure 3.8**
**(a)** A daisy-wheel printer creates an image by striking the raised image of characters against an inked ribbon. **(b)** Character enhancements available from a daisy-wheel printer.

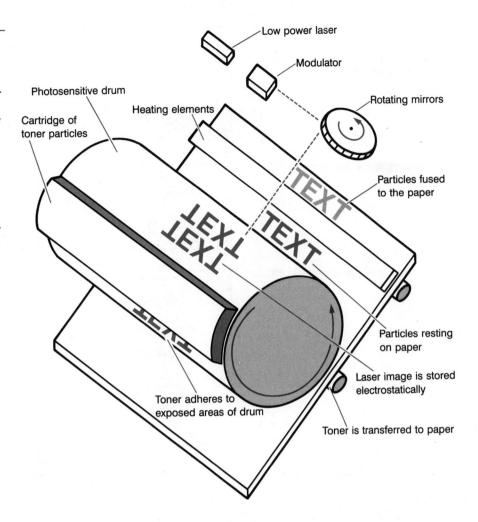

**Figure 3.9**
All laser printers operate in a similar way. The light from a low-power laser or LED (light-emitting diode) is directed by mirrors to a photo-sensitive drum. Electrically charged toner particles are attracted to the image, transferred to paper with pressure, and fused permanently in place with heat.

Low power laser

Modulator

Rotating mirrors

Photosensitive drum

Heating elements

Cartridge of toner particles

Particles fused to the paper

Particles resting on paper

Laser image is stored electrostatically

Toner adheres to exposed areas of drum

Toner is transferred to paper

Daisy-wheel printers generate high-quality output on normal paper, but they are slower than other printers. Typically, they print between 15 and 70 cps. And like other impact printers, daisy-wheel printers are noisy.

**Laser printers** offer some of the fastest, clearest printing available (see Figures 3.9 and 3.10). They come in micro and mainframe sizes, but they all work nearly alike. A laser beam traces the image on a photosensitive drum, which picks up ink particles. Single blank pages are fed in at one end of the printer; the paper rubs ink particles from the drum; and the particles are fused to the page as it emerges from the printer. The resolution is excellent, and to the casual eye, graphics and text look typeset. Typical speeds are six to eight pages per minute. Prices range from less than $2,000 to more than $6,000.

Since laser printers are nonimpact, they are limited to printing single copies. However, they are fast enough that multiple copies can be made from several print runs instead of from carbon copies. The main disadvantage of laser printers, to date, is their high cost. In the next few years, this cost should decline swiftly, making laser

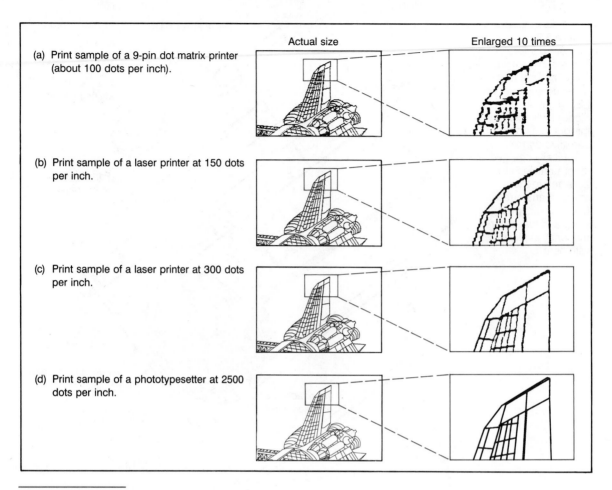

|  | Actual size | Enlarged 10 times |
|---|---|---|
| (a) Print sample of a 9-pin dot matrix printer (about 100 dots per inch). | | |
| (b) Print sample of a laser printer at 150 dots per inch. | | |
| (c) Print sample of a laser printer at 300 dots per inch. | | |
| (d) Print sample of a phototypesetter at 2500 dots per inch. | | |

**Figure 3.10**
The size and sharpness of a printer's dots determines the quality of printed image.

printers the dominant printer technology where medium- to high-volume printing is required.

Table 3.1 summarizes printer technology. Impact printers are today the most cost effective and versatile. However, they are not the most reliable, and they are limited by the laws of physics to modest print speeds.

The future of printing is in nonimpact technologies. Ink-jet printers will perhaps take over the low-cost end of the spectrum, and laser printers will likely dominate the high-cost end. For all, the goal is to produce typeset-quality output while increasing speed and reliability.

## Displays

The least costly **visual display unit** is a surplus television pressed into service as part of a home computer system. Hooked up between the computer and the television's antenna leads is an **RF modulator,** which converts (modulates) the computer's video signal into the *radio frequency* of a television channel. This

**Table 3.1**
**Some Printer Technologies**

| Mechanism | Resolution | Speed | Reliability | Cost |
|---|---|---|---|---|
| **Impact** | | | | |
| Typewriter | 300–800 | 15 cps | Medium | 150–1,000 |
| Daisy-wheel | 300–800 | 15–70 cps | Low | 400–2,000 |
| Dot matrix | 75–250 | 60–300 cps | Low | 200–1,000 |
| **Nonimpact** | | | | |
| Thermal | 75 | 30–120 cps | Low | 20–100 |
| Ink-jet | 75–200 | 200–300 cps | Medium | 200–2,000 |
| Laser | 300–600 | 600 lpm | High | 1,500–6,000 |
| Typesetter | 1,000–3,000 | 300–1,000 lpm | Medium | 30,000–150,000 |

arrangement works, but not well. Television sets were not designed to display text; they cannot display eighty readable characters per line.

If price is not an overriding concern, a video monitor is used. A **monitor** is basically a high-resolution television set that has been stripped of the speaker, channel selector, and radio-frequency receiver.

Both televisions and monitors generate images by bombarding the end of a phosphor-coated glass tube with electrons. The beam of electrons is created by an electron gun, or *cathode*; hence monitors are often called **cathode ray tubes (CRTs)**. Dots and lines are created by turning the electron beam on and off as it sweeps across the surface of the screen (see Figure 3.11). The image you see is actually a mosaic of glowing spots caused by bombarding a thin layer of phosphors with electrons. To refresh the quickly fading phosphors and keep a constant image on the screen, the electron beam must redraw the image fifteen to thirty times a second.

Before an image can be displayed on a screen, it must be stored in video RAM. We now look briefly at two ways of coding and storing this image: bit-mapped and character-oriented displays.

### Bit-Mapped and Character-Oriented Displays

In a **bit-mapped display,** images are produced by coloring each of thousands of **pixels**--*pic*ture *e*lements, the smallest display element on the screen--and storing the

**Figure 3.11**
Color and monochrome CRTs

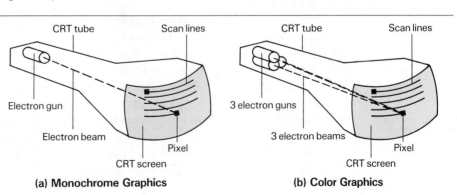

(a) Monochrome Graphics          (b) Color Graphics

status of each as one or more bits in RAM. This method of storing the screen image in memory is quite simple; each pixel on the screen has a corresponding bit or bits in memory. For a *monochrome display*, there is a one-to-one correspondence between bits in the bit map and pixels on the screen. A monochrome pixel will be black or white depending on whether its corresponding bit in memory stores a 0 or 1. A *color display* requires at least 2 bits per pixel to specify which of the pixel's three primary colors are turned on. Even more bits are required if many colors are to appear on the screen at once. For example, a color palette with 256 different colors requires 8 bits ($2^8$ equals 256) be assigned to each pixel.

In a **character-oriented display,** the screen image is produced by drawing characters on the screen. Each character to be displayed is assigned a pattern of pixels. The image is stored in RAM as a list of characters to appear on the screen, not as a list of individual pixels. The conversion between the character codes stored in memory and the dot patterns of characters on the screen is performed by a special circuit called a *character generator.*

A character-oriented display is not nearly as flexible as a bit-mapped display. In a character-oriented display, only a limited set of characters can be displayed, usually fewer than 256 (see Table 3.2). So there is not likely to be, for example, a character that looks like the mirror image of a question mark. Second, each character must appear in a fixed position on the screen. With a character-oriented display, you cannot shift a letter half of a column position left or right.

The difference between the coding schemes has important implications for the amount of memory required to store a screen image. In most character-oriented systems, each character takes 2 bytes to store: 1 byte specifies which symbol should appear in each character position, and 1 byte determines the character's display attributes, such as its color or whether it should blink on and off. Thus a 25-line-by-80-column screen requires 25 x 80 x 2 = 4,000 bytes of storage space. In contrast, a 640-by-480 pixel display with a palette containing 256 colors requires 640 x 480 x 8 = 2,457,600 pixels, or 307,200 bytes, to store an entire screen. In short, character-oriented displays require far less memory than bit-mapped displays.

Some display systems can generate either a bit-mapped or a character-oriented image. This allows them to use bit-mapped images for graphics programs and to save memory space by storing images in a character-oriented format for text-based programs.

## Liquid Crystal Displays

Portable, battery-operated computers cannot afford the size or power required for a CRT display. Instead, like digital watches, they often use a **liquid crystal display (LCD),** which rather than a bulky tube, is a flat panel—an excellent shape for portable or light-weight computers (see Figure 3.12).

An LCD does not generate any light itself; rather, it depends on reflected light. It has a liquid crystal material and a grid of wires sandwiched between two sheets of polarizing glass. When current is passed between crossing wires, the crystals shift position rendering the liquid opaque. The pattern of dark and light produces the image of a character. Because this works well in some light conditions and poorly in others, some LCDs use small built-in lamps to *backlight* the screen.

**Figure 3.12**
This laptop com-
puter has a 25-line
by 80-column liquid
crystal display (640
by 200 pixels).

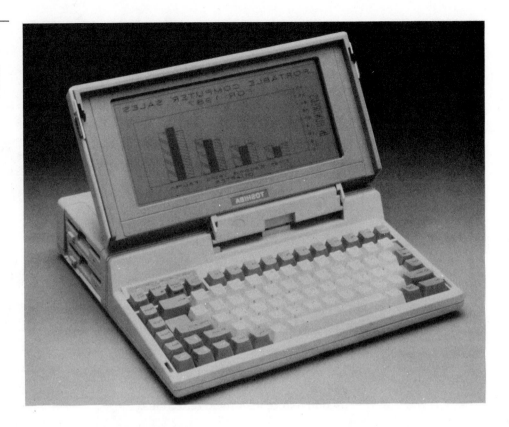

## Qualities of a Good Display

A good-quality monitor is important. No one wants to spend hours peering at a screen of blurry characters. Many factors influence a monitor's readability, including

- The color of the monitor. The phosphors in a **monochrome monitor** glow in only one color. The two most popular colors for monochrome monitors are light green and amber. Endless debates occur over which color is better. Apple Computer broke with tradition by choosing a black-and-white monitor for their Macintosh computer. A **color monitor** (or **RGB monitor**) breaks each pixel into three dots: *r*ed, *g*reen, and *b*lue. Color monitors create excellent graphics, but their characters are not quite as readable as those on monochrome monitors because the extra dots per pixel make each pixel fuzzier.

- The resolution of the screen. **Resolution** is measured horizontally and vertically. The number of scan lines determines the vertical resolution, and the number of pixels along each scan line sets the horizontal resolution. Low-resolution monitors have around 200 lines with 500 pixels. IBM's Personal Series/2 computers have 480 lines with 640 pixels. The full-page monitors used for desktop publishing or computer-aided drafting often have more than 1,000 lines and pixels.

**Figure 3.13**
A plotter converts
graphical informa-
tion into hard copy

• The reflective properties of the screen. Glare from a light bulb is annoying. Etched faceplates, mesh screens, or even a simple cardboard shade can be used to reduce unwanted reflections.

## Plotters

A **plotter** is a printerlike output device that prints pictures rather than alphanumeric information. Most plotters use a stylus or pen to draw an image on paper (see Figure 3.13). A plotter is used instead of a graphical printer when high-resolution drawings are needed. For example, commercial *flat-bed plotters* can move 10,000 steps per inch. A machine like this is indispensable for drawing electronic circuits or making precise mechanical drawings.

Pen plotters are not well suited for filling areas in a drawing because they *fill* an image by drawing many lines side by side—a time-consuming process. *Photoplotters* do not have this problem because they use a light source (often a laser) to draw high-resolution images on photosensitive paper. A special-purpose photoplotter (called a *typesetter*) was used to typeset this book.

## Other Output Devices

The most familiar output devices—printers, displays, and plotters—use paper or monitors to produce some type of image as output. If you wish to use some other media, there is likely an output device that will do the job. For example, a *COM* (computer *o*utput *m*icrofilm) device records computer output on microfilm instead of paper. Vast amounts of information can be compactly stored on microfilm. If you need presentation-quality slides, special cameras and slide makers are available that connect to the display screen of a personal computer or take pictorial information directly from memory and produce developable film. Making presentation-quality slides with these devices is as easy as taking a picture with your Polaroid.

In theory at least, just about anything can be hooked up to a computer and become an output device, even entire factories. For example, most paper products, such as paper plates, tissue paper, cups, and paper towels, are made automatically by computer-controlled machines. The computer senses temperature, moisture, and other characteristics of the pulp and directs the machinery during the paper-making process.

---

## Summary

We have surveyed only a few of the major input and output devices available; there are many more. Input devices convert events in a computer's environment into digital signals. The keyboard is the most common input device, although voice recognition devices should become practical in the near future. A computer's keyboard usually has more keys than does a typewriter's. Some of the extra keys on an IBM keyboard are function keys, cursor-control keys, and the control and alternate keys.

Output devices convert digital signals into actions. Printers and displays are the most common output devices. There are several different kinds of printers. Dot matrix printers print an array of dots that approximate a typewriter's font. These printers are less costly and faster than daisy-wheel printers, offer multiple fonts, and can print graphical images as well as text.

Carefully choosing the right I/O device is just as important as selecting the right computer. So keep in mind ease of use, speed, cost, versatility, quality, and reliability when you select I/O devices.

---

## Key Terms

| | |
|---|---|
| bit-mapped display | laser printer |
| cathode ray tube (CRT) | light pen |
| character printer | line printer |
| character-oriented display | liquid crystal display (LCD) |
| characters per second (cps) | monitor |
| color monitor | monochrome monitor |
| cursor | mouse |
| daisy-wheel printer | nonimpact printer |
| dot matrix printer | page printer |
| impact printer | pixel |
| ink-jet printer | plotter |
| keyboard buffer | puck |

raster
repeating keys
resolution
RF modulator
sonic pen

thermal printer
touch screen
touch tablet
visual display unit

## Discussion Questions

1. Can information be sent directly from an input device like a keyboard to an output device like a printer?

2. Which peripheral devices are strictly for output? Which are strictly for input? Which perform both input and output functions?

3. Other than speed, what characteristics would you use in comparing printers? Rank these in importance. Is speed the most important?

4. Suppose speech recognition devices are perfected for personal computers and are quite inexpensive. What effect would this have on the use of personal computers in business, education, or elsewhere? Who would still be likely to use the devices if they were expensive?

5. Personal computers offer great potential for handicapped persons. For various handicaps, such as blindness, describe the special input and output devices that would enable a person with the handicap to use a personal computer.

6. How does the QWERTY keyboard slow a typist down? Does this suggest another type of keyboard? How should this new keyboard be introduced?

7. What is meant by the term *letter-quality printing*? Can a dot matrix printer produce letter-quality printing? If so, how small would each dot have to be?

8. A touch screen has limited accuracy. What devices would allow you to point to an individual pixel, such as the dot in the letter *i*?

## Exercises

1. Determine how long it would take to print a fifteen-page report on a letter-quality printer at 30 cps and on a dot matrix printer at 150 cps.

2. If a 9-by-9-inch touch screen can only resolve the end of a 1/4-by-1/4-inch finger, how many "points" can be located on the screen with a standard finger?

3. Printers are rated according to their speed. If a typical printer for a personal computer can print 120 characters per second, how long will it take to print the contents of a page containing 66 lines of 80 characters each? Assume the speed rating does not include the time for a carriage return. What effect does this have on the actual time it takes to print the page?

4. Dot matrix printers use a form of printer graphics to print characters. Compare the character patterns of a bit-mapped display with the character patterns of a dot matrix printer.

5. Find and read a request for proposal (RFP) used in the past two years to buy equipment. Many schools and government organizations treat their RFPs and the vendors' responses as public documents.

# Operating Systems

In this chapter, we describe what you need to know about the operating system—the computer's master control programs—to begin computing. In the next chapter, we describe how to use application programs. Important now is getting an idea of how the operating system loads and controls other programs in a computer system and learning how to perform essential tasks such as running programs, managing files, and performing maintenance operations.

In the first section of this chapter, we explain how the parts of the operating system work together to control the computer system. We describe how the operating system schedules the tasks to be done, controls interactions with peripheral devices, manages main memory and the storage of files, and provides other useful services. In the last two sections, we explain the command-line and the visual operating system--that is, how to accomplish frequently performed tasks by either typing on the keyboard or using a pointing device like a mouse. Even though you might use just one of these systems, you should study both. The contrast helps illustrate the difference between form and function in computer programs.

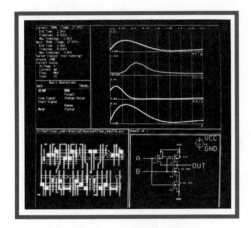

## UNDERSTANDING THE OPERATING SYSTEM

First of all, let us review where operating systems fit in the major categories of software. As we saw in Chapter 1, *application software* performs a specific task, such as word processing or spreadsheet analysis. All developmental software designed either to control the computer system or to help programmers is **system software** and includes operating systems as well as *interpreters, compilers, assemblers, debuggers,* and *editors*—the tools programmers use to write new programs. As Figure 4.1 shows, several layers of software normally insulate a user from a computer's hardware characteristics. The operating system occupies the innermost layers, and application, developmental, and communications software occupy the outer layer.

An **operating system** is a set of programs that govern the operation of a computer. Whenever the computer is running, the operating system provides the computer with the ability to manage automatically the use of its memory, interact with peripheral devices, and execute application programs.

We give examples from two operating systems: the Macintosh operating system and **MS-DOS** (*Microsoft-Disk Operating System*). The Macintosh operating system, developed by Apple Computer, is only for computers in the Apple Macintosh family. MS-DOS is for IBM PCs and compatibles.

The Macintosh operating system and MS-DOS have fundamentally different user interfaces. MS-DOS is a **command-line operating system;** commands are given by typing a line, such as TYPE LETTER.JIM. Command-line operating systems are by far the most common for all types of computers—micro, mini, and mainframe. Whereas command-line operating systems accept commands from a keyboard, the **visual operating system** used by the Macintosh accepts commands from a mouse. The commands are given by moving or selecting pictures (called *icons*) and items

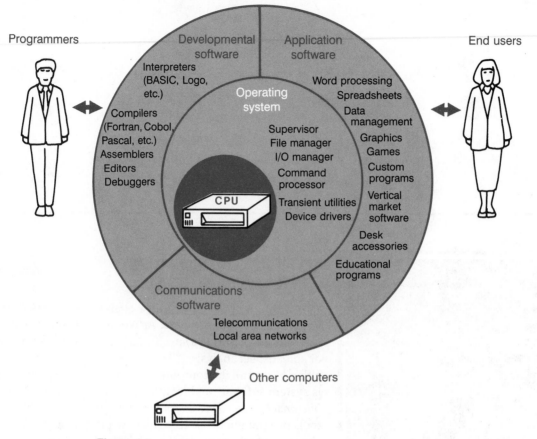

**Figure 4.1**
The layers of software in a computer system

---

from menus. Thus a visual operating system is said to use a *visual interface* between the computer and the user. In contrast, command-line systems use a *textual interface*.

## An Operating System's Components

Although the parts of an operating system vary, all operating systems have components that function as a (1) supervisor, (2) input/output manager, (3) file manager, and (4) command processor. Microcomputer operating systems also usually include transient utilities for infrequently performed tasks and device drivers for communicating with peripherals (see Figure 4.2). You do not have to know how these parts work to use a computer, just as you do not have to know how an engine works to drive a car. But learning what these parts do will give you th  background necessary to use the operating system with more authority and less confusion.

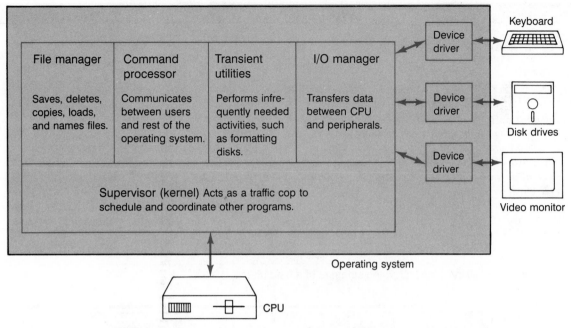

**Figure 4.2**
The parts of a microcomputer operating system

## Supervisor

At the heart of all operating systems is the **supervisor,** or *kernel*; it schedules and coordinates the activities of other programs. The supervisor is like a traffic cop who signals when each activity is permitted to take place. Whenever a computer is running, its supervisor is loaded in internal memory, directing and controlling.

## Input/Output (I/O) Manager and Device Drivers

In general, all data transferred to and from peripheral devices are filtered through the **I/O manager** and its **device drivers.** These are programs that insulate the rest of the programs in the computer system from the peculiarities of the peripherals. For example, most personal computer keyboards do not generate ASCII character codes (see Chapter 1) when their keys are pressed. Instead, they generate scan codes specifying the row and column of the key. Pressing a *b* might cause the keyboard to send the scan code (4,8), meaning the eighth key on the fourth row has been pressed. However, another keyboard available for the same computer might use an entirely different system of scan codes. Here, pressing a *b* might cause the keyboard to send the scan code 85. To resolve these differences, each keyboard needs its own device driver that tells the I/O manager how to translate the keyboard's scan codes into the ASCII character codes used by the rest of the computer system.

## A Word About ... *DOS Shells*

*"For the beginner, a DOS shell can mean the difference between complete bewilderment and the ability to make a system perform basic functions. For the advanced user, a DOS shell can either get in the way of normal business or provide a more efficient method to take care of business." —John Walkenbach*

For many PC users, having to type "copy a:file c:\path\subdirectory\file" is as pleasant as

shaving with cold water. This is especially uncomfortable when there is clearly a better way to do the job.

PC users can bypass DOS via programs called DOS shells, which let users switch back and forth between programs and customize their own integrated packages. While such programs generally cost less than $100, they can be priceless when it comes to improving the user productivity.

---

Xtree, a DOS shell that helps show the structure of a hard disk.

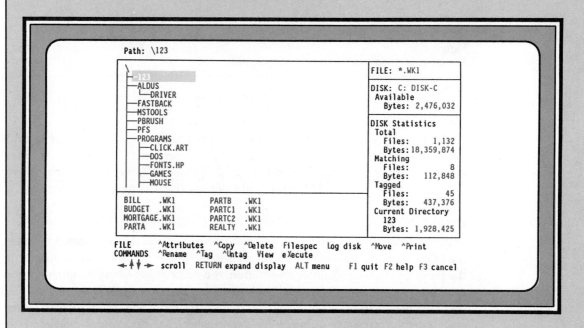

With a good operating system, it is possible to add a hard disk or faster printer to the computer system just by adding a new device driver—without making any changes to other software. This is called **device independence.** The device driver tells the I/O manager how the new hardware functions.

**Machine independence,** an even stronger form of hardware independence, allows application software to be moved from one member of a family of computers to another without making any programming changes. This can make it possible to

Noah Davids, a software developer for Honeywell, in Phoenix, uses the Norton Commander DOS shell extensively. "Almost everything I do is invoked from the Commander itself," he said. "It's reduced the amount of typing, and, as a result, the amount of typos. I use it for everything. I no longer use DOS commands."

Allen Cariker, director of computer systems for the Dallas Cowboys, in Irving, Texas, is a dedicated user of the Xtree hard disk manager. "Xtree gives me the power I need to do all the hard disk management," Cariker said. "It helps me locate a file, determine how many files need to be backed up, and then go through the tree structure."

This is especially useful for Cariker, who has a copy of every software package used in the Cowboy's organization on his hard disk. Anyone in the company with a question about a program comes to him, and he needs a quick way to find the right files.

Cariker agrees that DOS shells flourish because of a perceived deficiency in DOS, and that many of these capabilities should be in the operating system. But he feels "it has more to do with the business acumen of people who have generated them. The Norton Utilities was the first program that gave you control over file notation. Norton saw a business opportunity and filled that need. Xtree is in the same class as the original Norton Utilities, solving an obvious problem in a creative and efficient way."

replace a slow personal computer with a faster one made by a different manufacturer so long as both computers use the same operating system. Most MS-DOS personal computers can be interchanged in this way.

### File Manager

Everything on disk is stored in a file. Each file has its own name and stores one type of information—for example, a program or data. A *data file* might contain text for a last will and testament, a recipe for banana bread, or a digitized picture. A *program file* might contain a BASIC program or a word processor.

Whatever the contents of a file, the **file manager** is responsible for saving, deleting, copying, loading, naming, and renaming files. The file manager also provides a translation between our *logical* view of the file—the file name and type of data it stores—and the *physical* arrangement of data on a disk.

As we saw in Chapter 2, data on a disk are grouped into sectors, with each sector forming part of a track. The file manager provides this translation from file names to storage locations by maintaining a directory and a file allocation table in special areas on the outside edge of each disk. The *directory* is a list containing the name and number of each file on the disk. The **file allocation table** is an index showing the specific physical locations assigned to each file. Many file managers, by setting up *subdirectories*, allow files to be grouped in a hierarchical manner. In this case, the *root directory* lists the names of the files in the root directory and the names of the subdirectories.

Suppose the file manager is asked to copy 2,400 bytes from main memory to create a new file named BASEBALL.CAP on a disk with 512 bytes in each sector. Although the exact procedure for storing a file varies somewhat from one operating system to another, in general the file manager must

- Examine the disk's file allocation table to find five unused sectors.

- Modify the appropriate directory (or directories) and the file allocation table to include an entry for the new file, and list the sectors it occupies.

- Tell the I/O manager to copy the data file from main memory onto the five previously unused disk sectors.

### Command Processor

The **command processor,** or *shell*, communicates between the user and the rest of the operating system. It accepts commands from the user, makes sure they are valid, and then takes the appropriate action. For example, if you ask the computer to copy BASEBALL.CAP and call the new file GOLF.TEE, the command processor will translate the command and relay the request to the file manager. If the disk does not have enough room to store GOLF.TEE, the file manager sends a coded error message, which the command processor might translate to read: INSUFFICIENT FREE SPACE ON DISK—COMMAND ABORTED.

Many operating systems have more than one command processor available for different types of users. For example, programmers might prefer to use a command processor with a command-line interface, whereas casual users might choose to use one with a visual interface.

Sometime during a computer session you are bound to say to yourself, I have typed this series of operating system commands over and over again. Perhaps you must make a backup copy of a file with one command before you start word processing with another. This repetition can be avoided if your operating system's command processor allows you to establish batch files. A **batch file** is simply a file that contains a series (or batch) of operating system commands. For example, you might build a batch file containing one command to backup the file and another to start word processing. Then you can accomplish the work of two commands with a single command that tells the command processor to begin executing the batch file. The command processor will take commands one at a time from the batch file and execute them. This ability can make an otherwise unfriendly operating system seem reasonable to casual users because the obnoxious commands can all be hidden inside batch files.

### Transient Utilities

In some portable computers, the entire operating system is permanently stored in ROM, but in most computers, the operating system is too large to fit into main memory at once. Instead, the operating system is divided into two parts, the resident portion and a set of transient utility programs.

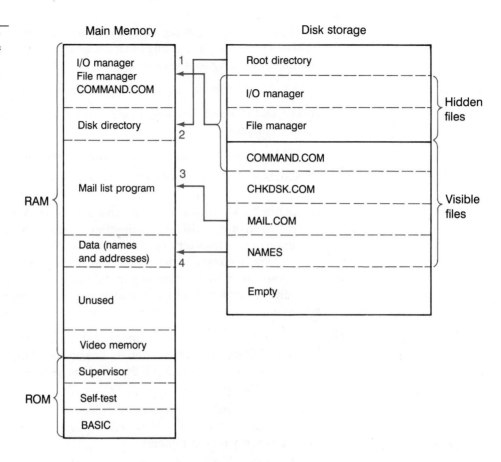

**Figure 4.3**
Several transfers of files from disk to memory are necessary before an application program can begin execution. The numbers indicate the sequence of these transfers.

The **resident** part of the operating system is loaded into memory as soon as the computer is turned on, a process called *booting* the computer. The resident part always contains the routines essential for controlling the computer and its peripherals—that is, the operating system supervisor, the I/O manager, and at least some of the file manager—and may contain some frills as well.

The **transient utility programs** remain on disk until one of the programs is requested. Then the requested program is transferred into memory. Commands that are resident in one operating system may be transient utilities in another; the choice is made by the operating system designer, not by the user. If the computer gives a command for a transient utility but cannot find the program on the disk, it makes a request for the **system disk** (a disk containing the operating system).

## Memory Management

How an operating system manages memory is best illustrated with an example. We will describe how MS-DOS manages a computer session in which a mailing list program prints names and addresses onto mailing labels. Figure 4.3 shows how main memory and the disk files might be laid out for this application. On the disk

- The two hidden files contain the file and I/O managers of the operating system. A *hidden file* is the same as any other file except that its name does not appear in directory listings of file names.

- COMMAND.COM contains the operating system command processor.

- CHKDSK.COM contains the transient utility program that implements the CHKDSK command.

- MAIL.COM contains the mailing list application program.

- NAMES contains the data file of names and addresses to be printed.

Before the machine is turned on, main memory is blank except for programs stored in ROM. In an IBM PC, ROM contains the operating system supervisor, some self-test programs, and a truncated version of Microsoft BASIC. When the computer is turned on, it looks for a system disk. If the system disk is not found, the computer generally responds with an error message and waits. Programs must be in memory before they can be executed. Thus four transfers from disk to memory are necessary before the mailing list program can print the mailing labels (see Figure 4.3).

1. Loading the I/O manager, the file manager, and the command processor (COMMAND.COM) into memory. You do this by switching on the computer, which activates instructions in ROM that load the resident part of the operating system from the disk.

2. Loading a copy of the disk's directory into memory. This allows the computer to read files from the disk faster. The operating system then displays a prompt, signifying it is ready for a command.

3. Loading the mailing list program into memory. You do this by typing MAIL NAMES. This command not only tells the operating system to load MAIL.COM into memory but also tells the mailing list program to use the data file NAMES.

4. Transferring names and addresses from NAMES to memory. MAIL.COM carries out this process, formats the names and addresses to look good on mailing labels, and sends them to the printer.

In this example, you had to give only one command to begin running the application program because the disk had been conveniently configured to store all the programs and data necessary for the application.

## USING A COMMAND-LINE OPERATING SYSTEM

When you begin using a personal computer, you will find the tasks you perform most often are

- Running an application program

- Copying and deleting files and other file operations

- Formatting new disks, backing-up disks, setting the system clock, and other maintenance tasks

In this section, we explain how to perform these operations on a computer that has a command-line operating system. Although specific commands vary from one command-line operating system to the next, the general approach is fairly standardized.

Command-line interfaces are not easy for beginners to use because the user must remember commands and type them exactly. The computer prompts a command by displaying a character like ? or A. Each command is typed on a new line and begins with a **keyword,** usually a verb such as TYPE, MOVE, or KILL. Normally, a keyword is followed by one or more **parameters,** or *arguments*, telling the keyword what to do. A parameter can be a file name, but it might be a number specifying how fast to send characters to the printer. A keyword and its parameters must be separated by a **delimiter,** generally a space or comma, to indicate where one part of the command ends and the next part begins. For example, in the command COPY DATA.OLD DATA.NEW, the keyword is COPY, the two delimiters are the blank spaces, and the parameters are the file names DATA.OLD and DATA.NEW. The number and type of parameters vary depending on the keyword and the action desired.

## Running a Program

Becoming proficient with MS-DOS takes time and practice. Each command begins either with the name of a program file or with a keyword. If it begins with a program filename, the operating system loads the program into memory and begins executing it. For example, to execute a word processing program stored on a disk as the file WORD.COM, you type WORD and complete the command by pressing the [Enter] key.

If the command begins with a keyword, the operating system executes the command. For example, if you type TYPE LETTER.JIM, the file named LETTER.JIM is displayed on the screen. After completing the command, the operating system shows it is ready for the next command by displaying a *prompt* such as B or A. Incorrectly typed commands elicit the error message BAD COMMAND OR FILE NAME, followed by another prompt.

Besides acknowledging that the computer is ready for the next command, the prompt designates the default drive. Disk drives are named by single letters; the **default drive** is the drive that MS-DOS searches to find a file if it is not told explicitly where the file is stored. If the prompt is A, MS-DOS will search drive A to find the file named BASEBALL.CAP, but it will search drive B to find the file B:BASEBALL.CAP. To change the default drive, you type the letter of the new default drive followed by a colon. For example, if the original prompt is B, you type A: to change the default drive to drive A. The prompt is then changed to A.

Most computer programs rely heavily on **default values** to reduce the amount of information that must be requested from the user. For example, the disk formatting utility will, by default, make *double-sided disks*—disks capable of storing data on both sides—unless you specifically request single-sided disks.

## File Names

In MS-DOS, you must follow some rigid rules when naming a file. A **file name** contains two main parts: a *primary file name* containing one to eight characters and an optional *extension* containing one, two, or three characters. For example, you might name three files JIM, CLIENTS.89, and FORMAT.COM. These files might contain, respectively, a memo to Jim Martin, a list of clients in 1989, and the transient operating system utility that formats new disks.

made in its early design and development no longer made sense. For example, although Intel's new microprocessors could access many megabytes of RAM, MS-DOS could only manage 640KB efficiently. Other significant limitations included its intimidating command-line interface and its inability to execute multiple programs concurrently.

These limitations are addressed by OS/2 (Operating System/2), yet another upwardly compatible version of MS-DOS released in 1988. OS/2 is designed to work with 80286- and 80386-based computers, such as the IBM AT or most of the IBM Personal System/2 computers. It supports up to 16MB of RAM and includes a Macintosh-like visual interface based on Microsoft Windows.

The size and complexity of microcomputer operating systems has grown by leaps and bounds. Early 8-bit personal computers such as the Apple II were limited to 64KB of memory. Every extra byte in the operating system meant less room for the application program and data,

so operating systems for these microcomputers provided only the bare essentials for controlling the computer. Because memory is less constrained in 16- and 32-bit machines, MS-DOS provided a wider range of functions and more convenience—at the cost of occupying about 50KB of RAM. OS/2 is quite a memory hog; its minimal system requirements are 1.5 MB of RAM and a hard disk.

Still, microcomputer operating systems are quite crude by the standards of mainframe computers, which use operating systems that occupy megabytes of memory and generally allow the computer to execute concurrent programs, allocate memory among many users, and manage large databases. This too may be a temporary limitation. IBM has announced its intention to release an Extended Edition of its OS/2 operating system. The Extended Edition will include a database management system using the same relational model as DB2, a popular database system for its largest computers.

---

One drawback of magnetic media is that people cannot sense magnetic signals directly and must rely on the computer system to report what a disk or tape contains. The short file names of MS-DOS do not help matters much: A file name like JIM may not jog your memory about what is in the file six months after you wrote it. This problem is exacerbated if you use a hard disk because it can contain more than a thousand files.

Fortunately, some standard conventions for naming files exist that make it easier to determine what is stored in each file. For example, one convention is that any file ending with the extension .COM is a machine language program. Some other conventions are

- .BAS contains a BASIC language program.

- .BAT is a batch file containing operating system commands.

- .DOC contains documentation—instructions about how to run or use a program.

- .EXE contains an executable program and is similar to a .COM file.

- .PAS contains a Pascal language program.

- .PIC or .PCX contains a picture or graphics file.

- .SYS contains system parameters used to initialize a program.

- .TXT contains a text file.

- .WKS or .WK1 contains a worksheet created with Lotus 1-2-3.

A complete file name includes two other parts that describe where the file is located. One part is the name of the drive storing the file. Thus the file A:ELMER.GLU is stored on drive A. On a two-drive floppy disk system, the left-hand (or upper) drive is usually named A, and the right-hand (or lower) drive is named B.

The other part of a complete file name identifies the subdirectories (if any) the file is located in. Remember, a subdirectory is similar to a file folder; it is an index file that contains the names and locations of other files. For example, the file name C:\LETTERS\1985\BIRTHDAY.MOM states that the BIRTHDAY.MOM file is stored inside the subdirectory named 1985, which in turn, is located inside the subdirectory named LETTERS, all of which reside on drive C. In this example, the C:\LETTERS\1985 part of the file name is called a **path** because it describes the route that must be followed to find the file. On hard disk systems, subdirectories are particularly important; without them, the root directory would contain all the entries for the disk's files. Imagine trying to find a file in a root directory with more than a thousand file names in it.

## File Management

The most important file management operations are

- Examining a root directory or subdirectory to see what files are in it
- Erasing files
- Copying files

In this section, we give examples of each of these operations. In all the MS-DOS examples in this chapter, characters typed by the user are shown in color, and output generated by the computer is shown in black.

### Examining Directories

Probably the most frequently used command is DIR, which extracts a list of file names, file sizes in bytes, and dates and times when files were created from a directory. The DIR command then formats the list as a report and sends it to the screen. The DIR command shown in Figure 4.4 displays the entries of the root directory on disk C. By substituting other parameters after the DIR command, you can see what files are stored in other directories. For example, the command DIR C:\WORDPERF would list the files in the WORDPERF directory of disk C.

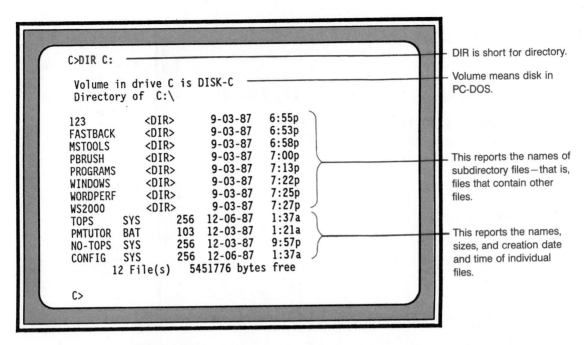

```
C>DIR C:                                           DIR is short for directory.

Volume in drive C is DISK-C                        Volume means disk in
Directory of  C:\                                  PC-DOS.

123        <DIR>      9-03-87   6:55p
FASTBACK   <DIR>      9-03-87   6:53p
MSTOOLS    <DIR>      9-03-87   6:58p
PBRUSH     <DIR>      9-03-87   7:00p              This reports the names of
PROGRAMS   <DIR>      9-03-87   7:13p              subdirectory files—that is,
WINDOWS    <DIR>      9-03-87   7:22p              files that contain other
WORDPERF   <DIR>      9-03-87   7:25p              files.
WS2000     <DIR>      9-03-87   7:27p
TOPS     SYS    256  12-06-87   1:37a
PMTUTOR  BAT    103  12-03-87   1:21a              This reports the names,
NO-TOPS  SYS    256  12-03-87   9:57p              sizes, and creation date
CONFIG   SYS    256  12-06-87   1:37a              and time of individual
        12 File(s)   5451776 bytes free           files.

C>
```

**Figure 4.4**
DIR (directory). This example shows how to request a listing of the file in the root directory of disk drive C.

The CHKDSK (check disk) command is a transient MS-DOS disk-management utility. It produces a report about the contents of a disk and the status of the memory. The report in Figure 4.5 indicates one of the hard disk drives is three-fourths full.

*Erasing*

Erasing files is straightforward. The command ERASE B:DRAWINGS.FEB deletes the file DRAWINGS.FEB from drive B. Actually, only the file name is deleted from the directories on the disk; the file's content is not affected until a later operation causes other data to occupy its space. But because MS-DOS does not provide an UNERASE utility to cancel the deletion, the practical effect is the same as if the file were instantly and permanently erased.

**Wild card characters** are used to specify a category of items. For example, with the asterisk (*), you can indicate several files with just one specification. Thus ERASE LETTERS.* erases every file on the default drive that has the primary file name LETTERS, regardless of the file extension (LETTERS.JIM, LETTERS.SUE, and so on).

Directories are more difficult to delete than normal files. Only empty directories can be deleted, so the first step is to delete any files or subdirectories stored in the directory you want to delete. Then you use the RMDIR (remove directory) command to delete the directory. For example, RMDIR C:\WORDPERF will remove the WORDPERF directory from disk C—if it is empty.

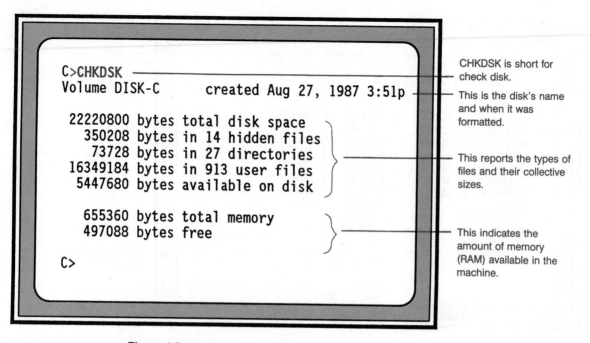

```
C>CHKDSK
Volume DISK-C        created Aug 27, 1987 3:51p

  22220800 bytes total disk space
    350208 bytes in 14 hidden files
     73728 bytes in 27 directories
  16349184 bytes in 913 user files
   5447680 bytes available on disk

    655360 bytes total memory
    497088 bytes free

C>
```

CHKDSK is short for check disk.

This is the disk's name and when it was formatted.

This reports the types of files and their collective sizes.

This indicates the amount of memory (RAM) available in the machine.

**Figure 4.5**
CHKDSK (check disk). This utility produces a short report about the contents of a disk (in this case, a 22MB hard disk) and the amount of memory in the machine.

## Copying

The COPY command is used to make copies of specific files. For example, COPY A:BASEBALL.CAP B:GOLF.TEE copies A:BASEBALL.CAP to drive B forming the file GOLF.TEE. Or, instead of copying one file at a time, you can copy many files with one COPY command by using a wild card character. For example, COPY B:*.DOC will take all the files on drive B that have the extension .DOC and copy them onto the disk in the default drive.

You can also copy a file into a specific directory by providing the destination directory's name after the name of the file to be copied. For example, COPY A:*.* C:\LETTERS will copy all files on drive A into the LETTERS directory on drive C. This example assumes the LETTERS directory already exists on drive C. If it does not exist, you must first use the MKDIR (make directory) command to create an empty directory named LETTERS.

MS-DOS does not have a MOVE command; instead, you must give separate commands to COPY and ERASE. To illustrate this procedure, let us explore how DOS commands can be used to reorganize the files on a hard disk. For example, Figure 4.6(a) shows a before and after view of a hard disk containing four data files. Two of the files, GOLF.TEE and BASEBALL.CAP, are to be moved into a new directory named PRODUCTS. Placing these files in new directories takes five commands: one command to create the new directory, two commands to make copies of the files, and two commands to delete the files from their original locations (see Figure 4.6b).

**Before**

Disk: C:\
├─Directory: LETTERS\
│  ├─File: MARTIN.JIM
│  └─File: GOLF.TEE
└─Directory: CONTRACTS\
   ├─File: WILSON.DON
   └─File: BASEBALL.BAT

**After**

Disk: C:\
├─Directory: LETTERS\
│  └─File: MARTIN.JIM
├─Directory: CONTRACTS\
│  └─File: WILSON.DON
└─Directory: PRODUCTS\
   └─File: GOLF.TEE
      File: BASEBALL.BAT

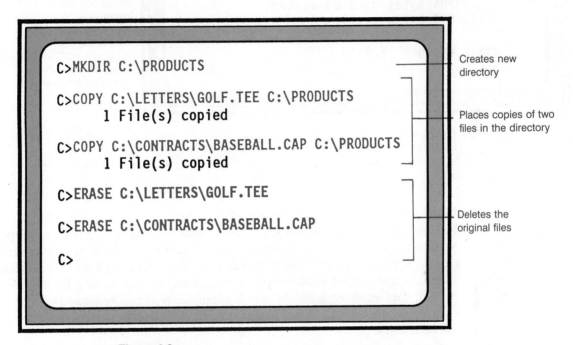

```
C>MKDIR C:\PRODUCTS                                    ──── Creates new
                                                            directory
C>COPY C:\LETTERS\GOLF.TEE C:\PRODUCTS
     1 File(s) copied
                                                       ──── Places copies of two
C>COPY C:\CONTRACTS\BASEBALL.CAP C:\PRODUCTS                files in the directory
     1 File(s) copied

C>ERASE C:\LETTERS\GOLF.TEE
                                                       ──── Deletes the
C>ERASE C:\CONTRACTS\BASEBALL.CAP                           original files

C>
```

**Figure 4.6**
Reorganizing the file structure of a hard disk by moving two files into a new directory.

---

If you find these examples confusing, you are not alone. MS-DOS's strange command names and difficult procedures have driven many users to buy and use a menu-oriented DOS shell.

## Maintenance Tasks

Important enough to warrant examples are two general maintenance tasks: formatting a disk and backing-up a disk.

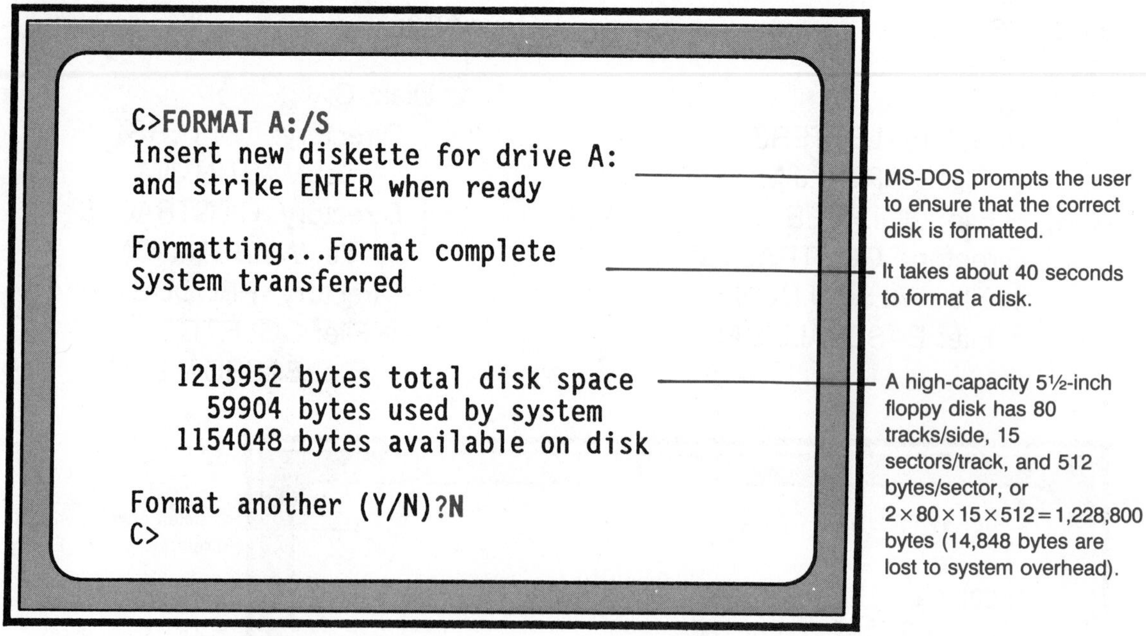

```
C>FORMAT A:/S
Insert new diskette for drive A:
and strike ENTER when ready

Formatting...Format complete
System transferred


   1213952 bytes total disk space
     59904 bytes used by system
   1154048 bytes available on disk

Format another (Y/N)?N
C>
```

MS-DOS prompts the user to ensure that the correct disk is formatted.

It takes about 40 seconds to format a disk.

A high-capacity 5½-inch floppy disk has 80 tracks/side, 15 sectors/track, and 512 bytes/sector, or $2 \times 80 \times 15 \times 512 = 1{,}228{,}800$ bytes (14,848 bytes are lost to system overhead).

**Figure 4.7**
Dialog of a typical disk-formatting operation

## Formatting Disks

**Formatting,** or *initializing*, a disk involves erasing the disk and giving it an empty root-directory file. Disks come from the manufacturer in a blank, or unformatted, condition; files, however, cannot be stored on an unformatted disk. Formatting should be approached with caution. A disk cannot be used until it has been formatted, but formatting a disk by mistake completely erases its contents. Accidentally formatting a hard disk can be disastrous if adequate backup procedures have not been followed.

Figure 4.7 shows the dialogue between the user and MS-DOS for disk formatting. The command line begins with the keyword FORMAT followed by the argument A:/S. The A: specifies that the disk to be formatted will be in drive A. The /S is an option switch that tells the format program to initialize the new disk with a copy of the operating system, making it a system disk. **Option switches** are used to override default values. Other option switches for the FORMAT command are /1, to create a single-sided disk, and /V, to write an electronic name on the disk.

## Backing Up Disks

An excellent idea is to periodically copy disks that store letters, reports, spreadsheets, and other data files. Then, if a file is destroyed—either by accidental erasure or by mechanical failure—you will have a copy of the information on another disk. For very important information, such as business records, you should follow a regular schedule of making backup disks. At least one set of backup disks should be stored away from the computer.

Floppy disks are copied with the DISKCOPY command, a nonresident utility. For example, DISKCOPY B: A: causes the operating system to ask that the disk to be copied be put in drive B and the target disk (the disk to be copied to) in drive A. After confirming that the correct disks are in the drives, MS-DOS copies the disk in drive B onto the disk in drive A.

Some application software developers copy-protect the disks they sell to try to prevent users from making unauthorized copies. A **copy-protected** disk is manufactured with an intentional defect that prevents a normal COPY or DISKCOPY utility from making copies of selected files. Generally, only program files are copy-protected. So even if you use copy-protected programs, you should make backup copies of the data files you create.

Hard disks also need to be backed-up because they can quit working without warning—just like a light bulb. MS-DOS includes a BACKUP command for copying files from the hard disk onto numerous floppy disks. Unfortunately, the BACKUP command is slow: It can take an hour or more to backup a 20MB hard disk onto floppy disks. Much faster, friendlier, and more reliable backup utilities are available from third-party software vendors.

---

# USING A VISUAL OPERATING SYSTEM

Even before games like Pong and PacMan popularized visual interfaces, computer scientists at Xerox's Palo Alto Research Center were developing a visual interface as the basis of an operating system. They decided to model the interface on a desk top, making the computer screen look like a desk on which papers could be piled on top of each other or placed in in-baskets, out-baskets, file folders, and trash cans. Pictures, or *icons*, on the screen represented these objects, as well as printers and pads of blank paper. In 1981, Xerox announced the first commercial computer featuring a visual interface (see Figure 4.8).

Immediately recognized by computer professionals as a technical masterpiece, the Xerox Star Information System received little attention from the general public because a typical workstation cost $30,000. The Apple Lisa, introduced in 1983, used a similar visual system at an introductory price of $10,000. Still, there were few buyers. Then in 1984, the introduction of the Apple Macintosh brought the price of a visual operating system down to less than $2,500. Finally, the cost of visual interfaces had become competitive with that of textual ones. It now appears that, within a few years, most personal computers will use a visual interface.

To illustrate how a visual operating system works, we use the Macintosh as an example. Although all Macintosh operating system commands can be given with the mouse or the keyboard, we explain only the mouse commands. You need to type only when you want to name a new file, rename an old one, or enter information to be stored. The mouse controls an arrow that is used to point at objects on the screen. By moving the mouse along a flat surface, you move the arrow on the screen.

**Figure 4.8**
The Xerox 8010
Star Information
System. The display
has a very high
resolution for its
visual interface.

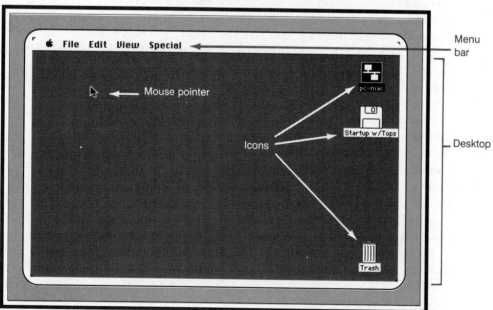

**Figure 4.9**
A nearly empty Macintosh screen display

## Running Programs

To run an application program, the first step is to switch on the power and slip a system disk into the drive. The appearance of the screen depends on what disk is inserted. Figure 4.9 shows one example. The gray area of the screen represents the desk top. The three icons represent the system disk in the Macintosh's floppy disk drive (labeled "Startup w/Tops"), a hard disk connected to the Macintosh via a local area network (labeled "pc-mac"), and a trash can sitting on the desk.

The next step is to open a disk to see its contents. The quickest way of doing this is to move the mouse until the arrow on the screen points at the desired icon and then click the button on the mouse twice (called **double-clicking**). This opens a **window,** a rectangular viewing area covering part of the screen, such as the pc-mac box in Figure 4.10.

The icons in the pc-mac window tell you what files are on the hard disk. Those in Figure 4.10 have the following meanings:

- MacWrite is a word processing program.

- MacPaint is a free-hand drawing program.

- MacDraw is a line-art drawing program.

- Office Layout and Steam Engine are data files created by MacDraw.

- System Folder is a subdirectory containing files that, in turn, contain most of the operating system. (Some of the operating system is stored in ROM.) The Macintosh operating system lets you organize the information on a disk by

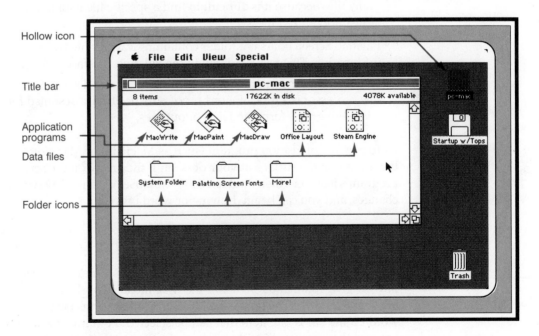

**Figure 4.10**
Window showing the contents of the pc-mac hard disk

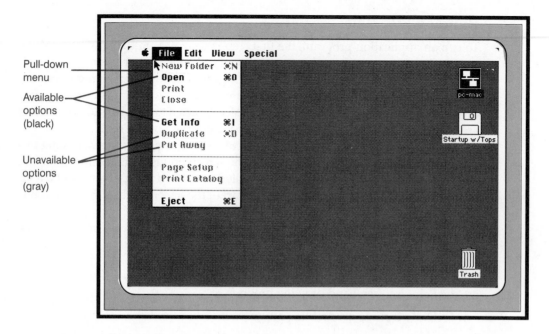

Pull-down menu

Available options (black)

Unavailable options (gray)

**Figure 4.11**
Second-level menus. These "pull down" from the menu bar.

putting files inside folders. Using file folders is important if the disk includes many files because it is difficult to find a specific file if all files are kept in one large unorganized mess.

- Palatino Screen Fonts is a folder containing various files filled with typeface information. This text is printed in the Palatino typeface.

- More! is a folder containing an outline processor and several data files. An outline processor is a type of word processor specifically designed for entering and editing well-formatted lists or outlines.

To run an application program (such as MacPaint or MacWrite), you just move the mouse on the surface of your desk until the arrow on the screen points at the program's icon, and then double-click the mouse. Within a few seconds, the screen changes, and you can begin drawing or word processing.

## Giving Commands

A slower method of opening a disk is also worth describing because it illustrates how to give commands by using the Macintosh's two-level menu system. Look again at Figure 4.9. The text at the top of the screen forms part of a **menu bar;** each word on the bar is one item that can be selected. Pointing at a word on the menu bar and then pressing and holding down the mouse button causes a **pull-down menu** to appear on the screen (see Figure 4.11); that is, a list of options appears below the word. Some items on the pull-down menu are not available for selection at this time. For example, if nothing has been opened yet, the Close option is written in gray. The available items appear black. You select one of these options by moving the mouse until the arrow points at the desired item on the menu and then releasing the button. Thus you can also open the pc-mac disk by selecting the File option from the menu bar and then selecting the Open option from the pull-down menu. The pull-down menu vanishes, and a window appears on the screen (Figure 4.10). Although this sounds complicated, with only a few minutes of practice it becomes surprisingly natural.

You can also give commands on the Macintosh by pointing at and moving icons with the mouse. For example, look again at Figure 4.10. To delete the Steam Engine file, you move its icon on top of the trash can icon. To do this, you point at the Steam Engine icon, "pick up" the icon by pressing and holding down the mouse button, drag the icon across the screen to the trash can by moving the mouse, and then release the button. When the button is released, the icon for Steam Engine disappears. This sequence takes many words to describe but only a second or two to do.

---

## Summary

In this chapter, we described the parts of an operating system and how the operating system controls the computer. Through the operating system's command processor, you have access to the file manager for manipulating files (copying, deleting, renaming, formatting, and so on) and to the supervisor for loading and executing application programs. Knowing how the operating system manages the computer's resources will help you understand the progress of any computer session, whether you are involved in word processing, data management, communications, or just playing games.

Command-line operating systems force you to type commands with keywords and parameters. It takes experience and practice to use a command-line operating system proficiently. Using a program with a command-line interface is similar to doing traditional computer programming. The main difference is that with computer programming the commands are accumulated in a file for later processing rather than executed as soon as they are typed.

Visual operating systems rely on icons, mice, and pull-down menus to let you give commands. Because visual operating systems are fairly easy to use, they are growing rapidly in popularity.

---

## Key Terms

batch file

bug

command-line operating system

command processor

copy-protected

default drive

default values

delimiter

device drivers

device independence

double-clicking

file allocation table

file manager

file name

formatting

I/O manager

keyword

machine independence

menu bar

MS-DOS operating system

option switch

parameter

path

pull-down menu

resident

supervisor

system disk

system software

transient utility programs

upward compatible

visual operating system

wild card characters

window

## Discussion Questions

1. What is the difference between application software and system software? What kinds of programs might fall in a gray area between the two?

2. Why are floppy disks sold blank rather than formatted?

3. What is a file? What conventions for naming files are used on your computer?

4. Why are wild card characters convenient? Think of some tasks that would be easier to perform with wild card characters than without them.

5. What happens if you make a typing mistake in a command-line system? If you make a typing mistake when giving a command, is the result likely to be a valid command?

6. What is the difference between device and machine independence?

7. What is the significance of upward compatibility? Is downward compatibility as important as upward compatibility?

8. In a command-line operating system, a batch file stores textual commands. How might a visual operating system store commands in a batch file?

9. Suppose the directory of your disk contains the following file names:

TICTAC.EXE          README.DOC

ALGEBRA.DAT         DEFAULT.TXT

STARTUP.BAT

What do you suppose each file contains? Comment on the importance of choosing meaningful file names.

## Exercises

1. Prepare a list of the operating system commands for your computer. Rank the commands according to how often you are likely to use them.

2. Determine which commands in your computer's operating system are resident and which are transient.

**3.** Make a copy of a disk with a DISKCOPY command; then make a copy by formatting a new disk and using the COPY command. Which method took longer? Which method is more reliable? More flexible?

# Application Software

In this chapter, we discuss application software—the programs that direct a computer to perform activities such as writing a letter, playing Space Invaders, or printing paychecks. Application software adapts a general-purpose computer to a specific task.

Some interesting similarities exist between using application software and driving a car. Just as you don't need to know how to build an engine to drive, so you don't need to know how to write a program to use a computer. As a driver, you need to know where you want to go, how to operate the car's controls, and how to read a map for guidance in unfamiliar areas. So too, as a computer user, you must know what you want to accomplish, how to interpret the screen and give commands, and how to read a manual for those times when you cannot figure out by trial and error how a program works.

It takes practice to learn how to drive, but once you have mastered driving in one car, transferring your skills to another car is reasonably straightforward. The same is true of using application software: After you learn a few "rules of the road," you will find it much easier to begin using new programs.

In this chapter, we describe some basic skills and techniques that will put you in control of application programs. These skills include how to use menu systems and give commands, how to manage the screen in programs that use windows, and how to ask for help. We also cover some principles that lie behind application programs, such as the way the screen can act like a porthole, giving you access to a much larger

# 5

underlying workspace. In the chapter's last section, we discuss some issues you should consider when selecting which application programs to use.

## USING MENUS

Nearly all application programs use a network of menus as their primary user interface. **Menus** simplify learning new software by presenting lists of program options. To give commands, you select options from the lists.

Menus come in every imaginable orientation, color, style, and type of network. Some menus pop-up on the screen when you press a specific combination of keys; others stay on the screen whenever the application program is running. A good menu system is unobtrusive and efficient, but a poorly designed system is likely to send you running to the manual to see if there are control-key options or other alternatives to hunting through the menus for the option you want.

Menus fall into two main categories: horizontal and vertical. We look at each category in turn.

### Horizontal Menus

Horizontal menus are called **menu bars** because they display choices across the screen on one or two lines. They are popular because they occupy little of the screen's real estate, leaving most of the screen for viewing data or other program functions.

Two types of menu bars are *keyword menu bars* and *one-letter menu bars*. Of the two, the one-letter menu bar takes less screen space because it displays only the initial letter of each command keyword (see Figure 5.1). Menu bars encourage software developers to invent new command keywords as a way of avoiding first-letter conflicts. If ERASE conflicts with EDIT, it is likely to be called ZAP. And it does not take many keywords like ZAP before remembering what the letters on a

```
 19|
 20|
> A1
Enter B,C,D,E,F,G,I,L,M,O,P,Q,R,S,T,U,W,X,Z,?
 2>/
       Function keys:   F1 = HELP ;   F2 = ERASE LINE/RETURN TO WORKSHEET
```

```
SuperCalc     AnswerKey (tm)  slash commands :
B(lank)-----> Removes contents of cells.
C(opy)------> Copies contents of cells.
D(elete)----> Deletes entire row or column.
E(dit)------> Allows editing the contents of a cell.
F(ormat)----> Change display format of cells, rows, or entire worksheet.
G(lobal)----> Change global display or calculation options.
I(nsert)----> Create new row or column.
L(oad)------> Read worksheet (or portion) from disk.
```

```
 19
 20
Arrange  Blank  Copy  Delete  Edit  Format  Global  Insert  Load  Move  Name
Output  Protect  Quit  Save  Title  Unprotect  View  Window  Zap  /more
 2>/
MENU   Sort spreadsheet (entire or partial) by column or by row
```

**Figure 5.1**
A comparison of the one-letter menu bar used by the original SuperCalc program (1981)
and the keyword menu bar used by SuperCalc4 (1987).

one-letter menu bar mean becomes difficult—not that remembering what they
mean is ever especially easy.

As the personal computer market has matured, keyword menu bars have displaced most one-letter menu bars. Many keyword menu bars require two screen lines to display all the options. For example, Microsoft's PC-based application programs use two-line keyword menu bars at the bottom of the screen.

Application programs often have more than one hundred commands. The keywords for all these commands cannot be displayed without filling up the screen, so most of the commands are hidden inside a multilevel menu system. The keywords in the main menu bar represent *categories* of commands; it is from submenus that specific commands are chosen. Thus choosing the right category from the main menu can be tricky. For example, beginners might suspect the correct choice from Microsoft Word's main menu to delete a file on disk is DELETE when actually it is TRANSFER, which only its submenu makes clear.

A good example of a multilevel menu system is Lotus 1-2-3, a spreadsheet program. Its main menu presents the program's categories of commands on one line at the top of the screen (see Figure 5.2).

To tell Lotus 1-2-3 to load a file from disk into memory, you first must activate the menu bar by typing a slash (/). (Other programs allow you to activate the menu bar by pressing [Esc] or by pointing with a mouse.) Two menu bars now appear at the top of the screen: Immediately below the main menu bar is a second-level (or subsidiary) menu bar that displays what the next set of options will be if the highlighted option on the main menu is chosen. You can select an option from the main menu in one of two ways.

- You can highlight the option you want using the arrow keys or space bar. When you use these keys, the submenu changes to let you examine the second-level choices associated with the highlighted option of the main menu. Pressing [Enter] selects the highlighted option.
- You can simply type the first letter of the desired option. For example, to select the File option, press the [F] key.

Whenever an option is selected, the appropriate submenu advances up the screen one line to become the current menu. This process may continue through several levels of menus to select all the options needed to complete the command.

When the command is completed, the menu bar usually disappears. But **sticky menus** stay on the screen, anticipating your need to use them again. To get a sticky menu to disappear, you must select its Quit option. Sticky menus are helpful for tasks requiring several closely related commands. For example, it can take many commands to establish all of the parameters for a print operation: setting the margins of the page, selecting the line spacing, and so on. For this reason, the Lotus 1-2-3 submenu for Print options is a sticky menu. Thus you can select many print options without bothering to reactivate the menu bar system and reselect the Print submenu.

## Vertical Menus

By their very nature, vertical menus occupy a significant chunk of the screen, but they are generally more informative than the letters or words found in a menu bar. Vertical menus come in several varieties: pull down, pop up, partial screen, and full

**Figure 5.2**
Loading a file into memory with Lotus 1-2-3, a spreadsheet program

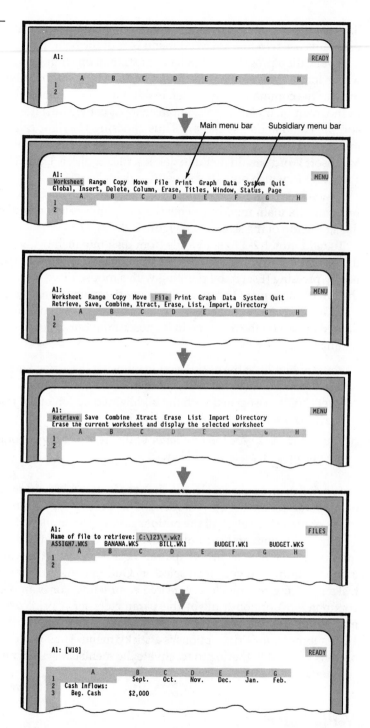

screen. Pull-down and pop up menus have the advantage of disappearing when you have finished using them, so the entire screen can be used for other tasks. Partial- and full-screen menus occupy large areas of the display; new users find them reassuring.

**Figure 5.3**
Pull-down menus—
like this one from
PFS:Professional
Write—make judi-
cious use of the
screen.

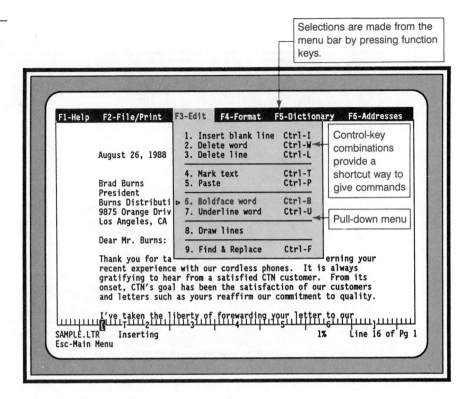

Selections are made from the
menu bar by pressing function
keys.

F1-Help   F2-File/Print   F3-Edit   F4-Format   F5-Dictionary   F6-Addresses

                                1. Insert blank line  Ctrl-I     Control-key
                                2. Delete word        Ctrl-W     combinations
August 26, 1988                 3. Delete line        Ctrl-L     provide a
                                                                 shortcut way to
                                4. Mark text          Ctrl-T     give commands
Brad Burns                      5. Paste              Ctrl-P
President
Burns Distributi ▷ 6. Boldface word    Ctrl-B
9875 Orange Driv                7. Underline word     Ctrl-U     Pull-down menu
Los Angeles, CA
                                8. Draw lines
Dear Mr. Burns:
                                9. Find & Replace     Ctrl-F
Thank you for ta                                      erning your
recent experience with our cordless phones.  It is always
gratifying to hear from a satisfied CTN customer.  From its
onset, CTN's goal has been the satisfaction of our customers
and letters such as yours reaffirm our commitment to quality.

I've taken the liberty of forwarding your letter to our
SAMPLE.LTR   Inserting                              1%    Line 16 of Pg 1
Esc-Main Menu

## Pull-Down Menus

Pull-down menus are submenus attached to a menu bar at the top of the screen (see Figure 5.3). The appropriate pull-down menu descends like a window shade whenever you select an option from the menu bar. This hybrid menu system works well: Pull-down menus intrude on the screen just enough to make room for the menu's contents; meanwhile, the menu bar remains on the screen to provide program context.

The pull-down menu system shown in Figure 5.3 is controlled from the keyboard. First an option is selected from the menu bar by pressing one of the function keys, causing a pull-down menu to appear. Then up and down arrow keys are used to highlight the desired pull-down option. Pressing [Enter] selects the highlighted option. Though not lengthy, this sequence can be bypassed entirely with control-key shortcuts. In Figure 5.3, the control-key shortcuts are listed on the right-hand side of the pull-down menu. For example, pressing [Ctrl]-[L] deletes from the document the entire line that the cursor sits on.

Microsoft Windows is an MS-DOS shell that uses a Macintosh-like pull-down system (see Figure 5.4). The widespread adoption of this visual interface is likely because Microsoft Windows is built into the OS/2 Presentation Manager used on IBM PS/2 computers.

Although Microsoft Windows can be controlled entirely from the keyboard, it works best with a mouse. Options are selected from the menu bar by pointing and holding down the mouse button. Then moving the mouse up and down highlights

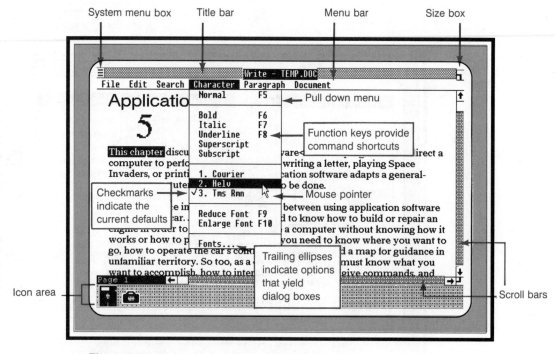

System menu box    Title bar    Menu bar    Size box

Pull down menu

Function keys provide command shortcuts

Checkmarks indicate the current defaults

Mouse pointer

Trailing ellipses indicate options that yield dialog boxes

Icon area

Scroll bars

**Figure 5.4**
Microsoft Windows provides IBM and compatible personal computers with a Macintosh-like visual interface, complete with pull-down menus, icons, and scroll bars.

options on the pull-down menu; releasing the mouse button selects the currently highlighted option. Function keys provide shortcuts for the most frequently used options.

If a pull-down menu option is followed by ellipses (...), selecting it causes a dialog box to appear (see Figure 5.5). Dialog boxes are special windows that appear temporarily and then go away. Many programs use dialog boxes to warn of dangers or keep you informed, but the dialog boxes associated with pull-down menus are used to collect information from you. For example, the Fonts dialog box shown in Figure 5.5 allows you to make decisions about the type size and style of characters in the document.

Dialog boxes can collect information in several ways. For example, the Fonts dialog box contains two list boxes and two text boxes for making selections. A list box lets you scroll through a list of options to see what choices are available. You choose an option by clicking on it with a mouse, causing it to be displayed in inverse video—that is, with reversed screen colors such as white letters on a black background. Alternatively, you can type entries into the text boxes. Either way, your selections become effective only when you close the dialog box by clicking the *button* labeled Ok or by pressing [Enter]. The Cancel button lets you abandon your selections—closing the dialog box without side effects.

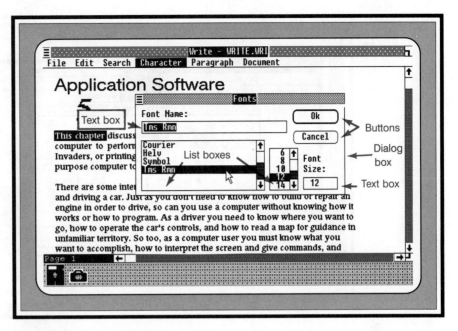

**Figure 5.5**
This dialog box appears when you select the Fonts option from the Character pull-down menu.

The Control Panel shown in Figure 5.6 illustrates several other ways to make selections. This dialog box lets you

- "Push" buttons by pointing and clicking on them. The buttons in Figure 5.6 adjust the sensitivity of the keyboard and mouse and determine other hardware options.

- Adjust the volume of the computer's speaker with a sliding *control arm*. To move the control arm to a new position, you point at it and depress the mouse button. Then you can drag the control arm up or down by moving the mouse. Releasing the mouse button fixes the control arm in its new position.

- Select the amount of memory assigned to the RAM Cache, a buffer between the CPU and the disk drives. Clicking the arrows in the RAM cache's scroll bar increases or decreases the RAM Cache's size. A large RAM Cache boosts the computer's overall speed by reducing the frequency of disk accesses. However, memory assigned to the RAM Cache is not available for use by application programs.

## Pop-Up Menus

**Pop-up menus** appear on the screen seemingly from nowhere. After you have made your selection from a pop-up menu, it disappears leaving no trace. This makes pop-up menus a popular choice for **memory-resident utility programs.** These programs are loaded into memory before any application programs are run, and they stay in this reserved memory even when other programs are executed. Normally memory-

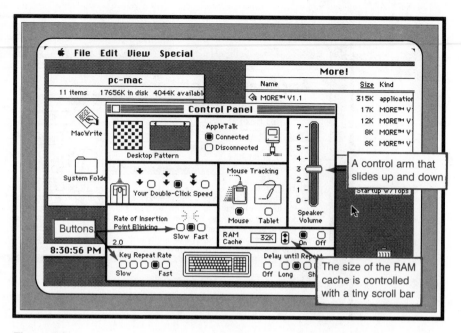

**Figure 5.6**
The Control Panel is a Macintosh dialog that adjusts characteristics of the hardware, such as the volume of the speaker or the repeat rate of the keys.

resident programs are inactive, allowing other programs to function without interruption. You activate them by pressing a special combination of keys, such as the [Ctrl] and [Alt] keys at the same time. Once activated, the memory-resident program suspends the current application program and presents itself through pop-up windows on the screen.

Figure 5.7 illustrates Sidekick, a memory-resident desk accessories program. (**Desk accessories** are instantly available tools, such as an electronic calendar, calculator, or note pad.) The screen shows a word processing session in which the user has activated Sidekick—possibly to do some quick arithmetic calculations with Sidekick's calculator. Sidekick's main menu is superimposed on top of the word processing display. Selections can be made from Sidekick's main menu in three ways: (1) by choosing an option with arrow keys and pressing [Enter], (2) by pressing one of the highlighted letters in the menu, or (3) by pressing a function key. For example, if you press function key [F3], Sidekick's main menu would be replaced by a pop-up window containing an electronic version of a four-function pocket calculator. Other Sidekick desk accessories include a monthly calendar 1901 through 2099; a phone directory for storing names, addresses, and phone numbers; an autodialer for placing phone calls (a modem is required to use this accessory); a note pad for jotting down notes and editing files; and an ASCII table for easy reference. Pressing [Esc] deactivates Sidekick, causing its windows to disappear and allowing the primary application program to continue from wherever you were when you activated Sidekick.

## A Word About . . . *User Interfaces*

*Firms must choose between speed and friendliness when they select the user interface for their software.*

Anyone who doubts the impact a user interface can have on a corporation's bottom line should talk to consultant Deborah Mayhew.

If a corporation with 40 microcomputer users saves just 10 seconds each day per employee due to a fast and efficient interface, it will save the company one employee's salary annually, said Mayhew, whose Medford, Massachusetts-based company, Deborah Mayhew and Associates, specializes in software interface design.

But speed isn't everything, according to Mayhew. For users intimidated by personal computers, a graphically oriented—but slower—interface can bring novice users and PCs together painlessly.

Whether an interface should emphasize speed or friendliness is a difficult choice facing many microcomputer managers, and the answer to that question, according to Mayhew, depends on two things: what users want and how much the company can afford.

Some corporations go to the trouble to develop custom user interfaces for all software used in-house; however, that adds a good 20 percent to the cost of the application's development, Mayhew said.

Because of that cost, most companies accept the interfaces found in off-the-shelf PC software. According to Mayhew, most corporations going this route must choose between two basic paradigms: a 1-2-3-like interface that is patterned after Lotus' popular integrated product, or a graphically oriented interface that is similar to programs run on Apple's Macintosh computer.

Source: Edward Warner, *Infoworld*, 12 January 1987, pp. 31.

Because the Lotus interface is character-based—rather than icon-based—it is faster than graphically oriented interfaces, said Michael Kolowich, director of marketing and development for Cambridge, Massachusetts-based Lotus.

Graphic interfaces, he elaborated, "don't run fast enough" and can't display data at the same speed as character-based programs.

Stanley Scott, senior manager at Peat, Marwick, Mitchell & Co., in New York, said that though good for first-time users, icons get in the way for more experienced employees.

"1-2-3's interface is going to win out," Scott said. "When people get a little more experienced, it's just as easy to put the cursor at the command or type the first letter [as it is to use icons]."

Office automation analyst Amy Wohl, however, believes that graphical interfaces using icons and windows represent the future of office automation software.

"Users see the Macintoshlike interface as more modern and as saving user training costs," according to Wohl, who is president of Wohl Associates Inc., located in Bala Cynwyd, Pennsylvania.

Wohl cited as an example IBM's Displaywrite 4, which offers a pop-up menu interface that she said improves upon the character-based interface of Displaywrite 3.

To help PC managers and developers choose the right interface for their users, consultant Mayhew has established a foremost rule for interface design: Know your user. User needs vary, she elaborated, pointing out that a mouse-driven icon interface is useless to even a novice airline reservation clerk because of slow performance and lack of adequate desk space.

**Figure 5.7**
Sidekick, a desk accessories program, announces itself with a pop-up menu as well as a line of instructions on the screen's bottom line. Here, the primary application is Microsoft Word. Sidekick obscures part of the document editing window, but Microsoft Word's two-line menu bar is still visible.

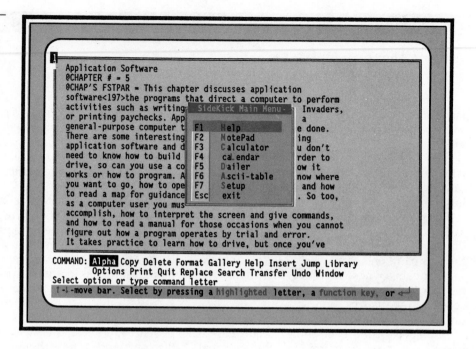

```
  Application Software
  @CHAPTER # = 5
  @CHAP'S FSTPAR = This chapter discusses application
  software<197>the programs that direct a computer to perform
  activities such as writing         Invaders,
  or printing paychecks. App    ┌─SideKick Main Menu─┐   a
  general-purpose computer t    │ F1   Help          │  e done.
  There are some interesting    │ F2   NotePad       │  ing
  application software and d    │ F3   Calculator    │  u don't
  need to know how to build     │ F4   calendar      │  rder to
  drive, so can you use a co    │ F5   Dialer        │  ow it
  works or how to program. A    │ F6   Ascii-table   │  now where
  you want to go, how to ope    │ F7   Setup         │  and how
  to read a map for guidance    │ Esc  exit          │  . So too,
  as a computer user you mus    └────────────────────┘
  accomplish, how to interpret the screen and give commands,
  and how to read a manual for those occasions when you cannot
  figure out how a program operates by trial and error.
  It takes practice to learn how to drive, but once you've
```

```
COMMAND: [Alpha] Copy Delete Format Gallery Help Insert Jump Library
          Options Print Quit Replace Search Transfer Undo Window
Select option or type command letter
↑↓-move bar. Select by pressing a highlighted letter, a function key, or ↵
```

## *Partial- and Full-Screen Menus*

**Partial-screen menus** stay put on the screen so that their options can be examined at any time. They are similar to menu bars although they occupy more of the screen. For example, Figure 5.8 shows a partial-screen menu used by WordStar to explain its control-key commands. (Note that ^ stands for the [Ctrl] key; in other words, ^E is a shorthand method of writing [Ctrl]-[E].) The menu's first four columns describe various cursor-movement and editing commands; the last column lists the submenus in WordStar's multilevel menu system. For example, to move the cursor to the beginning of the document, you might type [Ctrl]-[Q] to activate the Quick Functions menu, and then press [R] to select the Beg Doc (begin document) option from the Quick Functions menu. WordStar's poor command-key mnemonics are forgivable only because it was among the first word processors available for personal computers.

**Full-screen menus** take over the entire display, precluding you from using the screen for any other purpose. These menus not only show what options are available but also describe briefly what each option means. Generally, they itemize options down the center of the screen (see Figure 5.9). They work best for programs infrequently used, such as an end-of-the-month accounting program, or for programs designed for novices.

## WINDOW OPERATIONS

Recall that a *window* is a rectangular viewing area of the screen. Not all application programs allow you to use windows, but those that do have some distinct advantages. Windows give you control over the screen's real estate—always a precious

# Output:
# Displaying and Printing

*Like everyone else, you use computers to get output. Perhaps you want to look at information in a file. Or maybe you want to print a letter. Or you might need to control a blast furnace. Whatever the application, you need an output device to convert the computer's digital signals into a useful form. This photo essay will give you a better idea of how flexible output systems can be.*

1. Printers and monitors vary considerably in size, quality, speed, price, and convenience. It pays to consider options carefully before making a purchase.

# VIDEO DISPLAY

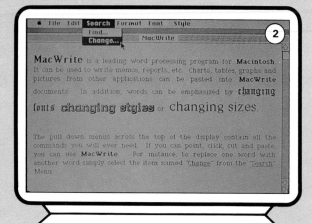

2. The Apple Macintosh uses a monochrome screen with a resolution of 512 by 342 pixels. Here the MacWrite word processing program is displaying several sizes and styles of text.

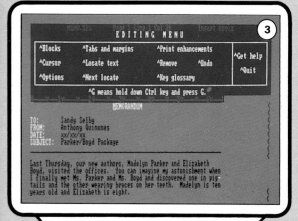

3. This picture was made with an IBM PC, a Tecmar Graphics Master color adapter card, and a 35-mm slide-maker camera system. Its resolution is 640 by 200 pixels, the same as that on a standard IBM PC color display. Because there are only 8 scan lines for each row, the characters look grainy. The memo in this screen is being edited with WordStar 2000.

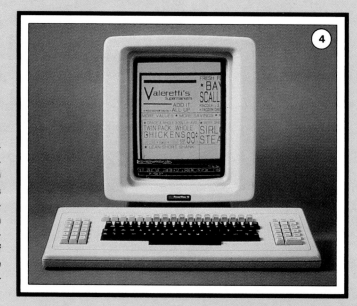

4. The trend in word processing systems is toward what-you-see-is-what-you-get display. This PowerView 10 terminal, produced by Compugraphic, is used to preview work before it is typeset. PowerView processes the screen image with an Intel 80186 microprocessor supported by one megabyte of memory. The screen image can be scrolled horizontally and vertically, reduced in size, or enlarged.

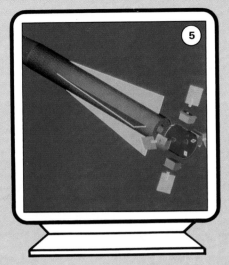

5. This image was produced by the IBM 5080 Graphics System, which is used primarily by design engineers. The screen has a viewing area 11.2 inches square and can display up to 256 colors with a resolution of 1,024 by 1,024 pixels. Today a display of this quality is too expensive for most personal computers—but in the future, who knows?

6. The 9-inch, flat-panel amber display on this portable computer has 512 by 255 pixels and an adjustable viewing angle for easy reading. Built into the top of the computer is a small ink-jet printer. The computer weighs only 25 pounds and costs less than $5,000.

7. Liquid crystal displays are popular for portable computers because they consume little power. For example, the battery in this portable computer can operate up to eight hours without recharging. Hidden in the side of the computer are two 3.5-inch 720KB diskette drives.

*window 3*

# PRINTERS

8. Most dot matrix printers can print both text and graphics. Dot matrix printers have captured an increasing share of the market as their cost has fallen and print resolution has increased.

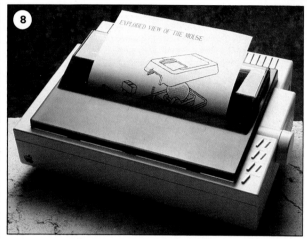

9. This color dot matrix printer has a 24-element printhead that provides 144 dot-per-inch (dpi) resolution. The suggested retail price is less than $270.

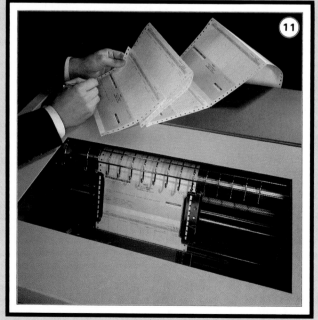

10. With daisy-wheel printers, raised images of letters are pressed into an inked ribbon and paper. They produce high-quality letters but are noisy, unable to handle graphics, and slow, printing just 10 to 80 characters per second.

11. Business documents are often created by filling in the blanks in preprinted forms.

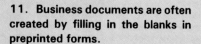

**12.** Like many recently introduced laser printers, Apple's LaserWriter is based on the print engine used in Canon's personal copiers. The printer is controlled by a Motorola 68000 microprocessor supported by 2 megabytes of internal memory. It produces 300-dpi output at rates up to 8 pages per minute, and it comes with a number of built-in fonts in a range of sizes.

Cut Here

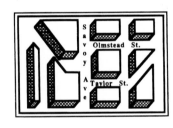

Our Newest
Watermill Restaurant
is located at 101 Savoy Ave.

The Watermill Restaurant is located
between Olmstead St. and Taylor St.
on Savoy Ave. Plenty of Free Parking.
Open 11am-12pm Mon. thru Sun.

First Class Mail

ANNOUNCING THE OPENING OF
THE WATERMILL RESTAURANT
AT 101 SAVOY AVE.

# G·R·A·N·D  O·P·E·N·I·N·G

**13.** This sample output, which is almost typeset quality, was created using a Macintosh application program and the LaserWriter printer.

# PLOTTERS

14. Pen plotters produce smoother lines than dot matrix printers, but they operate much more slowly. This inexpensive six-pen plotter prints by moving the paper back and forth while moving the pen from side to side, with 250 steps per inch. To fill in a region with color the pen must run back and forth many times, which is a slow process.

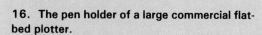

15. Engineering, architecture, and other design applications require large, high-resolution plotters. This drum plotter uses the same basic technology as the small plotter in photo 14, but it is much more accurate.

16. The pen holder of a large commercial flat-bed plotter.

17. Sample plot of an integrated circuit from an electrostatic plotter.

18. This stand-alone plotter was designed for drafters, engineers, and architects. From text entered on the keyboard, this system produces wet ink lettering for use on drawings and schematics.

19. This laser-driven photoplotter is accurate to 0.005 of an inch, which is far smaller than can be seen by an unaided human eye.

20. A close-up view of the photoplotter's printhead.

21. High-quality photoplotters have historically been very costly—more than $60,000. This photoplotter costs $25,000. It interfaces with microcomputers, such as the IBM PC/AT shown here, with an RS-232 interface and is used to create the precision artwork for printed circuit boards.

# OTHER OUTPUT DEVICES

*Anything that can be controlled with electrical signals or motors can be controlled by computer. This page gives three examples of very different types of computer output.*

22. Computers are increasingly being called on to perform mechanical tasks. This is an automated testing system that helps ensure the quality of circuits in some of IBM's mainframe computers.

23. This fully portable, electronically controlled printer can produce labels with both bar codes and human-readable information. Because the labels are printed on thermally coated paper with a thermal printhead, no ribbons are required.

24. The electron-beam exposure system shown here etches microscopic patterns on glass plates. The system translates data on a tape into physical form by shooting an intense beam of electrons at a chemically coated glass plate. Eventually the glass plates are used as masks to fabricate integrated circuits.

*window 3*

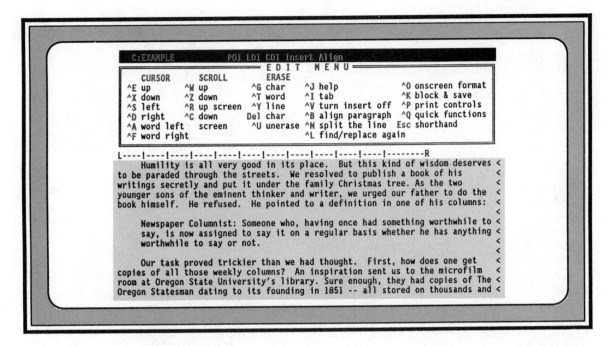

**Figure 5.8**
WordStar's Edit Menu is a fine example of a partial-screen menu. Note how related commands are grouped into columns.

**Figure 5.9**
File Express, a simple file management program, displays options on its full-screen main menu as if they were cards in a card file.

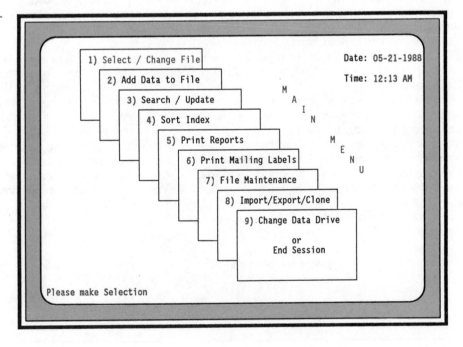

## A Word About . . . *Software Standards*

*Establishing corporate software guidelines can save time and money, but pitfalls abound for the unwary manager.*

Last year, Evan Carpenter advised the users in Litton's Areo Products Division to use Office Writer for word processing. A key department chose to use Wordstar 2000 instead. Now, Carpenter says, that department's files can't be shared directly with other departments, and its employees aren't easily moved to other areas.

Carpenter is the office systems manager for Litton's Information Systems Department, which supports 150 users in the Moorpark, California, division. Because users balked at a standard, he must face the decision of whether to transfer the department's Wordstar 2000 files into Office Writer files, a costly, time-consuming endeavor involving an estimated 70 megabytes of data. "Either way, it's definitely going to end up costing us," says Carpenter.

Like Carpenter, most micro managers consider companywide software standards a necessity of centralized computing centers. Limiting the number of programs in circulation can save time and money. "The bigger your company is, the more you can benefit from standards," says Cliff Hodges, supervisor of the computing services center at Chevron USA, in San Ramon, California.

Some managers insist that users uphold the corporate standard; others tell employees using unapproved software not to expect support. The reasons companies cite for software standardization are not new. Highest on the list remains support: The fewer programs used in a company, the easier it is for the microcomputer staff to support them.

"It would be an absolute nightmare if there were four or five programs out there," says

Sharon Lugo, who provides support for about 150 users of word processing and graphics software at Calcomp of Anaheim, California. "I couldn't hope to know them all."

Keeping up with software upgrades, a task Lugo describes as a "nightmare" for just one product, would be an even more enormous task if more products were used. "If we had four or five packages, all I'd be doing would be upgrading," she says.

Limiting the time needed for training is also a primary reason why companies establish software standards. At the Chicago Tribune, a job-posting procedure enables people to move between departments, according to Lewin. Employees can change departments and be up to speed faster if the software is the same from job to job, he says.

"The real cost of a piece of software is not the cost of the program but the time you have to invest before people become productive with it," according to Glenn Watts, director of the Office of Budget, Planning, and Analysis at the University of Wisconsin at Madison. "Through being able to share what employees know, you shorten the learning curve for the whole office," Watts says.

Despite these benefits, establishing companywide software standards—and then convincing users to adhere to those standards—remains a difficult task for corporate micro managers.

Chevron's Hedges says he has frequent problems with people wanting to continue to use their own program. "We are very concerned with things that threaten our standard," he says. "Without a good reason for not using the standard, we fight pretty hard."

Source: Laurie Flynn, *Infoworld*, 4 August 1986, pp. 31–32.

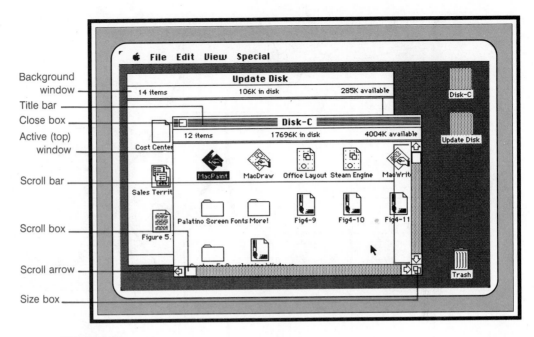

Background window
Title bar
Close box
Active (top) window
Scroll bar
Scroll box
Scroll arrow
Size box

**Figure 5.10**
Overlapping windows can be stacked on top of one another.

commodity. They let you compare or move things between files with ease. And they help you switch quickly from one application or activity to another.

There are several ways to handle windows in a computer system. The Macintosh uses the most common method, **overlapping windows,** as Figure 5.10 shows. Overlapping windows can be opened and closed, moved, resized, scrolled, and—on some systems—zoomed.

- *Open and close.* Once a window is opened, it remains open until you close it by clicking the close box, a tiny rectangle in the window's upper left-hand margin, or by selecting the Close option from the File menu.

- *Move.* You can move a window about on the screen. Pointing at any visible part of a window buried in the pile and clicking the button brings that window to the top (or foreground) so that you can see it and work on its contents. On the Macintosh, windows in the background are deactivated—or frozen in place—until activated again. The active window can be moved or dragged by pointing to its title bar, pressing the mouse button, and dragging it across the screen.

- *Resize.* You make a window larger or smaller by dragging its size box in the lower right-hand corner.

- *Scroll.* Because a window may not be large enough to display all its data, you may have to resort to *scrolling*, which means moving the contents of a window up, down, left, or right. You can scroll a window in several ways. Pressing a scroll arrow moves data slowly across the screen. A faster method is to click the gray area in a scroll bar; this scrolls by the windowful. If you want to

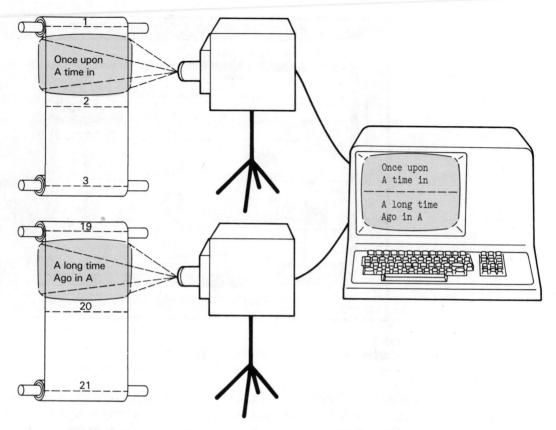

**Figure 5.11**
In word processing, the screen is usually split horizontally into windows.

jump quickly to a distant part of a directory or document, you can drag the scroll box to a place along the scroll bar that represents the approximate position you want to see. For example, to see the bottom of a document, you would drag the scroll box down the right edge of the window to the bottom of the scroll bar.

• *Zoom.* With many windowing systems, you can have the active window expand and occupy the entire screen, that is, *zoom in*. Later, if you *zoom out*, the window will return to its previous size and position on the screen. You should know that graphics programs usually define zooming differently. With these programs, zooming changes the size of data, not the size of windows. For example, if you select a Zoom-In option in a drafting program, the drawing will expand so that you can see a portion of it more clearly.

Instead of overlapping windows, some programs use **tiled windows** to divide the viewing screen into nonoverlapping regions similar to window panes. Since the windows do not overlap, the entire rectangular area of each window is visible at all times. Windowing requires powerful processors, and tiled windows conserve

**Figure 5.12**
WordStar 2000
splits the screen
into tiled windows of
equal size.

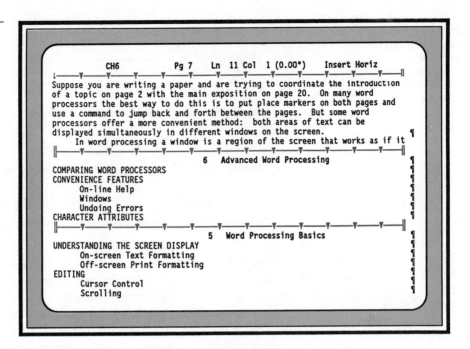

```
            CH6              Pg 7    Ln  11 Col  1 (0.00")    Insert Horiz
└───────▼────────▼──────▼────────▼────────▼──────▼─────▼──────▼────▼──┤
Suppose you are writing a paper and are trying to coordinate the introduction
of a topic on page 2 with the main exposition on page 20.  On many word
processors the best way to do this is to put place markers on both pages and
use a command to jump back and forth between the pages.  But some word
processors offer a more convenient method:  both areas of text can be
displayed simultaneously in different windows on the screen.                ¶
     In word processing a window is a region of the screen that works as if it ¶
╟──────▼────────▼──────▼────────▼────────▼──────▼─────▼──────▼────▼──╢
                           6    Advanced Word Processing                    ¶
COMPARING WORD PROCESSORS                                                   ¶
CONVENIENCE FEATURES                                                        ¶
     On-line Help                                                           ¶
     Windows                                                                ¶
     Undoing Errors                                                         ¶
CHARACTER ATTRIBUTES                                                        ¶
╟──────▼────────▼──────▼────────▼────────▼──────▼─────▼──────▼────▼──╢
                           5    Word Processing Basics                      ¶
UNDERSTANDING THE SCREEN DISPLAY                                            ¶
     On-screen Text Formatting                                             ¶
     Off-screen Print Formatting                                          ¶
EDITING                                                                     ¶
     Cursor Control                                                         ¶
     Scrolling                                                              ¶
```

processor speed and storage because they do not require the computer to save and then restore a hidden, overlapped part of each deactivated window. Thus switching from one tiled window to another is fast and memory efficient.

Many MS-DOS word processors and spreadsheet programs use tiled windows. Early versions of Microsoft Windows used tiled windows, but with version 2.0 in 1987, it changed to overlapping windows.

Tiled windows can be opened and closed and resized, but the procedures for performing these operations vary widely from program to program. This emphasizes why it is nice to have windowing built into the operating system: That way, all application programs use the same commands to control windows.

- *Open and close.* To open another window, you must cut an existing window in two. Closing a window causes another to fill in the void.

- *Resize.* An existing window is resized, but not moved, if you change the boundary between two windows.

A typical use of windows is to help organize the presentation of ideas in a word processing document. Suppose you are writing a paper and are trying to coordinate the introduction of a topic on page 2 with the main exposition on page 20. On some word processors, the best way to do this is to put *place markers* on both pages and use a command to jump back and forth between the pages. But if your word processor supports windows, each area of text can be displayed in its own window.

In word processing, a window is a region of the screen that works as if it had its own TV camera pointed at a scroll of text (see Figure 5.11). For example, WordStar 2000 can split the screen into three windows of equal size (see Figure 5.12).

**Figure 5.13**
Integrated software typically emphasizes one component, called the central component.

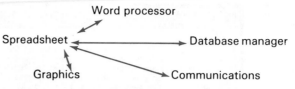

**(a)  Spreadsheet-based integrated software**

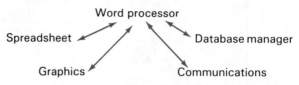

**(b)  Integrated software based on a word processor**

Windows are especially helpful for cut-and-paste operations. By scrolling the windows appropriately, you can put the source text in one window and its destination in another. Cutting and pasting between windows is the same as a regular, one-window cut-and-paste operation except that the pasting and cutting are done in different windows. Since the windows can look into separate files, windows make moving text among several files as easy as moving text within a single file.

## INTEGRATED APPLICATIONS

An **integrated program** is a collection of related programs, or **components,** combined into a unified package that provides a means of transferring data among the components. Integrated programs make sense when the programs perform related functions or similar tasks or when they use the same data. For example, an integrated accounting program may combine programs that take care of all the basic accounting systems maintained by a business—accounts payable, accounts receivable, inventory management, payroll, and general ledger. A trend in personal computer software is to integrate the functions of word processing, spreadsheet analysis, graphics, data management, and communications into an integrated package. As computer systems have increased in capability, we have seen steady increases in the integration of programs.

Programs are often integrated into one package to unify the user interface. When each program has a common user interface, learning to operate one part of the package makes learning the other parts easy because they share a common mode of operation.

In almost all integrated programs, one component is central, the basis for all the other components in two ways. First, one component is usually the center of data transfers. For example, Figure 5.13 shows two integrated programs, each of which includes spreadsheet, graphics, database management, word processing, and data communications components. An arrow points to a component if data can be transferred to it from another component. In Figure 5.13(a), data can be transferred from the spreadsheet to any other component and from any component to the spreadsheet, but data cannot be transferred directly between the other components. Thus in this case, the spreadsheet is the central component; this is a *spreadsheet-based integrated program.*

Second, the central component may determine the form of the data in all other components and thus exert a strong influence on the other components. For example, if the spreadsheet is the central component, all other components may adopt the spreadsheet's row and column format. The word processor may store text by expanding a spreadsheet column until it is as wide as the printed page, and the fields in the database manager may be equated to cells in the spreadsheet.

One major advantage of integrated programs is the ease with which data can be transferred between components. For example, if you are writing a letter (word processing) that contains a graph (graphics) illustrating a relationship you discovered with a numerical model (spreadsheet analysis), an integrated program may work better for you than an assortment of standalone programs. Data can be taken from one program and entered into another by a simple cut-and-paste operation. In contrast, moving data between standalone programs is often time consuming and bothersome. For example, to move part of a Lotus 1-2-3 spreadsheet into a WordStar word processing document, you must

1. Load Lotus 1-2-3 and the spreadsheet into memory.

2. "Print" the portion of the spreadsheet you want to transfer. Instead of printing to a printer, you must request the print operation to send its output to a disk as a data file.

3. Load WordStar and the document into memory.

4. Merge (also called *import*) the data file into the document with a Block-Read command.

These steps are necessary because WordStar cannot directly read Lotus 1-2-3 spreadsheet files, but it can read files that Lotus 1-2-3 has "printed" to a disk. This type of rigmarole is common when moving data between standalone programs because they usually store data in their own specialized formats on disk.

Another advantage of having integrated programs is the speed with which you can move from one processing activity to another. For example, you may begin a session by preparing a sales forecast with a spreadsheet, as Figure 5.14(a) shows; then use the graphics component to construct a bar graph showing your forecast; and then insert the graph into a memo in the word processing component, as Figure 5.14(b) shows.

Most integrated programs use a *clipboard*, a special file that holds data while it is being moved from one component to another. Used with windowing, a clipboard file can provide powerful methods of merging components. Programs usually provide a *copy-and-paste* operation that removes the data from the source window without destroying the original data. Copy-and-paste operations make static (dead) copies of the original data. If the original version of the data is modified after the copy has been made, the copy remains unchanged. A few integrated programs allow *copy-and-link* operations that create "live" linkages between components. For example, a portion of the spreadsheet window in Figure 5.14(a) is copied and linked

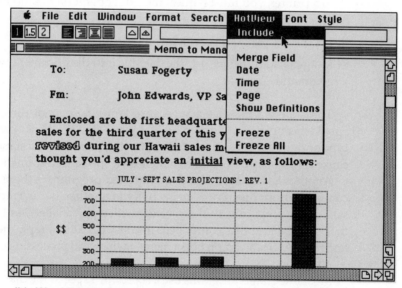

**Figure 5.14**
Using an integrated program to transfer information from a spreadsheet to a memo. Sales data in the spreadsheet window **(a)** is first transferred to a graph window, where it is transformed into a bar graph. Then the bar graph is copied and linked to a memo in a word processing window **(b)**.

**(a) Worksheet**

| | File | Edit | Window | Range | Tools | Font | Style | | |
|---|---|---|---|---|---|---|---|---|---|

270

D5

**Monthly Sales Forecast**

| | A | B | C | D | E | F | G |
|---|---|---|---|---|---|---|---|
| 1 | Sales Forecast | | | | | | |
| 2 | (in thousands) | | Inflation= | | 5% | | |
| 3 | | | | | | | |
| 4 | | | July | Aug | Sept | | Total |
| 5 | Sales | $245 | $257 | $270 | | $772 | |
| 6 | Costs | 86 | 129 | 135 | | $350 | |
| 7 | Profit | 159 | 128 | 135 | | $422 | |
| 8 | | | | | | | |
| 9 | Expenses | | | | | | |
| 10 | Auto | 24 | 26 | 27 | | $77 | |
| 11 | Phone | 12 | 13 | 14 | | $39 | |
| 12 | Wages | 37 | 39 | 41 | | $117 | |
| 13 | Taxes | 9 | 10 | 10 | | $29 | |
| 14 | Total | $82 | $88 | $92 | | $262 | |
| 15 | | | | | | | |
| 16 | Net | $77 | $40 | $43 | | $160 | |
| 17 | | | | | | | |

**(b) Word Processing**

| | File | Edit | Window | Format | Search | HotView | Font | Style |
|---|---|---|---|---|---|---|---|---|

Memo to Mana

To:        Susan Fogerty

Fm:        John Edwards, VP Sa

Enclosed are the first headquarte
sales for the third quarter of this y
revised during our Hawaii sales m
thought you'd appreciate an *initial* view, as follows:

Include

Merge Field
Date
Time
Page
Show Definitions

Freeze
Freeze All

JULY - SEPT SALES PROJECTIONS - REV. 1

$$

to a graph window to construct a bar chart, which in turn, is linked to the memo shown in the word processing window in Figure 5.14(b). Later, if you change the numbers in the spreadsheet, both the bar chart in the graph window and the copy of the bar chart in the word processing window will automatically reflect those changes.

# MODES IN SOFTWARE

Most programs have several **modes,** or states, but only a restricted set of operations can be performed in any particular mode. For example, if a word processor is in the text entry mode, any text typed on the keyboard is added to the document being created. But if the word processor is in a command mode, the same keystrokes may be interpreted as commands to erase, move, or reformat text. New users tend to get confused about which mode is active and are surprised when the program is unresponsive or does something different from what they intend.

Good programs use several techniques to help the user switch quickly between modes, recognize which mode is active, and operate effectively within each mode. Some of these techniques are to

- Display the current mode—such as Ready, Edit, Graph, or Menu—in a status indicator. For example, Lotus 1-2-3 displays its current mode in the upper right-hand corner of the screen (see Figure 5.2).

- Provide a **help system**—a display of explanatory information—at the touch of the help key. At its best, on-line help is like a reference manual that consistently opens to the right page. A *context-sensitive help system* silently observes which function is being used and stands ready to present information about that function and what can be done next—all at the touch of the help key. If the initial display is not helpful, most systems have menus from which you can select the topic for the next screen of information.

- Design the program to operate in a manner similar to systems that most people are already familiar with. For example, a file management program might mimic the operations of a Rolodex card file; an integrated package might simulate a clipboard in the way data is transferred among its component programs; and so forth.

- Use menus to prompt the user with choices of available commands and assign commonly used functions to the keyboard's function keys.

- Permit special selection devices, such as a mouse or touch screen, to be used to enter commands, allowing the keyboard to be reserved for entering data.

- Prompt for confirmation before performing destructive operations. For most operations, once a command is given, execution is immediate. But some operations are so destructive that application programs ask for a confirmation. For example, if you gave a command that would delete the entire document, a word processor might respond with

  DELETING ENTIRE DOCUMENT—TYPE Y TO CONFIRM.

- Provide an **UNDO command,** with which you can reverse the effect of the previous command. Pretend, for the moment, that instead of moving ten pages of text from one spot in memory to another, you accidentally delete all ten pages. An UNDO command would allow you to restore the lost pages to memory. Unfortunately, in practice, the UNDO command is not as helpful as it sounds. Most programs undo only the very last command. Typing a second UNDO command cancels the effect of the first one; it does not allow you to work your way back to correct a mistake made several commands ago. Being limited to reversing the effect of the last command is more serious than it first sounds. For example, Microsoft Word interprets insertion or deletion of a single character as a command. Thus you cannot undo a command that deleted ten pages if you bump the space bar while considering what to do. Clearly, the best defense against disaster is to make frequent back-up copies of your work.

## SELECTING SOFTWARE

Thousands of application programs have been written and are available for sale. Each is designed for a particular type of activity. If you cannot find a satisfactory prewritten application program, you can have a program written to your specifications. For example, a control program for a one-of-a-kind piece of machinery would need to be written from scratch. Although custom programs perform exactly as needed for a specific application, they require expensive and lengthy development. The trend in the computer industry has been away from custom programs and toward commercial application packages that can be bought and used immediately with little or no modification. This is particularly true of software for personal computers, where the cost of developing a substantial custom program is likely to exceed the cost of all the system's hardware.

### Application Packages

Using the right application package for a job is just as important as using the right tools to build a house. Many problems experienced by beginners can be traced to using the wrong program. For example, you could write and print a letter with a spreadsheet program, but doing that makes as much sense as cutting a two-by-four in half with a hammer. Choosing the right application program and learning to use it effectively are so important that the bulk of this book is about exactly that.

Commercial application packages normally include all the materials needed to use the program. Chief among these materials is **documentation**, the manual and other printed material that describes what a program does, how to use the program, what error messages a program generates, and so forth. As an example, let us look at what is inside Lotus 1-2-3, a $495 list price program that combines spreadsheet processing with the ability to produce graphs and perform limited data management activities. The package contains

- Six floppy disks, including two copy-protected system disks (original and backup), a tutorial disk that teaches how to use the package, and three disks filled with less frequently used programs (installation programs, utilities, device drivers, and so on).

- A 60-page *Getting Started* booklet that describes how to install the program and begin running it. Like most programs, Lotus 1-2-3 must be *installed* before you can use it the first time. The booklet uses cookbook-type instructions to explain how to make a backup copy of the original disks and how to use the installation programs to configure the program for your particular monitor, printer, and other hardware.

- A 12-page booklet explaining how to use Lotus 1-2-3 with a hard disk. This booklet is necessary because the copy-protection system makes it difficult to copy a working version of Lotus 1-2-3 onto a hard disk.

- A 172-page *1-2-3 Tutorial* written for people unfamiliar with computers and Lotus 1-2-3.

- A 344-page *Reference Manual* that contains a comprehensive description of the program's commands and procedures.

- A fistful of miscellaneous materials, including a 16-page *Quick Reference* guide, three plastic keyboard templates with definitions for the function keys, an offer of a free six-month subscription to *Lotus* magazine, and a sternly worded limited warranty and license agreement.

## Collecting Information

Because computers are normally bought to solve specific problems rather than to provide raw processing capabilities, software has fueled the sales of computers. For the same reason, choosing the software you want to use before deciding which computer to buy is a good idea. For example, a dietician may buy a particular computer because it runs a program that offers special features for producing diets customized to the needs of individual patients. Or a company may buy a computer because it runs a particularly good set of accounting programs. These decisions eventually make some computers a success and others a failure, depending on the software available for them.

Computers are virtually useless without software, so your search for information should focus first on the capabilities and limitations of high-quality programs. Many resources are available to help with this search.

- *Local computer clubs.* Computer clubs are an excellent source of help for beginners and advanced users. The members have wrestled with similar decisions, and they are eager to attract new people into the computer community. Their meetings usually include demonstrations of hardware and software. Many clubs have librarians who collect and distribute software in the public domain.

- *Hands-on experience.* Borrowing or renting equipment is another good source of ideas. With hands-on experience, the practical uses of a computer quickly become more evident.

- *Computer magazines.* Independent reviews in computer magazines are reliable and increase your knowledge of features to look for. A six-month subscription to *InfoWorld* will provide current information as well as improve any buying decision. In contrast to general-purpose computer magazines such as *Byte*, *InfoWorld*, and *Personal Computing*, many magazines cover only specific brands of computers. For example, *PC Magazine* is for IBM and compatible computers, *inCider* for Apple IIs, and *MacWorld* for Macintoshes.

- *Computer newsletters and indexes.* These publications can be found in many libraries and include *DP Directory, Microcomputer Software Newsletter, Microcomputer Index,* and *PC News Watch.* They are full of new-product reviews, summaries of articles, and references to reviews. On-line databases such as CompuServe and The Source as well as services such as *SOFSEARCH,* which locates software, also include references to reviews.

- *Software catalogs and directories.* These provide helpful listings of programs. Each entry usually includes the name of the program, address of the vendor, hardware and operating system required, price, and either a brief description of the program or a list of its features. Some catalogs are devoted to a particular brand of computer or particular application area such as games, business, or education. For example, the *Agricultural Computing Source Book* lists agricultural programs by area, such as farmer and agribusiness systems. Unfortunately, catalogs and directories become out of date as soon as they are published, but some (such as *Datapro Directory of Microcomputer Software*) publish monthly updates.

- *Professional associations.* Anyone who faced problems and decided to solve them with a personal computer has learned something in the process. Ask your professional associates what problems they had and how they solved them.

- *Retail outlets.* Although it may be necessary to visit retail outlets to see product demonstrations, beware of misinformation. Salespeople will emphasize the strong points of their products. It would be a coincidence if these were the features you need.

## Vertical Market Applications

This book is largely devoted to the features of general-purpose application programs—word processing, spreadsheets, data management, graphics, and communications—because these programs are useful to just about everyone and illustrate concepts relevant to all computer programs. But remember that these programs represent only a small portion of the software available for computers.

Software developers have produced a program for virtually every conceivable application. Literally tens of thousands of programs are aimed at small markets for special purposes, such as analyzing the strength of I-beams, controlling laboratory equipment, or copy-protecting disks. Using a special-purpose program will often provide a much better solution than adapting a general-purpose application program.

**Vertical market applications** is a catchall category for job-specific software. Programs in this category are diverse, as the following list illustrates:

- *Facilities scheduling* programs handle reservations for racquetball, tennis, golf, and so on.

- *Structural analysis* programs help compute the strength of walls, bridges, and other physical objects.

- *Process-control* programs monitor and regulate the equipment in factories, laboratories, and buildings.
- *Operations research* programs solve mathematical problems in which many variables are interrelated; for example, you might use an operations research program to find the shortest, quickest, safest, or most scenic route for a traveling salesperson.
- *Farm management* programs compute and record the yields of test plots for farmers.
- *Architectural* programs create preliminary architectural drawings, remodeling plans, and furniture rearrangements for homeowners and builders.

Vertical market applications are the most difficult programs to find. Computer stores are not likely to stock them because the sales volume is low, and specialized knowledge and training are needed to sell them effectively. The best sources of information about these programs are professional magazines and software catalogs. The prices for the programs vary about as much as their applications—from less than $100 to more than $100,000.

---

## Summary

Every computer program has its own set of commands that must be learned before the program can be used effectively. New users often find this disconcerting because there are few hard and fast rules to rely on when operating a computer. A command that works in one program is unlikely to work in other programs. The meaning of keyboard keys also changes from one program to the next. For example, in one program, pressing [S] may display an *S* on the screen, and in other programs, it might shoot a missile or store a file. Even the on-off switch can have different meanings. On most computers, it immediately disconnects the computer from all power; on some, it is merely a request for the computer to stop executing application programs, save all work in progress on the disk, and then turn off the power.

Which interface a program uses has a major influence on how long it takes a beginner to learn to use the program and how long it takes an expert to get tasks done. To a certain extent, there is an inverse relationship: The easiest method to learn may be the slowest method to use. Most programs sidestep this conflict by offering a combination of methods. For example, common commands may be assigned to function keys, and less frequently used commands might require making selections from menus.

Nearly all application programs are built around some form of menu system. Full-screen menus fill the entire screen with options. They are often used in complicated but infrequently run programs. Menu bars occupy just one or two lines on the screen to display the available options. Choosing an option from a menu bar often leads to a submenu, prompting another choice. Pop-up and pull-down menus do not obscure the view of the screen until they are needed. This makes them convenient for the user, but they are harder than other menu systems for programmers to create.

Software developers consume much time and energy debating the best user interface for programs. Some argue that a mouse or windows should be used to achieve a consistent interface. Others argue that technological devices are merely gadgets, that the easiest programs to use employ extensive menu systems. Still others argue that making an interface easy to use is less important than creating a responsive system that requires few keystrokes to issue commands. In this book, we show examples of how all these systems work.

An integrated program combines related programs, called components, into an integrated whole. Integrated programs make sense when the programs perform related functions or similar tasks or when they use the same data. Integration tends to make software more powerful, versatile, and complex. Increased power and versatility are certainly commendable, but increasing complexity may make software difficult to use.

It is impossible to overemphasize the importance of choosing software appropriate to the task to be done. Sometimes the best choice is to use a special-purpose program rather than adapt a general-purpose program or develop a program from scratch.

---

## Key Terms

| | |
|---|---|
| components | menu bar |
| desk accessories | mode |
| dialog box | overlapping windows |
| documentation | partial-screen menu |
| full-screen menu | pop-up menu |
| help system | pull-down menu |
| integrated program | sticky menu |
| inverse video | tiled window |
| memory-resident utility programs | UNDO command |
| menu | vertical market applications |

---

## Discussion Questions

1. How much on-line help should be provided by an operating system? An - application program?

2. Describe the features of an "ideal," easy-to-use interface for an airline reservation system. How might this interface differ from the ideal interface for a game? For a word processor?

3. What are the advantages of an integrated program over a collection of individual programs that perform the same tasks? What are the disadvantages?

4. Many computing problems can be solved with general-purpose software or with a vertical market program. What general rules or guidelines can you suggest for determining which type of software should be used?

## Exercises

1. Find the thirty top-selling application programs. What is the most popular category? Do the same thing for one year ago. Are there any differences?

2. Select a specific category of vertical market application software and find all the programs available for your personal computer in that area.

3. Compare three license agreements that accompany application programs. What activities do they proscribe?

4. Read the installation procedures accompanying a word processing or spreadsheet program. What types of equipment will the program accommodate? See if you can tell from the instructions what is being done when the procedures are followed.

# Word Processing Basics

In the early 1800s, most business correspondence was carefully handwritten by male clerks using quills and ink bottles. Good handwriting was a prerequisite for clerical employment.

A revolution of office procedures began in 1868, with the invention of the typewriter. Employers began testing clerical applicants to determine their typing speed and accuracy. The mark of business professionalism became the typewritten document, but the production of business letters remained expensive, tedious, and time consuming. Typographical errors were erased with correction paper or fluid that left behind a tell-tale blemish. Even minor editorial revisions required retyping the entire document and inevitably introduced new typographical errors. To verify a word's spelling, it was neces-

sary to stop and look up the word in a dictionary. To select an alternate word, a writer had to stop and consult a thesaurus.

Then along came *word processing*—the manipulation of text by computer. In 1964, IBM introduced a Magnetic Tape Selectric typewriter that stored text on small cassette tapes, but not until the early 1970s did screen-oriented word processing systems began to appear. An early version, introduced by Wang Laboratories in 1971, was a *dedicated word processing system;* this system was designed solely for word processing. Businesses formed centralized typing pools of word processing specialists to efficiently use the expensive new equipment.

The advantages of word processing did not become widely available until the 1980s with the appearance of low-cost, personal, computer-based word processing. Two of the first popular word processors were AppleWriter, introduced in 1978 for the Apple II, and WordStar, introduced in 1979 for CP/M-based computers. WordStar, which enabled the user of a personal computer to easily revise documents by adding, deleting, inserting, and moving blocks of copy on screen, soon sold more than a million copies and became the standard that other programs were measured by.

Since 1980, word processing vendors have competed to see who can pack the most useful features into their product. This "features war" has made it commonplace for a good word processor to offer a built-in dictionary to check the spelling of words, a thesaurus to suggest synonyms of words, an on-line help system, support for a wide range of printers, and the ability to edit several files at once in different windows—along with a host of other specialized features.

The vendors of dedicated word processing systems have not fared well; most of their original customers now buy personal computers and add word processing software to them. For example, MultiMate, a word processing program with more than 400,000 users, was introduced in 1982. It transforms an IBM PC into a word processor with a user interface and editing features similar to the Wang dedicated word processors.

People who need publication-quality results were not content with standard word processing programs. Most printed documents require several typefaces and typeface sizes. Some print jobs require a complicated page layout; for example, a newsletter may demand text, graphs, and pictures from different files be arranged in a newspaper-style page. These requirements led to the development of *desktop publishing software*—programs designed to produce typeset-quality documents with a personal computer system. Desktop publishing got its start in 1985 with a pair of new products: Aldus Corporation's PageMaker page composition program and Apple Corporation's Laserwriter printer. PageMaker provided a true what-you-see-is-what-you-get presentation of text along with the ability to compose multicolumn page layouts on the screen. The Laserwriter worked with Page-Maker to print near-typeset-quality output at a cost of a few cents a page. Together, these two products have revolutionized the way both individuals and businesses communicate their ideas.

Now, word processing vendors are integrating text editing capabilities with the on-screen typeface and page composition abilities of desktop publishing. Already, it is difficult to tell where word processing ends and desktop publishing begins.

Part II teaches about word processing and desktop publishing in three chapters. In Chapter 6, we provide detailed examples to explain the basic concepts used in creating memos, letters, or other typical documents. Basic editing and printing functions are introduced, and the features of five word processors are compared. In Chapter 7, we show how to format text and design the page layout to make your documents look attractive. We also describe the "bells and whistles" of advanced word processing. These features can check the spelling of words electronically, print form letters rapidly, and help you organize your thoughts in an outline. In Chapter 8, we explain what you can expect from desktop publishing. It describes page composition and various typesetting operations, as well as discussing all the steps in the desktop publishing process. We introduce you to desktop publishing hardware—laser printers and scanners—and two desktop publishing programs—PageMaker and Ventura Publisher.

# Word Processing Basics

It is a safe bet that word processing has sold more personal computers than any other application. Writers come to love their word processing systems because they eliminate most of the drudgery associated with traditional, paper-based methods of transforming thoughts into printed documents. Moving characters around on the screen allows words to be edited easily before they are committed to paper. It is possible to delete text, move paragraphs, or lengthen all the lines on a page with *at most* a few commands.

In this chapter, we describe commonly available word processing functions and how to use them. To help you understand how important it is to choose your word processor wisely, we begin by comparing five different word processing programs. Next, we describe the steps of a typical word processing session and explain how to interpret the parts of a word processing screen. We devote most of the chapter to detailed examples of common operations, such as moving the cursor, scrolling, simple editing, and moving blocks of text. We conclude with a discussion of ending a word processing session and an admonition to make back-up copies of your work.

## 6

## BASIC CONCEPTS

### Comparing programs

Word processing is such a big improvement over pencils and typewriters that even a poor word processor can impress a new user. Few people have the time or opportunity to test word processing programs, so most people choose their word processing program because it came with their computer system or was recommended by friends. As a result, the world is filled with computer owners who happily use an inferior word processing program or one inappropriate to their needs.

The first step in choosing a program is to define your writing needs. How often will you use it? How important is ease of use versus long-run convenience and advanced features? What type of documents will you create? Is the appearance of the printed document more important than ease of editing? Do you have any unusual writing needs, such as the need to print scientific equations containing Greek letters? What type of printer will you require?

After answering these questions, you need to know what types of features you can expect to find. One source of information is the reviews printed in trade magazines such as *InfoWorld* and *Personal Computing*. Comparison charts at the end of the articles often go on for pages with concise but cryptic labels for each feature. Today's word processors are full of time savers, writing aids, formatting tricks, and other helpful features. Some make life easier for beginners; others are essential for specific tasks; and still others sound better in advertisements than they work in practice.

Table 6.1 compares the features of five popular programs available for IBM PCs: PFS:Professional Write, WordStar 2000, WordPerfect, Microsoft Word, and Ventura Publisher. Many of the features listed in Table 6.1 may seem puzzling now, but they will become clearer after reading the next two chapters.

**Table 6.1**
**A comparison chart for five word processing products**

| Feature | PFS:Professional Write | WordStar 2000 | WordPerfect | Microsoft Word | Ventura Publisher |
|---|---|---|---|---|---|
| Primary user interface | Function keys, pull-down menus, dialog boxes | Control keys, partial-screen menus | Function keys, message lines | Mouse, keyword menus | Mouse, icons, pull-down menus, dialog boxes |
| Mouse support | No | No | No | Yes | Yes |
| Edit multiple files at once | No | 3 | 2 | 8 | Many |
| Newspaper-style columns | No | 3 | 24 | Many | Many |
| Lines per header or footer | 2 | Unlimited | Unlimited | Unlimited | 2 |
| Odd/even page distinctions | No | Yes | Yes | Yes | Yes |
| On-screen help system | Yes | Yes | Yes | Yes | No |
| On-screen tutorial system | No | Yes | No | Yes | No |
| Spelling checker | Yes | Yes | Yes | Yes | No |
| Automatic hyphenation | No | Yes | Yes | Yes | Yes |
| On-line thesaurus | Yes | No | Yes | No | No |
| Avoids widows and orphans | No | No | If desired | Always | If desired |
| Footnote placement | Manual | Automatic | Automatic | Automatic | Manual |
| Movable columns of text | No | Yes | Yes | Yes | No |
| Document chaining | Yes | Yes | Yes | Yes | Yes |
| Table of contents/indexing | No | Optional | Yes | Yes | Yes |
| Form letters (mail merge) | Yes | Yes | Yes | Yes | No |
| Style sheets (format files) | No | No | No | Yes | Yes |
| Outline processing functions | No | No | Some | Yes | No |
| User-definable macros | No | No | Yes | No | No |
| Prints proportional spacing | No | Yes | Yes | Yes | Yes |
| Prints multiple typefaces | No | Yes | Yes | Yes | Yes |
| Displays multiple typefaces | No | No | No | Some | Yes |
| Merges text and graphic files | No | No | No | No | Yes |
| Required memory | 320KB | 320KB | 320KB | 192KB | 512KB |
| Maximum file size | 64KB | Limited by disk | Limited by disk | Limited by disk | Limited by memory |
| List price | $199 | $495 | $495 | $450 | $895 |

The programs in Table 6.1 were chosen because they illustrate different approaches to word processing.

- *PFS:Professional Write* is a simple word processor designed for easy use by casual users. Its commands are prompted by pull-down menus followed by dialog boxes. Even someone unfamiliar with computers can productively use PFS:Professional Write after only an hour or two of practice.

- *WordStar 2000* is an extensive revision of the original WordStar program. Most of its commands require a combination of keystrokes, such as pressing [Ctrl]-[B] and then [B] to mark the beginning of a block of text. To become comfortable with the full range of WordStar 2000's commands takes days of practice, but once the commands have been learned, they are far less intrusive than the frequently appearing menus.

- *WordPerfect* is perhaps the most popular word processor for IBM PCs. Its commands require the frequent use of function keys. For example, pressing the [F3] function key begins the on-screen help system, and pressing [Ctrl]-[F2] begins the spelling checker. WordPerfect's function-key system takes some time to get used to but is convenient for experienced users. WordPerfect's extensive feature list includes all common word processing features as well as many obscure ones, such as sorting columns of text, statistical typing features, user-definable keyboard macros, and file security provided by optional passwords and data encryption.

- *Microsoft Word* is a state-of-the-art word processing program with many innovative features for quickly creating professional-quality documents. Although Microsoft Word's commands can be invoked from the keyboard, the program was designed to work best with a mouse. The mouse commands help beginners become proficient with Microsoft Word's many features, but "mousing around" can be distracting if you are a touch-typist because you must move a hand from the keyboard to use a mouse. Some of Microsoft Word's distinguishing features are up to eight documents can be edited simultaneously in different windows; an outstanding on-line tutorial system is built into the help system; special format files (known as *style sheets*) standardize and simplify laying out the appearance of documents; and an outliner helps organize ideas into a good-looking outline.

- *Ventura Publisher* is not normally considered a word processor at all; it is a screen-oriented desktop publishing program. It is discussed in this chapter because it illustrates many advanced text formatting abilities including professional page layout features that give text a typeset appearance. It also allows pictures and graphics to be merged with the text on the screen. Although it has simple text editing abilities, it is more often used to format and merge text files created by other word processing programs.

By now it should be clear that word processors are definitely not the same. Which one is best for you depends on the type of writing you do.

## Steps of a Typical Session

Let us assume you have selected your word processor and are ready to begin running the word processing program. On a personal computer, you might do this by turning on the computer, loading the operating system, typing the name of the word processing program, and waiting until the word processing program is loaded into memory and takes control of the computer. On a mainframe computer you must first log in.

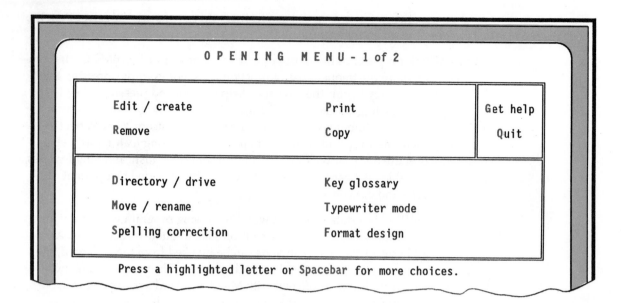

| Edit / create | Print | Get help |
|---|---|---|
| Remove | Copy | Quit |

| Directory / drive | Key glossary |
|---|---|
| Move / rename | Typewriter mode |
| Spelling correction | Format design |

Press a highlighted letter or Spacebar for more choices.

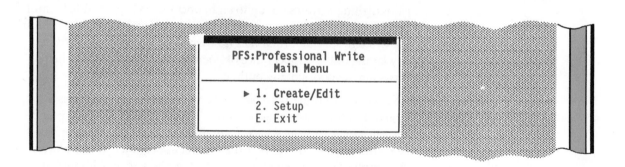

PFS:Professional Write
Main Menu

▶ 1. Create/Edit
2. Setup
E. Exit

COMMAND: **Alpha** Copy Delete Format Gallery Help Insert Jump Library
Options Print Quit Replace Search Transfer Undo Window
Select option or type command letter
Page 1    {}                              ?                    Microsoft Word:

**Figure 6.1**
The opening display of three word processors. **(a)** WordStar 2000's Opening Menu acts as the focal point for the creation and manipulation of document files. **(b)** PFS:Professional Write's Main Menu is quite limited in both options and usefulness. **(c)** Microsoft Word begins with the upper portion of the screen reserved for editing and the bottom lines reserved for help, status, and command information.

Most word processors begin with a full-screen menu as Figure 6.1 shows. Word-Star 2000's Opening Menu is of central importance to the program; it coordinates the file manipulation activities of creating, printing, copying, and deleting document files. In contrast, PFS:Professional Write's Main Menu acts as a minor barrier to getting anything done because the Setup and Exit options are rarely used.

As Figure 6.1(c) shows, some word processors jump immediately to their document editing screen, which is convenient if you want to begin editing quickly.

To edit an existing document, you must tell the word processor the name of the text file that contains the document. This causes some (or all) of the file to be transferred from disk to memory. Alternatively, you can edit an empty file, that is, create a new file.

The next step is to type and edit the document. You can correct typing mistakes by deleting, inserting, or replacing characters. Throughout the editing process, it is a good idea to periodically *save* the text—to transfer it from memory to the disk. This ensures that a temporary power failure will not create a major problem when it erases the contents of memory.

When you are finished editing, save the text to disk a final time. If you wish, you can print out the text by turning on the printer and typing the appropriate command to start the word processor's printing routines. Finally, end the session either by giving a command to leave the word processing program (thus returning to the operating system) or by turning off the computer.

## Understanding the Screen

Figure 6.2 shows a typical screen display while a letter is being entered and edited. The screen is divided into two areas: The bottom part shows the text being edited,

**Figure 6.2**
Typical screen display of a word processor while editing a letter

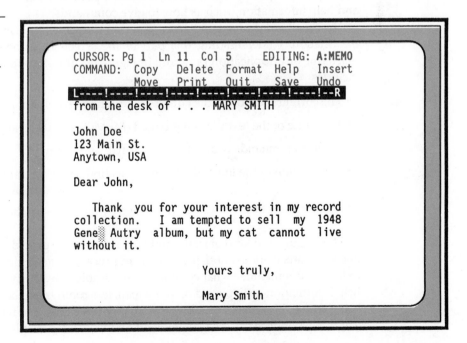

```
CURSOR: Pg 1  Ln 11  Col 5      EDITING: A:MEMO
COMMAND:  Copy   Delete  Format  Help   Insert
          Move   Print   Quit    Save   Undo
L----!----!----!----!----!----!----!----!--R
from the desk of . . . MARY SMITH

John Doe
123 Main St.
Anytown, USA

Dear John,

    Thank  you for your interest in my record
collection.   I am tempted to sell  my  1948
Gene  Autry  album, but my cat  cannot  live
without it.

                    Yours truly,

                    Mary Smith
```

**Figure 6.3**
The result of print-
ing the letter shown
in Figure 6.2

*from the desk of . . .* MARY SMITH

John Doe
123 Main St.
Anytown, USA

Dear John,

    Thank you for your interest in my record
collection. I am tempted to sell my 1948 Gene
Autry album, but my cat cannot live without it.

                    Yours truly,

                    Mary Smith

and the upper part gives status information, such as where the cursor is located, and help information, such as how to give commands.

Nearly all word processors reserve part of the screen to display status and help information. Understanding this part of the screen is a good first step toward mastering any application program. In Figure 6.2, the status and help information includes

- The current location of the cursor (page 1, line 11, column 5)

- The name of the text file being edited (MEMO) and its location (disk drive A)

- A list of commands (Copy, Delete, Format, and so on)

- The location of the left and right margins (indicated by L and R on line 4 of the screen)

- The positions of the tab stops (indicated by ! on line 4 of the screen)

The amount and kind of status and help information provided vary widely from one word processor to another. A few word processors use a large part of the screen to help you remember what commands are usable. Obviously, as more status and help information is displayed on the screen, less room is available to show the text being edited. New users usually want all the status and help information they can get, but experienced users usually want an uncluttered display showing as much

**Figure 6.4**
Typical screen display of a WYSIWYG desktop publishing program

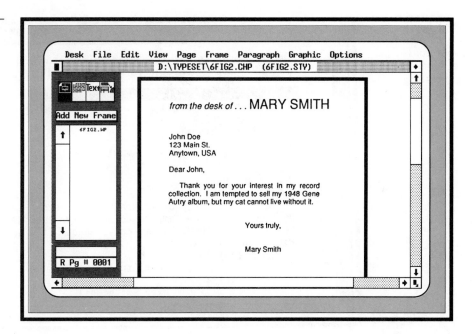

of their text as possible. This conflict is usually resolved either by allowing the user to choose how much of the screen will be devoted to each function or by using a pull-down or pop-up menu.

### WYSIWYG Word Processors

Figure 6.3 shows the result of printing the letter shown in Figure 6.2. Although the text in the two figures is identical, the printed letter looks better than the screen version shown in Figure 6.2. This is typical for word processors; often the differences are more dramatic.

The trend in word processing is clearly toward on-screen formatting known as WYSIWYG (pronounced "wizzy-wig"), an acronym for "what you see is what you get." A **WYSIWYG word processor** attempts to make the text on the screen appear just the way it would on paper. It is helpful, especially for a beginner, to see what the document looks like without printing it or using a separate print-preview operation. But building a perfectly accurate WYSIWYG word processor is an almost impossible technical challenge. One difficulty is the relatively low resolution of monitors—around 75 dots per inch (dpi). Even inexpensive printers provide resolutions from 150 to 600 dpi, so text looks coarser on a screen than on paper. For example, compare the clean-looking text of the printed letter (Figure 6.3) with the on-screen version (Figure 6.4). The versions look identical except for the resolution of the characters. It takes a good graphics monitor and elegant software to produce the image shown in Figure 6.4, and many computer systems do not have the necessary equipment. Thus, nearly all WYSIWYG word processors make compromises, they attempt to organize the screen like the printed page but reserve some formatting operations for the printing stage. For example, the on-screen image of bold,

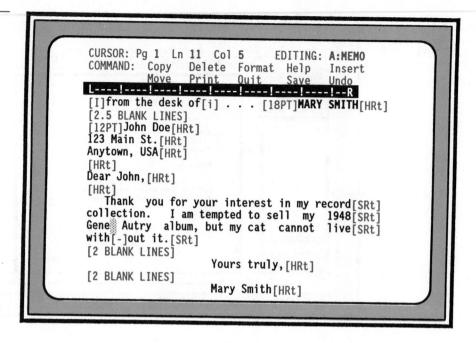

```
CURSOR: Pg 1  Ln 11  Col 5        EDITING: A:MEMO
COMMAND:  Copy   Delete  Format  Help   Insert
          Move    Print   Quit    Save   Undo
L----!----!----!----!----!----!----!----!--R
[I]from the desk of[i] . . . [18PT]MARY SMITH[HRt]
[2.5 BLANK LINES]
[12PT]John Doe[HRt]
123 Main St.[HRt]
Anytown, USA[HRt]
[HRt]
Dear John,[HRt]
[HRt]
    Thank  you for your interest in my record[SRt]
collection.   I am tempted to sell  my  1948[SRt]
Gene  Autry  album, but my cat  cannot  live[SRt]
with[-]out it.[SRt]
[2 BLANK LINES]
                    Yours truly,[HRt]

[2 BLANK LINES]
                 Mary Smith[HRt]
```

italic, and normal characters may all look the same. Or the lines on the screen may have the same number of characters as they will have when printed, but the spacing between words may be more uniform on paper than on the screen.

Differences between the screen version and the printed document can cause confusion while you are editing. For example, it certainly is not apparent from Figure 6.2 that the words "from the desk of" in the first line will be printed in italic. Normal and italic characters look the same in Figure 6.2, so how can you tell one from the other?

Most word processors deal with this problem by placing **format codes** in the document. These codes describe how the text will be printed or control how the text will be reformatted if you alter the document, for example, by changing the margins on the page. Usually these codes are hidden so that they do not clutter the screen. But if you wonder how something will be printed, you can give a command to have the codes displayed on the screen, as Figure 6.5 shows. Because the format codes in Figure 6.5 are shown in color, it is easy to distinguish them from the text in the document.

WordPerfect provides an instructive and unconventional method for you to view its format codes (see Figure 6.6). When you ask to see a document's format codes (by pressing [Shift]-[F3]), WordPerfect displays two windows: The top window shows text in the usual WYSIWYG format, and the bottom window shows the same

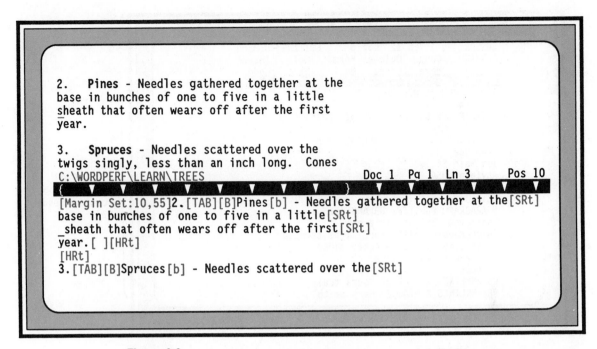

**Figure 6.6**
WordPerfect's reveal-codes screen displays text in two ways: The top window shows formatted text whereas the bottom window shows both the text and the normally hidden format codes.

text along with the format codes. This makes it easy to determine how the text's usual on-screen appearance is affected by the normally hidden format codes.

The use of format codes has not been standardized among word processors. For example, the word processor shown in Figure 6.5 uses the code [I] to mark the beginning of italic characters; another might use [ITALIC]; and still another might display italic characters in a different color from normal characters. This sort of variation among word processors makes people reluctant to switch from using one word processor to another, as learning new commands is time-consuming.

### Off-Screen Text Formatters

The oldest method of electronic word processing is **off-screen text formatting,** which relies on two steps to enter and print documents. In the first step, you enter special format commands along with the document's text. These commands describe how the text should look when printed. As you edit, the screen shows both the text and the format commands. Unlike WYSIWYG word processing, the text is not rearranged on the screen in an attempt to show how the document will look on paper. In the second step, after all the text and format commands have been entered in a data file, a *text-formatting program* reads the data file, strips the format com-

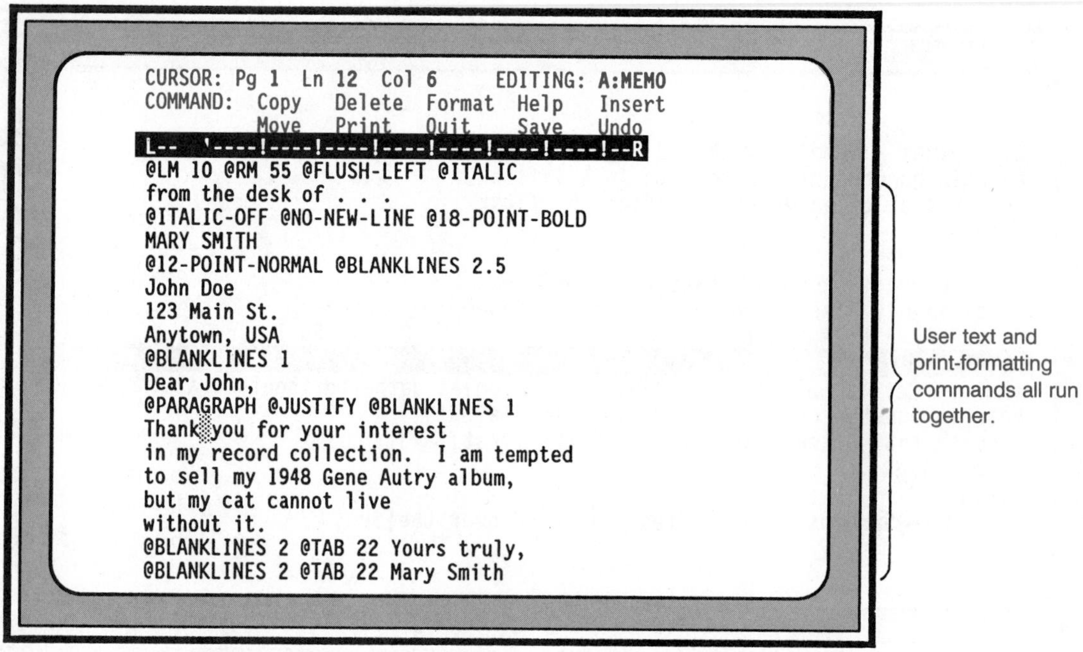

```
CURSOR: Pg 1  Ln 12  Col 6      EDITING: A:MEMO
COMMAND:  Copy   Delete  Format  Help    Insert
          Move   Print   Quit    Save    Undo
L--  '----!----!----!----!----!----!----!--R
@LM 10 @RM 55 @FLUSH-LEFT @ITALIC
from the desk of . . .
@ITALIC-OFF @NO-NEW-LINE @18-POINT-BOLD
MARY SMITH
@12-POINT-NORMAL @BLANKLINES 2.5
John Doe
123 Main St.
Anytown, USA
@BLANKLINES 1
Dear John,
@PARAGRAPH @JUSTIFY @BLANKLINES 1
Thank you for your interest
in my record collection.  I am tempted
to sell my 1948 Gene Autry album,
but my cat cannot live
without it.
@BLANKLINES 2 @TAB 22 Yours truly,
@BLANKLINES 2 @TAB 22 Mary Smith
```

User text and print-formatting commands all run together.

**Figure 6.7**
Typical screen display of an off-screen print formatter

mands from the text, and uses them as instructions on how to print the text. For example, when the data shown in Figure 6.7 is run through a text formatter, the printed result will look exactly like the letter shown in Figure 6.3.

Each text formatter has its own set of embedded commands. So complicated are some command systems that they resemble programming languages. Many text formatters require that the format commands be preceded by a special character—such as an at sign (@), a period (.), or a backslash (\)—to distinguish them from regular text. For example, the screen shown in Figure 6.7 contains format commands and text. The first line contains four of these commands.

- @LM sets the left-hand margin of the printed document to column 10.

- @RM sets the right-hand margin to column 55.

- @FLUSH-LEFT specifies that the following lines are to be printed flush with the left-hand margin.

- @ITALIC indicates that an italic typeface be used.

The obvious drawback of off-screen text formatting is that it is difficult to visualize how the text will look when printed. At times, this can lead to unexpected or disastrous results. Imagine, for example, that you decide to go to lunch while the text formatter sends a 120-page document to the printer. When you return, you discover you made only one misspelling, unfortunately, it was in the @NO-UNDER-

LINE command on the fourth page. The result is that every word in the last 116 pages is underlined! To avoid this sort of error many text-formatting systems have an on-screen print-preview feature that allows you to "print the document to the screen." The main drawback of this feature is that you cannot edit what you see on the screen.

Text formatters are time-consuming and prone to error, so they are no longer popular for simple word processing tasks. Still, they are important to know about. Many of the best scientific word processors, technical documentation systems, and typesetting systems use off-screen text formatting. For example, Figure 6.8 illustrates FormSet, a text formatter that produces custom business forms with a laser printer. Although FormSet can create sophisticated forms, it requires detailed, cryptic instructions much like those that a traditional programming language requires.

The dividing line between off-screen text formatters and WYSIWYG word processors is not entirely clear. The advanced features of most WYSIWYG word processors require the same two steps as text formatters: First format codes must be inserted in the document, and then the program reads the codes to know how the document is to be printed. Thus most word processors are hybrids having characteristics of both WYSIWYG and text-formatting systems.

Regardless of the type of word processor you use, you must know how to enter and edit text, which is the topic of the next section.

## EDITING

Editing is the fun part of word processing. It allows you to express your thoughts—by typing them into the computer—so that they can be seen on the screen. If you dislike what you see, you can use editing operations to quickly insert or delete words or sentences.

To enter and edit a simple document like a letter, you must learn only four editing operations.

**1.** Moving the cursor to where you want to make changes

**2.** Scrolling text on the screen so that you can view other parts of the document

**3.** Deleting text by removing characters

**4.** Adding text by inserting or replacing characters

After discussing these essential operations, we describe two techniques that make it much easier to revise a document: block operations and search-and-replace operations. *Block operations* manipulate entire groups of characters at once; for example, moving a paragraph. *Search-and-replace operations* allow you to locate occurrences of a group of characters (such as *Smith*) and, if you wish, replace them with another group of characters (such as *Smyth*).

### Cursor Control

The *cursor* is the indicator on the screen that shows where things will happen next. To make a change in the text, you must move the cursor to where the change is to

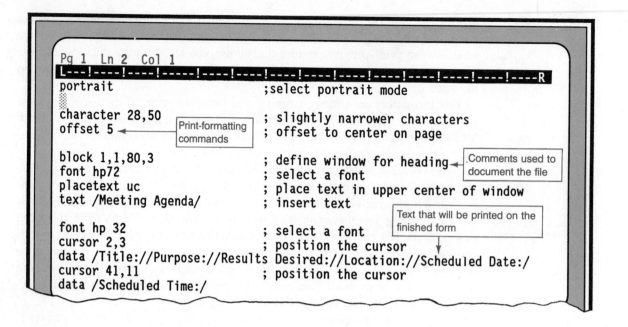

```
Pg 1  Ln 2  Col 1
L---!----!----!-----!----!----!----!----!----!----!----!----!----!----R
portrait                        ;select portrait mode

character 28,50                 ; slightly narrower characters
offset 5 ◄──[Print-formatting   ; offset to center on page
            commands]

block 1,1,80,3                  ; define window for heading ◄──[Comments used to
font hp72                       ; select a font                  document the file]
placetext uc                    ; place text in upper center of window
text /Meeting Agenda/           ; insert text
                                        [Text that will be printed on the
font hp 32                      ; select a font    finished form]
cursor 2,3                      ; position the cursor
data /Title://Purpose://Results Desired://Location://Scheduled Date:/
cursor 41,11                    ; position the cursor
data /Scheduled Time:/
```

**Figure 6.8**
Creating a form with FormSet. **(a)** Entering the description of the the form to be printed. **(b)**
The resulting form.

# Input:
# Entering, Editing, and Sensing

*To get useful results from a computer, you must first enter data into it. You might want to enter text, edit a computerized drawing, or have the computer automatically record data from a scientific experiment. Regardless of the task at hand, you will need an input device. If you have the right input device, the task will go smoothly or even effortlessly. The wrong device will make the entire computer system seem unfriendly. This photo essay illustrates how computers can collect data.*

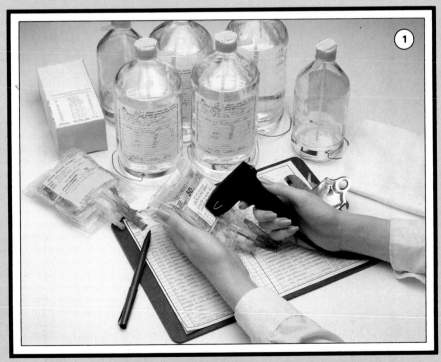

1.  Inventory records of medical supplies need accurate and timely maintenance. This optical character reader makes the task as easy as passing a wand over a preprinted label.

# KEYBOARDS

2-5. Anywhere you find a computer—dorm room, classroom, computer center, or automobile service center—you are likely to find a keyboard. The keyboard is undoubtedly the most common input device. Because of the importance of computers in our society, touch-typing has become a very useful skill.

6. With the appropriate interface you can attach a piano-style keyboard to a personal computer. Here an optional interface card in an IBM Personal System / 2 allows it to control a Musical Instrument Digital Interface (MIDI) keyboard and function as a versatile music synthesizer system.

7. The IBM Personal Computer AT keyboard has two columns of function keys on the left. On the right is a numeric key pad that can also serve as a cursor-movement key pad.

8. The operator is entering data from checks with the help of a cash receipts program. The white text on the screen represents a computerized business form; only the green fields can be modified by the operator. Notice that the operator has entered the word *EASTON* in the customer number field, causing the computer to change the field's color to orange and display an error message on the bottom of the screen.

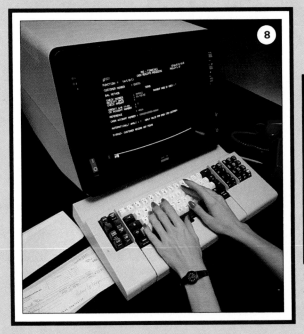

9. A typical data entry workstation. In the background is a Modular Composition System 8400 phototypesetter, the brand of typesetting machine that created the text you are reading.

*window 4*

# SELECTION AND POINTING DEVICES

*Steering wheels are standard equipment on cars; so you don't see cars with steering levers or joysticks. The computer industry has fewer standards than the automobile industry; so you can choose how you want to enter data into computers. You can use devices such as a joystick, trackball, light pen, touch screen, mouse, and graphics tablet to select and point.*

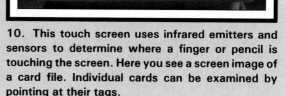

10. This touch screen uses infrared emitters and sensors to determine where a finger or pencil is touching the screen. Here you see a screen image of a card file. Individual cards can be examined by pointing at their tags.

11. Although touch screens appear convenient, they have limitations. Fingers are blunt instruments that leave an oily film on the screen. You cannot see through your finger, and after a while, your arm is likely to complain about using a touch screen.

12. A mouse is a pointing device that relays directional information to the computer as it is dragged across a flat surface. It takes little practice to become a proficient mouse user. Generally, you move the mouse to point or draw; you click a button to select or initiate actions.

13. An enthusiastic mouse user.

# GRAPHICAL DATA ENTRY

*Graphics design requires specialized input devices that are capable of digitizing—or tracing—points that indicate the shape of the design.*

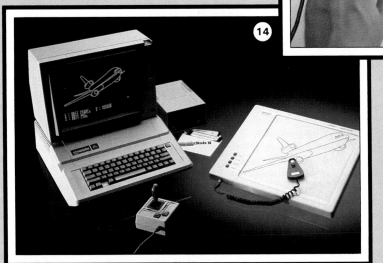

15. Designs can be digitized by placing the design on a graphics tablet and tracing it with the puck. The key pad on the puck is used to enter specific points and to issue commands.

14. A graphics design workstation. This system includes a joystick for positioning the cursor on the screen and a tablet with a hand-held puck for entering the outline of drawings.

16. A light pen can accurately sense where it touches a CRT screen. The upper and right edges of this screen represent an electronic key pad of commands. With a light pen you can quickly choose commands and draw on the body of the screen.

*window 4*

# COMMERCIAL INPUT DEVICES

*The market for commercial input devices is characterized by an extreme diversity of data collection equipment.*

17. An automatic teller machine (ATM) dispenses cash and conducts banking transactions. Banks have been putting ATM units where the customers are—high-volume retail outlets, airports, and hotels.

18. A fully programmable, portable data collection terminal. With up to 256 kilobytes of memory for data storage, this battery-powered terminal is able to collect extensive amounts of data with its keyboard and optical wand reader. Through a built-in modem, the terminal can send and receive data over ordinary phone lines to a host computer. It is designed for uses such as auditing shelf prices or keeping records of a delivery route—applications that require sophisticated data management by a hand-held unit.

19. Laser-powered bar code readers are able to automatically scan bar codes from as close as three inches, or as far away as three feet.

20. Wherever the movement of products must be recorded quickly and accurately, hand-held optical character readers are useful. These devices help with inventory control in stores, libraries, and assembly lines.

21. This compact OCR makes short work of entering data from utility bills.

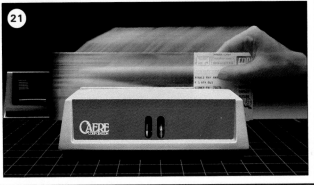

22. Membrane keyboards are inexpensive to manufacture and virtually indestructible. They perform well in harsh environments, such as restaurants where liquids might be spilled on them.

# OTHER INPUT DEVICES

*Anything that can be sensed electronically can become input to a computer.*

23. Voice input systems are frequently used in applications where the operator's hands are occupied with tasks other than data entry. These systems allow the computer to "listen" to a limited vocabulary of spoken words.

24. You don't need to know how to type to use this pressure-sensitive, battery-operated tablet. Just insert a standard 8 1/2-by-11 inch printed form, pick up a ballpoint pen, and fill out the form. As it recognizes your handwritten characters, they are displayed on the one-line liquid crystal screen and stored in memory. Later the characters can be loaded into any computer with an RS-232 serial port.

25. In the foreground is an optical character recognition reader. Because it can read the text on normal typed pages, it eliminates the need to enter documents manually into the computer system.

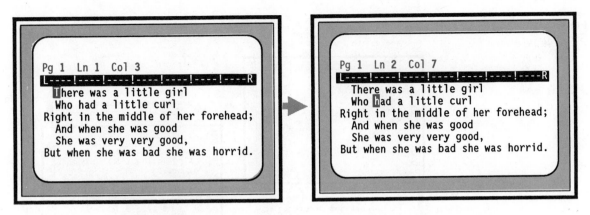

**Figure 6.9**
Effect of pushing the right-arrow key four times and the down-arrow key once

be made. Being able to efficiently move the cursor around the screen is therefore important.

Most keyboards have **cursor-movement keys** or *arrow keys*: the [←] key moves the cursor one position to the left; the [→] key, to the right; the [↑] key, up; and the [↓] key, down. For example, if you press the [→] key four times and then press the [↓] key once, the cursor moves over four columns and down one line, as Figure 6.9 shows. To move the cursor all the way to the end of a line, hold down the [→] key. The cursor will float across the line. When it reaches the last character on the line, it will jump to the beginning of the next line and begin floating across it. You can use the [←] key in the same way to move right to left across a line. When the cursor reaches the first character on the line, it will jump to the last character on the previous line.

## Scrolling

**Scrolling** moves lines of text up or down on the screen, allowing new parts of the text to be seen. It may be useful to think of scrolling as a process similar to the one shown in Figure 6.10. That is, scrolling moves the screen up and down but leaves the document fixed in place. The screen acts like a window, letting you view the document. As you scroll the screen up, lines of text disappear from the bottom of the viewing area and new lines appear on the top.

Holding down the [↓] key moves the cursor down the screen until it nears the bottom; then the text on the screen begins to jump up one line at a time. Most word processors begin scrolling the text before the cursor has reached the bottom line (see Figure 6.11). This guarantees that you can see at least one line of text below the line marked with the cursor (unless, of course, the screen is displaying the end of the document), which helps you understand the context of the area being edited. Naturally, only the text scrolls on the screen; any status or help information stays put.

**Figure 6.10**
Scrolling

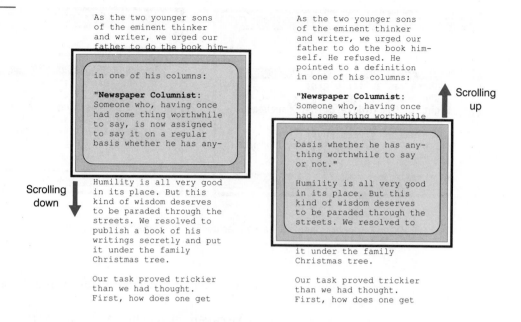

You can use the cursor keys to scroll one line at a time to the bottom of a document; however, if the document is long, doing this is time consuming and boring. Full-featured word processing programs offer an alternative: They provide several commands that quickly move the cursor from one part of the text to another. Commonly available cursor-control commands allow you to

- Move one word at a time, forward or backward
- Jump to the beginning or end of the current line
- Jump to the upper left-hand corner of the screen, which is the **home** position
- Jump to the bottom of the screen

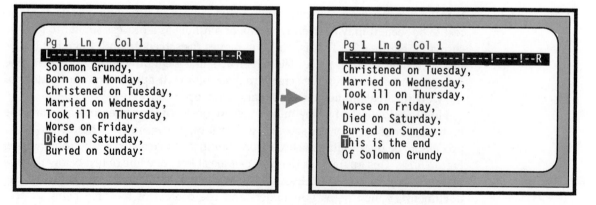

**Figure 6.11**
Scrolling two lines by pushing the down-arrow key twice

Even more powerful than these simple cursor-control commands are commands that

- Scroll up or down one line at a time.

- Scroll up or down one screen of text at a time, which is called **paging** through the document. Many keyboards have keys labeled [PgUp] and [PgDn] that allow you to page through a document.

- Scroll left or right. This **horizontal scrolling** is essential if you must create documents wider than standard 8 1/2-by-11-inch paper.

- Jump to where you have put a *place marker*—a kind of electronic bookmark.

- Jump to a specified page number.

- Jump to the beginning or end of the document. For example, the software designer may have designated the keystroke sequence [Ctrl]-[PgUp] as a command for jumping to the beginning of the document and [Ctrl]-[PgDn] for jumping to the end.

You might wonder why anyone would want to learn so many commands, all of which do essentially the same thing. If you want to write only one-page memos, you probably need not learn all these commands. But if you write longer documents, you will be glad your word processor has them. The ease with which you learned to use the program soon becomes less important than the number and power of a word processor's commands. It is surprising how quickly a person who buys a simple, easy-to-use program stops saying, "Gee, this is easy," and starts complaining, "Boy, it takes a long time to get anything done with this product."

## Deleting, Replacing, and Inserting

You will spend more time using the basic, one-character-at-a-time editing operations than you will spend using all other word processing commands put together. Thus you must have a good understanding of how to delete, replace, and insert characters in a document.

### Deleting Characters

A single character is erased by moving the cursor to the character to be deleted and typing a *character-delete command*. Although the exact command for this operation varies from program to program, it is always simple. Here, we assume your keyboard has a key labeled [Del], which is used to delete the character immediately under the cursor.

When you use an eraser or correction fluid to remove characters from paper, blank spaces remain. But when you use a word processor to delete a character, the rest of the line is shifted to the left to fill the void.

Holding down the [Del] key continues the erasing and shifting so that entire words and phrases can be deleted. If you want to delete an entire sentence, move the cursor to the beginning of the sentence and hold down [Del]. The characters in

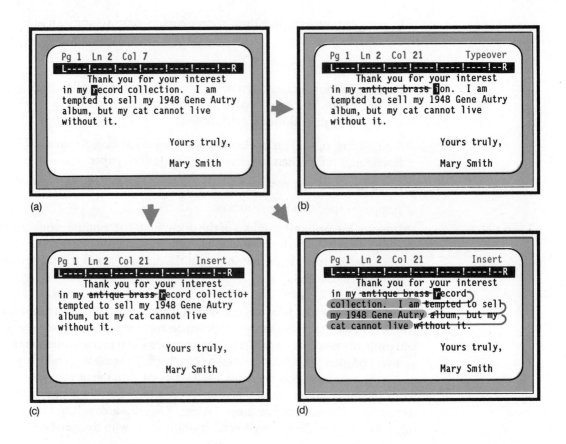

**Figure 6.12**
Three ways to insert text. **(a)** A word processor in typeover mode will replace existing text with whatever is typed. **(b)** A word processor in insert mode will shove existing characters to the right as new characters are typed. **(c)** A word processor with dynamic paragraph reforming will automatically shift words from line to line within a paragraph as you type to keep the paragraph within its assigned margins.

the sentence will shift and disappear one by one until the entire sentence has been deleted.

Most word processing programs have two character-delete commands, one for forward deletion and one for backward deletion. We just described *forward deletion*; it deletes characters in the direction we read. *Backward deletion* deletes the character to the left of the cursor, moves the cursor to the position vacated by the erased character, and shifts the rest of the line left to cover up the hole.

Backward deletion is useful when you decide to erase something you have just typed because you can do so without moving the cursor to the beginning of what you want to delete. Backward deletion is often used to remove typographical errors immediately after they are made. Forward deletion is usually used when you need to go back and edit the document for meaning or style.

Besides deleting individual characters, most word processors have specific commands for deleting the current word, deleting to the end of the line, and deleting an entire block of text.

### Insert versus Typeover Mode

Two general ways of entering new characters into a document are *insert*, meaning they are added between existing characters, and *replace*, meaning they are typed over existing characters. Usually the status portion of the screen indicates which method the program is using, as shown in the upper right-hand corners of the screens in Figure 6.12. When the program is in the **insert mode**, new characters are added to the text as they are typed.

When the program is in the **typeover mode**, new characters take the place of characters already in the text. Most programs begin in the insert mode because it is used more often.

The choice between insert and typeover modes is usually made with a **toggle switch,** which maintains a value until the switch is thrown. Household light switches operate this way. If you throw a switch to turn a light on, it stays on until you throw the switch again. Similarly, if you use a toggle switch to give a command to the computer, that command remains in effect until you throw the toggle switch again. Toggle switches are used for many commands in word processing programs.

Generally, the same command is used to toggle from one value to another. For example, most IBM PC-compatible word processors use the [Ins] key to toggle between the two modes. Thus each push of the [Ins] key causes the word processor to alternate between the insert and typeover modes.

For some tasks, such as fixing typing errors, it is quicker to replace characters than to delete the erroneous characters and then insert the correct ones. In general, the typeover mode is convenient when a change does not increase the number of characters in the document. Thus the typeover mode is more efficient than the insert mode if you are rearranging transposed letters, such as in changing *recieve* to *receive*.

When the insert mode is in effect, each character you type causes three things to occur.

- It pushes the rest of the characters on the line to the right.
- It inserts the character in the document at the current cursor position.
- It moves the cursor to the next column position.

These rules explain what happens when you insert characters in the middle of a line of text, but they do not explain what happens when the current line becomes too long to fit within its assigned margins. That is the topic of the next section.

## Making Words Fit within Margins

Word processors provide two features to confine text within its assigned boundaries: *word wrap* and *paragraph reforming*. Often it is appropriate to have the word processor hyphenate words as well. We discuss each feature in turn.

## Word Wrap

A typewriter's bell rings as the carriage nears the end of a line. If the typist fails to return the carriage, the typing soon stops with the carriage stuck against the right margin.

With a word processor, there is no need to listen for the typewriter bell or to peek to see if the next word will fit on the line. A word too long to fit at the end of a line is automatically moved to the next line. This feature is called **word wrap**. By eliminating the need to determine where to stop each line, word wrap increases the rate at which you can enter text.

To understand how word wrap functions, it helps to know that words, lines, and paragraphs have different meanings in word processing than in everyday life. In word processing, a *word* is a string of letters or numerals. Words are separated one from another by spaces, punctuation marks (commas, periods, question marks, and so on), and carriage returns. To a word processor, R2D2 is as valid a word as any other.

A *line* is one row of text on the screen or on paper. At the end of each line is a carriage return, which can be either hard or soft. A **hard carriage return** is a return generated by pressing [Enter] (or on some keyboards, [Return] or [↵]). **Soft carriage returns** are generated automatically by the word wrap feature. When a word extends beyond the maximum line length, word wrap moves the last word on the line to the next line and places a soft carriage return at the end of the preceding line.

A *paragraph* is a string of characters ended by a hard carriage return. Paragraphs can be quite short and do not necessarily form a complete thought. For example, if you type "Bananas" and press [Enter], then type "Apples" and press [Enter], and then type "Oranges" and press [Enter], you will place three one-word paragraphs in the document.

Some word processors tell you which lines end in a hard carriage return by placing a paragraph symbol (¶) in the rightmost column of the screen. Figure 6.13 illustrates another method of disclosing the same information: Each line ends with a format code, either [HRt] to indicate a hard return or [SRt] to indicate a soft return.

Figure 6.13 further illustrates how you can break a paragraph in two by pressing [Enter] to insert a hard carriage return in the middle of a paragraph and [Tab] to indent the beginning of the new paragraph. This is reversible: Most word processors allow you to delete format codes in the same way you delete other characters. Thus you can merge two paragraphs by deleting the hard carriage return at the end of the first paragraph. For example, to move from the right-hand screen in Figure 6.13 to the left-hand screen, you would push [Del] twice to delete the tab and the hard carriage return.

## Paragraph Reforming

Insertion, deletion, and other editing operations will shorten some lines and lengthen others. On a typewriter, the changed paragraphs would need to be retyped. But this is where a word processor shines. **Paragraph reforming** will shift words up to fill the shortened lines or move words down to trim the lengthened ones.

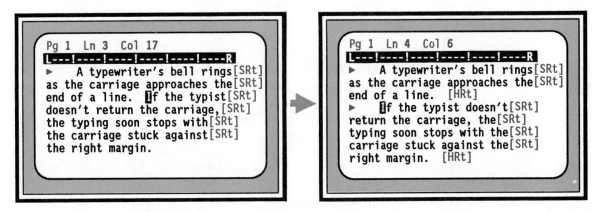

**Figure 6.13**
Breaking a paragraph in two by pressing [Enter] and [Tab]

To reform a paragraph, the word processor first removes the soft carriage returns and any other "soft" characters previously added by the word processor, such as **soft spaces**, which spread out the line so that it ends squarely with the right margin. Then the word processor determines which words fit on each new line. Finally, it adds soft carriage returns at the ends of the new lines (and possibly other soft characters).

Some word processors reform a paragraph only when you command them to do so. Figure 6.12(b) illustrates this situation: Inserting two words in the middle of the line has shoved the word "collection" past the paragraph's right margin and partly off the screen. You could view the end of the line by scrolling the screen horizontally to the right, but it is simpler to give the command to reform the paragraph. Then the paragraph containing the cursor would be shaped to fit within the current margins of the ruler line.

Many word processors use *dynamic paragraph reforming*, which means a paragraph is reformed whenever a change is made in it, as shown in Figure 6.12(c). As characters are inserted into a paragraph, words are moved off the end of the current line, which makes the rest of the paragraph ripple with action as the effect of the insertion trickles down. Although some people find this movement disconcerting, most people prefer dynamic paragraph reforming because it requires less work.

### Hyphenating Text

Reforming a paragraph can cause hyphenation problems. A long word that falls in the middle of a line before reforming might not quite fit after reforming. If the word is not moved to the next line, the current line must have either a large blank space at the end or big gaps between the words. Hyphenation is not essential for normal-width lines, but it can dramatically improve the appearance of narrow lines.

A word processor with **automatic hyphenation** will hyphenate long words if they fall at the end of the line. Usually you can turn automatic hyphenation on and off with a toggle switch. A **soft hyphen**, *optional hyphen*, or *discretionary hyphen* is a hyphen inserted by automatic hyphenation. A **hard hyphen** is part of a word, as in *one-upmanship*.

Any full-featured word processor will let you manually insert soft hyphens—for example, to insert a soft hyphen in WordPerfect, you type a control-hyphen (you hold down the [Ctrl] key and then press [-]). Soft hyphens are printed only if they happen to fall at the end of a line; hard hyphens are printed regardless of their location. If editing moves words around again, you do not have to delete the soft hyphens; they are not printed unless they fall at the end of a line. Soft hyphens do not show up on the screen of a WYSIWYG word processor unless they are needed at the end of the line or the screen is set to display the normally hidden format codes. For example, no soft hyphens are visible in Figure 6.2, but Figure 6.5 shows a soft hyphen in the word "with[-]out".

Automatic hyphenation routines vary in quality. Because English words do not always follow simple rules for where hyphens should be inserted, an automatic hyphenation routine that relies solely on predetermined rules will occasionally place hyphens in startling locations, such as in "Step-hen." The best hyphenation routines are used by typesetting machines; they rely on extensive **hyphenation dictionaries**—lists of correctly hyphenated words. A typical compromise is to use standardized hyphenation rules along with a small hyphenation dictionary that contains exceptions to the rules.

Several methods let you adjust the hyphens produced by an automatic hyphenation routine. For example, Ventura Publisher lets you create a supplemental hyphenation dictionary. This solution has the advantage of modifying the way the hyphenation routine works so that you will not encounter the same problem twice. WordPerfect, WordStar 2000, and Microsoft Word offer only temporary solutions, such as manually inserting and deleting soft hyphens in an incorrectly hyphenated word.

## Block Operations

If you want to move or delete a large number of characters, one-character-at-a-time operations are inefficient. Instead, **block operations** are used to manipulate many characters simultaneously. These usually involve two separate operations: First you mark off the block of characters; then you give a command to manipulate the block.

To mark a block of characters, you must identify both ends of the block. Normally, this involves four steps.

*1.* Move the cursor to one end of the block.

*2.* Issue a command to begin marking the block.

*3.* Move the cursor to the other end of the block.

*4.* Issue a command indicating your selection is complete.

Some word processors provide short cuts; they offer one-step commands for marking the current word, sentence, or paragraph. Still others allow you to select a block of text by pointing with a mouse.

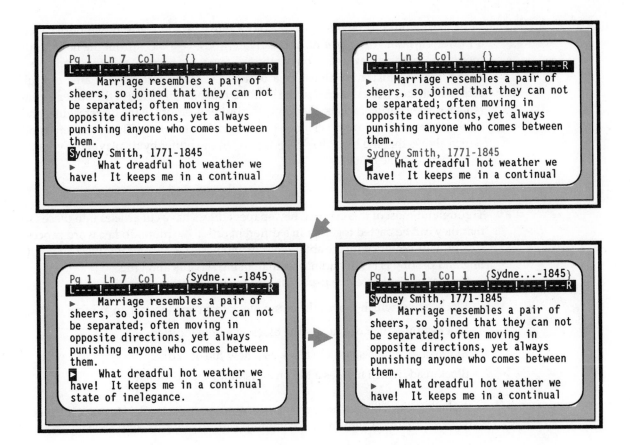

**Figure 6.14**
The steps of a cut-and-paste operation. **(a)** The first step is to move the cursor to one end of the block of text. **(b)** Then a block-marking command is given, and the cursor is moved to the other end of the block—in this case, a single line of text. **(c)** A block-cut command is given to remove the block from the document and place it in a buffer (shown between brackets on the top line). **(d)** The cursor is moved to a new location and an insert-from-buffer command is given to place a copy of the block in the document.

Generally, once the block is marked off, it is displayed differently from the rest of the text. For example, the line "Sydney Smith, 1771-1845" in Figure 6.14(b) is displayed in color to indicate it has been selected as a block. Some programs display a block in **inverse video**, reversing the screen colors in the marked area; others use **highlighting,** emphasizing the characters in the block in a different intensity.

## Deleting Blocks

Once you have marked a block, a block-delete command will remove it from the document. There are two possibilities for what happens to the deleted characters. First, the block may be thrown away permanently. Because a block may contain many pages of text, this method will not seem very friendly if you make a mistake.

Thus most word processors move the block into a separate area of memory called a **buffer**, *clipboard*, or *scrap area*. You can later retrieve a block from the buffer, but moving something new into a buffer throws away the buffer's previous contents.

Figure 6.14 illustrates the use of a buffer. The status information area of each screen indicates what is stored in the buffer by displaying some of the buffer's contents between curly brackets. Evidently the buffer is empty in the upper right-hand screen because there are no characters between the brackets. The lower left-hand screen shows that the block has been moved to the buffer by displaying "Sydne...-1845" between the brackets.

### Cut and Paste

Throughout most of this century, newspaper editors have cut articles into pieces so that they can be pasted together in a different order. No more. Today, word processors provide editors with the ability to "cut and paste" electronically. Electronic cutting and pasting is faster and neater than using scissors and glue.

Besides block-delete, the usual cut-and-paste operations are

- Block-move, which moves the entire block from one location to another
- Block-copy, which duplicates the block in a new location
- Block-save, which saves the block as a new file on a disk
- Block-read, which merges a file on a disk into the document

As in deleting a block, the first step in any cut-and-paste job is to mark the block to be manipulated. There are two common ways to move or copy a block.

1. In the simpler method, you place the cursor where the block is to be moved and then give the command to move or copy the block. The command to move the block transfers it from its original position to where the cursor is. Photos 13 through 16 of Window 5 illustrate this method of moving a paragraph. The command to copy the block leaves the block in its original position and places a copy in the document right after the cursor.

2. The second method follows the cut-and-paste analogy more closely. In the "cut" part, you give a command to move or copy the block into the buffer. In the "paste" part, you place the cursor where the block is to be inserted and give a command to restore the block, which copies the buffer's contents back into the document, as shown in Figure 6.14(d).

### Search and Replace

Any good word processing program will search a document to find a word or phrase. We will use PFS:Professional Write as our first example because its search-and-replace operations are easy to understand although not particularly flexible.

Pressing [Ctrl]-[F] begins the search; it produces an empty dialog box similar to the one in Figure 6.15(a) but without the colored text. Suppose you are searching for the word *June*. This is done by typing "June" after the **Find:** prompt, and then

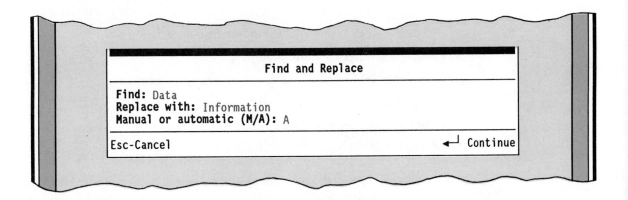

```
                    Find and Replace
_____
Find: Data
Replace with: Information
Manual or automatic (M/A): A
_____
Esc-Cancel                                 ⏎ Continue
```

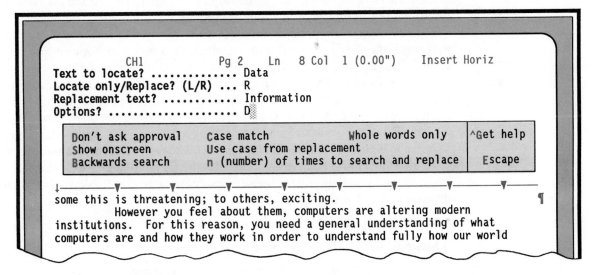

```
          CH1          Pg 2   Ln  8 Col  1 (0.00")    Insert Horiz
Text to locate? .............. Data
Locate only/Replace? (L/R) ... R
Replacement text? ........... Information
Options? .................... D
   ┌──────────────────────────────────────────────────────────┬──────────┐
   │ Don't ask approval   Case match           Whole words only │ ^Get help│
   │ Show onscreen        Use case from replacement             │          │
   │ Backwards search     n (number) of times to search and replace│ Escape│
   └──────────────────────────────────────────────────────────┴──────────┘
↓─────▼──────▼──────▼──────▼──────▼──────▼──────▼──────▼
some this is threatening; to others, exciting.                          ¶
        However you feel about them, computers are altering modern
institutions.  For this reason, you need a general understanding of what
computers are and how they work in order to understand fully how our world
```

**Figure 6.15**
Two ways to perform the same search-and-replace operation. **(a)** PFS:Professional Write uses a simple dialog box to determine the search and replacement phrases. **(b)** WordStar 2000 allows more options, such as searches that move backward from the cursor's current position to the beginning of the file.

pressing [Enter]. Then Professional Write searches the document, beginning at the cursor's location, to find the first occurrence of *June*. Because it ignores the difference between uppercase and lowercase letters in search operations, the first match it finds might be *JUNE* (or *june*). When a match is found, the program returns to the normal edit mode with the cursor at the beginning of the phrase it found.

Replacing one word or phrase with another is also a simple operation. Suppose the easiest way to write a July sales report is to make a copy of the June report and modify it. Rather than searching for *June*, this situation calls for replacing every *June* with *July*. This is done by

- Pressing [Ctrl]-[F] to display the Find-and-Replace dialog box
- Typing "June" after the **Find:** prompt
- Pressing the [Tab] key to move from one prompt to another
- Typing "July" after the **Replace with:** prompt
- Typing "A" after the **Manual or automatic** prompt
- Pressing [Enter] to begin the search

When [Enter] is pressed, Professional Write searches to the end of the document, changes every occurrence of *June* to *July,* and positions the cursor after the last occurrence it found. This is called *automatic search and replace* because the word processor did not stop to ask for permission to make the replacement each time it found a match. *Manual search and replace* pauses after each match is found and asks whether the current match should be replaced or ignored.

The automatic search and replace feature is handy, but it can lead to serious problems if the search phrase is more common than expected. For example, if you replace all occurrences of *too* with *to, tool* and *took* become *tol* and *tok.*

Like most full-featured word processors, WordStar 2000 offers many search-and-replace options. Its options are listed in the shaded area of Figure 6.15(b). For example, if you want to perform an automatic search and replace operation, you can select the **Don't ask approval** option by typing a "D" after the **Options?...** prompt, as shown in Figure 6.15(b). Alternatively, you could replace the first three occurrences of the search phrase by typing "3D" after the **Options?...** prompt.

Most programs allow you to choose from among several definitions of what constitutes a match. For example, the optional criteria might allow you to

- Match uppercase and lowercase exactly (so that *june* would not match *June*)
- Match whole words only (so that *jump* would not match *jumps*)
- Use format codes in the search phrase (so that you could find all the places where italic text is used)
- Use a search phrase containing wild card characters (so that *pre\** would match *predict, prefer,* and so on)

## PRINTING, SAVING, AND QUITTING

### Printing Options

After all the editing and formatting is done, it is time to print the document. Giving the print command usually produces a menu asking for last-minute printing instructions (see Figure 6.16). Most word processors ask for the range of page numbers to be printed. Thus if you make an editing change on the last page, you can reprint just the last page rather than the entire document. A related option is to pause after each page. This permits single sheets of paper (called **cut sheets**) or envelopes to be loaded one at a time. The menu may also ask for the desired number of copies.

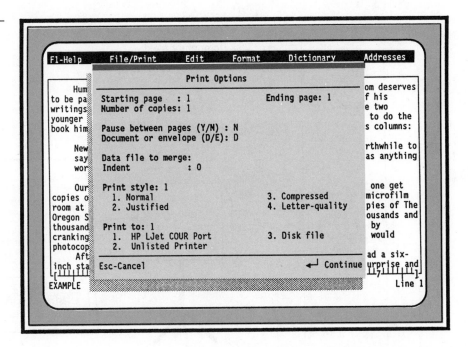

**Figure 6.16**
The print menu used in PFS:Professional Write

All word processors have a Stop-Print command, which is invaluable if the printed text turns out to contain gross errors, such as being single-spaced when a double-spaced document is desired.

Generally, a pause-print command can be embedded in the text to temporarily suspend printing. The pause can provide time for changing the print wheel to a new font, changing the ribbon to a new color, or grabbing a sandwich. Then a resume-print command will continue the printing from where it left off.

## Memory Management

Most word processors automatically mange the computer's memory so that they never have to give a message like: FATAL ERROR:  MEMORY FULL; REBOOT.

It is nice to know that the system will not crash because you attempt to enter more text than will fit into memory. Still, this does not mean you can afford to be ignorant about where your text is being stored. Understanding how your word processor manages memory is important if you want to write a long document or if you want to recover pages of a document that have been accidentally deleted.

### Disk-Based versus Memory-Based Word Processors

*Memory-based word processors* require that the entire document fit into memory while it is being edited. If a document becomes large enough to fill the available memory, it must be broken into pieces before more text can be added. Each piece is saved as a separate file on a disk. For example, on an IBM PC with 320KB of main memory, PFS:Professional Write limits each file to sixteen pages of text. Other examples of memory-based programs are MacWrite and Symphony.

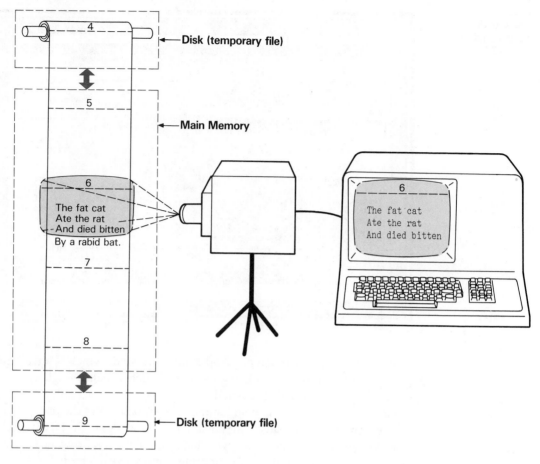

**Figure 6.17**
Disk-based document editing

Editing a long document on a memory-based word processor can be a chore, particularly if it is necessary to move text frequently from one of the document's files to another. *Disk-based word processors* are more convenient; they can edit files that are too long to fit into memory at once. Figure 6.17 shows how a disk-based word processor loads the text being edited into memory, while the rest of the document is stored in temporary disk files. As a result, the size of a document is limited only by the storage capacity of the disk. Examples of disk-based word processors are WordPerfect, WordStar 2000, Multimate, and Microsoft Word.

Scrolling through a large document with a disk-based word processor is occasionally interrupted while some of the text in memory is moved to the disk and replaced by new text. As with program overlays (see Chapter 3), the data transfers happen automatically and are noticeable only because of the noise of the drives and the delay. Sometimes the delay can be substantial. On many systems, the command to jump to the bottom of a 100-page document takes more than a minute to execute.

## Back-Up Copies

The best defense against a serious loss of data is to have extra back-up copies of the file stored on disk. That way, when something happens to the master copy, a back-up copy can take its place.

Almost all word processors provide some back-up automatically. When you edit a document, the changes alter the contents of memory or temporary disk files, but the changes do not immediately affect the master copy (if any) on the disk. If something drastic occurs, it is possible to abandon (*quit*) the current editing session without transferring (*saving*) anything to the disk, leaving the master file unmodified. Abandoning an editing session can be a mixed blessing. You are unlikely to be enthusiastic about losing the results of two hours of editing just because you accidentally deleted a paragraph.

Sometimes the word processor will abandon the current editing session without asking for your approval. A loss of electricity for a second or more causes this reaction. Less frequently, a bug in the word processing program sends the machine into never-never land until it is rebooted. The way to protect against these problems is to periodically save a copy of the edited text. A few word processors, such as Word-Perfect, can be set up to automatically transfer edited text to the disk after a specified length of time (or a specified number of keystrokes), but typically the operator must request the text be saved.

Most word processors retain the original master file as a back-up file after the document is saved. For example, assume you begin by editing a file named A:LETTER, causing a copy of the LETTER file to be transferred from disk drive A to memory. Now assume, after editing the text in memory, you save the revised text on the disk. Most word processors implement this command by first giving a new name to the old master file (perhaps calling it A:LETTER.BAK), and then saving the new, edited text as the file named A:LETTER.

We would be remiss if we did not emphasize again that disks are not as reliable a storage medium as paper. Crumpling a piece of paper, or even spilling coffee on it, is not likely to make its contents unreadable. Not so with disks. Important files should always be stored on two disks, and the disks should be stored separately.

---

## Summary

This chapter has covered a lot of ground, and perhaps you are beginning to feel that learning to use a word processor is difficult. That impression would be misleading. Some things—like brushing your teeth, riding a bicycle, or using a word processor—are harder to describe than they are to do.

Most of the time spent working with a word processor is spent on the four fundamental operations of entering and editing: (1) moving the cursor, (2) viewing the text by scrolling, (3) entering new characters of text (using either the insert or the typeover mode), and (4) deleting characters. You can become comfortable with these four operations with only an hour or so of practice.

The usual steps in creating a letter, memo, or other document are quite simple.

- Begin running the word processing program.
- Give a name to the file that will contain the document.
- Type the document in the insert mode. Correct simple typing mistakes by deleting and retyping characters.
- Scroll to view the document during proofreading and editing. For each correction, move the cursor to the appropriate location and make the change using the character-delete, insert, or typeover operations.
- Save the document on a disk periodically and immediately before quitting.
- Print the document by turning the printer on and giving the print command.
- Quit the word processing program.

There are two methods for specifying how to format the characters to be printed. WYSIWYG word processors do some on-screen text formatting. Off-screen text formatting ignores the screen appearance of text and uses special print-formatting commands embedded in the text to control the appearance of the printed document.

Word processors have a wide variety of convenient editing, formatting, and printing features. Word wrap automatically returns the carriage at the end of a line. Whole blocks of text can be deleted, copied, and moved anywhere. Phrases can be located and replaced throughout the document. Page layout options include headers, footers, page numbers, and forced page breaks. Most products permit the margin and tab settings to be viewed on the screen and changed if needed.

Electrical storage in main memory is less reliable than magnetic storage on disk. Both are less reliable than storing information on paper. Making copies of your work on a disk (and on paper) is like buying an insurance policy: Usually you do not need it, but when you do, it pays off handsomely.

---

## Key Terms

automatic hyphenation

block operations

buffer

cursor-movement keys

cut sheet

format code

hard carriage return

hard hyphen

highlighting

home

horizontal scrolling

hyphenation dictionary

insert mode

inverse video

off-screen text formatting

paging

paragraph reforming

scrolling

soft carriage return

soft hyphen

soft space

toggle switch

typeover mode

word wrap

WYSIWYG word processor

## Discussion Questions

1. Compare the capabilities of typewriters with those of word processors. What types of tasks would be easier with a typewriter?

2. When are you likely to use forward deletion? Backward deletion? Which are you more likely to use?

3. Would you prefer to use a full-featured off-screen text formatter or a simple WYSIWYG word processor? Why?

4. Describe the steps necessary to change the address in a letter stored on disk.

5. What happens if you accidentally turn off the computer while using your word processor? Is everything lost?

6. When is it more efficient to use block operations rather than one-character-at-a-time operations? How many keystrokes must you make to move a block on your word processor?

7. What is the difference between hard and soft characters?

8. Which type of paragraph reforming would you prefer—dynamic or manual?

## Exercises

1. Consult the manual for your word processor to find the keys to press for the following commands:
   a. Load the word processing program.
   b. Name the file containing the document.
   c. Move the cursor up, down, right, or left.
   d. Scroll up and down.
   e. Move the cursor to the beginning or the end of the document.
   f. Delete a single character at the cursor or to the left of the cursor.
   g. Toggle between the insert and the replacement modes.
   h. Save the document in a file.
   i. Print a document.
   j. Exit from the word processing program.
   k. Quit an editing session without saving the changes made during the session.

2. Determine what happens to the previous copy of a document when you save a modified version on a disk with your word processor.

3. Use your word processor to write a letter requesting an annual report from General Electric Corporation. Then request an annual report from Westinghouse. How much less time did you spend preparing the second letter?

4. Experiment with the word wrap feature of your word processor. How does it define a word? What effect do characters such as numerals or dashes have? What is the maximum word length?

5. Can you exit from your word processor without saving the document? Do you think a word processor should give you a message if you attempt to do this?

# Advanced Word Processing

**Text Formatting**
*Page Design Methods*
*Local Formatting Options*

**Outline Processors**

**Large Documents**
*Document Chaining*
*Indexes and Tables of Contents*

**Form Letters**

**Writing Aids**
*Spelling Checkers*
*Thesauruses*

In Chapter 6, we described the mechanics of writing and editing with a word processor. In this chapter, we cover text formatting and some important advanced features provided by most word processors. Text formatting features can help you create better-looking documents; any serious writer should understand them. With the advanced features described in this chapter you can

- Organize your thoughts by writing them down and rearranging them in an outline

- Number all the pages in a large document correctly, even if parts of the document are stored in many files

- Create an index or a table of contents, complete with accurate page numbers, as a by-product of writing the body of a document

- Quickly print hundreds of individualized letters by merging the names and addresses from one file into the appropriate places in a form letter in another file

- Proofread a document for spelling errors at 50,000 characters per minute

- Look up the synonyms of a word at the touch of a button

## 7

## TEXT FORMATTING

Most of what you have learned so far about word processing has been about editing—entering, deleting, and reordering characters. This section deals with **text formatting**—controlling the appearance of the document so that it looks good on paper.

The formatting options provided by word processors are adequate for most everyday documents, such as letters or reports. But professional-quality documents like newspapers, magazines, and advertisements may require multicolumn page layouts that artistically combine text and graphics. To produce these documents, it is usually best to use a *page composition program* to arrange the placement of text and graphics on the page. In this chapter, we discuss the formatting options offered by word processors; page composition we discuss in the next chapter.

Formatting activities fall into two interrelated categories: page design and local formatting options.

- *Page design* determines the **page layout**—the page size and initial settings for the format and appearance of text on the page. This nearly always involves choosing the top, bottom, left, and right margins of the page. Depending on your word processor, it may also include formatting instructions for items within the document, such as where to place footnotes or how to format different types of paragraphs.

- *Local formatting options* allow you to adjust the appearance of text within a portion of the document. They temporarily override the global page design settings. For example, you might use them to choose a shorter line length for a paragraph or to switch from one typeface size to another.

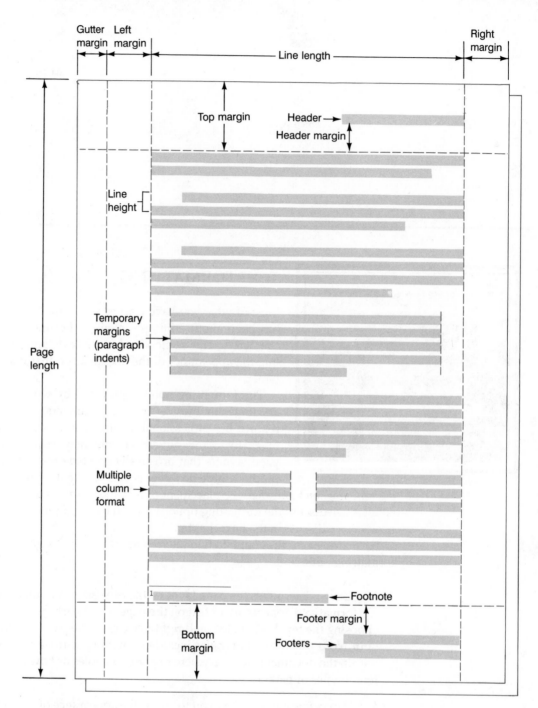

**Figure 7.1**
Page design terms

## Page Design Methods

For a word processor to print correctly, it must know the size of each piece of paper and how wide to make the margins. Most full-featured word processors provide page design options similar to those shown in Figure 7.1. Some of the terms in Figure 7.1 deserve further explanation.

- *Page length* is generally given in the number of lines per page. It can be set for standard 8 1/2-by-11-inch paper or for envelopes, mailing labels, odd-size pages, or extra-long sheets of paper. The most common setting is sixty-six lines, which allows six lines per inch on 11-inch paper.
- **Headers** and **footers** are the text at the tops and bottoms of pages. They are typed into the file only once; the word processor then places them on each page automatically. For example, headers and footers might be used to print the title at the top of each page and the page number at the bottom.
- Most programs define the *top* and *bottom margins* as the areas above and below the regular text. These programs print the header and footer lines inside the top and bottom margins, as Figure 7.1 shows. Other programs consider the header and footer part of the body of the page.
- Bound documents are usually printed on both sides of the paper, and they need different margins on odd and even pages because part of the page is hidden within the binding. The traditional way of doing this is to add a **gutter margin** to the right-hand side of even pages and the left-hand side of odd pages.
- *Left margin, right margin, gutter margin,* and *line length* are related to one another because they add up to *page width*. Some word processors arrive at an implied page width by letting you specify the margins and line length; others calculate the line length by subtracting the margins from the page width.

With this background, we are ready to compare the page design methods of three word processors: PFS:Professional Write, WordStar 2000, and Microsoft Word.

### Page Design with PFS:Professional Write

Despite its fancy-sounding name, PFS:Professional Write is a simple word processor that provides few formatting options. It is worth studying because its features are representative of the capabilities of many easy-to-use word processors.

Figure 7.2 shows the two dialog boxes PFS:Professional Write uses to establish a document's global format specifications. This method is easily learned but quite restrictive because these two dialog boxes control the page layout for the entire document—few of the global settings can be overridden with local format options. Among other things, this means the top and bottom margins must be the same for every page throughout the document.

The Margins-and-Page-Length dialog box is noteworthy because of the questions it doesn't ask. For example, it doesn't ask how many columns will be on each page because Professional Write doesn't create multicolumn documents.

```
┌─────────────────────────────────────────────────┐
│ ███████████████████████████████████████         │
│                                                 │
│           Margins and Page Length               │
│ ───────────────────────────────────────         │
│                                                 │
│   Left margin   : 10                            │
│   Right margin  : 70                            │
│                                                 │
│   Top margin    : 6                             │
│   Bottom margin : 6                             │
│                                                 │
│   Page length   : 66                            │
│                                                 │
│ ───────────────────────────────────────         │
│                                                 │
│  Esc-Cancel                   ←┘ Continue        │
└─────────────────────────────────────────────────┘
```

```
┌─────────────────────────────────────────────────────────┐
│ █████████████████████████████████████████████████████   │
│                                                         │
│                         Header                          │
│ ─────────────────────────────────────────────────────── │
│  Line 1: Chapter 2 -- Sally's Misgivings About David    │
│  Line 2:                                                │
│  Position (Center/Left/Right): C                        │
│  Style (Normal, Boldface, Underline, Italics): N        │
│  First header page: 1                                   │
│                                                         │
│                         Footer                          │
│ ─────────────────────────────────────────────────────── │
│  Line 1: Page *1*                                       │
│  Line 2:                                                │
│  Position (Center/Left/Right): C                        │
│  Style (Normal, Boldface, Underline, Italics): N        │
│  First footer page: 1                                   │
│                                                         │
│ ─────────────────────────────────────────────────────── │
│  Esc-Cancel                            ←┘ Continue       │
└─────────────────────────────────────────────────────────┘
```

**Figure 7.2**
Page design with PFS:Professional Write. **(a)** A simple dialog box establishes the boundaries of a page. **(b)** Another dialog box is used to set the headings and footings for the entire file.

The Header-and-Footer dialog box collects the information to print two-line headers and footers. Like any reasonable word processor, Professional Write will print page numbers as part of either the header or footer. The position at which page numbers are to be inserted is identified by surrounding a number with asterisks, as in *8*. For example, the dialog box in Figure 7.2 would cause "Page 12" to print in the center of the footer line of page 12 of the document.

**Figure 7.3**
WordStar 2000 asks a long series of questions—only some of them are shown here—to establish a format file containing page design specifications for a document.

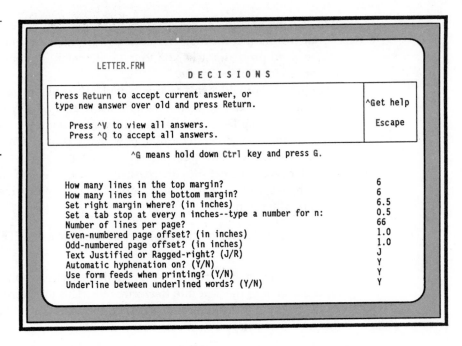

```
LETTER.FRM              D E C I S I O N S

Press Return to accept current answer, or              ^Get help
type new answer over old and press Return.
                                                        Escape
     Press ^V to view all answers.
     Press ^Q to accept all answers.

            ^G means hold down Ctrl key and press G.


How many lines in the top margin?                        6
How many lines in the bottom margin?                     6
Set right margin where? (in inches)                      6.5
Set a tab stop at every n inches--type a number for n:   0.5
Number of lines per page?                                66
Even-numbered page offset? (in inches)                   1.0
Odd-numbered page offset? (in inches)                    1.0
Text Justified or Ragged-right? (J/R)                    J
Automatic hyphenation on? (Y/N)                          Y
Use form feeds when printing? (Y/N)                      Y
Underline between underlined words? (Y/N)                Y
```

Professional Write is somewhat unusual in that it stores the header and footer lines as a global format setting. Thus if you want different headers or footers in each part of a document, you must break the document into parts and store each part in a separate file.

Professional Write does not provide an automatic method of distinguishing between odd and even pages, making it difficult to print well-formatted double-sided documents. For example, Professional Write doesn't have gutter margins to reserve space for a binding, and it can't vary the placement of page numbers in headers and footers to fall on the outside edges of opposing pages.

### Page Design with WordStar 2000

WordStar 2000 provides more flexibility for page design. Generally, the more sophisticated your word processing program is, the more choices you have to make to determine the document's design. For example, simple word processors don't allow documents to have more than one column per page, but full-featured word processors may require you to select the number of columns you want to use, specify the line length of each column, and choose the amount of margin to place between columns.

Because laying out the format of each document from scratch is tedious, many advanced word processors store your document design choices in a *format file* or *style sheet*. WordStar 2000 uses **format files**—files that contain page formatting instructions and also text (see Figure 7.3). In the next section on Microsoft Word, we discuss **style sheets**—files that contain instructions for page and paragraph formatting but not text. With either format files or style sheets, you can lay out the format of several types of documents and store the specifications for each type in a separate file. One file might store the design specifications for letters, another for legal contracts, and yet another for financial statements. Whenever you create a new document, the word processor asks you to indicate which file contains the formatting specifications for the document.

WordStar 2000 provides several predefined format files to make page layout easy for beginners. You can create your own format files or modify the predefined ones by answering a long list of formatting questions; Figure 7.3 shows some of these questions. Other questions determine how many columns are on each page, the spacing between lines, and so forth.

WordStar 2000's format files are particularly useful if you want to create documents with a consistent format. For example, if you wanted to create a series of business letters, you might

- Enter the page layout specifications into a file named LETTER.FRM, as shown in Figure 7.3.

- Create a skeleton of a letter by typing all the text that won't change from one business letter to the next into the format file. This might include the return address, part of the salutation, and the closing. You can edit a format file in the same way you edit a normal document file.

- Create a specific business letter by asking to edit a new document file named MARTIN.JIM. When WordStar 2000 asks which format file to use, choose LETTER.FRM. This would cause WordStar 2000 to make a copy of the LETTER.FRM file, name the copy MARTIN.JIM, and begin editing the MARTIN.JIM file. You would then flesh out the document file by typing in the name of the recipient and the body of the letter. This step would be repeated with different document file names for each business letter you wanted to produce.

WordStar 2000's format files, unlike Professional Write's dialog boxes, don't control the appearance of the entire document. Most of the global settings for the document's appearance can be reset with local format codes inside the document file. For example, you can insert local formatting codes to use a two-column page layout in one part of a document even if the rest of the document uses a one-column format.

## Page Design with Microsoft Word

Microsoft Word is well known for its extensive and powerful text formatting features. It lets you format a document with either direct formatting or style sheets. Direct formatting adjusts the appearance of the document by embedding formatting information directly in the document itself. In contrast, a style sheet stores formatting instructions in a separate file from the document. Either method can be used to format a document, or a combination of the two methods can be used. We explain both methods in turn.

*Direct formatting* attaches formatting instructions directly to selected text by using format commands. It is the simplest method of changing the appearance of a document. Each of Microsoft Word's format commands leads to a menu of formatting

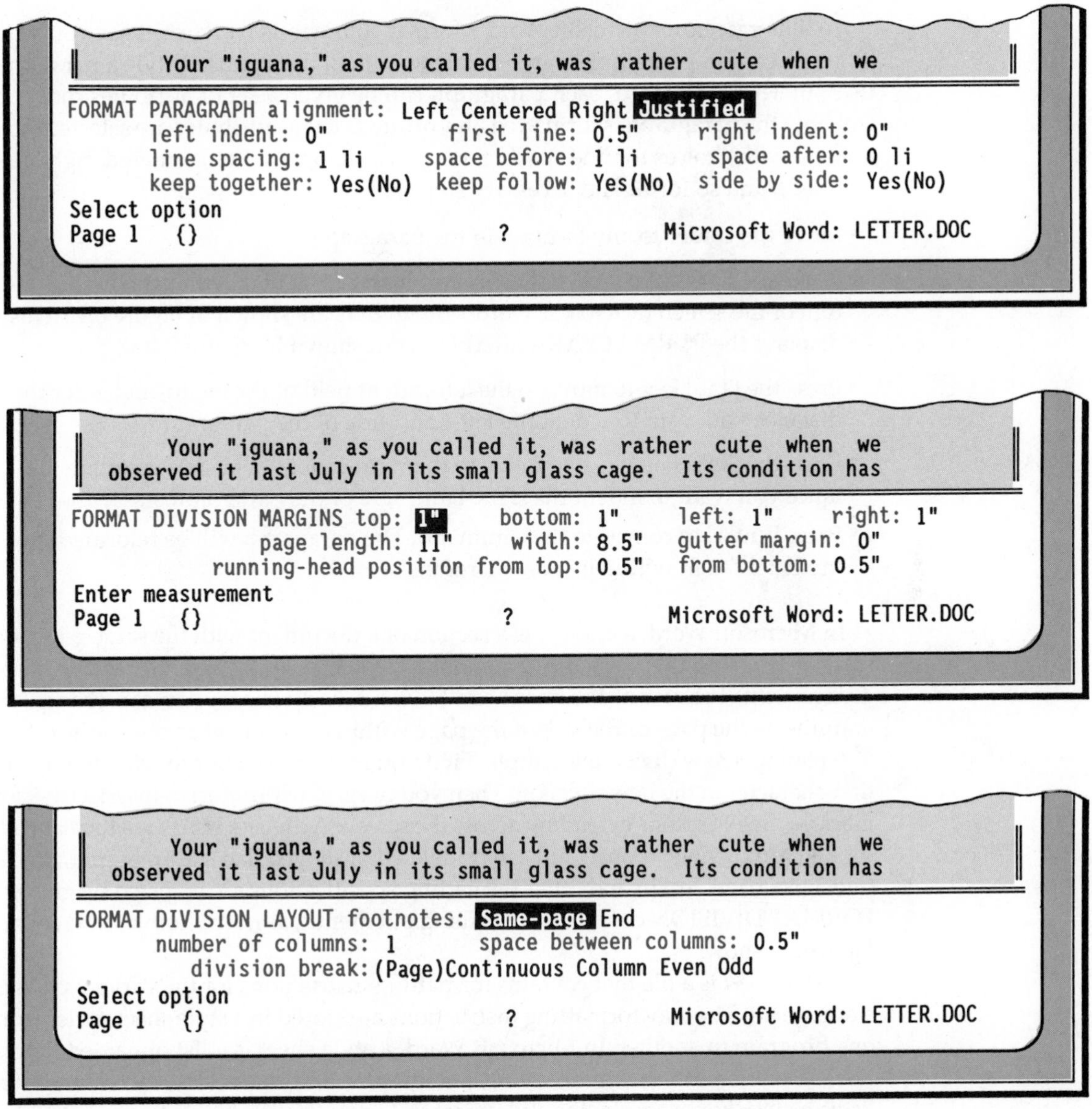

```
        Your "iguana," as you called it, was  rather  cute  when  we

FORMAT PARAGRAPH alignment: Left Centered Right Justified
        left indent: 0"          first line: 0.5"      right indent: 0"
        line spacing: 1 li    space before: 1 li      space after: 0 li
        keep together: Yes(No)  keep follow: Yes(No)  side by side: Yes(No)
Select option
Page 1    {}                              ?              Microsoft Word: LETTER.DOC
```

```
        Your "iguana," as you called it, was  rather  cute  when  we
   observed it last July in its small glass cage.  Its condition has

FORMAT DIVISION MARGINS top: 1"      bottom: 1"     left: 1"      right: 1"
                 page length: 11"      width: 8.5"   gutter margin: 0"
          running-head position from top: 0.5"     from bottom: 0.5"
Enter measurement
Page 1    {}                              ?              Microsoft Word: LETTER.DOC
```

```
        Your "iguana," as you called it, was  rather  cute  when  we
   observed it last July in its small glass cage.  Its condition has

FORMAT DIVISION LAYOUT footnotes: Same-page End
        number of columns: 1        space between columns: 0.5"
          division break: (Page)Continuous Column Even Odd
Select option
Page 1    {}                              ?              Microsoft Word: LETTER.DOC
```

**Figure 7.4**
Text formatting with Microsoft Word. **(a)** The FORMAT-PARAGRAPH command displays
this menu and allows you to adjust the appearance of a paragraph. **(b)** The FORMAT-
DIVISION-MARGINS menu establishes the page size and margins. **(c)** The FORMAT-
DIVISION-LAYOUT menu determines the number of columns on the page and the place-
ment of footnotes in the document.

choices. For example, the format commands for adjusting paragraphs and divisions
(page layouts) produce the menus shown in Figure 7.4. Other format commands
control the appearance of characters (bold, italic, and so on), set tab stops, or deal
with footnotes or headers and footers.

To illustrate how Microsoft Word's format commands work, suppose you want to give a certain paragraph margins narrower than the standard style a paragraph uses. In Microsoft Word, each paragraph can be given a set of attributes that control how the paragraph is formatted and printed. These attributes are selected from a menu with choices for line spacing, margins, alignment (left, centered, right, and justified), and so forth. The necessary steps are

- Move the cursor to any location in the paragraph.
- Select the FORMAT-PARAGRAPH command from the menu bars on the bottom of the screen (Microsoft Word's menu bars are shown in Figure 6.1.) This displays the FORMAT PARAGRAPH menu shown in Figure 7.4(a).
- Press the [Tab] key to move to the left-indent field of the menu, and enter the distance you want to indent the left-hand side of the paragraph.
- Press the [Tab] key twice to move to the right-indent field, and enter the distance you want to indent the right-hand side of the paragraph.
- Press [Enter] to complete the command. The paragraph will be reformed immediately to fit within its new margins.

In Microsoft Word, a *division* is a section of a document with the same page format, such as a chapter or table of contents. Most simple documents need only one division. But because a document can have many divisions, you can change the margins on the page or the size of the page within a document as often as you like.

Creating a new division is simple. First you move the cursor to what will be the first character in the new division. Then you press [Ctrl]-[Enter] to insert a division mark—a line of colons extending across the screen. A division mark is a format code (like a hard carriage return) and can be deleted or moved like a normal character. A division's page design and other formatting specifications are adjusted by giving a FORMAT-DIVISION command and filling out menus, as the bottom two screens of Figure 7.4 show.

A *style sheet* is a file that contains formatting instructions for the various parts of a document. The way formatting instructions are stored in a style sheet varies from one program to another. In Microsoft Word, a style sheet is a list of named definitions for different types of divisions, paragraphs, and characters. Each item in the list is a *style*. For example, the style sheet in Figure 7.5 lists six styles: two division styles, two paragraph styles, and two character styles. If the style sheet looks confusing, this is understandable. To make sense of the poorly labeled information in a Microsoft Word style sheet takes some experience. It helps to know that a style has three parts: a name (such as Paragraph 10), a *key code* that is used to identify the style quickly (such as Alt-Q), and a definition that contains the formatting instructions. Here is a partial explanation of two styles in Figure 7.5.

- The Division 2 style is invoked by pressing [Alt]-[X], its key code. It formats the pages in a division to have two columns on an 8 1/2-by-11-inch page.
- The Paragraph 10 style is invoked by pressing [Alt]-[Q]. It causes a paragraph to be preceded by two blank lines and to print in an italic Courier typeface with indented margins.

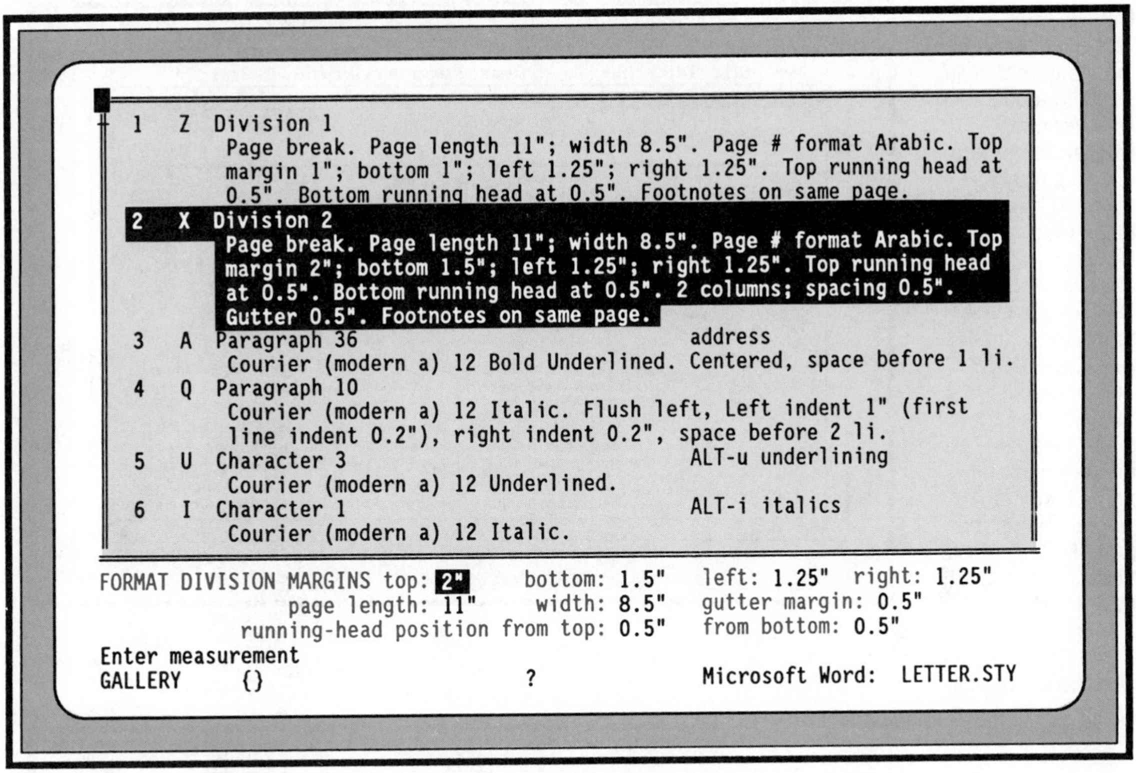

**Figure 7.5**
Editing a Microsoft Word style sheet

Microsoft Word is distributed with several sample style sheets. You can create your own style sheets or modify the sample ones by filling out the same format menus used with direct formatting. For example, the menu shown at the bottom of Figure 7.5 is adjusting the page layout instructions of the Division 2 style.

Creating a style sheet for a new type of document can be a substantial job because decisions must be made about how all the different parts of the document should look. Often it is easiest to create a new style sheet by modifying an existing one for a similar type of document.

In organizations, it is desirable that documents produced by different people have a consistent appearance. By having someone with an artistic flair create style sheets for the organization's letters, memos, reports, and other documents, and training people to use these style sheets, the documents will have a standardized look.

Creating a style sheet is the tough part; using it is easy. To use a style sheet, you give a format command to "attach" it to the document file—this tells the word processor which style sheet to use. Then you "tag" the parts of your document to tell the word processor where to apply the styles to the text. To tag text, first you select the text (perhaps by pointing and dragging with a mouse), and then you

**Figure 7.6**
The effect of attaching a different style sheet to a document with Ventura Publisher. Ventura allows paragraph styles to have meaningful names like Chapter Title, First Para, or Body Text. **(a)** This screen is formatted with the &BOOK-P1.STY style sheet. It centers the Chapter # and Chapter Title on the page and prints text in a single-column format. **(b)** This screen uses the &BOOK-P2.STY style sheet. It aligns the Chapter # and Chapter Title with the left margin and prints text in a two-column format.

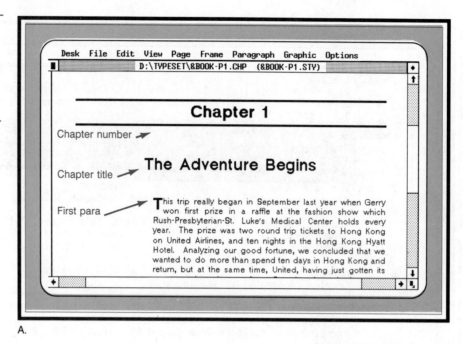

A.

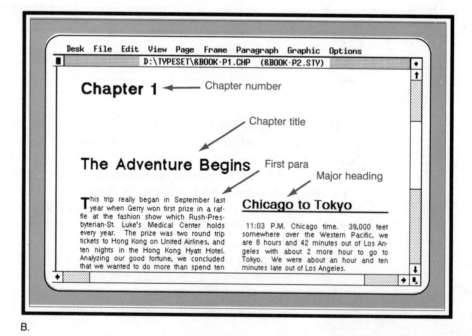

B.

identify which style definition you want to apply to the text (perhaps by typing the style's key code). For example, suppose you want to use the style sheet shown in Figure 7.5 to format a paragraph with an italic typeface and indented margins. The Paragraph 10 style matches this description, and its key code is Alt-Q. So you would select the paragraph—here moving the cursor to any location in the paragraph would be sufficient—and then press [Alt]-[Q]. Immediately, the paragraph would be reformed to fit the new margins and the other format instructions in the Paragraph 10 style. This illustrates one of the major strengths of style sheets: They provide a quick and easy way to reuse formatting instructions.

Style sheets provide another advantage over direct formatting: They let you change a document's format without editing it—you only need to attach a different style sheet. Figure 7.6 shows the effect of switching style sheets on a Ventura Publisher document. Although it takes only a single command to attach a different style sheet to a document, the change can give the entire document a different appearance. The ability to quickly reformat a document can be a godsend as it goes through development. For example, it may be important to edit double-spaced manuscript, provide reviewers with single-spaced copies, and publish a typeset version.

## Local Formatting Options

To give a document a polished appearance, it is often necessary to override the global page design that governs the usual placement of text on the page. For example, you may want to center a title on the page rather than place it flush against the left margin like the rest of the text. Or you may want to reserve an area of blank space so that a picture can be pasted in it later. This type of format change is made by giving local format commands that temporarily override the global format settings.

Word processors vary considerably in their ability to adjust a document's format from page to page. Advanced word processors are equipped with a myriad of local formatting options; simple word processors may not even let you change the settings for the margins on the page.

In this section, we explain what local format options are typically available and illustrate how they are used.

### Adjusting Page Breaks

A **page break** occurs when one page ends and another begins. Page breaks occur automatically when all the lines between the top and bottom margins are filled. A WYSIWYG word processor typically shows page breaks on the screen by displaying a line of characters, for example, hyphens or equal signs. An off-screen text formatter, however, gives no clue during editing of where page breaks will fall.

Adjusting page breaks so that they fall in the right spot can be difficult, especially when a document includes not only paragraphs but also footnotes, tables, figures, or section headings. Sometimes there is no good way to break a page short of rewriting the text. Two partial solutions offered by word processors are forced page breaks and conditional page breaks.

A **forced page break** starts a new page at a specific location rather than fill the rest of the current page. At the end of a chapter, it is traditional to force a page break. Nearly every word processor provides a method of doing this, and some methods work better than others.

You can ask PFS:Professional Write to force a page break by inserting a special format command, *NEW PAGE*, where you want the page break to occur in the document. Normally, Professional Write displays page breaks on the screen in the correct location, but like an off-screen text formatter, it does not consider the *NEW PAGE* command until printing, so all the page breaks after a *NEW PAGE* command are displayed incorrectly.

A more common method of forcing page breaks allows you to insert a **hard page break**, a format code similar to a hard carriage return. A hard page break signals the end of a page and takes effect immediately by displaying a page break on the screen. In contrast, **soft page breaks** are generated automatically by a WYSIWYG word processor and will shift to new locations if you edit or reformat the document. Most WYSIWYG word processors let you insert or delete hard page breaks just like other format codes. For example, WordPerfect lets you insert a hard page break in the document by pressing [Ctrl]-[Enter]; you can delete one by moving the cursor immediately before it and pressing [Del].

A **conditional page break** lets you protect a group of lines from being split by a page break. This is handy if you are reserving blank space for a figure or table to be inserted later. You can place the necessary blank space in a document by pressing the [Enter] key once for each blank line. But the blank space is not enough; you also need a guarantee that all the blank lines will be printed on the same page.

The simplest word processors, such as PFS:Professional Write, provide no special support for conditional page breaks. Although time consuming, you can work around this limitation, for example, just before printing, you could scroll through the document and insert forced page breaks before items that otherwise would be split inappropriately across two pages.

Many word processors provide a format code that establishes a conditional page break. For example, you can group lines together with WordPerfect or WordStar 2000 by inserting a conditional page break before the first line in the group. For example, the [KEEP 20 LINES TOGETHER] format code in WordStar 2000 will force an immediate page break if fewer than twenty lines remain on the page; otherwise, the format code is ignored.

Some word processors treat conditional page breaks as an aspect of a paragraph's layout. In Microsoft Word, for example, you can give attributes to paragraphs that determine how they will be positioned on the page. One of these attributes, the *keep* attribute (see Figure 7.5), keeps the paragraph in one piece, moving it as a unit to the next page if necessary.

A conditional page break can result in wasted blank space at the bottom of a page. The best solution for a figure or table that does not fit on the current page may be to fill the page with text and print the figure or table at the top of the next page. Few word processors can perform this formatting trick automatically, but most page composition programs can.

## Widows and Orphans

Sometimes an automatic page break places the first line of a paragraph at the bottom of a page, forming an **orphan**, or it may place the last line of a paragraph at the top of a page, forming a **widow**. It is generally agreed that widows and orphans are unsightly—particularly in documents with long paragraphs—but there is no entirely satisfactory way to get rid of them. From this book, most widows and orphans were eliminated from this book by adjusting the size and placement of illustrations or inserting blank space before headings. These techniques provide a pleasing page layout, but they require last-minute decisions and considerable work.

Many word processors ignore widows and orphans, making it a good idea to scroll through the document just before printing to eliminate them. An easy way to get rid of orphans is to add a blank line or a conditional page break before each of them. To remove widows, you might edit the paragraph, jam the last line of the paragraph into the bottom margin of the page, or insert a page break before the next-to-last line in the paragraph.

WordPerfect, Microsoft Word, and Ventura Publisher can be set to automatically "correct" widows and orphans. When this feature is turned on, these programs refuse to put a page break after the first or before the last line of a paragraph, instead, they shift lines to the next page, leaving the current page one or two lines shorter than usual. Moreover, when this feature is on, they never put a page break in a three-line paragraph—if it does not fit entirely on the current page, it is printed on the next page.

### Using Headers and Footers

Headers and footers help the reader identify the parts of a long document quickly. In books, the chapter title and book title are often placed in headers on facing pages. Page numbers are most commonly placed in footers. Telephone directories use headers to identify the first and last names on each page of the directory—forming a handy index. In all publications, headers and footers are likely to change from page to page.

Most word processors meet this requirement by placing the text of headers and footers inside special format codes in the document. The effect of these format codes is temporary: They determine what will be printed in the header or footer until the next header or footer format code supersedes it. This lets you change headers and footers page by page if necessary.

WYSIWYG word processors normally hide their format codes, so the headers and footers usually are not visible on the screen. Even if you ask to see the format codes on screen, you may find them unintelligible. For example, the WordPerfect format code [Hdr/Ftr:1,3;^B] causes the page number to print at the left margin of the header on even-numbered pages. With WordStar 2000, the equivalent format code is a little more understandable and looks like

```
[EVEN HEADER]
&%page&
[EVEN HEADER]
```

Some programs provide many options for controlling the format of headers and footers. Figure 7.7 illustrates some of the options provided by Ventura Publisher. Its Headers-&-Footers dialog box lets you establish different headers and footers for facing pages in a double-sided document. This feature is often used to place page numbers on the outside edge of each page, where they can be viewed most easily.

**Figure 7.7**
Establishing a head-
ing line with Ventura
Publisher

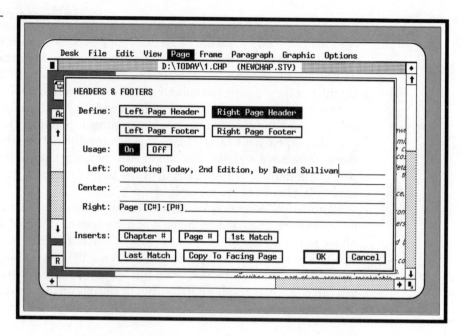

## Footnotes and Endnotes

**Footnotes** are placed at the bottom of the page, and **endnotes** are placed at the end of the document; both create their own special problems. Whenever a new footnote or endnote is added to a document, all subsequent notes must be renumbered (un-less referenced alphabetically, such as by the authors' names). The rules of style for footnotes and endnotes are full of exceptions, and simple word processors do not provide special features for handling them all. Common among word processors with special help are: automatic numbering of notes, bottom-of-page placement for footnotes, and end-of-document placement for endnotes.

If a word processor provides **automatic numbering**, regardless of how many notes are added or deleted, they are numbered sequentially throughout the docu-ment. Some programs offer automatic numbering for elements other than notes and page numbers, such as chapters, sections, theorems, figures, and tables. These programs may let you choose how each element should be numbered. For example, you might want the program to use roman numerals (I, II, III) for chapter numbers, arabic letters (a, b, c) for section numbers, and regular numbers (1, 2, 3) for every-thing else.

Bottom-of-page placement floats a footnote down until it is printed after the regular text on the page.[1] This feature saves time by eliminating the need to shift blocks of text before or after a footnote to print it exactly at the bottom of the page.

End-of-document placement prints endnotes in a group after the regular text in the document. Nearly all word processors print endnotes in the order they appear in the document. Unfortunately, this is the wrong order for an alphabetical bibliog-

---

1. This footnote illustrates bottom-of-page placement.

raphy. Few word processors offer the option of sorting endnotes alphabetically and then renumbering them according to their sorted order.

The procedure for inserting a footnote or an endnote into the document varies. With an off-screen text formatter, you identify notes by specially marking them in the text, as in `@FOOTNOTE(This footnote illustrates bottom-of-page placement.)`. Most WYSIWYG word processors place footnote and endnote text inside a format code. For example, the format code for a WordPerfect footnote looks like `[Note:Foot,2;[Note #]This footnote illustrates bottom-of-page placement.]`. Remember, format codes are normally hidden, so all you would see on the screen is the footnote number—unless you asked for the format codes to be displayed.

### Adjusting Text within Paragraphs

Suppose you want to distinguish a long quotation from the rest of a document by giving it narrower margins. To do this and similar tasks efficiently, being able to vary the margins of a paragraph independently from the margins of the page is important. Most word processors let you do this in conjunction with their **ruler line,** a horizontal line on the screen that displays the position of the cursor, location of tab stops, and position of paragraph indents or temporary margins (if any). Figure 7.8 illustrates the ruler lines used by PFS:Professional Write, WordStar 2000, and Microsoft Word; each program provides a different method of varying a document's margins.

Professional Write displays its ruler line immediately below the text-editing window. Its ruler line indicates several types of information.

- The cursor's position is shown in inverse video.

- Every tenth column position is indicated by a number.

- The document's left and right margins are indicated by brackets.

- A temporary left margin is indicated by a greater-than symbol (>).

- Each tab stop is indicated by a T for a typewriter tab or a D for a decimal tab. Typewriter tabs are usually used to align columns of text; decimal tabs align the decimal points in a column of numbers.

To indent a paragraph with PFS:Professional Write, you select the paragraph as a block with a pull-down Edit menu, causing the paragraph to appear in inverse video. Then you move the cursor to the column position where you want the temporary left margin and press [Ctrl]-[N]. Immediately, the text in the block is reformed to fit with the new left margin. One of PFS:Professional Write's significant limitations is it does not have a corresponding command to indent a paragraph's right margin.

WordStar 2000 displays a ruler above the text-editing window. WordStar 2000 also lets you adjust the document's margins or change the tab settings by inserting a new ruler in the document. The new ruler is actually a format code and, like other format codes, can be deleted, moved, hidden, or displayed. Each ruler you place in a document determines the location of tabs and margins until the next ruler. After

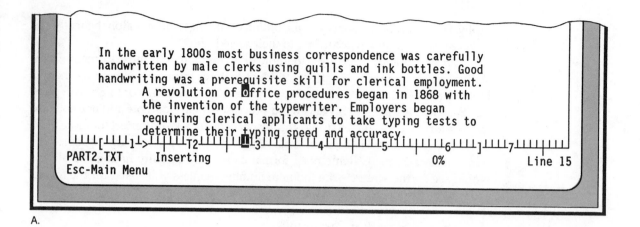

A.

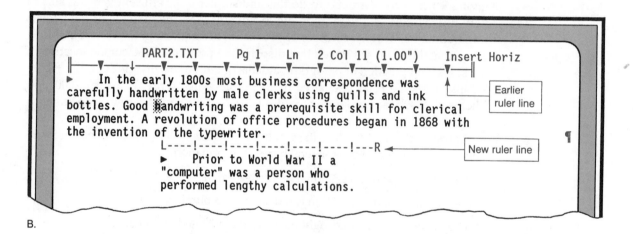

B.

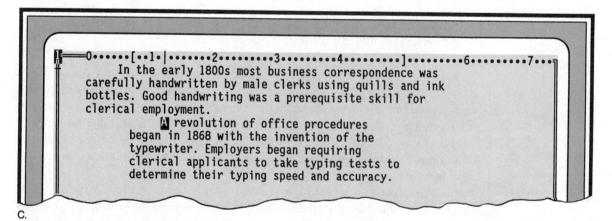

C.

**Figure 7.8**
The ruler lines of three word processors. **(a)** PFS:Professional Write's ruler indicates the position of the document's margins with brackets on the ruler. **(b)** WordStar 2000 allows ruler lines to be inserted in the document to temporarily adjust the margins or tabs. **(c)** Microsoft Word indicates the current paragraph's margins with brackets on a ruler at the top of the screen.

a ruler is moved, inserted, or otherwise edited, WordStar 2000 immediately reformats the document's text to reflect the changes.

Microsoft Word displays its ruler line at the top of the screen. This line indicates the current paragraph's margins with brackets. Earlier in this chapter, we saw that Microsoft Word allows you to change the margins of individual paragraphs or the entire page by using the Format menus shown in Figure 7.4 or by attaching new definitions from a style sheet.

## Using Tabs

Tabs are primarily used to format tables or other tabular information, but they can be used for such simple tasks as indenting paragraphs.

Most word processors have two basic types of tab stops: typewriter and decimal. A **typewriter tab**, as the name suggests, works more or less like a tab stop on a typewriter. Typewriter tabs are indicated by a special character such as !, T, or ∇ in the ruler line.

A **decimal tab** is usually indicated by # or D in the ruler line. Decimal tabs are convenient for lining up the decimal points in a column of numbers. As a number is typed at a decimal tab stop, its digits are shifted left until a decimal point is typed. Digits typed after the decimal point are placed after the tab stop. For example,

```
L--------------------T------------------D-----R
Derek Wakefield        503-74-8836         329.25
Trudy Vlastelica       548-75-5409       2,458.
Hugo Lamplighter       503-75-7934         14.85
```

There is a subtle but important difference between a table formatted with tabs and one laid out with spaces. Each time you tap the space bar or press the tab key, you generate a character code, and the character codes for tabs and spaces are different. Because tabs and spaces are not normally visible on the screen, thinking of them like other characters may seem strange. But they are inserted in and deleted from text as are other characters, and they take up the same amount of memory in the computer.

Most WYSIWYG word processors let you see the location of tabs when you ask to view the screen with the normally hidden format codes (for example, see Figure 6.6 or 6.13). A few simple word processors, such as PFS:Professional Write, let you establish and use tab stops but do not place tab characters in the document. Instead, they convert the tab character into spaces as soon as the cursor is moved from the tab stop.

Sometimes you can see the difference between a tab and a space in the way the cursor moves. If you use the right-arrow key to move the cursor across a line filled with tabs, the cursor will jump from one tab stop to another rather than float from one column to the next.

It may seem simplest to use spaces to lay out the columns of a table, but using tabs is generally better for two reasons. First, if the columns in a table are formatted with tabs, they can be shifted to new locations simply by changing the positions of tab stops. This allows you to adjust the size of columns without meticulously adding or removing spaces throughout the table.

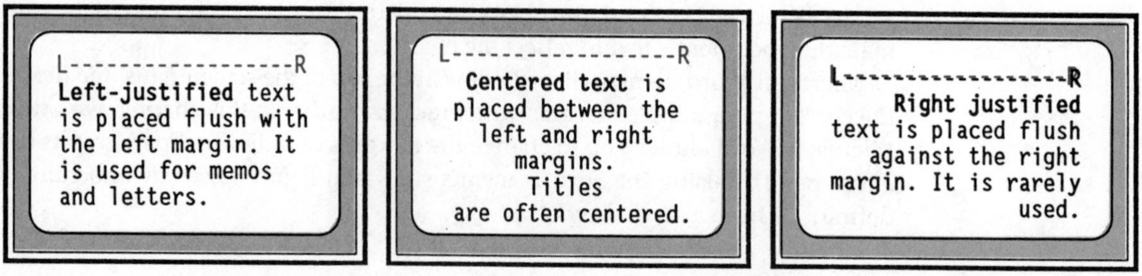

```
L-----------------R
Left-justified text
is placed flush with
the left margin. It
is used for memos
and letters.
```

```
L-----------------R
  Centered text is
 placed between the
   left and right
      margins.
       Titles
 are often centered.
```

```
L····················R
    Right justified
text is placed flush
   against the right
   margin. It is rarely
              used.
```

**Figure 7.9**
Samples of ragged-right, centered, and ragged-left text

---

Second, some typefaces make it difficult to line up columns exactly by inserting and deleting spaces because they assign different widths to each letter. For instance, the typeface used in this sentence gives an *M* more room than an *i* or a space.

## Line Spacing

Nearly all programs let you change the distance between lines from one paragraph to the next. Thus a page might be double-spaced except for a single-spaced paragraph in the middle.

Word processing programs offer a variety of line spacing choices.

- PFS:Professional Write limits the choice to single- or double-spacing.

- WordStar 2000 lets you adjust the line spacing by varying the height of each printed line, but the only allowable line height choices are two, three, four, six, and eight lines per inch. WordStar 2000 always single-spaces text on the screen, but the line height setting is correctly reflected in the position of on-screen page breaks and in the printed document.

- WordPerfect provides two ways to adjust the line spacing: height of each line can be set to six or eight lines per inch, and the line spacing can be varied by half-line increments, so line spacing values of 1.5, 3, or even 12.5 are acceptable. WordPerfect shows the correct line spacing on the screen to the nearest whole number. For example, if you set line spacing at 2.5, text appears triple spaced on the screen.

- Microsoft Word accepts line spacing measurements in lines or inches. For example, to print ten lines per inch, you would set the line spacing to 0.1 inch.

## Aligning and Justifying Text

Almost every word processor has a simple command for centering a line between the margins (see Figure 7.9). Centered titles stand out from the rest of the text.

Handwritten and typed documents have **ragged right** margins; that is, the right-hand edge is uneven. On most word processors, a ragged right margin is the default value.

**Figure 7.10**
Text justified with
fixed-width spaces,
microspacing, and
proportional spacing

```
L---------------R   L---------------R   L---------------R
```

Fixed-       width
spacing      allows
text         to    be
justified but can
leave   ugly   gaps
between words.

Microspaced text
spreads out the
gaps between words
so that they are
less noticeable.

Proportional spacing
places letters in fields
with different widths,
so "MMMM" takes
up more room than
"iiii."

Occasionally, ragged left lines are necessary; for example, some letter formats call for the date to be aligned with the right margin; that is, ragged left. Since most word processors do not have a specific command to create a ragged left margin, you must make individual lines ragged left by inserting spaces at the beginning of the line until the end of the line is flush with the right margin.

To **justify** text is to align it within boundaries. **Left-justified** text is placed flush against the left margin. Similarly, **right-justified** text is placed flush against the right margin (see Figure 7.9). The printing in newspapers and books is usually both left- and right-justified. Because "left- and right-justified" is a mouthful, text with straight left and right margins is simply said to be **justified**. Justified documents look professional, but studies have shown that documents with ragged right margins are easier to read.

Most word processors have a toggle that turns justification on and off. Text is justified in several ways, but all the methods involve varying the spacing between letters and words (see Figure 7.10).

- **Fixed-width spacing** pads out short lines by inserting full-size spaces between words. This method is often used for on-screen justification because some monitors are column oriented and cannot shift a character left or right less than a full column position. Even if fixed-width spaces are spread out as evenly as possible, they are noticeable, especially on narrow lines.

- **Microspacing** can make justified text look better by inserting tiny spaces between letters and words. For example, many printers can position the print head in 1/120-inch increments. If the word processing software and printer communicate correctly, these printers can spread enough 1/120-inch spaces between the letters and spaces to fill the line.

- **Proportional spacing** allocates a variable amount of space per character depending on the width of the character. This keeps the space between each letter the same, permitting more text to fit on each page without reducing the document's readability.

### Setting Character Attributes

The appearance of documents produced by a word processing system depends on the combined capabilities of the printer and software. Buying an expensive, versatile printer is a mistake if the software you plan to use does not have commands for selecting different sizes and styles of type. Similarly, buying a state-of-the-art desktop publishing package designed for typesetting make no sense if you use an inexpensive dot matrix printer. And there is another pitfall to avoid in choosing a

**Figure 7.11**
Samples of some of
the type styles avail-
able within MacWrite

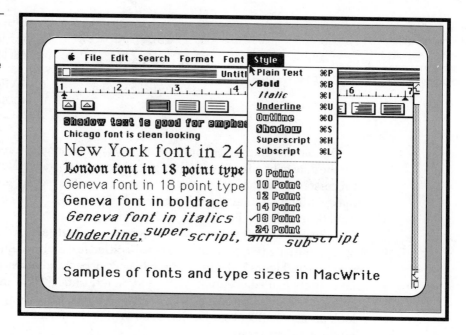

Samples of fonts and type sizes in MacWrite

printer and software: Even if the documentation for both the printer and software claim they accommodate a particular printing feature, different coding systems might describe the feature. Because the character codes for ordinary letters and numbers are standardized, getting a printer to work like a simple typewriter is not difficult. But most features, such as shifting from plain to italic text, have not been standardized, so you should check to be sure the software and hardware are compatible.

The appearance of a character is influenced by its size, typeface family, and style. Many programs give you control over each of these characteristics; others let you change only a character's style (bold, italic, and so on).

Type size is measured in *points*, and the spacing between characters on a line is called the *pitch*. A **point** is 1/72 of an inch. Typical point sizes are 10 or 12 points for typewritten characters, 6 to 8 points for the fine print in legal notices, and 24 to 48 points for the headlines in newspapers. For example, this paragraph is set in 11-point type. The **pitch** is a measure of how many characters fit within an inch. This measurement makes sense only for fixed-width type; proportionally spaced type is said to have a *variable pitch*. The pitch of many office typewriters can be set for either 10 or 12 characters per inch. Sometimes 17 pitch type is used by dot matrix printers to compress a 132-character line onto a 8 1/2-inch wide page.

The **typeface** determines the shape of each character. For example, Courier is the most common typewriter typeface, **Helvetica Bold** is often used for headlines, and Times Roman is a popular typeface for the text in books and newspapers. Typefaces are designed in "families" that usually include regular, bold, and italic styles and may include other styles such as outline, backslanted, or bold italic. Technically, a **font** is a set of characters in a particular typeface and size. Thus the Geneva Bold typeface in 12 point is one font, and the 14 point is another. But some word processing vendors use these terms more loosely—for them, the terms *typeface* and *font* appear to mean the same thing.

Some word processing program may require that all characters in a document be the same size and come from the same typeface family. For example, PFS:Professional Write limits the options on character styles to regular, bold, and underlined characters. Other programs offer a wider range of character enhancements, including subscripts, superscripts, strikeout, italic, compressed, and double-width type.

Figure 7.11 illustrates some of the typefaces that can be selected within MacWrite, a fairly simple word processor for the Apple Macintosh. To change the appearance of text with MacWrite, you first select the text to be affected with a mouse, and then from the Style menu, you choose the typeface and type size.

Many programs allow you to change fonts by inserting format codes in the document. For example, with WordStar 2000, the format code that requests a fixed-width, 12-pitch font looks like [NON PS 12]. The effect of a format code continues until another format code cancels it. So you must remember to place format codes before and after text that is to receive new attributes.

Style sheets provide a different way of selecting fonts. Remember that a style sheet is a list of formatting instructions for the parts of a document. Each part (or style) of the document can be given its own font, and this information is stored in the style sheet. For example, Figure 7.12 shows the dialog box that Ventura Publisher uses to assign a font to a paragraph style. In this illustration, the style named Firstpar is assigned the Times Roman typeface, 10-point type, normal character style, and black ink. As soon as this selection is made, all paragraphs in the document tagged with the Firstpar name are displayed with the appropriate font.

Whether character attributes are visible on the screen depends on the capabilities of the monitor and software. For example, if you use an IBM PC with a color monitor, Microsoft Word displays not only underlining but also double-underlining. But on the same monitor, WordPerfect represents an underlined character by changing its color. Neither program is able to display different type sizes.

## OUTLINE PROCESSORS

Sifting through a jumble of thoughts is easier if you write your ideas down in a list. You can organize your thoughts even more effectively if you arrange them into an **outline**, a *hierarchical* list of topics and subtopics.

Most people find that their outlines undergo considerable refinement: Topics are rearranged, edited, split in two, and shifted from one level to another. Doing this on paper inevitably leads to a confusing proliferation of erasures, cross-outs, inserts, and arrows. You can avoid this mess by using a word processor to enter the outline on a computer screen and rearranging the topics as necessary with block moves. But an *outline processor* makes the process simpler and less time consuming.

An **outline processor,** or *idea processor* or *outliner,* is a program with an array of special-purpose features for creating and manipulating outlines. For example, a generally available feature is a command that collapses the outline so that only the major headings are visible. And nearly all outline processors have single-keystroke

**Figure 7.12**
**(a)** A dialog box for selecting the typeface, size, style, and color of a paragraph's text. **(b)** Samples of the Times Roman typeface in various sizes.

A.

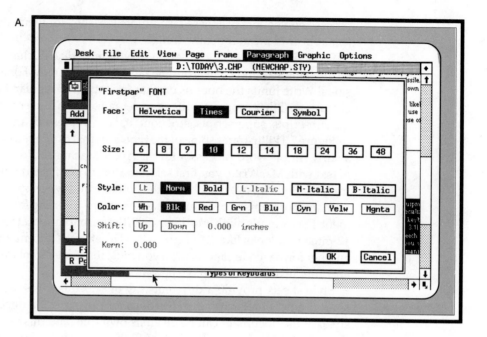

B.

Times Roman (6 point)

Times Roman (12 point)

# Times Roman bold (24 point)

# Times Roman bold (30 point)

commands that change the level of a heading, for example, to raise a minor heading to a major heading. There are at least four types of outline processors.

- *Standalone programs*, like ThinkTank, Max Think, and PC Outline, were the first type of outline processor to be developed. Although these programs gained immediate acceptance for organizing thoughts and lists, their limited word processing abilities make them inconvenient for outlining lengthy documents. However, standalone programs usually provide the most advanced outline processing features. For example, MORE (see Figure 7.13) is a standalone outline processor that can quickly switch the display of an outline among three views: outline, tree chart, and bullet chart.

- *Memory-resident outline processors*, such as Ready, Voila, and Pop-Up Partner, are readily accessible when you use other programs. Once they have been loaded into memory, a special keystroke causes them to pop up on the screen—even in the middle of a session with another program.

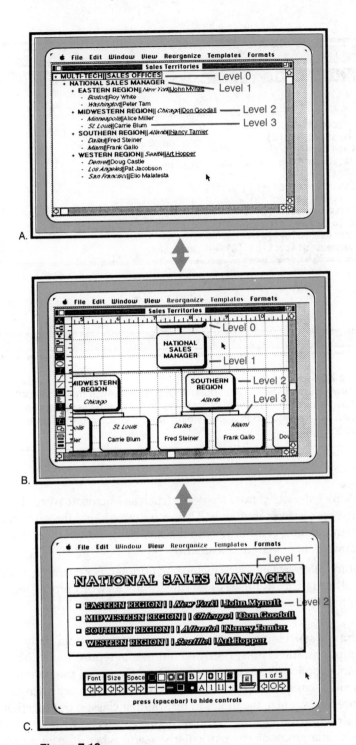

**Figure 7.13**
Three views of the same outline. **(a)** The outline view is used to enter and edit topics in the outline. **(b)** The tree chart view gives a graphical perspective of the relationships among topics. **(c)** The bullet chart view is used to transform the outline into bulleted lists for presentations.

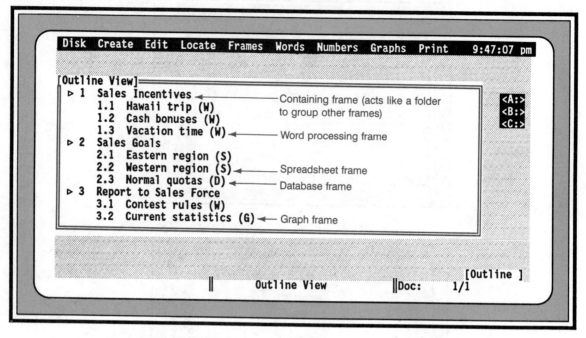

**Figure 7.14**
Framework stores data in a modular structure, and each module is called a frame. Individual frames can hold word processing text, a database file, spreadsheet, or graph. Frames can be grouped in a "containing frame," which organizes the individual frames in an outline form.

- Many *full-featured word processors* (such as Microsoft Word) have built-in outline processing commands. These programs blend the easy creation and manipulation of outlines with the capability to flesh them out into well-organized, book-length documents.

- Some *integrated programs* include an outliner. For example, Framework uses its outline facility as the basis for integrating its word processing, database, spreadsheet, and graphics components (see Figure 7.14).

Outline processing is used to create everything from daily "to do" lists to job descriptions, travel itineraries, and outlines of reports and books. This diversity of possible applications is exploited by Peter Gysegem, the training manager for MS Systems, a computer store in Corvallis, Oregon. He uses Microsoft Word's outline features to organize the topics in his training classes, put together business plans, and structure the logic of the computer programs he writes.

"Outline processing is particularly useful when I write *pseudocode* [which are English-language notes that programmers use to rough out programs]," says Gysegem. "The indentation shows part of the structure of the program and is especially important for languages like C and Pascal—languages that are heavily indented. I begin by dividing the program into three or four logical areas (major headings) and then work down to the second level. If something doesn't make sense, I can pop it into another section. Even though you can do all these things with a normal word processor, the tools here are more appropriate and powerful."

An essential feature of an outline processor is the ability to expand a heading to see the text in that section or to collapse the text so that you can see and manipulate the overall organization. For example, an outline processor enables you to reorganize a document by rearranging headings in the outline. Figure 7.15 illustrates these features.

1. Figure 7.15(a) shows a document with headings and text. The headings appear in color and are numbered according to their level and position in the hierarchy.

2. Figure 7.15(b) shows the same document in outline form, so only the headings are visible. The active heading (the one pointed to by the cursor) is shown in inverse video. Headings that have text hidden beneath them are indicated by a t at the left edge of the screen.

3. Figure 7.15(c) shows the active heading has been moved to a new location in the outline, and as a result, the headings are temporarily numbered incorrectly. Microsoft Word renumbers headings only when you give it a specific command to do so.

4. Figure 7.15(d) shows the expanded view of the document again. Because the text in the document is associated with headings in the outline, the text has been rearranged automatically to correspond to the new outline.

## LARGE DOCUMENTS

Large documents are much harder to create than letters or short papers. The problem is not simply that large documents have more pages but also that coordinating all the parts is more of a chore. As the document grows, its file size increases until it will not conveniently fit in one file. As soon as it is split into separate files, tasks like moving paragraphs cease to be simple operations. Instead, they require reading and writing in various files, changing disks, and the like. Even more bothersome are the chores of coordinating the page numbers among all the parts and creating an accurate table of contents and index. Managing a large document is simplified if your word processor supports document chaining and can automatically collect page references.

### Document Chaining

**Document chaining** allows information in several files to be merged and printed sequentially as if everything were in one large file. This way each file is kept to a manageable size, yet the whole document is printed at once with the pages numbered properly from start to finish.

Document files can be chained together in several ways, but the most common is to place a print-formatting command in a **master file** that suspends printing of

**Figure 7.15**
Outline processing
with Microsoft Word

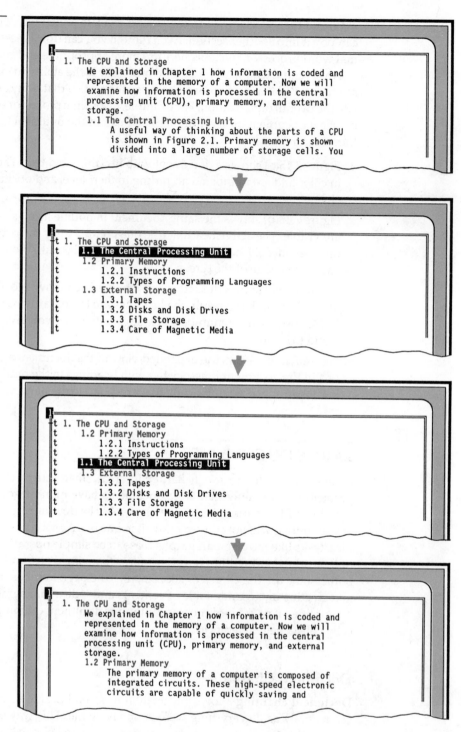

the master file, prints a second file, and then continues printing the master file. Think of the master file as a form to be completed that receives its information from other files. For example, in PFS:Professional Write, the document-chaining command is *JOIN followed by the filename and *. Suppose the master file contains

Tom appeared on the sidewalk with a bucket of whitewash and a
long-handled brush. *JOIN SAWYER.TOM* Thirty yards of board
fence nine feet high. Life to him seemed hollow, and
existence but a burden.

And the file SAWYER.TOM contains

He surveyed the fence, and all gladness left him and a deep
melancholy settled down upon his spirit.

Then printing the master file produces

Tom appeared on the sidewalk with a bucket of whitewash and a
long-handled brush. He surveyed the fence, and all gladness
left him and a deep
melancholy settled down upon his spirit.
Thirty yards of board
fence nine feet high. Life to him seemed hollow, and
existence but a burden.

Besides illustrating how document chaining works, this example shows PFS:Professional Write does not correctly reform paragraphs that contain a JOIN command. This is not a major flaw because most often document chaining is used to merge whole paragraphs or even larger units—not just sentences—with the master file. For example, a master file might include JOIN commands for each part of the document, as in

*JOIN B:TITLE.PG* *NEW PAGE*
*JOIN A:CHAPTER.1* *NEW PAGE*
*JOIN A:CHAPTER.2* *NEW PAGE*

.

.

*JOIN A:CHAPTER.9* *NEW PAGE*

Print-formatting commands are not the only way to provide document chaining. For example, Ventura Publisher lets you link many "chapter" files together to form a "publication" with the Multi-Chapter Operations dialog box shown in Figure 7.16. A Ventura publication is nothing more than a list of chapter files. Once the list is complete, you can use the commands in the dialog box to print, generate a table of contents, or create an index for the entire publication.

One use for document chaining is to customize letters by inserting **boilerplate**—prewritten passages. For instance, a politician might insert a standardized paragraph about his support for social security in letters to the elderly (with a *JOIN

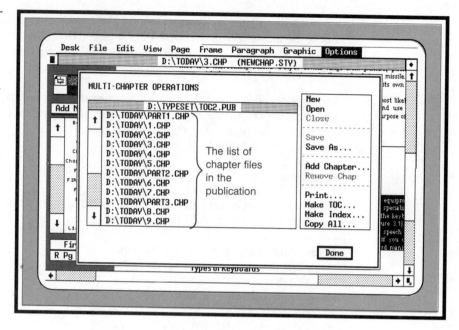

**Figure 7.16**
This dialog box allows Ventura Publisher to organize many "chapter" files into a "publication" that can be printed or indexed as a unit.

SECURITY.OLD* command) and a paragraph about his support for more jobs in letters to teenagers (with a *JOIN MORE.JOB* command). Lawyers often use boilerplate in writing contracts, wills, and other legal documents. Because storing each paragraph in a separate file is inconvenient, some word processors allow the boilerplate passages to be stored in a **glossary**, a data file designed to facilitate access to commonly used passages of text.

**Nested chaining** permits several levels of chaining, such as organizing sections into chapters and then consolidating the chapters into a single document. For example, with nested chaining, the master file might contain a *JOIN BEAM.JIM* command, and the BEAM.JIM file might contain a *JOIN CROW.OLD* command.

## Indexes and Tables of Contents

No matter how late in a document's development an index and table of contents are created, something inevitably comes up that changes the page references. Few tasks are more disheartening than reworking an index or a table of contents because a couple of pages have been added to or deleted from the beginning of a report—nearly every page reference must be changed. But if you have the right word processing products, a table of contents, list of figures, list of tables, bibliography, and index can be produced with relatively little extra effort as a by-product of preparing the document for printing. For example, as the printing routines send the main text to the printer, a program might keep track of the chapter titles and section headings and the page references for these. It might also automatically format this information and place it in a file that can be edited or printed. Not only does this feature eliminate the need to renumber all the page references manually when the document changes; it also results in fewer mistakes.

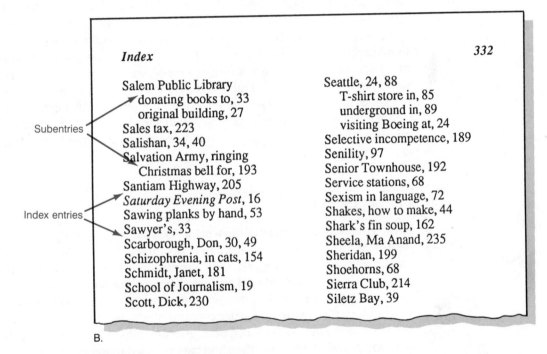

**Figure 7.17**
Creating an index with WordStar 2000. **(a)** This screen shows how an index entry for the *Saturday Evening Post* is inserted into a document. **(b)** This shows part of a 23-page index created by WordStar 2000 from the electronic version of a 337-page book.

None of these reference aids are created by magic. Each item must be marked in a way the word processor recognizes. For example, WordStar 2000 lets you place format codes in the document that contain the word or phrase to appear in the index (see Figure 7.17). The format codes for index entries are ignored when WordStar 2000 prints the document. But when you give the command to create the index, it scans through the document from top to bottom, extracting the index entries along with their page numbers. Then it sorts the information alphabetically, formats it, and puts the finished index in a file on the disk.

Often creating a table of contents is nearly effortless because the needed reference marks are already in the document. For example, if your word processor includes outline-processing abilities, the first step in writing a long document will probably be to enter the major titles and section headings as topics in an outline. Next, the text is written and inserted under the topic headings. After the document is complete, the word processor can prepare a table of contents by collapsing the document to an outline view that displays the appropriate page numbers after each heading in the outline.

Alternatively, if your word processor uses style sheets, the necessary reference marks are available as a by-product of formatting the document. Recall that when you use a style sheet, each paragraph in the document is tagged as a particular paragraph style. Chapter titles and headings are usually tagged as special styles because they are printed in large or boldface type. If this is the case, the paragraph tags can be used to tell the word processor which paragraphs contain headings that should appear in the table of contents. For example, this book was printed with Ventura Publisher, and the table of contents was produced by completing a dialog box similar to the one shown in Figure 7.18. The dialog box in Figure 7.18 asks Ventura to extract the text and page numbers of all the paragraphs tagged as Part Titles, Chapter Titles, Major Headings, and Minor Headings. It took Ventura about five minutes on an IBM AT to search through the ninety-five files containing this book and format the table of contents.

## FORM LETTERS

Form letters eliminate most of the work associated with printing standard business replies, and the ability to print them is invaluable for producing "personalized" mass mailings. If properly prepared, a computerized form letter is indistinguishable from a manually produced business letter, except possibly by its lack of errors.

A **form letter** is printed by merging data into a partially completed master letter in a primary file. The master letter contains all the text that does not change from one letter to the next as well as special insertion tags to indicate where the missing data will go. Most often, the insertion tags are used to insert names and addresses, but they can receive any information such as payments received, winning lottery numbers, or dates.

The insertion tags can be set up to receive data from the keyboard, a data file, or a combination of the two. In Figure 7.19, the missing data is supplied by a secondary data file, so we discuss that case first.

A data file with names and addresses can be created in several ways. If you must print thousands of form letters or if the data file will need frequent maintenance, you should consider building the data file with the help of a file management program (see Chapter 11). But for short, one-shot mailings, it is generally quicker to create a data file by typing information into an empty file with your word processor.

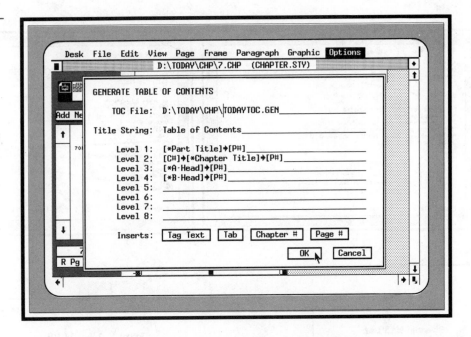

**Figure 7.18**
This dialog box tells Ventura Publisher what items to include in a publication's table of contents.

The information in the data file needs to be organized so that the word processor can identify the pieces. Each piece, such as a name or phone number, is called a *field*. All the fields related to one form letter are called a *record*. Several methods can be used to identify the ends of the fields and records. For example, Figure 7.19 illustrates the conventions used by WordPerfect: It expects each field to end with ^R, and each record to end with ^E. Many word processors expect the fields to be separated from one another by commas. Usually the end of each record is indicated by a hard carriage return or a blank line.

To print the form letters, the word processor needs to know which fields in the data file correspond with which insertion tags in the master letter. To accomplish this, the insertion tags are given names. WordPerfect uses a particularly simple naming convention: Insertion tag ^F1^ receives data from the first field of each record in the secondary file; ^F2^ receives data from the second field; and so on. The fields in the data file need not be in the same order as the insertion tags in the primary file. This allows two fields (^F3^ and ^F6^) in Figure 7.19 to be used twice in the master letter, whereas the field containing phone numbers (^F5^) is not used.

If the information to complete the master letter is supposed to come from the keyboard, each insertion tag causes the word processor to wait for an entry. For example, the dialog for producing the letters shown in Figure 7.19 might proceed as follows (the characters in color are typed by the user):

Enter data for FULL NAME: Mr. Jim Bassett
Enter data for STREET: 1045 Lone Pine Road
Enter data for CITY: Stayton
Enter data for STATE: Oregon 97345
Enter data for FIRST NAME: Jim
Please wait for printing to complete . . .
Enter data for FIRST: STOP

A.

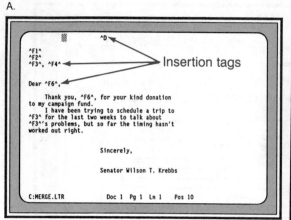

```
                              ^D
^F1^
^F2^
^F3^, ^F4^

Dear ^F6^,

      Thank you, ^F6^, for your kind donation
to my campaign fund.
      I have been trying to schedule a trip to
^F3^ for the last two weeks to talk about
^F3^'s problems, but so far the timing hasn't
worked out right.


            Sincerely,


            Senator Wilson T. Krebbs


C:MERGE.LTR          Doc 1  Pg 1  Ln 1   Pos 10
```

Insertion tags

B.

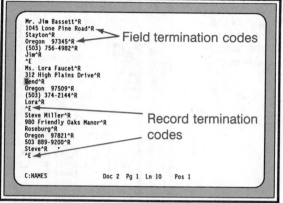

```
Mr. Jim Bassett^R
1045 Lone Pine Road^R
Stayton^R
Oregon  97345^R
(503) 756-4982^R
Jim^R
^E
Ms. Lora Faucet^R
312 High Plains Drive^R
Bend^R
Oregon  97509^R
(503) 374-2144^R
Lora^R
^E
Steve Miller^R
980 Friendly Oaks Manor^R
Roseburg^R
Oregon  97821^R
503 889-9200^R
Steve^R
^E


C:NAMES              Doc 2  Pg 1  Ln 10  Pos 1
```

Field termination codes

Record termination codes

C.

Steve Miller
980 Friendly Oaks M
Roseb

Dear

to my

Roseb
about
timir

Ms. Lora F
312 High P
Bend, Oreg

Dear Lora,

      Thank
my campaig
      I have
Bend for t
Bend's pro
hasn't wor

Senator Wilson T. Krebbs

April 13, 1988

Mr. Jim Bassett
1045 Lone Pine Road
Stayton, Oregon  97345

Dear Jim,

      Thank you, Jim, for your kind donation to
my campaign fund.
      I have been trying to schedule a trip to
Stayton for the last two weeks to talk
about Stayton's problems, but so far the
timing hasn't worked out right.


            Sincerely,


            Senator Wilson T. Krebbs

**Figure 7.19**
Producing form letters with WordPerfect. **(a)** The primary file contains the basic letter and includes insertion tags showing where information will be inserted. **(b)** The secondary data file contains the particular information about each individual letter. **(c)** The finished form letters.

The exact procedure for entering data varies from program to program. Most programs have handy features for customizing the prompts or for setting fields (such as the date field) to a fixed value for all copies.

## WRITING AIDS

Near every typewriter there is likely to be a pocket dictionary, and within arm's reach of many writers is a thesaurus. For the most part, these books are used mechanically: A word is looked up to verify its spelling or discover its synonyms. Mechanical tasks are what computers excel at, so it shouldn't be surprising that electronic dictionaries called spelling checkers and electronic thesauruses exist. Of the two, spelling checkers are more important because they remove most of the drudgery of proofreading for typographical errors.

### Spelling Checkers

A **spelling checker** performs the most time-consuming part of manual spelling correction: It identifies which words cannot be found in a dictionary. Checking and, if necessary, correcting words not in the dictionary still requires human intervention and is the most time-consuming part of computerized spelling correction.

A spelling checker works by comparing the words you type with an electronic dictionary of correctly spelled words. Any word not matching one of the words in the dictionary list is displayed as a *suspect word.*

There are several types of spelling checkers. Some memory-resident programs can check your spelling *as you type.* If you misspell a word, these programs alert you with a beep of the speaker. This sort of immediate feedback can be disconcerting. Most people prefer to spell check document files immediately before printing, which is most conveniently done if your word processor includes a built-in spell checker.

The dictionaries used by spelling checkers differ from traditional paper-based dictionaries because they do not have definitions. True electronic dictionaries, containing definitions, are available on CD-ROM disks, but they are not in common use because most computers lack a CD-ROM reader.

Some dictionary lists have more than 200,000 words, and most include between 80,000 and 140,000 words, so validly spelled words have a good chance of being in the dictionary. For example, in CorrectStar (a built-in spell checker in WordStar 2000), the main dictionary contains 103,000 words drawn from the *American Heritage Dictionary* and occupies 296KB of disk space—not particularly compact. Still, any program with a dictionary large enough to be useful will require a sizable amount of disk space.

Standard dictionaries do not include many of the words in your written vocabulary, such as the proper nouns you use frequently: your last name, the name of the street you live on, and so forth. Unless the electronic dictionary can be modified, these words will be displayed as suspect words again and again. Most programs adapt to your vocabulary over time by allowing you to add words to the main dictionary or an auxiliary dictionary.

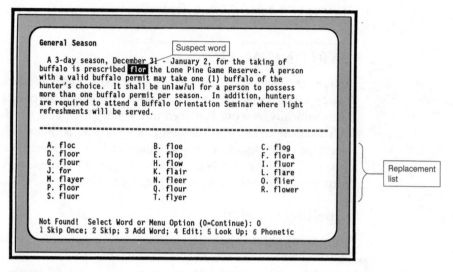

**Figure 7.20**
During a spell-check operation, WordPerfect does not find "flor" in its dictionary, so it provides a list of suggested replacement words.

What do you do when a dictionary program has found a suspect word? The options available for handling suspect words vary from program to program. As Figure 7.20 shows, you can tell WordPerfect to do any of the following:

* You can type the letter next to any of the words in the replacement list. This causes WordPerfect to replace every occurrence of the suspect word in the document with the suggested replacement and is handy for those pesky words that are consistently misspelled.

* The *Skip Once* option causes WordPerfect to ignore the current occurrence of the suspect word and continue checking words in the file.

* The *Skip* option ignores the suspect word for the duration of the spelling correction session.

* The *Add Word* option places the suspect word in an auxiliary dictionary so that the word will never again, in this or any future session, be classified as a suspect word.

* The *Edit* option allows you to correct the spelling of the suspect word. When [Enter] is pressed, the program verifies that the replacement is in the dictionary and continues spell checking.

* The *Look Up* option lets you search through the dictionary for words that match a pattern containing wild card characters. For example, entering "bl*ot" displays *blot*, *Blackfoot*, and *bloodshot*.

* The *Phonetic* option displays a list of replacement words that sound like the suspect word. For example, if the suspect word is *sicology*, this choice displays *psychology* and *sociology*.

**Figure 7.21**
Word Perfect's thesaurus displays this screen when it is asked to look up "base."

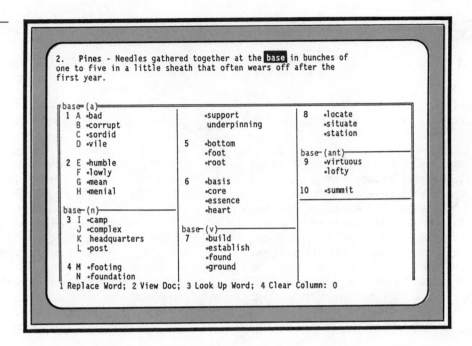

Dictionary programs are not proofreaders; they cannot tell when correctly spelled words are incorrectly used. They will not notice "that too errors are inn this quotation." After the dictionary program has caught the misspellings, it is best to carefully read the document for sense.

## Thesauruses

A **thesaurus** program provides a list of synonyms and antonyms for the word containing the cursor. A thesaurus program can spruce up your writing by finding the right word when the current one does not seem to fit.

A well-designed thesaurus program is one of the easiest programs to use. You simply move the cursor to the word you are uncomfortable with and press a particular keystroke combination, such as [Alt]-[F1]. Within seconds, a list of substitute words appears on the screen (see Figure 7.21). With another keystroke combination, you can remove the original word from the text and insert one of the synonyms. For example, to replace "base" with "foundation" in Figure 7.21, you would press [1] to select the Replace-Word option and press [N] to select "foundation" from the synonym list. The replacement word is given the same capitalization as the original.

A thesaurus program relies on an index and a dictionary. The *index* contains all the words synonyms are available for, and the *dictionary* lists the synonyms themselves. An index containing from 10,000 to 20,000 words is common; the dictionaries are larger and often have from 100,000 to 200,000 words or more.

If the word you've chosen isn't in the index, many thesaurus programs display an alphabetical list of nearby index entries, as shown in Figure 7.22. Word searches are more likely to work if the thesaurus can remove prefixes and suffixes to better

## A Word About . . . *Software for Writers. Helping the Bad, Hurting the Good?*

Simply processing words is passe.

The latest in personal-computer software tries to help people write better. It fixes misspellings, offers synonyms, catches sexist words, flags cliches and even rates a piece of writing against the Gettysburg Address.

For less-accomplished or careless writers, this software can prevent embarasing—uh, *embarrassing*—mistakes and polish poor prose. "I can't write for people—I had one paragraph that had 81 words in it, in one sentence," says David Englehart, a computer programmer at Ohio Edison Co. in Akron. Thanks to "style-checking" software, he broke up that sentence and otherwise improved a paper for a college course.

But for people who already write well, writing software isn't so good. Style checkers—software that evaluates writing style and syntax—"will make bad writing better but will make good writing worse," says Peter McWilliams, the author of several books on personal computers. Indeed, following rigid rules, the programs spew criticism of the Gettysburg Address and make snide remarks about Mark Twain's *The Adventures of Tom Sawyer*.

The problem is that all writing software works in the same simple-minded way. Words or phrases are compared with a list stored in the computer. When the computer sees a phrase that it is programmed to criticize, it does so.

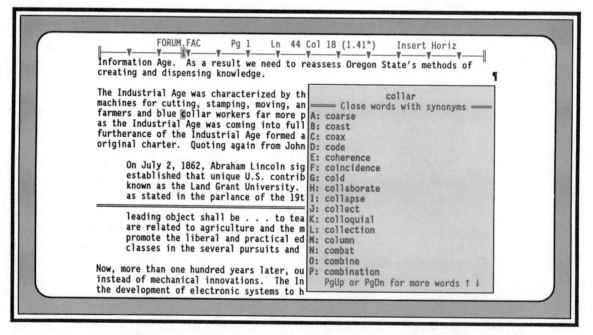

**Figure 7.22**
Borland's Lightning is a memory-resident dictionary and thesaurus program. When Lightning was asked to provide synonyms for the word "collar," it placed this pop-up window over part of the underlying WordStar 2000 screen.

Everything else is okay. "It's not artificial intelligence, just a computer program that recognizes certain patterns," says Reference Software Inc. of San Francisco, the maker of Grammatik II, an $89 style analyzer.

"This is a lot of software to tell us stuff that you can pretty well figure out for yourself: Active verbs are better than passive verbs, short words are better than long ones," says William Zinsser, the author of writing guides and the general editor of Time Inc.'s Book-of-the-Month Club. "On the other hand, a lot of people simply don't know these things. If the software can thin out the pomposity of writing in corporations, in bureaucracies, in government, it'll be a public service."

Style analyzers aren't always reliable. *PC Magazine*, a New York biweekly, estimates that the programs catch only 25 percent of the mistakes that a good human editor would find. Grammatik II notices the misuse of "affect" and "effect," but not always. It doesn't like the correct sentence: "He has a flat affect."

But style analyzers do catch common mistakes that are easily fixed. "I learned that I use 'very' too much," says Mr. McWilliams. Walter Davis, a Hollywood screen writer, marvels at the programs' unfailing ability to notice when he inadvertently types the same word twice. F. Ladson Boyle, a University of South Carolina law professor, says the software alerts him when sentences are too long. Also, after six months of using RightWriter, a $95 program by Decisionware Inc. of Sarasota, Fla., Mr. Boyle favors active verbs. "After it jumps you about the passive verbs for about the hundredth time, you start trying to avoid them," he says.

Unfortunately, the software doesn't always know when a writer's style works well. Grammatik pounces on Abraham Lincoln for saying, "Now we *are engaged* in a great civil war," scolding him for using the passive voice which the software dislikes.

The problem lies not with the rules that the software applies. Rather, the programs don't know when to break them. "They don't allow for personal style," says Stephen Levy, a New York nonfiction writer who has experimented with software for writing. Sometimes, he says, a sentence fragment works. Perfectly. But the software doesn't know that.

Style analyzers try to measure the quality of writing with all sorts of numbers, but most of them aren't much help in distinguishing good writing from bad. Grammatik calculates that the sentences in this story average 16.4 words and that a reader needs a ninth-grade education to understand this story. Grammatik says that compares with 11th-grade for the Gettysburg Address and fourth-grade for a Hemingway short story. Grammatik likes simple words and short sentences.

The numbers can be ignored. But Charles Spezzano, a Denver psychologist and writer, says the gimmicks of such software can be distracting. He explains, "You become more fascinated with what the programs do than with the writing itself."

Source: David Wessel, *The Wall Street Journal*, July 7, 1986.

identify the root word. For example, *undeniably* isn't in the index of WordPerfect's thesaurus, so it substitutes synonyms for *undeniable*.

## Summary

The mistakes people make when they select word processing programs are amazing. Any bare-bones word processor can handle a one-page letter or memo. But a bare-bones word processor is the wrong product to use if you must create a mailing with hundreds of "personalized" letters; a word processor that can use an electronic mailing list to print the letters automatically is much more efficient. Similarly, a casual user who plans to write short memos may not want to learn how to use a full-featured program.

In this chapter, we described a representative sample of the advanced features provided by word processing products. Our discussion should give you the strong impression that you should define your writing needs and select your word processing programs accordingly.

## Key Terms

| | |
|---|---|
| automatic numbering | nested chaining |
| boilerplate | orphan |
| conditional page break | outline |
| decimal tab | outline processor |
| document chaining | page break |
| endnotes | page layout |
| fixed-width spacing | pitch |
| footers | point |
| footnotes | proportional spacing |
| font | ragged right |
| forced page break | right-justified |
| form letter | ruler line |
| format file | soft page break |
| glossary | spelling checker |
| gutter margin | style sheet |
| hard page break | text formatting |
| headers | thesaurus |
| justified | typeface |
| left-justified | typewriter tab |
| master file | widow |
| microspacing | |

## Discussion Questions

1. What types of writing projects need an outline? When can you get by without one?

2. What outline processing features would be most useful for preparing daily "to do" lists? Would the same features be the most important ones for outlining an organization chart in a business or preparing an outline for a major report?

3. When is the best time to check the spelling of words: as you type them or just before you are going to print a document?

4. What features in a spelling checker would you expect to see in a "perfect" spelling checker?

5. What factors determine how a large document such as a book should be broken into separate files?

6. How would you design the specifications for an automatic index-generating program?

7. What is the difference between microspacing and proportional spacing? What types of documents require proportional spacing?

## Exercises

1. Prepare an outline of the steps you take to get dressed in the morning.

2. Design a user interface for an on-line dictionary system that includes definitions, synonyms, and antonyms.

3. Describe a window-based user interface for generating form letters.

4. You have been given the task of selecting a word processing system for a law office with four attorneys. Prepare a report that describes the likely word processing needs of the office, includes a requirements list for the purchase, and evaluates several software and hardware systems that satisfy the requirements list.

5. Determine the types and styles of characters that your printer can produce. Can your word processor use them?

6. Investigate what features would be required in a word processor for a language such as German or French. What additional features would be needed for Chinese or Japanese?

# Desktop Publishing

S tructural changes in our society occur slowly and often are hidden in a thicket of daily headlines about transient events. Determining which events represent a truly fundamental change is easier if you examine them from a historical perspective. History shows the progress of human culture is linked conclusively to advances in the technology of writing and publishing. From this viewpoint, desktop publishing promises to be one of the most important advances of our time because it opens new avenues of communication to ordinary people.

Author A. J. Liebling wrote, "Freedom of the press belongs to those who own one." As recently as ten years ago, publishing required a substantial capital investment and the expertise of specialized professionals. Today, any motivated person with an artistic flair can buy a $5,000 desktop publishing system and produce top-quality professional results.

What the long-term effects of this unusually abrupt shift in power will bring, no one knows, but even the short-term predictions are impressive. Dataquest, a market-research firm in San Jose, California, predicts the desktop publishing market will grow from $306 million in 1986 to $4.9 billion in 1990. Even at that level, Ajit Kapoor, Dataquest's director of Electronic Publishing Market Analysis, says, "$4.9 billion reflects that only 8 percent of the installed base of personal computers will be used for publishing by 1990. That's not a hell of a lot, so I think it will probably be much larger in the future."

Certainly the potential market for desktop publishing is huge. Virtually all businesses are engaged in some form of publishing—from price lists, brochures, and directories to newsletters, manuals, and financial reports. Corporations typically

spend between 5 and 10 percent of their gross revenues on publishing, according to David Goodstein, president of Inter-Consult, a market-research firm in Cambridge, Massachusetts.

It is generally agreed that the term *desktop publishing* was coined by Paul Brainard, founder of Aldus Corporation—the company that developed PageMaker. About the term's definition, there is less agreement. To some, desktop publishing is the application of personal computers to the publishing process. But software vendors take a conveniently broader view and tout any product that produces good-looking computer output as a desktop publishing solution. Suddenly, the words *desktop publishing* have acquired the same marketing magic for the computer field that the words *new and improved* have long held for selling soap.

But why has desktop publishing generated such widespread interest and appeal? Certainly the momentum behind it extends far beyond the traditional publishing community. Actually, major publishers still produce nearly all of their final copy with conventional typesetting systems and graphic artists, partly because converting established operating procedures is a bother but mostly because desktop publishing tools need more development before they can challenge high-volume publishing systems. The ground swell of support for desktop publishing has come from a broad spectrum of users—small businesses, churches, public relations firms, corporate in-house publication departments, and freelance writers and designers. The common element behind these new "publishers" is a desire to communicate ideas effectively. In the Information Age, presenting facts clearly, concisely, and even artistically is as important as having the facts in the first place.

In this chapter, we examine several aspects of the desktop publishing revolution. We first build a foundation of understanding by surveying the history of publishing and its influence on society. We then discuss the hardware involved in desktop publishing, emphasizing laser printers, the engines that made low-cost, high-quality desktop publishing possible. Finally, we examine page composition software and its ability to integrate text and graphics in a pleasing page layout.

**Figure 8.1**
A fifteenth-century printing press.

## A BRIEF HISTORY OF PUBLISHING

Since the Middle Ages, the power of publishing has shaped our destiny. The mass dissemination of the printed word broke the monopolistic power of the Roman Catholic Church and created the basis for democratic institutions and the importance of individualism that still dominates our culture.

Perhaps the greatest breakthrough in communication came with the invention of movable type around 1450 by Johann Gutenberg (see Figure 8.1). A piece of **movable type** is a metal block tipped with an embossed image of a character. One after another, the pieces of type were placed in rows to form words and lines; rows were packed into a rack to form a page. When the page was complete, rollers spread ink across the raised images, and paper was pressed onto the type to absorb the ink. After printing the desired number of copies, the type was disassembled and sorted into bins in preparation for setting the next page.

Movable type permitted the first mass printing of books by allowing the type to be reused again and again. Before this invention, books were copied tediously, one page at a time with sharpened quills laden with ink, by monks in monasteries.

The Chinese invented movable type hundreds of years before Gutenberg, but because of the complexity of their language, they could not use it to revolutionize their culture, as did Western civilizations. Written Chinese is not easily adapted to printing because it requires as many as 50,000 individually shaped characters.

The difficulty of assembling and disassembling pages of type remained a problem for hundreds of years. Samuel Clemens (pen name, Mark Twain) went

**Figure 8.2**
In its day, the Linotype Comet was the fastest typesetter in the world. With a Teletypesetter attachment, as pictured here, it could operate at speeds up to twelve lines a minute.

bankrupt financing the development of an automatic machine for this task. The eventual solution, the **Linotype machine** shown in Figure 8.2, was one of the world's most complicated mechanical devices. The Linotype machine molded complete lines of lead type from movable dies. Each die was tipped with the indented image of a character. As the operator typed on a keyboard, dies would drop from storage slots into a line. As soon as the line was full of words, wedge-shaped spacers were shoved between the dies to justify and fill out the line. Next, an image of the line was captured by pumping molten lead against the dies and allowing it to harden into a *slug*. The slugs were stacked into a *galley* that was used to make raised-image plates for the press. After the slug was formed, the Linotype used an identifying pattern of notches in the dies to mechanically sort and return each to its assigned storage slot for reuse. A competent Linotype operator could set four or five newspaper-length lines of type each minute.

As late as 1965, there were 40,000 Linotype operators in the United States. But today, only a few Linotype machines remain in use. They were replaced by offset presses and phototypesetters, neither of which requires movable type.

The offset press borrows technology from earlier developments in lithography and photography. Lithography uses the principle that oil and water do not mix to transfer a design onto paper. The inventor of lithography, Alois Senefelder (1771-1834), applied a thin layer of grease to some areas of a fine-grained, polished limestone and moistened other areas with water. When a roller spread oily ink across the stone, the greasy areas accepted the ink, but the wet areas did not. Pressing paper against this surface created a printed image.

**Figure 8.3**
Lithography (top) produces a printed image from an ink-receptive image drawn on a flat surface. In an offset press (bottom), the image is placed on plates that can be mounted on the press's rollers.

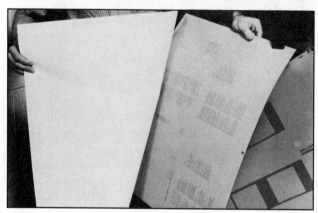

In an **offset press**, the lithographer's limestone is replaced by thin aluminum or plastic plates that can be wrapped around the press's rollers (see Figure 8.3). Photographic methods convert the image of a paper-based master copy into an ink-receptive pattern of chemicals on the printing plate. This has reduced the required setup for printing to simply preparing of one high-quality original. The upshot has been an explosion in the variety and quantity of printed material.

The difficulty of creating high-quality originals was reduced with the invention of the **phototypesetter**, a printer that uses light to write on a photographic material (see Photo 30 in Window 1). Early phototypesetters printed characters by shooting bursts of light through character patterns stored on a film wrapped around a revolving drum. This restricted them to printing a fixed set of characters at a time. Most modern phototypesetters are completely digital and build images from dots, the same as a dot matrix printer. Phototypesetters draw precise images on the photographic surface by flashing a xenon lamp or laser hundreds of thousands of times a second to print tiny dots—from 900 to 5,200 dpi (dots per inch). Aside from the resolution, the output has absolutely clean whites and pitch black blacks. The

## A Word About . . . *New Desktop Publishing Services*

*Going from disk to hard copy is easier than ever as on-line services and copy shops offer fast turnaround and professional results.*

Linda Ohde used to face a dilemma over the training manuals she helped produce every week for her employer, Echols and Pryor Technical Communication Inc.

The small Berkeley, California, firm frequently needed to produce manuals for its customized seminars on business and technical writing, but commercial typesetting shops took too long and were too expensive. Documents produced on a daisywheel printer were affordable but unprofessional looking, Ohde says. When the company lost its outside word processing help, she began to look for a better solution. Ohde found it at a local copy shop.

A few blocks away, Krishna Copy Center was renting time on an Apple Macintosh and Laserwriter printer. Ohde began bringing Microsoft Word files on a disk into the center, where she combined them with graphics and printed them. Now the quality of Echols and Pryor's documents is similar to typeset material, Ohde says, and by designing the manuals itself, the company avoids the time-consuming process of sending documents back and forth to outside help for corrections.

Echols and Pryor is just one of many firms that are taking advantage of such services. Users who own a computer can often take a disk into a quick-print or typesetting shop for printing, send in their documents over phone lines via a modem, or, in some areas, upload documents onto a print shop bulletin board or network. Those who don't own a computer can often rent time on one. Prices range from 30 cents per page for laser printing to $70 for one-on-one desktop

publishing training courses to $35 an hour (and up) for full design and printing services.

Desktop publishing services are being used not only by small companies that have never typeset their documents before, but also by departments within larger companies that need a faster turnaround than their corporate publishing departments can offer. "Publishing departments often have a backlog problem similar to the MIS [management information systems] problem," says Brian Skidmore, director of the Publishing/Computer-Aided Publishing group of the Boston Computer Society. "The department is overwhelmed."

Vince Swanson of Dalmo Victor Inc., of Belmont, California, for example, may opt to use a desktop publishing printing service rather than the defense contractor's publishing department for an upcoming contract. As the senior technical writer, he wants a faster turnaround time and also would like to maintain more control over the design of his documents, he says. Documents sent through in-house channels take up to three days to be completed, he says, and often contain errors that have been introduced through the rekeying required for the company's word processing equipment. "With a service, you have precise control," Swanson says.

Such desire for control, fast turnaround, and professional results without professional typesetting costs appears to ensure the continuing growth of desktop publishing services for some time to come.

"Our documents are much more professional looking now," says Ohde. The company may even consider purchasing its own Laserwriter in the future, she says. "The desktop publishing services have been convenient, but it's getting crowded down at Krishna Copy Center."

Source: Karen Sorensen, *Infoworld*, 1 September 1986, pp. 25–26.

**Figure 8.4**
This full-page display shows Superpage, a professsional-level page composition program. The display has 1,008 scan lines from top to bottom with 736 pixels on each line.

photographic material is usually a roll of resin-coated paper, but it can also be photographic film or even an offset plate. A fast phototypesetter can print seven hundred 2-inch lines per minute and costs about $200,000. Slower typesetters may cost no more than $15,000.

Computers have been controlling typesetters since the early 1970s. Usually a typesetter is sold as part of a system that includes a front-end computer and terminals for operators to enter and format text from. Since each manufacturer developed a different set of format codes to control **composition**—the selection of type sizes and styles and the positioning of type on the page—a print file created for one manufacturer's phototypesetters cannot be printed by another's.

Until the arrival of desktop publishing, typeset documents were invariably prepared by specialists. If you wanted typeset-quality output, the first step was to mark up the text to indicate its position on the page along with the typeface sizes and styles to be used. This was submitted to a typesetting service bureau where an operator would keyboard the text and the needed formatting codes into the front-end computer and print a **galley proof** (draft copy) for you to review. Proofreading would usually reveal mistakes, so a second (or third) pass would be necessary to get an acceptable version. Each step required passing paper back and forth and affected the overall schedule. The completed page would cost twenty dollars or more, depending on the amount of text and the number and extent of revisions.

## DESKTOP PUBLISHING HARDWARE

A good desktop publishing system begins with a powerful microcomputer system. The computer must have enough memory to run large programs and enough speed to reformat and rehyphenate a document. This involves more work than you might

# Application Software: A Professional's Tools

*White-collar workers are rapidly abandoning conventional office products in favor of more powerful tools. Typewriters are being replaced by word processors. Pencils, multicolumn paper, and calculators are giving way to electronic spreadsheets. Information in filing cabinets is being moved into hard disks controlled by data management programs. Letters are traveling through electronic mail systems. Graph paper remains unused as graphics programs transform lists of numbers into instant charts and graphs. This photo essay will give you a clearer view of the capabilities of these new software products.*

**1.** In this screen each of six programs is given its own window in which to display information. Windowing makes it easy to switch quickly between different tasks.

# WINDOWS

*A window is a region of the screen dedicated to a particular activity. Programs that use windows give you control over how the area of the screen is to be used.*

2. Two types of windows are in common use: overlapping and tiled. This display shows tiled windows; the viewing area is broken up into nonoverlapping regions called tiles. With tiled windows, if you want to create a new window, you must split an existing window in two. And if you want to make a window larger, you must make one of its neighbors smaller by moving the boundary between them.

3. The Macintosh II—like all Macintosh computers—has support for overlapping windows built into its operating system. But unlike other Macintosh computers, it uses a color display with a 640 by 480 pixel resolution and can accept six expansion circuit boards.

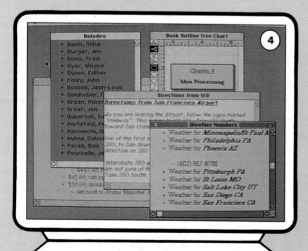

4. Windows appear to sit on this Macintosh screen in the same way pieces of paper can pile up on a desktop. Overlapping windows can be created, moved, or resized without affecting existing windows. You can bring any window to the top of the stack by pointing at it and clicking the mouse button.

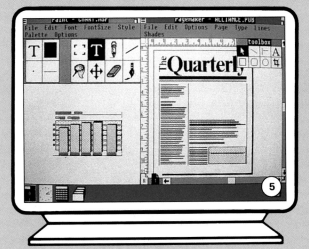

# VISUAL OPERATING ENVIRONMENTS

*A visual operating environment uses windows, pull-down menus, and icons to create an understandable interface between the user and computer. The features of a visual operating environment can be built into the operating system. Alternatively, they can be added on top of an operating system by another program, such as the way Microsoft Windows or the GEM Desktop add visual capabilities to MS-DOS.*

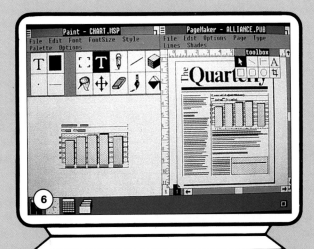

5–6.  A visual operating environment can help integrate normally separate programs in two ways. First, it can allow them to appear in different windows so that switching between applications is fast and efficient. Second, it can help move data between applications by providing a *clipboard* or *buffer*. For example, a graph has been prepared in the left window of photo 5, and a newsletter is being laid out in the right window. Then, a copy of the graph is placed on the operating environment's hidden clipboard. The finished newsletter is shown in photo 6, complete with the graph retrieved from the clipboard.

7.  Early versions of Microsoft Windows used tiled windows (shown in photo 5 and 6), because they require less memory and processing than overlapping windows. But in late 1987 Microsoft Windows began using overlapping windows (shown here) to give the user more control over the size and placement of windows.

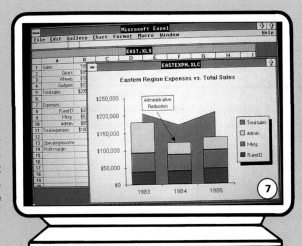

# DESK ACCESSORIES

*Desk accessories are readily available tools that can be used even in the middle of a session with another application program. They appear in pop-up windows that lie on top of the primary application program. This page shows how Sidekick, a desk accessories program, might be used while using a word processor.*

8–11.    While writing a letter, a question arises about what is stored in another file. Instead of closing one file in order to open another, Sidekick's Notepad feature is used to view the second file in a pop-up window. In photo 9 the Notepad is brought to the screen by pressing [Ctrl] and [Alt] at the same time—producing the Sidekick Main Menu—and pressing function key [F2] to select the Notepad. Next, a number in the Notepad window needs to be verified by recomputing it. This calls for another Sidekick feature, the electronic calculator shown in photo 10. In photo 11 a calendar window is opened on top of the other windows to find out what day of the week May 17th falls on in 1988. Eventually, Sidekick's pop-up windows are closed—one at a time—by pressing [Esc] repeatedly.

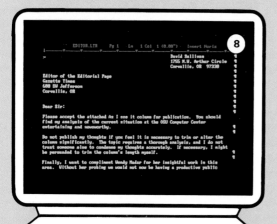

# WORD PROCESSING

12. It is likely that more people have learned to use word processing than any other computer application. Word processing frees writers from the tyranny of paper when making revisions.

13-16. This sequence shows how a paragraph is moved with WordStar. The first step (photo 13) is to move the cursor to the beginning of the paragraph and to insert a marker in the document. In photo 14 the cursor has been moved to the end of the paragraph and another marker has been inserted, causing the paragraph to turn green on the screen and the first marker to disappear. In photo 15 the paragraph has been transferred to its new location. Finally, in photo 16 the markers are removed.

17. A typical WordStar 2000 screen display. WordStar 2000 is an enhanced version of the original WordStar program and is primarily designed for use on personal computers with hard disks.

18. Normally WordStar 2000 hides the formatting codes it uses which control how the document will be printed. But in this screen the formatting codes have been made visible so they can be examined or changed. For example, *MEMORANDUM* will be centered on the printed page because it is preceded by the [Center] formatting code.

19. A spelling checker looks up each word in the document in its own dictionary. Words that aren't found in the dictionary are highlighted as suspect words. In this screen the spelling checker can't find the word *plase* in its dictionary, so it suggests the word *place* instead.

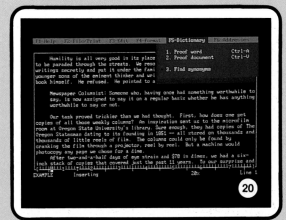

20

**A thesaurus program allows you to find synonyms at the touch of a key. You might use one to spruce up your writing with more descriptive words or to verify that you understand the meaning of a word correctly.**

21

**20–21.** PFS:Professional Write includes a built-in thesaurus program. To use it, you begin by moving the cursor to the word you are curious about. Pressing function key [F5] produces the pull-down menu shown in photo 20. After you select the Find Synonyms option from this menu, a pop-up window containing synonyms appears.

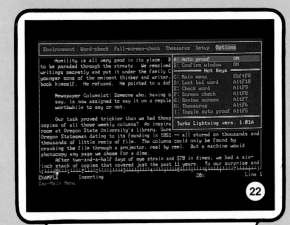

22

**22–23.** For word processors that don't have a built-in thesaurus program, you might want to use a *memory-resident program,* such as Turbo Lightning. A memory-resident program is loaded into memory and remains there even when other application pro-

23

grams are running. To use Lightning to verify the spelling of a word or find a word's synonyms, you can activate Lightning's pull-down menu system (shown in photo 22) by pressing Shift-[F8]. Then you can select an option from one of the pull-down menus. Alternatively, you might use one of Lightning's, shortcut commands to bypass the pull-down menu system. For example, pressing Alt-[F6] provides synonyms for the word containing the cursor, as shown in photo 23.

*window 5*

# OUTLINE PROCESSING

*An outline processor is a program with features designed to let you create and revise well-formatted lists quickly.*

24. Microsoft Word is a full-featured word processor with built-in outline processing features. For example, the chapter and section titles in a report can be "tagged" as headings in an outline. Then, with a simple command, the text in the report can be collapsed so that only the headings are visible.

25-27. Framework is an integrated program with word processing, data management, spreadsheet, graphics, and communications components. It stores information in windows called *frames.* Framework uses outline processing as the basis for organizing the information created by its components. A new frame can be created with the pull-down menu system, as shown in photo 25. The outline frame shown in photo 26 lists the frames it contains; word processing frames are labeled with a (W), spreadsheet frames with (S), and graphics frames with (G). In photo 27 a graphics frame overlaps a spreadsheet frame and an outline frame.

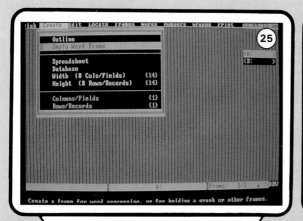

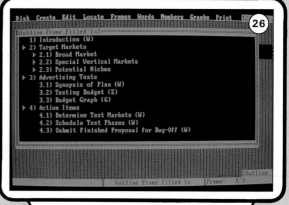

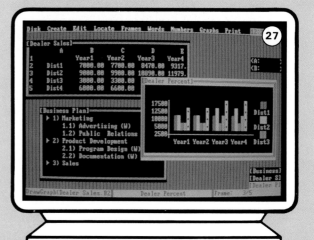

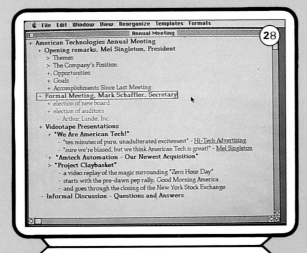

*The photos on this page were created with MORE, a stand-alone outline processor with the ability to transform an ordinary outline into a tree chart or a bullet chart.*

28. This is the normal text-editing view used to enter and edit the headings in an outline. Headings can be rearranged, deleted, promoted (raised to a higher level in the outline), or demoted to reorganize an outline.

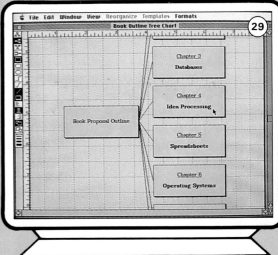

29. The tree chart view changes an outline instantly into a tree diagram. The icons along the left edge of the screen determine what kind of tree chart MORE creates.

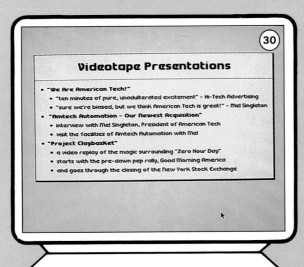

30. The bullet chart view can turn an outline into professional-quality overhead transparencies or slides.

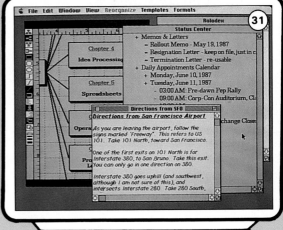

31. Several MORE windows can be open on the screen at the same time.

*window 5*

# DESKTOP PUBLISHING

*Desktop publishing takes simple word processing several steps further by giving the user control over the size and style of type as well as merging graphics with text on a page. It is one of the hottest areas in computing.*

32. A complete desktop publishing system is likely to include a laser printer (foreground), a scanner (middle), and a fast personal computer with a high-quality display.

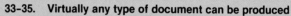

33–35. Virtually any type of document can be produced with desktop publishing. However, the color separations of photographs still need to be prepared with traditional equipment.

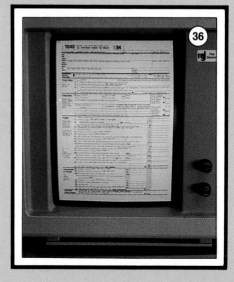

36. With a high-resolution display you can preview a full page and still read the small type sizes. For example, this tax form is displayed on a monitor with 736 by 1008 pixels.

# PAGE COMPOSITION PROGRAMS

*A page composition program combines text and graphics from various sources to form a finished page. They are an essential part of a complete desktop publishing system.*

37. Aldus PageMaker was one of the first personal computer-based page composition systems to provide an interactive display of what the final page layout would look like. This facing-pages view allows the user to determine whether a two-page spread will look balanced. The text in this screen is *greeked*—represented by straight lines—to save time while redrawing the screen.

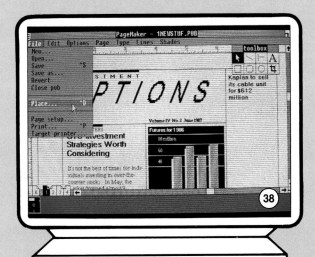

38-39. The IBM version of PageMaker, introduced in 1987, uses Microsoft Windows to provide the same sort of visual operating environment found on the Macintosh version. Commands are selected from pull-down menus. The icons in the toolbox provide tools for cropping graphics, entering text, and drawing boxes, lines, and circles.

*window 5*

# ELECTRONIC SPREADSHEETS

*Electronic spreadsheet programs automate the process of editing and manipulating worksheets containing numbers. Spreadsheets have evolved through several generations since Visicalc, the first spreadsheet program, was introduced in 1979.*

40. Visicalc was so important to the early success of the Apple II computer that some people called it the Visicalc machine. By today's standards Visicalc had very crude features. For example, it displayed numbers without commas and had no on-line help system. Despite Visicalc's shortcomings, it ushered in an entirely new way to manipulate numbers.

41. Visicalc soon had scores of copycat competitors, known as "Visi-clones." Most of these products offered better features, a lower price, or both. This screen shows SuperCalc, one of Visicalc's strongest competitors in 1981. SuperCalc introduced an excellent help system and can be displayed in color.

42. Multiplan won *InfoWorld* magazine's 1982 Software Product of the Year award. Multiplan provided a host of improvements including complete words in its menu, the ability to establish up to eight windows on the screen, and a way to link numbers between worksheets so that changes in one worksheet would automatically affect other worksheets.

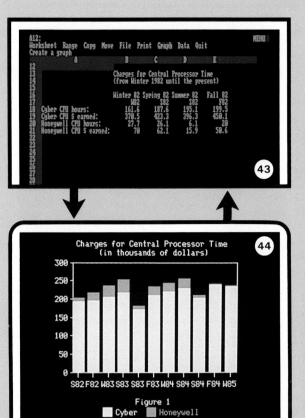

43. Lotus 1-2-3 became the best-selling personal computer program within a few months of its introduction in late 1982. Its instant success resulted from combining an excellent spreadsheet with limited graphics and data management in one easy-to-use package.

44. A Lotus 1-2-3 bar chart. Once numbers are in a 1-2-3 worksheet, it takes only a few keystrokes to convert them into a simple pie chart, bar chart, or line graph. To create a graph, you must point out which numbers are to be graphed, and you need to select the type of graph you want. Although 1-2-3 can't display a graph and the worksheet simultaneously on one screen, it takes only five keystrokes to switch from the worksheet to the graph and back to the worksheet again.

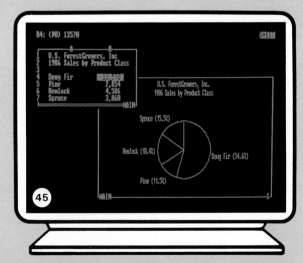

45. In mid-1984 Lotus Symphony combined Multiplan's windowing abilities with an improved version of 1-2-3's spreadsheet. Also included in the package are simple graphics, record management, word processing, and telecommunications. This screen shows a small spreadsheet window and a larger graph window. If a number in the spreadsheet window is changed, the graph is immediately redrawn to reflect the change.

# DATA MANAGEMENT SOFTWARE

46. Businesses rely heavily on data management systems to do their record keeping. Most data management systems allow business forms to be displayed on the screen, making it easy to enter, revise, or query data about a particular transaction.

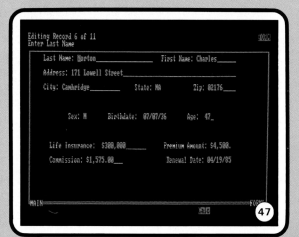

47. Lotus Symphony provides single-file data management but not database management. This means Symphony can manipulate information in one file conveniently but cannot extract or process information from several files at once. This sort of simple data management system is well suited for such everyday tasks as keeping a calendar of appointments, maintaining a Christmas card mailing list, or recording the names, addresses, and phone numbers of clients.

48. SuperCalc4 is another spreadsheet-based integrated program with single-file data management abilities. In this example, SuperCalc4's ability to store and execute commands in *macros* has been used to create a customized data management system for maintaining the inventory in a wine cellar. Notice how the menus at the bottom of the screen apply specifically to managing an inventory of wines.

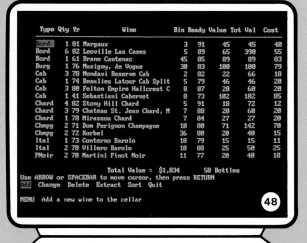

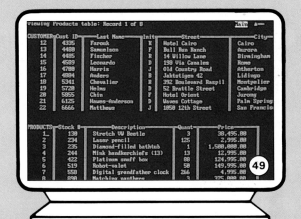

**49.** Paradox, a relational database management system, stores data in tables and can manage many tables at once. This provides much more flexibility and power for performing complex data manipulation activities than single-file data management programs. In this screen, the user can scroll through and compare the data in two different tables.

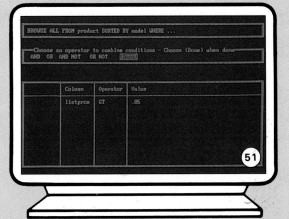

**50–51.** Instead of looking at data in a table, you may want to work with one record at a time by using a form. The form shown in photo 50 was created automatically by Paradox. However, if you don't like the default form, you can create your own custom forms to rearrange the data any way you like, such as the Customer Information Form shown in photo 51.

**52.** Paradox lets you ask questions or manipulate tables by filling out a query form. Queries are used to join tables together, select subsets of a table, and answer questions like, How many departments have a travel budget greater than $5,000? This query is a request for a list of all the clients living in Oregon.

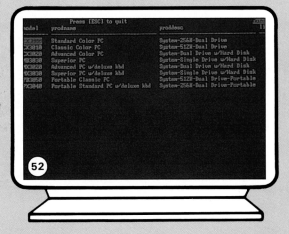

53. WordStar 2000 provides context-sensitive help; so it often seems to work like a user manual that automatically falls open to the right page.

54. Lotus Symphony has one of the best help systems on the market today. Because it is context-sensitive, it will provide spreadsheet information if you are working on a spreadsheet, graphing information if you are constructing a graph, and so on. But Symphony's help system goes one step further; it provides a list of related topics on the bottom of each help screen. You can view the help screen for a related topic by moving the highlighted cursor box onto the name of the topic and then pressing [Enter].

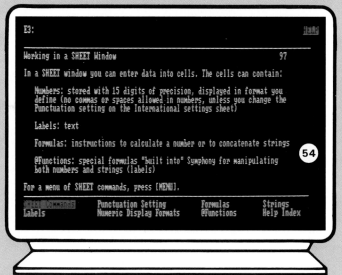

expect. For example, a WYSIWYG page composition program must determine each character's position precisely and then draw a bit-mapped replica of it on the screen. These tasks generally require at least an 8-megahertz processor and a megabyte of memory. You can get by with less only if you do not mind taking a ten-second break every time the machine needs to repaint the screen.

The screen must be able to accurately display how your document will look when printed; color is not as important as resolution. The best displays for desktop publishing let you edit a full page of text at once (see Figure 8.4). This requires at least a thousand scan lines from the top to the bottom of the screen. On displays with less resolution, you will need to scroll up and down and left and right to read an entire page (see Figure 8.5).

Other components of a desktop publishing system are likely to be a hard disk, mouse, laser printer, and scanner. Laser printers and scanners are important enough to warrant further discussion.

**Figure 8.6**
An original Hewlett-Packard LaserJet (top) is shown receiving a new toner cartridge. The newer LaserJet Series II printer (bottom) is smaller, more reliable, and can accept more memory.

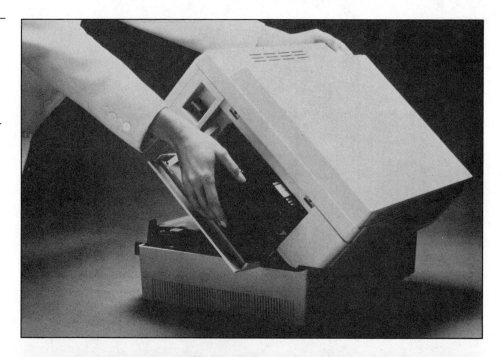

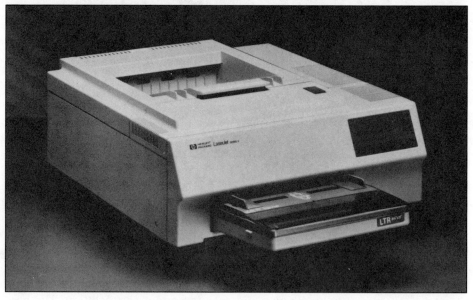

## Laser Printers

Low-cost laser printers, first introduced in 1985, are credited with ushering in the new age of desktop publishing. Laser printers are faster and quieter than daisy-wheel and dot matrix printers. But best of all, their 300-dpi resolution and ability to mix various styles of text with graphics produces output that looks almost as good as typeset documents.

**Figure 8.7**
A *bit-mapped font*
(left) defines letters
as a pattern of dots.
An *outline font*
(right) defines letters
by their shape, in
this case, by line
segments and arcs.

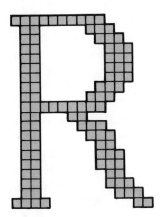
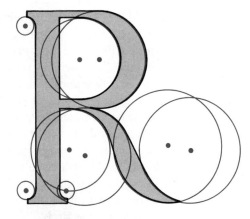

The Apple LaserWriter, *InfoWorld*'s 1985 Product of the Year, offered 1.5MB of RAM for image processing, thirteen built-in type fonts (drawn from the Courier, Times Roman, and Helvetica families), and a host of graphics features at an initial price of $6,995. Because of these features and its ability to scale the size of characters, it acted as a catalyst on the entire desktop publishing market. In 1986, Apple lowered the LaserWriter's price and introduced the LaserWriter Plus with six additional families in ROM: Avant Garde, Bookman, New Century Schoolbook, Palatino, Zapf Chancery, and Zapf Dingbats.

Despite the LaserWriter's popularity among desktop publishing enthusiasts, Hewlett-Packard captured the lion's share of the laser printer market with its Laser-Jet printers. Although the LaserJets are much less capable, their lower price (a basic model cost $3,500 in 1985) prompted many people to buy them as a replacement for daisy-wheel printers. In 1987, Hewlett-Packard discontinued the LaserJet and introduced the LaserJet Series II printers (see Figure 8.6). A basic LaserJet Series II printer has 0.5MB of RAM and costs $2,595.

Both the LaserWriter and LaserJet printer families share some important traits. Both are built from Canon "print engines" that use the same xerographic printing methods as Canon's Personal Copiers. Both are reliable because the most error-prone parts—the belt and photosensitive drum—are housed inside a $100 replaceable toner cartridge. Both use a Motorola 68000 microprocessor to execute commands and control printing. And both fostered a host of "me-to" competitors that emulate their features.

Despite their many similarities, it soon became apparent that the LaserWriter and LaserJet printer families are fundamentally different. The differences arise from the software they use to manage fonts and accept instructions.

### Bit-Mapped versus Outline Fonts

The most significant limitation of the LaserJet printer family is the way it handles type fonts. The fonts are stored in the printer's memory as a *bit map*—a pattern of dots (see Figure 8.7). Each font specifies the patterns for a particular size, style, and orientation of characters, such as 10-point Courier characters in the *portrait* (upright) orientation. A font's size is fixed because the machine cannot change the size of the dot patterns to get larger characters. Several crude fonts are built into the printer's

ROM, but for desktop publishing tasks, additional fonts must be loaded into the printer, either by plugging a font cartridge into the printer or by downloading fonts from a disk in the personal computer. Whenever fonts are loaded into the printer's memory, less memory is available for printing graphics.

Memory is another limitation of the LaserJet printers; most of them do not have enough memory to print a full page of 300-dpi graphics. This problem arises because laser printers are *page printers;* that is, they cannot pause while printing a page. So quickly do they print—more than a million dots per second—that the information for an entire page must be in the printer's memory before printing begins. An 8 1/2 by 11-inch page requires about a megabyte of memory at 300 dpi. Laser printers with less than a megabyte of memory must print full-page graphics at either 75 or 150 dpi, about the resolution of a dot matrix printer.

Taking an entirely different approach to type fonts is the Apple LaserWriter. It stores fonts as descriptions of the outline or shape of the characters rather than as a fixed dot pattern. Each character is defined as a mathematical model of the character's outline, so it can be scaled to any size or rotated to print sideways or at an angle. This flexibility makes outline fonts far superior to the bit-mapped variety for desktop publishing.

There is a drawback to outline fonts, however. Before a page can be printed, the printer must determine which dots on the page fall within the outlines of the characters. This makes the LaserWriter print text more slowly than printers with bit-mapped fonts.

## Page Description Languages

The most significant difference between the LaserWriter and LaserJet printers is in the languages they use to control their actions. LaserJet printers use Hewlett-Packard's Printer Control Language (PCL), whereas LaserWriter printers use Post-Script, a page description language created by Adobe Systems of Palo Alto, California.

Hewlett-Packard's PCL is a simple language designed to load bit-mapped fonts and bit-mapped graphics into the printer. Fonts cannot be scaled or manipulated in any way, such as printing white letters on a black background. The language has no commands for rotating, scaling, or clipping graphics or for drawing curves or other geometric figures. Thus the LaserJet requires that the personal computer and its application software perform these functions. Each bit in a graphics image must be calculated inside the personal computer and then loaded into the printer, which can be painfully slow. Of even more importance, however, is that PCL adheres to none of the emerging graphics standards, making life difficult for application software developers. Unless they write a special LaserJet printer driver, their programs will not print on a LaserJet.

In contrast, a **page description language (PDL)** is a programming language with specialized instructions for describing whole pages to a printer. That is, a PDL's role is to let an application program tell a printer how to build a page from a combination of text, fonts, lines, arcs, and other graphics images. With a PDL, the marks to appear on the page are described by a series of instructions and parameters rather

**Figure 8.8**
The Linotronic L300 combines laser technology and PostScript image processing to produce reproduction-quality output on photographic media, such as resin-coated paper. The L300, priced at $56,000 to $77,000, prints images with 635, 1,270, or 2,540 lines per inch.

than indicated by every spot to be inked. Then it is up to the printer to interpret the instructions and translate them into the marks that will appear on paper.

Although PostScript is not the only PDL, it is the best known and most widely supported. Other PDLs include Xerox's Interpress and Imagen's DDL (Document Description Language). All three are descendants of research on printer languages conducted at Xerox Corporation's Palo Alto Research Center (PARC).

The Apple LaserWriter was the first of many printers to adopt PostScript. Other PostScript lasers include units from QMS, DEC, Texas Instruments, NEC, Quadram, Dataproducts, and IBM. For people demanding typeset-quality output, Allied Linotype introduced the first PostScript-compatible phototypesetters in 1985. First came the Linotronic L100, which costs from $32,000 to $40,000 and produces a resolution of 1,270 lines per inch. Other PostScript-compatible models include the faster, higher-resolution L300 (see Figure 8.8) and the L500, which allows for a wider image area. In 1987, even Hewlett-Packard adopted the emerging standard by announcing a PostScript option for its laser printers.

PostScript provides a standardized way for application programs to communicate with printers. Figure 8.9 illustrates how this works. An application program with a PostScript device driver, such as a word processor or drafting program, can send an output file to *any* PostScript printer. The application program does not need to know whether the actual printer is of the dot matrix, laser, or typesetter variety because every PostScript printer can accept the same instructions. Obviously, a high-resolution printer will produce a clearer, sharper rendition of the instructions than a low-resolution printer, but otherwise the output will look the same. This frees

**Figure 8.9**
PostScript is a page description language that insulates application programs from printers. The device driver translates text and graphics into PostScript language statements. Then any PostScript-compatible printer can interpret the statements without further modification.

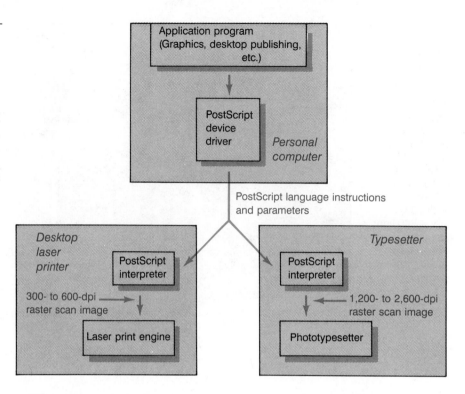

software developers from the need to write another device driver whenever a new printer is marketed. It also allows users to use one device to print draft copies and another higher-resolution device to print the final copy.

In just this way, PostScript formed the first convenient link between typesetters and personal computer-based systems. By using a PostScript-compatible desktop publishing program and an Apple LaserWriter, people began to design and print documents that appeared typeset to the casual eye—at a cost of five cents a page! But if true typeset quality was required, the output files could be sent directly from a Macintosh to a Linotronic phototypesetter over an AppleTalk local area network. Or the files can be sent by disk or telecommunications to a service bureau that operates a Linotronic typesetter. Because these PostScript output files could be printed immediately—without additional format codes or editing—the cost of this sort of typesetting is around six dollars a page, much lower than conventional typesetting.

Most people who use a PostScript printer have never seen a single PostScript instruction. Normally, the instructions are created by application programs and sent directly to the printer. But if you own a PostScript printer and you feel so inclined, you can write PostScript programs for your printer to execute. This can give you a better understanding of what a PDL is all about. For example, the screen in Figure 8.10 shows a file with PostScript instructions that tell the printer what text to print, what font and type size to use, what lines to draw, and where to place all these objects. This simple example shows only a few of the instructions you might encounter if you look at the print files created by an application program. Other instructions

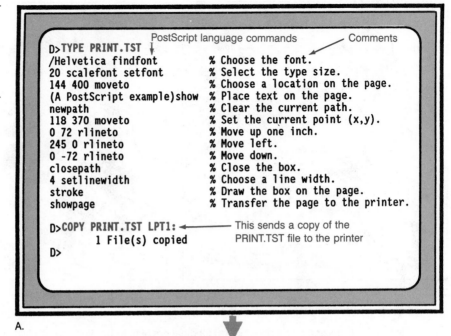

```
                         PostScript language commands          Comments
D>TYPE PRINT.TST
/Helvetica findfont              % Choose the font.
20 scalefont setfont             % Select the type size.
144 400 moveto                   % Choose a location on the page.
(A PostScript example)show       % Place text on the page.
newpath                          % Clear the current path.
118 370 moveto                   % Set the current point (x,y).
0 72 rlineto                     % Move up one inch.
245 0 rlineto                    % Move left.
0 -72 rlineto                    % Move down.
closepath                        % Close the box.
4 setlinewidth                   % Choose a line width.
stroke                           % Draw the box on the page.
showpage                         % Transfer the page to the printer.

D>COPY PRINT.TST LPT1:           This sends a copy of the
        1 File(s) copied         PRINT.TST file to the printer
D>
```

A.

# A PostScript example

B.

PDLs typically provide draw curves, rotate text, fill areas with patterns or colors, make decisions (Is the current line full?), or establish loops to repeat a section of instructions.

## Scanners

Drawings and photographs add life to the published page. But before paper-based artwork can be manipulated with desktop publishing software, it must be **digitized**, or converted into a digital format. Digitizing is done with a **scanner**, a special, light-sensitive device that converts photographs, black-and-white drawings, or other visual images into bit-mapped images. Scanners provide a quick way to enter images into a computer. Then you can use a graphics editor or page composition program to modify, stretch, shrink, crop, or erase parts of the image.

Figure 8.11 shows the result of digitizing a black-and-white drawing using the Macintosh and a light-detector scanner called ThunderScan. ThunderScan replaces the ribbon in the Apple ImageWriter dot matrix printer—thus making the Image-Writer read from the paper rather than print on it. This low-cost scanner is simple:

A.                                     B.

**Figure 8.11**
Digitizing a line drawing. **(a)** Original drawing to be digitized. **(b)** Digitized image captured
by ThunderScan and printed by an ImageWriter.

A light is cast onto the paper, and the reflected light is registered by a light-sensitive detector. When a position is examined by the scanner, the detected light is converted into a bit-mapped image, sent to the computer, and displayed on the screen.

Because ThunderScan relies on the paper-movement mechanism of a dot matrix printer, its images are not very sharp. The resolution of the digitized image shown in Figure 8.11 is about 75 dpi.

**Figure 8.12**
The HP ScanJet, a
flat-bed desktop
scanner

**Figure 8.13**
Scanning Gallery, an application program provided with the HP Scan-Jet, lets you capture and edit images within Microsoft Windows.

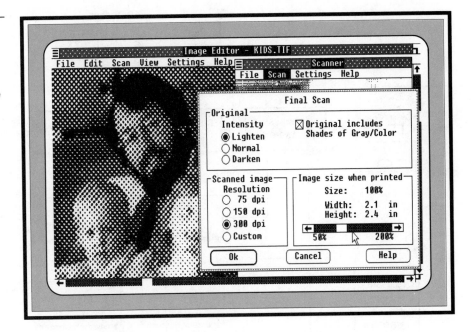

Another way to capture images is with a flat-bed document scanner (see Figure 8.12). Although these units cost more—from around $600 to more than $3000—they can capture images at 300 dpi or more, matching the resolution of laser printers.

Most scanners are sold bundled with software to help control their functions. For example, Figure 8.13 shows some of the selections you can make while using Scanning Gallery, the application program Hewlett-Packard provides to control the HP ScanJet. Before you scan the original, Scanning Gallery lets you adjust the scanner's resolution, select the size of the scanned image to be produced, and set the brightness level. After the image has been captured, you can preview it on the screen, cut and paste parts of the image, and convert the image into any of several graphics formats.

Scanners are used to capture all kinds of information: typed text, line drawings used for logos or illustrations, letters to be mailed electronically, and photographs or other images containing colors or grays. Each type of information needs to be treated differently (see Figure 8.14).

The photosensitive detector in most scanners can sense several levels of light for each spot examined. For example, the HP ScanJet uses 4 bits to record how bright each spot is, resulting in sixteen gray-scale levels. But for some tasks, such as scanning text or line art, the gray scale information is an unnecessary complication. In this case, the scanner's software is used to convert the gray-scale image into a binary image where each spot is either white or black. This conversion is simple: Any spot darker than a fixed value becomes black, and everything else becomes white.

If the original image is a photograph, a more sophisticated conversion is necessary. Laser printers and phototypesetters can print only black spots; they cannot print gray. But a photograph would look terrible if all its dark gray areas became black and its light gray areas white. The conventional way of solving this problem

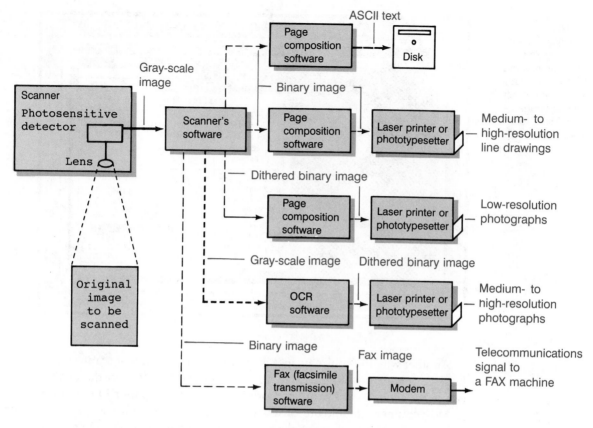

**Figure 8.14**
A good scanner captures images in a gray-scale format. Then application software converts the gray-scale image into the type of information desired by the user.

is to convert the photograph into a **halftone**—a pattern of dots of varying sizes—by rephotographing it through a special etched screen. However, if a scanner is used, the solution is to **dither** the photograph, that is, to approximate the levels of gray in the original with a carefully chosen pattern of white and black spots that are all the same size.

Dithering involves a tradeoff between contrast and resolution. If a large grid pattern is chosen, there is considerable flexibility in producing shades of gray. Conversely, a smaller grid pattern reduces the size of each **grain,** or dithered area, allowing more detail to appear in the photograph. Another factor to consider is the pattern of spots to use within each dithered grain. For example, the dither pattern shown in Figure 8.15 arranges the spots along one side of each grain, forming what appear to be vertical lines. This works well for photographs with smooth contours, such as faces but is unacceptable for photographs that have vertical lines before digitizing.

The quality of the printed image depends on the resolution of the scanner, the size of each grain, and the power of the printer. A 300-dpi scanner and laser printer

# A Word About . . . *Dithering and Halftoning*

*The image captured by a scanner is best at reproducing line art where everything is either black or white. This insert describes some techniques used to capture and print gray-scale images.*

Dithering is an image processing technique that allows printers and computer displays (which support only two tone levels, black and white) to produce documents that appear to have continuous shades of gray. In other words, dithering allows most available printers and computers displays to produce images that look like ordinary black and white photographs.

As a consequence of dithering, some detail on the original black and white photograph may be lost. Usually, however, the additional simulated gray information makes up for the loss of detail.

The human eye and brain have the ability to look at an area of closely spaced dark dots on a white background and perceive them as a gray tone. The eye and brain fill in and average the black and white data and transform them into gray information. For example, looking at [a dithered photo] from a distance, it appears as a normal continuous tone image even though, when looked at closely, it appears as a series of closely spaced black dots.

Dithering is similar to a technique used by newspapers and magazines known as halftoning. Halftones simulate shades of gray by varying the size of circular black dots on a fixed grid pattern. Dithering accomplishes the same purpose as halftoning, but does so by making use of fixed black squares and changes the number of adjacent black squares in small regional areas to control the apparent level of gray.

Note that the word "halftone" is often used as a synonym for "dither." to the untrained eye, the output produced by the two processes can look similar. They really are two different processes with the same goal.

Courtesy of Hewlett Packard. Publication number: 5958-4194.

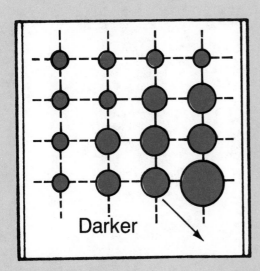

**Figure 8.15**
Gray scale in a photograph can be represented by various dither patterns. This screen illustrates a *vertical line* dither pattern. Compare it with the *coarse fatting* dither pattern shown in Figure 8.13.

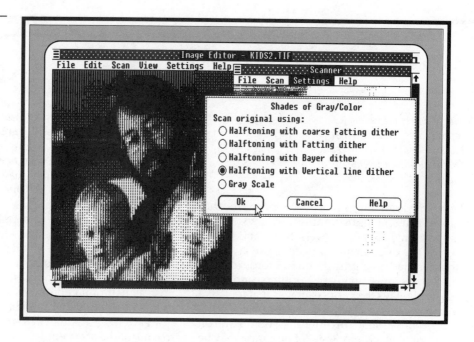

**Figure 8.16**
These two views of David Sullivan and his daughters, Mary and Molly, compare **(a)** a low-resolution dithered image (40 grains per inch) with **(b)** a conventional halftone (150 grains per inch).

are capable of printing images with 40 to 80 grains per inch (see Figure 8.16). This is slightly worse than the quality of an average newspaper photograph. However, magazine-quality work is well within the capability of a desktop publishing system if the gray-scale information of a 300-dpi scanner is dithered by a page composition program and sent to a phototypesetter.

Scanners can also be used to enter text into the computer without rekeying it. Yet another conversion is necessary to translate the scanned image of text into a format that can be used by a word processor. **Optical character recognition (OCR)** software converts the binary image of typed text into the equivalent ASCII characters. Thus a scanner equipped with OCR software can convert an ordinary typewriter into a computer input device. Scanners used in this manner often are equipped with a sheet feeder so that they can automatically digitize and read a whole stack of papers.

Finally, scanners can function as the input device of a fax system. **Fax** is short for facsimile transmission, a method of sending documents across phone lines. (For more details on fax, see Chapter 14.)

## PAGE COMPOSITION

A **page composition program** or *page layout program*, controls page makeup and assembles the elements of the printed page. This software, the heart of a desktop publishing system, lets you place and move text and graphic elements on the page. Most of these programs offer a WYSIWYG display, that is, show on the screen what the page will look like when printed. Page composition programs provide a variety of special tools to revise the page layout quickly, mix different typefaces, and control the spacing of text and the sizing of graphics. Other features may allow you to zoom in to see part of the page more clearly or zoom out to see whether a two-page spread looks balanced.

Almost any document can be prepared with a page composition program and a desktop laser printer.

- The *Queen Elizabeth II* uses PageMaker to prepare an eight-page daily newspaper. The news, culled from the pages of *The International Herald Tribune*, is put together in London with PageMaker and then transmitted by satellite to the luxury liner, which then prints 1,200 copies for its passengers.

- Caterpillar, a $7 billion ground-moving equipment manufacturer, has begun using Ventura Publisher for many of its shorter documents: service manuals, sales proposals, software documentation, and dealer bulletins. Because Caterpillar depends heavily on style sheets to standardize the appearance of its documents, it selected Ventura as its main desktop publishing program.

- Hesston Corporation, a farm equipment manufacturer, uses PageMaker to turn out all its operator's manuals, assembly instructions, parts catalogs, and department forms with minimal paste-up time. In fact, desktop publishing has allowed the technical publications group to continue to meet its publication schedule despite the loss of three people.

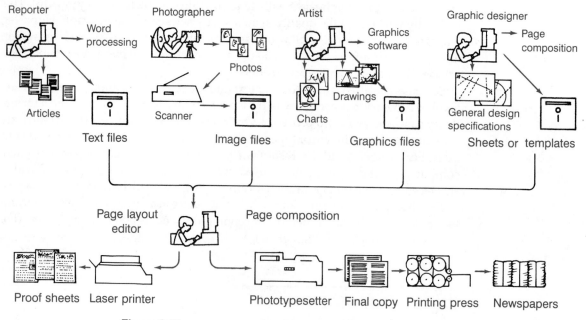

**Figure 8.17**
Producing a newspaper with desktop publishing methods

Page composition programs are particularly suited to the last-minute changes demanded by the newspaper field and are used by many college newspapers. Figure 8.17 illustrates how a newspaper staff might coordinate activities by feeding text and graphic files to the page layout editor's personal computer.

- The reporters write their articles with an assortment of word processing programs—most page composition programs can accept text in several formats. The text files are transferred to the page composition program either by disk, telecommunications, or a local area network.

- Photographs are digitized with a scanner and pasted on the page electronically.

- Artists prepare free-hand drawings, charts, and graphs with graphics programs. Graphics can also be bought from vendors of electronic clip-art files.

- The graphic designer establishes the design specifications for the document, including the margins, typeface sizes, width of ruling lines, spacing of text, placement of headings, and a host of other factors. Most of these specifications can be incorporated into a style sheet or **template**—a partly completed document— to make the day-to-day page layout process go more smoothly.

## Page Composition Programs

The most popular page composition programs offer on-screen page makeup and cost less than $1,000. These programs have been available on the Macintosh since early 1985 and on IBM and compatible computers since mid-1986. Two of the first programs for the Macintosh were PageMaker from Aldus ($495) and ReadySetGo from Manhattan Graphics (now available from Letraset at $395). Programs for IBM and compatible microcomputers include Ventura Publisher from Xerox ($795), PageMaker for the PC ($695), and PFS:ClickArt Personal Publisher from Software Publishing ($185). All these programs rely on word processing and graphics programs to create most of the source material; then they take over and automate the paste-up and final formatting.

Professional typographers require more features, precision, and control than these page composition programs offer. However, systems that suit their needs are expensive. For example, a permanent license for Superpage II from Bestinfo costs $7,000—beyond the means of everyone except publishing professionals. Superpage, a copy-protected page layout and typesetting program that runs on IBM microcomputers, provides a WYSIWYG display of text and graphics as well as excellent composition on a wide range of output devices. Although not a desktop publishing program, it appeals to magazine and newspaper publishers with exacting standards and pressing deadlines.

Even more expensive are corporate electronic publishing systems (CEPS). For example, a complete Interleaf system with a Sun Microsystems workstation, 86MB of disk storage, tape backup unit, and laser printer sells for around $46,000. These are **turnkey systems**; that is, they come with all the hardware and software needed to begin using them immediately.

Not all page composition programs let you see the page interactively on the screen. Some of the most accurate programs use embedded text formatting codes to give the user precise control over the composition of text. For example, the typesetting programs of most large computerized typesetting systems can be controlled by placing special formatting commands inside WordStar documents. This approach can make sense if you must have access to a conventional typesetting system or if you need to typeset a lengthy but fairly simple document, such as a paperback novel. The vendors of these systems argue that once you get used to it, coding a document in this manner is a more precise, faster way of formatting. If this were true for the average print job, desktop publishing would not have waited for the arrival of WYSIWYG programs to become popular.

## Using a Page Composition Program

In this section, we explain the usual steps involved in using a page composition program. Figure 8.18 shows the typical relationship a page composition program has to other programs in a desktop publishing system. Each activity—writing, creating graphics, and laying out the page—is shown associated with a separate application program. The next generation of desktop publishing software may change this situation by bundling good word processing, graphics, and page composition into one integrated program. It is also likely that word processing programs will evolve to have more page layout features, lessening the need for a standalone page composition program.

Desktop publishing is a fluid process, so few hard and fast rules exist about the order of events in the publishing cycle. Ordinarily, one of the first steps is creating

## A Word About . . . *Desktop Publishing and the Production of this Book*

*"If the text in this boxed insert looks fuzzier than the rest of the book, it is because the master copy was printed by a laser printer in my home. The rest of the book was typeset by a Linotronic phototypesetter from files created by my personal computer. Each step in the process of preparing the manuscript for typesetting is explained below."*
— David Sullivan

Despite the hoopla that desktop publishing receives, most textbooks are still typeset in the traditional fashion: A copyedited and marked-up version of the author's manuscript is keyed into a typesetting system.

That didn't happen with this book—the manuscript was written with word processing programs; then, the word processing files were prepared for typesetting by a desktop publishing program.

The first step was to select the desktop publishing software. Finding and evaluating programs took about six months. Seven programs were reviewed extensively. Some were so difficult to use they made conventional typesetting look appealing. Others would work fine for a one-shot or small-scale publishing project but

weren't suitable for a lengthy manuscript that would go through numerous revisions. We finally settled on Ventura Publisher, a $895 desktop publishing program that runs on a standard PC.

The next step was to select the hardware. At that time, my primary computer system included an IBM AT-compatible computer with a fast 40MB hard disk, a mouse, an EGA (enhanced graphics adapter) color display, and a Hewlett-Packard LaserJet Series II printer. The computer was adequate, but the printer and monitor needed to be upgraded. The LaserJet would not print the exact sizes of type needed for the book, so it was supplemented by a $5,000 PS Jet+ (PostScript) laser printer. The EGA monitor was acceptable for text editing, but it had only 350 scan lines from the top to the bottom of the screen—not enough to display a clear view of how the typeset pages would look. Consequently, when the book was being paginated, it was necessary to buy a higher resolution monitor.

Next, a professional graphic artist was assigned to determine the page layout and select the typefaces, sizes, and styles of type for the book. The initial specifications filled seven typed pages and included fourteen pages of ex-

**Figure 8.18**
The typical relationships among desktop publishing tasks

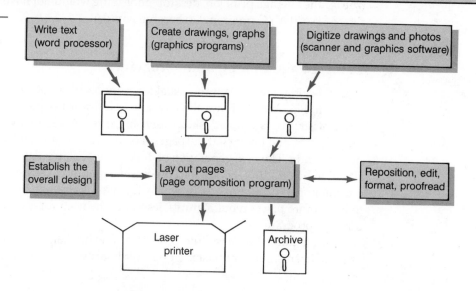

amples. It took me about a week to translate these specifications into a series of Ventura style sheets. For example, one style sheet was used to format boxed inserts, like this one; others controlled the appearance of the table of contents, chapters, part openers, and so on.

Over the next six months the design of the book continued to evolve. Adjustments were made to the type size, the layout of the chapter opening pages, and most other aspects of the book's appearance. As the design consultants changed their minds and revised the specifications, I entered the changes into the Ventura style sheets.

Another important step was to organize the manuscript files. The first edition of this book was written with WordStar and WordStar 2000, and each program has its own data file format. These file formats were no longer appropriate because WordStar has become out-dated, and the WordStar 2000 files are incompatible with Ventura. So a utility program was used to convert them into WordPerfect format.

Although the writing and editing for this book was done with WordPerfect, nearly all the printing was done with Ventura. This meant that the WordPerfect data files contained a fair number of Ventura print-formatting codes. For example, a major heading would be preceded by @A-HEAD = to tell Ventura which paragraph style to use. These codes were a minor distraction while writing.

Each draft of the manuscript popped out of the printer looking just like the final book—with the same margins, footers, and typefaces. The only differences were caused by the lack of artwork and the lower resolution of the laser printer.

Reviewers, copy editors, and proofreaders all contributed their comments and improvements. As these were received, I would type the changes into the WordPerfect files, print a fresh copy with Ventura, and express mail it off for further critique and review.

Eventually, it was time to determine the exact location of page breaks. Among other steps, this involved using Ventura to reserve blank space on the pages to receive artwork. Finally, Ventura's output files were sent to a Linotronic phototypesetter to print the master copy of the book.

This all would have taken much longer with conventional publishing methods. But from an author's viewpoint, the most significant improvement was being able to see exactly how the book would look *while it was being written*.

the raw material to be assembled on the page. Each item—a drawing, graph, photograph, or unit of text—is prepared with an application program and stored on disk in a format compatible with the page composition program.

Another early step is designing the overall look, or format, of the publication. First, you must determine the basic structure of every page. How large is the paper? Will the page be printed in the **portrait** orientation (tall and narrow) or in the **landscape** orientation (short and wide)? Where will the margins be? Will the pages be double-sided (printed on both sides) or single-sided? Other questions determine which design elements, if any, should appear on every page. What should appear in running headers or footers? What logos, lines, or boxes do you want to be consistent throughout the document? The design also includes selecting the fonts, size, and style of type for headings, body text, captions, and other text elements.

An effective design is often the key to a successful publication. Catching and holding a reader's attention is difficult in this busy world, so publishing professionals work hard to display ideas attractively. The typed text produced by a typewriter is inadequate for most printing jobs; it does not look good enough. **Typesetting** makes documents more attractive and easier to read by converting text into well-defined character forms and carefully controlling the positioning of letters. Because typeset characters are more legible, smaller sizes of type can be used. This can pack 30 to 50 percent more text on each page—saving a considerable amount of paper for high-volume print jobs.

Typesetting can pay off in other ways as well. Studies have shown that typeset documents are more credible than typewritten ones. Readers tend to believe an article more just because its text looks better.

Arriving at an acceptable overall design requires a combination of artistic judgment and experience. For a newcomer to publishing, the potential for disaster is quite real. A common error is to get carried away with the new typographic controls, perhaps by sprinkling the page with many incompatible fonts or crowding the page with too much text. The result can be a garish-looking page or one so imposing that people do not bother to read it. One way to avoid these problems is to model your document after the design of a similar professionally produced document. This is perfectly legal; copyright laws do not protect the overall design specifications used in a publication, such as the size and spacing of type or use of white space to provide visual relief. Only the content—the tangible expression of ideas—is protected.

Once the design specifications and the text and graphic files are at hand, you are ready for the page composition program. On-screen page layout means no more scissors and glue, no more missing scraps of paper, and no more problems placing items squarely on the page. The page composition program assembles the text and graphics created by other programs and helps you paste them in position (see Figure 8.19). Page layout is done on the screen, so you can make last-minute changes to reposition items, edit text, stretch or crop graphics, or even change the format of the entire document. When the final pages roll off the laser printer or typesetter, they are ready for the print shop.

To give you a feel for how page composition programs work, in the next two sections, we compare PageMaker with Ventura Publisher. Although these programs use entirely different methods of setting up a document, they have certain aspects in common. Both programs are designed around a Macintosh-like user interface and work best with a mouse. Commands are hidden on pull-down menus where they are readily available but unobtrusive. Like most page composition programs, they use the screen as a window to show you the document in any of several different views. The facing-pages view lets you contemplate a two-page spread. Then you might zoom in to see the current page as it appears when it just fits in the window; zoom in again to see a life-size part of the page; and zoom in yet again for an enlarged, highly detailed view. Scroll bars along the edge of the window let you roam around the page when the view is too magnified to show the whole page at once.

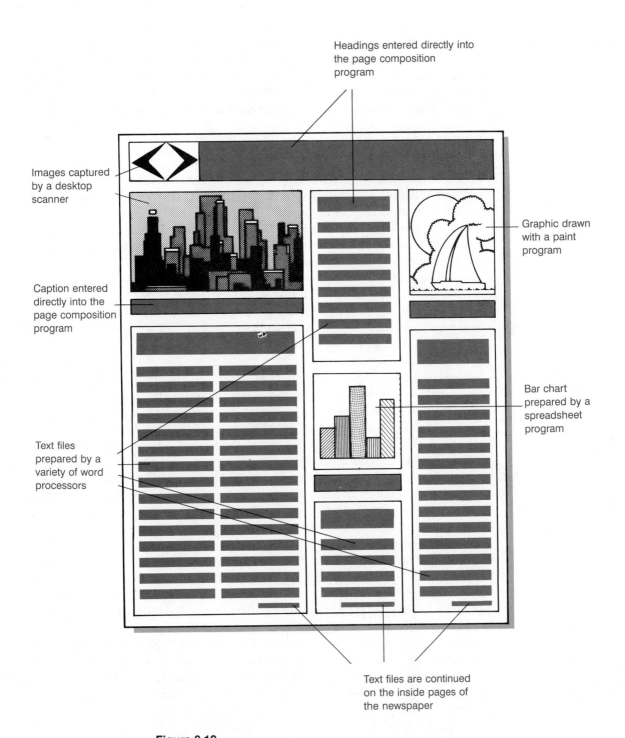

Headings entered directly into the page composition program

Images captured by a desktop scanner

Graphic drawn with a paint program

Caption entered directly into the page composition program

Text files prepared by a variety of word processors

Bar chart prepared by a spreadsheet program

Text files are continued on the inside pages of the newspaper

**Figure 8.19**
A page composition program gives you control over each area of the page, integrating the text and graphics files from numerous sources.

Although both programs can perform limited text editing, they lack many useful word processing features, such as search and replace and spell checking. Their text-editing ability is best reserved for entering minor elements such as headlines or for simple revisions. Fortunately, both programs can import text in a variety of formats, so you are likely to find they are compatible with your word processor.

## Using PageMaker

PageMaker was released in July 1985 by Aldus Corporation only eighteen months after the company was founded. Designed initially for the Macintosh and the Apple LaserWriter, PageMaker launched desktop publishing and set the standards with which similar programs are compared. In February 1987, Aldus introduced a PC version of PageMaker that duplicates the interactive environment that made the Macintosh version such a success. Although differences between the two versions exist, their basic features and user interface are largely the same.

PageMaker organizes the working area like an artist's pasteboard complete with a toolbox full of design aids for page composition. For example, in Figure 8.20, the pasteboard holds the current page and a drawing of three mice. The dithered photo in the page looks much worse on screen than it would look when printed; its poor appearance is the result of interference between the screen's pixel pattern and the photo's dithered dot pattern.

Some tasks are remarkably easy in PageMaker. You can jump directly to another page by clicking the appropriate numbered page icon at the bottom left-hand corner of the screen. A graphic image can be moved to a new location simply by dragging it with the mouse. You can stretch or shrink a graphic like a rubber band by grabbing one of its handles—small dots along the edges—and dragging the handle.

With PageMaker, you lay out pages by placing margin and column guides in position; then you fill the columns with text. The margin guides define the outside boundaries of the image area for every page in the document. They are fixed in place with the Page Setup dialog box (found on the File menu), which also establishes the size and orientation of the page, the number of pages in the document, and whether the pages are single- or double-sided.

With PageMaker for the PC, a publication can have up to 128 pages, with a maximum size of 17 by 22 inches per page. If the document you wish to create has more than 128 pages, you must break it into separate publications and format each separately. When you save a PageMaker publication on disk, all its text and graphics images are stored in one combined file.

Column guides serve as boundaries for text, and each page can have as many as 20 columns. Although PageMaker automatically creates equal columns, you can change a column's position or width by dragging its column guides. Column guides can be set up page by page, but it is easier to define them on a master page.

Text, graphics, and guides repeated on every page in the document are put on a master page. Open a master page by clicking on the L or R page icon at the bottom left-hand corner of the screen, then fill out the master page like a regular page. PageMaker overlays the corresponding master page on the regular pages, so you can use master pages for setting up running heads, automatic page numbering, and elements that will appear on every page (such as hairline rules between columns).

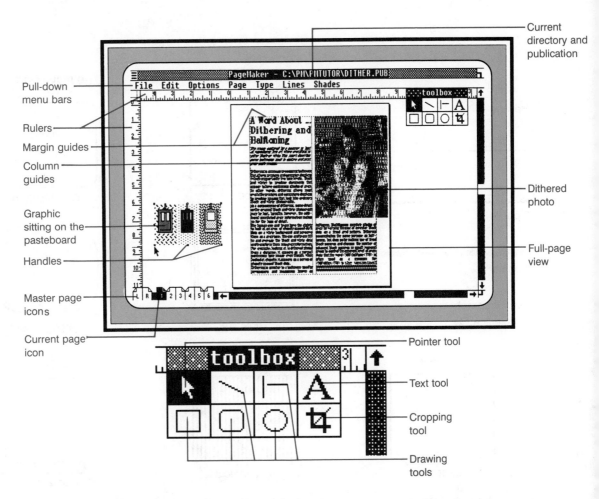

**Figure 8.20**
PageMaker provides the same types of tools found on an artist's pasteboard: rulers for measuring, open areas for storing graphics, and a toolbox with tools for selecting items, drawing lines, editing text, creating boxes and circles, and trimming graphic images.

The usual way of adding text and graphics to the page is to use the Place command from the File menu. This command produces a dialog box showing the text and graphics files available on the disk. After selecting a file from the list, the mouse pointer changes to show it is "loaded," ready for you to place the item on the page by clicking wherever you want the item's upper left-hand corner to be. If the pointer is loaded with a block of text, text will flow down the current column from the pointer's position until it runs into the bottom of the page or a graphic. Each column to receive text must be filled individually; PageMaker cannot automatically fill the columns on a page and continue filling pages until the block of text is exhausted.

Other ways of filling out a document are available. You can use the clipboard to cut, copy, and paste items within PageMaker or from other programs into PageMaker. For short documents, such as an overhead transparency or an advertisement, you might use PageMaker's built-in text editor to enter and format the text.

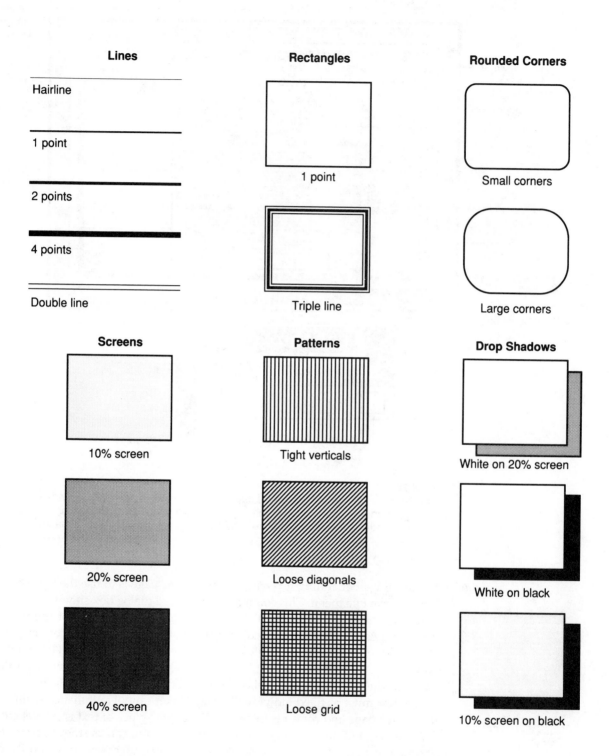

**Lines**

Hairline

1 point

2 points

4 points

Double line

**Rectangles**

1 point

Triple line

**Rounded Corners**

Small corners

Large corners

**Screens**

10% screen

20% screen

40% screen

**Patterns**

Tight verticals

Loose diagonals

Loose grid

**Drop Shadows**

White on 20% screen

White on black

10% screen on black

**Figure 8.21**
PageMaker's drawing tools can create a variety of lines, shapes, and patterns.

**No leading with 9 point type**

I am the voice of today, the herald of tomorrow . . . I coin for you the enchanting tale, the philosopher's moralizing, and the poet's visions . . . I am the leaden army that conquers the world—I am TYPE.

From: *The Type Speaks*

**1 point leading with 9 point type**

I am the voice of today, the herald of tomorrow . . . I coin for you the enchanting tale, the philosopher's moralizing, and the poet's visions . . . I am the leaden army that conquers the world—I am TYPE.

From: *The Type Speaks*

**3 points leading with 9 point type**

I am the voice of today, the herald of tomorrow . . . I coin for you the enchanting tale, the philosopher's moralizing, and the poet's visions . . . I am the leaden army that conquers the world—I am TYPE.

From: *The Type Speaks*

The toolbox window at the top right-hand corner of the screen determines what mode the program is in. If the pointer tool is active, you can select and move graphics and blocks of text, but you cannot edit text. You must select the text tool before you can edit text. The drawing tools allow you to draw lines, rectangles, boxes with rounded corners, ovals, and circles. A cropping tool is available if you want to trim or crop graphics. These modes help organize the program's functions. But if you don't select the right mode, the results are unpredictable.

PageMaker's drawing tools are convenient because they create graphics right on the page (see Figure 8.21). Lines are useful to set off a heading from the body text, separate columns, or create simple drawings. Boxes draw attention to figures and can establish a focal point on the page. Any box, circle, or oval can be filled with a **screen** (tiny pattern of dots) or pattern to give it added emphasis. A **drop shadow,** which is created by stacking two boxes almost on top of each other, gives a box the feeling of depth, as if it sits slightly above the rest of the page.

When you use PageMaker's drawing tools, no line is ever crooked, and every corner meets precisely. Some operations, such as drawing rounded corners on a box, are far easier to do electronically than with border tape and an X-Acto knife.

PageMaker offers many features for **copyfitting,** that is, getting text to fit within the available area. If the text in a file does not fit within its assigned area on a page, the remaining text can be made to flow to another page, similar to the way a newspaper article can be continued on another page. Or the available area might be increased by moving the column margins or adjusting the top and bottom guides. More text can always be packed in an area by using a smaller type size or by reducing or eliminating the **leading,** the extra space between lines. These techniques, however, may damage the document's readability (see Figure 8.22).

PageMaker also gives you control over the average amount of space placed between words and letters, letting you squeeze text together or stretch it out. **Kerning** is another way of adjusting the spacing; it takes advantage of the way specific pairs of letters fit together because of their shape. For example, the arm of a capital $T$ can be slid over the top of a lowercase $o$ to save a bit of space. Kerning is not very noticeable in small type sizes, but the letterspacing in headlines can look uneven without kerning, as Figure 8.23 shows. With PageMaker, you can kern individual letters by shifting them one at a time, and you can set PageMaker to automatically kern pairs of characters preselected by the font designer. Despite all these fancy options, often the best copyfitting strategy is to delete the extra text.

# WATER WAY
A.

# WATER WAY
B.

## Using Ventura Publisher

Xerox Corporation's Ventura Publisher is perhaps the leading page composition program for the PC. It is a suitable choice for formatting short flyers, business forms, and newsletters. But it excels in preparing long documents that need to go through extensive revisions.

Perhaps the most notable difference between Ventura and PageMaker is the way they store information on disk. Instead of merging all a document's text and graphics into a single PageMaker-like publication file, Ventura builds a "chapter" file that contains instructions for assembling the document from the original text and graphics files (see Figure 8.24). The chapter file contains only pointers to the

**Figure 8.24**
Ventura Publisher uses two special files to assemble and format a document from text and graphics stored in other files. The *chapter file* contains pointers to the other files; it describes how to assemble the document from its components. The *style sheet* is a list of formatting instructions that controls the appearance of the various types of paragraphs, from body text to major heading.

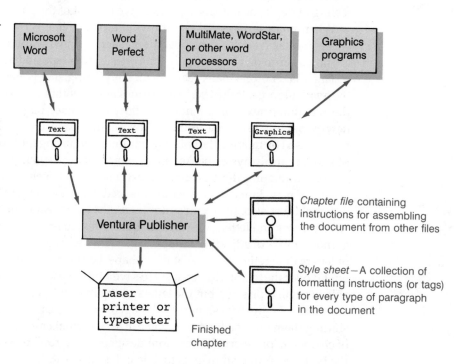

document's other files and some formatting information. Thus, for example, if you move a graph from page 6 to page 2, Ventura merely rearranges the pointers in the chapter file.

Documents that go through extensive revisions benefit from Ventura's file storage system. For example, after you have written a rough draft of a document with a word processor, you can use Ventura to link and format the document's text files. Next, the formatted document can be viewed and edited with Ventura's text editor. When you leave Ventura, it saves all of your editing changes in the original word processing files. This means that a text file can be created with WordPerfect, formatted and edited with Ventura, then edited more extensively with WordPerfect.

Besides a chapter file, each document is attached to a style sheet. A Ventura style sheet is a collection of formatting instructions (or tags) for each type of paragraph used in the document. That is, the style sheet tells Ventura what the body text, chapter titles, footnotes, and other paragraph styles should look like. You can attach a different style sheet to a document (to give the entire document a new look), or you can make changes in the current style sheet (see Chapter 7).

PageMaker uses a toolbox to group its functions; Ventura uses four icons near the top left-hand corner of the screen for the same purpose (see Figure 8.25).

- The Frame Setting icon allows you to manipulate frames (boxes) that are used to hold text and pictures. Basic document layout is accomplished in this mode by opening, moving, resizing, and deleting frames. A frame can hold information from only one text or graphics file, so if you want to add a bar chart to a page, you must open up a new frame for it. Creating the new frame is easy (see Figure 8.26). While in the Frame Setting mode, you click the Add New Frame button, move the pointer to where you want a corner of the frame, and hold down the mouse button while dragging the mouse to the opposite corner—stretching the frame as you go. Later you can use the frame's handles to adjust its size or position on the page.

- The Paragraph Tagging icon provides a speedy way to adjust the appearance of paragraphs by tagging them with a paragraph name defined in the style sheet. When the Paragraph Tagging mode is active, the Selection box on the left of the screen lists the available tags by name. To tag a paragraph, first you highlight it with the mouse, then you click on the tag name. For even faster paragraph tagging, you can assign tag names to function keys.

- The Text Editing icon lets you use Ventura's built-in text editor.

- The Graphics Drawing icon gives you access to the same sort of drawing tools found in PageMaker's toolbox.

In addition to placing text in frames that sit on top of a page, text can also be attached to the underlying page. When a text file is attached to the underlying page, any remaining text will flow automatically to succeeding pages, snaking its way around any frames in its path. On long documents, this can save plenty of time because you do not have to lay out the document page by page.

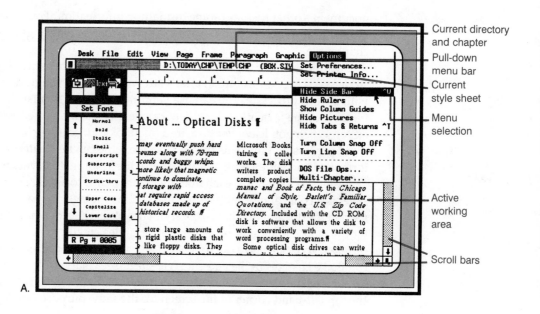

Current directory and chapter

Pull-down menu bar

Current style sheet

Menu selection

Active working area

Scroll bars

A.

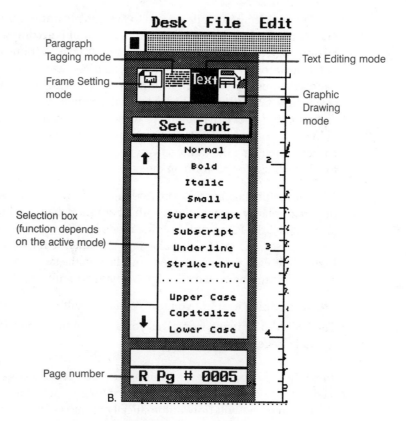

Paragraph Tagging mode

Frame Setting mode

Text Editing mode

Graphic Drawing mode

Selection box (function depends on the active mode)

Page number

B.

**Figure 8.25**
Ventura Publisher uses pull-down menus and four icon-modes (near the top left-hand corner) to control most of its features.

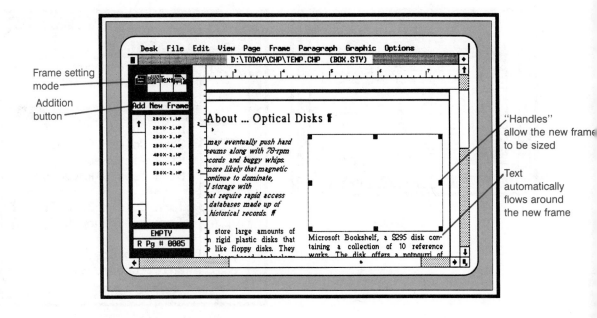

Frame setting mode

Addition button

"Handles" allow the new frame to be sized

Text automatically flows around the new frame

**Figure 8.26**
An empty frame sits on this page waiting for a text or graphic file to fill it. The text in the underlying page has automatically flowed around the new frame.

Like PageMaker, Ventura can **scale** a graphics image electronically to change its size or **crop** an image to trim off unwanted areas (see Figure 8.27). By using different scaling factors for the horizontal and vertical directions, images can be distorted to make them fat or skinny—a design trick tough to duplicate with conventional publishing. Of course, if a bit-mapped image, such as the one shown in Figure 8.27, is increased markedly in size, it will begin to look grainy. Many graphics programs create *line art* images that are stored mathematically, and like outline fonts, line art images can be scaled without introducing graininess.

## Summary

Desktop publishing is the most recent in a long series of advances in the technology of printing and publishing. Printing began with the invention of movable type—an invention that created the new problems of setting type in pages and of disassembling and resorting the pieces of type. An interim solution was the Linotype machine; it automatically transformed the operator's keystrokes into finished lines of lead type. The ultimate solution, offset printing, entirely eliminated the need for printing plates with raised images. Along with computer-controlled typesetters, offset printing sponsored an explosion in the variety and quantity of printed material over the last thirty years.

Desktop publishing got its start in 1985 with advances in laser printing and software. Desktop laser printers slashed the cost of producing near-typeset-quality

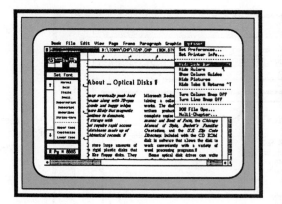

**Figure 8.27**
These two views of the same graphics file were prepared by capturing an electronic image of Ventura on a CRT screen. Then Ventura was used to manipulate its own image. On the left, the image was *scaled* until it fit inside a border consisting of two boxes. On the right, the image was *stretched* and *cropped* to highlight the pull-down menu. The images and the boxes surrounding them were printed with an HP LaserJet printer and placed directly on the final paste-up to reproduce this book.

text to a marginal cost of five cents a page. Desktop scanners have played a lesser role; they convert visual images into digital bit-mapped images that can be manipulated inside a computer.

Two software developments have had the most influence: page description languages and page composition programs. Page description languages allow application programs to describe the objects to be printed rather than specifying each spot to receive ink. Page composition programs have placed the same sort of typographic and page makeup capabilities available to professional printers in the hands of ordinary people.

A final word of caution about desktop publishing is in order. Just because you have access to a set of tools does not mean you will be able to use them appropriately. In fact, unwary users often become so dazzled with the newfound capabilities that they spend their time playing with a document's format instead of organizing their ideas. You may find it tempting to become heavy-handed with graphics, which can overwhelm the copy. Another common mistake is to place too many different fonts on a page, diverting the reader's attention to the document's format rather than its content. Along with the newly acquired control over the production process comes a responsibility to understand the basic rules of page design and aesthetics.

## Key Terms

composition

copyfitting

crop

digitize

dither

drop shadow

fax

galley proof

grain

halftone

kerning

landscape

leading

Linotype machine

movable type

offset press

optical character recognition (OCR)

page composition program

page description language (PDL)

phototypesetter

portrait

scale

scanner

screen

template

turnkey system

typesetting

## Discussion Questions

1. What will be the ultimate impact of desktop publishing? Is it a passing fad, or will it rank with movable type as one of history's most notable milestones?

2. When is an X-Acto knife and glue a reasonable substitute for a page composition program?

3. What advantages does desktop publishing have over conventional publishing methods? Which method would you choose for producing a newsletter, technical manual, or four-color sales leaflet?

4. What percentage of the documents you read are typeset? What percentage are prepared by desktop publishing? How might you determine these percentages?

## Exercises

1. Determine whether the campus publications you read are produced with desktop publishing. Find out how they are prepared and printed.

2. Find two examples of typeset documents: one that you like and one that you do not. Write a critique comparing the two, pointing out their design flaws as well as their strengths.

3. Dot matrix printers and laser printers use a form of printer graphics to print characters. Compare the character patterns of a bit-mapped display with the character patterns of a dot matrix and a laser printer.

# Spreadsheets

Our ability to understand the world in terms of numbers is the result of a series of advances affecting how numbers are represented and processed. Even in prehistorical times, people needed help manipulating numbers; the scratch marks on cave walls are evidence of our ancestors' limited memory. The introduction of clay tablets and paper made numerical records more portable and erasable. The abacus, the first mechanical aid, increased the speed and accuracy with which numbers could be added and subtracted. The invention of a symbol for zero and the Hindu decimal system made arithmetic easier and led to many advances in higher mathematics. Logarithm tables and slide rules eliminated most of the work of multiplying and dividing. The early part of this century saw the widespread use of mechanical and electromechanical adding machines; in the last two decades,

these have been replaced by electronic desktop and hand-held calculators. The last major step in this progression occurred with the introduction of the first spreadsheet program, VisiCalc, in 1979.

The first version of VisiCalc used only 16KB of memory and stored data on tape cassettes. Despite its initial limitations, VisiCalc did something no program had done before: It made a computer's numerical processing abilities available to people who had no previous computer experience. Since VisiCalc's introduction, literally hundreds of competitive spreadsheet programs have been written, and spreadsheet processing has become one of the most popular applications for personal computers.

A spreadsheet program provides for numerical work what a word processor does for writing: flexibility, convenience, and power. Spreadsheet programs include many features to help users enter, move, label, and display numbers. But the real advantage of spreadsheet programs is their ability to store not only numbers but also formulas for calculating numbers. When critical numbers are changed, the entire model is recalculated, updating other numbers as needed to keep everything self-consistent and in balance.

This ability to do instantaneous what-if recalculations lets people experiment with the relationships among numbers in a manner previously impractical. For example, if the sales estimate in a typical five-year financial plan is changed, adjustments must be made in manufacturing costs, overhead costs, and many other items. A spreadsheet program makes these changes automatically, but in the past, it could take hours of error-prone, tedious figuring on paper to predict the implications of changes in a forecast's basic assumptions. This arduous work discouraged experimentation and limited how many assumptions about the future were explored.

Part III teaches you about spreadsheet processing in two stages. In Chapter 9, we discuss simple models and show detailed examples of common features and concepts. In Chapter 10, we discuss the advanced features that allow spreadsheet programs to construct sophisticated applications.

# Spreadsheet Basics

A **spreadsheet** program transforms the computer into a "number-crunching" tool capable of solving problems once tackled with a pencil, scratch pad, and calculator. It is especially useful for time-consuming tasks such as performing the same calculations with different starting assumptions or choosing among several alternatives.

Like any other powerful tool, spreadsheets have their own terminology and basic operations that must be mastered before sophisticated applications can be undertaken. In this chapter, we explain the concepts necessary for typical spreadsheet applications and describe features that all spreadsheet programs provide in one form or another. We explain each step in a simple session and describe the basic operations: how to view the worksheet, edit and enter cells, rearrange portions of the worksheet, and give simple commands.

234

## 9

## BASIC CONCEPTS

Figure 9.1 illustrates how a spreadsheet program stores and displays data. Data is stored and edited in an enormous sheet built out of small rectangular storage bins called **cells**. Some programs call this sheet the **worksheet** and reserve the term *spreadsheet* to describe the application program. For clarity, we use this terminology, but many people use *spreadsheet* to apply to either the program or the worksheet.

The size of the worksheet depends on the program. A minimal size is 64 columns wide by 256 rows long; most worksheets have hundreds of columns and thousands of rows. Because the display is much smaller than the worksheet, only a tiny rectangular part of the worksheet shows in the display's window. Using the cursor keys, a mouse, or another pointing method, you can scroll the window horizontally and vertically to view any part of the worksheet.

Data in a worksheet cell passes through several layers of processing before it appears in the display window. These layers can be thought of as processing filters that calculate the cell's value and convert the value into the desired format for display. Each cell stores a **value rule** that tells the spreadsheet how to calculate the cell's value. The value rule might simply be the value itself, such as the number 689.55 or the label Sales; or it might be a *formula*, which is an expression stating how the value is to be calculated. Each cell also has one or more **format rules** that tell the spreadsheet how to display the value. For example, a format rule might cause the value 689.55 to appear on the display as $690.

Although Figure 9.1 labels both the rows and columns with numbers, most programs label the columns with letters. But if there are sixty-four or more columns, they cannot all be designated with just the twenty-six letters of the alphabet; it's necessary to use two letters to designate the later columns. This means the first twenty-six columns are labeled A to Z and the later columns AA, AB, . . . AZ, BA, BB, and so on until the end of the worksheet.

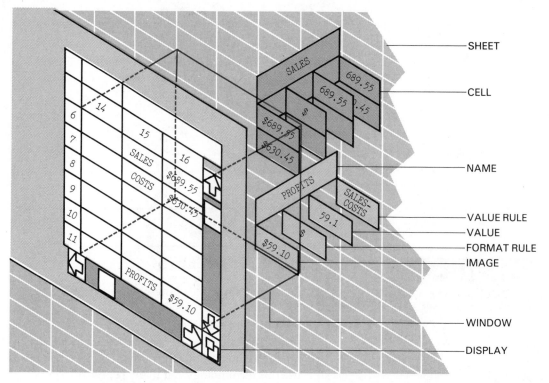

**Figure 9.1**
A worksheet is an aggregate of cells that can get values from one another. You can think of each cell as having several layers in front of the sheet that compute the value of the cell and determine the format of the presentation. For example, each cell has a value rule, which can be the value itself or a way to compute it, as well as a format rule, which converts the value into a form suitable for display. A cell's image is the formatted value, as displayed in the rectangular part of the sheet appearing in the window. Adapted from "Computer Software," by Alan Kay. Copyright (©) 1984 by *Scientific American*, Inc. All rights reserved.

In most programs, the name of a cell is the cell's column letter(s) followed by its row number, as in R2, D2, Z80, AD1989, or A1. Some programs label both the rows and columns with numbers; these products need a way to indicate whether a number refers to a row or column. One way of doing this is to precede row numbers with an *R* and column numbers with a *C*. Thus instead of referring to the upper left-hand cell of the worksheet as cell A1, you would call it cell R1C1. An advantage of this convention is that it can be adapted to three-dimensional worksheets. For example, if a spreadsheet allows information to be stored on more than one worksheet at a time—like a pad of paper—the third dimension might be preceded with a *P* for "page." Then cell R5C2P8 is the cell at the intersection of the fifth row and the second column of the eighth page in the worksheet tablet. However, most spreadsheet programs allow only one worksheet (or page) in memory at a time. In our examples, we use letters to designate columns and numbers to designate rows.

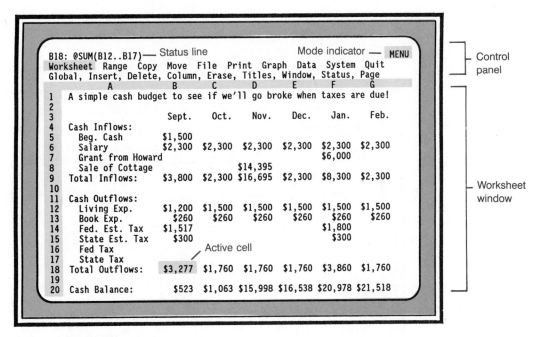

```
B18: @SUM(B12..B17)── Status line                  Mode indicator ── MENU
Worksheet Range Copy Move File Print Graph Data System Quit
Global, Insert, Delete, Column, Erase, Titles, Window, Status, Page
                A         B       C       D       E       F       G
1   A simple cash budget to see if we'll go broke when taxes are due!
2
3                        Sept.    Oct.    Nov.    Dec.    Jan.    Feb.
4   Cash Inflows:
5     Beg. Cash          $1,500
6     Salary             $2,300  $2,300  $2,300  $2,300  $2,300  $2,300
7     Grant from Howard                                  $6,000
8     Sale of Cottage                    $14,395
9   Total Inflows:       $3,800  $2,300 $16,695  $2,300  $8,300  $2,300
10
11  Cash Outflows:
12    Living Exp.        $1,200  $1,500  $1,500  $1,500  $1,500  $1,500
13    Book Exp.            $260    $260    $260    $260    $260    $260
14    Fed. Est. Tax      $1,517                           $1,800
15    State Est. Tax       $300                             $300
16    Fed Tax                   Active cell
17    State Tax
18  Total Outflows:      $3,277  $1,760  $1,760  $1,760  $3,860  $1,760
19
20  Cash Balance:          $523  $1,063 $15,998 $16,538 $20,978 $21,518
```

Control panel

Worksheet window

**Figure 9.2**
Lotus 1-2-3 separates the worksheet window from the control panel with a highlighted border of row and column labels. The most interesting part of this worksheet lies off the screen in the column for April, the month when taxes are due.

Most spreadsheets allow you to assign names to cells. For example, you might give cell C5 the name Sales and cell C6 the name Costs. A cell's name is different from a cell's value; for example, the cell named Sales might store the number 689.55. Formulas are easier to write and understand if cells have been given logical names; Sales – Costs makes more sense than C5 – C6.

## Understanding the Display

Spreadsheet programs assign different parts of the display to two tasks: The **control panel** displays status and help information, and the *worksheet window* lets you see what is in the worksheet. The control panel is like a car's dashboard; that is, it shows you what the product is doing, tells you what options are available, and lets you control the activity. You should understand everything the control panel says.

Like dashboards, control panels vary from one product to the next (see Figures 9.2 and 9.3). The examples in this chapter are drawn from two spreadsheets: Excel from Microsoft Corporation ($395) and Lotus 1-2-3 from Lotus Development Corporation ($495). Excel, introduced in 1985, is the leading spreadsheet for the Macintosh and recently became available in an IBM version that runs under Microsoft Windows. Lotus 1-2-3 has been the dominant spreadsheet for IBM microcomputers since early 1984. These programs use very different command systems. Excel uses

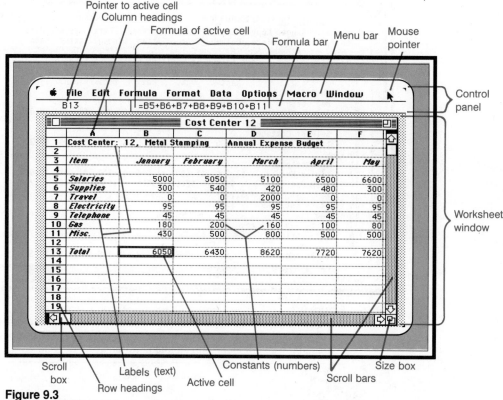

**Figure 9.3**

With Microsoft's Excel, you control the worksheet window with scroll bars (to view other areas of the worksheet) and a size box (to make the window larger or smaller). Several worksheets can be open on the screen at a time, each in their own window.

pull-down menus, dialog boxes, multiple worksheet windows, and a mouse in its user interface; whereas Lotus 1-2-3 relies on typed commands and a system of nested menu bars to accomplish the same tasks, though usually in a more convoluted fashion.

The **active cell** is the cell available for immediate use or modification. It is marked on the screen so that it stands out from the rest of the cells. Lotus 1-2-3 highlights the active cell; Excel puts a border around it.

Nearly all spreadsheets have one or more lines in their control panel devoted to two major functions.

• The **status line** (or in Excel, the *formula bar*) tells you the coordinates of the active cell and displays its value. Whenever you make an entry to an empty cell or edit the contents of a full one, you type on this line.

• The **menu bar** shows you what categories of commands are available. This area is also used in Lotus 1-2-3 to display prompts or ask questions.

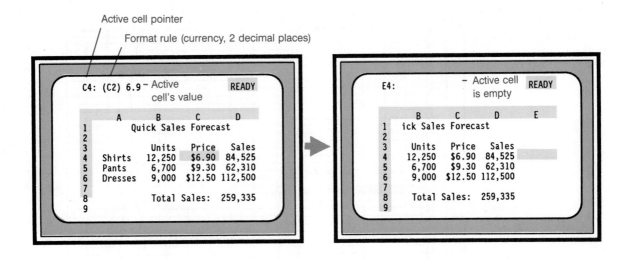

**Figure 9.4**
Pressing the right-arrow key [→] twice causes this reduced-size Lotus 1-2-3 worksheet to scroll.

## Moving around the Worksheet

Whenever you begin editing an empty worksheet, cell A1 is the active cell. You can mark any cell in the window as the active cell by using the arrow keys or mouse. Whereas in most programs the arrow keys move the cursor, in spreadsheet processing they change which cell is the active cell by one column or row at a time.

If you try to move the active cell off the edge of the window, the window scrolls to a different part of the worksheet, as Figure 9.4 shows. Scrolling does more than shift the contents of the window: The window's borders are also relabeled, and the coordinates of the active cell shown in the control panel are adjusted. If you hold down the cursor keys, the repeat-key feature is invoked, and scrolling continues until the window runs up against an edge of the worksheet; then the scrolling stops. Most spreadsheets beep if you try to scroll past the edge of the worksheet—in effect saying, "You can't go there."

In theory, you could use the cursor keys to scroll the window to show any part of the worksheet. But this would take a long time indeed on either Lotus 1-2-3 or Excel because their worksheets are enormous. A Lotus 1-2-3 worksheet has 256 columns and 8,196 rows; Excel's are even larger at 256 by 16,348. If each cell is 1 inch wide and 1/4 inch high, a complete printout of an Excel worksheet would be 21 by 340 feet.

Fortunately, there are other, quicker methods to move the worksheet window. Most spreadsheets have special commands for **paging** through the worksheet one

**Figure 9.5**
Paging down
through a Lotus
1-2-3 worksheet by
pressing [PgDn]
twice

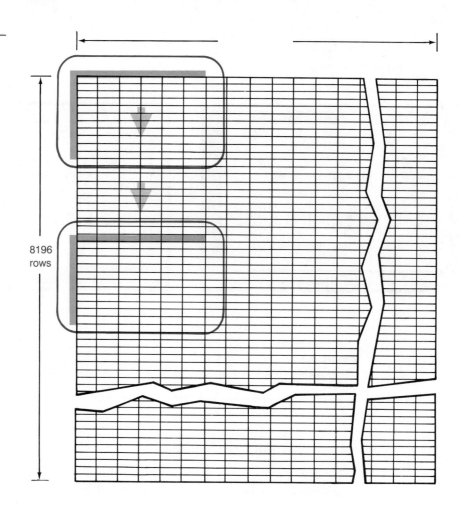

8196
rows

full screen at a time (see Figure 9.5). For example, paging up and down with Lotus 1-2-3 is done with the [PgUp] and [PgDn] keys. The equivalent action with Excel is to click in the gray area of the vertical scroll bar.

For moving long distances with Lotus 1-2-3, the fastest method is to jump between points. The procedure is to press function key [F5] (labeled GOTO on a plastic keyboard template supplied with the program), causing the prompt "Enter address to go to:" to appear in the control panel. Then you tell Lotus 1-2-3 where to go by typing a cell's coordinates, such as BJ4516, and pressing [Enter]. Immediately, the window displays a region of the worksheet containing the requested cell. With Excel, you can jump to a new location by selecting the Goto option from the Formula menu and then typing a cell's coordinates or choosing a named area (such as Balance_Sheet or Budget_1992) from a list box. Usually it is faster, however, to drag the scroll box along the scroll bar to a place that represents the approximate position in the worksheet you want to see.

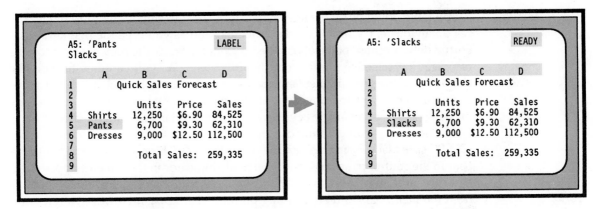

**Figure 9.6**
The left-hand screen shows the display while an entry is being typed. The right-hand screen shows the entry's effect after the [Enter] key has been pressed.

## ENTERING AND EDITING

Moving around the worksheet soon becomes second nature. Your attention will quickly shift to entering and editing the contents of cells because that is how you get to see the results of calculations. But before we give examples of editing cells, we should describe the modes of operation encountered during spreadsheet processing and the methods used to shift between modes. To get caught in an unexpected mode is disconcerting because, without much warning, the keys have different meanings.

Every spreadsheet has three basic modes of operation, which we call the *ready mode*, *entry mode*, and *command mode*. The program begins in the ready mode, which is used to move around the worksheet. The entry mode lets you put new information in the active cell. The command mode lets you change the format of a cell, save a worksheet on the disk, or perform any of a hundred or more other actions.

Typing a letter (A to Z), number (0 to 9), or one of a few special symbols (quotation mark, plus sign, minus sign, at sign, or left parenthesis) shifts Lotus 1-2-3 into the entry mode. The characters of the new entry appear on the status line of the control panel as they are typed (see Figure 9.6). While in the entry mode, you cannot scroll the screen or do anything other than type and edit a new entry for the active cell. You can use the left- and right-arrow keys to move the cursor back and forth across the entry to insert or delete characters. The normal way to exit from the entry mode is to press the [Enter] key, which discards the old contents (if any) of the active cell, stores the new entry in the active cell, and returns the program to the ready mode. Once [Enter] is pressed, the old entry is gone and cannot be recovered. But if you have not pressed [Enter], you can escape from the entry mode without affecting the contents of the current cell by pressing the escape key [Esc].

Anything you type on the keyboard causes Excel to shift to the entry mode. The cell's previous entry (if any) is discarded as soon as you type the first keystroke. Fortunately, for those of us who make frequent mistakes, the previous entry can be recovered by selecting Undo from the Edit menu. As you continue to type, the characters of the growing new entry appear in the control panel and in the active cell itself. When you are satisfied with the entry, you return to the ready mode by pressing [Enter] or an arrow key or by selecting another cell with the mouse.

The normal way of entering command mode with Lotus 1-2-3 (and most other IBM PC spreadsheet programs) is to type a slash (/). This causes a menu bar to appear in the control panel and shifts the mode indicator in the screen's upper right-hand corner from READY to MENU. To complete the command, you select options from the menu bars and answer any prompts that appear. However, a few commands are so important they are assigned to function keys. We've already seen that jumping is one such command; others include asking for help or viewing graphs built with 1-2-3's graphics component.

With Excel, you enter the command mode by holding down the mouse button while pointing at an item on the menu bar, causing a pull-down menu to descend. Then you highlight the choice you want from the pull-down menu and release the mouse button. Some commands—such as Cut, Copy, and Paste—are completed as soon as the button is released, but many commands require you to fill out a dialog box requesting more information.

## Labels versus Numbers and Formulas

The value rule in each cell can store one of three types of information: a label, number, or formula. A **label** is a string of normal text characters, such as Smith, Dresses, 123 Main Street, and Pro-Forma Income Statement. Labels help identify the items in the worksheet. A number might be the integer 4 or the number 3.14159. A **formula** is generally an instruction to calculate a number, although both Excel and Lotus 1-2-3 allow formulas to process text. For example, 5+4 is a valid Lotus 1-2-3 formula. All Excel formulas start with an equal sign, so the equivalent Excel formula is =5+4. Either way, this trivial formula reads "five plus four" and causes the number 9 to appear on the screen. Formulas may be quite complex and are the most powerful part of spreadsheet processing.

Cells that store numerical data can be used in mathematical formulas; cells that store labels cannot. For example, a formula can add the values of a group of cells storing numbers. But to add labels, such as Pants and Dresses or apples and oranges, makes no sense.

As soon as you type the first character of an entry, Lotus 1-2-3 decides whether the entry will store text (a label) or numerical data (a number or formula). If the first character is a letter, the entry is assumed to be a label, as Figure 9.7 shows. If the first character is a number or an arithmetic symbol (such as a plus sign, minus sign, or a left parenthesis), the entry is assumed to be either a number or a formula.

Because most entries beginning with a letter are labels, and most other entries are numbers or formulas, having Lotus 1-2-3 guess which type of entry is being made saves time. But for some entries the guess is incorrect. For example, although

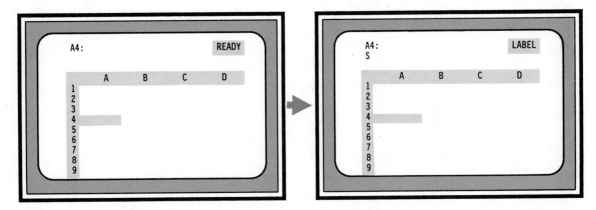

**Figure 9.7**
Default assumption. When you begin to enter "Shirts" by typing an S, Lotus 1-2-3 signals that it assumes the entry is a label by changing the mode indicator to say "LABEL".

123 Main Street and the social security number 543-64-9856 do not begin with letters, they must be stored as labels. The "123" of 123 Main Street should be stored as the character 1, followed by the character 2, followed by the character 3. This string of three characters is not a number; it is merely three characters in a row. (If you are curious about how the keystroke [7] could be stored as a number or text character (label), read the Appendix, "How Computers Process Information.")

These examples indicate the need for a way to override Lotus 1-2-3's default assumption that all labels begin with letters. The usual procedure is to begin the label by typing a quotation mark (") or an apostrophe ('). The spreadsheet interprets either of these symbols as a command to begin the entry mode and enter a label regardless of the characters that follow. Then when the label is displayed on the screen, the quotation mark or apostrophe is suppressed; instead, it is used to tell Lotus 1-2-3 whether to left- or right-justify the label within the cell.

Excel uses a different method to determine whether an entry is a label, number, or formula. It waits until you complete the entry to decide. Then anything beginning with an equal sign becomes a formula; anything Excel can interpret as a number becomes a number; and everything else becomes a label. For example, Excel will accept 123, 1,234, and even $1,234 as numbers. But because 123 Main Street contains text, it becomes a label.

Excel is more flexible than Lotus 1-2-3 in the way it accepts numbers. With Excel, you can enter a number in whatever format you want it to have on the screen. With Lotus 1-2-3, you cannot enter numbers containing commas, such as 89,500. If you enter a number with illegal punctuation—such as a comma or letter—Lotus 1-2-3 beeps and flashes ERROR in the mode indicator. This can be particularly frustrating for novice users who attempt to enter a number in the way it is supposed to appear. Although the integer 89500 might be displayed on the screen as $89,500, it must be entered and stored in the worksheet without the comma. Later, a separate formatting operation can be used to change the number's on-screen appearance.

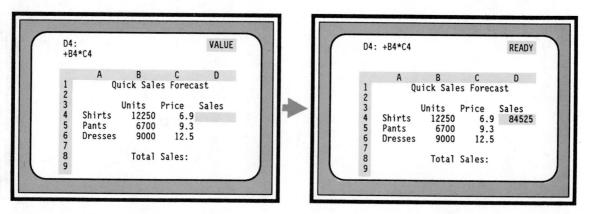

**Figure 9.8**
Entering a formula into the worksheet

## Entering Labels and Numbers

To make our discussion as concrete as possible, let's suppose you want to build a worksheet like the one in Figure 9.3 to forecast sales for a clothing manufacturer. Your first step is to turn on the computer, load the operating system and the spreadsheet in memory, and begin editing an empty worksheet. You type the labels and numbers in the sales forecast into the worksheet one at a time by repeatedly

- Marking a particular cell as the active cell with the arrow keys
- Typing an entry
- Pressing the [Enter] key

Figure 9.7 shows the very beginning of this process. When all the labels and numbers have been entered, the window showing the worksheet would look like the left-hand screen in Figure 9.8. The sales figures and the total have not been entered because they will be calculated by formulas.

The information in Figure 9.8 is poorly formatted in comparison with the same information in Figure 9.3. The column headings are not aligned with the numbers beneath them, and the numbers do not have commas, dollar signs, or even the correct number of digits after the decimal point. Obviously, the spreadsheet has made some assumptions about how the entries should look that are inappropriate for this forecast, such as left-justifying all labels and right-justifying all numbers. Later in this chapter, we discuss how to change the appearance of entries. For now, it is enough to know that entering data and formatting data to look good are often separate steps.

## Entering Formulas

If a spreadsheet could only record labels and numbers in a grid of cells, it wouldn't have much practical use—a simple text editor would be more convenient and just

**Table 9.1**
**Arithmetic Operators**

| Symbol | Operation | Precedence | Example | Value |
|--------|-----------|------------|---------|-------|
| ^ | Exponentiation | First (Highest) | 3^2 | 9 |
| * | Multiplication | Second | 4*3^2 | 36 |
| / | Division | Second | 4*3^2/12 | 3 |
| + | Addition | Last (Lowest) | 5+4*3^2/12 | 8 |
| - | Subtraction | Last (Lowest) | 5+4*3^2/12-6 | 2 |

as powerful. A spreadsheet is useful because it can store formulas—instructions for calculations—inside the cells.

As an example, look again at Figure 9.8. Suppose you want cell D4 to show the result of multiplying the units of shirts in cell B4 (12,250) times the price per shirt in cell C4 ($6.90). In spreadsheet arithmetic, an asterisk means multiply; a slash means divide; a plus means add; and a minus means subtract. Therefore, you might type the formula 12250*6.9 into cell D4. But since the numbers in cells B4 and C4 have already been entered into the worksheet once, there is no need to enter them again for the formula in cell D4. Instead of telling the spreadsheet which numbers to multiply, you can tell it which cells contain the numbers. Typing the formula +B4*C4 into cell D4 causes the spreadsheet to find the value of cell B4, multiply it by the value of cell C4, and display the result in cell D4, as shown in the right-hand screen in Figure 9.8.

The plus sign in the formula +B4*C4 is very important for Lotus 1-2-3. Let's suppose it had been omitted and B4*C4 had been typed into cell D4 instead of +B4*C4. Since the first character of the entry is now a letter, the entry would be stored as a label, not as a formula. Labels are treated as text and are not processed to see if they make mathematical sense; thus the window would now display B4*C4 for cell D4. The same problem can occur with Excel if you forget to begin a formula with an equal sign.

A few early spreadsheet programs carried out operations from left to right across a formula. With these programs, the formula 2+2/4 equaled 1 because the addition was done first. Today, nearly all spreadsheets respect the normal order of operations assumed in algebra or computer programming: multiplication and division are done before addition and subtraction (see Table 9.1). These programs evaluate 2+2/4 as equal to 2.5.

For some formulas, the normal order operations are performed in is inconvenient. For example, if you want to find the average of the values in cells B2, B4, and B6, it is confusing to write +B3/3+B4/3+B6/3. To simplify this sort of formula, use parentheses; whatever is enclosed in parentheses is done first. With the help of parentheses, the formula to compute the average becomes (B2+B4+B6)/3. If appropriate, parentheses can be nested, as in ((5+8)*(13+7)+3)/2. When there are nested sets of parentheses, the operations in the innermost set of parentheses are done first.

The spreadsheet stores the formula, but it displays the result of computing the formula. The difference is important. When you look at a cell in the worksheet window, you do not see the cell's contents as they are stored in the worksheet itself. Instead, you see a processed version, which is the value that results from evaluating the formula. The processed version of a label might vary from the stored version by being right-justified or centered in the cell or by being truncated. You can check to see what is stored in a cell by making it the active cell and looking at the control panel.

## Specifying Ranges of Cells

Our sample worksheet in Figure 9.8 also calls for the total sales to be given. To obtain this figure, you might put the formula +D4+D5+D6 in cell D8. But clearly, this approach would be cumbersome if the sales forecast had forty or fifty sales items. A more reliable method is to specify a range of cells to be added. A **range** of cells is a rectangular group of cells treated as a unit for some operation. A range can be as small as a single cell, or it can be part of a row or column, an entire row or column, or even a large rectangular region of cells (see Figure 9.9).

For most commands and functions used in spreadsheets, you must indicate the range of cells to be processed. For example, you can

- Save a range of cells on a disk as a file

- Print a range of cells on the printer

- Use a function to add, average, or find the largest value in a range of cells

- Change the appearance of cells in a range, such as right-justify all the labels in a range

- Use a command to copy, move, or delete a range of cells

The method for specifying a range varies from program to program. For example, to select a range of cells with Excel, you move the mouse pointer to one corner of the range, hold down the mouse button, and drag the pointer to the opposite corner. As the pointer moves across the worksheet, a growing area is marked in inverse video. If you try to drag the pointer off the edge of the screen, the worksheet will begin scrolling to let you select an even larger range. Lotus 1-2-3 has a similar procedure for pointing out the corners of a range that involves using the arrow keys.

Both Excel and Lotus 1-2-3 also allow you to enter the coordinates of a range from the keyboard. The usual procedure is to type the name of the upper left-hand cell in the range, a delimiter (either a colon or a series of periods), and the name of the lower right-hand cell. For example, the range that includes cells D4, D5, and D6 is entered as D4:D6 with Excel or as D4..D6 with Lotus 1-2-3. A range of cells within one row has the same row number for both endpoints of the range, as in the range A20..Q20. One specification can encompass an entire worksheet, as in A1:IV16384.

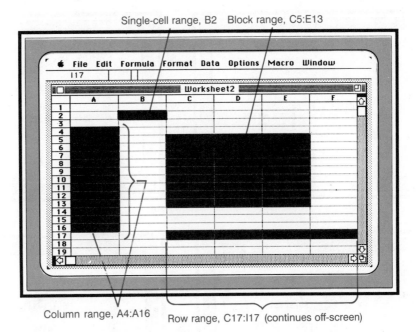

Single-cell range, B2   Block range, C5:E13

Column range, A4:A16   Row range, C17:I17 (continues off-screen)

**Figure 9.9**
A range can be a cell, part of a row or column, or a rectangular area.

## Entering Functions

Whenever you find it tedious or difficult to write a formula, you should check to see if a function would make the task easier. **Functions** are special-purpose calculating tools built into the spreadsheet that let you do complex tasks quickly and easily. For example, a function can total a column of numbers or compute the average of the values in a range. Although you could perform these computations with simple arithmetic operators, a function is less bulky and more reliable. Other activities, such as finding the largest number in a column or searching through a table for a particular value, require functions because they cannot be achieved with ordinary formulas.

Some functions are nothing more than powerful operators. Just as the + operator adds two numbers, the SUM function totals a series of numbers. And just as the * operator multiplies one number by another, the NPV function finds the net present value of a series of payments.

The rules for using arithmetic operators are the same from one spreadsheet to another, but unfortunately, the use of functions hasn't been standardized. For example, the function that computes the average of a list is called AVG in Lotus 1-2-3 and AVERAGE in Excel. Lotus 1-2-3 functions must be preceded by an at sign (@) to identify them, whereas Excel's functions don't need a special identifier. With both programs, a function is used by typing its name into a cell and then giving the

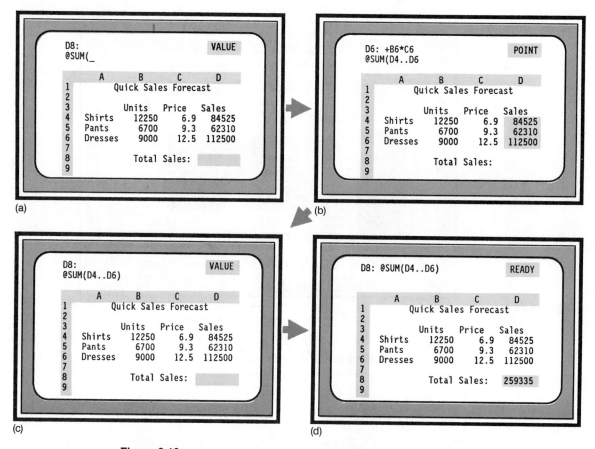

**Figure 9.10**
Using the SUM function to add three cells with Lotus 1-2-3. **(a)** The name of the function is entered in cell D8. **(b)** Arrow keys are used to highlight the range to be added. **(c)** Typing a right parenthesis accepts the highlighted range. **(d)** Pressing [Enter] completes the entry.

function's arguments (if any) inside parentheses. For example, the function that computes the total of the first fifty cells in column D is @SUM(D1..D50) with Lotus 1-2-3 and =SUM(D1:D50) with Excel.

Figure 9.10 illustrates how you can enter the SUM function into a Lotus 1-2-3 formula with the assistance of the arrow keys. An equivalent method is to type the entire formula without using the arrow keys. Most people find "pointing" at the cells with the arrows keys is easier than typing their coordinates.

A formula can consist of a single function or several functions or built-in functions, and arithmetic operations can be mixed in the same formula. Thus functions can run in with the rest of the formula, as in =8+AVERAGE(2,4,6)+12, which is a valid Excel formula equal to 24.

In general, you can put a function in a formula wherever a number would be valid. For example, assume that the sum of the numbers in cells D9..F9 is 20. Then the Lotus 1-2-3 formula 2+(@SUM(D9..F9)/10) is equal to 4. Even nested functions

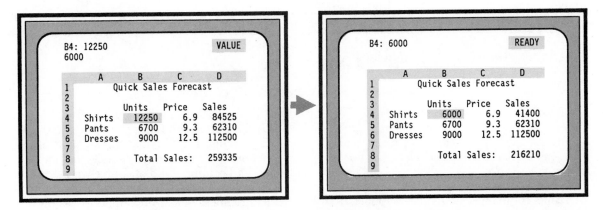

**Figure 9.11**
What-if analysis. Changing the number in cell B4 shows what will happen to sales if fewer shirts are sold.

are acceptable in a formula. For example, @COS(@SUM(A1..A5)) takes the cosine of the sum of the values in cells A1 through A5.

There are many ways to obtain the same mathematical result with spreadsheets. For example, the following two formulas will both find the average value of all non-blank cells in the range from cell B4 to cell B152:

@AVG(B4..B152)
@SUM(B4..B152)/@COUNT(B4..B152)

The first formula assumes the existence of a built-in function that finds the average of a range of cells directly; nearly all spreadsheets have a function like this. The second formula goes the roundabout route of totaling the range of values, then counting the number of nonblank cells, and finally dividing the two numbers to obtain the average.

## Automatic and Manual Recalculation

The advantage of using cell references rather than absolute numbers in formulas becomes apparent when a worksheet is modified. Consider Figure 9.10 again. If the formula in cell D4 is 12250*6.9, no matter what changes are made to cells B4 and C4, the display for cell D4 stays the same. Thus if the number of shirts sold (the value of cell B4) is changed from 12,250 to 6,000, the value of the sales displayed in cell D4 is not changed accordingly. Of course, you could edit the formula in cell D4 to reflect the change, but you can avoid this unnecessary work by writing formulas with cell references instead of absolute numbers. Then, whenever the value in a cell is entered or modified, every formula in the worksheet is automatically recalculated.

Most spreadsheets evaluate every formula in the worksheet whenever any entry is changed; this is called **automatic recalculation**. For example, Figure 9.11 shows how the sales for shirts (cell D4) and the total sales (D8) are recalculated when the

# A Word About . . . *Spreadsheet Products*

*Unlike other markets for personal computer software, which have become segmented into different levels of capabilities to accommodate users' varying expertise, the spreadsheet market has only one tier.*

While companies will often support two or three word processing programs for different levels of users, for example, most companies have standardized on a single spreadsheet program—often Lotus Development Corp.'s 1-2-3—for all their spreadsheet users.

But does the spreadsheet market need to become segmented? Should there be one set of spreadsheets for the bulk of users who require relatively few functions and another set for accountants and MBAs? It depends on who you ask.

"I think we'll see more software with two tiers, one tier for the guy who does basic functions, and doesn't have the master's degree needed to run every function of the really powerful programs, and one tier for the guy who needs all 7,000 functions available on the program," said Rick Richardson, national director of microcomputer technology at New York-based Arthur Young.

"This means that the aim of the MIS manager is to find the software with both tiers, one in which the files from one tier can be used in another. Spreadsheets are a natural for that. So manufacturers have two choices: They can either produce two products that share the same files, or one product that appeals to all users. Corporate buyers want the latter," Richardson said.

Seafirst Bank, in Seattle, Washington, currently uses Microsoft Corp.'s Excel and Multiplan spreadsheet programs for its 2,100 Macintosh computers and Lotus 1-2-3 for its 200 IBM PCs. "We use Multiplan at the low end of the functionality scale for people who just rack up rows and columns, and of course we use Excel, which has gotten rave reviews for its tremendous richness and functionality," said Tim Turnpaugh, senior vice president of technology services at the bank. "In my opinion, Excel is to the Macintosh what 1-2-3 became to the IBM PC."

When asked what criteria he used in his decision to purchase Excel, Turnpaugh explained, "We were clearly looking for functionality, and our preference was to have no more varieties around than we had to. So for the PCs and the Macs we were looking for something from a well-established vendor, good support, someone who can deal with large corporations, and of course price and economics. We try to pick the package with the best price/performance, which is really the name of the game. We keep Multiplan around for people who don't need much."

But many people believe that Lotus 1-2-3 already satisfies the needs of users at both ends of the spectrum. Paul Romesburg, for example, standardized on Lotus 1-2-3 three years ago at the Barnett Bank, based in Fort Myers, Florida. As assistant vice president of credit and administration, Romesburg teaches 1-2-3 to people at the bank.

"We don't teach people about computers, we teach them about 1-2-3. I bring in people who know nothing about computers, and in eight weeks we have them writing macros. That's the nice thing about Lotus, it allows you to rise to your own level," Romesburg said.

Source: Rochelle Garner, *Infoworld*, 10 November 1986, p. 51.

number of shirts (B4) is changed. Spreadsheets encourage people to experiment with different assumptions—known as **what-if analysis**—because it is fun to see the effects of a change ripple across the numbers in the window.

A worksheet can have hundreds or thousands of formulas. Evaluating all the formulas takes time, especially if some of the formulas involve heavy-duty calculations, such as logarithms or statistical functions. If the worksheet is large and complicated, it can take five or ten minutes to complete the job. Obviously, this is too long to wait between making entries. Setting the spreadsheet to manual recalculation avoids these delays. With **manual recalculation,** formulas are evaluated only when you give the command to recalculate. In Lotus 1-2-3, this command is given by pressing function key [F9]. In Excel, you can select the Calculate Now command from the Options menu.

## REVISING, REARRANGING, AND COPYING

When you first enter data into a small worksheet, the cycle of repeatedly marking the active cell and typing an entry works well enough. Although theoretically possible to use this method to "copy" entries—by retyping them into other cells—it is faster and more accurate to use the spreadsheet's copy command. And when it becomes necessary to rearrange information already in the worksheet, you will find the spreadsheet provides efficient methods of moving information.

These commands make it possible to redesign the layout of the worksheet by changing the order that entries appear in. Within limits, this lets you divide the construction of a worksheet into two phases. In the first phase, you concentrate on entering data and building formulas until the computations have been completed. In the second phase, you rearrange everything, enter additional labels, and adjust the worksheet's format rules until the visual layout is appropriate for a report.

The procedure for copying entries is basically the same as that for moving them, but copying is used for a different purpose. Generally, you move entries to revise the worksheet, and you use copy commands to fill out the worksheet quickly. Copy commands are a real time-saver when you are constructing worksheets: A single copy command can duplicate a row of formulas to complete the entries for an entire table.

Spreadsheets use two fundamentally different ways of moving information: inserting or deleting and cutting and pasting. When you insert or delete an area, the cells below or to the right of the area are shifted to new locations. With cut-and-paste techniques, you can move or copy information without shifting other cells around. Both methods have pitfalls you need to avoid, so understanding them clearly and using them correctly are essential.

### Inserting and Deleting

One of the most common revisions to a worksheet is adding or removing a line item from a list. Perhaps a new part number needs to be added to an inventory status report or a student needs to be dropped from a class grade worksheet. With Lotus

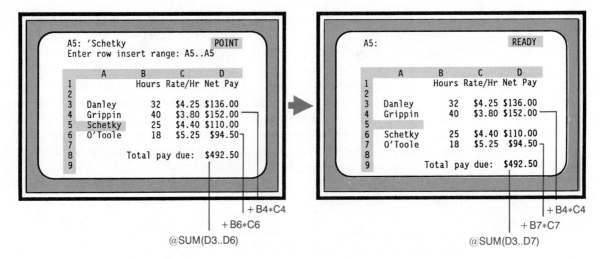

**Figure 9.12**
**(a)** After selecting the Worksheet-Insert-Row command, Lotus 1-2-3 asks which rows should be inserted. **(b)** Pressing [Enter] at this point inserts a new row 5.

1-2-3, the easiest way to perform these operations is to insert or delete entire rows or columns.

When you insert a new row, all the following rows are moved toward the bottom of the worksheet to make room for the new blank row. When you add a column, the following columns are shifted to the right, creating a blank column. Therefore, throwing away old information to make room for new information isn't necessary.

Inserting rows or columns has another important effect: All the formulas in the worksheet are automatically adjusted to refer to the correct entries *even though the entries may now be in new cell locations*. Study Figure 9.12 to see what the effect of inserting a new row 5 is on the worksheet's formulas. When the entries in row 6 are shifted to row 7, the spreadsheet automatically changes all cell references from row 6 to 7. The references to cells B4, C4, and D4 are not changed because inserting the new row did not affect row 4.

Similarly, whenever a row or column is deleted, the spreadsheet attempts to adjust the remaining formulas to refer to the correct entries. For example, if column F is deleted, the formula @AVG(A12..S12) will be changed to @AVG(A12..R12).

Deleting an area of a worksheet can have an unexpected side effect if formulas elsewhere in the worksheet contain references to the deleted entries. Such a formula is rendered invalid because it refers to an entry that no longer exists. For example, in Figure 9.13, the formula that calculates the total payroll due is rendered invalid when one of the rows that the formula is based on is deleted. When a formula is invalid for this reason, the worksheet window displays a terse error message, such as ERR, @ERROR, or #REF!.

When you insert a row with Lotus 1-2-3, you begin by selecting the Worksheet-Insert-Row command from the menu bars. Only after you have made these selections does Lotus 1-2-3 allow you to choose which rows to insert. These steps are

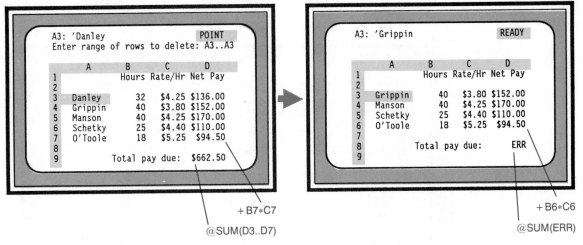

```
A3: 'Danley                    POINT          A3: 'Grippin                   READY
Enter range of rows to delete: A3..A3

        A      B     C      D                         A      B     C      D
1            Hours Rate/Hr Net Pay            1            Hours Rate/Hr Net Pay
2                                             2
3   Danley    32   $4.25 $136.00              3   Grippin   40   $3.80 $152.00
4   Grippin   40   $3.80 $152.00              4   Manson    40   $4.25 $170.00
5   Manson    40   $4.25 $170.00              5   Schetky   25   $4.40 $110.00
6   Schetky   25   $4.40 $110.00              6   O'Toole   18   $5.25  $94.50
7   O'Toole   18   $5.25  $94.50              7
8                                             8         Total pay due:      ERR
9         Total pay due:  $662.50             9
```

                                    +B7*C7                              +B6*C6

                              @SUM(D3..D7)                          @SUM(ERR)

**Figure 9.13**
When row 3 is deleted from the worksheet, the formula for the total payroll becomes invalid because the formula referred to row 3.

---

reversed when you use Excel. Before you can insert, rearrange, or format part of an Excel worksheet, you must select the area to be affected. Then you choose a command to manipulate the area. For example, to insert a new row 6, you click the number 6 in the worksheet border as shown in the top screen of Figure 9.14. This selects the entire row and marks it with inverse video. Then when you select the Insert command from the Edit menu, the new row is inserted.

This difference between Lotus 1-2-3 and Excel is consistent. Lotus 1-2-3 always makes you wait until the end of a command to select part of the worksheet; Excel always makes you select first. Neither method is clearly superior. However, because Excel leaves the selection highlighted when a command is completed, its approach can save time when several operations must be done to the same area.

How Excel adjusted the two formulas in Figure 9.14 is worth examining. In the top screen, both formulas total the values in rows 5 through 11. In the bottom screen, the formulas are no longer equivalent: The SUM function still totals the whole column, but the other formula lacks a reference to the new row containing cell C6. What effect will this have on the accuracy of the worksheet if the new row is filled in with figures for payroll deductions? Notice how easily this hidden problem crept into the worksheet. This example shows formulas with functions are more adaptable and reliable than "equivalent" formulas without functions. It also illustrates that no worksheet should be trusted until thoroughly tested.

Deleting a row or column removes unwanted material from the worksheet, but deleting entire rows or columns can cause unwanted side effects. For example, suppose a worksheet filled with financial information has an income statement in the area bounded by cells A1 and F50 and a balance sheet in the range H1..Z50. Deleting a row removes the *entire* row from the worksheet. This means the seemingly innocent operation of deleting a line from the income statement will also remove material from the balance sheet.

With Excel, you can usually sidestep this sort of problem by inserting a partial row or column of blank cells. Doing this is simple. First you mark off an area the

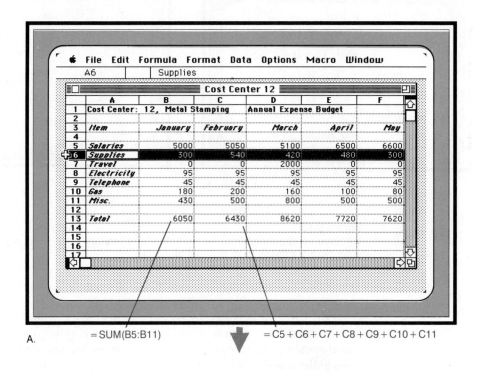

A.　= SUM(B5:B11)　　= C5 + C6 + C7 + C8 + C9 + C10 + C11

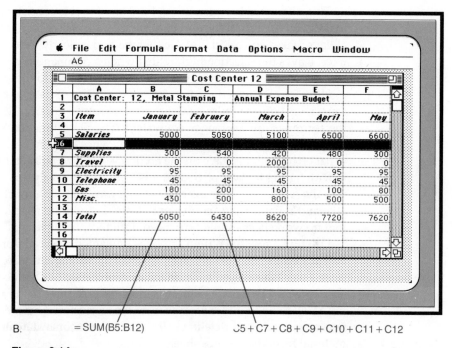

B.　= SUM(B5:B12)　　C5 + C7 + C8 + C9 + C10 + C11 + C12

**Figure 9.14**
Inserting a new row with Excel. **(a)** The first step is to click on the row number you want to insert. **(b)** To insert the row, you select the Insert command from the Edit menu.

**Figure 9.15**
Adding a partial row
to an Excel
worksheet

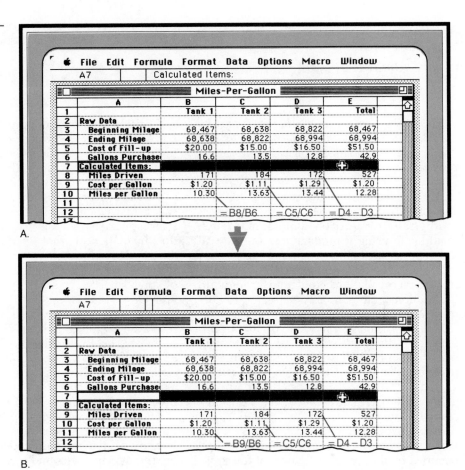

size you would like to have added to the worksheet by selecting it with the mouse. You can select a partial row, as in Figure 9.15, a partial column, or even a range containing many rows and columns. Then you select the Insert command from the Edit menu, which presents a dialog box asking you to choose whether to shift existing cells down or to the right. Your choice tells Excel how to open up a hole for the new cells. For example, if you want to insert a partial row without affecting other cells on that row, you would choose to shift existing cells down. When you complete the dialog box, Excel inserts the same number of cells as you selected before beginning the command. If you want to delete an area from the worksheet, you use the same procedure except you select the Delete command from the Edit menu.

## Erasing

Every spreadsheet has a command for erasing a range of cells. This command lets you quickly clear out a region without shifting other cells in the worksheet to fill up the hole.

# A Word About . . . Finding Spreadsheet Errors

*Spreadsheet programs are reliable, but how much should you trust the worksheets you develop? Experienced spreadsheet users know an untested worksheet is a recipe for disaster.*

One of the strongest selling points of today's spreadsheet software is ease of use. Any user, vendors claim, can learn one almost immediately and begin using it productively. But now a hidden downside to this benefit may be emerging. As millions of computerized models and spreadsheet calculations proliferate throughout organizations, human errors seem to be proliferating along with them.

Donald N. Roark, president of Intelligent Machines Training in Sherman Oaks, California, says, "I can immediately think of 20 or 30 cases [in various companies] where major decisions were based on spreadsheets that later turned out to contain errors. Some of the decisions proved disastrous."

Anyone who uses a spreadsheet can all too clearly imagine the specter of human errors magnified by the speed and power of the computer. An error—leaving out a line item or perhaps assigning the wrong formula to a cell—is passed on from manager to manager until the tainted data reaches the chief executive officer.

"You can get the same errors if you handwrite the spreadsheet," protests Jeff Ehrlich, manager of product technology for General Electric Co's Information Systems Division. "It's nothing new, and it's not tied to the spreadsheets themselves."

"People using PCs just have to relearn the dangers that mainframe people learned 20 years ago," he says. "There will be some of these problems until they do."

Dale Christensen, product manager for Microsoft Corp.'s Multiplan spreadsheet, also advises caution. "A spreadsheet is a really complex analytical tool," he says, "and, as with any tool, you can make errors."

Christensen identifies "a point on any large spreadsheet where you lose control." Furthermore, he insists, "Anyone who says they understand a spreadsheet more than 100-times-100 cells is fooling themselves."

Part of the problem, according to Christensen, is that when people hand in the results of their spreadsheets, they do not include the documentation of what went into the models. "We tend to be much more careful about reviewing the logic of programmed applications than of spreadsheets," he says. "Nobody does code reviews of spreadsheets."

One attempt to catch these errors before they reach the bottom line is an auditing program such as The Spreadsheet Auditor and The Spreadsheet Analyst from Cambridge Software Collaborative. These packages offer features akin to the spell checkers that come with word processing software.

The auditing packages operate on the files produced by spreadsheet software, performing a variety of logic and parameter checks, displaying cell dependencies and formulas and checking range references and other potential problems.

Tim Gustafson, product manager for The Spreadsheet Auditor, cites several studies that show more than half of all spreadsheets contain errors. "Virtually everyone in the market admits this," he says. But he claims most errors are common, simple mistakes an auditing program can catch.

"One common error is copying a formula across a row and later typing a number on top of one formula cell. Now, when you change data, that value remains fixed," Gustafson says. "A spreadsheet auditor lets users highlight all the formulas copied from an original formula. If one cell in the row is not highlighted, users can tell the pattern has been interrupted.

"Other common errors are to reference blank cells in a formula or to specify only part of a full range," Gustafson declares. "Auditing software sees these kinds of errors and reports them, so the user can verify that is what he wants or can fix the mistake before it creates a problem."

While these features may help spreadsheet error checking, some users are unconvinced that auditing packages offer the complete solution.

"Who says the auditing software is right?" asks Jeff Ehrlick, manager of product technology for General Electric Co's Information Systems Division. "The ultimate responsibility stays with the person delivering the answers. If the auditor helps them, it's all to the good. But there is as much danger with the auditor as without it, because it can give users a false sense of security."

James A. Wick, director of applications planning for Lockheed Corp., points out, "If the errors are a result of a defect in the design of the model itself—as they commonly are—it is not very likely that the audit program will catch them. It would be pretty tough to picture an artificial capability to offset an individual's thought process that is flawed or mistaken in its assumptions."

Even without spreadsheet auditing features, users can employ some simple techniques to validate their spreadsheet results. For example, more users try a check for reasonableness. They enter fairly simple numbers and perhaps vary them in predictable ways to check the results.

A variation on this is to use old numbers, in which the results are already known, and check that the new spreadsheet provides the same answers.

Another error checking technique is cross-footing—adding rows and columns that should balance out and comparing answers to make sure they do. A more elaborate approach is to perform calculations two ways in a spreadsheet and compare the answers for agreement.

Source: Robert Moskowitz, *ComputerWorld*, 4 May 1987, pp. 35–40.

If you use Lotus 1-2-3, be sure to use the Range-Erase command to erase an area. Don't select the nearby Worksheet-Erase command (which erases the entire worksheet from memory!) unless you want to throw everything away and start with a fresh worksheet.

To erase an area with Excel, you begin (as always) by selecting the area with the mouse. Then you choose the Clear command from the Edit menu, producing a dialog box that gives you three choices of what to clear: All, Formats, or Formulas. If you choose All, everything in the area is erased. You choose Formats if you want to retain the area's values and formulas but want their on-screen appearance to revert to the default format. Choosing Formulas removes the area's values and formulas without affecting the format rules attached to the area's cells. After the area is erased, you can retrieve the erased information by selecting the Undo command.

Lotus 1-2-3 doesn't have an Undo command, so be cautious whenever you erase, delete, or move data. If you are the least bit unsure of how to do one of these operations, save a copy of the worksheet on disk before you experiment. That way, if you destroy the worksheet in memory, you can load another copy from disk.

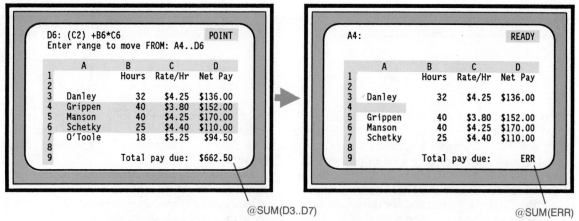

```
D6: (C2) +B6*C6                POINT          A4:                         READY
Enter range to move FROM: A4..D6

         A       B      C       D                     A       B      C       D
1               Hours  Rate/Hr Net Pay      1                Hours  Rate/Hr Net Pay
2                                            2
3  Danley       32     $4.25   $136.00       3   Danley       32     $4.25   $136.00
4  Grippen      40     $3.80   $152.00       4
5  Manson       40     $4.25   $170.00       5   Grippen      40     $3.80   $152.00
6  Schetky      25     $4.40   $110.00       6   Manson       40     $4.25   $170.00
7  O'Toole      18     $5.25   $94.50        7   Schetky      25     $4.40   $110.00
8                                            8
9              Total pay due:   $662.50      9              Total pay due:    ERR
```

@SUM(D3..D7)                                                          @SUM(ERR)

**Figure 9.16**
Moving the entries in cells A4..D7 to the range whose upper left-hand corner is cell A5

## Cutting and Pasting

For a complex worksheet with many pages of information, you may be forced to move areas just to add new items to a list or place new columns in a report. For example, it may not be possible to insert a new row—or even a partial row—in a worksheet without damaging the organization of other areas.

As you fill out and revise a worksheet, its shape changes, and you may become dissatisfied with its appearance. One part may seem too far from another, or you may want to reposition areas to line them up squarely. Again, these tasks call for moving areas of the worksheet.

With Lotus 1-2-3, you use the Move command from the main menu bar to move entries from the cells in a *source range* and place them in the cells of a *destination range*. Thus the move command removes the entries from a group of cells (leaving a blank area behind) and inserts them in a new location. You can move the entries to a wholly different part of the worksheet, or you can shift them only one row or column. With this command, you can open up room for a new row or column in a localized region without the long-distance side effects of inserting an entire row or column.

The entries you move to the destination range overwrite its previous entries. For example, in Figure 9.16, twelve cells are cut from A4..D6 and pasted in one row down from their previous location. The destination range is A5..D7, but you need to specify only the upper left-hand cell of the destination range, cell A5. This operation opens up a blank line for a new employee between the lines for Danley and Grippen, but it also destroys the payroll information for O'Toole and invalidates the formula for total pay due by erasing the previous entry of cell D7. For the operation to be successful at opening up a new row without side effects, the source range must have a blank line below it; otherwise, it will obliterate useful information when placed back in the worksheet. Moving entries into completely blank areas of the worksheet is safest; Lotus 1-2-3 gives you no warning or recourse when it tosses out the previous contents of the destination range.

**Figure 9.17**
A cut-and-paste
operation

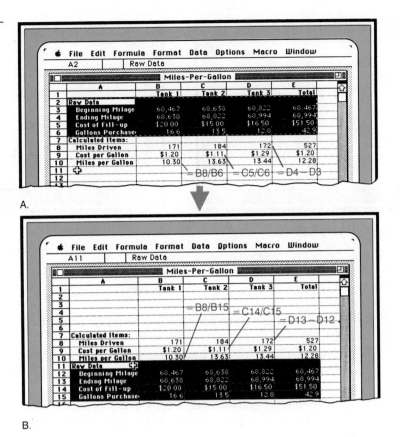

Excel moves areas with a two-step cut-and-paste operation. In the "cut" step, you use the mouse to select the range of cells to be moved and choose the Cut command from the Edit menu. This step outlines the "cut area" with a dotted line, as shown in the top screen of Figure 9.17, but does not actually move it anywhere. In the "paste" step, you tell the spreadsheet where to place the entries by selecting a single cell with the mouse. Then, when you choose Paste from the Edit menu, Excel matches the upper left-hand corner of the cut area with the cell you have selected, and fills the rest of the range down and to the right.

## Copying

The major technical difference between moving and copying entries is when you move entries, the source cells are left blank, but when you copy entries, the source cells remain unchanged. Both methods take existing cell entries and place them in other cells, tossing out whatever the destination cells may have previously held.

The practical difference is more profound. Move commands are usually used to rearrange data. But by copying entries, you can dramatically reduce the number of keystrokes needed to complete most worksheets and decrease the likelihood of hidden errors. Spreadsheets excel at making projections because once a relationship

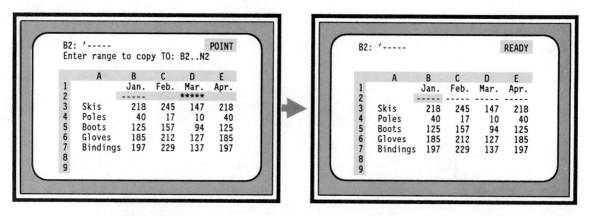

**Figure 9.18**
Copying a label from cell B2 to the cells B2..N2 affects cells C2, D2, and E2 on the screen and cells F2..N2 off the screen's edge.

has been entered for one period, it can be copied across rows or columns to see the effect over time.

Once you have learned how to move entries, you are well on the way to copying them. With Lotus 1-2-3, you begin a copy command by selecting Copy (located next to Move) from the main menu bar; then you fill out the same prompts that apply to moving entries. Excel's copy-and-paste operation is virtually identical to its cut-and-paste operation; you simply select Copy instead of Cut from the Edit menu.

The easiest cells to copy are those that contain only labels or numbers. For example, in Figure 9.18, a cell full of hyphens is copied across a row to emphasize a heading. In this example, the entry from a single cell is copied into a range of cells. The asterisks in cell D2 of the left-hand screen are overwritten by the hyphens. Again, there is no way to recover a cell's previous contents unless the spreadsheet has an Undo command.

Copying formulas is more complicated than copying labels and numbers because you rarely want the spreadsheet to perform *exactly* the same calculation in two different places of the worksheet. Normally, you want a set of similar computations to be done—with appropriate adjustments in the formulas to reflect their new locations. For example, many worksheets have a total column that adds the numbers in earlier columns, as in Figure 9.19. If the formula in row 6 of the total sales column is @SUM(B6..E6), it doesn't make sense to copy this formula unchanged into row 7 or 8 of the total column. In row 7, you want the formula @SUM(B7..M7) so that the formula in row 7 totals the numbers in row 7. Similar changes must be made to the formula as it is copied into succeeding cells down the total column.

To make these changes in the new formulas, you must tell the spreadsheet that the cell references in the source formula are **relative cell references**, which means they should be interpreted *relative* to the formula's current position. With relative cell references, when a formula is copied into a cell two rows down and three columns to the right of its original location, all row numbers in the formula will be

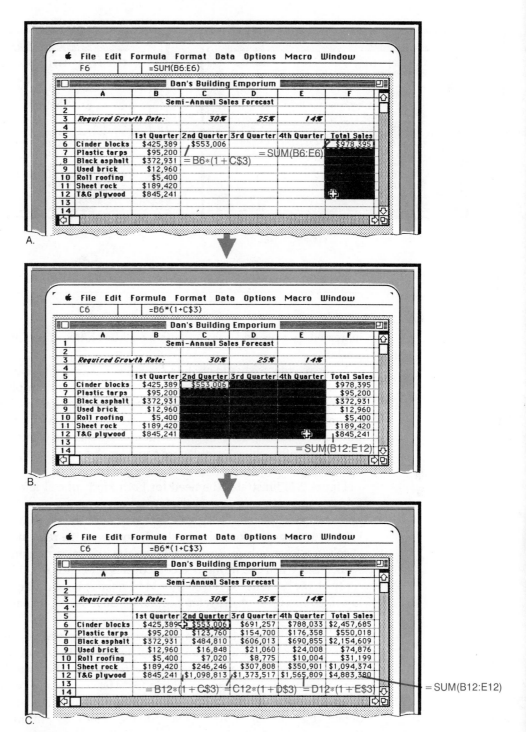

**Figure 9.19**
Completing a worksheet with two copy operations. **(a)** Cell F8 has been placed on the clipboard, and the range F6:F12 is selected. **(b)** Choosing the Paste command from the Edit menu fills out column F. Then cell C6 is copied to the clipboard, and the range C6:E12 is selected. **(c)** Choosing Paste again completes the worksheet.

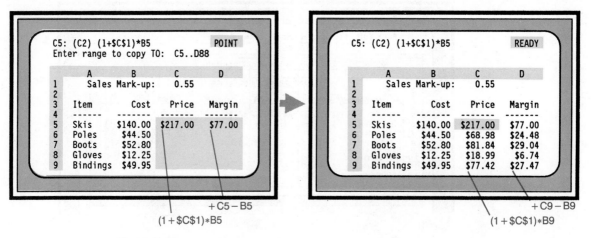

**Figure 9.20**
Copying the formulas in C5..D5 to C5..D88 using both relative and absolute cell references

increased by two, and column letters will be shifted three letters through the alphabet.

Some references should not be adjusted when a formula is copied from one location to another; these are **absolute cell references**. For example, a good way to organize a projection is to place all of its critical assumptions in cells in a well-labeled area of the worksheet. If you are analyzing the cash flow from an apartment complex, these assumptions might include the occupancy rate, inflation rate, and several tax rates. When formulas are copied in this worksheet, references to the cells containing assumptions should not be adjusted.

Figure 9.20 illustrates the need for both kinds of cell references. With a single Copy command, you can copy the formulas in a row range (C5..D5) down a rectangular range (C5..D88), filling an entire region of the worksheet in one operation. When you copy the formula in cell C5, you want the reference to cell C1 to be an absolute reference because the cell contains the sales markup rate for the entire worksheet; when the formula is copied, this reference should not be changed. In contrast, the reference to cell B5 should be relative because it contains the cost of an item for a specific row; this reference should therefore be changed when the formula is copied.

Different spreadsheets distinguish absolute from relative references differently. A few spreadsheets wait until the final step in the Copy command to ask you to choose—reference by reference—whether the parts of the formula should be treated as relative or absolute. Lotus 1-2-3 and Excel lets you label a cell as absolute or relative when you enter a formula. With both programs, cell references are relative by default, but they allow you to override the default by putting dollar signs before the row number and column letter of a cell. For example, the reference to cell C1 in the status line in Figure 9.20 is written $C$1 to indicate it is an absolute cell reference. Similarly, the formula @SUM($B$1..$D$1) will add the contents of cells B1, C1, and D1 regardless of where the formula is copied.

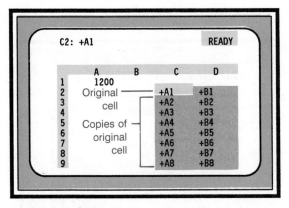

(a) Relative references

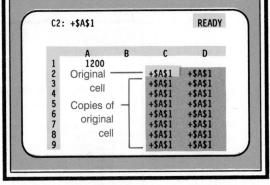

(b) Absolute references

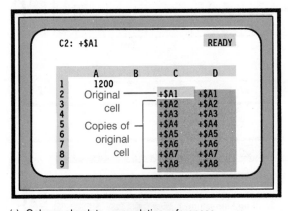

(c) Column-absolute, row-relative references

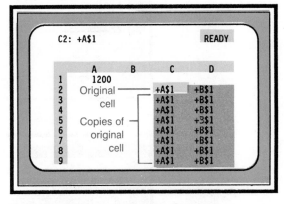

(d) Column-relative, row-absolute references

**Figure 9.21**
The way a formula is copied from one location to another depends on whether it contains relative, absolute, or mixed cell references.

Two dollar signs are needed to specify an absolute cell reference because you can also create **mixed cell references**, which are half absolute and half relative (see Figure 9.21). For example, the formula @SUM($B1..$D1) will be copied without changes if it is copied across a column, but it will read @SUM($B2..$D2) if it is copied into the cell immediately below its original location. Mixed cell references are useful if you have a row full of assumptions for a single type of item, such as the Required Growth Rate shown in row 3 of Figure 9.19. In this situation, any reference to the row number should be absolute, but a reference to the column letter should be relative.

## FORMATTING

The way a spreadsheet displays labels and numbers is determined by format rules stored inside each cell along with the cell's value rule. Format rules change the

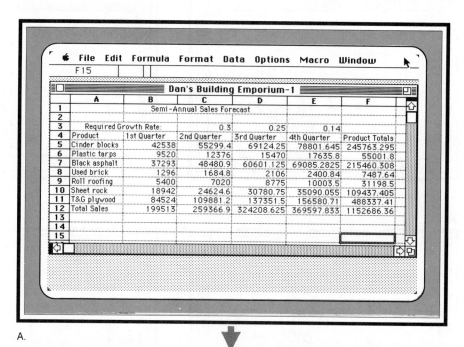

A.

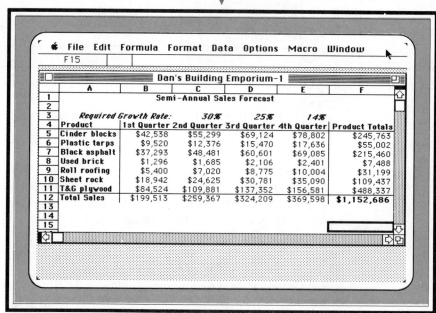

B.

**Figure 9.22**
Two views of the same data. **(a)** An unformatted worksheet: Numbers appear in the default format, labels are left-justified, and all columns have the same width. **(b)** A formatted worksheet: Numbers appear in either the percentage or currency format, column headings are right-justified, columns have varying widths, major items are highlighted with bold or italic type, and solid-line borders divide the worksheet into logical areas.

appearance of the worksheet without actually modifying the worksheet's underlying values. Most spreadsheets let you examine the active cell's format rules by displaying them in the control panel. For example, in Figure 9.20, the status line shows the contents of cell C5 as (C2) (1+$C$1)*B5, but the worksheet displays $217.00 for cell C5. The (C2) portion of the entry is a format rule; it instructs Lotus - 1-2-3 to use *currency format;* that is, to display numbers with a leading dollar sign, commas between thousands, two digits after the decimal point, and parentheses for negative numbers.

Spreadsheets have more commands to create and adjust format rules than any other command category. This emphasis is appropriate; format rules give your worksheets a professional appearance and make them easier to read and use. For example, in Figure 9.22, the worksheets in both screens contain the same formulas and numbers, but the top worksheet has been stripped of format rules, making it quite difficult to interpret. Its headings and totals blend into the background, and its numbers have an inconsistent number of digits past the decimal place.

Format rules come in two major varieties: A **global format rule** affects the entire worksheet, whereas an **individual format rule** applies to a single cell, range, or column. You can think of a global format rule as a special filter that sits between you and the worksheet, sort of like a giant sheet of colored cellophane. But instead of changing colors, global format rules do things like making all the columns wider, rounding all the numbers to the nearest integer, or removing the grid of dots that outlines each cell. Individual format rules are smaller filters that you can place in front of specific areas. They can be used to align column headings with the numbers below them, make certain columns wider, and change specific numbers into percentages.

Early spreadsheets had crude formatting abilities, but each succeeding generation of spreadsheets has had more formatting options. With Lotus 1-2-3, numbers can have commas in the appropriate places, leading dollar signs or trailing percent signs, and a user-specified number of digits after the decimal point. To apply format rules to cells with Lotus 1-2-3, you begin by selecting the format rule you want from the menu bar system. For example, you would choose the menu bar sequence RANGE-FORMAT-FIXED-0 to cause numbers to appear as integers that do not have embedded commas. You complete the command by pointing out the area to be affected and pressing [Enter]. The procedure for giving a global format rule is similar except you begin the command sequence by selecting WORKSHEET, and you don't need to select the area to be affected at the end of the command.

Because global format rules affect the entire worksheet, changing the global column-width setting simultaneously adjusts the width of all columns. An individual format rule overrides a global format rule. Thus changing the global column-width setting will not affect a column that has been given its own individual format rule with a previous command. If a worksheet has many narrow columns for numbers and a few wider columns for labels, the quickest way to set up the worksheet is to use a global command to make all the columns narrow, and then widen the label columns with individual column-width commands.

Some spreadsheets have a three-level hierarchy for format settings. For example, you might use the integer format (123) as the global setting for numbers, the

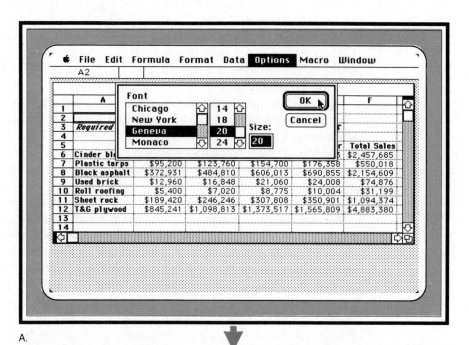

A.

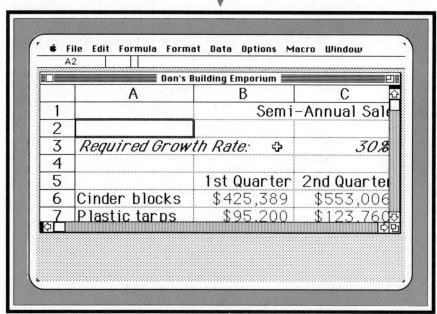

B.

**Figure 9.23**
Changing the font of an Excel worksheet causes it to look different on-screen and on paper.

**Figure 9.24**
Giving a user-
defined format rule
to the cells in
column B

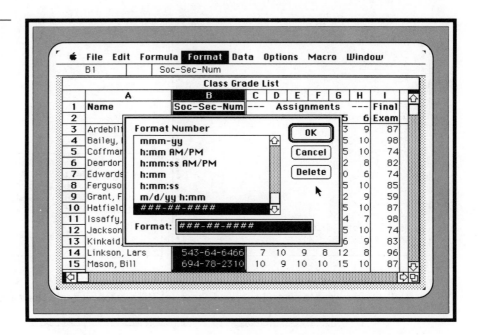

currency format ($123.45) as the setting for column D, and the general format (123.45) as the setting for cell D4. Individual cell settings override column or row settings, which in turn, override the global setting.

Excel's global format rules are listed on the Options menu. For example, selecting Font from the Options menu leads to the dialog box shown in the top screen of Figure 9.23. Other global format rules determine whether the worksheet will have visible grid lines, whether the row and column borders will be displayed, and whether the worksheet will display formulas in the cells instead of the values they produce.

Excel is unusual because it lets you create your own numeric formats. For example, you might want all numbers in column B to look like social security numbers by inserting hyphens at the appropriate places. This is not a standard Excel format, but you can easily create a new format for just this purpose. As always with Excel, the first step is selecting the area to be affected. In this case, it is enough to click on the label for column B in the window's border, causing the entire column to appear in inverse video. Then when you choose FORMAT-NUMBER from the pull-down menu system, Excel displays a dialog box containing a list of predefined number formats and an entry line that you can use to construct your own format (see Figure 9.24). Once you create a new format, such as ###-##-####, it becomes part of the Excel format list and can be used to determine how numbers appear on the screen.

Spreadsheets have definite formatting limitations. Occasionally, you will be unable to adjust the worksheet to look exactly as you want. Perhaps a number should appear centered in its cell, but the spreadsheet's manual doesn't list an option for centering numbers. You might try entering the number into the worksheet as a label, but then you can't refer to it in formulas. Or suppose you want the columns in a

```
B1:  "Units
C1:  "Price
D1:  "Sales
A2:  'Shirts
B2:  (,0) 12250
C2:  (C2) 6.9
D2:  (C0) + B2*C2
A3:  'Pants
B3:  (,0) 6700
C3:  (C2) 9.3
D3:  (C0) + B3*C3
A4:  'Dresses
B4:  (,0) 9000
C4:  (C2) 12.5
D4:  (C0) + B4*C4
B6:  '     Total Sales:
D6:  (C0) @SUM(D2..D4)
```

```
             Units    Price    Sales
Shirts      12,250    $6.90    $84,525
Pants        6,700    $9.30    $62,310
Dresses      9,000   $12.50   $112,500

                     Total Sales: $259,335
```

**Figure 9.25**
Two ways to print a Lotus worksheet. **(a)** The worksheet printed as it is stored in memory.
**(b)** The worksheet printed as it looks on the screen.

report to be staggered on the page. Although manuals rarely mention this limitation, in all spreadsheets, a column must have the same width from the top to the bottom of the worksheet. This poses a dilemma when you lay out a worksheet: Should columns be made wide enough to display their widest entry, or should some entries be truncated (or rewritten) in the interest of saving space?

Often, it is best to live with the formatting limitations and accept a report that isn't laid out character for character the way you would design it by hand. If every character must be in exactly the right spot, it may be necessary to transfer the information to a word processor so that editing can proceed without the limitations inherent in a cellular worksheet.

## PRINTING

You can print a report at any time during a spreadsheet session. Spreadsheet programs give you a great deal of control over the layout and appearance of the report by offering several print options. But usually the first step is to insert format rules into the worksheet to make it look good on the screen. Unless you choose special print options, the worksheet's cells will appear in the report just as they appear in the worksheet window.

Here are some typical choices you can make to determine how the report is formatted.

- Which cells are to be printed? You specify the range of cells to be printed by giving the upper left-hand and lower right-hand corners of the range.
- Should the cells be printed as they appear in the display or as they are stored in memory? Figure 9.25 shows both types of report. Printing the cells as they

**Figure 9.26**
This Page Setup
dialog box lets you
control where the
worksheet is printed
on the page, how
large the type is,
what the page
header and footer
are, and whether
the worksheet is
printed with a bor-
der labeling the
rows and columns.

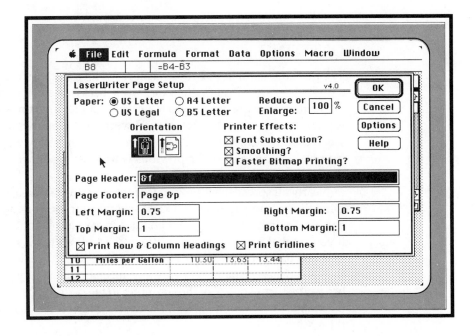

are stored in memory allows the formulas to be audited for accuracy, but normally reports are printed to show cells as they appear in the worksheet window.

- How big is the page, and where are the margins on the page? The spreadsheet will automatically split the region of the worksheet to be printed into smaller units, each of which fits on a single page. This is called **pagination**. To paginate correctly, the spreadsheet must know the length and width of the paper and the margin settings of each page (see Figure 9.26). Usually there is an option to suppress page breaks so that a model prints out in one continuous strip. Some programs allow the model to be printed sideways (in landscape mode) so that more columns can fit on one page.

- What headers or footers should be printed on each page? These help identify the model and often include the page number, the worksheet's filename, and the date.

- What special characters should be sent to the printer before printing the report? These characters, or *printer setup string*, allow the user to select special printer features. For example, the printer setup string might cause the report to be printed with compressed characters, allowing a 132-column report to fit on an 8 1/2-inch wide piece of paper.

- Should the report have a border identifying the rows and columns of the work-sheet? When you create and troubleshoot a model, it is probably best to print reports with borders, but the final report will look cleaner without borders.

- Should the report be "printed" to a disk rather than on paper? This creates a file usable by other programs and is the logical choice if you want to include some of the worksheet in a word processing document.

# LOADING, SAVING, AND QUITTING

The first command in most spreadsheet sessions loads an existing worksheet from a disk. You can edit more than one worksheet in a session, but few spreadsheets allow more than one worksheet to be active at the same time. Excel is a notable exception; it allows you to open several worksheet windows and to have a different worksheet in each. But with most programs, when a new worksheet is loaded into memory, the contents of the previous worksheet are either erased or merged with the contents of the new worksheet.

Nearly all spreadsheet programs store the active worksheet in memory. Keep in mind that memory is volatile. To lose several hours of work because of a power outage is extremely discouraging. Periodically save a copy of the worksheet on a disk if you are making useful modifications or additions to it.

If you have made changes in the worksheet that have not been saved on a disk, the spreadsheet usually will give you a final opportunity to save the worksheet before it returns control of the computer to the operating system. Thus the last two commands in a session are likely to save the revised worksheet on a disk and end the session.

## Summary

Spreadsheets manipulate information by storing it in a large grid of cells. Most of the time spent working with a spreadsheet is spent moving the active-cell marker around the screen, entering data to be stored in a cell, and giving commands to change the formatting information stored in cells. While you are working with a spreadsheet, the screen will display a control panel, which helps you use the program and allows you to see entries as they are stored in memory, and a worksheet window, which shows you a processed version of the worksheet's contents.

Each cell of the worksheet stores a number, label, or formula; many also store some formatting information. The formulas can perform arithmetic operations on three types of data: absolute numbers, cell references, and built-in functions, which are special tools that perform a specific type of processing, such as adding a column of numbers or computing the standard deviation of a range of values.

Many spreadsheet programs still use command systems that hark back to the original VisiCalc program: Commands are given by typing a slash (/) and then making selections from menu bars and responding to questions. More recently developed programs tend to use pull-down menus to issue commands. Regardless of whether menu bars or pull-down menus are used, several selections are necessary to complete most commands. Spreadsheets have many commands that can help you edit cells and rearrange the worksheet. These commands allow you to redesign the worksheet without entering information into the worksheet a second time.

You can increase the power of both functions and commands by specifying a range of cells to be processed. This allows one operation to affect an entire region of the worksheet.

Spreadsheets vary widely in their ability to format and print reports. Most format rules can be given as either global rules, which affect the entire worksheet, or individual rules, which affect only one cell or column. Important format settings include those that determine the width of columns and how numbers and text are formatted. The crudest spreadsheets do little more than dump the contents of the screen to the printer; the best systems generate good-looking reports with page breaks and page headers.

You do not need prior experience with a computer to use a spreadsheet, but some training and study are required. A general rule of thumb is that it takes forty hours of reading, practice, experimentation, and mistakes before a person feels proficient with most of the advanced features of a spreadsheet, though it shouldn't take more than an hour or two to begin building simple models. Some spreadsheets are easier to master than others either because they have fewer features or because they are better designed.

## Key Terms

| | |
|---|---|
| absolute cell reference | menu bar |
| active cell | mixed cell references |
| automatic recalculation | pagination |
| cell | paging |
| control panel | range |
| format rule | relative cell references |
| formula | spreadsheet |
| function | status line |
| global format rule | value rule |
| individual format rule | what-if analysis |
| label | worksheet |
| manual recalculation | |

## Discussion Questions

1. Is using a spreadsheet more like programming the computer or like using a word processor?

2. What types of tasks would a manufacturing accountant use a spreadsheet for? A personnel manager? A civil engineer? Would their needs for computational support differ?

3. How should the cells in a worksheet be labeled? Why?

4. What information would be useful in the control panel? Would the time of day be useful? The number of entries made in a session?

5. Why do spreadsheets have several modes of operation? Would spreadsheets be easier to use if they had more modes? What additional modes might there be?

6. This chapter gave examples of several types of menu bars. Which would be easiest for a beginner? Which quickest for the expert?

7. What could a three-dimensional worksheet do that a two-dimensional worksheet could not do conveniently?

8. Suppose you are working with information in three separate areas of a worksheet. How should these areas be positioned in the worksheet so that inserting or deleting rows or columns in any one of the areas will not disturb the other two areas?

## Exercises

1. Refer to the illustration of SuperCalc in photograph 41 of Window 5. Identify which cells contain labels, numbers, and formulas. Write the formulas necessary to complete the worksheet. Then try entering the worksheet to see if your solution works.

2. Determine the maximum number of rows and columns in your spreadsheet program. How much memory would it take to fill each cell with the word *overflow*?

3. Give formulas for each of the following:
   a. Add cells A1, B2, C3, and D4.
   b. Multiply the sum of the first twenty columns of row 6 by the sum of the first ninety rows in column 6.
   c. Add the average of columns 3, 4, 7, and 9. Assume the first 120 rows of each column contain useful information.

4. Suppose the formula in cell A4 is 13+B2 and in cell D5 is 6*B2. If the value in cell B2 is 3, what are the values of cells A4 and D5? Find the new values if the formula in cell D5 is 6*A4.

5. You are a stockbroker and the following table presents the portfolio of one of your clients:

| Stock | No. of Shares | Purchase Price (per share) | Market Price (per share) |
|---|---|---|---|
| Control Datum | 200 | $53.50 | $40.00 |
| Dow James | 350 | $8.75 | $12.125 |
| Bandon Ltd. | 100 | $98.00 | $59.25 |
| Peavy Inc. | 2000 | $5.25 | $4.375 |

a. Use a spreadsheet to generate a report that shows the information in this table. Provide columns for the market value for each stock and the percentage of gain or loss for each stock. Include a line that shows the total market value of the portfolio and the total gain or loss for the portfolio.

    *b.* Experiment with the model to find out what market price of Dow James would make the current market value of the entire portfolio equal to its purchase price.

6. Discover what happens in a MOVE or COPY command when the source is larger than the destination and when the source is smaller than the destination.

7. Assume your worksheet contains the names of the fifty states in cells B2 to B51, their populations in cells C2 to C51, and their areas in cells E2 to E51. Give the commands and formulas to place each state's percentage of the total population in cells D2 to D51 and each state's percentage of the total area in cells F2 to F51.

# Advanced Spreadsheet Processing

In Chapter 9, we described the mechanics of solving common mathematical problems with a spreadsheet. In this chapter we cover the advanced features necessary to implement more sophisticated applications. For simple projections or one-shot calculations, you usually can get by without the features described here, but for complex worksheets or for applications that require many people to interact with the worksheet, they are essential. With the features described in this chapter, you can

- Protect some cells from being accidentally modified
- Hide parts of the worksheet from view and require a password be given before they can be seen or modified
- Use part of the worksheet as a form that guides the user through the process of entering data
- Keep title lines or columns frozen in one place on the screen when the rest of the worksheet is scrolled

- Divide the display window into panes that look into separate areas of the worksheet
- Alter the order the spreadsheet recalculates formulas in
- Consolidate information from several worksheets
- Have the current date loaded into a cell each time the worksheet is recalculated or perform calculations on dates stored in cells
- Build tables of information into the worksheet and include formulas that "look up" the appropriate entry in the table
- Store commands so that a long series of them can be implemented by a single keystroke

Learning about these features is a prerequisite to becoming adept at solving problems with a spreadsheet.

## BUILDING TEMPLATES

Spreadsheets reduce the need for computer programmers because people who do not understand programming languages can develop spreadsheet applications. Still, there is often a reason for having a professional design the worksheet: One knowledgeable professional can design a high-quality solution for many users. Here are some examples.

- A financial manager might design a worksheet to be used by the managers of a firm's departments. The worksheet could help each manager complete a detailed budget consistent with the firm's budget policies.
- An industrial engineer might design a worksheet that predicts for other engineers the size of motor required to accelerate a given mass through a specified distance in a fixed time while being affected by friction and inertia.

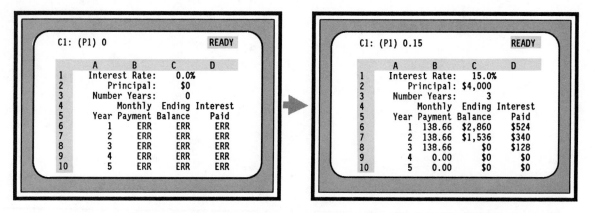

```
C1: (P1) 0                    READY            C1: (P1) 0.15                   READY

         A      B      C     D                         A      B      C     D
  1  Interest Rate:    0.0%                      1  Interest Rate:   15.0%
  2      Principal:     $0                       2      Principal: $4,000
  3  Number Years:       0                       3  Number Years:      3
  4         Monthly Ending Interest              4         Monthly Ending Interest
  5  Year Payment Balance   Paid                 5  Year Payment Balance   Paid
  6    1     ERR    ERR     ERR                   6    1  138.66 $2,860    $524
  7    2     ERR    ERR     ERR                   7    2  138.66 $1,536    $340
  8    3     ERR    ERR     ERR                   8    3  138.66    $0     $128
  9    4     ERR    ERR     ERR                   9    4    0.00    $0      $0
 10    5     ERR    ERR     ERR                  10    5    0.00    $0      $0
```

**Figure 10.1**
The left screen contains an empty template. In the right screen, the template has been completed by filling in the values for cells C1 through C3.

- A tax accountant might design a worksheet to help customers predict the effects of alternative tax strategies.
- A construction expert might design a worksheet to help clerks prepare estimates of construction costs based on the amount of materials required for a job.

In each example, the application is developed by one person who is knowledgeable about both the spreadsheet and the task to be done and who tries to make the worksheet useful to people who know little about either the spreadsheet or the necessary calculations. This usefulness is achieved by creating a worksheet containing the labels that identify the items in the application and the formulas that perform the calculations but having blank cells where the data for the application will go. A half-completed worksheet like this is a **template** because it contains rules that guide how the data is to be processed, but it does not contain the data.

Figure 10.1 illustrates the difference between a template and a completed worksheet. The template in the left screen of Figure 10.1 contains the labels and formulas needed to calculate the monthly payments, year-end balances, and interest on a loan. All the calculated cells in the template display the error message ERR because the template does not include data for the interest rate, the principal, or number of years the loan will run. In the right screen of Figure 10.1, the template has been completed by typing these numbers in cells C1 through C3. A loan officer in a bank could use a more detailed version of this template to generate a customized loan report for each new client.

A good template guides the user in entering data and prevents the user from modifying the template's formulas. It is bullet proof, impervious to the numerous errors made by beginners. Many methods are used to construct bullet-proof templates, including changing the widths of columns, protecting some of the worksheet's cells from modification, entering processing commands known as *programmable macros* into cells, and creating forms that help guide data entry.

## Changing Column Widths

Columns naturally need different widths because they are used for different types of information. In most worksheets, the leftmost column identifies the contents of the rows with labels such as names, items for sale, or months of the year. These labels nearly always require more room than the numbers in the following columns. For example, a list of names requires a column approximately twenty characters wide, but the scores from a midterm exam fit in a column only four characters wide.

The number of characters that a single cell can contain varies from one spreadsheet to the next, but a typical number is around 250—many more characters than the usual column width. Thus you can type a long label into any cell without regard to the cell's column width. But keep in mind that what a spreadsheet displays as a cell's contents and what is stored in memory may differ. Early spreadsheets truncated labels in the display, showing only the portion that fits inside the cells in the worksheet window.

Current spreadsheets allow a long label to extend past the right edge of its cell if the cell to the right is empty. This means you don't need to chop headings and other lengthy items of text into cell-width units before entering them into the worksheet. Instead, you can type the text into one cell and leave the cells to its right empty. A label will not extend into a neighboring cell that appears empty but actually contains some blank spaces.

Changing the column width can also affect numbers. The high-order digits of a number are not truncated to make a number fit in its cell. But depending on the format rules in effect, the digits past the decimal point might be rounded (causing 4.55 to become 5), or a long number might be converted into scientific notation (causing 12,000,000,000 to become 1.2 E +10). Otherwise, if a number is too long to fit, the cell on the screen is filled with a warning character, such as !!!!!!, *******, or ######. If you widen the column, the number will appear.

Most spreadsheets store numbers internally with the equivalent of eleven to fifteen decimal digits. Thus if you type the number 1.234567890123456789 into a cell, the spreadsheet might store the number as 1.23456789012. The number stored is used in any calculation regardless of how the number is displayed on the screen. Sometimes this can lead to surprising results, as Figure 10.2 shows.

## Protecting Cells

In certain situations, you may want other people to use a worksheet without being able to make accidental or unauthorized changes in it. This is usually done with a PROTECT command that gives protected status to a range of cells. A **protected cell** cannot be edited, deleted, or moved unless the cell's protected status is first removed with an UNPROTECT command. In effect, protecting a cell is the same as locking the cell's contents from further modification. The UNPROTECT command acts as a key that unlocks cells.

Figure 10.3 demonstrates how cell protection can prevent the formulas in a loan analysis from being accidentally modified. Three cells are unprotected and are shown in color; the interest rate, principal, and length of the loan are entered into

**Figure 10.2**
Because the worksheet's values are rounded before they are displayed, the total is "incorrect."

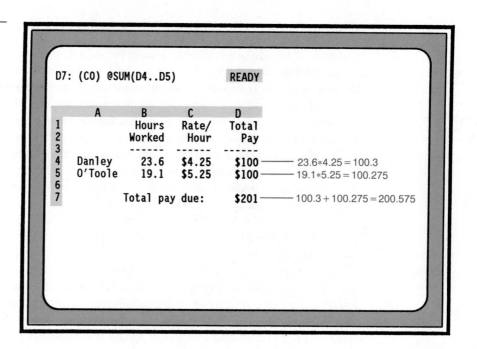

these cells. Any attempt to modify other cells in the worksheet produces an error message, as shown in the right-hand screen.

To make the development process smoother, most spreadsheets have a two-level protection system—one level for each cell plus a global protection system. A two-level system gives each cell its own protected or unprotected status and also allows the entire protection system to be enabled or disabled. While the worksheet is being developed and tested, the protection system is left disabled. During this time, the status of individual cells is adjusted so that all the cells are protected except those the user will employ to enter data or need to modify. When the worksheet works

**Figure 10.3**
Only the three cells in color are unprotected. Thus an attempt to enter the number 420 in cell D7 produces an error message.

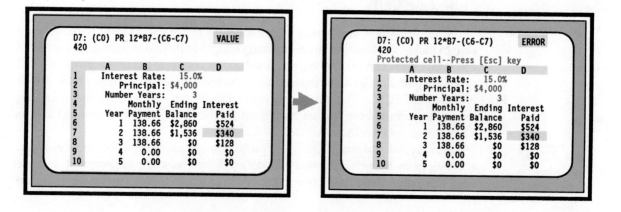

as desired, the global protection system is activated so that only the unprotected cells can be modified.

Excel permits an additional level of protection: It allows a password to be established. If a password is established when the global protection system is turned on, the spreadsheet will not turn off the protection system without asking for and receiving the password again. Obviously, it would be a serious mistake for the worksheet's developer to forget the password because then there would be no way to modify the protected cells.

## Hiding Cells

Another useful way of protecting cells from unwanted modification is to hide them from view. Both Lotus 1-2-3 and Excel let you give cells a format rule that hides them. With Lotus 1-2-3, a hidden cell's value won't appear in the worksheet window, but you still can see its value or formula if you select it and look at the control panel. This is handy if you want to clean up a worksheet by hiding areas that compute intermediate results. Excel hides cells differently. The values of its hidden cells are visible in the worksheet window, but you can't see their formulas in the control panel. This allows you to hide the logic contained in a worksheet without hiding its results.

Excel provides a way to hide entire columns: You can set a column's width to zero. With Excel, the usual way to adjust a column's width is to drag the line at the right edge of its column heading in the border, causing the column to expand or contract as you move the mouse. To hide a column, you drag this line until it overlaps the line from the previous column. A column whose width is zero doesn't show in the display or on printed reports. You can tell if a column is hidden by looking for its letter in the border. For example, if column D is hidden, the border will list columns A, B, C, E, and so on. A hidden column's cell entries remain in memory, and calculations in the hidden entries can affect the cells displayed.

You can also hide entries by placing them in a remote, unused part of the worksheet. Because the area available in most worksheets is enormous, this can be an effective strategy for hiding entries. A possible problem is that many spreadsheet programs require a few bytes of memory for every cell in the active area of the worksheet, even for cells that appear to be empty. Generally, the worksheet's **active area** is the rectangular region that extends from cell A1 in the upper left-hand corner, to the nonblank cell farthest to the worksheet's right, to the nonblank cell farthest toward the bottom. As a result, placing an entry in a remote cell can create a very large active area and therefore require most of the computer's main memory; it can even produce a memory-full error message. With these spreadsheets, it is important to pack all cell entries into as small a rectangle as possible in the upper left-hand corner of the worksheet.

## Creating Forms

Almost all businesses use standard forms to record transactions. A form speeds up the process of entering data by providing blanks for each data item. It also increases

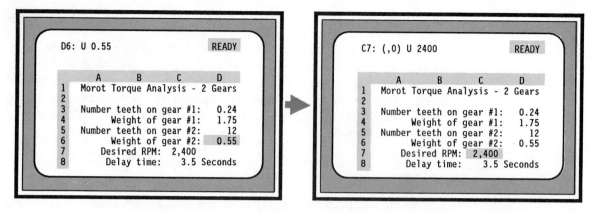

**Figure 10.4**
Pressing the down-arrow key [↓] while entering data into a form moves the active-cell marker to the next unprotected cell—in this case, cell C7.

the accuracy with which data is entered by clearly labeling each blank and ensuring every data item is entered. Computerized forms have another advantage: As soon as an entry is placed in one blank, the cursor jumps to the next blank. Since the blanks in a form are not necessarily on adjacent lines or in adjacent cells, this can eliminate many cursor-movement keystrokes.

Generally, spreadsheets construct forms by giving protected status to all cells except those that are blanks in the form. When data items are entered in the form, the active-cell marker jumps directly from one unprotected cell to the next. This is shown in Figure 10.4, where pushing the down-arrow key [↓] moves the active-cell marker from cell D6 to the next unprotected cell, C7.

Forms are used extensively by most data management systems, so it is not surprising that the spreadsheets that do the best job managing forms are part of integrated programs combining spreadsheet and data management functions. For example, Figure 10.5 was prepared with Jazz, a Macintosh program that combines record management and spreadsheet components with word processing, telecommunications, and graphics modules. Figure 10.5 shows a form that can be used to add, view, or modify records in a customer list. Once data is in the list, it can be analyzed with formulas to answer such questions as, What is the average age of my customers?

## WINDOWING TECHNIQUES

Windows are like portholes through which you view a small part of the underlying worksheet. Until now, we've shown only one worksheet window on the screen at a time. But some spreadsheets let you open several windows and control them separately; thus you can view isolated areas of a worksheet at once or compare several worksheets by placing each in its own window. Other spreadsheets, though

**Figure 10.5**
On-screen business forms are used to add, view, and modify records in lists.

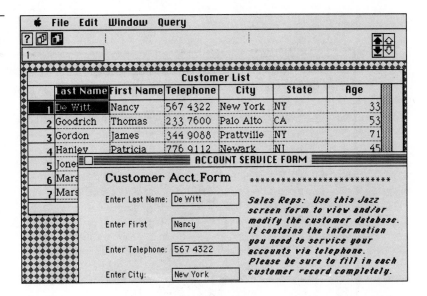

they let you open only one worksheet window, let you split the window into *panes* that you can scroll independently. Both methods are worth examining.

Worksheets often hold lists of information that have more columns or rows than fit on the screen. A worksheet might store monthly sales projections for a hundred products, the assignment and examination scores for ten classes of students, or the growth rates for five hundred experimental varieties of Douglas fir seedlings. Exploring one of these worksheets is easier if you split the window into **window panes** that look into different parts of the worksheet. For example, the full-year budget in Figure 10.6 occupies columns A through N and is roughly twice as wide as the worksheet window. The most important columns are columns A and N, which label the rows and give the totals. Jumping back and forth between these columns is inconvenient. But by splitting the window into two panes, you can position the panes so that both columns are visible at once.

Almost all spreadsheet programs let you split the worksheet window either horizontally or vertically to form two panes. With Excel, you can create four panes by splitting the window both horizontally and vertically. Creating window panes with Excel is easy. For example, to split the window as shown in Figure 10.6, you point at the vertical split bar and drag it from the left edge of the horizontal scroll bar to a location in the middle. Each of the new window panes has its own horizontal scroll bar and can be scrolled left or right independently of the other pane. So by scrolling the right-hand pane to column N, you can view the totals without disturbing your view of column A in the left-hand pane.

Another technique for keeping important rows or columns on the screen is to fix them in place with a TITLE command. This command freezes a part of the worksheet so that it won't scroll regardless of how the rest of the worksheet window is moved. You might think of the TITLE command as a way to expand the border

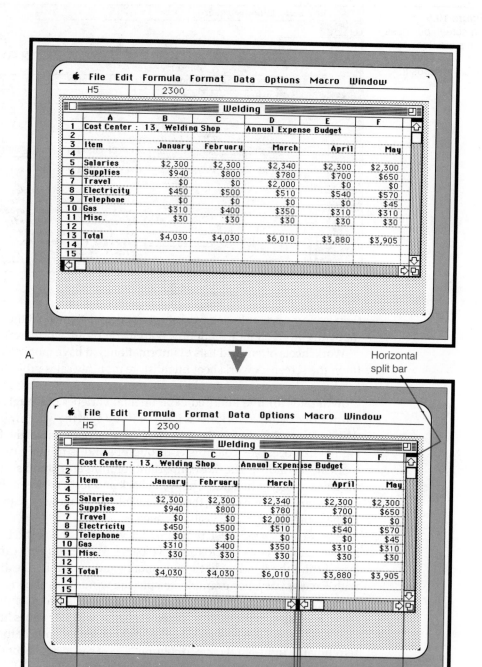

**Figure 10.6**
Creating window panes with Excel by dragging the vertical split bar across the scroll bar at the bottom of the window

## *A Word About . . . Building Better Models*

*Here are some simple rules to help you create spreadsheet models of lasting value.*

**Begin with a plan.** You are more likely to build a useful model if you clearly identify what you want it to accomplish before you begin. Decide what you want the model to compute, what data it needs, and how you want to see its results.

**Organize your use of the worksheet.** A good worksheet groups related information so it is clear what each part does. For example, you might list all the model's basic assumptions in one area, perform the processing in another, and display the results in a third. If the model is too big to fit in one screen, try to organize it down the left edge of the worksheet. This makes it easy to find all the parts by paging up and down and lets you insert rows without inadvertently damaging other areas.

**Build in flexibility.** Make sure the model's assumptions are displayed where they can be reviewed and changed. Avoid putting these values inside formulas where they will be hard to locate and change later. Instead, put them in their own cells and label them appropriately. If you follow these rules consistently, your formulas will contain few numbers and many references to other cells. As a result, your model will be able to answer many more what if types of questions.

**Start small, build gradually.** By building a tiny model or prototype, you can test out your ideas before you have invested a lot of time in one approach. You are also more likely to notice logical errors in a small model than in a large and complex one. Once everything seems to be working, you can expand the prototype by inserting rows and columns and by copying formulas.

**Label everything thoroughly.** Take the time to label the numbers and formulas so that they are clearly identified. Spreadsheet models tend to be used sporadically, so it is easy to forget how they work and what they do. You will thank yourself later if you place a few lines of documentation in the upper left-hand corner of the worksheet.

**Give names to cells and ranges.** Spreadsheet formulas are tough enough to understand without having to fight through the alphabet soup of unnamed cells. A formula like =Sales–Gross_Margin is much easier to interpret than =B21–E40.

**Use the copy command liberally.** The obvious reason to use the copy command is to save time. But there is an even stronger reason: You are less likely to make mistakes if you copy formulas than if you retype them. For example, if you copy a formula down a column, you can determine whether the copies are working correctly by testing one or two of them. But if you retype each formula individually, every formula is a candidate for a potentially disastrous typing error.

**Use white space liberally.** Worksheets are far larger than most models, so there is no reason to crowd everything together. Use blank rows to separate logical areas.

**Test and audit your results.** It is surprising how many spreadsheet models work incorrectly; all it takes is a small error in one formula to produce the wrong answer. Errors are easily overlooked when you examine the formulas themselves. At a minimum, you should experiment with the model and confirm that its behavior and answers are reasonable. A more reliable method is to compare the spreadsheet's output with answers that are known to be correct. It may be a pain to prepare test data and calculate the results with a calculator, but the alternative may be to rely on fictitious answers.

**Protect the worksheet.** Even a thoroughly debugged worksheet can be corrupted by inadvertently typing a value into a cell that is supposed to contain a formula. You can protect against this by turning on the worksheet's cell protection feature. Then unlock only those cells that contain assumptions or other values to be changed by the user.

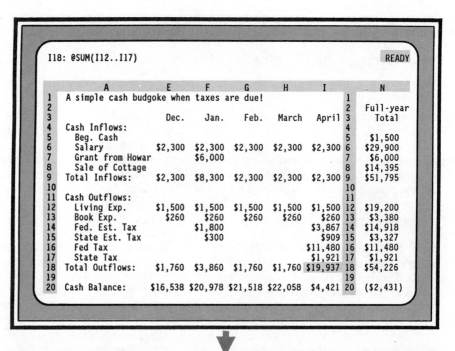

| | | A | E | F | G | H | I | | N |
|---|---|---|---|---|---|---|---|---|---|
| | 1 | A simple cash budgoke when taxes are due! | | | | | | 1 | |
| | 2 | | | | | | | 2 | Full-year |
| | 3 | | Dec. | Jan. | Feb. | March | April | 3 | Total |
| | 4 | Cash Inflows: | | | | | | 4 | |
| | 5 | Beg. Cash | | | | | | 5 | $1,500 |
| | 6 | Salary | $2,300 | $2,300 | $2,300 | $2,300 | $2,300 | 6 | $29,900 |
| | 7 | Grant from Howar | | $6,000 | | | | 7 | $6,000 |
| | 8 | Sale of Cottage | | | | | | 8 | $14,395 |
| | 9 | Total Inflows: | $2,300 | $8,300 | $2,300 | $2,300 | $2,300 | 9 | $51,795 |
| | 10 | | | | | | | 10 | |
| | 11 | Cash Outflows: | | | | | | 11 | |
| | 12 | Living Exp. | $1,500 | $1,500 | $1,500 | $1,500 | $1,500 | 12 | $19,200 |
| | 13 | Book Exp. | $260 | $260 | $260 | $260 | $260 | 13 | $3,380 |
| | 14 | Fed. Est. Tax | | $1,800 | | | $3,867 | 14 | $14,918 |
| | 15 | State Est. Tax | | $300 | | | $909 | 15 | $3,327 |
| | 16 | Fed Tax | | | | | $11,480 | 16 | $11,480 |
| | 17 | State Tax | | | | | $1,921 | 17 | $1,921 |
| | 18 | Total Outflows: | $1,760 | $3,860 | $1,760 | $1,760 | $19,937 | 18 | $54,226 |
| | 19 | | | | | | | 19 | |
| | 20 | Cash Balance: | $16,538 | $20,978 | $21,518 | $22,058 | $4,421 | 20 | ($2,431) |

I18: @SUM(I12..I17)   READY

J18: @SUM(J12..J17)   READY

| | | A | F | G | H | I | J | | N |
|---|---|---|---|---|---|---|---|---|---|
| | 1 | A simple cash budg taxes are due! | | | | | | 1 | |
| | 2 | | | | | | | 2 | Full-year |
| | 3 | | Jan. | Feb. | March | April | May | 3 | Total |
| | 4 | Cash Inflows: | | | | | | 4 | |
| | 5 | Beg. Cash | | | | | | 5 | $1,500 |
| | 6 | Salary | $2,300 | $2,300 | $2,300 | $2,300 | $2,300 | 6 | $29,900 |
| | 7 | Grant from Howar | $6,000 | | | | | 7 | $6,000 |
| | 8 | Sale of Cottage | | | | | | 8 | $14,395 |
| | 9 | Total Inflows: | $8,300 | $2,300 | $2,300 | $2,300 | $2,300 | 9 | $51,795 |
| | 10 | | | | | | | 10 | |
| | 11 | Cash Outflows: | | | | | | 11 | |
| | 12 | Living Exp. | $1,500 | $1,500 | $1,500 | $1,500 | $1,500 | 12 | $19,200 |
| | 13 | Book Exp. | $260 | $260 | $260 | $260 | $260 | 13 | $3,380 |
| | 14 | Fed. Est. Tax | $1,800 | | | $3,867 | | 14 | $14,918 |
| | 15 | State Est. Tax | $300 | | | $909 | | 15 | $3,327 |
| | 16 | Fed Tax | | | | $11,480 | | 16 | $11,480 |
| | 17 | State Tax | | | | $1,921 | | 17 | $1,921 |
| | 18 | Total Outflows: | $3,860 | $1,760 | $1,760 | $19,937 | $1,760 | 18 | $54,226 |
| | 19 | | | | | | | 19 | |
| | 20 | Cash Balance: | $20,978 | $21,518 | $22,058 | $4,421 | $4,961 | 20 | ($2,431) |

along the top or side of the screen so that it includes several rows or columns of the window. For example, suppose you use the TITLE command to expand the border in a monthly budget to include column A (see Figure 10.7). Then when you scroll to see the middle of the budget, column A will remain on the left edge of the window.

Several commands must be mastered to use window panes successfully, and they vary from one spreadsheet to the next. Knowing the command that jumps the active

## Figure 10.8

These two windows show the same area of the same worksheet. The Miles-Per-Gallon:2 window displays the worksheet's values, and the other window displays the worksheet's formulas.

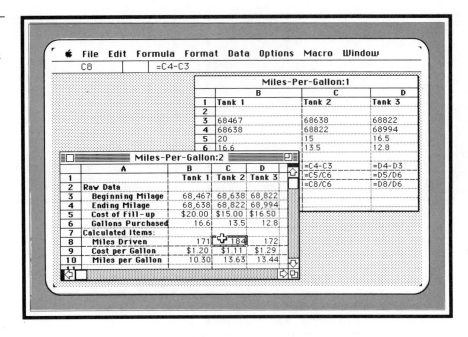

cell from one pane to another is important. (With Lotus 1-2-3, you push function key [F6] to jump back and forth between window panes; with Excel, you click anywhere in the pane you want to use.) The cursor-movement keys will not move the active cell out of the current pane; instead, when the active cell is moved against the edge of the pane, the pane begins to scroll. If the panes are **synchronized**, scrolling one pane causes the other pane to scroll in the same direction. Generally, there is a command that toggles from synchronized scrolling to independent scrolling and back again.

The major limitation of window panes is that each pane looks into the same worksheet. Excel is one of a few spreadsheet programs that lets you open more than one worksheet window. Thus even though one worksheet is already open, you can open a second window showing another worksheet. In fact, you can continue opening windows until the computer's memory becomes full. Windows can be stacked on top of one another, moved, closed, resized, and zoomed to fill the screen. These abilities are particularly helpful if you must move or copy information between worksheets. Excel's cut-and-paste operations work the same way between windows that they do within one window. To transfer information between worksheets, you cut or copy the cells from one window and paste them into another.

Most spreadsheets allow each window or window pane to have its own formatting rules. Thus if the same cell appeared in two windows, it might not look the same in each window. This can be used to compare the worksheet as it normally appears on the screen with the worksheet's formulas as they are stored in memory. For example, you might open two windows into the same worksheet and position them to show the same area (see Figure 10.8). Then by setting one window to display formulas, you can compare the windows to see whether the formulas work as expected.

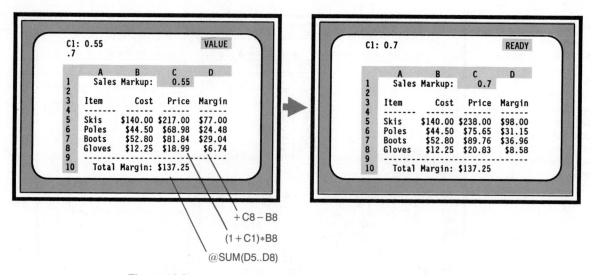

```
C1: 0.55                    VALUE          C1: 0.7                    READY
.7

       A      B      C      D                    A      B      C      D
  1  Sales Markup:   0.55                   1  Sales Markup:   0.7
  2                                         2
  3  Item   Cost   Price  Margin            3  Item   Cost   Price  Margin
  4  ------ ------ ------ ------             4  ------ ------ ------ ------
  5  Skis   $140.00 $217.00 $77.00          5  Skis   $140.00 $238.00 $98.00
  6  Poles   $44.50  $68.98 $24.48          6  Poles   $44.50  $75.65 $31.15
  7  Boots   $52.80  $81.84 $29.04          7  Boots   $52.80  $89.76 $36.96
  8  Gloves  $12.25  $18.99  $6.74          8  Gloves  $12.25  $20.83  $8.58
  9  ------------------------------         9  ------------------------------
 10   Total Margin: $137.25                10   Total Margin: $137.25
```

+ C8 − B8

(1 + C1)*B8

@SUM(D5..D8)

**Figure 10.9**
When column-oriented recalculation is used, changing cell C1, the sales mark-up, leaves the total margin in cell C10 inconsistent with the rest of the worksheet—unless the worksheet is recalculated twice.

## RECALCULATING FORMULAS

When a critical assumption in the worksheet is modified, you can sometimes see the changes ripple across the window. But how does the spreadsheet determine which formulas to evaluate first? And how often are they evaluated? Not surprisingly, the answers depend on the spreadsheet program you use and the recalculation commands you give it. Visicalc and other early spreadsheet programs used a simple recalculation order: After evaluating the active cell, they would evaluate the formulas in column A by working down the column one cell at a time, then evaluate column B, column C, and so forth. This is known as **column-oriented recalculation**.

You cannot assume that all the numbers on the screen represent stable values just because the worksheet has been recalculated. For example, suppose you type the formula +1+A1 into cell A1. This formula turns cell A1 into a counter that displays how many times the worksheet has been recalculated. Every time the worksheet is recalculated, the number in cell A1 is increased by 1, and a new number is displayed. This formula will not converge to a stable value; instead, it will continue counting.

Some worksheets require several recalculations before the numbers they display become stable. For example, the worksheet in Figure 10.9 must be recalculated twice before a change in the sales markup (cell C1) is reflected in the total margin (cell C10). On the first recalculation, the formula in cell C10 is evaluated before the numbers in column D have been adjusted to reflect the new sales markup. After the second recalculation, everything is self-consistent again.

One way of avoiding the need for two recalculations is to move the formula for the total margin from cell C10 to cell D10. That way the margin for each item would be calculated before the total margin. Another solution is to use **row-oriented recalculation,** which evaluates formulas in the worksheet from left to right across each row, starting with the top row in the worksheet. Row-oriented recalculation works well for the example in Figure 10.9 because the Margin numbers are in earlier rows than the Total Margin number.

Lotus 1-2-3, Excel, and most recently developed spreadsheets do not blindly follow a fixed recalculation order. Instead, they postpone calculating a formula until all the cells it depends on have been evaluated. Thus if the formula in cell B4 depends on the values in cells C8 and F9, the contents of cells C8 and F9 are processed before cell B4. This is called a **natural recalculation order** because it respects the natural relationships among cells.

Some spreadsheet programs let you choose the order of recalculation: natural, row oriented, or column oriented. However, since natural recalculation is by far the preferred order, this may be an unnecessary complication in their command systems.

Excel exploits the relationships among formulas to speed up recalculating the worksheet. Most spreadsheet programs blindly recalculate all the worksheet's formulas every time you make a cell entry. For large worksheets, this can be time consuming, forcing you to use the manual recalculation mode so that simple editing changes can be entered quickly. Excel, on the other hand, uses the natural recalculation order to determine which formulas need to be recalculated; then it evaluates only those formulas. For example, if you enter the formula =C8+F9 into cell B4 of an Excel worksheet, and then make a change to cell F9, Excel will evaluate cells F9 and B4 and any formulas that refer to cells F9 and B4. Although this may seem like the obvious way to do things, Lotus 1-2-3 and most other spreadsheet programs are more mechanical in the way they recalculate worksheets.

If cells depend on each other in a circular manner, there is no natural recalculation order. The simplest example of a **circular reference** is a cell whose formula refers to the cell's own value.

Figure 10.10 provides more complicated examples of circular references. It shows the income statement of a profit-sharing company that gives employees a bonus based on net profit. This situation naturally requires circular references: The formula for the employee bonus in cell B6 is calculated as 30 percent of net profit (0.3*B7), and the formula for net profit in cell B7 is calculated as the prebonus profit minus the bonus (+B5−B6). Thus cell B6 depends on cell B7, but cell B7 depends on cell B6. When the formula for cell B6 is entered, the bonus becomes 1,800 (calculated as +.30*6,000), and the net profit becomes 4,200 (calculated as 6,000−1,800). After another recalculation, the numbers for bonus and net profit become 1,260 and 4,740, respectively. It takes eight more calculations for the numbers to stabilize at their final values of $1,384.62 and $4,615.38.

A helpful feature for worksheets with circular references is an option that lets you specify how many times the formulas should be evaluated when the worksheet is recalculated. For example, both Lotus 1-2-3 and Excel allow you to enter an itera-

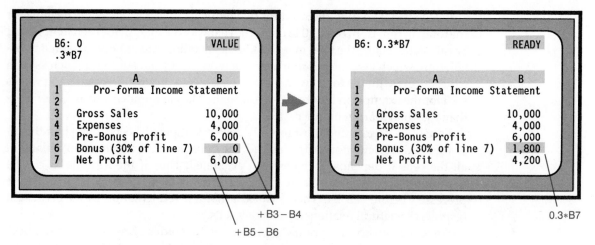

**Figure 10.10**
Entering a circular reference. When the formula for cell B6 is entered, the bonus depends on the net profit, which in turn depends on the bonus.

tion count that will determine the number of calculation cycles made per recalculation pass. Lotus 1-2-3 lets you specify only 50 iterations; Excel lets you set the Maximum Iterations count as high as 32,767. Excel also lets you enter a Maximum Change value that determines how small the changes in worksheet values must become before the recalculation stops.

Some circular references converge to a stable set of values quickly; others never produce a set of self-consistent numbers. A few spreadsheets will warn you if the numbers on the screen are not consistent with the worksheet's formulas, but most will not. Instead, you must rely on your common sense and your knowledge of the underlying relationships in the worksheet.

## CONSOLIDATING INFORMATION

Spreadsheets use a two-dimensional worksheet format, but many applications are best solved with a three-dimensional format for reports. For example, consider the task of creating expense budgets for a firm with fifty small operating units called cost centers. Let's assume the budget for each cost center has twelve months of expenses for thirty expense categories. The budget for a single cost center will have a variety of identifying labels and about four hundred numbers (thirty expense categories times twelve months, plus various total figures). The final budget report for the firm will require more than fifty pages—one page for each cost center and at least one summary page for the firm's aggregate expense budget.

The three dimensions in this report are months, expense categories, and cost centers. You could make the report fit on one two-dimensional worksheet by placing each cost center's budget in a different area of the worksheet, but this is an inconvenient solution. The worksheet would include twenty thousand numerical entries (fifty cost centers times four hundred numbers per cost center). It would be hard to coordinate the entry of so many numbers into one giant worksheet, and many personal computers don't have enough memory to create a worksheet with twenty thousand numerical entries.

Probably the best way of handling this budget is to use a data management program (see Chapters 11 and 12). Budgeting is characterized by a large amount of data and limited arithmetic computations—just the type of problem that data management programs solve best. Another option is to use a financial modeling program. Still, you can handle this budget with a spreadsheet program if you place each cost center's budget in its own worksheet and then consolidate these worksheets into other worksheets to obtain total budget figures. We now review two common methods of consolidating information from several worksheets: copying or merging information from one worksheet to another and linking worksheets so that changes in one worksheet affect the contents of another.

## Copying and Merging Worksheets

Almost all spreadsheets allow information to be copied from one worksheet to another, but the procedure varies from one program to the next.

For example, Lotus 1-2-3 allows information to be read directly into the current worksheet from a worksheet stored on a disk. First you move the active cell to the upper left-hand corner of the region to receive the new information. Then you give the FILE-COMBINE-COPY command. Either an entire worksheet or just a part can be copied from the disk into the current worksheet. Cells copied into the current worksheet replace any previous entries. Thus positioning the active cell carefully before giving the COPY command is important; a careless command can destroy an entire worksheet.

Information isn't aggregated by copying it from one worksheet to another; it is merely transferred. That is why most worksheets provide a command that merges the contents of two worksheets by adding the numbers in them together. For example, Lotus 1-2-3 aggregates worksheets with the FILE-COMBINE-ADD command. The only difference between this command and the FILE-COMBINE-COPY command is in how the incoming cells are merged with the current worksheet. The FILE-COMBINE-ADD command does not transfer labels and empty cells from the worksheet on disk; it takes only values (numbers and the results of formulas). The rules for merging an incoming value into the current worksheet depend on the type of cell it is merged with.

- Number cells have their value added to the incoming value so that the sum of the two values is displayed.
- Empty cells acquire the value of the incoming value.
- Label and formula cells are not affected by the incoming value; they retain their original contents.

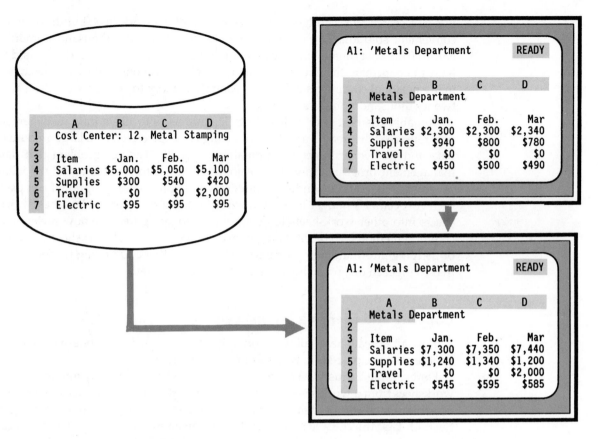

**Figure 10.11**
The effect of a FILE-COMBINE-ADD command, which merges the numbers from a
worksheet on disk with the worksheet in memory.

Figure 10.11 shows one step in using the FILE-COMBINE-ADD command to summarize cost-center budgets into a department budget. The first step is to create a template for the department budget that has empty cells (or zeros) where the expense values belong. The next steps are to use FILE-COMBINE-ADD commands to add the values in the cost-center worksheets stored on disk to the template for the department budget. With a similar procedure, you could aggregate the department budgets into a budget for the entire firm.

In contrast, Excel lets you merge worksheets as a variation of its usual copy-and-paste operations. You begin by opening the source and destination worksheets in separate windows. Then you copy a region of the source worksheet onto the clipboard and select the cell in the destination worksheet at the upper left-hand of the region to receive information (called the *paste area*). At this point, you have a choice. You can complete the command by choosing Paste from the Edit menu, which replaces an area of the destination worksheet with the information on the clipboard. Or if you want to merge the clipboard's information with the destination worksheet,

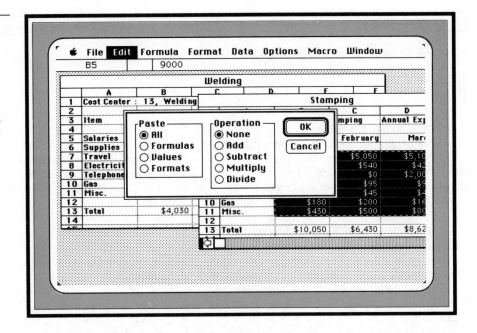

you can choose Paste Special from the Edit menu, producing the dialog box shown in Figure 10.12. The choices listed under Paste in this dialog box give you control over what information in the clipboard is transferred: All transfers everything (formulas, values, and format rules); Formulas transfers only the formulas in the cells; Values transfers only the values that appear in the cells; and Formats transfers only the format rules of the cells. The choices listed under Operation give you control over how the information is combined with the cells in the paste area: None replaces the cells in the paste area; Add adds the values in the selected parts of the clipboard to the paste area; Subtract subtracts values from the paste area; Multiply multiplies the paste area cells by the corresponding values in the clipboard; and Divide divides the paste area cells by values in the clipboard.

Collectively, these options give you full control over what information is transferred and how it is copied or merged. The options are useful for tasks other than consolidating information. For example, you might enter formulas into an area and then decide to replace the formulas with their values. To do this, you would cut (or copy) the area to the clipboard and then use Paste Special to paste only the values back into the area. Text and numbers would come through this copying process without change, but only the results of the formulas would remain, not the formulas themselves.

## Linking Worksheets

A destination worksheet that information is copied to or merged into is not affected by subsequent changes to the source worksheets. Anyone who has been through a budgeting process knows how serious this limitation can be; budgets inevitably go

*As data processing use of undocumented spreadsheets mushrooms and as the management decisions made from them become more important, the opportunity for critical errors multiplies. This has lead to the use of modeling programs that build large time series models more easily.*

The virtue of spreadsheets—that users can quickly and easily move about them making changes and then copy the changes into other cells—makes documenting them devilishly difficult. The data and the logic are homogenized so well that separating the two becomes nearly impossible.

If I build a spreadsheet for you to use, you would be hard-pressed to sort out why and how it works. Users cannot see the logic behind the sheet, only the results of the calculations as they are displayed. A single calculation error—a cell copied one too many times, for example—often leads to false results. Spreadsheets have become an MIS manager's nightmare.

Enter financial modelers: a class of programs designed to rectify some of these spreadsheet problems. A modeling program, in the broadest sense, is any program that allows a user to simulate real events or to test hypothetical situations on a computer. Spreadsheets can be used as modeling programs, as can a broad range of other generic programs. However, since the

newer financial planners specialize in creating models, they generally document model logic more lucidly than spreadsheets.

The following characteristics further set modeling programs apart from generic financial planners:

- Built-in programming languages
- Flexible data view and report capability
- Complete separation of data and logic
- Easy path to consolidation

Modeling programs usually have their own programming languages. It may be either a fully developed procedural or nonprocedural language or simply a collection of modeling techniques such as sensitivity analysis, goal seeking, multiple regression, and so on. The language has one distinctive feature, though: It was designed to make the evaluation of events over time less complex. Time series analysis—a series of numbers that represent values for a variable at different points in time—is integral to almost all business models or simulations. Most modeling programs have a wealth of time series functions or commands that simplify conversions from one time series to another.

Business modeling programs also offer considerably more flexible approaches to viewing and reporting data. Whereas spreadsheets are

through many revisions before everyone is satisfied. This disadvantage can be removed by permanently linking the worksheets.

For example, formulas in an Excel worksheet can obtain values from other worksheets as easily as they obtain them from cells in the same worksheet. References to cells or names on other worksheets are called **external references.** You insert an external reference in a formula as follows:

*1.* Open the worksheet you want to refer to so that it is visible in a window on the screen.

*2.* Start the formula as you usually do.

printed from top to bottom, left to right, modeling programs permit selective viewing and printing of values. A user can choose to work with subsets of the model, such as selected rows and columns in any order, without losing the relationships between variables.

The most telling difference between spreadsheets and modeling programs lies in the area of data manipulation. Spreadsheets force the user to work with all the data all the time. Modeling programs separate data and logic. Normally, models are expressed as variables in English-like statements. The same logic in a spreadsheet is referred to as cells, that is, A1 – B1 = C1. In a modeling program, the variable "Sales" can have multiple data sets, since the variable has no value permanently associated with it. In a spreadsheet, however, the values represented by the cell locations are tied directly to that location. The cells cannot function as variables, but merely as containers.

For example, a typical small model logic file could look something like this:

```
Sales = GROW(1000 @ Jan 86,.05)
Cost of Goods Sold = Sales * .36
Gross Margin = Sales – Cost of Goods Sold
General & Administrative = GROW(150 @
```

```
Jan 86,.02)
Marketing = Sales * .04
Profit = Gross Margin – SUM(General & Administrative + Marketing)
```

With very little effort one can figure out that sales are expected to start out at $1,000 in January 1986 and grow by 5 percent each month thereafter. The GROW function is just one of many functions in modeling programs that make it easy to project into the future. By contrast, a spreadsheet would copy a formula, multiplying the previous cell by 1.05 into the range the user wished to predict. If the user changed a growth rate, he would have to remember to change each cell individually. In the modeling program he makes just one change, to the growth rate. The change is automatically extended into the future.

When comparing this logic with similar spreadsheet logic, it rapidly becomes apparent that modeling programs offer a much more understandable picture of what is happening. The cell designations found in a spreadsheet say nothing about the reasonableness of the model, while the modeling program actually gives an understandable description of what is happening.

Source: Shawn Bryan, *Computerworld*, 15 September 1986, pp. 47–48.

3. Click the worksheet you want to refer to, and select a cell or cell range in it by pointing with the mouse.

4. Finish building the formula in the usual way.

References to cells in other worksheets have longer names: First comes the name of the other worksheet, then an exclamation point, and then the row and column (or name) reference. For example, the Metals Department worksheet in Figure 10.13 links corresponding cells in the Stamping and Welding cost center worksheets. So cell B5 in the Metal Department worksheet contains the entry =Stamping!B5+Welding!B5.

**Figure 10.13**
Linking worksheets.
The expense num-
bers on the work-
sheets for Cost
Centers 12 and 13
are linked to the
budget worksheet
for the Metals
Department.

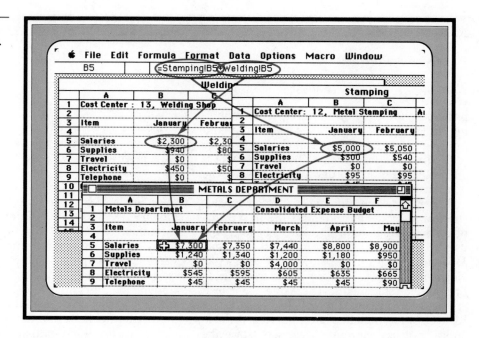

Once a worksheet is linked to supporting worksheets, changes in the supporting worksheets are automatically reflected in the dependent or destination worksheet. For example, if the number in cell B5 of the Stamping worksheet is changed from 5,000 to 3,000, the number in cell B5 of the Metals Department worksheet will drop from 7,300 to 5,300. Excel's method of linking worksheets works best if all the supporting worksheets for a dependent worksheet are loaded into memory and reside in their own window.

## ADVANCED FUNCTIONS

Spreadsheets provide short cuts for common financial, statistical, mathematical, and other processing tasks through built-in functions. Whenever you are having a particularly difficult time constructing a formula, check a reference manual to see if a function for the task exists. Most spreadsheets offer dozens of built-in functions; they often spell the difference between struggling with a clumsy formula and finding an instant solution.

To give you a sense of the variety of tasks that functions can perform, we look at examples of Lotus 1-2-3's functions. These examples are representative of the functions offered by other spreadsheets, but the number and type of functions vary from program to program. Even if the name of a function is the same in two programs, there may be differences in syntax between them. For example, one program's function may give you more options, forcing it to require more arguments.

A function's **arguments** are the values it uses to produce a new value. Arguments are separated by commas and enclosed in parentheses. They can be constants, cells, ranges, or other formulas. An argument can even be another function, as in @ROUND(@SUM(2,3,5)), which is equal to 3.

**Figure 10.14**
Examples of mathe-
matical functions

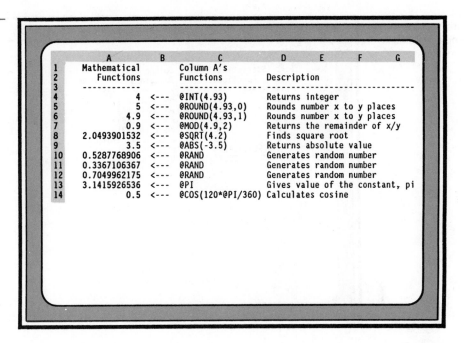

Each function expects a certain type and number of arguments. For example, the SUM function expects a list of numbers. The numbers can be constants (such as 5.24/7), but it is generally better to provide references to cells that contain numbers. For example, @SUM(A1,B2,D1..E5) references twelve cells to be totaled. If you have given names to the cells in your worksheet, you can refer to them by name. For example, @SUM(SALES) would total all the cells in the range named SALES. If you make a mistake and provide a function with the wrong number or type of arguments, as in @SUM("Apples"), Lotus 1-2-3 will flash ERROR in the mode indicator and refuse to enter the formula into the active cell until you correct the problem.

## Mathematical and Statistical Functions

Mathematical functions perform various types of arithmetic on data in the worksheet (see Figure 10.14). Most mathematical functions accept a single number, perform a mathematical transformation on it, and return a single number. For example, the INT function truncates the fractional part of its argument and returns the integer part, so @INT(4.9) is equal to 4. Many people are surprised to find, with spreadsheet logic, @INT(-3.2) is equal to -4, not -3.

A few mathematical functions take two arguments. For example, the ROUND function's second argument determines where to round the first argument. If the second argument is positive, the number is rounded after the decimal point. Thus @ROUND(15690.83,1) is equal to 15,690.8. But you can also use this function to round numbers before the decimal point. For example, @ROUND(15690.83,-3) is equal to 16,000. This is particularly handy for eliminating unwarranted detail from forecasts.

**Figure 10.15**
Examples of statistical functions

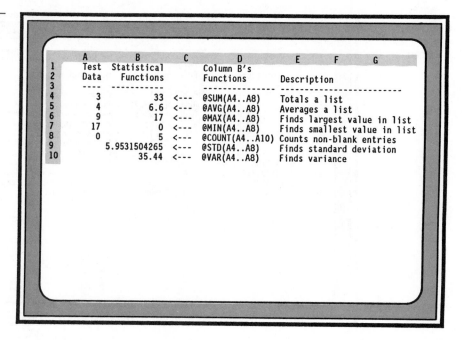

```
      A      B         C        D           E      F      G
 1  Test  Statistical          Column B's
 2  Data  Functions            Functions   Description
 3  ----  -----------          ---------------  ------------------------
 4     3           33  <---  @SUM(A4..A8)     Totals a list
 5     4          6.6  <---  @AVG(A4..A8)     Averages a list
 6     9           17  <---  @MAX(A4..A8)     Finds largest value in list
 7    17            0  <---  @MIN(A4..A8)     Finds smallest value in list
 8     0            5  <---  @COUNT(A4..A10)  Counts non-blank entries
 9     5.9531504265  <---  @STD(A4..A8)     Finds standard deviation
10           35.44  <---  @VAR(A4..A8)     Finds variance
```

Statistical functions provide summary statistics; thus they accept a list of items to summarize. Figure 10.15 shows some examples.

**Matrix operations** are closely related to statistical functions. (*Matrix* and *array* are mathematical terms that correspond to *range* in spreadsheet terminology.) One of the simplest matrix operations is to add or multiply all the numbers in one matrix by the corresponding numbers in another. For advanced statistical analysis, the most useful matrix operation is to *invert* a matrix, a complex transformation extremely difficult to do by hand. Lotus 1-2-3 supports several matrix operations, including matrix inversion. Each time you want to use one of these operations, you must give a special menu bar command. Excel lets you place matrix operations in formulas stored in the worksheet. This is certainly convenient, but Excel lacks a function for inverting a matrix.

## Financial Functions

Accountants and financial managers solve problems that require fairly extensive calculations. Although the typical sales transaction can be recorded with nothing more complicated than addition, transactions that take a long time to complete are affected by interest rates. Financial functions calculate the effect of interest rates on sums of money over time (see Figure 10.13).

Even for some seemingly simple business problems, the required computations can be onerous to do by hand. For example, suppose you have the opportunity to invest $8,000 in a project that will pay you $5,000 at the end of the year and another $5,000 one year later. Certainly, the $8,000 cost is less than the $10,000 return, but would you do better at a bank? One way to find out is to calculate the investment's

**Figure 10.16**
Examples of financial functions

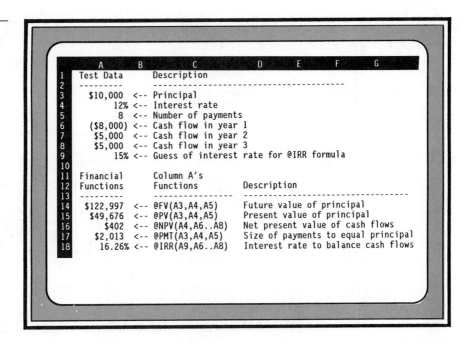

```
          A        B           C              D       E        F        G
  1   Test Data           Description
  2   ---------           ------------------------------------------------
  3     $10,000   <-- Principal
  4          12%  <-- Interest rate
  5           8   <-- Number of payments
  6    ($8,000)   <-- Cash flow in year 1
  7      $5,000   <-- Cash flow in year 2
  8      $5,000   <-- Cash flow in year 3
  9          15%  <-- Guess of interest rate for @IRR formula
 10
 11   Financial           Column A's
 12   Functions           Functions        Description
 13   ---------           ----------------  ------------------------------------
 14    $122,997   <-- @FV(A3,A4,A5)        Future value of principal
 15     $49,676   <-- @PV(A3,A4,A5)        Present value of principal
 16        $402   <-- @NPV(A4,A6..A8)      Net present value of cash flows
 17      $2,013   <-- @PMT(A3,A4,A5)       Size of payments to equal principal
 18      16.26%   <-- @IRR(A9,A6..A8)      Interest rate to balance cash flows
```

implied interest rate, known as the *internal rate of return*. Then you could compare this investment's interest rate with the interest rates quoted by banks. Unfortunately, there is no simple way to calculate an internal rate of return. The only method is to make a guess of an interest rate and then test to see if the guess was too high or too low. Each new guess is likely to bring you closer to the correct answer. But with a spreadsheet's internal rate of return function, all this work is avoided. For example, the bottom line of Figure 10.16 shows the $8,000 investment earns 16.26 percent over the life of the project. The IRR function uses two arguments: a guess of the interest rate and a list of periodic cash flows. The guess is used only to help the spreadsheet get off to a fast start at performing the calculations; a poor guess will delay each recalculation but will not affect the answer (except in those rarely encountered, perverse cases where there are several correct solutions).

## Logical Functions and Operators

Logical functions are used to determine the status of cells or to choose between two values for a cell. For example, you can use the @ISNUMBER function to see if a value in a cell is numeric (see lines 19 and 20 of Figure 10.17). If the value is numeric or the cell empty, @ISNUMBER returns the value 1 (true). Otherwise, the condition is false, and @ISNUMBER returns the value 0.

Most logical functions use **logical operators** to test whether a condition is true or false. For example, the condition A3>100 uses the logical operator > (greater than) to compare the value in A3 with the number 100. If A3 contains a value greater than 100, the condition has the logical value true; otherwise, it has the logical value false. Other frequently used logical operators include < (less than), <= (less than or equal

**Figure 10.17**
Examples of logical
functions

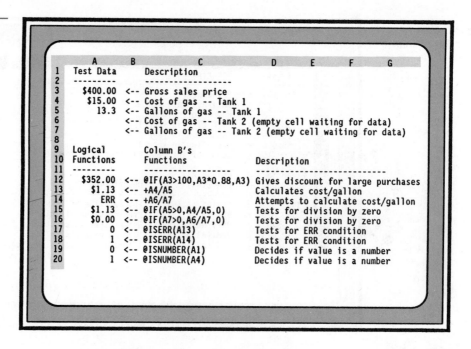

```
        A       B          C              D      E      F      G
1   Test Data        Description
2   ---------        -------------------
3     $400.00  <-- Gross sales price
4     $15.00   <-- Cost of gas -- Tank 1
5      13.3    <-- Gallons of gas -- Tank 1
6               <-- Cost of gas -- Tank 2 (empty cell waiting for data)
7               <-- Gallons of gas -- Tank 2 (empty cell waiting for data)
8
9   Logical          Column B's
10  Functions        Functions              Description
11  ---------        -------------------    ----------------------------
12    $352.00  <-- @IF(A3>100,A3*0.88,A3)  Gives discount for large purchases
13    $1.13    <-- +A4/A5                  Calculates cost/gallon
14    ERR      <-- +A6/A7                  Attempts to calculate cost/gallon
15    $1.13    <-- @IF(A5>0,A4/A5,0)       Tests for division by zero
16    $0.00    <-- @IF(A7>0,A6/A7,0)       Tests for division by zero
17       0     <-- @ISERR(A13)             Tests for ERR condition
18       1     <-- @ISERR(A14)             Tests for ERR condition
19       0     <-- @ISNUMBER(A1)           Decides if value is a number
20       1     <-- @ISNUMBER(A4)           Decides if value is a number
```

to), >= (greater than or equal to), and <> (not equal to). Occasionally, you may need to test compound conditions; for example, to determine if the values in cells B3 and C3 are both greater than 200. Compound conditions are written with the #AND# and #OR# operators, as in B3200#AND#C3200. When the #AND# operator is used, the compound condition is true only if both of its parts are true. The #OR# operator makes the compound condition true if either of its parts is true.

The real power of testing conditions lies in the ability to choose between two values in an @IF function. For example, suppose the owner of a clothing store wants to give a 12 percent discount on all purchases over $100. If the gross sales price is entered in cell A3, the net sales price can be selected by testing the condition A3>100. This condition appears in the @IF function shown on line 12 of Figure 10.17. Because the condition is true ($400 is greater than $100), the value for cell A12 is obtained from the function's second argument, A3*0.88. But when the value in A3 is less than or equal to $100, the function's value would be obtained from the third argument, A3.

Logical functions perform tests that cannot be accomplished in other ways. Suppose some of the formulas on the screen display ERR, and after some analysis, you discover the source of the problem is the formula +A6/A7. Although this formula uses valid syntax, it makes sense only if A7 contains a numeric value other than zero. When A7 is blank, the formula will display ERR, and every formula that references it—either directly or indirectly—will also display ERR. The @IF function in cell A16 of Figure 10.17 sidesteps this problem. This function reads, "When the value in A7 is greater than 0, divide A6 by A7; otherwise, display 0."

Another way to stop one formula from invalidating many others is to use the @ISERR function (see rows 17 and 18 of Figure 10.17). It tests to see whether its argument is a valid formula. A typical way of using this function is to nest it inside

# Communications: Transporting Data

*The development of microprocessors brought machine intelligence to previously dumb products. Terminals became personal computers, cash registers became point-of-sale terminals, wrist watches became digital alarm chronometers, and, unfortunately, some household appliances learned to talk, saying things like, ''Beep, your coffee's done.'' The first intelligent products had little or no ability to communicate, but that has changed. Today intelligent office products are linked into integrated office systems. Satellites, microwave links, and telephone transmission systems provide widely dispersed equipment with access to databases managed by large host computers. This photo essay gives you a glimpse into the consolidation of two fields: communications and computing.*

**1.** New telephone systems encode and transmit voice messages as digital signals rather than analog signals. As a result, both voice and data can be transmitted conveniently by one communications systems.

2. Large antennas allow RCA Americom's Satellite Operations Control Center to monitor and control up to eight communications spacecraft in orbit. Without frequent earth-based supervision, communications satellites would soon wander out of position and become useless. Two small microwave relay antennas are visible near the skyline.

3. The control console inside the RCA Satellite Control Center.

# SATELLITES

*Satellites provide high-speed digital communications among widely dispersed locations. They allow large amounts of computer-generated data to be transmitted quickly between data processing centers.*

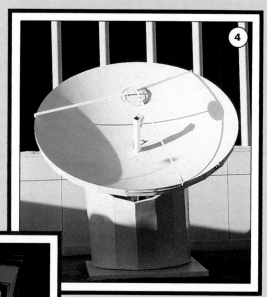

4. A satellite earth station located in Dallas, Texas, forms a major hub in the EDS Corporation's nationwide communications network.

5. The EDS communications control center.

# FIBER OPTICS

*Optical fibers transmit data as pulses of laser light, not as electrical signals. They are extremely fast, compact, insensitive to electrical disturbances, and secure from eavesdropping. Despite these advantages, conventional twised-pair wire and coaxial cable are used more often than optical fibers because of their lower cost.*

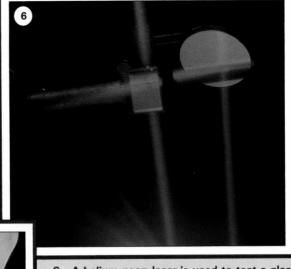

6. A helium neon laser is used to test a glass preform before it is drawn into optical fiber.

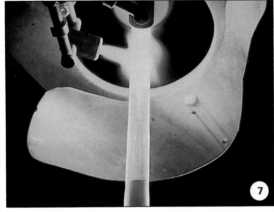

7. In one step in the production of glass fiber, an oxygen-hydrogen flame travels the length of a quartz tube, causing chemical reactions at the point of heat.

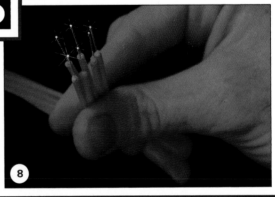

8. Although the finished glass fibers are tiny, they can transmit hundreds of telephone conversations at once.

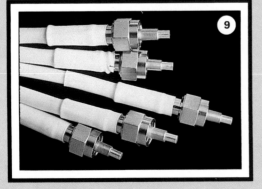

9. Tandem uses five fiber-optic strands in each FOX system link between its computers. The fibers are connected to the system with screw terminations for easy installation.

*window 6*

# INFORMATION SERVICES

*Business information is a precious commodity. It can be stored and shared effectively by centralized data processing centers in conjunction with telecommunications networks.*

10. Row upon row of hard disk drives are a common sight in large computer centers. This view shows one of three "supercenters" maintained by GE Information Services, the world's largest commercially available teleprocessing network.

11. Although a commercial hard disk drive stores from 100 megabytes to more than 5 gigabytes (100 million to 5 billion characters), large installations require many drives. Hard disk drives provide fast data retrieval; access times are measured in milliseconds (thousandths of a second).

12. Telex's MIS (management information systems) Center in Tulsa expedites communication between corporate headquarters and other Telex operations.

**13.** Tapes are used to store infrequently used data and to back-up data stored on disk drives in case of disk failure. Only one reel of tape can be mounted at a time on each tape drive.

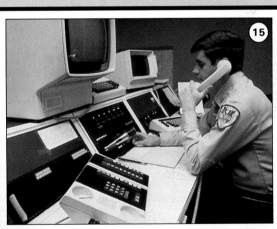

**14.** Most magnetic tapes are *off-line,* meaning they cannot be read by the computer unless they are mounted on a tape drive by a computer operator. Storing data on tape is inexpensive; a 2,400-foot tape costs about $20 and can store over 100 megabytes.

**15,16.** Law enforcement and health-care workers need quick answers from large databases. Usually these requirements are met by connecting desktop terminals to a central host computer. The connection can be made with a dedicated wire running directly between the two, with a permanently leased telephone line, or with dial-up telephone service. Often the terminal and the host computer are linked by a number of intermediary communications devices such as concentrators, modems, and local area networks.

# LOCAL AREA NETWORKS

**Local area networks allow devices in a limited area to be connected so that any device on the network can communicate with any other device.**

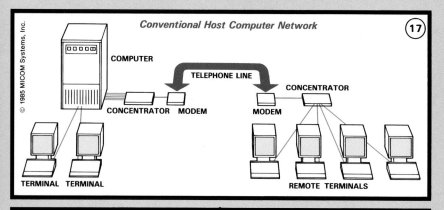

### Conventional Host Computer Network

© 1985 MICOM Systems, Inc.

COMPUTER

TELEPHONE LINE

CONCENTRATOR

CONCENTRATOR   MODEM   MODEM

TERMINAL   TERMINAL

REMOTE TERMINALS

**17.** In a conventional computer network, all peripheral devices are connected to the host computer. If you want one terminal to talk to another, the message must pass through the host computer first. To use the telephone lines efficiently, concentrators and other communications devices splice messages from several terminals onto one telephone line.

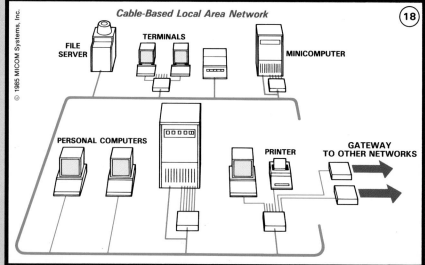

### Cable-Based Local Area Network

© 1985 MICOM Systems, Inc.

FILE SERVER   TERMINALS   MINICOMPUTER

PERSONAL COMPUTERS   PRINTER   GATEWAY TO OTHER NETWORKS

**18.** In a cable-based local area network, all devices are connected to one cable. Often the cable is similar to the coaxial cable used in cable TV systems. Local area networks use a number of methods to prevent the electronic "voices" of the devices from colliding. Local area networks are very reliable; unless the cable is cut or damaged, the entire network cannot fail.

**19.** With a local area network, an office work group using personal computers can share a hard disk drive and printer. Networks also allow users to send and receive electronic mail.

# TELEPHONE TERMINALS

*Nowhere is the consolidation of communications and computing more evident than in the development of telephone terminals.*

**20.** This personal communications terminal combines a powerful terminal and a full-featured telephone in one unit. The phone features a built-in speakerphone for hands-free calls, the ability to enter and revise a phone list with 200 entries using the retractable keyboard, and a built-in calculator. The unit can also emulate a DEC VT100 terminal or an IBM 3270 terminal.

**21.** This telephone unit has all the capabilities of the terminal shown in photo 20, but it also contains a personal computer compatible with an IBM PC. Mostly hidden by the man's arm are two floppy disk drives. Inside the unit are a microprocessor that can run IBM PC software for business applications and 512KB of memory.

**22.** A sales clerk telephones the National Data Corporation (NDC) to obtain credit card authorization for a customer. NDC's network links the consumer, the bank, and the merchant for fast and efficient credit service.

**23.** A waitress in a Tokyo restaurant uses CATNET, a nationwide credit verification system introduced by IBM in Japan.

# OTHER TERMINALS

25. You can temporarily convert virtually any personal computer into an intelligent computer terminal by adding a modem and a communications program. This allows the personal computer to be connected to a host computer to run applications such as order entry, electronic mail, or electronic funds transfer.

24. This hand-held portable data terminal can be connected directly to telephone lines with a standard RJ11 snap connector for data transmissions with a host computer. Its clock can "wake up" the terminal and automatically dial a telephone number at a preset time, allowing transmissions to occur unattended late at night, when long distance rates are low. Data can be entered through the keyboard or with a variety of bar code readers. The terminal operates for up to a hundred hours on four AA alkaline batteries. It provides up to 16KB of data storage.

26. Researchers at RCA Labs are testing teletext systems. These systems can be used to display news and weather information, present stock market quotations, or advertise shopping specials. A teletext system transmits data to television sets by encoding it in the vertical blanking interval (the black bar visible when vertical hold isn't working) of a video frame. Then a teletext decoder in the television decodes the data into text and graphics to be displayed on the screen.

**Figure 10.18**
Examples of string
functions

```
            A         B          C          D        E      F       G
 1  Test Data
 2  ------------
 3  Tom Wolfe
 4  TOM  WOLFE
 5  89 2/3
 6
 7  String              Column A's
 8  Functions           Functions      Description
 9  ----------          --------------- --------------------------------------
10  Tom          <--- @LEFT(A3,3)       Extracts left portion of string
11  Wolfe        <--- @RIGHT(A3,5)      Extracts right portion of string
12  Tom  Wolfe   <--- @PROPER(A4)       Converts to "proper" capitalization
13  TOM WOLFE    <--- @TRIM(A4)         Removes embedded blanks
14  Tom Wolfe    <--- @TRIM(A12)        Removes embedded blanks
15  tom wolfe    <--- @LOWER(A3)        Converts to lower case
16          84   <--- @CODE(A3)         Converts first letter to ASCII code
17  -=-=-=-=-=   <--- @REPEAT("-=",5)   Makes n copies of string
18  89.66666666  <--- @VALUE(A5)        Converts a label into a number
19           3   <--- @FIND(" ",A3,1)   Finds first occurance of a character
20           9   <--- @LENGTH(A3)       Returns the length of string
```

an @IF function, as in @IF(@ISERR(100*B9),0,100*B9). This imposing formula anticipates the possibility that cell B9 might contain a text that cannot be validly used in a numeric formula. The formula reads, "If 100*B9 evaluates to a valid number, display the number; otherwise, display 0."

## String Functions

String functions manipulate text. After looking through Figure 10.18, you might decide that string functions are rather silly; after all, it is much easier to truncate Tom Wolfe's name with the backspace or [Del] key than to write a string function to do it. But this perspective overlooks the way string functions are normally used; they are placed inside spreadsheet instructions called *macros* that execute automatically. Used this way, string functions allow the spreadsheet to test the responses entered by the user, to truncate them to fit in their destination cells, or to extract the first names from a column holding complete names.

## Date and Time Functions

Date and time functions allow you to calculate with dates and times as easily as with any other numbers. To help Lotus 1-2-3 do its math, dates are assigned consecutive integers, starting with January 1, 1900, as the number 1. (SuperCalc4 counts from March 1, 1900, and Excel counts from January 1, 1904.) Times are assigned fractional numbers, starting with midnight as the number 0.0 and noon as 0.5. Thus June 15, 1988, at 6:38 P.M., is stored as 32309.776393. Fortunately, you never have to look at dates or times in this way. By selecting an appropriate format rule, you can

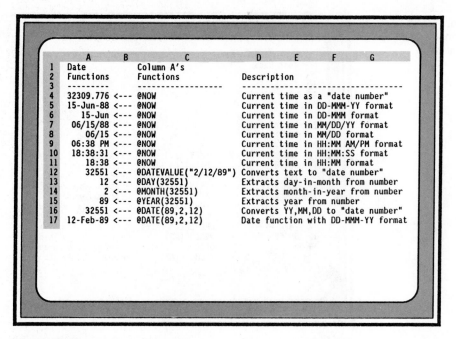

```
       A        B          C            D      E      F      G
 1  Date             Column A's
 2  Functions        Functions             Description
 3  ---------        ------------------    -----------------------------------
 4  32309.776 <--- @NOW                    Current time as a "date number"
 5  15-Jun-88 <--- @NOW                    Current time in DD-MMM-YY format
 6     15-Jun <--- @NOW                    Current time in DD-MMM format
 7   06/15/88 <--- @NOW                    Current time in MM/DD/YY format
 8      06/15 <--- @NOW                    Current time in MM/DD format
 9   06:38 PM <--- @NOW                    Current time in HH:MM AM/PM format
10   18:38:31 <--- @NOW                    Current time in HH:MM:SS format
11      18:38 <--- @NOW                    Current time in HH:MM format
12      32551 <--- @DATEVALUE("2/12/89")   Converts text to "date number"
13         12 <--- @DAY(32551)             Extracts day-in-month from number
14          2 <--- @MONTH(32551)           Extracts month-in-year from number
15         89 <--- @YEAR(32551)            Extracts year from number
16      32551 <--- @DATE(89,2,12)          Converts YY,MM,DD to "date number"
17  12-Feb-89 <--- @DATE(89,2,12)          Date function with DD-MMM-YY format
```

**Figure 10.19**
Examples of functions that manipulate dates and time. Cells A4..A11 all contain the same value, but they look different because they have been assigned different format rules.

instruct the spreadsheet to display them in a variety of traditional formats (see Figure 10.19).

Because dates are stored as numbers, they can be compared to see which is larger. With logic functions, this could be used to search a list of insurance policies for those that have expired. Using date arithmetic, you can add and subtract dates to calculate periods. This would be useful to determine whether a 180-day warranty period had expired before a warranty claim was received.

The most common use for date functions is to print the current date automatically in reports. Placing the @NOW function in a cell causes the spreadsheet to retrieve the current time from the computer's clock whenever the worksheet is recalculated. The @NOW function might display 06/15 or 6:38 PM; the result depends on the current time in the computer's clock and the format rule assigned to the cell containing the function.

## Look-Up Tables

A look-up function allows you to retrieve an entry from a table. This is useful for retrieving taxes from a tax table or assigning letter grades to students based on the points they have earned in class. The class grade list example is a common one in academic settings and is worth exploring.

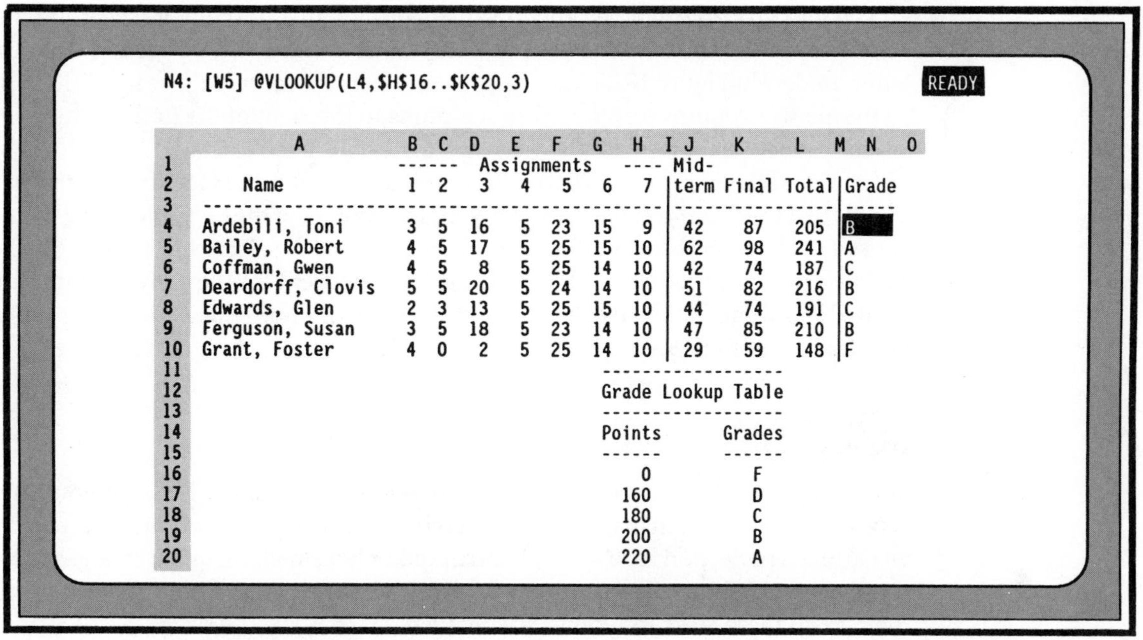

```
N4: [W5] @VLOOKUP(L4,$H$16..$K$20,3)                                    READY

                  A     B C D   E   F   G   H I J   K     L  M N   O
           1                ------ Assignments ---- Mid-
           2      Name      1 2   3   4   5   6   7 |term Final Total|Grade
           3      -------------------------------------------------- -----
           4      Ardebili, Toni    3 5  16   5  23  15   9 | 42   87   205 |B
           5      Bailey, Robert    4 5  17   5  25  15  10 | 62   98   241 |A
           6      Coffman, Gwen     4 5   8   5  25  14  10 | 42   74   187 |C
           7      Deardorff, Clovis 5 5  20   5  24  14  10 | 51   82   216 |B
           8      Edwards, Glen     2 3  13   5  25  15  10 | 44   74   191 |C
           9      Ferguson, Susan   3 5  18   5  23  14  10 | 47   85   210 |B
          10      Grant, Foster     4 0   2   5  25  14  10 | 29   59   148 |F
          11                                       ------------------
          12                                       Grade Lookup Table
          13                                       ------------------
          14                                       Points      Grades
          15                                       ------      ------
          16                                           0         F
          17                                         160         D
          18                                         180         C
          19                                         200         B
          20                                         220         A
```

**Figure 10.20**
The letter grades in this table are determined by a look-up function that searches through the Grade Look-up Table at the bottom of the screen.

Many classes use a point system to determine the students' grades. The cornerstone of this system is a grade look-up table containing cutoff values for each grade bracket. For example, assume an instructor wants to assign grades to students based on the following point scheme:

| Points | Letter Grade |
|---|---|
| 0 to 159 | F |
| 160 to 179 | D |
| 180 to 199 | C |
| 200 to 219 | B |
| 220 or more | A |

When everything has been graded and totaled, each student's point total must be compared to the table and converted into a letter grade. Having taught many large classes, we know that when this is done by hand, it is a time-consuming, error-prone process. The alternative is to have a spreadsheet do this conversion automatically with a look-up function.

With Lotus 1-2-3, the appropriate function is named @VLOOKUP. It uses three arguments to tell it how to search a vertical table. The first argument is the value to be looked up, in this case, the student's point total. The second argument specifies the range containing the table, and the third argument tells where the answer column (containing grades) is in relation to the table's first column.

The look-up table can be typed into any empty area of the worksheet. Its first column contains the cutoff points, and any other column can be used to hold the letter grades. In Figure 10.20, the grade look-up table occupies the range H16..K20, so the answer column is shifted three columns to the right of the first column.

The table look-up formula that calculates Ardebili's grade in cell N4 is @VLOOKUP(L4,$H$16..$K$20,3). It searches down column H looking for the pair of cells that bracket the value in cell L4, 205. The smaller of the two bracketing values is used (200), so in this case, the entry to be returned is selected from row 19. The function's third argument is 3, telling the spreadsheet that the answer column is located in column K, three columns past the first column. Thus Ardebili's grade is selected from cell K19, resulting in a grade of B.

## MACROS

Spreadsheet applications often involve repetitive commands. Perhaps you must type the same phrase in many cells. Or maybe you must give the commands to print an earnings projection repeatedly, interrupted only by making quick changes to the model's assumptions. Because computers are best at repetitive activities, expecting them to do these tasks for you is reasonable.

Many spreadsheets let you write a script of commands describing a sequence of tasks. This script is then assigned to a single key on the keyboard and played back at the touch of that key. The script of commands is called a **macro,** or *keyboard macro.* When the macro's key is pressed, the keystrokes are automatically typed one at a time; the spreadsheet interprets them just as if you had typed them yourself.

The simplest keyboard macro types a word or phrase whenever the macro is invoked. For example, a macro might type the fifty-seven–keystroke phrase

Computing Today: Microcomputer Concepts and Applications

whenever [ALT]-[C] is pressed. More complicated macros associate a series of commands with a single key.

- [ALT]-[F] might display a business form on the screen and prompt the user through the process of entering a business transaction.
- [ALT]-[M] might invoke a macro that merges parts of several worksheets on a disk into the current worksheet.
- [ALT]-[P] might establish the line length, margins, heading, and footing for a report and send the report to the printer.
- [ALT]-[S] might save a copy of the current worksheet on disk and move the active cell to cell A1.

The procedure for using a macro varies widely depending on the program, but it usually requires three basic steps.

*1.* Store the macro. Generally, you do this by storing the keystrokes that make up the macro as entries in cells. For example, you might type "Computing Today~" in cell Z8 of the worksheet. (The character ~ in this macro represents a carriage return.)

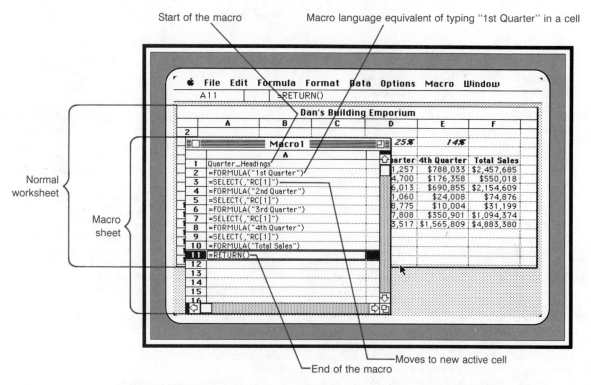

Start of the macro

Macro language equivalent of typing "1st Quarter" in a cell

Normal worksheet

Macro sheet

Moves to new active cell

End of the macro

**Figure 10.21**
Excel records and stores keyboard macros in a special *macro sheet*. Whenever the Quarter_Headings macro shown in this macro sheet is invoked, it enters a row of five column headings for a quarterly forecast into the active worksheet.

2. Associate the macro with a key. Generally, you do this by giving a special name to the cells that store the macro. For example, cell Z8 might be given the name \C. In Lotus 1-2-3, this would assign the keystrokes stored in cell Z8 to the [ALT]-[C] key.

3. Invoke the macro. Usually this is done by typing the key associated with the macro. For example, pressing [ALT]-[C] would cause Lotus 1-2-3 to type "Computing Today" followed by a carriage return into the active cell.

There is both an easy and a hard way to create keyboard macros. Excel illustrates the easy way; it has a *recorder* that you can use to teach it exactly what the macro is to do. You "record" a macro by starting Excel's recorder, then you carry out the actions you want the macro to perform. In addition to executing your commands as you type them, Excel silently records your keystrokes in a special worksheet called a *macro sheet* (see Figure 10.21). Once the procedure is recorded, it can be edited, given a name, and used like any other macro.

# A Word About . . . *Macro Processing*

*Macro languages are a powerful and effective tool to create programs, but they are limiting in three major ways. First, too many of them exist. Each specific application has its unique macro language, creating problems for those who must learn several different macro languages. Second, each macro language is bound to an individual application. No existing macro language lets you call routines from several different applications. Third, macro languages do not have the power and flexibility of traditional programming languages. With a traditional language, you can access the hardware directly and perform data manipulation down to the bit level. You can't do either of these tasks with existing macro languages.*

Macro languages appear in every type of application, and each has a unique syntax and set of commands. Programming in macro languages has become popular due to the high level of embedded functionality they provide.

Macro languages are not a recent development, nor are they unique to spreadsheet applications. One of the first popular applications with a macro language was dBASE II [a database management program], which offered users both a forms orientation and a *programming environment*. Not all macro languages look like a programming environment.

You can find macro languages in communications packages and word processors. Many communications packages provide an *auto-login* feature that is a form of macro language. Microsoft Word has a form of macro language called the style sheet. You can assign a name to various formatting characteristics. Then, by selecting and applying the name to a paragraph or document, you can reformat the text. Perhaps the best known macro language is the Lotus 1-2-3 spreadsheet program. While the 1-2-3 macro language was not the first, it might be the most widely recognized.

Each of these macro languages adds considerable functionality to its application. Unfortunately, each is unique. This causes problems in creating and using macro programs. You have to learn a new set of keystrokes or commands with each new application. You cannot use macros created for one application in another. This forces you to start from scratch with each application and eliminates any concept of a general-purpose macro program library.

Being bound to a single application is the most limiting factor of the present macro-language architecture. Within each application, you can write programs using the power and functions of that specific application. You cannot write programs to combine the unique strengths of several applications.

Macro languages are evolving toward traditional programming languages. They incorporate many features of traditional programming languages. Branching constructs and file input and output are now standard.

Macro-language syntax is also evolving from a keystroke orientation to a keyword orientation. Many of the original macro-language programs were files containing a series of keystrokes. The application would simply *play* the stored keystrokes at the user's request. To simplify the creation of macros, applications frequently included a *record* mode. When turned on, the record mode would capture all the subsequent keystrokes and store them in a file. A user would later ask the program to replay the file. Users never needed to know what was in the file. Even without a record mode, the programs were easy to create because the programming commands were identical to the program's commands.

The drawbacks of a keystroke syntax are difficulties in the readability and maintenance of macro programs. An example from a keystroke-style program might be /RNCdatabase. This calls the Range, the Name, then Create menu choices and creates a new range named database. Small programs using this syntax would be easy to create and modify. But a large program of these macros would be difficult to create and maintain.

Traditional languages use a keyword-oriented syntax. Each procedure and function is accessed by a command or keyword. An example from a keyword-style program could be SET.NAME ("database", C1:D15). This command names cells C1 through D15 "database."

The evolution of keystrokes to keywords and the addition of branching and file I/O can be seen in the differences between the macro syntax of Lotus 1-2-3 versions 1A and 2 (see Figures 1 and 2).

Macro languages are popular because of their high level of embedded functionality. The application becomes a rich subroutine library that the macro program can access. You don't have to write all the routines from scratch. Complex routines such as sorting, formatting, and table lookup are already available. Many programs are much shorter and easier to create using a macro langauge.

The 14-line macro program from Microsoft Excel (see Figure 3) demonstrates a table lookup program. The same program in any traditional language would be much longer.

| | |
|---|---|
| /XI | is equivalent to the IF command |
| /XG | is equivalent to the BRANCH command |
| /XQ | is equivalent to the QUIT command |
| /XC | is equivalent to the SUB-ROUTINE_NAME command |

Figure 1
Macros in Lotus 1-2-3 version 1A.

| | |
|---|---|
| {BEEP} | {LOOK} |
| {BLANK} | {MENUBRANCH} |
| {BRANCH} | {MENUCALL} |
| {BREAKOFF} | {ONERROR} |
| {BREAKON} | {OPEN} |
| {CLOSE} | {PANNELOFF} |
| {CONTENTS} | {PANNELON} |
| {DEFINE} | {PUT} |
| {DISPATCH} | {WRITELN} |
| {FILESIZE} | {QUIT} |
| {FOR} | {READ} |
| {FORBREAK} | {READLN} |
| {GET} | {RECALC} |
| {GETLABEL} | {RECALCCOL} |
| {GETNUMBER} | {RESTART} |
| {GETPOS} | {RETURN} |
| {IF} | {SETPOS} |
| {INDICATE} | {SUB-ROUTINE_NAME} |
| {LET} | |

Figure 2
Macros in Lotus 1-2-3 version 2.

Figure 3
A Microsoft Excel macro program called Animal_Babies. Animal_Babies is a guessing game where the program displays an animal randomly selected from a table named "animals" and asks the user to guess what the offspring is called.

```
Command Animal_Babies
WindowTitle="Names of Animal Babies"
continue    ="Try another (Y or N)?"
correct     ="That's right!!!"
            =SET.NAME("animals",D1:E8)
select      =INT(RAND()*8)+1
animal      =INDEX(animals,select,1)
baby        =INDEX(animals, select,2)
prompt1     ="What is the name of the offspring of "&animal&"?"
answer      =INPUT(prompt1,2,WindowTitle)
wrong       ="Wrong... The name of a "&animal&" 's offspring is "&baby&"."
prompt2     =IF(answer=baby,correct,wrong)&continue
next        =MID(input(prompt2,2,WindowTitle),1,1)
```

Source: Bill Gates (chairman of Microsoft Corporation), excerpted with permission from the 1987 Bonus Summer Edition of BYTE magazine, pages 11–12. © McGraw-Hill, Inc., New York, NY 10020. All rights reserved.

In contrast, Lotus 1-2-3 illustrates the hard way to create macros: You must type the macro directly into a normal worksheet's cells. Although this is not too difficult for simple macros, it is hard to remember the exact sequence of keystrokes necessary for a complicated procedure. Most people find that they must work through the procedure once at the keyboard, carefully writing down each keystroke. Then they type the keystrokes into cells where they are given a name and made into a macro.

With Lotus 1-2-3 and most other spreadsheets, you can use only the macros stored in the current worksheet. This is inconvenient if you use a macro for a task like setting up the printer. Either you must copy this macro into each new worksheet—increasing every worksheet's size and preventing you from modifying the macro easily—or it won't be available when desired. Because Excel stores macros on a separate macro sheet, you can build a library of macro commands and use them with any of your worksheets.

Most spreadsheet macros are created for one of two reasons. First, a macro can relieve the tedium of entering the same lengthy set of commands over and over again. Second, for infrequently given commands, such as those to print reports or consolidate data, a macro remembers the commands better than people do.

If you are developing sophisticated templates, there is a third reason to create macros: They can allow the spreadsheet to make decisions. Most macro languages include programming commands that can be embedded inside a macro to make IF..THEN.. tests, GOTO jumps, and SUBROUTINE calls (these are control structures familiar to any programmer). These commands convert a spreadsheet program from a simple calculating tool into an application development environment complete with a powerful programming language. By placing an IF..THEN.. command inside a macro, for instance, you can write a macro that erases a range of cells if the value in cell B5 is equal to 0 and does something else if the value is not equal to 0. Other macro programming commands allow a macro to display messages on the prompt line of the screen, pause for inputs from the keyboard, and store the inputs in specified cells. For example, Photo 48 in Window 5 shows how a system of macros can customize SuperCalc4's menu system and adapt its functions to the task of managing an inventory of wines.

Programmable macros provide the ultimate in power and versatility for spreadsheet applications, but they are not for the novice or the faint-hearted. In the hands of a motivated professional who is knowledgeable about spreadsheet applications, programmable macros can create interactive templates that help walk the user through the steps to complete the application.

---

## Summary

Most of the time spent interacting with a spreadsheet is not spent constructing formulas; it is spent entering data to obtain the results of calculations. Frequently, one person constructs a template that contains the formulas, and other people use the template. A substantial amount of knowledge can be built into a template. If a template is constructed carefully with protected cells, hidden entries, input via forms and menus, and helpful macros, the user needs little understanding of how the spreadsheet program or template works to obtain impressive results.

Macros not only save keystrokes for the expert user, they also make a template much easier for a beginner to use. Simple macros are fairly easy to construct; they eliminate repetitive typing. Advanced macros can turn a spreadsheet into a programming language. This provides the tools a professional needs to build powerful and easy-to-use applications; however, these tools are not for a novice spreadsheet user.

Advanced format settings can have a major effect on how information is presented on the screen. Chief among these settings is the width of columns. Other settings determine how many window panes are in the window, whether some rows or columns are frozen as titles on the window, and how numbers and text are formatted.

Three ways of recalculating the worksheet are to evaluate formulas column by column, row by row, or in a natural order that postpones evaluating a formula until the cells it depends on have been processed. Circular references set up a mathematical paradox in the worksheet; the paradox may or may not resolve itself with repeated recalculations.

Worksheets can be consolidated to transfer information or to summarize data. The consolidation can occur by copying information from one worksheet to another, by adding the values in two worksheets with a merge operation, or by permanently linking worksheets.

Built-in functions make it much easier to construct formulas for statistical, mathematical, and financial calculations. In addition, they can make it possible to process text inside a formula, perform calculations on dates and times, and look up values in a table.

---

## Key Terms

| | |
|---|---|
| active area | matrix operations |
| arguments | natural recalculation order |
| circular reference | protected cell |
| column-oriented recalculation | row-oriented recalculation |
| external references | synchronized scrolling |
| logical operators | template |
| macro | window panes |

---

## Discussion Questions

1. What might be some design and style rules for constructing templates to be used by clerical personnel?

2. Why might the numbers in a spreadsheet seem to "add up" incorrectly? How could this be avoided?

3. Can you suggest a scheme that would prevent a user from accidentally destroying information when copying or merging worksheets?

4. Suppose a worksheet is linked to several other worksheets, and each time it is loaded, the calculations take five minutes. This is rather awkward if no changes have been made to the other worksheets. What are some ways to avoid this problem?

5. Name some applications that can be solved with a spreadsheet that includes a macro programming ability. What sort of projects might be more easily solved with a traditional programming language?

6. When should you link cells instead of merging values? When is a copy-and-paste operation more appropriate?

7. Rank the following features according to their importance for developing spreadsheet applications: protecting cells, hiding cells, varying column widths, using forms to prompt the user for input, or building macros.

8. Describe how to merge a part of a worksheet into another worksheet if the part to be merged is not a rectangular-shaped group of cells.

9. Besides convenience, what are some other advantages of spreadsheet functions?

10. If macros are stored on a normal worksheet, where should they be placed? Would you prefer to store them on a separate, special sheet? What disadvantages might there be with this approach?

11. Who should decide who knows the password for a worksheet? Who should be able to change the password?

---

## Exercises

1. Create and test a template that accomplishes the same task as Figure 10.1 on page 276.

2. Design a template for a professor's grade book. Have the template compute the final grades from a grade look-up table. Use the COUNT function to prepare a frequency distribution of the resulting grades. For extra credit, design the worksheet so that it automatically modifies the cutoff values in its look-up table to give 20 percent of the students A's, 20 percent of the students B's, and so on.

3. Design a template for a state or federal long-form tax return that links the various schedules to the main form. Alternatively, search the literature to find out how to order a good set of tax templates.

4. Compare the cell-protection and keyboard macro features of three spreadsheet programs.

5. Find formulas that give circular references to two cells and do not converge to a set of stable values.

6. Compare the functions in a spreadsheet such as Lotus 1-2-3 with the functions in a programming language such as Fortran, Basic, or Cobol.

7. Design a worksheet to record the frame-by-frame bowling scores for a five-person bowling team bowling a three-game series. Display each person's scores for the three games, each person's total score, and the total team score.

# Data Management

In the early days of computing (around 1950), computers were used exclusively to compute formulas. Then, in 1957, the hard disk drive was invented and rapidly installed in computer systems. A hard disk could store more information than the computer's main memory and was much faster than magnetic tape. Its invention made it possible to store large amounts of information within a computer system and to retrieve the information quickly. This led to a shift in how computers were used—away from numerical calculations and toward transaction processing and information retrieval.

As the use of computers grew, so did the number of data files stored by organizations. By the late 1960s, a typical data processing department main-

tained thousands of data files, and, not suprisingly, keeping track of them was becoming unmanageable. The most obvious problem was the effort that was required to keep track of all the filenames and to catalog the types of data that was stored in each file. Another problem was redundant data. For example, some of the data in a payroll file might be the same as that in a personnel file—a clear waste of storage capacity. A more subtle problem resulted from the direct link between programs and the data files they used: Each time the layout of a data file was changed—to add a new field or expand the width of an existing one, for example—all programs that used the data file had to be modified to reflect the new structure. Thus data processing departments spent most of their programming time modifying old programs (called *program maintenance*) instead of developing new ones.

These problems led to the development and use of *database management systems (DBMS)*—software for controlling, reading, and updating the information in a collection of files. A DBMS acts as a buffer between programs and data in the same way that a data processing department acts as a buffer between the computer user and mainframes. The database management system helps keep track of where data are stored. More important, a DBMS solves many of the problems of redundant data and program maintenance by separating the physical storage locations of data from the logical structure of data as seen by programmers—a division at the root of database management software.

The first database management systems were designed to meet the needs of data processing departments; these first systems were difficult to use. Full-time professionals called *database administrators* had to lay out the structure of databases and contend with the complexities of the software. To circumvent the need for programmers and database administrators, software developers invented file management software. A *file management system* (also called a *file manager*) is a collection of programs for managing data stored in a single file. File managers emerged in the 1970s to make it easy to set up a data file, enter and edit the data in the file, and print reports from the file. A file manager is not a complete database management system but a simple yet elegant solution for most applications that use only one file at a time.

In the 1980s, microcomputers with relatively large-capacity disk drives became widely available. These computers could easily manage large lists when equipped with data management software, but they aggravated the problems of the 1970s: They either required programming expertise to be used effectively or were limited to single-file applications. For example, PFS:Professional File, a popular file management program, can be mastered in a few hours. But early versions of dBASE II required a programmer to set up the database and write dBASE II file processing programs.

Today, most popular database management programs for personal computers are miniature duplicates of programs for mainframe computers. R:BASE System V was derived from RIM (Relational Information Management System), a database management system developed to track parts for NASA, and dBASE II and III evolved from programs for mainframe computers at the Jet Propulsion Laboratory. These programs handle multiple files and include various methods for instructing the computer to process the data stored in these files. At first, they were essentially scaled-down mainframe programs, so a programmer or someone familiar with database management was needed to fully utilize their features. Recent versions of these programs are easier to use than their earlier counterparts. Eventually, full-featured database management systems may be as easy to use as simple file managers.

Part IV introduces you to data management software in two steps. In Chapter 11, we describe file management systems, and in Chapter 12, we describe database management systems. File management systems, the simplest form of data management, are used to keep any large list that must be quickly retrieved and displayed. Their main purpose is to extract information in the form of a printed report. A DBMS can do everything a file manager can do, but it can do these things to two or more files simultaneously. A DBMS also usually incorporates many more features than those in a file management system.

# File Management Systems

File management is the simplest form of data management. The main purpose of a **file management system** is to extract information in the form of a printed report, a document containing data from your computer files. Although file managers can handle only one file of information at a time, they provide one of the best ways to organize and process a large volume of data. With them, you can easily enter, look up, modify, and delete information. You need not be concerned with how data are stored in files, how the information is arranged internally, or how the programs process the data stored on disk. The file manager insulates you from the details of information storage and retrieval.

## THE USER INTERFACE

The first step in understanding a file manager is to determine the underlying model assumed by the people who designed your software. The model is visible in the user interface—the prompts, menus, and other screen displays that appear when the program is run. File managers use various models.

Perhaps the simplest model is that of a piece of paper containing a written list. In the case of a file manager, the "piece of paper" is the display screen, as Figure 11.1 shows, and the list is scrolled on the screen. Each row in the list corresponds to a record in the file, and each column corresponds to a field. (Recall that a *record* is a collection of related data items, and a *field* is a part of a record reserved for a particular item or type of data.)

Other file managers use the business form as their model. This model is easily understood because we are all used to filling out business forms in everyday life. **On-screen forms** are templates that capture and display data by providing blanks

for each field. Figure 11.2 shows how the information in Figure 11.1 appears when displayed in a form. File managers that use the business form as their model let you design a form to appear any way you want. You may design the data entry form by "drawing" it on your screen when the file is initially set up. In many systems, defining a file and defining a form are identical; that is, defining the form also defines the contents of the file.

Lists and simulated Rolodex files not only provide logical ways to look at your data but also can establish boundaries on what you do with the system. For example, an electronic Rolodex system typically can do only what a manual Rolodex system does: look up information, add new entries, and so forth. A system built around the model of a business form is usually more flexible and might be able to check the input data to guarantee it is within certain bounds (greater than zero, for example) or verify all the blanks in the form have been completed before it accepts the form for storage.

A powerful file management system will provide the flexibility to let you view the data in several different ways. For example, Figure 11.3 shows a screen from Reflex (a popular, inexpensive file management system that has been marketed by Borland International since 1985) with three windows: The Form window places data in the blanks of a form; the List window displays data in a table; and the Graph window summarizes data in a pie chart, bar graph, or line graph. With Reflex, you can also select options that summarize data in a tabular format or lay out and print reports.

## FILES AS LISTS

Nearly everyone keeps some kind of list. For example, a teacher keeps a grade book, and a salesperson keeps a list of sales leads. If these lists are large or require frequent maintenance, sorting and updating them can be a tedious job to do by hand. File managers provide an alternative. Any list can be converted from a paper format to

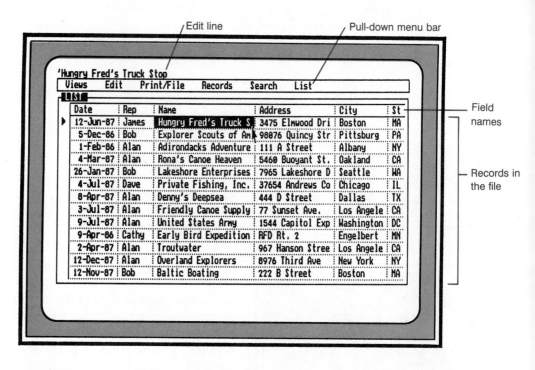

**Figure 11.1**
A list is one of the simplest ways to view a file. The list can be scrolled vertically to see different records or horizontally to see different fields.

**Figure 11.2**
A form displays only one record from the file at a time. In this form, the Name field contains the entry Hungry Fred's Truck Stop.

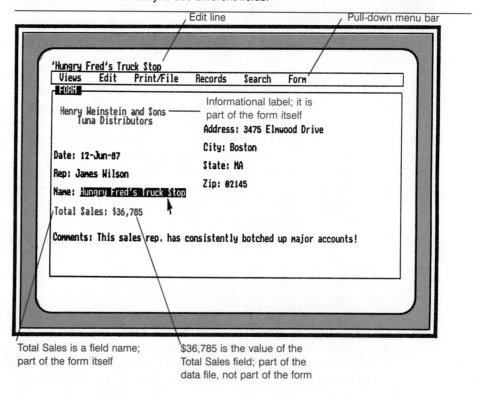

Total Sales is a field name; part of the form itself

$36,785 is the value of the Total Sales field; part of the data file, not part of the form

**Figure 11.3**
Three ways to view the same file. The Form option from the Views menu displays one record at a time; the List option shows records in a tabular format; and the Graph option summarizes the whole file with a bar chart.

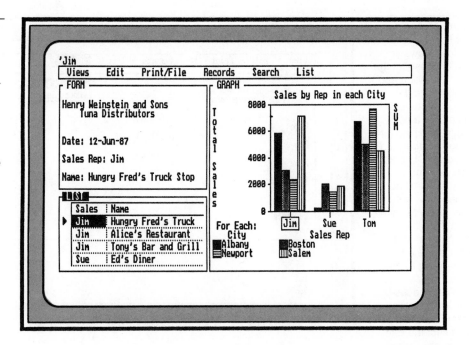

an electronic data file. Each row in the list becomes a record, and the items on a row are stored in the record's fields.

Laying out a file is a simple matter. You must tell the system the name of each field and the type of information it will contain. Most file managers allow fields to have variable lengths, but some require that all fields have a fixed width. Thus if the contents of a field will vary in length, you should select the most likely maximum width for that field.

Programs differ in how they let you set up a file and design its layout. One common method involves simply typing each field name followed by the type of data the field will store and the size of the field. The order you type the field names in determines their order in the record. Using this method, you might lay out the file shown in Figure 11.1 as follows. (In all the examples in this chapter, characters shown in color are typed by the user; characters in black are generated by the computer.)

Enter a command: BUILD

Enter the filename you wish to build: CLIENTS
Enter each field name, its data type, and format.
Example: ZIPCODE,Numeric,#####
Enter STOP when done, or press [Esc] for help.

DATE,Date,dd-mmm-yy
REP,Text,XXXXXXXXXXXXXXXXXXXXXXXX
NAME,Text,XXXXXXXXXXXXXXXXXXXXXXXXXXXXXXX
[ ... ]
TOTAL SALES,Numeric,$###,###,###.##

**Figure 11.4**
This Form Design window allows you both to construct the on-screen form and to determine the file's field names. You create a field simply by typing its name anywhere on the screen. Labels, such as Tuna Distributors, must be preceded by an apostrophe to distinguish them from field names. The form can be edited by dragging names or labels around the screen as necessary. When everything is complete, you select the Exit Design option from the menu bar.

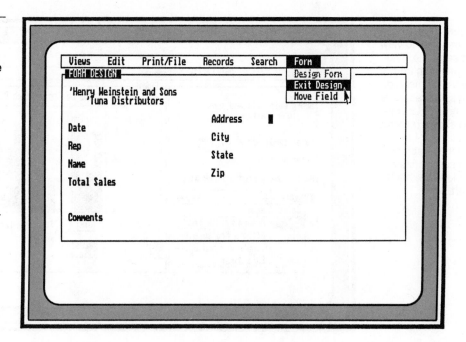

Because this method is fairly cumbersome, many recently developed systems let you design the file on the screen. For example, in Reflex, you create a new file by constructing a form for it, as Figure 11.4 shows. The parts of the form can be typed in and moved around the screen with the cursor-movement keys or a mouse until a pleasing layout is obtained. At this point, the form can contain only two types of entries: labels and the names of the file's fields. Labels merely comment on the form and are identified by an initial apostrophe, as in the 'Tuna Distributors entry of Figure 11.4. All other entries are assumed to be the file's field names. Once the file layout has been determined, you are ready to enter data into the file. To do this, you simply type entries in the fields, using the [Tab] or [Enter] key to move from field to field.

Reflex allows three basic types of fields: text, date, and numeric. It uses the first entry you make in a field to determine that field's type. For example, if you enter 6/12/87 into a field, Reflex makes that field a date field. (This procedure is similar to the way most spreadsheet programs determine whether an entry is a label or a number based on the first character of the entry.) Once the field type is determined, Reflex requires that new entries be of the correct type. This means "Smith," for example, can't be entered into a date field.

Most file managers allow you to set up computed fields. The value of a **computed field** is based on the values of other fields in the same record. You must give the file manager a formula for each computed field. For example, if the formula for a Total_Cost field is (Unit_Cost * Quantity), the file manager would multiply the values in the Unit_Cost and Quantity fields to obtain the value for the Total_Cost field. Computed fields can eliminate many manual calculations and can even be used to construct miniature spreadsheetlike models.

```
 Views    Edit    Print/File    Records    Search
            SEARCH CONDITIONS
 Method of entry:  ☐ Cell    ☒ Table

  Field   | Condition              | OR          | OR
  Date    | BTWN (1/01/87, 4/01/87)|             |
  Sales Rep| 'James Wilson'        | 'Jim Wilson'|
  Name    |                        |             |
  Address |                        |             |
  City    | 'Boston'               |             |
  State   |                        |             |

 Use:  ☒ Conditions as Entered   ☐ Opposite of Conditions

         [ Proceed ]   [ Cancel ]
```

# FILE PROCESSING OPERATIONS

All file managers provide a variety of essential file processing operations that let you look up, insert, delete, or modify a record; select a group of records; and either sort or index the file. You will spend more time doing these basic tasks than any other file processing activities. The file manager should therefore make each of these activities simple and quick to perform.

A *look-up operation* finds and displays a particular record on the screen. For example, you might want to retrieve the first record that includes Jim Wilson in the Name field. With a list-oriented system, you could hunt for the record directly by scrolling through the file. But for files containing thousands of records, this strategy amounts to looking for a needle in a haystack. A more effective method is to give the file manager a description of the record and have it find the record for you. Figure 11.5 illustrates how to do this by entering **search conditions** in a dialog box. Other systems let you enter the search conditions directly into the blanks of an empty form. Still other systems require that search conditions be typed in a command-line format. Look-up operations become imposing if you must use a command-line format; for example, a command-line equivalent of the search in Figure 11.5 is

DATE BTWN(1/01/87,4/01/87) AND (SALES REP = 'James Wilson'
OR SALES REP = 'Jim Wilson') AND CITY = 'Boston'

A *select operation* finds and marks records that match the search conditions. (The corresponding operation in word processing is marking a block of text.) A select operation precedes any activity that will affect an entire group of records at once. For example, you might want to examine all records with positive balances in the Past Due field. A select operation could mark these records; then you could scroll through them without having to view other records. Select operations can also be used to delete unwanted or obsolete records quickly or to select a subset of the file for printing.

An *insert operation* adds another record to the file. For example, you might add a new subscriber to a magazine's mailing list. With a form-oriented system, you begin this operation by asking for a blank form. Then you fill out the form by typing entries in fields, using the [Tab] or [Enter] key to move from field to field. With a list-oriented system, you need to request a new row before you can begin entering data, but otherwise the process is similar. Both types of systems let you correct spelling errors and edit the fields until the record is correct. In most systems, the records you insert are added to the end of the growing file.

A *delete operation* removes a record from the file. For example, you might remove Jason Wilkins from a mailing list when his subscription ends. To delete a record, you must first use a look-up operation to display it; then the delete operation removes it from the file.

A *modify operation* changes one or more fields in a particular record. For example, you might want to change the fields that hold Martha Tildon's address and zip code because she has moved. To modify a record, you must first use a look-up operation to retrieve it. Then you tab to the fields you wish to edit and make the changes.

A *sort* or *index operation* is used to place records in a particular order for viewing or printing. A file manager will either sort records or index them; it will not do both. We explain both methods in turn.

You tell a *sort-oriented file manager* how to organize the file by selecting the primary and secondary sort fields and by choosing whether to sort these fields in ascending or descending order. The **primary sort field** is used first in sorting the records. The **secondary sort field** resolves how records with the same primary field values should be ordered. For example, if you want to print a sales report organized by customers, the primary sort field would be the field that holds the customers' names. If some customers have made several purchases, you might choose the date field as the secondary sort field. This would cause each customer's purchases to be listed by date.

A file manager sorts by moving records or adjusting pointers that identify where records are stored. Either approach is tedious, even for a computer. Sorting a file with 10,000 records can take from five minutes to an hour or more on a microcomputer. Because a file can be in only one order at a time, you may need to sort the file often to view or print it differently. This can be a major disadvantage of a sort-oriented file manager.

An *index-oriented file manager* allows you to establish one or more indexes for a file. A book's index contains keywords and their location (page number) in the book. Similarly, a file's index is a list of field values and their location (record number) in the file. For example, consider the following two indexes for a file with only seven records:

| NAME INDEX | | ZIP INDEX | |
| --- | --- | --- | --- |
| Value in the Name field | Record # in the file | Value in the Zip field | Record # in the file |
| Adams | 1. | 10755 | 3. |
| Baker | 7. | 39588 | 6. |
| James | 4. | 43210 | 5. |
| Jones | 3. | 55143 | 2. |
| King | 6. | 65001 | 7. |
| Smith | 2. | 86501 | 1. |
| Thomas | 5. | 99123 | 4. |

The file manager could use these two indexes to read the file in alphabetical order by name (by retrieving records 1, 7, 4, 3, 6, 2, and 5) or in numerical order by zip code (by retrieving records 3, 6, 5, 2, 7, 1, and 4). Thus with indexing, it is not necessary to resort the file just to retrieve the records in a different order.

Index-oriented systems have some disadvantages. Indexing forces the file manager to do more work each time a record is added or deleted from the file: Each index must be updated; each index takes storage space; and finally, if you need to establish a new index for a file, you must wait while the index is constructed.

## REPORT GENERATION

A **report generator** or *report writer* is a program for producing reports from lists stored in one or more files. Data management systems vary greatly in the flexibility and capability of their report generators. Any report generator can print columnar reports with fields arranged as columns across the page. Most can also print mailing labels by arranging the fields of each record so that they occupy several rows of the page.

A good report generator will let you select which fields are printed, where they appear on the page, and what their column headings say. For example, you might want to print only the names and departments of employees who have worked for the company for more than twenty years or who earn more than $50,000 per year. To carry out these tasks, you must specify which records qualify for printing. With most report generators, the method for identifying these records is the same as the procedure for specifying the search conditions for a look-up operation.

Most report generators can also provide totals and subtotals. For example, sales transactions could be totaled and printed at the bottom of the Sales column. Subtotals could also be printed for groups of records; this is done in reports that contain breaks. A **report break** is a position in a report where a prespecified field changes value from one record to the next. For example, the report shown in Figure 11.6(b) has a report break based on the Date field. This report break occurs when the value

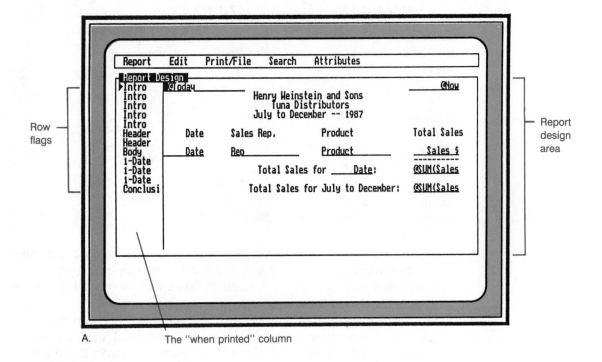

Row flags

Report design area

A.

The "when printed" column

**Figure 11.6**
Using **(a)** an on-screen report generator to print **(b)** a report from a data file.

Parts of report

Variables used in report

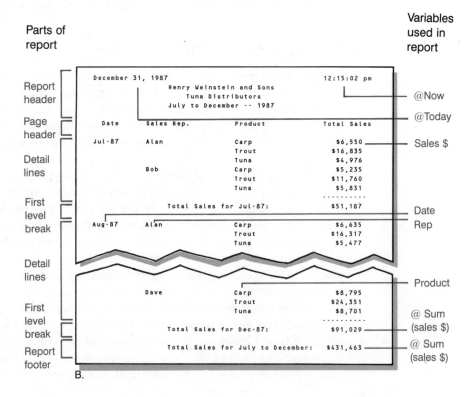

Report header

Page header

Detail lines

First level break

Detail lines

First level break

Report footer

@Now

@Today

Sales $

Date

Rep

Product

@ Sum (sales $)

@ Sum (sales $)

B.

in the Date field changes from one record to the next; the report break is used to print monthly subtotals for the Sales column. Some reports have several levels of report breaks. For example, suppose a report contains subtotals for each sales office in a firm, each salesperson within a sales office, and each product sold by a salesperson. In this case, the first-level break would be based on the Product field, the second-level break on the Salesperson field, and the third-level break on the Sales Office field.

Report generators also vary in how they allow you to lay out the report. As in many other areas of the computer field, there is a tradeoff here between power and convenience. The most powerful report generators require you to learn a command language to describe how the report should look. These systems provide commands for positioning fields on the page, establishing report breaks, performing calculations on field values before printing, and making decisions based on the values being printed. These features can be invaluable if you need to print an unusual or complicated report; for example, an apartment manager might want to print a few extra lines on invoices for tenants who still owe rent for past months. By testing the value in the Past Due field, a command-language report generator could print a standard invoice for most renters and an expanded invoice for slow-paying renters.

Forms-oriented report generators are much easier to use than those that rely on a command language. With a forms-oriented report generator, you draw a template on the screen of how the report should look, and the report generator uses the template to print the report. Figure 11.6 illustrates this process. The Report Design area in Figure 11.6(a) contains the template that describes all aspects of the report. Each line in this area describes one type of line in the report. The underlined items are variables that receive their values from fields in the data file when the report is printed. All other items are labels used to improve the report's appearance and readability.

Once you have specified how a report should be laid out, you should be allowed to save the specifications for later use. After several report specifications have been created and stored, requesting any report should be a simple matter—whether you want to print a report of past-due accounts, a report in mailing-label format, or a report listing recent entries to the file.

---

## Summary

Lists are used in a wide variety of businesses to keep track of subscriptions, sales leads, inventory, client names, and so on. No matter what the application is, all lists are processed by performing operations: data entry, look up, modify, delete, insert, and report generation. Most lists are kept in some kind of order to speed information retrieval. The order can be obtained by sorting the list or by constructing one or more indexes. Lists can be kept manually, but a computer file is generally the best way to manage lists when they become very long or when processing becomes complicated or time consuming.

A file management system simplifies rudimentary data processing operations. These include file setup and data entry as well as look-up, insert, delete, and modify operations and additional processing steps, such as sorting, indexing, and report generation.

Columnar reports are printed outputs in which each field of a record is printed in a separate column. A report generator lets you design your own headings, footings, date, page numbers, and column headings.

Forms add power to a file management system by increasing access control, extending the ability of the file management system to perform calculations, and making the file management software easier to use. A system that manages multiple forms can do much more than a single-form file system. One form is designated for each operation to be performed throughout the file-processing cycle. For example, one form may be used to enter data and another to print records. Records can be retrieved easily when search values are entered into a form. Matching conditions such as equal, greater than, and not equal are commonly used in file management software.

## Key Terms

| | |
|---|---|
| computed field | primary sort field |
| file management system | report break |
| on-screen form | report generator |

## Discussion Questions

1. How should you choose between using a spreadsheet or a file manager for an application? Do you know any examples of people making this choice poorly?

2. What model does the user interface of your file manager employ?

3. What rules can you give for determining whether a list should be computerized or handled manually?

4. If you were to design a file manager, how would you let the user specify the search conditions for a look-up operation?

5. Most spreadsheet programs have sort operations, and most file managers allow calculated fields. Are these two types of products likely to become more similar?

## Exercises

1. Design an on-screen form for a newspaper subscription department to use in entering data. Assume subscribers have the following options:
    a. Newspaper: morning, evening, or Sunday
    b. Billing: weekly, monthly, every six months, or annually
    c. Delivery: carrier or mail

2. Design a file management system for a health club's billing system. Assume the membership classes and monthly dues are family, $45; single adult, $25; and junior, $20. The club initiation fee is $500 for a family, $300 for a single adult, and $150 for a junior. The initiation fee may be paid either in a lump sum on joining (minus a 10 percent discount) or monthly over a three-year period.

# Database Management Systems

A database management system (DBMS) is a collection of programs that provides convenient access to data stored in a **database,** which is merely a logical grouping of one or more data files. The primary difference between a DBMS and a file management system is a DBMS allows simultaneous access to multiple files. A DBMS is also likely to have better features for restructuring and maintaining files and for automatic file processing. A DBMS can do more than a file management system.

In this chapter, we explain by example how most DBMS programs work. We show in these examples how to set up a database, use it to retrieve specified data, and process the information in one file to obtain new information stored in another file. For example, you can direct a DBMS to compute a total from a field in one file and then add the total to a balance in a master file.

The management information systems (MIS) departments in major corporations use mainframe computers with full-scale DBMS systems, which are more complex and comprehensive than the DBMS software found on most personal computers. In many instances, a personal computer DBMS is a scaled-down version of a mainframe DBMS. R:BASE System V, dBASE II or III, Revelation, Informix, and most popular DBMS systems for personal computers originated on large computers. The

# 12

major difference between DBMSs for mainframes and those for personal computers is the size and sophistication of their application-development tools.

A complete DBMS can provide many different views of the database, print reports from multiple files, make backup copies of existing files, and convert data from one format to another. These and other features are important to understand when selecting a DBMS. We devote an entire section of this chapter to the necessary and desirable features of a DBMS.

## BASIC CONCEPTS

### Overall Structure of a DBMS

A computer-based DBMS in some ways resembles a public library where people can share books, magazines, films, and newspapers. Access to the library's thousands of documents is possible because the items are cataloged logically, such as with the Dewey decimal system or the Library of Congress system. It's easier to retrieve a document by using a catalog than by browsing through the entire library because card catalogs provide a standard way of accessing information. If we use the terminology of database management systems to describe a public library, we would call the entire collection of documents the *database*, and the card catalog the *logical schema*.[1]

In a computer, a **logical schema** is a standard way of organizing information into accessible parts, just as the card catalog of a library is a standard way of organizing documents. Schemas contain machine-processable descriptions of the contents of

---

1. The *American Heritage Dictionary* defines *schema* as "a summarized or diagrammatic representation of something; an outline." Furthermore, according to this dictionary, *schemata* is the plural of *schema*. Computer terminology has historically abused the English language, and this is no exception—most DBMS experts use the word *schemas* when discussing more than one schema. We adopt this common usage.

| Organizational Structure | Systematic Structure | | | Technological Structure |
|---|---|---|---|---|

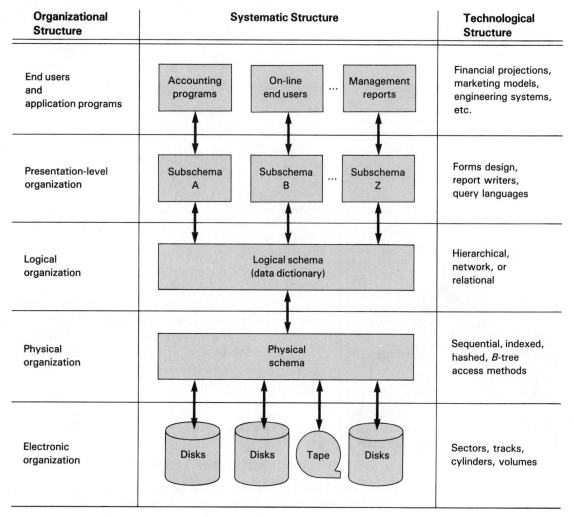

**Figure 12.1**
Organizational, systematic, and technological structures in a large database management system

the database so that users can easily browse and retrieve data from the database. The logical schema is separate from the **physical schema**, which describes how data are actually stored on a disk. The data might reside in thousands of files spread across many disks or tapes, but this isn't apparent because the logical schema insulates you from the physical schema; physical data access is handled by the DBMS. In this respect, a DBMS is better than a library. If a library were as convenient to use, librarians would instantly retrieve your card-catalog selections from the shelves.

Figure 12.1 shows the overall relationships among people, machines, and processes in a large DBMS as they might occur in a major corporation; but even a DBMS for microcomputers incorporates the fundamental ideas of the figure. This chart is best understood by reading it from left to right and from top to bottom, like a page in a book. The top row shows the people and programs that feed data into and receive information from the DBMS, as well as examples of the technology they might use to collect and analyze that information. A large DBMS can interact with many users at the same time, and the "users" can be people sitting at a terminal or application programs running in a multitasking computer system. Thus at a certain time, the DBMS might be sending payroll information to an accounting program, receiving sales transactions from clerks, and printing management reports. Financial projections, marketing models, statistical analyses, engineering calculations, or other technology may be incorporated into an application program or employed by an end user to collect and analyze information. In the following section, we examine some of the other structures depicted in Figure 12.1.

## Subschemas

The second row of Figure 12.1 indicates how the data in a database are filtered, formatted, and rearranged as appropriate for each group of users. In a large DBMS, each user can "see" only a small part of the entire database; most of the data are shielded from view. This illustrates another similarity between a DBMS and a library. Most people use only a small part of the library, and they have different ways of viewing it. An artist probably thinks of the library as a place to find copies of rare and beautiful paintings; an engineer views the library as a source of technical data, such as mathematical tables and engineering journals; and a business executive might use the library to read stock market reports. These different views may result in different ways of retrieving books, newspapers, and magazines, yet the underlying information is stored in the same way for all users of the library.

Using the terminology of database management systems, we would call each individual view of the library a **subschema**. Each description of how a database should look from a particular user's perspective is stored in a subschema. Subschemas also include information used by the DBMS to design forms, produce reports, and process queries. Because many data management systems for personal computers are designed to be used by a single user, some do not support the creation of subschemas.

As an illustration of the role of subschemas in a DBMS, consider a simple database for a small company. Assume the database contains the following:

| *Fields in database* | *A sample employee's information* |
|---|---|
| Name | Steve Johnson |
| Address | 1755 NW Arthur Circle, Corvallis, OR 97330 |
| Phone | (503) 753-1143 |
| Hiring Date | 8/15/81 |
| Birth Date | 12/17/51 |
| Salary | $43,000 |
| Soc-Sec-Num | 543-64-6466 |

The logical schema for this database would include the name of each field (Name, Address, and so on) and the type of data stored in each field (text, date, integer, and so on). The database might be used by many people in the corporation. For example, the payroll department needs salary information to print paychecks, and the personnel department needs to know when employees are eligible for retirement. To accommodate these different needs, the following two subschemas might be established:

*Payroll subschema*

Display format:
  DEFAULT
Fields:
  Name
  Soc-Sec-Num
  Salary
Password:
  ALPHA12

*Personnel subschema*

Display format:
  SCREEN FORM #482
Fields:
  Name
  Hiring Date
  Age
  Soc-Sec-Num
Calculations:
  Age = Today's Date – Birth Date

The syntax here is merely representative of how the subschemas might be laid out; database management systems vary greatly in how schemas and subschemas are constructed. The important point is that each subschema tells the DBMS how to accept and present data for a particular set of users or application programs. Thus when a payroll program uses the payroll subschema and provides the necessary password, the DBMS might respond with

Steve Johnson        543646466        43000

Alternatively, if, in May of 1987, a clerk uses the personnel subschema, the DBMS might display

EMPLOYEE                SENIORITY DATA
Name: Steve Johnson     Hiring Date: 8/15/81
Age: 35                 Social Security Number: 543-64-6466

The DBMS calculates the employee's age by subtracting the employee's birth date from today's date (the date in the computer system's clock). This example illustrates some fundamental characteristics of how a DBMS shares information among users. Subschemas can be used to create different, personalized views of the same data. Information might be arranged in a different order and presented in different formats. A subschema can be used to hide sensitive information (such as salaries) from view simply by omitting fields from the subschema's description. It can also create new information from the physical information in the database by performing calculations.

A subschema effectively shields its users from the details of how data are organized in files or stored on disk. The payroll program will work equally well if the database stores the information it needs in one large file, two smaller files, or some other manner. The payroll subschema specifies exactly how data are to be passed to the payroll program, so how data are actually stored doesn't matter to it.

This illustrates one of the most important consequences of the DBMS approach to managing information: **data independence.** The physical structure of the database is isolated from users and application programs; they do not see it at all. Data independence is extremely important to programmers and system analysts because it allows file maintenance operations to be performed without requiring modifications to existing application programs. Moreover, application programs can be written in different programming languages, view the data differently, or be modified without destroying other users' access. For example, the payroll program's view of data in the database can be changed without affecting the personnel program *even though they may both access the same information.*

## Logical Structure

The third row of Figure 12.1 refers to the logical organization within a DBMS. The way the logical schema is constructed influences the behavior of the entire DBMS because it controls what data are stored in the database and how the data may be retrieved. Here are some typical goals for the design of the logical schema.

- Data should not be stored redundantly in the database. For example, if names are paired with social security numbers in one part of the database, they should not be stored a second time in another part. Redundant storage wastes space and opens up the possibility of inconsistencies. For example, if Steve Johnson's social security number were stored twice in the database, once as 543-64-6466 and once as 432-53-5355, it would be a *data inconsistency.*

- The methods of organizing data should be understandable. You shouldn't need an advanced degree in software engineering to construct queries to determine, say, how many employees work in the Los Angeles sales office.

- The methods of accessing data should be efficient. The DBMS should quickly dispense with routine processing, such as posting a day's sales transactions to an accounts receivable master file.

- The logical schema itself should be flexible and expandable. It should adapt gracefully as your needs for storing and retrieving data change.

These goals often conflict; for example, the most efficient structure for processing may be the least flexible. Balancing these goals successfully can be tricky. This is one reason large database systems are often developed by professional *database administrators.*

Three dominant technologies are used to construct logical views of a database: hierarchical, network, and relational. Any particular DBMS will use only one of these methods to organize data. These methods accomplish the same basic task of cataloging the data in the database, but they use different models to describe the data.

### Hierarchical Databases

A **hierarchical database** establishes a top-to-bottom relationship among the items in a database, much like the relationships among members of a family on a family tree. Each member of the tree has a unique parent, or "owner"; to reach a member, you must pass through the owner. Figure 12.2 shows how a database for a class list

**Figure 12.2**
A hierarchical
database with a one-
to-many access
path between
classes and students

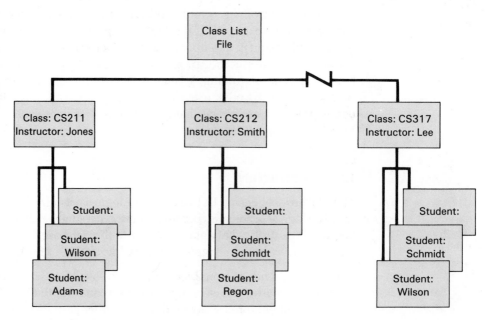

might appear in a hierarchical schema. This structure seems quite natural because all students for a given class are grouped under that class.

When a hierarchical model is used, the relationship among items in the database is established when the schema is constructed. This means that the hierarchy is static and can't be changed easily once the database is set up. This fixed structure makes some tasks far easier than others. For example, it's a trivial matter to read from Figure 12.2 the names of the students in class CS212, but the entire class list must be searched to determine the classes being taken by Schmidt.

Business data naturally have a hierarchical structure: Transactions belong to specific accounts, clients belong to sales regions, and so forth. The rigid structure of a hierarchical model makes it extremely easy to enter or update routine business transactions quickly, but it isn't convenient for answering specific inquiries. This efficiency of processing is a major reason most large transaction-processing systems today use the hierarchical model. Another major reason is historical: The first database management systems for mainframes were hierarchical, and large corporations find it difficult to convert from one database model to another.

### Network Databases

A network database is similar to a hierarchical database—with one important difference. Instead of restricting the structure to a one-to-many relationship between owner and members, a **network database** permits many-to-many relationships. For example, as Figure 12.3 illustrates, many students may be enrolled in many classes, and many instructors may teach many students; a network schema can reflect these relationships. Once established, these relationships are static and cannot be changed easily.

Many network databases have been implemented on mainframe computers. In fact, CODASYL (Conference on Data Systems Languages) recommends using net-

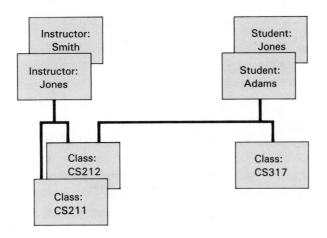

**Figure 12.3**
A network database consisting of a many-to-many access path between students and classes and between instructors and classes

work schema, and network databases are sometimes called CODASYL databases. Network databases are more flexible than hierarchical databases, but because the owner-coupled sets are fixed when the database is designed, the use of network databases has decreased.

### Relational Database

A **relational database** stores data in tables, as Figure 12.4 shows. Each table is called a *relation*; each row of a relation is a *tuple;* and each tuple is divided into fields or *domains*. Most people find it natural to organize and manipulate data with a relational database because it relies on the familiar model of a table containing records and fields.

**SCHEDULE Relation**

| CLASS | INSTRUCTOR |
|-------|------------|
| CS211 | Jones |
| CS215 | Franklin |
| CS317 | Lee |
| CS201 | Feldstein |
| . | . |
| . | . |
| . | . |

**REGISTRATION Relation**

| CLASS | STUDENT |
|-------|---------|
| CS212 | Adams |
| CS317 | Schmidt |
| CS211 | Wilson |
| CS212 | Schmidt |
| . | . |
| . | . |
| . | . |

**Figure 12.4**
A relational database stores data in tables called relations.

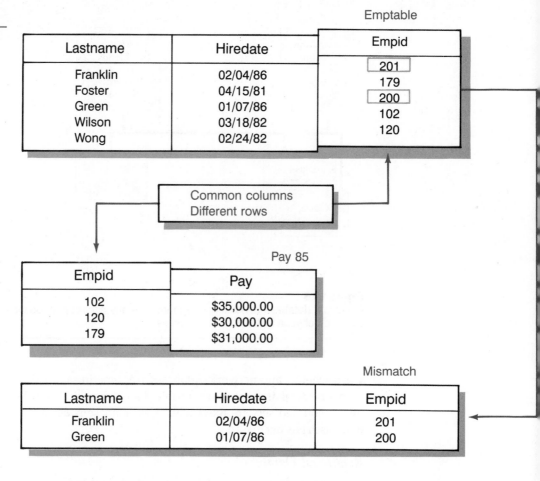

Emptable

| Lastname | Hiredate | Empid |
|----------|----------|-------|
| Franklin | 02/04/86 | 201 |
| Foster | 04/15/81 | 179 |
| Green | 01/07/86 | 200 |
| Wilson | 03/18/82 | 102 |
| Wong | 02/24/82 | 120 |

Common columns
Different rows

Pay 85

| Empid | Pay |
|-------|-----|
| 102 | $35,000.00 |
| 120 | $30,000.00 |
| 179 | $31,000.00 |

Mismatch

| Lastname | Hiredate | Empid |
|----------|----------|-------|
| Franklin | 02/04/86 | 201 |
| Green | 01/07/86 | 200 |

Unlike hierarchical and network databases, a relational database imposes little structure on the data at the time they are stored. For example, it is not immediately apparent from the REGISTRATION relation in Figure 12.4 what classes Schmidt is taking, nor is it obvious what students are in class CS212. The rows in the REGISTRATION relation are not automatically linked either by classes (as in a class list) or by students (as in a student schedule). Instead of permanent linkages among items, a relational database allows temporary relationships to be established by *query commands,* instructions given to the DBMS to look up, retrieve, calculate, move, copy, print, and so forth. A *query* is a miniature program that tells the DBMS what to do. For example, in the query

JOIN Schedule WITH Registration FORMING Temp-Rel.
DISPLAY Instructor FROM Temp-Rel WHERE student = "Joe Schmidt".

the first line directs the DBMS to merge the data in the SCHEDULE relation (Figure 12.4) with the data in the REGISTRATION relation, creating a new relation called TEMP-REL. The TEMP-REL relation will have three fields: Class, Instructor, and Student. The second line of the query tells the DBMS to display the name in the

Instructor field for all the rows in TEMP-REL whose Student field contains Joe Schmidt. The effect of these two commands is to display the names of Joe Schmidt's instructors.

One of the most powerful features of a relational DBMS is the ease with which tables can be manipulated. These systems have many commands for such tasks as extracting, joining, intersecting, and selecting tables. Taken together, these commands constitute a relational **query language** for processing multiple tables. For example, as Figure 12.5 illustrates, if you give the command

SUBTRACT pay85 FROM emptable FORMING mismatch

a table called MISMATCH is formed from all the records of EMPTABLE that don't have corresponding records in PAY85.

In the last ten years, relational database management systems have become very popular, particularly among users of personal computers. Relational systems provide more flexibility in manipulating data than either hierarchical or network systems because they offer powerful query languages that aren't limited by a fixed set of relationships among data items. The chief complaint about relational database systems has been their poor processing efficiency. But as the speed of relational systems improves and the cost of computing declines, this complaint is becoming less valid.

## Physical Structure

The last two rows of Figure 12.1 show the physical organization and electronic structure of a database system. Normally, the DBMS hides the details about where and how data are stored in the computer system so that users can concentrate on their application rather than on the details of the physical storage and retrieval of files.

Common physical structures for files in a DBMS include hashed, sequential, indexed, and B-tree files. Each file structure has definite advantages and disadvantages that depend on the storage device's characteristics, the importance of fast access versus compact storage, the types of queries the file must answer, and a host of other factors. Despite these important technical issues, you should remember that even if the DBMS (or, in some cases, the database administrator) chooses an inappropriate file structure for your files, the only effects noticeable to you should be slower response times or larger storage requirements. To emphasize the difference between a logical view and a physical view of the data, we discuss one type of physical structure: hashed files.

**Hashing** is a way of assigning the records in a direct-access file to specific tracks and sectors of a disk in a way that allows each record's location to be determined quickly. In a hashed file, the location of a record is determined by a *hashing function*, a mathematical formula that transforms a file key into a record location. An example of a simple hashing function is the so-called *shift-fold function*, which adds part of a key together to come up with the record number. For example, a social security number might be a key that is transformed into the location of a hospital patient's medical record by hashing the social security number. The shift-fold function partitions the social security number into three-digit numbers, the numbers are totaled, and the least significant three digits are taken as the location of the medical record.

Social security number:  542-22-4455
Shift-fold hash:  542 + 224 + 455 = 1,221
Record location:  221 (retain only the three least significant digits)

This hashing function transforms social security numbers into record locations ranging from 0 to 999. If 1,000 disk tracks are assigned to store the medical record file, the output of the hashing function can be used directly to point to a single track location for both storage and retrieval.

To use hashed files, the DBMS must also establish overflow storage areas and be able to restructure the hashed file. Overflow storage areas are necessary because several different social security numbers might hash into the same record location, creating the need to store some of these records on overflow tracks. As the number of records in the file grows, the number of overflow tracks will grow until the file must be completely restructured. Restructuring normally means modifying the hashing function, allocating more storage area to the file, and copying all the records from the old file structure to the new file structure.

# RELATIONAL DBMS PROGRAMS: CONCEPTS AND EXAMPLES

Relational DBMS programs for personal computers continue to grow in number and sophistication. For this reason, and because they reflect a well-developed theory, in this section, we examine the procedure for setting up and manipulating tables with Paradox, a relational database management system.[2]

Paradox uses menu bars to organize the program's major operations. The options on the main menu bar are

- *View* lets you view information in a table.
- *Ask* lets you build queries to select or manipulate information in a table.
- *Report* lets you design or print a report from information in a table.
- *Create* lets you define the structure (field names and types of data) for a table.
- *Modify* lets you restructure a table (for example, to add, delete, or modify a field in a table). Modify also lets you sort or edit a table.
- *Image* gives you control over the arrangement of information on the screen, such as width assigned to display a field or the order fields appear in.

---

2. Some of the text and illustrations in this section were adapted from *Query-by-Example in the Paradox Database Management Program,* a technical brief prepared by Ansa Software, a Borland company. Courtesy of Borland International, Inc.

**Figure 12.6**
Defining the structure of a new table with Paradox. For each field in the table, you enter its name and the type of data it will hold.

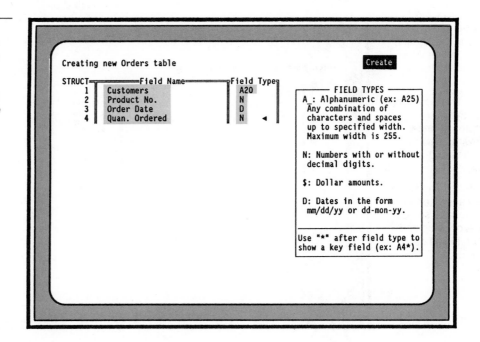

Creating new Orders table                                    Create

STRUCT⌐──────Field Name──────⌐Field Type⌐
  1 ‖ Customers              ‖ A20        ⌐──── FIELD TYPES ────┐
  2 ‖ Product No.            ‖ N          A_: Alphanumeric (ex: A25)
  3 ‖ Order Date             ‖ D             Any combination of
  4 ‖ Quan. Ordered          ‖ N  ◄          characters and spaces
                                             up to specified width.
                                             Maximum width is 255.

                                          N: Numbers with or without
                                             decimal digits.

                                          $: Dollar amounts.

                                          D: Dates in the form
                                             mm/dd/yy or dd-mon-yy.

                                          Use "*" after field type to
                                          show a key field (ex: A4*).

- *Forms* lets you create custom forms to display or enter information in the table one record at a time.

- *Tools* contains a grab bag of miscellaneous features. For example, you would select Tools to export information to other computer programs, delete a table, or rename a report.

- *Scripts* gives you access to Paradox's keyboard macro facility. It lets you record a sequence of keystrokes and play them back later. More important, Scripts is the gateway to the Paradox Application Language (PAL). By linking Paradox scripts together, you can build sophisticated database-oriented application programs.

- *Help* gives you access to an on-line help system.

- *Exit* returns control to the operating system.

## Creating, Viewing, and Editing Tables

Like other relational database programs, Paradox presents information in tables, with columns for categories of information and rows for individual records of people or things. Each table groups information logically for easy viewing and inspection. For example, a product orders table might list customers, products they ordered, dates the orders were placed, and quantities ordered.

Before you can use a table to store data, you must tell Paradox how the table is laid out. You define the structure of a table by selecting the Create option from the main menu. After Paradox asks for the new table's name, it displays the screen

**Figure 12.7**
Data in the Orders table can be viewed and edited in two basic ways.

**(top)** The table view displays many records at once, allowing you to scroll through the table.

**(bottom)** The forms view shows only one record, so you must page up and down to see other records.

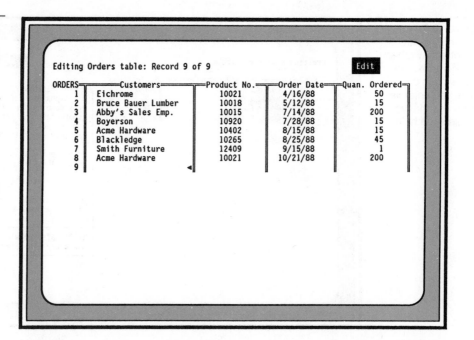

```
Editing Orders table: Record 9 of 9                    Edit

ORDERS        Customers        Product No.    Order Date    Quan. Ordered
   1    Eichrome                10021          4/16/88           50
   2    Bruce Bauer Lumber      10018          5/12/88           15
   3    Abby's Sales Emp.       10015          7/14/88          200
   4    Boyerson                10920          7/28/88           15
   5    Acme Hardware           10402          8/15/88           15
   6    Blackledge              10265          8/25/88           45
   7    Smith Furniture         12409          9/15/88            1
   8    Acme Hardware           10021         10/21/88          200
   9                              ◄
```

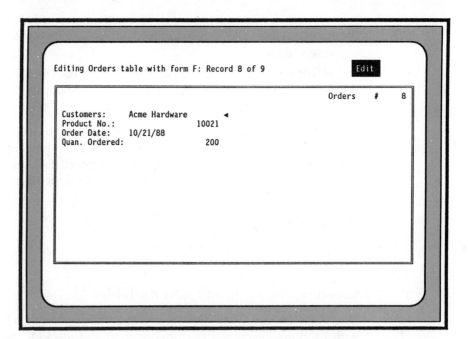

```
Editing Orders table with form F: Record 8 of 9           Edit

                                           Orders      #      8

Customers:      Acme Hardware        ◄
Product No.:                  10021
Order Date:     10/21/88
Quan. Ordered:                  200
```

shown in Figure 12.6. For each field you want in the table, you enter a name, field type, and whether it is a key field.

A **key** *uniquely* identifies a record in the table. Key fields are strictly optional with Paradox; the Orders table in Figure 12.6 does not have one. If you give a table a key field, Paradox will not allow two records to have the same value in the key field.

**Figure 12.8**
Designing a custom data entry form. The menu bar at the top of the screen provides options for positioning fields on the form, drawing borders, and moving and highlighting areas.

```
Put  Erase Border Move Style Form Help DO-IT! Cancel   Form ◄ Ins 1/1
Place a field on the form.


             DATA ENTRY FORM FOR THE "ORDERS" FILE
             ======================================


        ┌─────────────────────────────────────────┐
        │  Customer Name:      --------------------│
        │                                          │
        │  Product Number:     ------              │
        │                                          │
        │  Order Date:         --------            │
        │                                          │
        │  Quantity Ordered:   --------            │
        └─────────────────────────────────────────┘


           Record Number:      ------
```

For example, if the Orders table had an additional field named Order Number, you might want to establish that field as a key to prevent two records from having the same order number. When a key is made up of several pieces of information, it is a **compound key,** or *composite key.* Compound keys are useful whenever it takes two or more fields to identify a record. For example, in a table containing a telephone directory, the compound key might consist of the Area Code and Local Phone Number fields.

Once a table's structure has been defined, you can select the View or Modify options from the main menu to examine or edit the table's records. By pressing function key [F7], you can toggle between the *table* and *forms* views of the data (see Figure 12.7). When the Edit mode is active (the table is not protected from changes), pressing [Ins] inserts a new, blank record in the table; pressing [Del] deletes the current record. You can tab from field to field with either the [Tab] or cursor-movement keys.

The form in the bottom part of Figure 12.7 shows the standard form that Paradox creates automatically for the Orders table. If the standard form doesn't meet your needs, you can use the Forms option from the main menu to design a custom form that does (see Figure 12.8). A custom form can help highlight a table's important fields (by placing a border around them), present fields in a order different from how they appear in the table, and have calculated fields that aren't actually in the table. As many as ten forms can be defined for each table.

## Asking Queries

Paradox can be distinguished from most other database programs by its query-by-example (QBE) method of manipulating information in tables. QBE offers a power-

## A Word About . . . *Designing a Relational Database*

*When you design a relational database, don't try to put all the information in one table. Because tables can easily be linked together, simple tables are usually easier to work with than tables with many fields.*

Suppose you are the sales director for a national corporation. Your market is currently divided into four regions, East, Central, South, and West. Each region is divided into territories made up of between one and three states. Each territory is assigned one sales representative, who works out of the regional office and reports to the regional manager.

If you're like many database users, the great temptation is to put all the information you need to know into one large table (see the *Staff* table below).

Although all the relevant information is in the *Staff* table, it may not be easy to retrieve or update as the department grows and changes. For example:

1. What if you hire a second employee named Milford? How will you tell them apart?
2. Suppose the eastern region relocates from Boston to New York. You'll have to change the location and phone number of every employee and rep in the region.
3. Suppose you want to know who's respon-

sible for customers in Arkansas. First you'll have to remember whether its abbreviation is AR or AK. Then you'll have to search for this code in three separate fields (State1, State2, and State3).
4. What if you redraw the boundaries so that Maine, New Hampshire, Vermont, and Massachusetts form a single territory? You'll have to restructure the table to include a State4 field.
5. Suppose several sales representatives resign. Once you remove them from the database, you'll have no record of how their territories were constructed.

You can see how it might be inconvenient to use and maintain this database.

The problem with the large *Staff* table is that it's undifferentiated. It contains information about several different classes of things: employees, regions, territories, and states.

Instead of creating one huge table, you could create a few small and discrete tables:

- *Employee* contains information about all employees, including ID number, name, position, and salary
- *Region* contains the code number, name, location, phone number, and manager ID for each region

The "kitchen sink" approach to database design

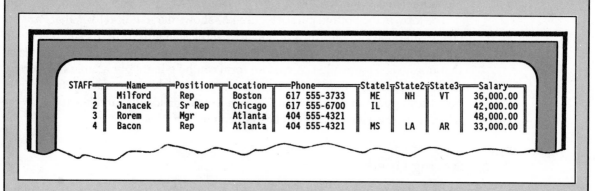

| STAFF | Name | Position | Location | Phone | State1 | State2 | State3 | Salary |
|---|---|---|---|---|---|---|---|---|
| 1 | Milford | Rep | Boston | 617 555-3733 | ME | NH | VT | 36,000.00 |
| 2 | Janacek | Sr Rep | Chicago | 617 555-6700 | IL | | | 42,000.00 |
| 3 | Rorem | Mgr | Atlanta | 404 555-4321 | | | | 48,000.00 |
| 4 | Bacon | Rep | Atlanta | 404 555-4321 | MS | LA | AR | 33,000.00 |

- *Terr* identifies each territory by a code number, and tells which region it is in and which representative it is assigned to
- *State* identifies each state by code and name, and tells which territory it is in

The four tables in which the information about the sales staff is now divided are small, simple, and much easier to work with. If you want to work with information spread over several tables, you can join or link them together.

Notice how the rows in the table have a unique identifying key field. This helps to avoid confusion among similar records, and makes it easy to relate the information in one table to that in another.

Consider how this differentiated database solves the problems we encountered with the *Staff* table:

1. Two employees named Milford can be differentiated by their employee code numbers.
2. If the eastern region moves to New York, you can simply change one location and phone number in the *Region* table.
3. To find out who's responsible for Arkansas, join the *Employee, State,* and *Terr* tables. You can learn the territory code from *State,* the rep code from *Terr,* and the salesperson's name from *Employee.*
4. If you redraw territory boundaries, simply change the territory codes for the affected states in the *State* table.
5. Territory divisions are stored in *State* and are not affected by changes in *Employee.*

This kind of division of information is called **normalization.** A normalized table is small, simple, and discrete, and contains a minimum of redundant information. Each field contributes additional and necessary information. Changes can be made easily.

Normalized tables

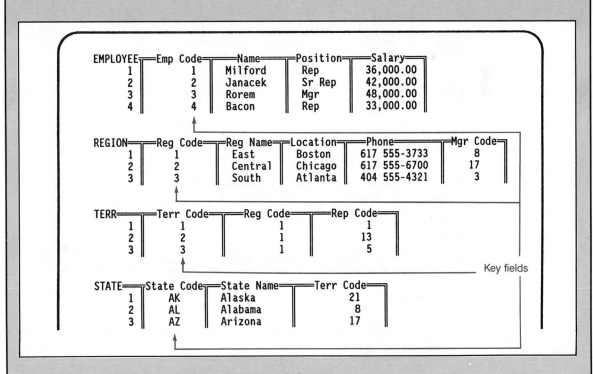

Source: *Paradox User's Guide,* pp. 215–217, © 1986 by Ansa Software.

**Figure 12.9**
Query-by-example lets you ask questions about data by filling out query forms on the screen.

**(top)** Filling out a query form involves typing into its fields to choose which fields you want to display (by putting check marks in them) and which records you want to select (by specifying search conditions).

**(bottom)** Once the query form is filled out, pressing function key [F2] causes Paradox to perform the query you have specified.

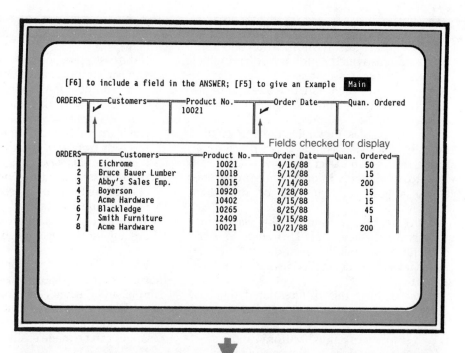

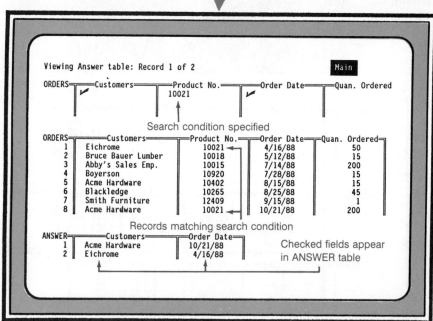

ful yet easy-to-use alternative to the query languages used by conventional database management programs.

QBE was originally developed in the mid-1970s at the IBM Research Laboratory at Yorktown Heights, New York. Commercial versions have been available for some

**Figure 12.10**
Complex query statements can select only those records that meet certain exacting conditions.

**(top)** This query selects all the records where the value in the Product No. field is equal to 10021 *and* the value in the Quan. Ordered field is greater than 100.

**(bottom)** This query selects all the records where the value in the Order Date field is greater than 9/1/88 *or* the value in the Quan. Ordered field is greater than 100.

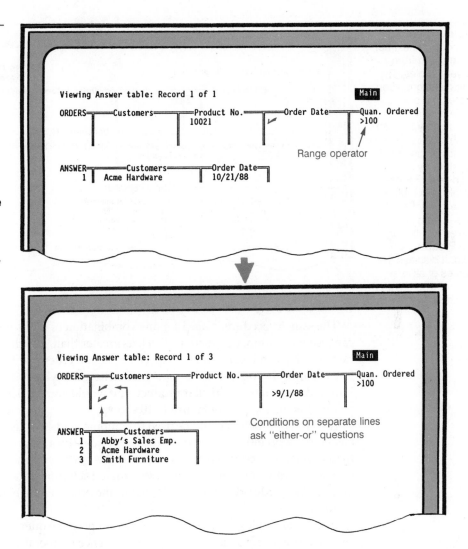

time on mainframe computers, but Paradox is the first microcomputer software to fully implement QBE.

To ask a question of a table, you call up a query form for the particular table by choosing the Ask option from the main menu. The query form displays the field headings of the actual table, but the columns have been left blank. You enter appropriate selection criteria into the columns and check off (insert a check mark in) those fields to be shown in the answer.

Suppose you want to find the names of all customers ordering a certain product and the dates their orders were placed. Using Paradox, you call up a query version of the Orders table. Then you enter the product number in the product number column and check off the two columns to contain answers—the Customers column and Order Date column (see Figure 12.9). Pressing [F2], labeled Do-it! on the function key template, produces the solution: an answer table listing the customers' names and the dates they ordered the particular product on.

**Figure 12.11**
Queries can extract information from several tables. To ask questions about more than one table, you must fill out a query form for each table, and you must link the tables together by a common field. For example, this multi-table query links the Orders and Stock tables together by the Product No. field. It displays the names of all customers who have ordered screwdrivers.

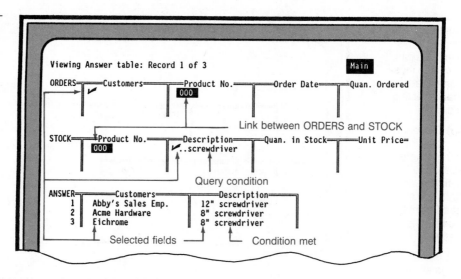

The same procedure is used for any combination of fields within the table. You can also use arithmetic functions (such as greater than, less than) and logical functions (such as and, or) to further specify selection criteria within particular fields. For instance, if you want the names of customers who ordered more than one hundred units of the particular product, you would enter 100 in the Quan. Ordered column, as the top part of Figure 12.10 shows.

A logical or function could be used to combine fields to select, for instance, those customers who either ordered a product in quantities greater than 100 *or* placed their order after a certain date. To construct this query, you check off the Customers field in two rows, entering the quantity ordered selection criterion (100) in one row and the date ordered criterion (9/1/88) in the other, as the bottom part of Figure 12.10 shows.

In these examples, little typing is needed to pose the query, no memorization of commands is needed, and no particular sequence of operation is needed. The formulation of the query is apparent from the graphical context.

Often, queries demand information that spans multiple tables. QBE simplifies such "relational" queries through *linking*. To link two tables for a relational query, you must ask Paradox to display a query form for each of the two tables; then you place example elements in corresponding fields in the query forms. As many as twenty four different tables may be linked at a time.

To extend an earlier example, suppose you want to know the names of customers who ordered a particular type of product, say, screwdrivers. The Orders table lists only product identification numbers, whereas another table, called Stock, lists product numbers and product descriptions. You begin by requesting two query forms, one representing the Order table and the other the Stock table (see Figure 12.11). Then you check off the fields that should be shown in the answer table—the Customers field from the Orders table and the Description field from the Stock table. Next, you insert the qualifier "screwdriver" in the Description field, signifying those records whose product descriptions contain the word *screwdriver* are to be recalled.

# A Word About . . . *Flat File versus Relational Databases*

*They call it "the wall": the steep learning process needed to jump from an easy-to-use product or a simple file manager, such as PFS File, to a powerful, flexible database manager, such as R:BASE System V or dBASE III Plus.*

Industry observers said that while some products are helping users scale the wall, there's a lot of room for more such products. Plenty of unsophisticated users could profit from managing data with simpler, so-called flat-file managers (database software that can manage only one file at a time) on their IBM PCs.

Users often face pressure from computer dealers who are afraid of "underselling" software, and thus heap on features, price, and complexity by claiming that users will never outgrow it, according to Rick Sherlund, vice president of investment research at Goldman, Sachs & Co.. of New York. "But often the all-in-one product is so complex it sits on the shelf while users continue to manage data either manually or clumsily though a spreadsheet," he said.

Yet another pressure on users is the management information system (MIS) manager enamored of powerful fully relational database managers. Some managers push a program through as the corporate standard without realizing that users don't want to kill a fly with an atom bomb. "There are ways for the MIS manager to solve that problem by giving users prepackaged name and address lists for such powerful products," said Paul Cubbage of Dataquest Inc., in San Jose, California. "But I don't know how many MIS directors are that clever."

Still other analysts think the trend toward buying high-end databases will continue. "Even if products like dBASE are underused as flat-file data managers, that's still OK because they provide greater flexibility," said Michael

Orsak, senior research analyst at Input of Mountain View, California. "Even if you only use 10 percent of the power, you can select which 10 percent you want, and if you need some additional functions or features in some other area, it's going to be there."

Orsak said it is true that the flat-file managers are often easier to learn and use than high-end databases. "But it's certainly not true for all applications," he said. "If you start your application as a single file, then have to switch to a relational product, you're going to make a significant investment in retraining."

In the near term, though, there will be a place in the market for flat-file mangers. "There's still a segment of users who don't want to learn even Paradox, which is a combination of power and ease of use," Orsak said. "For that class of users, there is still demand for a flat-file database."

In dollar share, the database market is overwhelmingly dominated by relational database products, Orsak said. In installed units, the number of PFS File and Report users still rivals that of dBASE II and III combined.

When asked what kind of product he would like to see, Orsak said, "It should be focused on flat-file applications, perhaps with some programming capability that's not as sophisticated as dBASE III. It should have a user interface oriented toward more Macintosh-type operations, with pull-down menus. The real selling point should be that it's dBASE III compatible—files that have already been developed under dBASE III should be able to be moved over.

Most industry observes believe that the distinctions between flat-file managers and relational database managers will continue to blur as the flat-file programs gain more features and the relational database managers become easier to use.

Source: Scott Mace, *Infoworld*, 8 September 1986, pp. 29–30.

To link the two tables, you must insert an example element in a field common to both tables, in this case the Product No. column. The product number is not an item of interest, and the specific example chosen need not apply to the products being described. The example used can be anything—000, 13, or xxx. It simply serves to cross-reference the Customers and Description fields across the two tables.

As before, a single keystroke elicits the answer: a table listing customers and descriptions of the types of screwdrivers they ordered.

Query-by-example methods also simplify other operations, including aggregate functions such as counts, sums, averages, maximums, and minimums. For example, to calculate the total number of units of all products ordered by each customer, you simply check off the Customer column and type "calc sum" in the Quan. Ordered column. This provides an extremely accessible way of asking and solving such questions as, "How many customers ordered product 125?" "What is the average monthly order by customer X?" and so on. The QBE method and table format can also be used to add new records, delete records, change values within a record, and manage collections of tables within a database.

## FEATURES OF A DBMS

Now that you have had a brief introduction to what a DBMS can do and how to set up a DBMS, we look more closely at the features every DBMS should provide. These include a data dictionary, query facility, forms management facility, report generator, file restructuring facility, data interchange facility, and data integrity facility. Understanding these features will help you recognize and use them in whatever DBMS you choose.

### Data Dictionary

A **data dictionary**, a special file containing the names of all fields in all files maintained by the DBMS, is a major component of the database's logical schema. For example, you create a new file by adding a new entry into the data dictionary. For each file in the database, the data dictionary always includes the name of each field, type of data stored in each field (such as text, numeric, date, or dollars), and width of each field.

A data dictionary also helps provide other features. Here are some ways a data dictionary can make a DBMS more powerful and convenient.

- *Better data editing.* A DBMS may make data entry easier and more reliable with the help of *editing attributes*, rules that govern the way data are entered into the database. These attributes are stored in the dictionary as part of the description of the fields. For example, a numeric field might be given upper and lower limits. As data is entered into the DBMS, these limits in the data dictionary are used to ensure that only values falling within certain limits are accepted. A more complicated situation arises if a field in another file must be searched to validate a data entry. For example, an editing attribute might require that the

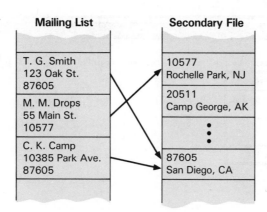

**Figure 12.12**
A compressed mailing list file and its associated secondary file

**Mailing List**

T. G. Smith
123 Oak St.
87605

M. M. Drops
55 Main St.
10577

C. K. Camp
10385 Park Ave.
87605

**Secondary File**

10577
Rochelle Park, NJ

20511
Camp George, AK

87605
San Diego, CA

customer numbers of entries to a transaction file be valid numbers in a customer account file.

- *Password security.* A password is often kept for an entire file to prohibit unauthorized access. Additionally, the data dictionary may contain many passwords: one for read-only access, another for data entry, and still another for updating the file.

- *Compressed information.* The data dictionary helps promote data compression by making it easy to store data in a coded format. For example, a mailing list can be compressed by eliminating the City and State fields from all records, as Figure 12.12 shows. Because the zip code uniquely identifies which city and state are intended, the data dictionary need only reference the city and state in a second file.

- *Data integrity control.* The date and time of the last access, the date and time of the last backup, and the date and time of the most recent modification to the file may be kept in the data dictionary. This information is useful for maintaining control over your information and becomes extremely helpful if there is a system failure.

## Query Languages

The *query facility* is the method the DBMS provides to request data. A good query facility allows nonprogrammers to process and update information stored in the database. This facility is especially important in a relational DBMS because relationships among fields are established by query commands.

Today, most microcomputer database systems rely on their own query language. Queries written for one DBMS, say, R:BASE System V, will not work on another, say

**Figure 12.13**
The opening screen
of The Assistant, a
menu-based user in-
terface for dBASE
III Plus.

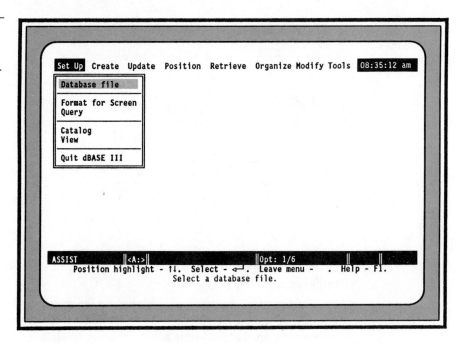

dBASE III, because each system has its own query commands. For instance, here is a short dBASE III query program.[3]

```
.USE Money INDEX Last┘
.LIST FOR Owing┘
.CLEAR┘
.LIST FOR Owing .AND. Pastdue┘
.CLEAR┘
.SUM Amount_due for Owing┘
.SUM Amount_due FOR Owing .AND Pastdue┘
.REPORT FORM Gimme FOR Owing PLAIN TO PRINT┘255
.REPORT FORM Scrooge FOR Owing .AND. Past due PLAIN TO PRINT┘
.USE┘
```

This routine extracts a list of people from a database file and prints two reports about them. Writing a routine of this complexity is beyond the inclination and abilities of most users.

As an alternative to using a formal query programming language, microcomputer DBMS programs usually give you some sort of menu-based or near-English option. For example, dBASE III's alternative, The Assistant (see Figure 12.13), provides access to many dBASE III features via pull-down and pop-up menus; however, some activities, such as building complex queries, can be accomplished

---

3. *Programming with dBASE III Plus*, © 1986, Ashton-Tate, p. 2.

only with the dot command language. With other programs, you can build queries from near-English commands, such as

> For each part supplied, find PNO and the names of all LOCATIONS supplying the part.
> Find SNO and STATUS for suppliers in London.

Natural-language inquiries, such as Find, How many, and What are common in many relational DBMS programs, but updating files by using natural-language inquiries is difficult. Thus command language and visual interfaces, such as QBE, that use pictures and diagrams are the most prevalent methods of giving commands to a DBMS.

Within the next couple of years, most high-end microcomputer database products should support **SQL** (*Structured Query Language*). SQL was defined by Chamberlin and others at the IBM Research Laboratory in San Jose, California, in the early 1970s. Although by name SQL is a query language, it is actually an entire database manipulation language. It is at the heart of IBM's mainframe database system, DB2 (for IBM Database 2), and used in many other relational products. A proposed SQL standard is being considered by a subcommittee of ANSI, the American National Standards Institute. Because of SQL's broad acceptance for mainframe and minicomputer relational database systems, it is being built into most high-end DBMS systems for microcomputers as well. Ashton-Tate, for example, has announced its intention of providing an SQL interface to dBASE III, the leading microcomputer database program.

In one way, SQL is similar to these other command-based query languages: Setting up and implementing a typical query command is difficult to do without some training. Most people hire an expert to design, set up, and implement the steps in DBMS processing. The query commands are entered into the DBMS and stored for execution later. Frequently, the expert will use menu-based prompting and selection methods to combine file processing queries and on-screen data entry forms. Then even a clerk who knows nothing about database processing can use the system without further assistance from the expert.

## Forms Management

The *forms management facility* of a DBMS lets you define forms for data entry; other forms for printing; and still other forms for look-up, insert, and delete operations. Moreover, any form can shield information from view by preventing certain fields from being displayed. An important feature is the ability to display and edit information from several files in a single form. For example, a form for entering orders might accept payment information and place it in the RECEIVABLES file and accept product information for the SHIPMENTS file. Forms can also control access to confidential fields by enforcing password protection.

Forms are often stored in a *forms library*, a file that can store many forms to make access to them convenient. A forms library makes it easy for programmers to use the same form in different programs.

**Figure 12.14**
A screen-oriented report generator lets you build a template of what the report should look like on the screen (above) and then preview the report (below).

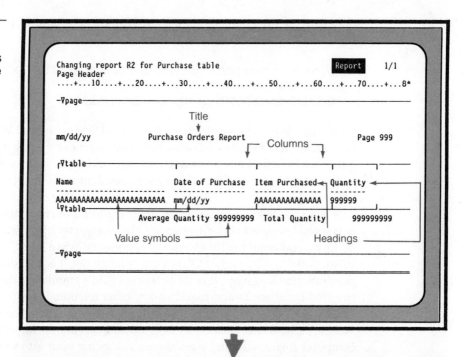

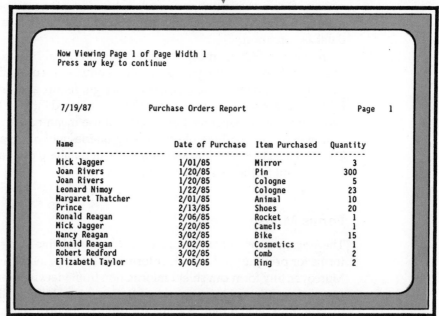

## Report Generators

Broadly, a report generator is a special kind of query facility. Instead of processing files to update another file, a *report generator* processes files to print the results on paper.

## A Word About . . . *The Output Side of Databases*

*Preparing output from a database involves placing specific information in the order you need it and getting the data in a presentable report you can distribute.*

Alas, getting information out can be every bit as tedious as getting it in. You must confront some questions—lots of them—before you get answers: Which records do you want to include in this report? Which fields? How should they be arranged on the page? Are there figures to be calculated? Will there be a title and subtitle? Headers and footers? Do you need one copy or several? Is that regular or compressed type? And the list goes on.

Ideally, database programs would ask these questions of you and alert you to possible oversights. ("Are you sure you want the report entries sorted by record number, and not by last name?") They do not. Not yet, anyway. This process of culling information and sensibly presenting it on paper therefore involves a great deal of trial and error. You may find it takes several hours to generate the summary you require if you're new to the reporting maze. And it can be a slow, repetitive routine even for old hands.

It's easy to regard the process of producing reports as merely a cantankerous formatting or printing problem to be ironed out—and it is certainly part that. But reporting is inexorably linked with the fundamentals of searching and sorting, those electronic filtering commands that are the primary movers and shakers of database information. Reporting axiom number one is: Before you decide what goes where, you must define the scope of "what." What data is pertinent to this report? What is not?

Selectively retrieving a group of records and sequencing them by one or more aspects of the information they contain is a vital part of the reporting process. It is crucial, therefore, that you fathom how to filter through your database files. Exactly how much you really need to know depends on the complexity of the reports you desire. A simple Sort command may suffice for an alphabetized listing of all records. However, culling a list of clients that reside in southeastern states and maintain annual incomes of $50,000 or more requires that you know how to use mathematical operators (equal to, greater than, etc.) and logic connectors (and, or) to seek out the right subset of records; and then know how to apply sorting commands or index files to sequence them properly.

Arranging the details of a report layout—the titles, margins, spacing, headers, footers, and so on—is usually, the least oblique part of the process. Nevertheless, getting your report to appear just so on the printed page can be tricky. If your report entries are one character too wide for the space allotted, for example, a single letter or number moves down to the next line. Page breaks are another source of frequent trouble. There's no substitute for a little experimentation here. Use small files, or small sections of files, and crank out a sample report several times, tweaking it each time to get a feel for what works and what doesn't.

Comfortable with the basics? Then it's time to begin saving the fruits of your labor so you can use them again. Boilerplate report formats, like boilerplate documents or spreadsheet models, can save you a lot of time. By saving report designs, you can quickly run off a report as often as updated information demands. The result: fast, fresh copy—ideal for weekly or monthly reports.

Source: Christopher O'Malley, *Personal Computing*, July 1987, pp. 89–97.

Report generators come in several varieties. A *screen-oriented* report generator lets you build the report specification by positioning and moving the report's elements on the screen (see Figure 12.14). This type of report generator is often just an extension of the forms management system that has special features for arranging information on paper.

Other report generators get their report specifications by asking a long series of questions. A typical dialogue with this type of report generator might appear as

```
FILE NAME:  PURCHASE
PAGE NUMBERS (Y/N)?  YES
DATE OF REPORT (Y/N)?  YES
HEADING, LINE 1:  Purchase Orders Report
HEADING, LINE 2:  Sorted by Invoice Number
```

At this point, the specifications for the report date, heading, and pagination have been completed. Later questions would determine which fields are to be included in the report's columns, where the report breaks should fall, how the report should be sorted, and what items should be totaled.

The most flexible report generators are based on a programming language. (For more details on report generators, see Chapters 11 and 17.)

## Restructure Ability

If you owned a gasoline service station in 1979, you would appreciate the importance of being able to restructure database files. In 1979, the price of gasoline went over $1.00 per gallon for the first time. Many databases had to be changed because the price field was not wide enough to accommodate the additional digit. But if you tried to rectify the problem by simply modifying the entry in the data dictionary, it would no longer be compatible with the actual data stored in the corresponding file. The only answer was to restructure the file so that it could hold the larger value.

With many DBMS programs, you must copy all the data from the original file into a new file to restructure it. The new file might be created with more fields than the original file, the fields might be in a different order, or some of the fields might be wider or narrower. After the data has been copied into the new file, the original file can be deleted, and the name of the new file can be changed to that of the original file.

## Data Interchange

A good DBMS provides ways to move data between the DBMS files and other programs. The most typical interchange is transferring information between the DBMS and a spreadsheet, word processing, or graphics program. For example, you may use a spreadsheet to perform calculations in a financial model and then cut these calculations out of your spreadsheet and paste them into a DBMS file. Or you may want to select a record from your DBMS file and move it into a part of a spreadsheet. Data in a DBMS file are normally made available to other programs through the *data interchange facility* of the DBMS.

Depending on the conversion programs being used, transferring data can be as easy as posting and removing a piece of paper from a clipboard, or it can be quite difficult. Every program that produces output to a disk file uses a format that may or may not be compatible with the output files of other programs. The simplest format is a sequential file containing ASCII text. The records of an ASCII file vary in width depending on the length of each line of text stored.

A worksheet file produced with Lotus 1-2-3 is written in the WKS format; Multiplan worksheets are written in SYLK format; and documents from MultiMate, MacWrite, and other word processor programs include codes that control the printer and character fonts. These files must be preprocessed to remove the special printer codes or to rearrange the data so that they match the arrangement expected by the DBMS. Whether this is easy or even possible depends largely on the capabilities of the file conversion programs provided as part of the DBMS.

## Data Integrity

One of the most overlooked features of a good DBMS is the *data integrity facility*. It consists of routines for backing up and restoring files, special controls on files shared with other users, and other programs to ensure the safety of your data.

There are several reasons to periodically make backup copies of your files, but the most obvious is to protect your valuable investment of time and effort. A single disk can hold thousands of records and, in an instant, lose those records. A backup copy is your best protection against lost data. Backup copies also provide some less obvious benefits. For example, if you have a backup copy of a file, you can restore previously deleted records and retrieve information for an audit trail.

An **audit trail** is the recorded history of the insertions, deletions, modifications, and restorations performed on a file. It is one of the simplest methods of guaranteeing the validity of information stored in a file, which is a necessity in most business applications. (Other methods that can provide these guarantees include cross-checking and balancing debits and credits.) One way of obtaining a satisfactory audit trail is to periodically produce a dated report containing all records in the file and to print all modifications to the file as they are made. The report and printed transactions together constitute a reasonable audit trail. A backup copy can also be part of an audit trail because it provides a dated copy of all records at a certain point in the life of the file. A history of the file can then be reconstructed from periodic backup reports and records of modifications.

Data integrity is particularly difficult to maintain whenever two or more users share access to a file. In particular, the DBMS may be susceptible to a **race condition,** that is, a condition where two concurrent activities interact to cause a processing error. For example, suppose one user of the file is modifying a record while a second user tries to look up the same record. Does the second user obtain the new version of the record or the record as it was before the modification? This outcome for the second user is uncertain.

## Table 12.1
## A Comparison of Three Popular Database Programs

| Product | DataEase | dBASE III PLUS | R:BASE System V |
|---|---|---|---|
| **List Price** | **$600** | **$695** | **$700** |
| **File Structure Limits** | | | |
| Number of fields per record | 255 | 128 | 400 |
| Record size (bytes) | 4,000 | 4,000 | 4,096 |
| Number of records per data file | 65,635 | 1 billion | Unlimited |
| Number of records per | 65,890 | 10 billion | Unlimited |
| Field size (bytes) | 255 | 254 | 4,092 |
| **Data Types and Sizes** | | | |
| Numeric | ● | ● | 1,500 |
| Money | ● | ○ | ● |
| Logical (Boolean) | ● | ● | ○ |
| Long text | ○ | ● | ● |
| **Data Entry and Editing** | | | |
| Range testing | ● | ○ | ● |
| Default values | ● | ○ | ● |
| Requires specific values | ● | ○ | ● |
| Look-up to external data tables | ● | ○ | ● |
| Double-entry verification | ○ | ○ | ● |
| Required fields | ● | ○ | ● |
| Must fill field | ● | ○ | ● |
| Forced uppercase | ○ | ● | ○ |
| Automatic incrementing fields | ● | ○ | ○ |
| Unique fields | ● | ○ | ● |
| Automatic data entry | ● | ○ | ● |
| **Data Manipulation** | | | |
| Number of index files | Unlimited | Unlimited | 400 |
| Compound indexes | ○ | ● | ○ |
| Sorting | ○ | ● | ○ |
| Number of sort fields | Infinite | 100 characters | None |
| Ascending order | ● | ● | ○ |
| Descending order | ● | ● | ○ |
| Maximum number of open files | 255 | 10 | 80 |
| Maximum number of tables merged | 40 | 2 | 2 |
| **Input Facilities** | | | |
| Screen definition: Automatic | ○ | ● | ● |
| Programming | ○ | ● | ● |
| Number of screens per file | 16 | Unlimited | Unlimited |
| Number of files per screen | 40 | 10 | 80 |
| Prompt messages for fields | ● | ○ | ● |
| **Output Facilities** | | | |
| Report generation: Statistical functions | ● | ○ | ● |
| Report definition methods: Painting | ● | ○ | ○ |
| Form layout | ○ | ● | ● |
| Automatic | ● | ○ | ● |
| Programming | ○ | ● | ● |
| Footers | ● | ○ | ● |
| Printer setup facility | ● | ○ | ○ |

●—Yes  ○—No  *Network support is about to be announced.  †At extra cost.
Reprinted from *PC Magazine*, January 27, 1987. Copyright © 1987 Ziff Communications Company.

Now consider what happens if the first user retrieves a record just before a second user modifies one of the fields in the record. The first user may decide whether to modify the record on the basis of values that were changed by the second user—without knowing the second user has modified the record. Again, a race condition occurs because the outcome is uncertain.

These are only two of the problems associated with multiple access to a shared file. To overcome these problems, the DBMS must be able to lock the file whenever modifications are performed. A file is **locked** if only one user is allowed access to it. The shared file must be locked before any user can modify, delete, or insert a record into the file. Some systems use a *record lock* so that simultaneous modifications can occur elsewhere in the file, but not to the locked record.

## Comparing Systems

Most DBMS programs accomplish the same basic functions, but they differ in myriad ways when you consider their extra features. Table 12.1 compares the features of three popular database systems; it includes an excellent list of factors to consider if you are selecting a DBMS for a personal computer. Remember to consider other features also, including the flexibility of the report generator, effectiveness of error handling and recovery, quality of documentation, simplicity and power of the query language, and processing speed.

Two goals of a DBMS are to eliminate the need for a programmer and to provide an easy-to-understand model of data. Menus, forms, report generators, and query languages are used to eliminate programming; a DBMS schema makes the DBMS general yet easy to understand. But neither of these goals is fully achieved by today's DBMS programs. Some programs are easier to use but less powerful than others. Powerful programs tend to be complex and difficult to understand. At the root of the difficulty is the likelihood that an application will be intrinsically complex because of the complex nature of its task.

*Summary*

A database management system (DBMS) can coordinate the storage and retrieval of information from many files. DBMS software maintains a comprehensive logical schema so that a uniform, consistent, and correct structure is always ensured; it maintains a physical schema so that the disk location of specific data items can be determined; it maintains separate subschemas so that independent users and programs can retrieve and interpret the data in their own way; and it provides a variety of functions to users, such as report generation, file conversion, query processing, and password protection.

A hierarchical database imposes a one-to-many relationship on data items when they are stored and works on sets of data. A network database imposes a many-to-many relationship on data items when they are stored. In practice, hierarchical and network models are more complex and difficult to use than relational models, in which the relationships among data are established only after data are stored. A relational database uses tables as the schemas for data. Tables, rows, and columns of fields are processed by giving query commands to the DBMS. These commands establish the relationships among files, records, and fields.

Every DBMS must have a data dictionary to hold the database's structural information. Some systems include additional editing features in their data dictionary such as upper and lower bounds on numeric input and forms.

A DBMS must also provide some way to process, update, and retrieve information. Typically, a query language provides these directions for processing files. A forms management facility lets users define forms for data entry, printing, and other operations. A querylike language can be used to generate reports on the screen. A report generator produces printed output, however, rather than updating a file.

A good DBMS also provides ways to share information with other software—for example, transferring information from a database file to a spreadsheet, word processor, or graphics file. A DBMS also should be able to transfer data from one file format to another format within the DBMS itself, allowing files to be restructured without resorting to manual reentry of data.

Finally, a DBMS must allow you to protect the database from damage in the event of a power outage or other failure leading to loss of information. A variety of methods for backing up files is part of any good DBMS.

---

## Key Terms

| | |
|---|---|
| audit trail | logical schema |
| compound key | network database |
| database | normalization |
| database management system (DBMS) | physical schema |
| data dictionary | query language |
| data independence | race condition |
| hashing | relation |
| hierarchical database | relational database |
| key | SQL |
| locked | subschema |

---

## Discussion Questions

1. How can you tell the difference between a file manager and a database management system? Is there a gray area between them?

2. What are the differences among hierarchical, network, and relational database systems?

3. What would be the most important features in the check list of DBMS features for a church that uses volunteers to keep track of its books? For the payroll department of a 1,000-person corporation?

4. What safeguards should be used to prevent the loss or accidental change of information in the two situations described in the preceding question?

## Exercises

1. For your data management program find the maximum number of
   a. files that can be open at a time
   b. records per file
   c. fields per record
   d. characters per field
   Determine also the types of data allowed and the formatting options for displaying them.

2. Diagram a relational database containing three files: PARTS, SHIPMENTS, and SUPPLIERS. The PARTS file has fields for Part Num, Part Name, Color, Quantity, and Weight. The SHIPMENTS file has fields for Part Num, Date, Ship Qty, Supply Num, and Price. The SUPPLIERS file has fields for Supply Num, Supply Name, and Address. Diagram how the database might look in a hierarchical model. Repeat the exercise for a network database. How do the hierarchical, network, and relational databases differ?

3. Give some examples of the applications and subschemas that might be used to design a management system for student registration and transcript information.

# *Other Applications*

In 1915 Lee De Forest and his associates stood trial for mail fraud after trying to sell stock in a manufacturing company. De Forest claimed he had invented a device that would make transatlantic telephone conversations possible. De Forest narrowly escaped prison, but his associates were convicted when the prosecutor persuaded the judge that transatlantic telephony was impossible. Two years later De Forest successfully applied the audion tube (the first vacuum tube) to transatlantic broadcasting. Since those days the audion tube has made possible modern radio, radar, television, first-generation computers, and ultimately, Silicon Valley.

Nowadays, few people are skeptical of advances in computer technology; in fact, we rather expect constant, exciting innovations. Hardware advances

such as speech synthesis, voice recognition, seeing-eye cameras, and touch-sensitive screens are being developed with increasing rapidity. Larger memories and faster processors are opening the door to advances in software such as picture programming, natural-language inquiry, and expert systems that give advice on a variety of topics. These capabilities will soon be expected of the lowliest personal computer.

Part V examines the frontiers of communications and graphics. These are among the most dynamic areas of computing because no dominant software or standard hardware has emerged.

In Chapter 13, we describe computer graphics—an area that, until recently, was stunted by the high cost of internal memory and color displays. But today, most personal computers have a monitor with the ability to display bit-mapped graphics. The new hardware capabilities have resulted in a profusion of graphic applications, from converting numbers in a spreadsheet into quick graphs, drawing free-hand sketches, and preparing presentation-quality charts and diagrams to creating highly detailed architectural drawings.

In Chapters 14 and 15, we examine how communications hardware and software are weaving computers into a world-encompassing web the like of which has never before been seen. In Chapter 14, we explain how information can be exchanged among computers over ordinary telephone lines. Telecommunications provides a convenient and simple method of sharing information across long distances. In Chapter 15, we take a broader view and compare the various types of computer networks, with a particular emphasis on *local area networks*, which operate over a limited geographical area. Local area networks can link all kinds of computers in a high-speed network to share information and resources, such as expensive printers or plotters. Local area networks are transforming the role of personal computers from standalone machines into workstations that are part of a larger, more capable computing environment.

# Graphics

In 1962, Ivan E. Sutherland built a computer system that enabled the user to draw on a televisionlike screen. His device was slow, expensive, and not very sophisticated, but it was the beginning of modern computer-generated graphics. During the 1970s, techniques for drawing on an electronic screen improved while the cost of computer hardware declined. Then, in the 1980s, low-cost RAM chips appeared, making it possible to store and quickly access a vast amount of information in a very small box at a very low cost. These chips gave graphics its biggest boost. Low-cost memory is ideal for graphical computing because "a picture is worth a thousand words" of storage.

We discussed earlier one use of computer graphics: Computers with *visual operating environments* rely on pictures instead of text to communicate with users. In this chapter, we describe other uses of computer graphics. We see how you can display information as a graph or chart and how you can draw pictures, print them, save them in a disk file, and retrieve them for later use. Specifically, we examine presentation graphics and graphics editors. We discuss both the technology and the usefulness of computer graphics. But before you continue reading this chapter, you should examine Window 7 on graphics.

# 13

## BASIC CONCEPTS

### Graphics Applications

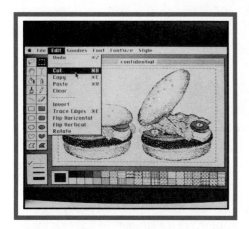

As Figure 13.1 shows, there are three main uses of graphics: entertainment, presentation graphics, and computer-aided design. Entertainment is a catchall category that includes many applications in art, education, animation, and games.

**Presentation graphics** describe high-quality graphs, charts, and diagrams that present facts, trends, and comparisons in a report, meeting, or convention. Presentation graphics turn numbers into pictures so that they can be easily understood. Often, the ability to produce presentation graphics is built into spreadsheet, database, and word processing programs to help analyze trends and other relationships in the data they store. For example, you might plot numbers from two rows of a spreadsheet to see the relationship between two sets of data, or you might plot the numbers from one field of a database file against those from another to reveal the relationship between the two fields. In either case, you might then move the resulting graph to a word processor document for inclusion in a report. Some people, considering this type of presentation graphics a separate category, call it **analytic graphics** because the resulting charts are less sophisticated than those produced by standalone graphics programs and are used to analyze data.

A third use of graphics is for computer-aided design. For this type of computer graphics, you need a **graphics editor**, which is like a word processor except that it helps you edit pictures instead of text. A graphics editor is used to create drawings on the screen with electronic tools, such as a simulated paintbrush, eraser, and pencil. With a graphics editor, you can then edit the sketch by moving, rotating, enlarging, and so on. Once you have obtained the desired design, the sketch can be printed. MacPaint and MacDraw are examples of graphics editors for the Apple Macintosh; PC Paintbrush, Publisher's Paintbrush, and Dr. Halo are examples of graphics editors for IBM and compatible microcomputers.

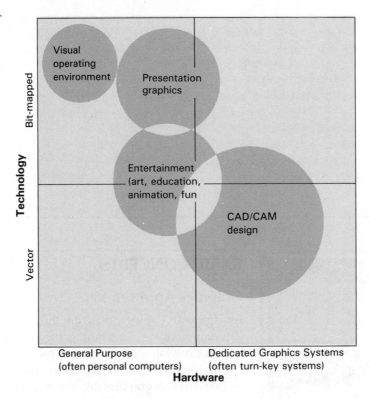

**Figure 13.1**
Applications of computer graphics using bit-mapped and vector graphics technology

Technology

Bit-mapped

Visual operating environment

Presentation graphics

Entertainment (art, education, animation, fun

Vector

CAD/CAM design

General Purpose (often personal computers)

Dedicated Graphics Systems (often turn-key systems)

**Hardware**

## Bit-Mapped and Vector Images

Figure 13.1 also classifies graphics applications according to whether they use bit-mapped or vector technology. Recall from Chapter 3 that a *bit-mapped* image is made of thousands of pixels, which are dots or points. In contrast, a *vector* image is made of **graphics primitives,** such as straight-line segments and arcs. The difference between these technologies is narrowing, but it still affects what you can do and how you can do it.

A monitor is designed to generate either a bit-mapped image or a vector graphics image. A **raster scan monitor** displays a bit-mapped image by moving the electron beam horizontally back and forth across the screen in a regular pattern along *scan lines*. In a **vector graphics monitor,** the electron beam is not limited to traveling along scan lines; instead, it draws straight lines from point to point.

Figure 13.2(a) illustrates the vector graphics method. A circle is constructed by drawing a polygon. Each side of the polygon is a straight line (called a **vector**). If three sides are drawn, the result is a triangle; if more straight lines are drawn, an eight-sided or a sixteen-sided polygon is produced. If hundreds of very short straight lines are drawn, the polygon will look like a true circle.

Now look at the approximations of a circle shown in Figure 13.2(b); they illustrate the raster scan method. Each box in Figure 13.2(b) represents one position on the screen and is a pixel. The raster scan method approximates the circle, not by a collection of straight lines, but by filling in certain pixels. A low-resolution image is obtained by filling in a few large pixels, whereas a high-resolution image is obtained

# Computer Graphics: From Art to Computer-Aided Design

*Most people think of a computer as a text and number processor, not as an image processor. This stereotype is changing quickly. Because manipulating images requires healthy amounts of storage and processing, the earliest users of computer graphics were draftsmen, cartographers, design engineers, and other professionals who could afford the expense. Only in the 1980s have low-cost memories and capable microprocessors brought computer graphics into wide use. Continued improvements in hardware will undoubtedly lead to even wider use of computer graphics. This photo essay provides a glimpse into the "state of the art" of computer graphics.*

1. The architectural firm, Davis and Marks of Boston, Massachusetts, created this three-dimensional model of a lobby on an Intergraph color workstation for the Liberty Mutual Insurance Company. It shows several advanced features, including shadows and nonfaceted shading of curved surfaces.

# DRAWING PROGRAMS

*Drawing programs allow you to paint on an electronic canvas (the screen) with electronic brushes, pencils, spray-paint cans, rollers, and erasers. You create a drawing by selecting tools one at a time and then using them to draw. For example, to spray part of the screen with paint, you first pick up the spray-paint can from a toolkit shown on the screen. Then you move the can to the screen's drawing area and hold down the mouse's button. Picking up tools and using them is normally done by pointing with a mouse and clicking the mouse's button, but many programs also accept keyboard commands. When the drawing is finished, a printer or plotter is used to transfer the screen image to paper.*

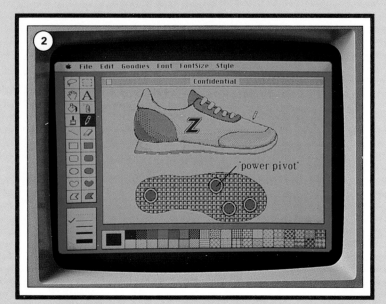

2. The MacPaint program from Apple has been a major reason for the popularity of the Apple Macintosh. MacPaint is fun to use and can produce extremely professional drawings.

3. This employment form was created using MacDraw and printed on the Apple LaserWriter printer.

## The Watermill Restaurants, Inc.

125 West Broadway
Personnel, Suite 300
Cambridge, Ma. 02142

**PERSONNEL REQUISITION**

REQUISITION NO.

EMPLOYMENT SPECIALIST

| JOB TITLE | DATE NEEDED |
|---|---|

| DEPARTMENT NAME/NUMBER | JOB LOCATION |
|---|---|

| SHIFT □ DAYS □ SWING □ GRAVEYARD | SALARY RANGE | □ EXEMPT □ NON-EXEMPT |
|---|---|---|
| □ PERMANENT □ TEMPORARY (DURATION) | | PAY GRADE |
| □ ADDITION TO HEAD COUNT □ REPLACEMENT (NO ADDITION TO HEAD COUNT) | NAME OF EMPLOYEE REPLACED | |

CAUSE OF REPLACEMENT

| TO WHOM WILL EMPLOYEE REPORT? | WHO WILL CONDUCT INTERVIEW |
|---|---|

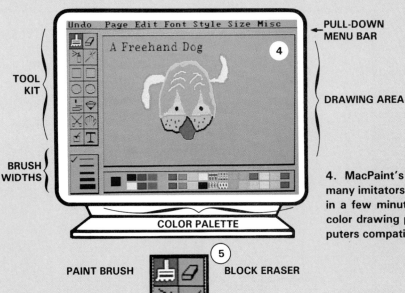

TOOL KIT

BRUSH WIDTHS

PULL-DOWN MENU BAR

DRAWING AREA

COLOR PALETTE

4. MacPaint's success has spawned many imitators. This drawing was created in a few minutes using PC Paintbrush, a color drawing program that runs on computers compatible with the IBM PC.

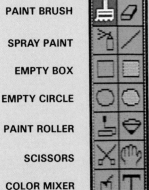

| PAINT BRUSH | BLOCK ERASER |
| SPRAY PAINT | LINE |
| EMPTY BOX | FILLED BOX |
| EMPTY CIRCLE | FILLED CIRCLE |
| PAINT ROLLER | PALETTE ERASER |
| SCISSORS | MOVE PAGE |
| COLOR MIXER | TEXT |

5. The PC Paintbrush toolkit. Electronic tools often perform better than their physical counterparts. For example, brightly checkered, plaid, or paisley paint can be sprayed from an electronic spray can.

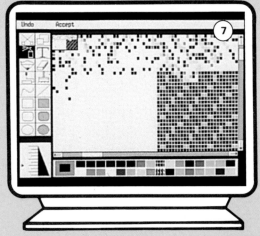

6. MacPaint and its imitators use pull-down menus to give access to the program's commands. For example, if you choose Brush Shapes from this menu, you can change the shape of the paintbrush's tip.

7. In this screen the drawing has been greatly enlarged so that the house's chimney fills the lower-right portion of the drawing area. This enlarged display is created when you choose the option labeled Zoom In; it allows you to make editing changes conveniently.

*window* **7**

# BUSINESS GRAPHICS

8. Graphs can help a business manager in two ways. First, a quickly generated *analysis graph* helps a manager find patterns and trends in otherwise meaningless tables of numbers. Second, a well-labeled *presentation graph* helps communicate a message to other people. This graph was sent to a plotter by Graphwriter, a graphics package for microcomputers that is designed expressly for preparing high-quality presentation graphics.

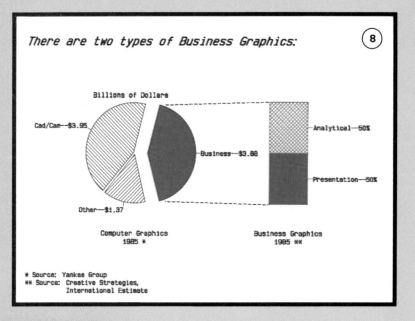

There are two types of Business Graphics: ⑧

Billions of Dollars

Cad/Cam—$3.95

Business—$3.88

Other—$1.37

Computer Graphics
1985 *

Analytical—50%

Presentation—50%

Business Graphics
1985 **

\* Source: Yankee Group
\*\* Source: Creative Strategies,
International Estimate

9. Many spreadsheet programs come with the ability to produce analysis graphs. This screen shows two columns of numbers stored in a spreadsheet created by Lotus Symphony. Symphony is a spreadsheet-based program that can produce line graphs, bar charts, pie charts, and stock market graphs.

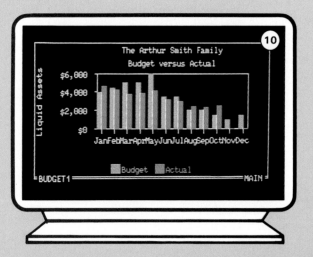

10. In this screen the Symphony program has converted the numbers from the spreadsheet into a bar graph. If the necessary raw data is already in the spreadsheet, it takes only a minute to create a graph of this complexity.

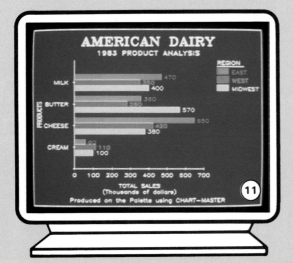

**11,12.** These presentation-quality graphs show better labels than most graphics packages can produce. Designing and entering high-quality presentation graphs require some skill and patience.

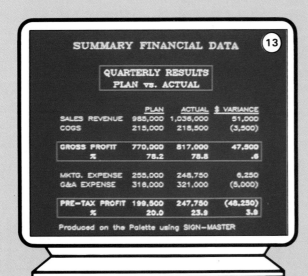

**13.** Text charts are useful for presenting lecture outlines, but surprisingly, many graphics packages can't create good-looking text charts.

**14.** Once a graph looks OK on the screen, it can be reproduced on a variety of media. For example, the graph might be printed on paper, plotted on an over-head transparency, or photographed on a 35-mm slide.

# ARCHITECTURE

Graphics and architecture have always been inseparable, but it has taken recent improvements in graphics hardware and software to bring computer-based methods into all phases of architectural design.

15. A CalComp computer-aided design system. Shown on the display, and on the pen plotter, is a drawing of a checkpoint for airport security.

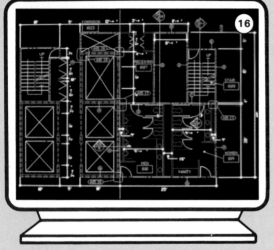

16. Complete floor plans can be displayed and modified before they are committed to paper.

17. Solids-modeling software can provide a three-dimensional view of a proposed design.

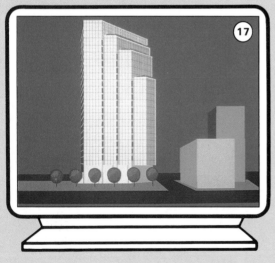

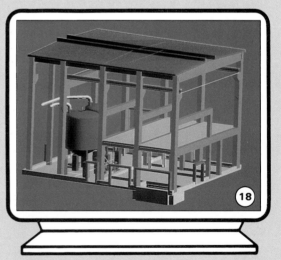

18. Three-dimensional views of the construction of a processing plant make it easy to see how pipes, equipment, and steel fit together.

# CARTOGRAPHY:
# THE ART OF MAKING MAPS

*Digital mapping starts by capturing large geographical data sets in a map database. Then map analysts identify and correct errors and convert the data sets into useful maps.*

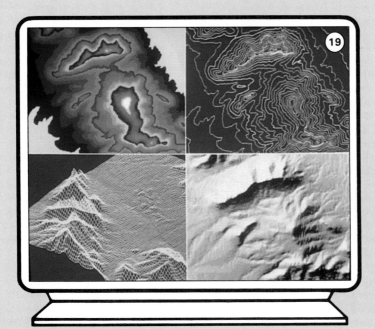

19. Once inside the computer, geographical data can be displayed in many ways. Here terrain is depicted by using (clockwise from upper left) color-coded elevations, contour lines, shaded relief, and rotated profiles.

20. This is a color-coded, shaded relief view showing features of the terrain as if they were illuminated from a light source above the screen. Shaded relief perspectives can even be displayed in stereo for viewing with 3-D glasses.

# COMPUTER-AIDED MANUFACTURING

Numerically controlled machines and robots can execute very long sequences of movement commands precisely and quickly. But developing accurate sequences of commands is not an easy task. The process is accomplished more quickly and more reliably if the sequences can be simulated on a computer screen before they are tried on the actual machines.

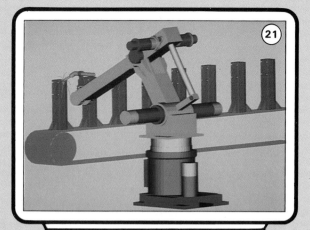

21. A simulated spot-welding operation.

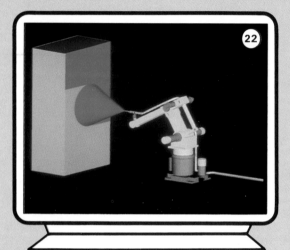

22. A simulated painting operation.

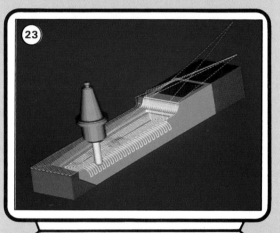

23. A simulated, numerically controlled milling sequence.

24. This crankshaft is modeled with Intergraph Sculptured Surfaces software.

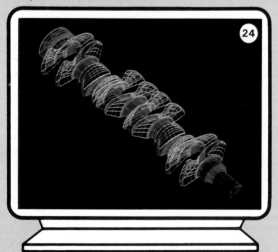

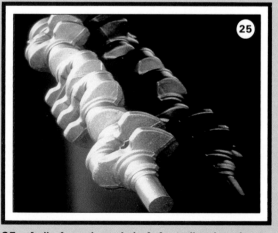

25. A die-forged crankshaft for a diesel engine.

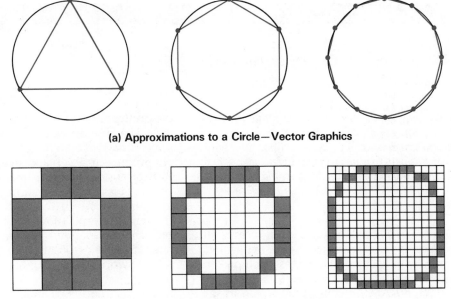

**Figure 13.2**
Vector versus bit-
mapped graphics

**(a) Approximations to a Circle—Vector Graphics**

**(b) Approximations to a Circle—Raster Scan**

by filling in many small pixels. The ratio of horizontal to vertical pixels is called the **aspect ratio** of the monitor and determines the shape of each pixel. If the aspect ratio is not 1, circles and diagonal lines may be distorted.

Vector graphics monitors produce extremely accurate line drawings. Because it takes more time for the electron gun to draw vectors than to horizontally scan the screen in a fixed pattern, vector graphics monitors are not good at filling in areas of the screen. As a result, an image with many dense objects will cause the screen to flicker noticeably. Vector graphics monitors are used in applications requiring a high-quality graphical display, such as computer-aided design and drafting (see Photo 51 in Window 1).

Raster scan monitors are less expensive and far more common than vector graphics monitors; all televisions and personal computers use raster scan monitors.

## PRESENTATION GRAPHICS

Usually, a presentation graph is prepared for viewing by decision makers who want information in a compact but meaningful form. The information may be obtained from any source and can be entered from the keyboard. In a personal computer, the most likely electronic sources are spreadsheet, database, or word processor files. To use presentation graphics programs, you must also own a graphics display device. In addition, a graphics printer or plotter is needed to obtain a hard copy of the resulting charts. In the following sections, we describe three ways to prepare presentation graphics: with the graphics component of an integrated program, with a stand-alone graphics program, and with a project management program.

Integrated programs frequently offer graphing routines that allow data to be converted into simple on-screen graphs with minimal effort. For example, let's suppose you are using a spreadsheet program that can produce graphics, and your worksheet contains financial information about computer companies. To convert data in the worksheet into a crude graph, takes only two steps: (1) asking for the graphics option of the program, and (2) pointing out the graph's data.

The order you perform these steps in depends on the program you use. If you use Microsoft Excel, the first step is to point out the data by selecting an area of the worksheet. You do this with the mouse, causing the area you select to appear in inverse video. For example, in Figure 13.3, the range containing cells A2:B6 has been selected from the Biggest DP Companies worksheet. The second step is to open a

## Graphics Standards (cont.)

if available and shades of gray if not.

Thus, on a screen with only 60 dpi, a graphics primitive for a circle will yield a rough-looking curve. The user can manipulate the jagged circle, secure in the knowledge that when the time comes to put it on paper, the driver for a laser printer will take the same primitive and create a smoothly executed 300-dpi circle. In a way, graphics primitives do for graphics what the ASCII character code does for text.

Graphics primitives alone, though, are not always sufficient. For example, if you describe a square with graphics primitives, you will define four separate lines. A program that looks at the graphics primitives will recreate the square but has no way of "knowing" that the four lines are actually a single entity that should be operated on together. But a "higher-level graphics" format can group the primitives to create complete objects.

Because programs are designed for so many different purposes, standardizing higher-level graphics descriptions is not easy. Nevertheless, some standards have been proposed or established in specific application areas, such as IGES (*Initial Graphics Exchange Specifications*) and PHIGS (*Programmer's Hierarchical Interactive Graphics Standard*) in computer-aided design, which run mainly on engineering workstations rather than microcomputers. The most popular higher-level graphics descriptions on micros have been established by the success of specific software packages, such as AutoCAD.

However flexible, no set of primitives can create every possible image. Some images, such as a photograph of a real scene, do not decompose into graphics primitives readily. Such images are best handled as bit maps, so any comprehensive graphics standard must also allow for this method as well. The resolution and other characteristics of the bit map depend on its origin and ultimate use; the main sources will be television images, facsimile machines, and scanners. In some cases, software can analyze a bit-mapped image and create a graphics primitive description. At present this capability is largely limited to converting cleanly made line drawings into line primitives.

Source: Cary Lu, *High Technology*, March 1986, pp. 23–24.

**Figure 13.3**
A simple pie chart prepared with Excel. Data in the Biggest DP Companies worksheet window is linked to the pie chart in the 5 Biggest Companies chart window.

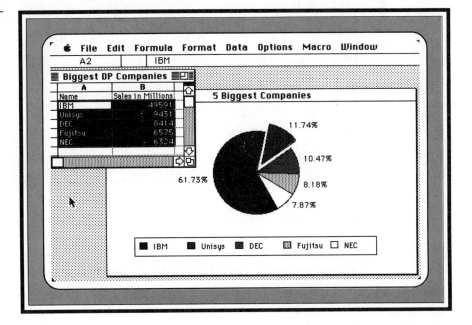

**Figure 13.4**
A stacked-bar chart
prepared with Lotus
1-2-3

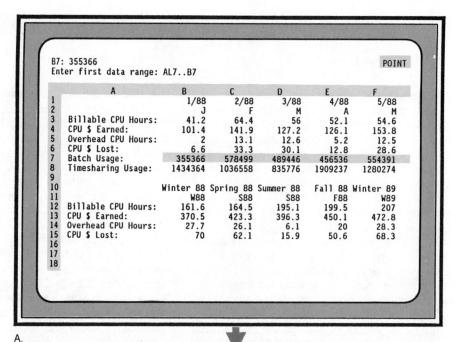

A.

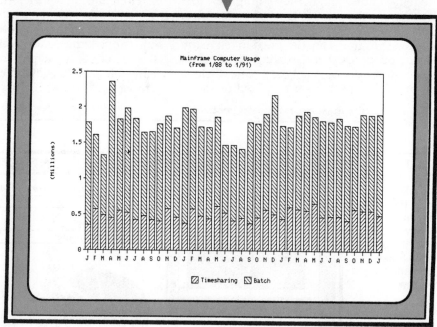

B.

*chart window* by choosing the New Chart option from the File menu. When the chart window appears on the screen, it contains a graph linked to the data in the worksheet window. Depending on how the default graphics values for Excel have been set, the graph might look like the pie chart shown in the 5 Biggest Companies chart window of Figure 13.3. Because the chart window is linked to the worksheet window, if you change the values of cells in the worksheet, the graph will be redrawn to reflect the changes.

If the initial graph doesn't look right, you can give additional commands to change it into another type of graph or to spruce it up by adding labels, legends, headings, and the like. For example, you might want to drag one of the wedges to a new location to separate it from the others and emphasize it.

Lotus 1-2-3 reverses the order commands are given in. First you select the GRAPH command from the main menu. Then you point out the data to be graphed and choose the type of graph. Suppose you want to use 1-2-3 to compare the amount of timesharing and batch computer usage that occurred in each month during the last three years on a certain mainframe computer. Figure 13.4(a) shows how the range of cells containing the batch usage numbers can be selected for graphing by pointing with the cursor-movement keys. But to create the stacked-bar chart shown in Figure 13.4(b), you must select three ranges of data: One range contains the labels for the horizontal axis, and the other two ranges contain the values for batch and timeshared computer usage. The finished graph lets you see and compare the relationships among seventy-four numbers that would not otherwise fit on the screen at once.

Spreadsheet graphics allow you to plot any row or column of data against any other row or column of data. You can choose various types of displays (such as bar, line, or pie) as well as various combinations (such as stacked bar or line bar). You can also save the graphical representation of the data in a disk file and retrieve it as you would retrieve a word processing document.

Producing a graph with a database program is similar to preparing one with a spreadsheet. The major difference is that with a database program, you select one or more fields of each record to be plotted, whereas with a spreadsheet, you select cells from a worksheet.

Most integrated programs offer a prepackaged set of graph types. For example, Figure 13.5 shows icons representing the types of graphs Excel can produce. You can change from one type of graph to another by selecting a different icon from the appropriate menu. Although this lets you try out different ways of displaying numbers quickly, it can be limiting if you want an entirely different type of graph from the prepackaged selections.

In most cases, you must spend some time tinkering with the program's options and experimenting before you arrive at an effective graph. Choosing an appropriate type of graph for the data at hand is one of the most important tasks. For example, the graph in Figure 13.6 compares the revenues and income of six computer companies. This combination chart superimposes a line graph on top of a bar chart. As a result, each company's revenue-to-income ratio is clearly apparent. Equally important is the selection of logarithmic scales for the vertical axes. Because IBM is more than a hundred times the size of Microsoft and Lotus, its statistics would dominate the chart without the compression provided by a logarithmic scale.

A *curve-fitting graph*, another useful type of combination chart, superimposes a mathematical curve on the data. Depending on the graph, the curve might be used to predict future data points or make an underlying relationship among the data points more apparent. The curve is often constructed with a mathematical technique

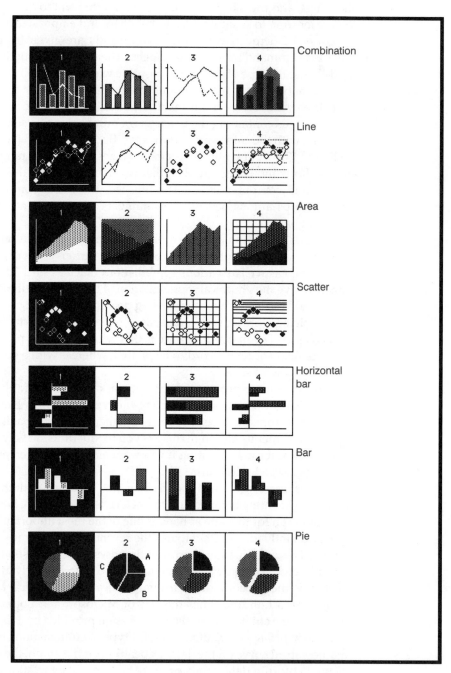

**Figure 13.5**
The types of charts produced by Excel

**Figure 13.6**
A combination line
and bar chart using
logarithmic scales

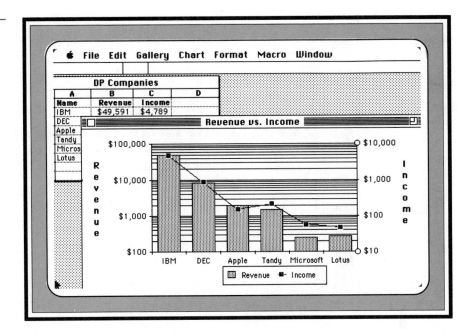

called *regression analysis*. Spreadsheet programs are particularly good at creating curve-fitting graphs because you can use the calculating abilities of the worksheet to compute and try out several mathematical functions. Usually one function results in a closer fit to the data than the others.

• Linear functions draw a straight line through the raw data.

• Weighted average functions smooth out variations in the data by computing a weighted average of the last *n* data points.

• Exponential functions draw exponentially increasing (or decreasing) curves through the data.

• Power curve functions draw a curve through the data by using the mathematical formula $\log y = b \log x + \log a$.

*Area-fill charts*, like simple line graphs, are used to show the relationship between variables. But an area-fill chart includes some texture in the area under the line graph to increase the effectiveness of the presentation. For example, Figure 13.7 is an area-fill chart showing ups and downs in a company's revenues and cost of sales.

*Scatter charts* are used to show the distribution of data values. You might use a scatter chart to show how different types of consumers buy different types of products or how one kind of data is clustered around certain regions of the graph, as Figure 13.8 shows.

Symbols are used in line graphs or scatter charts to identify different sets of data. For example, the legend in Figure 13.8 shows solid diamonds identify the sales of coffee, hollow diamonds the sales of hot cocoa, and solid squares the sales of iced tea. Each graphics program has a different set of symbols available to represent items. Figure 13.9(a) shows the symbols available with Excel. Some programs come

**Figure 13.7**
Area-fill chart

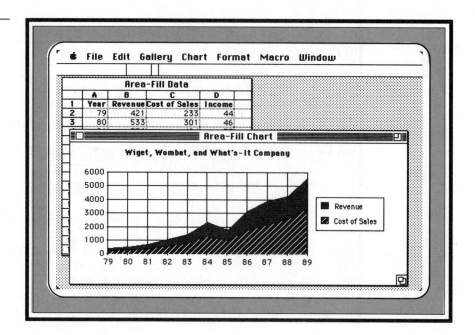

with extensive symbol libraries or allow you to build your own symbols, thus making it possible to represent the sales of iced tea with tall glasses and the sales of hot cocoa with steaming mugs.

A *simple bar chart* shows the variations in one set of values; a *multiple bar chart* shows the relationship between variations in several sets of values. Depending on the visual effect you want and the options provided by the graphics program, you might choose a simple bar chart, a chart with clustered or stacked bars, or a chart

**Figure 13.8**
Scatter diagram

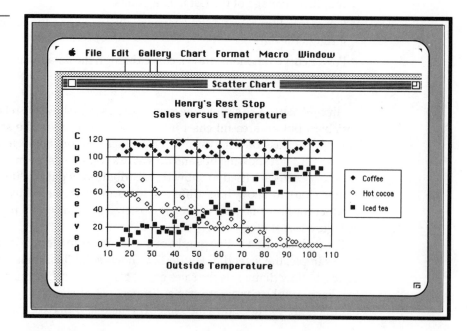

**Figure 13.9**
Excel's dialog boxes make it easy to choose hatch patterns and symbols for the various parts of a graph.

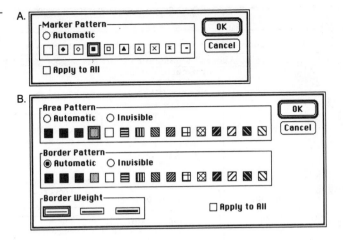

with bars displayed in a three-dimensional perspective. Figure 13.10 shows a clustered bar chart in which two sets of data are compared by overlapping one set of bars with another set. Clustered bar charts make it easy to contrast sets of values. Excel allows another variation in bar charts: The horizontal bar chart. Turning the chart on its side may make it easier to understand, or it may simply be the best way to print the chart. A three-dimensional bar chart is like a clustered bar chart, except that the bars in each cluster group are projected onto a three-dimensional cube. Your printed output will give the impression of depth: the clustered bars are placed one behind the other rather than next to each other.

Bar charts, pie charts, and area-fill charts usually use different hatch patterns or colors to distinguish each set of values. A *hatch pattern* is a graphical texture used to

**Figure 13.10**
A clustered bar chart that includes a note explaining the unusual height of one of the bars.

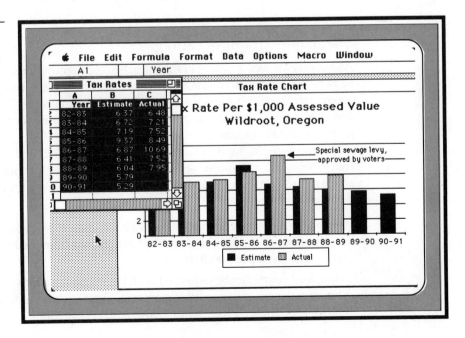

**Figure 13.11**
An organization chart produced by MORE, an outline processing program. The icons at the left of the screen determine the basic format of the chart.

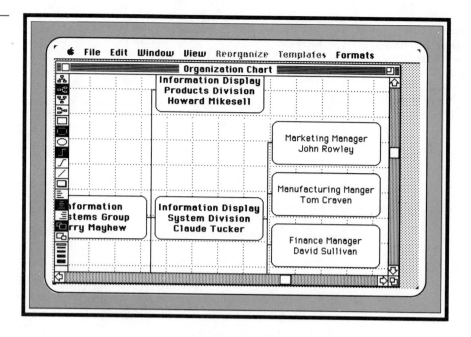

give an area a distinctive look. Most programs let you choose the hatch pattern to be used for each part of the graph. Figure 13.9(b) shows the hatch patterns available with Excel.

Outline processors sometimes have a graphic component that produces tree charts or other text charts. A *tree chart* is a series of boxes connected in a hierarchical fashion. *Text charts* convert the items in an outline into an attractive format for an overhead transparency. For example, Figure 13.11 shows part of an organization chart that was created by converting an outline into a tree chart.

## Standalone Graphics Packages

Although graphics components of spreadsheet programs like Lotus 1-2-3 and Excel have become the most common form of presentation graphics, standalone graphics programs can create more sophisticated and polished graphs. This added flexibility comes at a price: Standalone programs generally require far more effort than the graphics routines contained in integrated programs.

As an example, Lotus Freelance Plus sells for $395 and requires an IBM or compatible microcomputer with a minimum of 384KB, an appropriate graphics adapter card and monitor, and either a plotter or graphics printer. It has the following characteristics:

- Freelance's chart option provides five basic chart types: text, pie, bar, line, and scatter. Figure 13.12 shows how data are entered from the keyboard to create a standard Freelance pie chart.

- Standard charts can be enhanced with free-hand drawings or by adding building blocks called graphic elements. These include text, lines, arrows, rectangles, circles, slices, bows, markers, and polygons.

A.

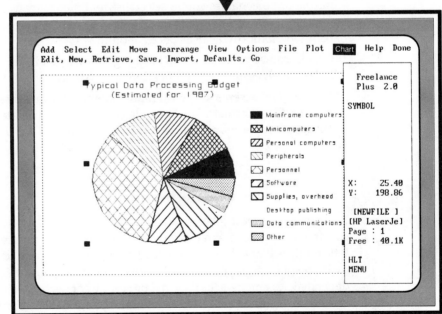

B.

**Figure 13.12**
Producing a pie chart with Lotus Freelance Plus. **(a)** Data for the pie chart is entered by completing an on- screen form. **(b)** The resulting pie chart.

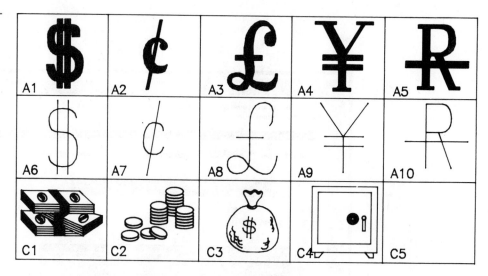

**Figure 13.13**
Symbol libraries, such as this one, allow previously stored drawings to be added to any graphic by pressing only a few keys. Symbol libraries containing maps are particularly important for creating presentation graphs based on geographical information.

- Graphics elements can be joined into a single object, or symbol. Symbols are organized in libraries where they are easily available. Over sixty libraries come with the program, but you can create symbols and build your own libraries or buy additional libraries for special purposes (see Figure 13.13).

- Output can be adjusted for paper, overhead transparencies, and film. A batch output option enables you to select, list, and plot as many as thirty-six completed drawings at a time. This is useful for creating large print jobs that can be run periodically, such as once a month.

- Graphs can be produced with hatching, color, legends, headers, several built-in font families, unlimited font sizes, and axis scaling.

- The program accepts keyboard input and imports data files in either Lotus 1-2-3 or dBase formats. Freelance also imports charts created by GraphWriter, 1-2-3, or Symphony, as well as ASCII files created by word processors.

## Project Management Software

A *project management program* analyzes and displays the activities of production, construction, or development projects. Although these programs incorporate analytic routines that fall outside the field of presentation graphics, their output is normally displayed as charts or diagrams. For example, a **PERT chart** shows the dependencies among activities in a project by connecting activity boxes with lines (see Figure 13.14). The *critical path* running through a PERT chart shows the activities that can't slip without affecting the project's entire schedule.

To create a PERT chart with MacProject, you begin by drawing task and milestone boxes on the screen and giving them labels. Then you add dependency lines by dragging the mouse from a box to a box that depends on it. Finally, you add task information, such as the number of days it will take to complete each task or the

# A Word About . . . *Project Management Software*

*"Two people using Microsoft Project cut the time needed to plan the project from ten days to two hours." —Kenneth Anderson, Chief Programmer and Analyst, Blue Cross/Blue Shield*

The first project management tools developed 30 years ago by the U.S. Navy were strictly manual methods using paper and pencil. Not long after these manual methods became popular among military planners, they also caught on with private industry, especially construction.

The specialized methods and highly structured planning techniques of project management eventually became computerized on mainframes and minicomputers. These programs for large computer systems typically cost between $25,000 and $200,000, and support virtually every function, method, analytic technique, and reporting style that you possibly could want in a project manager.

Large systems also give you access to large corporate databases and built-in multiuser capabilities, enabling professional project managers to evaluate the scope and progress of a project in considerable detail. Over the years, project management programs have also migrated to the personal computer.

The largest initial market for PC-based project management packages has been professional project managers—full-time specialists who spend their days designing, tracking, and coordinating large-scale complex projects. These project managers in turn provide the technical support for the middle-level managers directly responsible for the project. As PC-based project management software gets better, more powerful, faster, and easier to use, other professionals are likely to find that it solves their management problems as well.

Many of today's personal computer-based programs were converted from existing mainframe and minicomputer implementations, and their prices reflect that orientation (they cost more than $1,000). Other programs come from some of the industry leaders in microcomputer software publishing. These programs typically cost less than $500 and tend to be integrated within the vendor's complete productivity software family.

Each project management program we tested uses either the critical path method (CPM) or the program evaluation review technique (PERT) of project management. (Many use both.) CPM, which uses Gantt charts, concentrates on the resources needed to complete the project—assuming that the duration of the tasks can be estimated accurately—and analyzes and reports the compromises necessary to balance the cost of a project with the time needed to finish it.

PERT takes a broader view of the concepts inherent in project planning and management. This method allows you to chart each phase of a project and its links to other phases. Most of the tested programs offer PERT methods, which are much more useful in illustrating the network of relationships involved in project planning.

All of the programs tested here provide the minimum set of project management tools. They let you plan projects, create activities, assign resources (people and equipment) to those activities, apply the costs of those resources, decide which activities to schedule first, and set milestones (critical points in a project that must be attained at the time scheduled or the entire project will slip). These project managers also let you modify your plans to see how the changes will affect the overall project schedule and costs, produce reports that summarize work in progress, and generate graphical representations of the entire project.

None of these programs is as intuitive to use as other microcomputer software. You shouldn't forget that. Learning to use them is simply not as easy as learning a word processor or a database or a spreadsheet because the tasks of automated program management aren't as intuitive as the tasks of these other programs.

Source: Don Crabb, *Infoworld*, October 6, 1986, pp. 48–49.

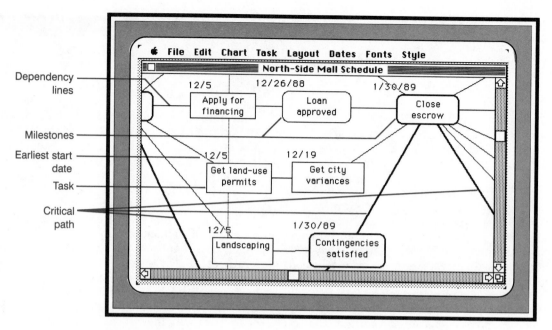

**Figure 13.14**
Project-scheduling information displayed as a PERT chart

resources they will require. The project management program does the rest automatically by calculating the critical path and producing a PERT chart like that in Figure 13.14.

A **Gantt chart** plots the activities of a project against a time line to provide a different visual representation of the project schedule. The Gantt chart in Figure 13.15 displays the starting date, earliest completion date, and number of slack days for each activity throughout the project. Most project management programs can also provide cash flow tables, resource usage charts, and status reports.

## A Summary of Features

A presentation graphics package should let you enhance a graph by emphasizing certain phrases or headings through the use of different sizes and styles of type. Moreover, a good graphics program can fit lines or curves to the points plotted in a graph, an especially important feature if you want to make projections.

Some graphics programs are especially good for making overhead transparencies. A typical program lets you print or display part or all of a picture—sometimes in color—so that you can copy it onto a transparency. Plotters will plot directly on a transparency with the use of special pens. Laser printers can also print directly on a transparency, but you must use special heat-resistant transparencies, or the heat from the fusing rollers will melt the transparency and gum up the machine.

A *slide show facility* lets you play back a series of pictures directly from the computer's screen. It also lets you determine the delay between the presentation of

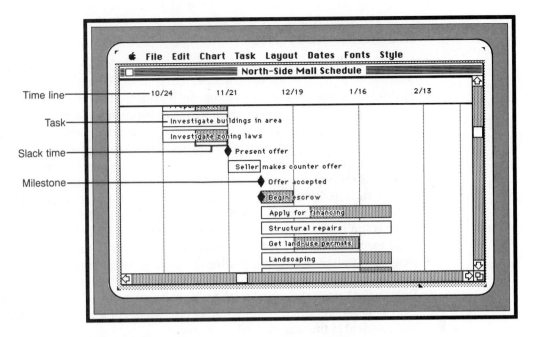

**Figure 13.15**
Part of a typical Gantt chart produced by MacProject

each slide or to step through the slides with keyboard commands (perhaps by using the [PgUp] and [PgDn] keys).

Because the extent and versatility of presentation graphics programs continue to grow, selecting the most suitable program can be confusing. Before buying one of the hundreds of programs now available, you should consider the following features:

| | |
|---|---|
| Number of fonts | Transparency facility |
| Number of pen colors | Slide show facility |
| Number of text sizes | Data interchange |
| Number of hatching patterns | Math functions |
| Size of symbol library | Title lines |
| Ability to add notes | Legends |
| Ability to reposition elements | Footnotes |
| Help facility | Chart types |
| Regression lines |    Bar (stacked, clustered, 3-D) |
|    Linear |    Line |
|    Exponential |    Scatter (XY) |
|    Logarithmic |    Pie |
|    Parabolic |    Area |
| Memory required |    Text charts |
| On-screen preview |    Special (Pert, Gantt, and the like) |
| Printer support |    Combinations |
| Support for graphic input devices | Compatibility with graphics standards |

# GRAPHICS EDITORS

A graphics editor is a program that draws graphical images by interpreting commands entered from a keyboard, mouse, touch tablet, or light pen. Two fundamentally different types of graphics editors are bit-mapped and vector graphics.

*Bit-mapped editors* store the screen image in memory as a grid of memory cells representing individual pixels. The screen image is constructed and modified by changing the values stored in the bit map. Using a bit-mapped editor is similar to drawing on paper. In contrast, *vector graphics editors* build a mathematical model in memory of the objects to appear on the screen. The model consists of interconnected objects, such as lines, circles, cylinders, boxes, and arcs, and the screen image provides a view of how the mathematical model looks. Using a vector graphics editor is similar to constructing a model out of building blocks.

Bit-mapped editors excel in artistic applications, but they aren't suitable for analytical applications such as finding an object's center of gravity, rotating a three-dimensional model to view it from the side, or calculating the strength of a bridge. Thus "paint" programs usually take a bit-mapped approach to graphics, whereas analytic programs take a vector graphics approach. These different approaches become evident in the way each editor operates.

## A "Paint" Graphics Editor

In this section, we describe a simple, general-purpose graphics editor. Although the details differ from one graphics editor to the next, the general techniques remain the same. This example adopts a paint, or bit-mapped, approach similar to that used by MacPaint or PC Paintbrush.

Because a graphics editor processes pictures instead of text, it may at first seem unusual. Most graphics editors are driven by a menu of icons (called *tools*), descriptive pictures that show what commands the editor can perform (see Figure 13.16). You tell the editor what to do by selecting an item from the menu, for example, by pointing with a mouse. The following list describes a few of these commands:

- Lasso. Select an object on the screen to move, duplicate, or erase it.
- Select. Select a region of the screen to move, duplicate, or erase it. The difference between Lasso and Select is that, by using Lasso, you can select an object within a region without also selecting the background surrounding the object (even though the background is within the region selected).
- Pan. Move your viewpoint around the drawing area. Since the drawing area may be too large to fit within the screen, Pan lets you roam around a larger area than you can see on your screen at any one time.
- Text. Enter characters, numbers, or whatever you want from the keyboard.
- Fill. Add color, shade, or hatch patterns to an enclosed region by filling it in with a pattern or color.
- Spray. Spray a mist or pattern on the screen.
- Paint. Draw a line or brush stroke on the screen.

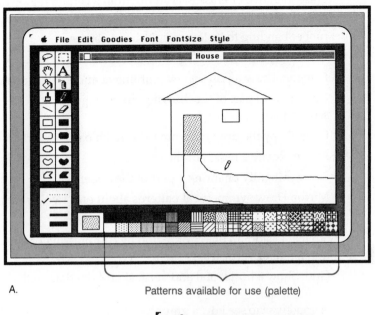

A.

Patterns available for use (palette)

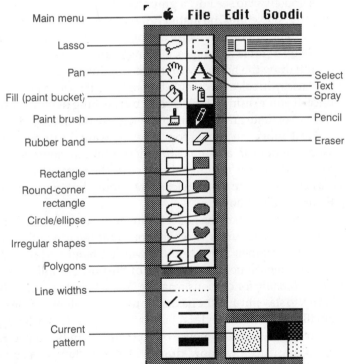

B.

**Figure 13.16**
MacPaint's icon menu. Each command is represented on the screen by a picture of a tool.

- Rubber band. Draw a straight line from point A to point B. The line stretches from point A, like a rubber band, as you move its endpoint to point B.
- Erase. Remove or erase everything from a certain region on the screen.
- Rectangle. Draw a rectangle by selecting its upper left-hand corner and then rubber banding to its lower right-hand corner.
- Circle. Draw a circle by defining its center and radius.
- Polygon. Draw a polygon by pointing at and selecting its vertices.
- Cut. Remove part of the drawing from a region of the screen and save it in the scratch pad.
- Paste. Copy the drawing from the scratch pad to a certain region of the screen.
- Rotate. Rotate a region of the screen.
- Zoom. Magnify or shrink a part of the screen.
- Mirror. Draw symmetrical patterns about one, two, or more axes.
- Drag. Move a region or object across the screen.
- Stretch. Distort an object or region by compressing or stretching it along the horizontal or vertical axis.
- Grid. Show a horizontal and vertical grid overlaid with the drawing.

A good way to see how a graphics editor works is to use it to draw a very simple picture. All pictures, no matter how simple or complex, are made up of many trivial graphical components. For example, the house shown in Figure 13.16 is actually made up of three rectangles, a triangle, and a free-hand drawing.

You draw the house by first selecting Rectangle from the menu. If you're using a mouse, you select Rectangle by pointing at its icon and clicking the mouse button once. If you're using a tablet, point by touching the surface of the tablet. If you don't have a separate graphics input device, use the keyboard's arrow keys.

Next, move the pointer to where you want the upper left-hand corner of the rectangle to appear, and hold the mouse button down while you drag the mouse toward the lower right-hand corner of the rectangle. When the lower right-hand corner has been reached, release the mouse button; the rectangle stays in place, as Figure 13.17(a) shows.

To put the roof on the house, as in Figure 13.17(b), select Polygon from the menu. Next, move the cursor to where you want the top of the roof, and click the mouse button once; then move to the lower left-hand vertex of the triangle, and click a second time. Notice how the edge of the polygon follows the cursor—this is called *rubber banding* for obvious reasons. At each vertex, a click of the mouse causes the vertex to stay put and the next edge to stretch following the movement of the mouse. Finally, when the triangle is closed at the top vertex (you've gone all the way around the triangle), click the mouse button twice to indicate you're done.

To construct a window, draw a second rectangle (a square) inside the first rectangle, as Figure 13.17(c) shows. The rectangular door shown in Figure 13.17(d) requires an additional touch. After you draw it, select Fill from the menu. Fill usually gives you a choice of patterns to use when filling in an enclosed polygonal area.

**Figure 13.17**
Building a simple
house using a
graphics editor

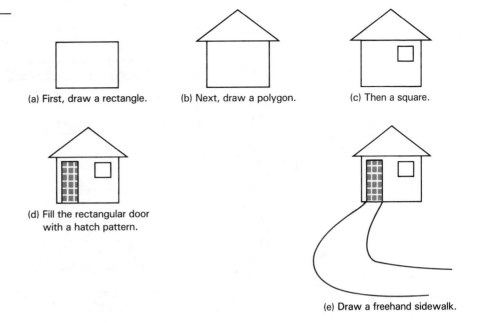

(a) First, draw a rectangle.    (b) Next, draw a polygon.    (c) Then a square.

(d) Fill the rectangular door
with a hatch pattern.

(e) Draw a freehand sidewalk.

Select a hatch pattern like the one in Figure 13.17(d), move the cursor to any point inside the rectangular door, and click the mouse button once. The entire door area will be filled in with the hatch pattern.

To draw the sidewalk shown in Figure 13.17(e), select Paint. When you use this command, shape and design depend on a steady hand. Hold the mouse button down while moving the mouse to draw the outline of the sidewalk. Your drawing may not be very smooth because the shape of the sidewalk follows the path of the moving mouse.

If you make a mistake or want to reenter an object, select the Undo command, and your last action will be undone. Alternatively, you can remove parts of the picture by selecting Erase. Most graphics editors offer many other options that we haven't illustrated, such as aids for drawing straight lines, French curves, shading, and texture.

## A Vector Graphics Editor

In most of this chapter, we discuss bit-mapped graphics because it is the most common technology in the personal computer world. But most commonly used for professional design and drafting on larger computers are vector graphics editors. Recall that a *vector* is defined by coordinates, such as the locations of the endpoints of a straight line. A vector graphics editor makes it possible for a computer to calculate mathematical properties of the objects on the screen, present different views or perspectives of the objects, and store drawings in much less memory space and perform operations that require greater precision and accuracy than is possible with a bit-mapped graphics editor.

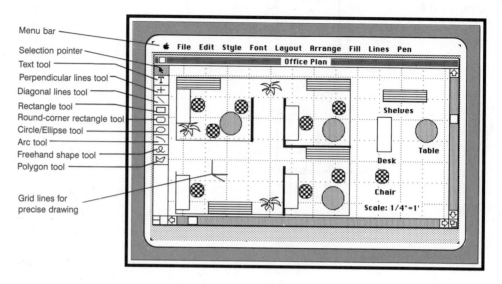

**Figure 13.18**
MacDraw tools and drawing board showing grid lines

Vector-oriented editors can display their models on either raster scan or vector graphics monitors. Graphical objects such as straight lines, circles, rectangles, and arcs are stored internally as vectors, but they can be displayed as bit-mapped regions on a raster scan monitor. Macintosh's MacDraw is a popular example of a vector-oriented editor that runs on a raster scan computer system.

The tools provided by a vector-oriented graphics editor are similar to the tools of a paint graphics editor, but they behave differently. Figure 13.18 shows the tools provided by MacDraw; text, lines, rectangles, circles, and polygons are all represented by small icons at the left of the drawing area. To draw an object, first click a tool with the mouse, and then place the object on the drawing board.

Vector-oriented editors are used to obtain very precise drawings (for architectural, engineering, and design work). For this reason, the MacDraw drawing board can be calibrated in either inches or centimeters. To help align items accurately, you can display rulers across the top and down the left side of the document window (see Figure 13.19). Crosshairs on these rulers move to display the pointer's horizontal and vertical coordinates. For even more precise alignment, MacDraw provides an invisible alignment grid that can be used to control the size and placement of objects. When the alignment grid is turned on, objects that you draw automatically "snap" to the nearest grid lines.

Selecting the Drawing Size option from the Layout menu allows you to set the size of the drawing board in 8-by-10-inch pages. Figure 13.20 shows how to select the number of pages used in your electronic drawing board.

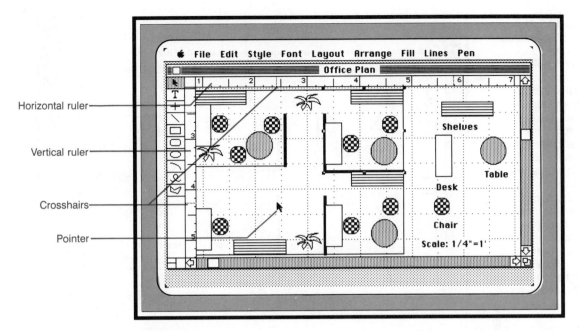

Horizontal ruler

Vertical ruler

Crosshairs

Pointer

**Figure 13.19**
Rulers along the edge of the screen help create scale drawings. In this drawing, 1/4 inch
equals 1 foot.

**Figure 13.20**
Your drawing board can be up to twelve pages wide by five pages long. Each page is 8
inches wide by 10 inches long, thus permitting accurate drawings up to 100 inches wide
by 50 inches long.

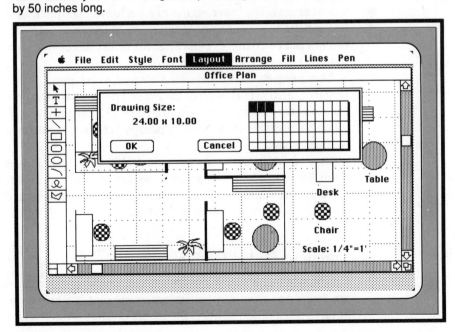

**Figure 13.21**
Vector objects can be picked up, moved, deleted, stretched, or shrunk. In this screen, one of the tables has been stretched from a small circle into an ellipse. First, the table was selected by pointing at it and clicking the mouse, thereby exposing its "handles" (the black spots around its edge). Then, dragging one of the handles caused the table to stretch.

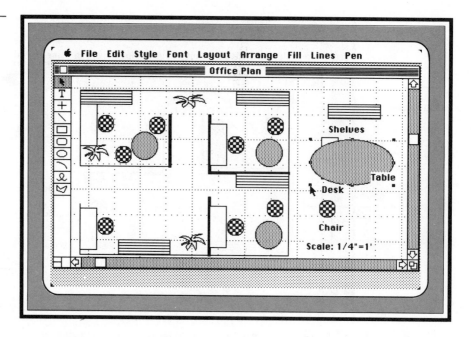

Each tool produces a graphical object that is described by one or more vectors. In Figure 13.21, the circle/ellipse tool was used to draw the table, the perpendicular-lines tool drew some of the walls, the round-corner rectangles tool drew the chairs, and the rectangle tool drew the desk and shelves. A line is defined by the locations of its endpoints, and a rectangle by the locations of its corners. Even though these objects are displayed on a bit-mapped screen, they are manipulated as vectors.

You can't erase part of a vector, move part of it, or merge it with another vector object. Instead, the entire vector is moved, overlapped with other objects "behind" it, and erased. The inner region of a vector can be filled, as shown by the checkerboard pattern of the chairs or the strips of the shelves in Figure 13.21. The texture of lines can be changed, even after the object has been drawn, by selecting the object and then choosing a pen texture.

Vector objects can be measured, rotated, overlapped, printed, and mathematically "smoothed." When stored, they take up less space than bit-mapped images. For example, the examples shown in Figure 13.21 require less than 2KB of disk space when MacDraw is used, but they occupy 12KB when converted into a MacPaint bit-mapped image.

Because vectors are mathematical objects, calculations can be performed on them. For example, vector graphics editors are used to prepare the models of physical objects submitted to finite element analysis programs to determine the object's strength, flexibility, or other properties. (See Photos 36–42 in Window 1.)

## Computer-Aided Design

**CAD/CAM** (*c*omputer-*a*ided *d*esign and *c*omputer-*a*ided *m*anufacturing) programs are developed especially for designing and manufacturing new products. The heart of all CAD/CAM systems is the graphics editor, which lets you enter, manipulate,

**Figure 13.22**
A designer using a
puck to enter very
precise graphical
data into a
CAD/CAM editor

and store images in the computer system. However, most CAD/CAM graphics editors use special-purpose hardware and software as part of a **turn-key system,** a complete system of hardware and software that the user need only "turn the key" to start. Turnkey CAD/CAM systems aren't cheap; they cost from $10,000 to more than $100,000 per workstation.

A CAD/CAM graphics editor uses a mouse or puck the way a word processor uses a keyboard. Both input devices control what goes in the computer. A mouse or puck can be used to draw lines, circles, boxes, and so forth, much as a keyboard is used to enter characters and numbers. Figure 13.22 shows a designer using a puck to enter graphical data.

Powerful computers equipped with high-resolution displays are needed in solids modeling. Figure 13.23 shows a **solids modeling** graphics editor that can display three-dimensional images and cross sections of images in solid form. Notice the

**Figure 13.23**
Display from a
solids-modeling
editor

*For millions of engineers, whose stock in trade is precision drawings, the desktop computer revolution is just beginning.*

We expect computers to be good at dealing with words and numbers. The idea is so ingrained in the corporate world that IBM threw graphics into the design of the original PC as an after-thought—in case someone wanted to play games. Nevertheless, there are times when no amount of words and numbers will get the point across. How do you explain how the doohickey works, how the pieces of the puzzle fit together, or what the definitive widget should look like? Draw me a picture.

When business people need a picture, they hire a designer, architect, engineer, or illustrator. Until now, the main market for computer-aided design and drafting (CADD, or CAD if you mean either design or drafting) has been graphic arts professionals. There is no replacement specialized expertise. But there are times when a quicker and simpler drawing must do.

Until now, making acceptable technical drawings on a microcomputer has been costly. In 1985 you could expect to pay $2,500 for a competent drafting program, at least $1,400 for a high-resolution color graphics card and monitor, several hundred dollars for a pointing device (mouse or digitizer), and $2,000 for a small plotter. This adds up to $7,000—not counting the computer and peripherals you already own. Today you can put together an acceptable configuration for $300 to $1,200, which includes the computer.

**Essential CAD Features**
CAD programs have often been called "word processors for drawing." It's a good analogy, but it doesn't go far enough. In addition to being able to edit extensively without redrawing, CAD cuts drafting time in many unique ways. The most fundamental of these is the ability to use "objects" as a drawing element. Objects are groups of lines, arcs, and circles welded together so they can be used in a drawing as a single entity. Objects can be as simple as an interior door or as complex as a microchip. Thanks to objects, CAD means you never have to draw anything twice.

"Zoom" gives you virtually infinite magnification of all parts of the drawing without loss of resolution. In practical terms, infinite zoom lets you enter any imaginable degree of precise detail into a drawing, regardless of the sharpness of your eyesight, the steadiness of your hand, or the clarity of your monitor. One of the demonstration files for Autocad is a map of the Milky Way. The file zooms in on the solar system, then earth, then the United States,

contrast and texture that can be produced by using a solids modeling graphics editor. Figure 13.24 shows a nonsolid display of a three-dimensional drawing. The computational requirements of the editor used to create Figure 13.24 are much less demanding than those of the editor that created the image in Figure 13.23.

The ultimate in CAD/CAM is the CAM—computer-aided manufacturing—portion, which helps produce manufactured goods. For example, after a designer perfects a circuit board, a CAM system can guide the production of the circuit

California, then San Francisco, then the Transamerica Pyramid, and finally through one of the pyramid's office windows to a monitor displaying the Autocad logo.

Finally, placement and measurement using a CAD program are both faster and more accurate compared to manual methods. CAD programs let you work in 1-to-1 (real-world) measurements, then automatically scale the drawing for you. You can specify intervals for a drawing grid and optionally "snap" the start and end points of drawing entries to its intersections. In imitation of the T square, there should be an option to force lines to be absolutely vertical or horizontal.

A full list of features found in most any CAD manual would fill several pages. Many of these features are just more ways to skin the same cat; they give a program its personality. Attributes that appeal to one user may frustrate another. On the other hand, certain advanced features are especially worthwhile because they save valuable time.

The first group of commands to look for are those that expand the list of drawing construction elements beyond the basic line, arc, and curve. The ability to draw parallel lines makes it easy to draw walls, piping, and anything with equilateral sides. Ellipses can be drawn by combining arcs, but it's tedious. It's even harder to build complex curves with arcs—look for an automatic curve-fitting command. Varying line widths can make a drawing far more readable.

About 80 percent of the drafting done on microcomputers is two-dimensional. The contractor for the final product understands how to read a 2-D technical drawing. The benefits of 3-D drawing emerge mainly in the areas of marketing and concept visualization. 3-D capabilities can eliminate some of the need for traditional model building. That can result in more competitive fees for the designer and speedy design approval by the client.

Source: Ken Milburn, *Infoworld*, 11 August 1986, pp. 28–29.

**Figure 13.24**
Arcad's interactive design system provides a library of two thousand standard symbols to use in architectural drawings.

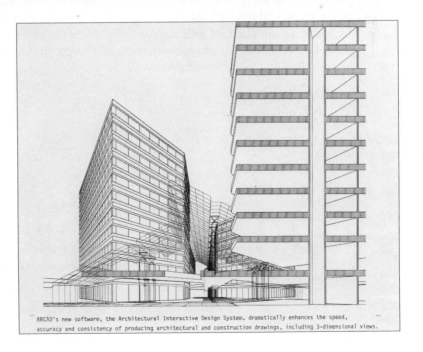

ARCAD's new software, the Architectural Interactive Design System, dramatically enhances the speed, accuracy and consistency of producing architectural and construction drawings, including 3-dimensional views.

boards by controlling machinery, creating parts lists, and generating the production artwork masters. CAM systems are often integrated with numerically controlled machines. For example, the CAM system might produce a list of instructions to be loaded into an automatic lathe or a welding robot. Parts are then manufactured and tested and adjustments are made until the production line is perfected.

## Art and Animation

Both computer art and animated graphics have exploded onto the technological scene since the invention of low-cost personal computers. High-resolution graphics systems have replaced canvas, brush, and paint with electronic stylus and color monitor. The computer has given artists an extremely fast and versatile tool.

Animation is only one of the many possible uses of computer-aided design, but it is perhaps the most intriguing. For more than half a century, cartoonists in the motion picture industry have been producing animations in which images appear to move if a series of still-frames is shown in rapid succession. The same idea is used in producing computer animation. A picture is *animated* on a computer by moving, rotating, translating (moving to a new location), or both rotating and translating one or more objects on the screen. If the motion is fast enough to simulate life, we say the animation is in **real time**. Real time animation usually involves more complex motion than simple rotation and translation. For example, a picture of a person walking across the screen requires movement of the whole object (body), movement of parts of the object (legs), and fluid coordination of the object and its parts (body and legs).

Suppose you want to animate a flying bird, as shown in the still-frames in Figure 13.25. The still-frames are made by reproducing the bird's body and changing the position of the wings. Frames (e) through (g), are identical to frames (a), (b), and (c). But in frames (a) through (d), the wings move down; in frames (e) through (g) the wings move up. The bird will appear to fly when the still-frames are rapidly displayed, erased, moved, and subsequently displayed on the screen. The animation is controlled by a sequence of commands similar to

```
DRAW FRAME (a)
ERASE
MOVE
DRAW FRAME (b)
ERASE
MOVE
DRAW FRAME (c)
ERASE
MOVE
```

You can repeat the sequence for as long as you want. To achieve more realistic animation, you would have to draw more complex sequences, but the concept is basically the same.

**Figure 13.25**
Still-frames of a flying bird

(a)           (b)

(c)           (d)

(e)      (f)      (g)

## Summary

There are three general categories of graphics programs: (1) presentation graphics for drawing charts, graphs, and diagrams; (2) graphics editors for doing CAD, CAM, and generalized drawing; and (3) educational and entertainment graphics.

Presentation graphics are frequently produced by graphics components of spreadsheets, word processors, and database managers. Another alternative is to produce them with a standalone graphics program. Both types of program produce specialized graphs and charts of communication and analysis.

Graphics editors often work along with programs for designing new products, tools, or parts. They work with such input devices as a mouse or puck and with such output devices as plotters and graphical printers.

The simplest graphics editors simulate an artist's tools in the way they draw on the screen. These paint programs store the screen image as a bit map in memory. The most sophisticated CAD/CAM graphics editors use vector graphics technology to store the object being drawn as a mathematical model in memory. Vector graphics programs are more difficult to use when drawing free-hand pictures, but they are more accurate for lines and other well-behaved mathematical shapes like cylinders and ellipses. Another advantage of vector graphics editors over bit-mapped graphics editors is their ability to store images compactly on disk.

Special-purpose programs are used along with graphics editors for CAD/CAM applications and to create entertainment graphics, such as animated sequences. These programs are used in games, education, and artistic applications that require special effects.

## Key Terms

analytic graphics

aspect ratio

CAD/CAM

Gantt chart

graphics editor

graphics primitive

PERT chart

presentation graphics

raster scan monitor

real time

solids modeling

turnkey system

vector

vector graphics monitor

## Discussion Questions

1. Presentation graphics can be created with the graphics option of a word processor, spreadsheet, or database manager or with a standalone presentation graphics program. Discuss when you might prefer to use each of these programs to create a bar chart.

2. What are Pan and Zoom? What is the difference between Fill and Spray?

3. How might rubber banding work with Rectangle, Circle, and Polygon commands?

4. Vector graphics is a much older technology than bit-mapped graphics. Explain why advances in RAM technology have made bit-mapped graphics dominant in personal computers. What are the advantages and disadvantages of each?

## Exercises

1. Use a graphics program to duplicate the spreadsheet graph shown in Figure 13.3. Count the number of keystrokes needed to modify a single cell of the spreadsheet and to redraw the graph.

2. Use a database manager to create a file containing the following information:

| Year | Barrels |
|------|---------|
| 1983 | 1,051,345 |
| 1984 | 1,967,002 |
| 1985 | 835,981 |
| 1986 | 955,300 |
| 1987 | 1,000,382 |
| 1988 | 1,499,999 |
| 1989 | 2,044,678 |
| 1990 | 2,894,053 |

Construct a bar chart plotting barrels versus year and then a pie chart in which each slice shows the percentage of the total number of barrels in a year.

3. Suggest how a word processor could be designed to handle both text and graphs within the same document. What problems with disk space do you suppose would be encountered for the word processing files?

4. Become familiar with a bit-mapped graphics editor. What is the difference between the Paint and Draw commands?

5. Show how a stick figure is animated by drawing a six-frame sequence of still-frames. Use a graphics editor to draw the six frames.

# Telecommunications

In the past ten years, three trends have combined to create a turbulent and dynamic environment in computer communications. First, the quantity of information stored in computers has more than quadrupled, a change that, in turn, has expanded the need to share information among computers. Second, the entire field of communications—from telephones and television to music recording—has begun switching from analog to digital storage and transmission methods, which is causing the fields of computing and communications to merge. Third, a shift in the relative costs of computing equipment has erased the cost advantage of centralized mainframes and is encouraging the use of personal computers.

Computer communications is also a field of many market niches, specialized pieces of equipment, and weak standards for hardware and software. It is an exciting environment, that leaves communications specialists divided about what the future will bring and how to prepare for it.

In this chapter, we introduce computer communications by explaining how a personal computer or terminal can be linked by telephone to any of thousands of

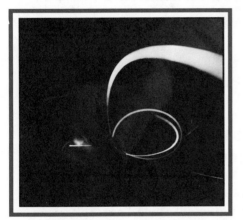

other computers. We explain the technology of sending data over telephones, the software used to link personal computers to other computers, and the types of tasks that can be accomplished with a personal computer and a telephone.

In Chapter 15, we generalize the concepts in this chapter to the entire field of computer communications. In it, we discuss communications media (wires, cables, airwaves, and so forth), how these media are used efficiently, and how computers can be linked in various types of networks.

## BASIC CONCEPTS

**Telecommunications** generally refers to any transmission of information over long distances by using electromagnetic signals like those used in telephones and radios. When used in discussions of personal computers, the term *telecommunications* usually means attaching a personal computer to the telephone system to move data from computer to computer. With this kind of telecommunications, you can

- Read the day's headline stories or search the last few months of news for articles on a particular topic
- Send letters to be printed and delivered by the post office
- Receive mail that was deposited instantly in your electronic mailbox by correspondents living across town, across the continent, or abroad
- Order books, cameras, and other items at a substantial discount
- Match wits with klingons in a Star Trek game
- Search libraries of bibliographic references for citations that match your query
- "Download" free public domain programs to be used later or swap files with out-of-town friends
- Use a mainframe or supercomputer to run programs and solve problems beyond the capability of your personal computer

**Figure 14.1**
Two methods of transmitting information through wires. In digital signaling, each bit is represented by the presence or absence of a voltage at a specific time. In frequency modulation, each bit of data is represented by a tone during a period.

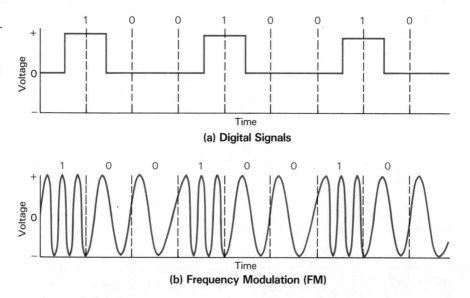

(a) Digital Signals

(b) Frequency Modulation (FM)

• Send a list of today's sales to your firm's head office or order inventory to be delivered for tomorrow's sales

• Request financial or stock market information about a specific company

• Post and read messages on a free computer bulletin board

To begin telecomputing, you must solve three problems. First, your personal computer must be physically attached to the telephone lines. This requires a hardware interface that allows your computer to "talk" on the phone lines. The connection to another computer is made by dialing the appropriate telephone number. Second, you need communications software to control your computer while it is sending and receiving data. Third, the communications software on your computer must be set to the protocol used by the other computer. The **protocol** is a set of rules that controls how messages are passed between machines. It establishes such important parameters as how fast characters are sent and whether characters are sent one at a time or in groups called *packets*.

## TELECOMMUNICATIONS HARDWARE

To understand how a computer transmits information through the telephone system, you must learn something about the methods used to encode data into electrical signals. All the parts in a computer (disk drives, CPU, printer, and so on) talk to each other by sending digital signals, as Figure 14.1(a) shows. *Digital signals* change from one voltage to another in discrete, choppy jumps. Generally, the presence of a positive voltage at a specific time represents the binary digit 1; the absence of a voltage represents the binary digit 0. In contrast, *analog signals* represent information as variations in a continuous, smoothly varying signal wave. Analog transmission methods dominated every aspect of the communications field before the invention of the transistor. **Frequency modulation (FM)**, illustrated in Figure 14.1(b), is one of several methods of analog signaling. It encodes data as changes in the frequency (or pitch) of the signal and is the transmission method used in FM radio. It also forms the basis for the relatively slow, but common, Bell System 103 method of transmitting computer data over phone lines. When frequency modulation is used to transmit binary data, a high-pitched tone during a given unit of time represents the digit 1, and a lower-pitched tone represents the digit 0.

Digital signals have two major advantages over analog signals. First, digital signaling allows faster transmission. Electrical circuits can encode and decipher bits as digital pulses more quickly than they can represent bits in a signal wave. Second, digital signaling is more accurate because transmission errors can be detected and corrected. For example, assume the digital signal for a binary 1 is to be encoded as +5 volts, and a binary 0 is to be encoded as 0 volts. Now assume that a signal is sent out at +5 volts but is received at +4.5 volts because of transmission errors. In this case, the receiving circuit will correctly interpret the incoming signal as a binary 1 because +4.5 volts is closer to +5 volts than to 0 volts. Analog transmissions do not have a comparable method of correcting errors.

For these reasons, telephone systems are rapidly converting from analog to digital transmission methods. Unfortunately, few telephone exchanges allow home phone lines to use digital signals. This means the digital signals of a personal computer must be translated into analog signals before they can be sent through most telephone systems.

For computers to send and receive messages over analog telephone lines, they must be able to convert digital signals into analog signals and back again. Converting digital to analog signals is called **modulation;** whereas converting analog to digital signals is called **demodulation**. A **modem** (short for *mo*dulate and *dem*odulate) is a device that can perform both functions. Modems modulate data transmissions at fairly high frequencies so that they can send and receive data as quickly as possible over telephone lines. Knowledgeable people avoid eavesdropping on telephone conversations between computers because all they make is a continuous, high-pitched shriek.

As Figure 14.2 shows, the appearance of modems varies substantially. Most portable computers come from the factory with built-in modems. Desktop personal computers usually have expansion slots in which an optional circuit board containing the modem can be inserted. Alternatively, it is almost always possible to connect an external modem to a personal computer through a serial interface (an RS-232 port) on the computer. External modems—also called *stand-alone* or *free-standing modems*—have the advantage of working with a wide variety of personal computers, but they require their own electrical power plug, often cost more than built-in modems, and make the computer system less portable.

Today, nearly all modems are **direct-connect modems;** they plug directly into telephone jacks (see Figure 14.3) and therefore make a very reliable electrical connection to the telephone system.

**Figure 14.2**
Comparison of an
external modem
and an internal
modem, which is
shown with its com-
munications
software and user
manual

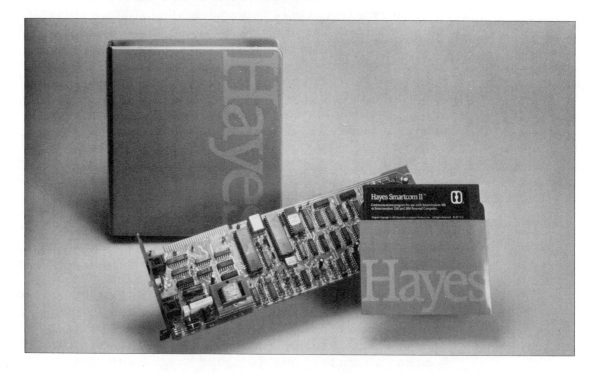

**Figure 14.2**
Comparison of an external modem and an internal modem, which is shown with its communications software and user manual

Modems range in price from well under $100 to more than $2,000 for commer-
cial-grade, high-speed modems. The least expensive modems are compatible with
the Bell 103 standard, meaning they follow a widely accepted standard for frequency modulation, which is limited to transmitting 300 bits per second (bps). It normally takes 10 bits to transmit one character. Thus a 300-bps modem will transmit about
thirty characters per second (cps), taking more than a minute to fill a 24-line-by-80-
column screen. Most people read faster than 30 cps. Modems operating at 1,200 bps

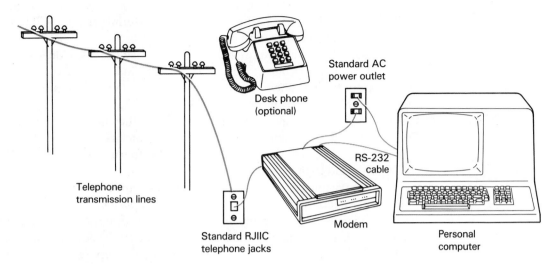

**Figure 14.3**
Typical cabling arrangements for a direct-connect external modem

(120 cps) transmit text as fast as most people read. They have dropped rapidly in price, from more than $2,000 a few years ago to about $100 in 1987. During this time, they have become the most popular type of modem. In 1987, several 2,400-bps modems selling for less than $200 were introduced. If current trends continue, in a year or two, more 2,400-bps modems will be in operation than 1,200- and 300-bps modems. Even faster modems are available. Several manufacturers sell modems with transmission speeds from 9,600-bps to 19,200-bps over ordinary phone lines. These modems are expensive—often more than $1,000—but expense isn't their only problem: High-speed modems use protocols that vary from one manufacturer to another and are incompatible. Thus, a 9,600-bps modem from company X cannot talk at high speeds to a 9,600-bps modem made by company Y.

Communications speeds are often given in a **baud rate,** the number of data signals the communications line transmits each second. Technical purists point out that the baud rate and bits per second are not the same because some elegant coding schemes pack two or more bits into each signal. But most people use the terms *baud rate* and *bits per second* interchangeably.

## COMMUNICATIONS SOFTWARE

### Terminal Emulation

The simplest type of communications software, a *terminal emulator,* makes a personal computer pretend it is a computer terminal. Although many types of computer terminals exist, the most common type is an *ASCII terminal* (a reference to the character code used by the terminal), a *Teletype* (historically, the most common type of electromechanical terminal), or simply a **dumb terminal,** an ASCII terminal that has no processing abilities of its own.

Understanding what a dumb terminal does is easy, because it does so little. Every time you press a key on the keyboard, the terminal sends the key's associated character out through the input/output port. Whenever the communications port receives a character, the terminal displays the character on the screen. Although these are a dumb terminal's important activities, they also do a few other things. For example, they contend with backspace characters and requests to beep the speaker. If desired, they also produce a **local echo**; that is, they send characters typed on the keyboard to the screen.

For most personal computers, a programmer competent in BASIC can, in a few hours, write a terminal emulator adequate for simple communications. A program like this can be as short as twenty lines. Still, few people write their own communications programs, instead, they use a commercial or public domain communications package. Nearly all these programs use the personal computer's processing abilities to provide convenient features not available on dumb terminals. Some of the public domain and shareware programs are excellent and can be acquired from computer-user groups for a nominal fee (see Figure 14.4). Commercial programs tend to come with better documentation and marketing support; their prices range from around $20 to more than $200. Often a communications program is sold as part of a package with a modem.

## Transferring Files

The most important feature in a communications package is the ability to upload and download files. **Uploading** means sending a file from your personal computer's primary memory or disk to another computer. **Downloading** means retrieving information and storing it on a disk as a file.

This ability to transfer files is important for several reasons. For some applications, such as exchanging computer programs, it is the reason for communicating in the first place. Other activities, such as sending and receiving electronic mail, are completed faster when information is transferred as a file. Completing tasks quickly can save money; most forms of telecomputing involve charges based on the length of the phone call.

## Frills for Convenience

Communications programs also offer frills, such as the ability to do limited editing, copying, or deleting of files without leaving the communications program.

Another popular feature, *auto-dialing*, allows you to dial telephone numbers by typing them on the keyboard. Auto-dialing isn't possible unless you have a **smart modem**—a modem capable of accepting commands, such as dialing instructions, from your computer. Another useful feature requiring a smart modem is the ability to create and use **dialing directories**, files that store the telephone numbers and communications parameters of remote computers and make it easy to log on to

**Figure 14.4**
ProComm, a shareware communication program with a suggested donation of $35, provides a typical range of features. **(a)** The HELP screen lists the program's major functions. **(b)** The DIALING DIRECTORY lets you store the telephone numbers and communication parameters for various remote computers so that you can log on to any of them easily.

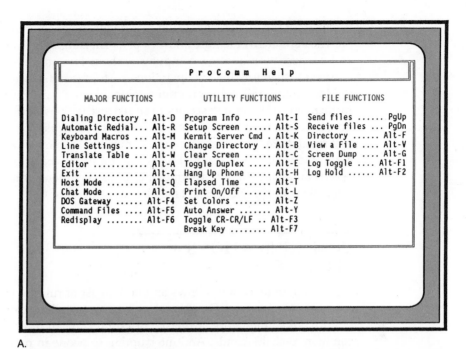

A.

B.

them. (Recall that *logging on* is simply identifying yourself to a computer; often it involves typing a user identification number and password.) Good dialing directories store and issue your user ID, password, and the entire log-on sequence. If you want to log on to a remote computer, you just select the computer's name from a list. Then the software-smart modem combination takes over—dialing the number, listening for the carrier signal, and issuing whatever commands are needed to log on. The **auto-answer** feature allows a personal computer to answer incoming calls and connect with another computer without human assistance. This feature is needed for such unattended operations as storing and forwarding messages.

Many communications programs, taking the dialing directory concept one step further, can work through **scripts,** or stored instructions. Scripts allow you to record how to connect to a remote computer, wait for particular prompts from the remote system, and respond to each prompt. Commercial communications packages generally come with preset scripts for logging on to the major on-line utility services. Scripts automate making routine data transfers among computers and can even schedule your connections to take place at preset times.

# COMMUNICATIONS PROTOCOLS

Human communication follows an informal set of rules, which could be called a *communications protocol*. For example, when you're talking to a group of people, it's best to look at them, not at the sky or ground. When meeting someone new, it's common to shake hands. And interrupting someone in midsentence is generally considered impolite. Computers also use communications protocols, but their protocols are more formal than those people use. Moreover, computers using different protocols cannot speak directly to each other. One of the most fundamental levels of a computer communications protocol regulates when each computer is allowed to transmit.

## Half-Duplex or Full-Duplex

Human beings communicate best when only one person talks at a time. In the computer field, this is **half-duplex** transmission, which limits communication to one direction at a time. If the computer on one end of the line is transmitting, the computer on the other end cannot respond until the entire message is sent. More often, personal computers use **full-duplex** connections, which allow simultaneous two-way transmission. Each end of the line is assigned a different frequency for speaking so that the "voices" don't interfere with each other.

Long-distance telephone connections are often poor, and static on the line can garble characters. **Remote echoing,** or *echo-plex,* provides a simple way to double-check the accuracy of the transmission. The remote computer echoes every character as it is received. Each letter you type travels to the remote computer, is echoed back, and eventually appears on your screen. If the letter you receive isn't the one you typed, you can backspace and type it again. Depending on the remote computer's workload, the round-trip transit time can be quite noticeable. (Be warned, too, that often—though technically incorrect—the term *half-duplex* is used for local echo, and *full-duplex,* for remote echo.)

Occasionally, you may log on to a computer that doesn't echo your characters. This can be disconcerting—your typing won't appear on the screen. On the other hand, you may get both local and remote echoes. In this case, everything you type shows up on the screen twice, as in "HHEELLLLOO." To correct these problems, you must be able to switch the local echo feature on and off.

## Asynchronous or Synchronous

Perhaps the most important distinction in transmission mode is between asynchronous and synchronous. **Asynchronous protocols** transmit data one character at a time. The transfer of data is coordinated by preceding each character with a *start bit*—a signal that transmission of a character has begun—and ending it with one or more *stop bits*. **Handshaking** is the ritual of preceding and following data with start bits, stop bits, and other control data. Remote echoing is also frequently used in asynchronous communication.

**Synchronous protocols** send and receive characters at agreed-on times, at a fixed rate. Normally, they send packets of characters instead of only one character at a time. Synchronous communication is faster and more complex than asynchronous methods. Personal computers rarely use synchronous communication except to interface with IBM host computers or local area networks.

## Error Correction

Even the best modems and telephone lines occasionally garble characters, producing errors in the information received. As long as this happens rarely—say, for one in ten thousand characters—the errors probably won't bother the average user of electronic mail. However, garbled characters are intolerable when program files—as opposed to data files—are transmitted. If even 1 bit in a 20,000-byte program file is received incorrectly, the program is likely to be useless.

Transmission errors can be avoided if both computers use *error detection and correction software*. To detect errors, the transmitting computer sends characters in packets with a **check figure** at the end of each packet; this figure is a mathematical function of the characters in the packet. The receiving computer calculates the same mathematical function on the packet it receives. If the result matches the check figure sent by the transmitting computer, the receiving computer acknowledges successful receipt of the packet; otherwise, the packet is retransmitted. In short, error detection is accomplished by sending characters in packets with a check figure; error correction is accomplished by retransmitting packets that contained errors.

For error correction and detection to work, both computers must be using the same error-checking protocol. For personal computers, one of the most popular protocols is Xmodem. It was developed and placed in the public domain by a Chicagoan named Ward Christianson—which says something about the grassroots spirit of the early days of personal computer communications. Most standards in the computer world are set by large corporations or international committees.

## Making the Connection

Dialing the telephone number of a computer is the easy part of establishing communications between computers. The hard part is setting your communications software to use the same protocol as the remote computer. Generally, this is done by making selections from a menu for such items as

- Baud rate. This depends primarily on the capability of the modems. Typical baud rates are 110, 300, 1,200, and 2,400.
- Number of start and stop bits. Most asynchronous links use one start bit and two stop bits per character.
- Parity setting. A **parity bit** is a redundant bit of information that allows the receiving computer to determine whether a character has been garbled in transmission. For example, if the parity setting is *even*, the sum of all the character's bits plus the parity bit should be equal to an even number. The possible parity settings are even, odd, and no parity.

Once all the necessary settings have been determined, they can be stored in a dialing directory. Reestablishing communications is then much easier than making the initial connection.

## WHOM TO TALK TO?

There is a bewildering diversity of computers and most of them—particularly larger systems—can be reached by telephone. To describe all the applications of telecomputing would be impossible, but we'll touch on the major ones related to personal computing.

## Bulletin Board Systems

A relative newcomer to the telecommunications world is the *public access message system*, commonly called a **bulletin board system (BBS)**. Almost anyone who uses a personal computer can set up and operate a bulletin board system. All you need is a personal computer, a telephone line, a smart modem with auto-answer capabilities, and one of the many public domain BBS programs. Just place messages on the BBS in your area, then load the program in your computer and let it answer the incoming calls.

A BBS responds to an incoming call by sending a welcome message and instructions on how to use the system. The instructions are usually easy to follow, though often they are quite condensed to save experienced users time. Having an adventurous spirit helps. Typically, you choose an option from a menu of possible commands listed on the screen (see Figure 14.5). For example, typing M might allow you to leave a message on the bulletin board; R, to read messages; and D, to download a program. In case you become confused, most systems display help information if you type ? or H.

```
+----------------------------------------------------------------+
|    M ... Select a msg area                                     |
|    R ... Read         S ... Quick List       I ... Search      |
|    E ... Enter        K ... Kill (delete)                      |
+----------------------------------------------------------------+
|    Z ... stats        C ... Change nulls, "more?", etc         |
|    X ... Xpert on/off U ... List users                         |
|    B ... Read Bulletins                                        |
+----------------------------------------------------------------+
|    F ... FILES subsystem                                       |
+----------------------------------------------------------------+
|    Q ... Questionaire Y ... Yell for sysop                     |
|    G ... Goodbye (logoff)                                      |
+----------------------------------------------------------------+
| FURTHER HELP: Enter  ?,  then  a semicolon,  then a  command   |
|              listed above. Examples:  "?;R"   "?;F"   "?;Y"    |
+----------------------------------------------------------------+

M,B,S,I,R,E,K,Q,F,Y,X,C,Z,U,G, or ? for help:
```

**Figure 14.5**
The main menu from a bulletin board system

Public messages can be read by anyone who wants to browse through them. Some systems allow private messages to be routed to specific recipients. Usually, as soon as you've logged on, the system informs you of private messages with a statement like

```
YOU HAVE 3 PIECES OF IN-COMING MAIL.
```

More than 1,500 bulletin board systems are in the United States. Exactly how many there are, no one knows because they can come and go at the flick of a switch. Don't be surprised if your first few calls to a bulletin board result in busy signals. The systems are popular, and most can communicate with only one user at a time.

All bulletin board systems are not alike. Some cater to users of particular types of machines, especially Apple IIs, CP/M machines, Macintoshes, and IBM PCs. Others are operated by manufacturers or vendors to promote their products. A few specialize in religious or sexual messages (DIAL-YOUR-MATCH). But because there is no charge for using a BBS—except for the cost of the phone call if it is long distance—most systems are used by a wide range of people.

A main use of a BBS is to leave messages for people to read later instead of talking in "real time." Some people use a BBS to jot graffiti; others, to discuss technical developments in computers. Most messages are heavily sprinkled with computer jargon. And bulletin board systems are used for more than just sending and receiving messages. Some systems allow you to play games. Many can upload and download programs. Still others allow you to order products or services from the system operator.

## Other Personal Computers

Contrary to what the ads for the overnight delivery services say, the fastest way to move documents across the country is not to stuff them into an expensive air-delivered pouch. Instead, they can be transmitted quickly over ordinary phone lines between two personal computers. Each end needs a personal computer, a modem, and software that supports the uploading and downloading of files. At 300 bps, a double-spaced, ten-page report can be sent in slightly less than ten minutes. At 2,400 bps, it should take about one minute.

Personal computers don't have to be the same model or brand to communicate over the phone. In fact, telephone links between computers can be used to sidestep the compatibility problems of floppy disks. Most of today's personal computers use the same type of floppy disks (5 1/4 inch), but many different recording formats are used. As a result, disks frequently can't be used to exchange information between different personal computers. For example, without a special program, neither an Apple II nor an IBM PC can read files written by the other, even though both accept the same blank disks. But characters traveling along a telephone line are represented in standardized codes and can be interpreted by the receiving computer regardless of the brand name of the transmitting computer. Communication by phone thus offers a way around the compatibility problem. Although it might seem strange to have an Apple II phone an IBM PC sitting on the other side of an office, it is often the most convenient way to transfer information between the two.

A word of caution is in order. Just because it's possible to exchange files between different machines doesn't mean the files will be useful after they have been transferred. Most programs that execute on an IBM PC will not execute on an Apple II, and vice versa. It makes more sense to transfer data files, such as a spreadsheet template or a word processing document, but even these files can be incompatible, depending on the application programs involved. For example, WordPerfect uses a different format to store documents than does WordStar; to transfer documents between them, you must use a file conversion program.

## General-Purpose Mainframes

A personal computer's ability to emulate a terminal allows you to tap the storage and computation resources of mainframe computers. Perhaps you need to analyze census data stored on magnetic tape. This requires access to a tape drive and good statistical programs. Chances are good that your personal computer doesn't have either. But with the right software, your computer can emulate a terminal so that you can use a mainframe. Many universities have mainframes with tape drives, excellent statistical programs, and the ability to number-crunch large data sets quickly, solving statistical problems in minutes that would take your personal computer hours or days to solve—if it could solve them at all.

Linking personal computers with mainframes can transform communications in companies that have many branch offices. For example, a personal computer in each sales outlet can be programmed to phone the company's mainframe at predetermined times at night, when long-distance rates are low. Each personal computer might upload the last day's sales activity. After a minute of processing, the mainframe could download a list of replacement parts being shipped and a list of back-ordered parts. Then both computers could hang up, ready for the coming sales day.

## Information Utilities

Companies that sell time on their timeshared mainframe computers have developed innovative services to attract customers. Called **information utilities** or *on-line services*, these companies offer services such as electronic mail, news stories, investment services, biorhythms, and travel guides. Three of the largest information utilities are The Source, operated by the Source Telecomputing Corporation; Compuserve, an H&R Block company; and the Dow Jones News/Retrieval Service, operated by Dow Jones & Company, publishers of *The Wall Street Journal*.

Rates for using the services of information utilities are based mostly on **connect time**, the time you are logged on to the utility. The charges are from $5 an hour to more than $100 an hour. Rates are higher during "prime time," which usually coincides with normal business hours. You may be billed at a higher rate if you use a 1,200- or 2,400-bps modem instead of a 300-bps modem, but a high-speed modem may pay for itself if you can do your work faster. Other fees can include one-time registration fees, monthly minimum usage fees, data storage charges (based on the number of bytes stored, if any), added charges for reading newsletters or searching databases, and charges for mailing letters and telegrams.

Here are a few of the services offered by The Source.

- Communications—Allows sending electronic mail to the computer mailboxes of other subscribers, "chatting" with another subscriber through a keyboard-to-keyboard conversation, participating in on-line computer conferences, posting and reading messages on public bulletin boards, sending Western Union Mailgram messages, and mailing first-class letters

- Business and investment—Includes instant quotations of stock and bond prices, portfolio analysis, employment services, and an electronic version of the *Washington Post*

- News and sports—Stores news from a variety of wire services, including United Press International (UPI), for seven days

- Consumer services—Offers electronic catalog shopping for everything from air conditioners to Zenith utility software; also includes movie reviews

- Travel services—Includes complete airline schedules for all domestic and most international flights, as well as Mobil Restaurant and Hotel Guides

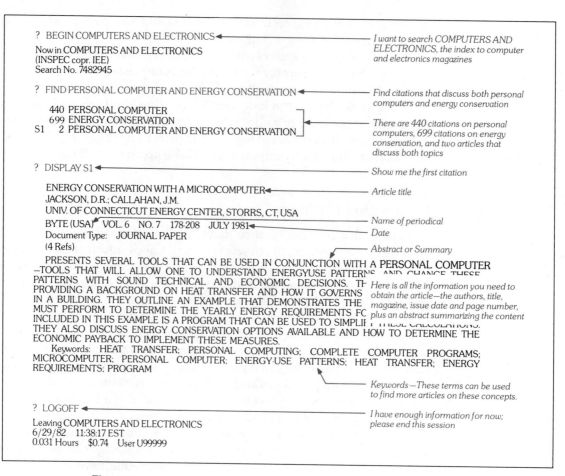

**Figure 14.6**
A sample search of KNOWLEDGE INDEX, a bibliographic database

One unique service provided by information utilities is the ability to search quickly through large volumes of information and find all items that match the criteria you specify. Information utilities that specialize in storing and searching information are often called *encyclopedic databases, bibliographic databases,* or *on-line databases.* More than 2,700 on-line databases exist. Most cater to specific types of information—legal, medical, business, and so on. Figure 14.6 illustrates how powerful this type of service can be. It shows the result of a search of KNOWLEDGE INDEX, a bibliographic database operated by Dialog Information Services. In less than two minutes, KNOWLEDGE INDEX searched more than 500,000 citations from 2,300 journals and magazines to find two articles discussing both personal computers and energy conservation.

But searching an on-line database isn't as easy as Figure 14.6 might lead you to believe. Asking the proper queries requires knowledge of the database's command structure and experience with what requests are likely to produce useful results.

Beginners tend to ask questions that yield either no matches or hundreds of matches. Neither result is particularly useful. Costs can accumulate quickly when you're paying from $20 to $100 an hour to do searches. Some searches are, therefore, best left to trained professionals, such as librarians or consultants. However, some on-line databases offer not only manuals but also excellent training courses on how to use their system.

### Packet-Switching Networks

Telecomputing can be expensive, especially if you make long-distance calls during the day when rates are high. Instead, hobbyists do most of their telecomputing locally or in the evenings and on weekends. But there's another way of reducing telephone charges: You can use a **packet-switching network** such as GTE's Telenet or Tymshare's Tymnet, which sends information in the form of *packets*.

Using a packet-switching network is just like dialing a remote computer directly—except that the response time is slightly slower, the log-on procedure more complicated, and the cost usually lower. In major cities (and some smaller ones), firms like GTE and Tymshare have local numbers that you can dial to connect your computer to their network. If you don't live in an area served by a packet-switching network, you make a toll call to the nearest city. Once connected to the network, you type the identifier of the remote computer you want. Then the packet-switching network takes over and routes information through the network between your personal computer or terminal and the remote computer.

Packet-switching networks aren't free, but using one is cheaper than making a long-distance call of the same length. The networks can charge less than the regular long-distance rates because they use the telephone system more efficiently than ordinary telephone calls. Most of a conventional telecommunications call is spent waiting while the computer user is thinking, reading, or typing at a slow rate. Packet-switching networks overcome this handicap by sharing the same communications channel among more than one user. Information is sent through the network in packets that include the packet's source and destination. Routing decisions are made by concentrators that send packets to each other over semipermanent telephone connections based on the addresses contained in the packet.

Using a packet-switching network with the major information utilities is particularly convenient. Because these utilities have prior agreements with packet-switching networks, you don't need a contractual arrangement with the network; the utility does the billing. Most utilities bundle the cost of using the network into their basic rate; others charge for it as a separate item on your monthly bill.

## FACSIMILE TRANSMISSION

Facsimile transmission, or **fax**, is a well-established method of transmitting images over phone lines. Facsimile transmission is especially useful when an exact image, say, of a bank check, prescription, drawing, page layout, or signed contract, is needed. In these cases, a printout of text created by a normal modem link-up just isn't acceptable.

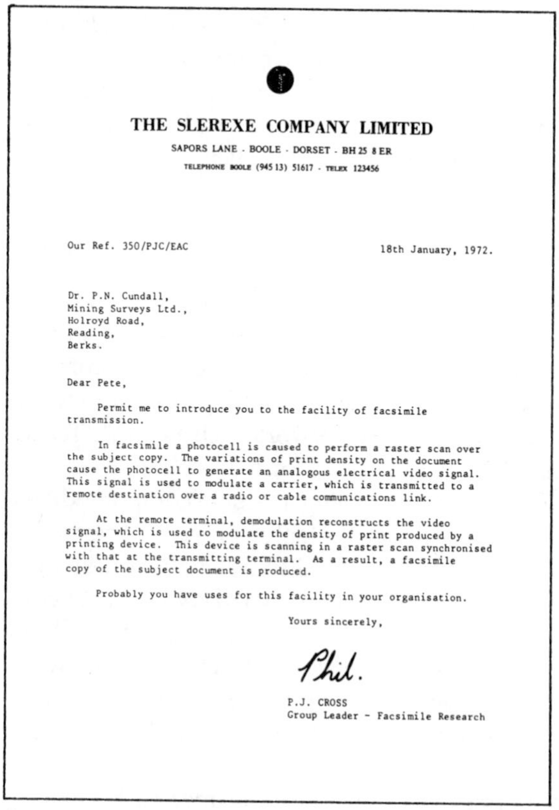

THE SLEREXE COMPANY LIMITED

SAPORS LANE · BOOLE · DORSET · BH 25 8 ER

TELEPHONE BOOLE (945 13) 51617 · TELEX 123456

Our Ref. 350/PJC/EAC                    18th January, 1972.

Dr. P.N. Cundall,
Mining Surveys Ltd.,
Holroyd Road,
Reading,
Berks.

Dear Pete,

    Permit me to introduce you to the facility of facsimile
transmission.

    In facsimile a photocell is caused to perform a raster scan over
the subject copy.  The variations of print density on the document
cause the photocell to generate an analogous electrical video signal.
This signal is used to modulate a carrier, which is transmitted to a
remote destination over a radio or cable communications link.

    At the remote terminal, demodulation reconstructs the video
signal, which is used to modulate the density of print produced by a
printing device.  This device is scanning in a raster scan synchronised
with that at the transmitting terminal.  As a result, a facsimile
copy of the subject document is produced.

    Probably you have uses for this facility in your organisation.

            Yours sincerely,

            Phil.

        P.J. CROSS
        Group Leader - Facsimile Research

THE SLEREXE COMPANY LIMITED

SAPORS LANE · BOOLE · DORSET · BH 25 8 ER

TELEPHONE BOOLE (945 13) 51617 · TELEX 123456

Our Ref. 350/PJC/EAC                    18th January, 1972.

Dr. P.N. Cundall,
Mining Surveys Ltd.,
Holroyd Road,
Reading,
Berks.

Dear Pete,

    Permit me to introduce you to the facility of facsimile
transmission.

    In facsimile a photocell is caused to perform a raster scan over
the subject copy.  The variations of print density on the document
cause the photocell to generate an analogous electrical video signal.
This signal is used to modulate a carrier, which is transmitted to a
remote destination over a radio or cable communications link.

    At the remote terminal, demodulation reconstructs the video
signal, which is used to modulate the density of print produced by a
printing device.  This device is scanning in a raster scan synchronised
with that at the transmitting terminal.  As a result, a facsimile
copy of the subject document is produced.

    Probably you have uses for this facility in your organisation.

            Yours sincerely,

            Phil.

        P.J. CROSS
        Group Leader - Facsimile Research

A.                                      B.

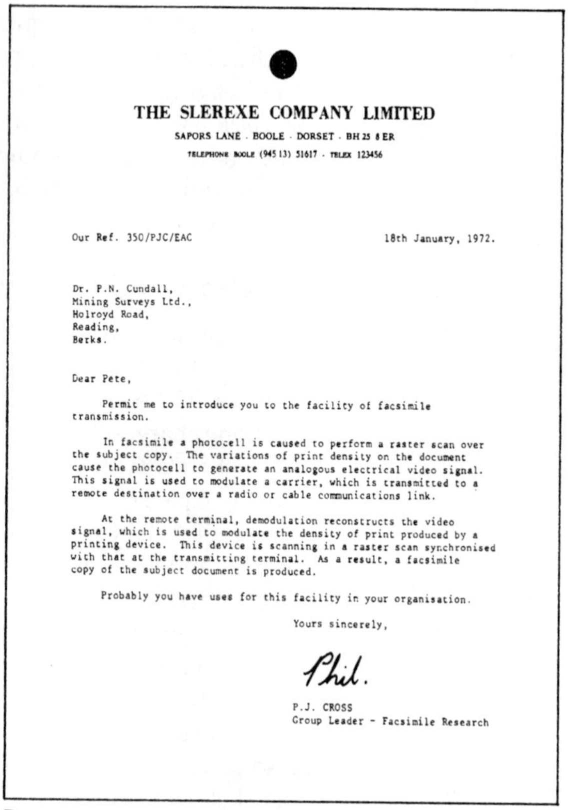

**Figure 14.7**
Two views of the CCITT Test Chart Number 1: **(a)** the original test chart, and **(b)** the test chart as it looks after facsimile transmission at 203 lines per inch.

A *fax machine* is a copier-sized box that contains a built-in scanner, printer, and high-speed modem. The sending fax machine scans the original document and converts it line by line into a continuous stream of information. Using data compression and modems that operate up to 9,600 bps, a typical page can be transmitted over a dial-up phone connection in less than sixty seconds. The receiving fax machine automatically answers the phone, receives the transmission, decompresses and prints it, and hangs up and waits for the next phone call. A large part of the appeal of fax machines is their ease of use; they are almost idiot-proof and don't require supervision to receive documents.

Fax is becoming increasingly important in business. More than 600,000 fax machines are in the United States, and the number is growing at more than 200,000 machines a year. To some, having a fax phone number on a business card has become a status symbol.

Facsimile transmission has been around a long time; newspaper wire photos have been sent by facsimile transmission since the 1930s. But its widespread use in business is a recent phenomenon based on dramatic performance and cost improvements. In the mid-1970s, a state-of-the-art fax machine cost more than $15,000 and

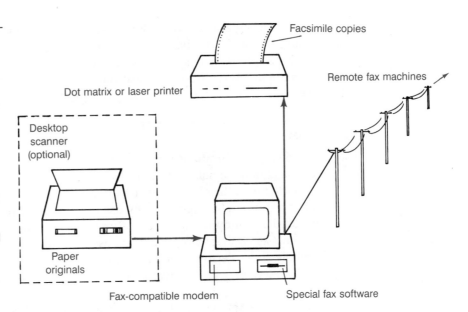

**Figure 14.8**
A personal computer-based fax system requires a printer, personal computer with a fax-compatible modem, and special software. The personal computer can create fax images directly by converting normal data files into a fax format, or it can convert the output of an optional desktop scanner into fax format. The modem is used to send and receive fax transmissions. Either a dot matrix or a laser printer can be used to print incoming fax transmissions.

Facsimile copies

Dot matrix or laser printer

Remote fax machines

Desktop scanner (optional)

Paper originals

Fax-compatible modem

Special fax software

took six minutes to transmit a page. In 1987, a fax machine selling for less than $2,000 could transmit the same image in thirty to sixty seconds. Prices are expected to continue falling; a basic fax machine should sell for less than $1,000 by 1990.

Another factor in the popularity of fax machines has been the establishment of standards by the CCITT, an abbreviation for the French rendering of the International Cooperative Committee for Telephone and Telegraph. This organization, which is part of the United Nations, adopted the Group 3 standard for facsimile transmission in 1980. The Group 3 standard is compatible with the earlier Group 1 and Group 2 standards and can transmit digital images with 203 dots-per-inch resolution (see Figure 14.7). Except for a few odd-ball holdouts, like IBM's faxlike ScanMaster for mainframe computers, all fax machines today adhere to this standard. Thus fax machines can talk to each other regardless of whether they were manufactured by the same company.

Facsimile transmission promises to be particularly important to personal computing (see Figure 14.8). Adding fax capabilities to a personal computer system costs less than buying a fax machine. For example, several companies market expansion cards for IBM PCs that contain a fax-compatible high-speed modem. These cards typically sell for less than $1,000 and come with software that causes the PC to double as a fax machine. Hardcopy output of fax transmissions can be obtained on any dot matrix or laser printer. If it is necessary to send copies of paper-based originals, an optional desktop scanner is required. But many users find the images they want to send are already stored in the personal computer as text or graphic files. With the help of the fax software, these files can be converted into a fax format and transmitted to remote fax machines.

PC-based fax systems have other advantages over dedicated fax machines. A PC-based system allows you to edit images on the screen, either before or after transmission. PC-based systems are easily programmed to send transmissions to remote fax machines starting at night when long-distance rates are low. And fax images created from data files have a better apparent resolution than scanned images. The reason for this improvement is the computer can optimally place each dot to give the sharpest apparent resolution. But a scanner must make do with whatever it is fed, so scanned characters often have fuzzy or jagged edges.

## Summary

The goal of telecommunications is to transmit information over long distances by using electromagnetic signals. Through telecommunications, a personal computer can be connected over the phone lines to virtually any other computer.

Data are transmitted through wires by using digital and analog signals. Digital signals are used in computers, in most local area networks, and in some parts of the phone system. Generally, analog signals are used for computer transmissions over ordinary phone lines. Personal computers can be attached to the public telephone system with a modem, which converts signals back and forth between digital and analog.

Communications software makes a personal computer behave like a terminal. Along with enabling personal computers to emulate dumb terminals, an important capability of communications software is uploading and downloading files.

The purpose of a communications protocol is to establish a set of rules for computing equipment to follow while transmitting and receiving data. The protocol determines whether data are transmitted with full- or half-duplex operation, synchronously or asynchronously, with or without error detection and correction, in packets or one character at a time, and with local echoing or remote echoing.

## Key Terms

asynchronous protocols

auto-answer

baud rate

bulletin board system (BBS)

check figure

connect time

demodulation

dialing directory

direct-connect modem

downloading

dumb terminal

fax

frequency modulation (FM)

full-duplex

half-duplex

handshaking

information utility

local echo

modem

modulation

packet-switching network

parity bit

protocol

remote echoing

scripts

smart modem

synchronous protocols

telecommunications

terminal emulator

uploading

## Discussion Questions

1. How does digital communication differ from analog communication?

2. What are some situations in which uploading or downloading capabilities might be important?

3. How does a protocol control the exchange of information between computers? What protocols are used by personal computers?

4. What type of remote computer would you telephone if you wanted to
   a. Try out telecommunications at the least cost?
   b. Determine the price of gold on December 13, 1987?
   c. Run a 10,000-line simulation program written in FORTRAN?
   d. Send a first-class letter to your grandmother in Alaska that will arrive within two days?
   e. Exchange computer programs with another personal computer user?
   f. Find out the final score of a basketball game that ended about an hour ago?

5. Why can a packet-switching network charge rates lower than those for normal long-distance calls?

6. How much of an effect do you think telecommunications and facsimile transmission will have on the usage of first class mail by 1999?

## Exercises

1. Examine the manual provided with a communications package. List the package's features and rank them according to which features you feel would be most useful.

2. Light travels at 186,000 miles per second. Suppose a satellite has an average distance of 24,500 miles from the surface of the earth.
   a. If two computers next to one another transmit through a satellite directly overhead, how long does it take for one computer to receive one 8-bit byte of asynchronous data from the other computer? Assume transmission speeds of 9,600 bits per second. Because the transmission is asynchronous, each byte must be accompanied by 2 bits—a start and a stop bit.
   b. Now, assume each byte must be acknowledged by the satellite, leading to a two-way handshake between the sender and the satellite and another two-way handshake between the satellite and the receiver. Assume a single bit is transmitted in each acknowledgment. How long does it take to copy 10,000 bytes from one computer to the other?

3. Find out what bulletin board systems are available in your local area and the types of services they provide.

4. Ask some information utilities for information on their services and rates; they generally have toll-free telephone numbers for sales information. You might begin by looking at "Buyers Guide for On-Line Services" in the November 8, 1986, issue of *Infoworld*.

# Networks

In Chapter 14, we limited our discussion of computer communications to simple point-to-point transmissions. A point-to-point communications link is like a conversation between two people. In contrast, a computer **network** links computers together in a web that allows transmissions among many devices. A computer network is a collection of communicating computers and the communications media connecting them.

For example, a **local area network (LAN)** links computers with other computing equipment within a limited area, for instance, within one building or industrial plant. By connecting computers, a LAN can bridge the gap between several personal computers, minis, mainframes, printers, and large-capacity storage disks. Some local area networks are set up to let many personal computers share an expensive peripheral device, such as a large hard disk or a high-quality printer. Other networks are established so that information can be shared conveniently, as in an interoffice electronic mail system.

A network is characterized by the media it uses to carry messages (wires, cables, microwaves, and so forth), the way the network links devices (in a star, ring, or other pattern), and the expansiveness of the network (whether it is limited to one building or spans a continent). Moreover, the network's communications protocols determine how and when devices can communicate. In the first part of this chapter, we explore these issues that determine a network's architecture and hardware.

Quite often, the users of a local area network have no idea what type of hardware is used to construct the network. A network's hardware and architecture is usually hidden behind layers of software that regulate the flow of information and the

sharing of network resources. For this reason, in the chapter's last section, we describe the typical features of a local area network from a user's viewpoint. This includes activities like assigning and using passwords and accessing information on a remote hard disk.

## NETWORK ARCHITECTURE AND HARDWARE

Before exploring the technical details of network hardware, we describe a basic shift in the costs of communicating and computing that encouraged the development of computer networks.

### The New Economics of Computing

From the 1950s to the 1970s, it was substantially less expensive to buy one large computer than to buy two smaller computers that, combined, have the same processing power. To get the most from their computing dollars, organizations consolidated their purchases by centralizing data processing operations. Large host computers were timeshared among many users. Early systems hooked all equipment to the central computer, which was responsible for controlling all communications. In this way, early corporate users spread the cost of expensive mainframes over many users, who shared access to the same equipment and information. Most large computer systems still follow this pattern, but as Figure 15.1 shows, the cost of the links needed by centralized computing centers hasn't been falling as rapidly as the cost of computing. Thus the cost of providing each user with a personal computer is less than the cost of connecting an equivalent number of terminals to a timeshared mainframe.

The rush to buy personal computers instead of terminals has created a major shift from centralized to decentralized, or distributed, computing. In a **distributed computing** environment, geographically separate computers are connected in a

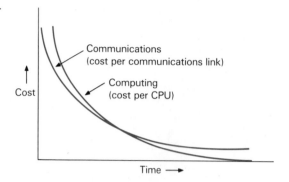

**Figure 15.1**
The relative costs of communications and computing

Communications
(cost per communications link)

Computing
(cost per CPU)

Cost

Time →

network to work on a common task. This shift toward personal computers wasn't caused exclusively by economics; personal computers have many advantages over timeshared computing, including greater control to the user, friendlier operation, and a faster response for most tasks.

But decentralized personal computers have a major disadvantage: They are harder to link to share information and peripheral devices. As the cost of the actual computer has plunged, the cost of the peripheral devices has grown as a percentage of the total system. Expensive laser printers; high-precision graphical devices, such as plotters, digitizers, and color displays; and the relatively high cost of storage devices have contributed to the need for interconnected workstations rather than separate personal computers. The economics of computing has dictated a new way to think about computing: Share the peripherals and data, but disperse the processors to the people who need processing time and instantaneous response.

## Communications Media

Many characteristics of a computer network—its speed, cost, and physical range—are determined largely by the media it uses to transmit messages.

Most telephone systems use **twisted-pair wire** to connect phones to the central switching station. Twisted-pair wire is inexpensive and easy to run through the walls in an office building. Its major disadvantage is its relatively low **bandwidth**; that is, its low capacity for carrying information. Twisted-pair wire is used in low-speed LANs (1 megabit per second or less).

A **coaxial cable** is a round cable in which one wire is a sleeve shielding another wire, like cable television wire. Coaxial cable offers much greater speed (up to 100 megabits per second) and is impervious to external electrical signals. It is used in high-speed networks where the cost of the cable isn't an overriding concern.

A **fiber-optic cable** is a bundle of strands of glass, which conduct laser light. Fiber-optic cables are rapidly replacing metal cables because they are lighter, cheaper, and capable of extremely high transmission speeds. A standard coaxial cable can transmit 5,000 voice conversations at once, whereas a fiber-optic cable can transmit ten times as many.

Wires and cables are suitable for connecting computers and devices when they are in the same room or building, but what about geographically distributed computer networks? Telephones and modems provide a low-speed method of connecting remote computers, but large corporations use other methods as well. A **dedicated line,** or *leased line,* is a special telephone line that connects a pair of computers. The advantages of a dedicated line are increased speed and continuous availability. No dialing is required, and a busy signal is impossible. A dedicated, point-to-point line is useful when large amounts of information are to be transmitted continually.

**Microwave relay stations** are used to transmit data and voice signals between distant locations. *Microwaves* are extremely short radio waves that have a high bandwidth, but they cannot bend to the earth's curvature. A series of relay stations can connect, say, corporate headquarters with dozens of branch offices. Renting time on microwave relay stations may be cheaper than renting a dedicated line.

A **ground station** may be used to send and receive information by satellite. Computers are excellent users of communications satellites because of their fast and constant transmission rates. Mainframes communicate around the world through communications satellite *transducers,* which are similar to radio antennas. Because each communications satellite has many transducers, it is possible to rent one just as a company might rent a dedicated telephone line.

## Transmission Efficiency

Most high-speed transmission methods, such as microwaves or satellites, cost the same amount of money regardless of whether the entire transmission capacity is used; for example, it isn't possible to install *half* a satellite ground station. This has led to developing clever ways to use the transmission capacity of high-speed communications links.

A **multiplexer** is a communications device that spreads the cost of a high-speed line over many users. A multiplexer timeshares the communications line by merging data from many users into the same line. There are two types of multiplexers: *time division* and *frequency division.*

A **time-division multiplexer** combines many low-speed channels into one high-speed transmission by interweaving them in time slots. Channel 1 is allocated time slot 1; channel 2, time slot 2; and so forth. The time slots are strung together like beads in a necklace and sent as one high-speed signal. When the signal is received, the low-speed signals are split again and sent to their destinations. A **frequency-division multiplexer** divides the high-speed signal into frequency bands, like the frequencies used by FM radio stations. Each channel is assigned a certain band, and the composite signal is sent. At the receiving end, the different channels are split out from their frequency bands and sent to their destinations.

**Broadband** transmission uses frequency-division multiplexing to transmit text, data, and video or audio signals simultaneously. This allows computers to handle a two-way video conference with a dispersed group of people who want to display computer-generated graphics as well as hear one another talk. In contrast, in **baseband** transmission, the entire communications spectrum is dedicated to one form of information.

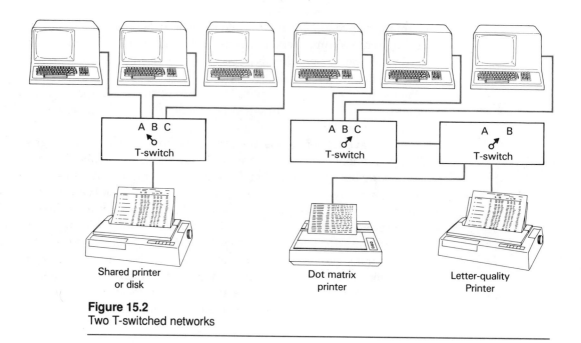

**Figure 15.2**
Two T-switched networks

A **concentrator** is an "intelligent" multiplexer; it can perform preliminary operations on data before they are multiplexed and sent to another computer. Thus it is an I/O device that unburdens the mainframe computer by taking care of many details of message transmission.

A step beyond a concentrator in intelligence is a **front-end computer,** a small computer located between a mainframe and other devices communicating with it. It handles all the communications chores of the mainframe. For example, it acknowledges receipt of a message, does multiplexing and demultiplexing, and checks for transmission errors. Some front-end computers also perform rudimentary text processing.

## Network Topology

The efficiency, reliability, and cost of a computer network are also affected by its **network topology,** or *interconnection pattern*. For example, a simple point-to-point network topology connects a pair of computers together with a cable.

A more flexible point-to-point topology is obtained by linking computing equipment with a T-switch and cables (see Figure 15.2). With a **T-switch,** you can rearrange the connections between computing equipment by turning a dial on the T-switch instead of unplugging and plugging cables. T-switches are inexpensive, ranging from $40 to more than $300. Their most common application is to let several personal computers or terminals share a peripheral device, such as a printer or plotter. Printers are often shared in this way because they are used intermittently. By using a T-switch, it is often possible for several people in an office to share one laser or daisy-wheel printer with little inconvenience. T-switched networks require

**Figure 15.3**
A star network. A
central network serv-
er controls the net-
work.

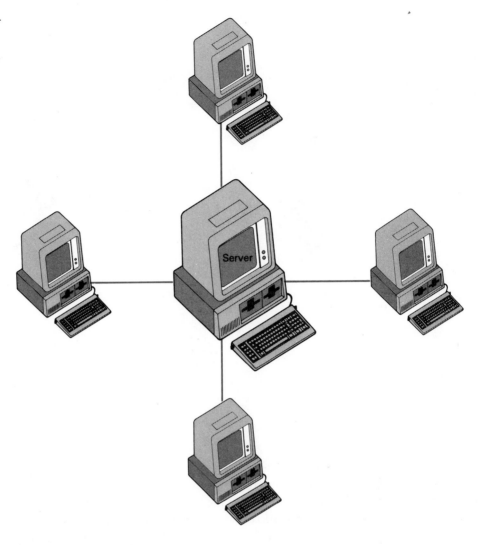

human intervention to route signals to their destination. Most people don't call T-switches a computer network, reserving the term for collections of computers and cables that can route messages automatically among devices.

A **star network** consists of a central computer surrounded by one or more satellite computers (see Figure 15.3). The central computer is sometimes called the hub, or *central server*, because all requests for data must go through the central computer. Star networks are simple but not very reliable. If the central server breaks down, the entire network is disabled in the same way the failure of a timeshared computer system disables all users. Star networks are the dominant topology for mainframe computers and their peripherals as well as for telephone systems.

A **ring network** consists of a cluster of computers connected in a ring (see Figure 15.4). In a ring network, the failure of one computer does not prevent the other computers from interacting with one another. Rings are sometimes used along with a *token-passing protocol* to coordinate access to the network. A **token** is a control signal

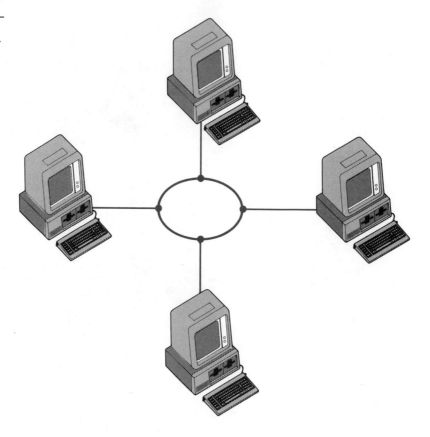

that determines which computer is allowed to transmit information. The token is passed from one computer to another, enabling each to use the network. Because only one token exists in the network, only one computer can use the ring at a time.

A **bus network** contains a single, bidirectional cable connecting two or more computers (see Figure 15.5). Information is passed between any two computers, one pair at a time, by seizing control of the common wire, or *bus*, transmitting a message, and then releasing the bus. Buses do not use the transmission media as efficiently as other network topologies because traffic congestion can delay use of the bus.

Bus networks often use a **CSMA** (*c*arrier-*s*ensed *m*ultiple-*a*ccess) **protocol** to direct traffic on the bus. A CSMA protocol is similar to a party line in a rural telephone system. On a party-line phone, everyone is allowed to make calls on the same line, as long as no one else is using the line. In a CSMA network, each device has access to the network when the network isn't busy. Two methods are commonly used to prevent devices from transmitting messages at the same time. With a CSMA/CA protocol (CA stands for collision avoidance), special circuitry in the LAN ensures only one device can transmit at a time. In contrast, a CSMA/CD protocol (CD stands for collision detection) allows devices to begin transmitting any time the network isn't busy. Occasionally, two or more devices might begin to

**Figure 15.5**
A bus network. Messages vie for time on the shared bus.

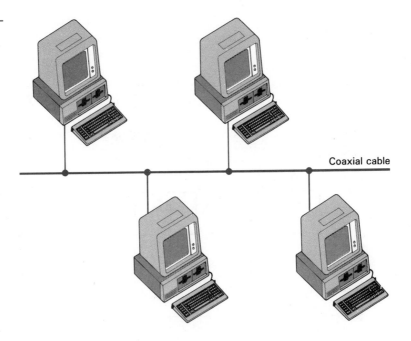

Coaxial cable

transmit messages at the same time, causing the messages to be garbled. If this happens, each device stops transmitting and generates a random number specifying how long it must wait before it can try transmitting again. The difference between these two protocols is subtle, but a CSMA/CA protocol becomes more efficient as greater demands are placed on the LAN.

Bus networks offer more flexibility in how devices are wired together than star or ring networks. The simplicity of CSMA protocols (such as the Ethernet standard developed by Xerox) has made the bus topology very popular for small networks.

## Local Area Networks (LANs)

As we mentioned, a LAN is used to share peripherals and data among computers in proximity. The LAN automatically routes messages among the devices on the network. A unique address is given to each device connected to the network. When one computer sends a message to another computer, the message is formatted into one or more packets in a manner roughly similar to that used by packet-switching networks. The packet contains the address of both the source and the destination so that the LAN will know where to send the message.

Figure 15.6 shows one LAN configuration: All the network's devices, or *nodes*, are coupled to a common bus. The AppleTalk network shown in Figure 15.7 is another example of such a network. The network in Figure 15.6 includes the following:

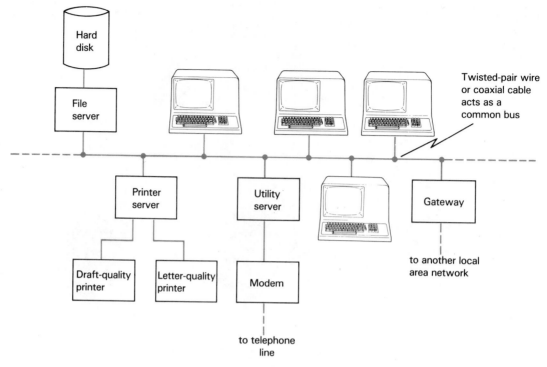

**Figure 15.6**
A local area network based on coupling devices to a common bus

- **File server**. A file server controls a hard disk and connects it to the network (see Figure 15.8). The file server is likely to establish a private storage space on the disk for each user, as well as areas for public files. It may also keep track of passwords for files.

- **Utility server**. A utility server allows everyone on the network to use several peripheral devices, such as a modem or plotter.

- **Printer server**. A printer server shares access to the network's printers among all users. It likely includes a memory buffer so that files can be accepted faster than the printer can print them.

- **Gateway**. A gateway allows devices on one network to communicate with devices on another.

The functions of network servers can be performed by specialized hardware devices or by an ordinary personal computer executing a special software program. For example, the file server on many networks is a personal computer with a large hard disk. A special program in the personal computer controls network access to the hard disk. If the personal computer has a modem, it might also act as a gateway to another network by sending and receiving packets of information between networks with a modem connection. On large networks, the personal computer acting

**Figure 15.7**
An AppleTalk network allows up to thirty-two devices to be connected to a SCMA/CA local area network limited to 230 kilobits per second. On the top, several Macintosh computers are sharing access to a LaserWriter printer. Because the Apple-Talk network uses a serial interface built into every Macintosh, all that is needed to connect a Macintosh to the network is a $75 cable and connector (shown on the bottom).

**Figure 15.8**
Connecting an Omni-Drive file server to a Corvus Omninet involves plugging the end of a twisted-pair wire into a socket. OmniDrive disk systems range in size from 11MB to 126MB versions. An Omninet network can support up to sixty-four devices with a data transmission rate of 1 megabit per second.

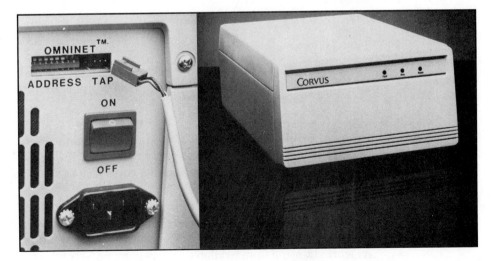

Network Architecture and Hardware    **421**

## A Word About ... *The Coming of Age of the Local Area Network*

*Local area networks have gone through several stages of development since 1981.*

The first IBM Personal Computer local-area networks (LAN), following close on the heels of IBM's debut of the PC in 1981, were unimpressive collections of cabling and interface boards that enabled a group of IBM PCs to share peripherals such as hard disks and printers.

While a few adventurous companies installed the early offerings of vendors such as Corvus Systems, Inc., 3Com Corp. and Nestar Systems, Inc., the vast majority felt that any potential savings from peripheral sharing were offset by the expense and hassle of installing and maintaining these systems. A 1984 report by Framingham, Mass.-based research firm International Data Corp. found that 15,800 PC LANs were shipped in 1983. Considering that 1983 IBM PC shipments totaled $1.5 billion, according to Future Computing, Inc., a very small percentage of PCs were being networked a few years ago.

Three developments that occurred in 1984 and 1985 made PC LANs a far more viable alternative to business users:

- The emergence of two standard network operating systems: MS-DOS 3.1, introduced by Microsoft Corp. in the fall of 1984, and Net-

ware, which Novell, Inc. released in November 1983. IBM PC software vendors could then develop versions of their packages that, by interfacing with MS-DOS 3.1 or Netware, could operate over all the network products that support either of those operating systems.

- The appearance of powerful file servers that let PCs concurrently access and update the same files—in contrast to early servers that just let users store their data on dedicated, floppy-size partitions of the same hard disk. The servers turned PC LANs into viable departmental systems, permitting users to share data and peripherals and exchange electronic mail.
- The emergence of gateways and bridges. Gateways gave users access first to IBM Systems Network Architecture and recently to IBM System/36 and 38 processors. Bridges link local networks into a corporatewide system.

"Companies can increase user productivity by making mainframe information available on PCs," says Merv Adrian of the New York PC Users Group. "It's much cheaper to do it via a LAN, because you only need to equip one PC, the gateway server, with a terminal emulation board."

Source: Elisabeth Horwitt, *Computerworld*, 3 November 1986, p. 15.

---

as a network server is *dedicated*, meaning it cannot be used for other tasks. But on small networks, the network server may be asked to do double duty. A *nondedicated server* used in this fashion can simultaneously act as both a network server and PC workstation.

Because local area networks use digital transmission and cover a limited physical range (usually less than several miles), they can provide fast transmission rates. Less expensive, lower-speed networks use twisted-pair wiring. Even these networks transmit from 50 kilobits to 1 megabit per second—much faster than the usual speed of telecommunications over public telephone lines. Faster networks, using the same coaxial cable used in cable television, provide transmission rates from 1 to 100 megabits per second. At 10 million bits per second, all the text in this book could be transmitted in 1 second. Ultrafast transmission rates are important if many devices must send or receive large files at about the same time.

To increase the speed of the network, some LANs use a **cache**, a memory buffer. The cache stores copies of the most recently retrieved records—hoping to save a transmission and a disk read operation. For software to use file records more than once during a file-update cycle is common. If the desired record is in the cache of the computer that wants it, the overhead associated with message transmission and file retrieval is avoided.

## Network Layers

Because networking is a rapidly changing area, it is filled with nonstandard parts, diverse approaches, and general confusion. For this reason, the International Standards Organization has proposed the ISO Reference Model for Open System Connection, or simply, **ISO layers**, as a standard for describing and categorizing network components. The ISO layers are seven levels found in all networks: physical, link, network, transport, session, presentation, and application.

- The *physical layer* defines the electrical characteristics of signals passed between the computer and communications devices, such as a modem or a network interface adapter. The voltage levels, baud rate, and so forth are determined at the physical level.

- The *link layer* controls error detection and correction, transmission over a single data line between computers, and the nature of the interconnection, such as whether it is synchronous or asynchronous.

- The *network layer* constructs packets of data, sends them across the network, and unpacks the message at the receiving end.

The first three layers are wrapped together when the telephone and a modem are used. The network layer is the collection of telephone lines and switching equipment maintained by the telephone company. The link and physical layers are embedded in the modem and telephone sets at either end of the telephone connection.

- The *transport layer* transfers control from one computer to the next across the network.

- The *session layer* establishes, maintains, and terminates logical connections for data transfer called virtual circuits. A **virtual circuit** temporarily links two devices in the network in a manner analogous to the way a telephone call links two telephones. The session layer also enciphers data for security purposes (if needed) and establishes the necessary handshaking such as full-duplex and message formatting.

- The *presentation layer* defines control codes, how data should be formatted, and other attributes of the message being transmitted. For example, the presentation layer defines a control code to clear the screen. It may also define how data is to be formatted to conform to the format expected by the receiving computer's software.

- The *application layer* consists of software being run on the computer connected to the network. The operating system software of a personal computer falls into the application layer as far as the network is concerned. Thus copying a file from one computer to another computer on the same network is an application-layer operation.

As an example of how these layers interact, consider the problem of reading a record from a file on a remote computer's disk. Suppose the request to read the file comes from a database management program on a personal computer; thus it originates at the application level. The read request is passed to presentation-level software on the personal computer and is converted into the format defined by the technology is well-proven and the system is very robust," Yundt said.

Network integrity is maintained with uninterruptible power supplies, giving the network 40 minutes of emergency power, and with redundant connections between Ethernets. So, with some exceptions, Sunet can operate even after a major cable has been damaged. "There are only two places on campus where a convergence of cables is within six inches of the surface," Yundt recalled, "and so of course we had some sprinkler installers who chose one of these spots to jackhammer through the sidewalk, causing major damage to four cables. Still, system routers moved data around the break and only one subnet was lost on the network."

About 930 PCs and computer-based workstations are now directly attached to the networks, including 180 Sun workstations, 170 IBM PCs, and 236 Macintoshes. Sunet has 2,000 RS-232C serial ports to supports PC users who dial in, as well as dumb terminals. Stanford treats Sunet as a free service to the educational community, much like the university library. Service between buildings and mainframe computers is free, to encourage use of the system, but individual departments and schools are responsible for providing their own networks and connections within buildings.

In addition to data, Sunet provides campus-wide video, with service possible both to and from any of 300 campus buildings. The dozens of video channels include commercial and satellite networks, the Stanford Instructional Television Network, live Soviet television, and a student-run channel (prime time offerings include a soap opera, "General Dormitory.")

Beyond connecting more of Stanford's 8,000 PCs directly to Sunet, future emphasis will shift to making the system more friendly to novices. "Most network interfaces are designed by computer science people for computer science people," said Yundt. With simplification in mind, each of the more than 1,000 computers directly attached to Sunet has an individual name like Argus, Lear, or Portia. So if a Stanford student wants to reach a specific Sun workstation in the Department of Music, he can either access device 36.53.00.11 or just ask Sunet for a connection to the polish Prince, Bobby Vinton.

Source: Mark Stephens, *Infoworld*, 29 June 1986, p. 10.

presentation layer of the network being used. The formatted read request is passed on to the session-layer control program, which translates the logical name of the remote computer (such as drive F) into a physical name (such as device 12,539), selects the protocol to be used (full- or half-duplex), and passes the message on to the transport layer. The transport and network layers work together to form one or more packets out of the message. The transport and network control programs guide the packet through the network. When the transport layer guides the packet containing the read request to the remote computer, it uses the link and physical layers. The link layer simply establishes an error-free connection from the sender to the receiver. Link control on a CSMA network would involve collision detection or avoidance, error detection, and retransmission of messages received in error. The read-request packet is passed through physical circuitry that obeys the physical laws of electronics—transmission rates, coding conventions, and protocol. Once the packet reaches the remote computer, the transport and network software running on the remote computer unpack the message and pass it on to the session layer. The message works its way through the presentation layer to the application layer of

**Figure 15.9**
A standard personal
computer connec-
tion to a local area
network is shown by
the diagram on the
left. All requests for
access to disk
storage are filtered
through the network
shell, which deter-
mines where the re-
quested data are
stored.

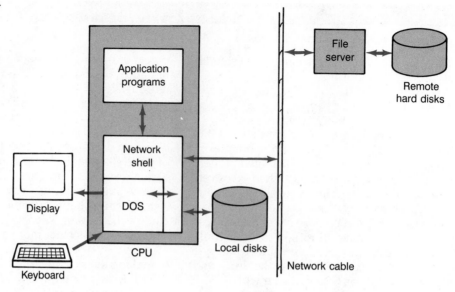

the remote computer, where the read operation is done. Finally, the process is reversed to return the file record to the requesting computer.

All future computer networks are likely to follow these ISO layers. This should make it easier to connect equipment from different manufacturers to the same network and for messages to be transferred from one type of network to another. But the techniques, performance, and cost of each new network will vary depending on the cleverness of the implementation.

# USING A LOCAL AREA
# NETWORK

From a user's viewpoint, the complexity of the LAN's communications protocol and cabling methods is hidden by a layer of software (see Figure 15.9). The *LAN software* is usually an extension of the computer's normal disk operating system (DOS). This extension, labeled network shell in Figure 15.9, is loaded into memory after loading DOS. It serves two purposes. First, it provides a variety of services directly to the user. For example, you would give special commands to the LAN software to find out what resources are available on the network or to submit a job for printing on a printer server. Second, the LAN software examines all requests for access to hardware resources and routes them to the appropriate hardware devices. For example, suppose your computer has two floppy disk drives (drives A and B), and the LAN has a hard disk file server (drive F). To copy a file from one of your disks to the file server, you would use the same COPY command that you use to copy a file from one floppy to the other. Instead of copying from drive A to drive B, you might copy from drive A to drive F. The network software in your personal computer would automatically route information for drive F to the appropriate file server and disk directory on the network.

**Figure 15.10**
Two views of the same disk directory. The directory is stored on a hard disk inside an IBM AT that acts as a network file server.

**(top)** When the directory is viewed from a Macintosh connected to the network, the files appear as icons in a desktop window and can be manipulated with the mouse, for example, by dragging them to the trash can.

**(bottom)** When the directory is listed on the IBM AT, the filenames are truncated to accommodate the restrictive file naming conventions of PC-DOS, and the files are manipulated with typed PC-DOS commands, such as ERASE.

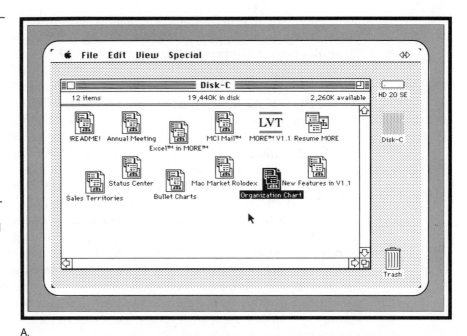

A.

```
C>dir

    Volume in drive C has no label
    Directory of  C:\MAC

    .             <DIR>      5-06-88   1:22a
    ..            <DIR>      5-06-88   1:22a
    DESKTOP           0      8-02-88   1:49a
    !README!      15925      8-02-88   1:52a
    ANNUALMO       2522      8-02-88   1:52a
    BULLETCO      33494      8-02-88   1:52a
    EXCELINO      10938      8-02-88   1:52a
    MCIMAILO       6993      8-02-88   1:52a
    MOREV10  1        0      3-30-88   7:59p
    RESUMEMO         56      8-02-88   1:53a
    SALESTEO        668      8-02-88   1:53a
    STATUSCO       6697      8-02-88   1:53a
    MACMARKO       3373      8-02-88   1:53a
    ORGANIZO        770      8-02-88   1:53a
    NEWFEATO 1     4021      8-02-88   1:53a
       15 File(s)   2312192 bytes free

C>
```

B.

LAN software makes remote disks and printers on the LAN appear to be connected directly to your computer. For this reason, many LANs are no more difficult to use than a standalone personal computer. They simply provide each user with access to the LAN's resources, such as large disk drives and fast printers.

LANs can also help communicate among different types of computing equipment. For instance, two of the authors (Lewis and Sullivan) have a mixture of IBM and Apple computers in their offices at home. Unfortunately, IBM and Apple computers use different floppy disk formats, making it difficult to use floppy disks to move files from one computer to another. To solve this problem, they installed tiny LANs among their computers. For example, Sullivan's LAN connects only three devices to an AppleTalk network: an IBM AT, a Macintosh SE, and a PS Jet laser printer. The IBM AT is connected to a modified AppleTalk network with a special interface card and software sold as a package by Centram Systems West. The software allows the IBM AT to act as a file server for the network. Once this system is installed, transferring files across the network is remarkably easy (see Figure 15.10). For example, while using a Macintosh, files can be transferred from one computer to another by dragging their icons from one desktop window to another.

LANs make it convenient to share network services, but in a multiuser environment, there are times when conflicts arise. For instance, one user might want some of his files to be readable but not modifiable by a certain group of other users. Another user might want all of her files hidden from everyone else's view. Still another user might have jobs that must be printed immediately, without waiting for other jobs in a printer server's queue to print first. These situations call for various forms of network security and user privileges. For most networks, the security system and user privileges are maintained by a LAN administrator who decides how the network's capabilities are used.

As an example, the LAN used by the College of Business at Oregon State University (OSU) connects an IBM-compatible personal computer in each faculty member's office with the computers in three student laboratories. One hundred eighty-five personal computers on the network are served by three high-speed file servers with 800MB of disk storage, three printer servers, an electronic mail server, and gateways to the university's other networks. Access to the network is controlled by Greg Scott, the LAN administrator. He uses the Novel Netware operating system running on the file servers to assign each user a *user name* and *password* (see Figure 15.11). Each user name and password combination is associated with a *user profile* that defines the user's access privileges on the network.

An important use of a LAN is to share application software. For example, the OSU College of Business LAN makes it almost effortless to begin running application programs like WordPerfect, Lotus 1-2-3, R:BASE System V, and Reflex. After logging onto the network (by typing in a user name and password), a user is greeted with a pop-up menu system similar to the one in Figure 15.12. An application program is run by highlighting its name in the Application Menu and pressing [Enter]. This loads a copy of the application program into the personal computer's memory from one of the network file servers, and the program begins executing on the user's personal computer. Thirty users can concurrently run R:BASE System V, a database management program, even though only one copy of the program is stored on the network's file servers. This reduces the amount of network disk space needed because only one copy of most programs needs to be stored regardless of how many users will be using them. It also eliminates most floppy disk shuffling and simplifies the task of upgrading from one version of a program to another.

If a network is easy to use, it is usually because the LAN administrator has carefully set up the network. The administrator uses special commands to configure the

**Figure 15.11**
Novel's Netware operating system provides a pop-up menu system for the LAN administrator to use while setting up or modifying the LAN. The top screen shows the major categories of commands. For example, selecting User Information causes a list of user names to appear in a new pop-up menu (bottom screen). Then, by selecting a name from this list, the administrator can find out information about a specific user or change a user's privileges.

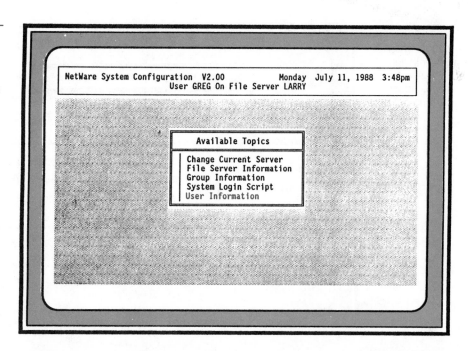

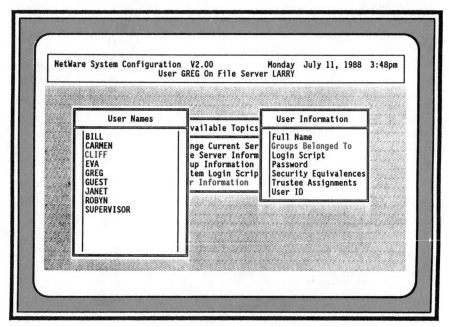

network by creating user directories on the file servers and assigning passwords. Using these commands, the LAN administrator writes batch files, or *scripts*, that organize user areas, maintain applications software, and perform other administrative chores. For example, Figure 15.13 shows part of the "login" script used by the OSU College of Business LAN. Whenever a user logs onto the network, this script

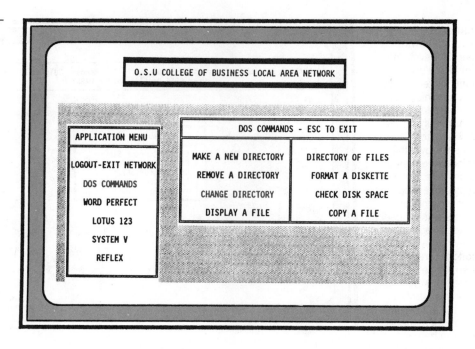

**Figure 15.12**
After logging onto the OSU College of Business LAN, a user is greeted by a pop-up menu system.

displays a message and tells the network where to find common application programs. Other scripts would set user privileges, establish individualized working environments for particular users, or perform maintenance tasks.

Special software for LANs can turn your computer into a mailbox for sending and receiving memos or a calendar for scheduling appointments. For example, if you want to schedule a meeting with three other people, you might run a special program on your computer that copies their appointment files to your computer, searches all four files (yours and the three others) for a mutually agreeable time, and then updates the files with the meeting's time and place.

Print spooling is another software feature of networks that helps save time. Normally, when two or more computers want to use the same printer, one must wait while the other uses the printer. But with **print spooling**, the second computer is allowed to continue as if it were also using the printer, by *spooling* its output into a disk file. Then, when the first computer finishes with the printer, the spooled print file is copied to the printer. In the meantime, the second computer can continue without waiting.

LANs are so powerful that they threaten to take many of the conventional functions of timeshared mainframes within large organizations. Because each computer in a LAN has its own memory and processor, a LAN that connects 150 personal computers can provide more computing power than a small mainframe computer. But you should also keep in mind the limitations of LANs. A LAN is restricted in size, and LANs can become as bogged down as mainframes can if too much activity is on the network.

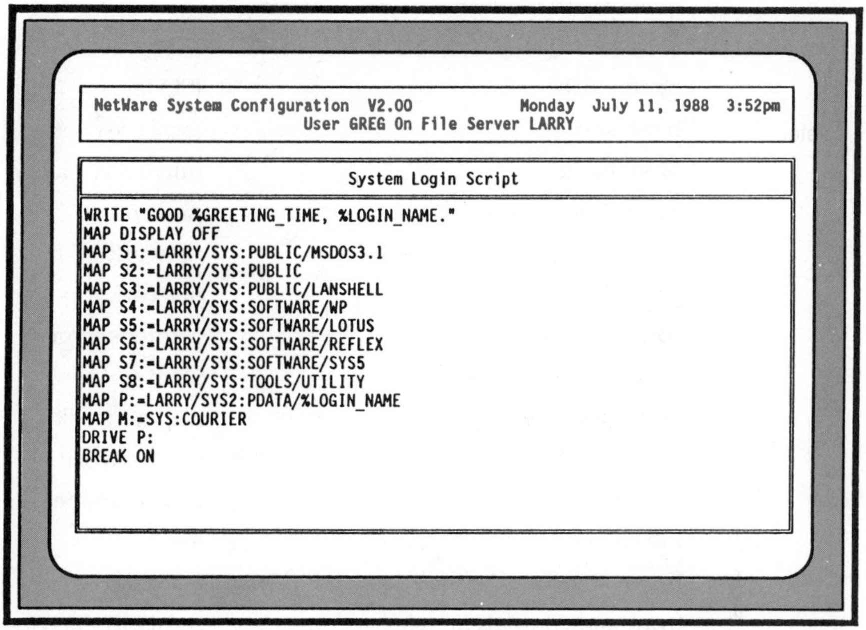

**Figure 15.13**
A script is a special type of batch file that stores network commands. This script displays a message to users when they log onto the network and establishes a list of drives to search when a requested file cannot be found in the user's default directory.

```
NetWare System Configuration  V2.00           Monday  July 11, 1988  3:52pm
                        User GREG On File Server LARRY


                              System Login Script

WRITE "GOOD %GREETING_TIME, %LOGIN_NAME."
MAP DISPLAY OFF
MAP S1:=LARRY/SYS:PUBLIC/MSDOS3.1
MAP S2:=LARRY/SYS:PUBLIC
MAP S3:=LARRY/SYS:PUBLIC/LANSHELL
MAP S4:=LARRY/SYS:SOFTWARE/WP
MAP S5:=LARRY/SYS:SOFTWARE/LOTUS
MAP S6:=LARRY/SYS:SOFTWARE/REFLEX
MAP S7:=LARRY/SYS:SOFTWARE/SYS5
MAP S8:=LARRY/SYS:TOOLS/UTILITY
MAP P:=LARRY/SYS2:PDATA/%LOGIN_NAME
MAP M:=SYS:COURIER
DRIVE P:
BREAK ON
```

## Summary

Computer networking has been heavily influenced by the relative cost of various types of computers. Until about 1985, it was cheapest to buy large mainframe computers and hook up many terminals to them. Thus the first computer networks were designed to connect terminals to a central computer that controlled all the network's activity. These networks were based on a star topology and were inherently unreliable because whenever the central computer failed, the entire network was brought down.

But the emergence of powerful, low-cost microcomputers has created a new economics of computing. Now mainframe computers are primarily used for data management tasks, leaving as many other processing tasks as possible for mini and microcomputers. This change toward decentralized computing has led to networks that can pass messages directly between any two nodes on the network. Thus most recently developed network systems use a ring or bus topology. A node on one of these networks can fail without bringing down the rest of the network. Generally, bus and ring networks are easier to install than star networks because you can tap into them at any point without running a new wire back to the central server.

Computers in a limited physical area can be coupled with other electronic equipment in a local area network. These networks allow resources such as disks, printers, plotters, minicomputers, and modems to be shared among the workstations attached to the network. LANs also provide methods of coordinating activities to prevent users from unintentionally destroying one another's data or trying to individually control the entire system.

## Key Terms

bandwidth

baseband

broadband

bus network

cache

coaxial cable

concentrator

CSMA protocol

dedicated line

distributed computing

fiber-optic cable

file server

frequency-division multiplexer

front-end computer

gateway

ground station

ISO layers

local area network (LAN)

microwave relay station

multiplexer

network

network topology

printer server

print spooling

ring network

star network

time-division multiplexer

token

T-switch

twisted-pair wire

utility server

virtual circuit

## Discussion Questions

1. What is the difference between a concentrator and a multiplexer?

2. How does a CSMA/CA protocol compare with a party-line telephone connection?

3. What are the major reasons for establishing a local area network?

4. In what ways might a local area network promote software piracy? How might one be used to prevent software piracy?

## Exercises

1. Frequency-division multiplexing can be used to combine slow transmissions to form a high-speed transmission. How might a two-channel broadband network be used to transmit voice and computer data simultaneously? How might this be useful for two people at distant locations who want to discuss a computer graphics display?

2. If a LAN transmits at 1 megabit per second, and ten computers are using it at the same time, what is the worst possible delay in copying a file across the network? Assume each of the ten computers is trying to do the same thing: copy a 50,000-character file from one computer to another on the same network.

3. Ask three companies that sell local area networks for information about their networks. Write a report comparing their strengths and weaknesses.

4. Find a local area network and determine the security features it provides. What flexibility does it give the LAN administrator to set user privileges?

# Computing Perspectives

Before World War II a "computer" was a person who performed lengthy calculations. An entire room of human computers was needed to complete the design of a skyscraper, bridge, or ship; some calculations went on for months. Today, a single desktop computer holds the computational power of thousands of human computers. A trained accountant, engineer, or scientist can calculate complex formulas, manipulate large databases of facts, and plot graphs at the touch of a few keys. Modern methods of computing and the low cost of electronic computers have changed the way people work.

To understand how these changes have occurred, we must understand software's central role in computing. Software adapts a general-purpose computer to a specific task. For most everyday computer tasks—writing let-

ters, preparing graphs, performing calculations, and managing lists—it is best to use off-the-shelf application packages like those discussed earlier in this textbook. This places the burden of developing software on computing professionals and leaves you free to concentrate on getting results. As long as your processing needs fit within the limits of available software packages, this solution works well.

Occasionally, you will run across a job that isn't appropriate for one of the application areas we've discussed so far. You should keep in mind that software developers have produced tens of thousands of programs aimed at small markets for special purposes, such as analyzing the strength of I-beams, controlling laboratory equipment, or copy-protecting disks. Often, using a special-purpose program will provide a better solution than adapting a general-purpose application program.

But what if the task you want to do requires judgment and experience? Today, most computing applications perform routine processing tasks and aren't directly applicable to general decision-making activities. This traditional allocation of tasks is being challenged by recent advances in *artificial intelligence*, the field of computing devoted to developing computer systems that display characteristics that we associate with human intelligence--such as reasoning, solving problems, understanding language, and learning. Artificial intelligence has led to seeing-eye robots that adapt to changes in their environment, decision support systems capable of anticipating the needs of human decision makers, voice recognition systems to capture the spoken word, and a host of other developments.

In Chapter 16 we pay particular attention to the *expert systems* branch of artificial intelligence. An expert system simulates the experience of a human decision maker in a particular subject area. Although expert systems have existed for more than a decade, they were initially limited to applications that could support the high cost of developing an entire expert system from scratch. However, with the appearance of inexpensive microcomputer-based *expert system shells* in 1984, the popularity of expert systems has soared. An expert system shell helps construct expert systems in roughly the same way a spreadsheet program helps construct worksheet templates. To build an application with a spreadsheet, you must supply your own labels, numbers, and formulas. But to build an expert system, you must supply the expert system shell with decision rules and facts.

In Chapter 16 we discuss the basic concepts of expert systems—situations that are applicable to development of expert systems, expert systems that are in use today, and the history of expert systems. We also take you through the development of a small expert system, MARKET ANALYST. Then we discuss advantages and limitations of expert systems.

Sometimes the best software solution is to develop a brand new program. In Chapter 17, we survey the diverse software tools available to solve problems unique enough to require programming. We discuss two broad aspects of programming: programming languages and programming techniques—in particular, the techniques of structured programming. The strict rules of structured programming described in Chapter 17 establish ground rules for how to solve problems efficiently. Because no programming language is best for all applications, we also present a few of the more popular programming languages, the differences among them, and guidelines for choosing the best language for your application.

Many interesting events contributed to the transition from human to electronic information processing. In Chapter 18, we review some of these events, including the early days of computing and the first electronic computer, developed during the 1940s; the four generations of mainframe computers; the introduction of the personal computer in the mid-1970s; and computers in the present day. We also make some informed predictions about the changes the future will bring.

Personal computers are admittedly powerful, but what about their social and legal ramifications? Have you inadvertently become one of the new breed of "outlaws" because you copied a friend's program disk? How can software authors protect their works from theft? In Chapter 19, we discuss the important issues of an evolving "computer morality."

# Expert Systems

**A**rtificial intelligence (AI) is the part of computer science that investigates systems displaying the characteristics we associate with human intelligence—reasoning, solving problems, understanding language, learning, and so on. One of the major successes of artificial intelligence has been the development of systems that duplicate the performance of human experts in solving particular problems; for instance, several of these systems advise doctors on diagnoses. In this chapter we explore expert systems in depth, including how they are constructed and tested and when they are appropriate. Several expert systems in use today are described—one of them, MARKET ANALYST, in detail. These examples help us project what the role of expert systems might be in the future.

## BASIC CONCEPTS

**Expert systems** are programs that reproduce the knowledge and thought processes of human experts in certain narrow, well-defined fields. Because they depend so

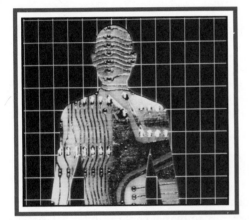

completely on an organized collection of knowledge, expert systems are sometimes called *knowledge-based systems*. Much like a skilled human consultant, an expert system questions the user to determine whether a problem falls within its scope, weighs the user's choices, and selects a course of action. Users can interact in a consultative dialogue with an expert system just as they would with a human expert—asking questions, requesting explanations, and suggesting possible solutions. Within narrow problem areas, the best expert systems can perform about as well as the best human experts. Expert systems ought not to be viewed as a replacement for human experts, but as a source of assistance to them.

Expert systems can store vast amounts of knowledge about their subject. Moreover, they frequently ask questions, make recommendations, and provide reasons for their suggestions in normal everyday language. Explanatory information is displayed on screens and menus, which allows users to select from various descriptions of the problems. Most expert systems can function even when the user does not provide a complete set of facts.

To offer these advantages, expert systems require a special kind of programming. Conventional data processing systems manipulate data in simple ways, recording and summarizing transactions or automating repetitive clerical tasks. Their processing is guided by complex *algorithms*, step-by-step procedures that ensure the same answer will be reached every time. In contrast, expert systems are developed to solve highly complex problems that do not always have only one answer. They produce intelligent problem solving or the selective and efficient choice of a solution from among many possible alternatives. The expert's knowledge and experience, encoded as a collection of facts and rules in the expert system's *knowledge base*, help the system to quickly spot useful data and pursue it, while eliminating extraneous information. Table 16.1 summarizes the differences between conventional software and expert systems.

**Table 16.1**
**Common Characteristics of Conventional Software and Expert Systems**

| Conventional Software | Expert Systems |
|---|---|
| Only one solution exists for any given set of data. | Many answers may be acceptable. |
| Standard problems can be solved by formulas. | Problem may not be cleary defined. |
| If too much data is missing, a solution cannot be reached. | Information is subjective and sometimes inconsistent; requires judgement. |
| The way to solve a problem is generally accepted. Correct answers can be verified. | Experts may disagree on how to solve a problem or on what constitutes a good answer. |
| Problem does not change much. | Problem is never quite the same. |
| Data can be represented by numbers and/or formulas. | Data is conceptual and cannot be represented by numbers. |
| Human expertise is abundant. | Human expertise is scarce. A late or poor decision is very costly. |

## Applications for Expert Systems

Expert systems are well suited to two types of problems. First there are those with which direct brute force methods produce an unmanageable number of possibilities. For example, even the fastest computers in existence today could not evaluate all the possible outcomes of one chess move in a thousand years. A chess game has more than $10^{120}$ possible moves. Other examples of this type of problem include determining the shortest driving route between two points and buying the least expensive bag of groceries that will provide a decent meal. People normally deal with these problems by arbitrarily eliminating all unlikely possibilities. That approach doesn't guarantee the best solution, but it does produce a quick solution.

The second type of problem expert systems handle well is the interpretation of huge amounts of data. For example, monitoring the sensors and evaluating the measurements from a space flight would overwhelm anyone. Nobody has all the needed expertise. But an expert system can integrate the data and make corrective decisions quickly.

Expert system applications also may be categorized by their general purpose. Feigenbaum and McCorduck, in *The Fifth Generation*, suggest expert systems are appropriate for the following business tasks:[1]

---

1. Edward A. Feigenbaum and Pamela McCorduck, *The Fifth Generation* (Reading, Mass.: Addison-Wesley, 1983).

### A Word About . . . *Expert System Shells*

*Since its modest beginning in 1984, the commercial market for expert system tools has gained strength—and vendors.*

With the arrival of personal computer-based expert system tools, the market divided into two distinct sectors based on the kind of hardware upon which expert system tool software operates. By the end of 1985, some 15 vendors of high-end tools had shipped products; add another 22 vendors of PC-based tools that were delivered to customers, and the expert system tools market includes over 35 vendors—with more on the way.

At present, these two sectors do not compete with each other, although there are indications that this may change, as tools developed on large symbolic processors are ported to smaller but increasingly powerful machines, such as Apple Computer, Inc.'s Macintosh and the impending generation of PCs based on 32-bit microprocessor chips.

Buyers of expert system tools tend to be large corporations and government agencies that use them to build expert systems for proprietary, in-house purposes.

According to our recent market research, the heaviest nonacademic users of expert system tools are manufacturing firms and those doing work in defense or other government contracts. Together, these users account for 60 percent of expert system tool usage. But interest in expert system tools has been increasing in such realms as banking, insurance, and finance as newly competitive companies in these industries look for ways to develop a strategic edge over their rivals.

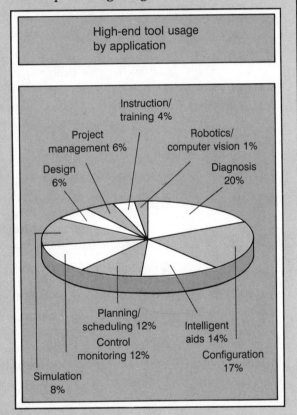

High-end tool usage by application

Instruction/training 4%
Robotics/computer vision 1%
Project management 6%
Design 6%
Diagnosis 20%
Planning/scheduling 12%
Control monitoring 12%
Intelligent aids 14%
Configuration 17%
Simulation 8%

Source: Susan Messenheimer, *Computerworld*, 14 July 1986, p. 52.

• Capturing, replicating and distributing expertise. Suppose a new market is developing nationwide. Several of your company's sales representatives have the knowledge and expertise to pursue it, but most of them do not. With conventional methods, it would take years for the few knowledgeable salespeople to train the others to take advantage of this opportunity. Small- and medium-sized companies face this problem frequently. Since expert systems contain both the necessary knowledge and the ability to explain their reasoning, they are excellent teachers within small domains. And they can get the job done much faster.

- Combining the knowledge of many experts. To accomplish some tasks, one needs the expertise of many different specialists working together. Expert systems can provide the necessary integration of knowledge bases even in the experts' absence. They provide *institutional memory,* the preservation of the cumulative experience and thinking of the best people in an organization. In industries where high turnover or shifts in personnel are common, this feature of expert systems is critical.

- Managing complex problems. Some problems have so many possible solutions they are almost unmanageable by conventional methods. For example, contracting for large one-of-a-kind projects usually requires a great deal of trial and error. Hypotheses must be formed, data analyzed, designs made, and design flaws diagnosed. Time constraints inevitably restrict the number of options that planners can explore. Expert systems increase them.

- Managing changes in knowledge. This problem is likely to crop up in emerging industries, where frequent price changes, new products, and changing market strategy require almost instant communication between managers and salespeople. In this setting, the usual sales and information meetings will not keep the sales force current. Expert systems can organize and disseminate information in the face of rapid technological change.

- Gaining a competitive edge. In a well-established and stable industry, everyone uses the same approach. Any idea that yields even a small improvement in performance will increase a company's market share. In such situations, expert systems can serve as a rich source of innovation. George Polya, in studying the behavior of his fellow mathematicians, noted that the use of heuristics was the key to the discovery of new ideas. And decision-making experiments have demonstrated conclusively that innovation and heuristic thinking—the special strength of expert systems—are related.

We have examined the types of problems expert systems can be applied to. In the next two sections, we describe some specific examples of successful expert system applications.

## Early Expert Systems

MYCIN, the most famous of the pioneer expert systems, is designed to help physicians diagnose infectious blood diseases and prescribe antibiotics for them. It contains the expertise of the foremost experts in the field of infectious blood diseases. The system diagnoses the causes of an infection using knowledge of the patient history, symptoms, and laboratory test results. Then it recommends the type of drug and dosage according to accepted procedures in infectious disease therapy. MYCIN has been used since 1979 at the Stanford Medical Center, and its performance has been found to equal that of the best experts.

MYCIN's conclusions are not always certain. After all, even human physicians are not always sure of their diagnoses. If after requesting additional information from the examining physicians, MYCIN still cannot make a reliable diagnosis, it lists all the conclusions consistent with the evidence, ranked by certainty factor. This is an important system feature for two reasons. First, since the conclusion is uncertain, the physician will want to check the other possibilities as well. And second, the patient may have more than one infection.

Another early expert system, PROSPECTOR, acts as a consultant to geologists exploring for ore deposits. Given field data about a region, PROSPECTOR estimates the likelihood of finding particular minerals, including lead, zinc, copper, nickel, uranium, and molybdenum. The system contains models of the types of terrain favorable to finding these minerals, constructed from extensive interviews with experts on the characteristics of favorable mining or drilling sites. As field data is fed in, the program checks it against its stored models from promising resemblances. PROSPECTOR can sift rapidly through observational data on a large number of sites, eliminating the majority and identifying the most likely. The system has found a molybdenum deposit worth $100,000,000.

Another expert system, DENDRAL, can identify the molecular structure of unknown chemical compounds. The system uses a special algorithm developed by Nobel Prize winner Joshua Lederburg to compute all the possible molecular structures. Then it prunes the list of possibilities to a manageable size using heuristics. DENDRAL has proved helpful in identifying dangerous pollutants. Before scientists can determine where a pollutant comes from and what to do about it, they must determine its chemical structure. The procedure is time consuming because literally millions of atomic combinations could be explored, and in a crisis, there is no time to sift through them all. For some tasks, DENDRAL has actually proved more able than any human expert.

## Current Expert Systems

By the late 1970s and early 1980s, the success of the prototype systems just described had established the commercial practicality of expert systems. Recent expert systems have proved cost-effective as well as useful in solving problems. For instance, Pacific Bell now runs a set of twenty expert systems that diagnose local area network (LAN) problems. Each of the twenty systems handles a particular domain related to problem. The system, which recommends solutions to the problems, can be run on a microcomputer and requires no special training to operate.

The Boeing Aerospace Company has pioneered a series of expert systems designed to preserve human expertise. The project began when Boeing's managers realized that several of the company's top tool-design engineers were about to retire. Transferring their experience and expertise to young engineers would be time consuming and costly. Moreover, there appeared to be a shortage of highly skilled engineers to draw on for future design needs. In effect, the company needed a permanent library of design principles to train new engineers with. Boeing's current expert systems include a trouble shooter for airplane engines, a space station designer, and a helicopter repair advisor.

Another system, DRILLING ADVISOR, assists oil rig supervisors in freeing trapped drilling mechanisms. When a drill bit gets stuck, the entire operation has to shut down—at a cost of $100,000 a day—to wait for the arrival of one of the few experts worldwide who know how to free it. DRILLING ADVISOR, which was developed by the French company Elf-Acquitane, took only a short time to recover its development costs.

Finally, State Farm Insurance Company is developing an expert system that models its best claim adjusters. Apparently, the difference in claim costs can vary widely between experienced adjusters and those new to the job. In the insurance industry, reducing rates and staying competitive requires carefully monitoring all costs. Preliminary calculations indicate the system should pay for itself in less than a year.

## DEVELOPMENT OF AN EXPERT SYSTEM: *MARKET ANALYST*

Expert systems are built through very deliberate interactions between *knowledge engineers* and **domain experts,** humans experts who are knowledgeable about the system's problem area. In the words of Paul E. Johnson,

> An expert is a person who, because of training and experience, is able to do things the rest of us cannot; experts are not only proficient but also smooth and efficient in the actions they take. Experts know a great many things and have tricks and caveats for applying what they know to problems and tasks; they are also good at plowing through irrelevant information to get at basic issues, and they are good at recognizing problems they face as instances of types with which they are familiar. Underlying the behavior of experts is the body of operative knowledge we have termed expertise. It is reasonable to suppose, therefore, that experts are the ones to ask when we wish to represent the expertise that makes their behavior possible.[2]

The other half of the development team, the **knowledge engineer**, is generally a computer professional. The knowledge engineer converts the expert's knowledge into forms the computer can accept, usually IF-THEN rules. Together, these rules comprise the system's **knowledge base,** or collection of facts and rules within the expert's subject area.

The acquisition and conversion of information can be an extremely lengthy process because experts often have difficulty explaining how they reach conclusions. Whereas conventional programmers usually interview the user only once,

---

2. Paul E. Johnson, "What Kind of Expert Should a System Be?" *The Journal of Medicine and Philosophy,* Vol. 8, pp. 77–97, 1983.

at the beginning of a job, knowledge engineers must interview the domain experts many times. After the first meeting, they develop a prototype of a system containing just a few facts and rules. They then test the system on a problem to see how it works. Based on the results, they return to the experts to ask more questions, and then refine or increase the knowledge base. Building an expert system, then, is an exploratory activity, a series of approximations. To illustrate the process, we examine the development of MARKET ANALYST, a small expert system.

### The Task

Although most businesses want to improve their profitability, they normally try not to compete directly with one another. Direct competition reduces their profit margins (the difference between revenues and expenses). If one business begins to infringe on the markets or territory of another, therefore, the second business may react with or without warning, dropping its prices or introducing a new product. In most industries, businesses try to avoid these shocks by announcing their moves ahead of time to see if competitors might react. This form of testing is called market signaling. According to Michael Porter, "A market signal is any action by a competitor that provides a direct or indirect indication of its intentions, motives, goals, or internal situation. Some of these signals are bluffs, some are warnings, and some are earnest commitments to action."[3]

Recognizing and accurately reading market signals is of major significance in choosing a defensible competitive position. Yet only experienced observers can make the subtle judgments about competitors needed to distinguish a true signal from a bluff. Although businesses usually signal intentionally, an astute observer with a great deal of experience in watching competitive behavior may also detect indirect signals. No two situations are the same. Considering the subtleties involved in making these judgments, market signaling is well suited to use of an expert system.

### Designing the System

In the design of this expert system, the domain expert would probably be a marketing consultant. The knowledge engineer could be anyone experienced in building expert systems. The first meeting between the knowledge engineer (KE) and domain expert (DE) might produce the following conversation:

KE: Suppose a competitor announces that it intends to look for a larger warehouse and retail facilities. Would you consider that a threat and expect more intense competition?

---

3. Michael Porter, *Competitive Strategy (Free Press, 1980), Chapter 4.*

DE: That depends on a number of factors. First, I would look at where the announcement was made. If it were widely publicized, it's probably serious. But the size of the investment is also important. Although the news might be widely spread, if we're not talking about a large investment, it could be a bluff.

KE: What are some of the other major indicators you evaluate?

DE: Well, it also would depend on what kind of announcement it was. Some are actually defensive. They indicate, "Don't worry, we won't retaliate." But some are very aggressive. They appear to be real, direct, competitive threats. You need to look at other factors, though, to be more certain.

KE: I am curious about bluffing; do competitors ever signal a move just to see what your response would be?

DE: Actually, companies often bluff. They're testing to see how serious and how sensitive you are about your markets. Or often they're auditing whether you're strong enough to fight back. To judge these gambits, you have to look at several of the variables I've mentioned at once.

KE: From another viewpoint, are there any signals that indicate a major attack on a company's markets or customers?

DE: Preemptive signals, indicating actions that have never been tried before, are cause for serious concern. They occur when a sizable investment is being made together with a widely announced public statement of intentions. Often there's a long-run profitable benefit to the signaler as well.

KE: Here's a rule that I think captures your explanation about preemptive signals. Tell me what you think.

> IF the signaler is making a major investment,
>   AND the media announcing it are broad and widely read,
>   AND the signaler expects long-term profitability from the action,
>
> THEN competitors in this market are sending preemptive signals and
>   intend to follow through with their announced actions.

DE: Uh, (long pause). Yes, that begins to capture it. But, of course, if the media used is not widely read, then they may be bluffing, although the other conditions are present.

KE: I see. Well, let's add that information to the knowledge base and see what it looks like.

To develop rules from this conversation, the knowledge engineer would first catalog the recurring variables mentioned by the domain expert. They were

- Type of market signal: accepting, aggressive, defensive, or divergent

- Size of the investment: minor or major

**Table 16.2**
**Summary of a Domain Expert's Rules for Analyzing Market Signals**

| Type of Signal | Major Characteristics of Signals | | | | Possible Meanings of Signal |
| | Size of Investment | Competitors' Reactions | Public Medium for Signal | Benefits to Company | |
|---|---|---|---|---|---|
| Divergent | Major | Neutral Mild reactions | Broad | Lasting | Preemptive Divergent |
| Aggressive | Major | Mild rebuke Major reactions | Narrow | | Aggressive Testing response |
| Acceptance | Major Major | | None | Lasting | Aggressive Threatening |
| Aggressive | Major | Neutral Mild reactions | Broad | Lasting | Preemptive Expanded role |
| Agressive | Major | | Narrow | Minor | Defensive Bluffing |
| Defensive | Minor | | Broad | Minor | Defensive Reaction |
| Acceptance | | Neutral | Broad | Lasting | Nonthreatening Accommodation |
| Defensive Acceptance Acceptance | Minor Minor | Nonneutral | Narrow None | | Insufficient information |
| Divergent Aggressive | Minor Minor | | None | | Inconsequential information |

- Competitors' reactions: neutral, mild rebuke, or major rebuke
- Medium used to signal: narrow, broad, or none
- Benefits that might accrue to the initiator: lasting or minor

The knowledge engineer would then list combinations of these variables according to their meaning, as in Table 16.2. Once listed this way, the domain expert's diagnoses can be easily converted into rules for insertion into the knowledge base. For example, the top row might be restated as

IF the market signal indicates divergent behavior,
    AND the magnitude of the proposed investment is considerable,
    AND competitors reactions are neutral or mildly negative,
    AND the intended audience for the signal is broad,
    AND by signaling a competitor could gain lasting benefits,

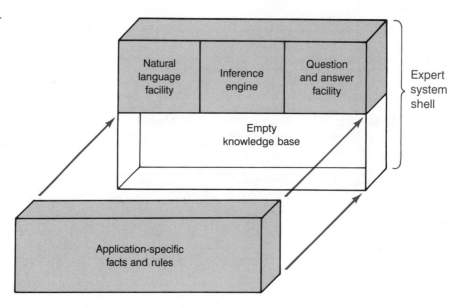

**Figure 16.1**
Components of an expert system. Most expert systems are developed using an expert system shell, which includes a ready-made natural language facility, inference engine, and question-and-answer facility. An empty knowledge base allows users to plug in application-specific facts and rules.

THEN competitors in this market are sending preemptive signals and intend to deviate from current industry practices.

As the knowledge engineer and domain expert continue to work together, they begin to establish a common language. Then, in that language, they identify the facts and relationships that the expert uses to understand a problem and search for solutions. The knowledge engineer encourages the expert to think aloud; that is, to work on an actual problem, talking about hunches as they occur. Slowly, the knowledge engineer builds a model of the system, expressed in the form of IF-THEN rules.

Finally, the knowledge engineer designs a menu-based interface to collect information from the system's user. MARKET ANALYST's user interface might offer a different menu for each column in Table 16.2. The menu corresponding to the column "Competitors' Reactions" might read

Reactions by others in the industry to competitors' or your intentions has been
a. No response
b. The usual industry responses
c. Indications of displeasure with your intentions
d. Announcement of a possible countermove not as damaging or threatening as possible
e. A direct counteraction to your intentions

Once a set of rules and menus has been designed, the knowledge engineer is ready to construct the prototype system.

**Figure 16.2**
Using a knowledge
editor to change a
rule. The left side of
the screen shows
the THEN part of a
programmed rule.
To change it, the
knowledge engineer
selects another
statement from the
right side of the
screen.

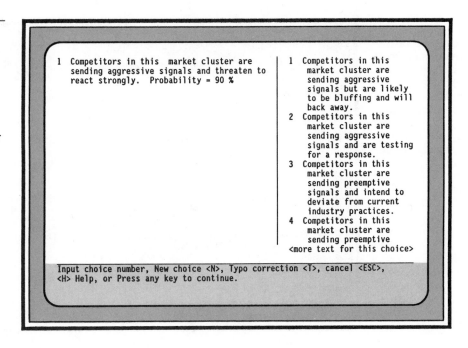

```
 1  Competitors in this  market cluster are        1  Competitors in this
    sending aggressive signals and threaten to         market cluster are
    react strongly.   Probability = 90 %               sending aggressive
                                                       signals but are likely
                                                       to be bluffing and will
                                                       back away.
                                                    2  Competitors in this
                                                       market cluster are
                                                       sending aggressive
                                                       signals and are testing
                                                       for a response.
                                                    3  Competitors in this
                                                       market cluster are
                                                       sending preemptive
                                                       signals and intend to
                                                       deviate from current
                                                       industry practices.
                                                    4  Competitors in this
                                                       market cluster are
                                                       sending preemptive
                                                       <more text for this choice>

  Input choice number, New choice <N>, Typo correction <T>, cancel <ESC>,
  <H> Help, or Press any key to continue.
```

## Building and Testing the System

Expert systems are not usually constructed from scratch. Instead, they are built using an **expert system shell,** the portion of an expert system that remains after all application-specific rules and user interfaces have been removed. As Figure 16.1 shows, most shells have four major components:

*1.* A **natural-language facility** that communicates with and collects facts from the user. Many expert systems use menu systems to moderate this dialogue, but others use command languages, icons and mice, or even spoken English.

*2.* An **inference engine** that generates inferences from the system's IF-THEN rules and the facts supplied by the user.

*3.* A **question-and-answer facility** that explains the system's reasoning.

*4.* An empty knowledge base to store the application-specific facts and rules in.

Expert system shells may be bought as part of commercial packages that include special "tools" for entering rules in the knowledge base or building the user interface. Figure 16.2 illustrates a **knowledge editor,** a tool that displays a menu of possible THEN clauses the knowledge engineer may choose from.

After the rules and user interface information have been incorporated into the shell, the new prototype system can be tested and refined. The domain expert checks the accuracy and consistency of the rules and the usefulness of the system's advice by feeding it case histories, and then refines the rules where necessary.

**Figure 16.3**
Using a question-and-answer facility. This display, which appeared in response to a user's command WHY, explains the reason the system asked for more information.

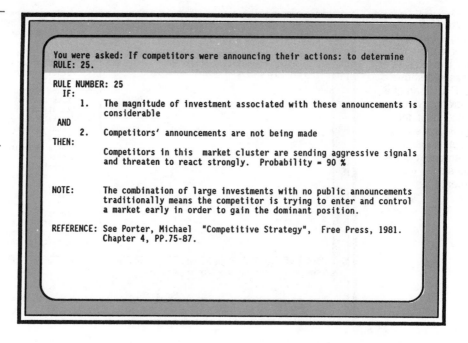

```
You were asked: If competitors were announcing their actions: to determine
RULE: 25.

RULE NUMBER: 25
   IF:
        1.    The magnitude of investment associated with these announcements is
              considerable
   AND
        2.    Competitors' announcements are not being made
   THEN:
              Competitors in this  market cluster are sending aggressive signals
              and threaten to react strongly.  Probability = 90 %


   NOTE:      The combination of large investments with no public announcements
              traditionally means the competitor is trying to enter and control
              a market early in order to gain the dominant position.

   REFERENCE: See Porter, Michael  "Competitive Strategy",  Free Press, 1981.
              Chapter 4, PP.75-87.
```

## Using the System

When the MARKET ANALYST is run, it asks a series of multiple-choice questions. The user enters the letters indicating the choices that correctly finish the statement. (If a question has more than one correct choice, the user should enter correct choices.) After each question has been answered, the inference engine determines which rules apply. If the user's choices agree with all the IF portions of a rule, the THEN clause must be true. But if even one IF clause does not match, the system rejects the rule. Once the inference engine has determined that one rule is true, it may use that rule's THEN clause to determine whether other rules apply.

The order of questioning reflects the system's inferencing procedure. The system begins by asking questions that will eliminate the need to search large areas of the knowledge base. The exact order the questions are posed in, therefore, depends on the user's responses. Each time the system is run, the sequence of questions is likely to be different.

At any time, the user may ask for an explanation of the system's reasoning by typing WHY. The question-and-answer facility will reply, as Figure 16.3 shows, with an answer that includes the rule the system is checking, a note stating additional details, and a reference. This feature opens the system to inspection, instructs the user about how the system functions, and increases the user's confidence in the system. Users must be able to ask why a conclusion or procedure has been recommended or why a particular question is being asked. Reasoning that cannot be explained to an end user is unsatisfactory, even if it's as good as or better than a human expert's.

When the system has reached a solution, it will display an ordered list of conclusions with their probabilities, as shown in Figure 16.4. The first conclusion has a

**Figure 16.4**
Conclusions
reached by
MARKET ANALYST.
When an expert sys-
tem comes to a con-
clusion about the
possible solutions to
a problem, it ranks
them according to
probability level.

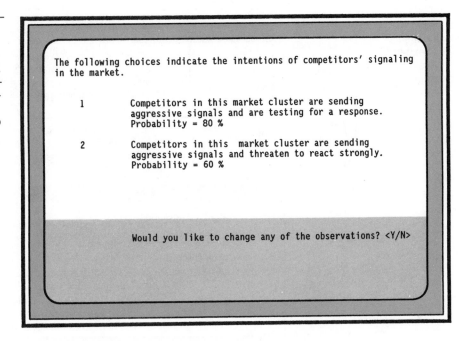

The following choices indicate the intentions of competitors' signaling in the market.

1        Competitors in this market cluster are sending aggressive signals and are testing for a response. Probability = 80 %

2        Competitors in this market cluster are sending aggressive signals and threaten to react strongly. Probability = 60 %

Would you like to change any of the observations? <Y/N>

higher probability and is therefore more likely to be correct. But the second answer also has a fairly high probability and should be considered by the user.

Even with the help of an expert system shell and its associated tools, building an expert system is not a speedy process. Although the final version of MARKET ANALYST contained only about twenty-five rules, it took more than two weeks to develop.

## ANATOMY OF AN EXPERT SYSTEM

Figure 16.5 shows a diagram of a typical complete expert system. Some of the parts of this system have already been introduced in connection with MARKET ANALYST; others need more explanation. In particular, we discuss how knowledge bases are constructed, how inferences are made from rules, and the various features of expert system development packages.

### The Knowledge Base

A knowledge base contains facts and rules. Facts include short-term information that can change even during the course of a consultation. Rules are directions about how to generate hypotheses or solutions from known facts. For example, here is an IF-THEN rule with two possible conclusions:

IF sales within the industry are growing rapidly,
    AND the basis for competition is not price or service or is undetermined,

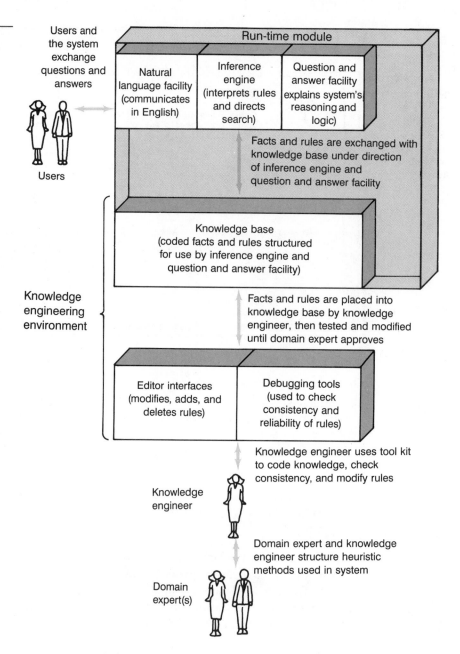

**Figure 16.5**
Basic components of a typical expert system development package

Users and the system exchange questions and answers

Users

Run-time module

Natural language facility (communicates in English)

Inference engine (interprets rules and directs search)

Question and answer facility explains system's reasoning and logic)

Facts and rules are exchanged with knowledge base under direction of inference engine and question and answer facility

Knowledge base (coded facts and rules structured for use by inference engine and question and answer facility)

Knowledge engineering environment

Facts and rules are placed into knowledge base by knowledge engineer, then tested and modified until domain expert approves

Editor interfaces (modifies, adds, and deletes rules)

Debugging tools (used to check consistency and reliability of rules)

Knowledge engineer uses tool kit to code knowledge, check consistency, and modify rules

Knowledge engineer

Domain expert and knowledge engineer structure heuristic methods used in system

Domain expert(s)

THEN the conditions described suggest an emerging industry .87;
OR the conditions described suggest a fragmented industry .13.

The two tentative conclusions in this rule are "reasoned" from the information provided in the IF clause. Until more facts can be assembled, one conclusion is much more probable than the other.

Knowledge bases are not the same as databases. The difference is best explained by analogy. Suppose an emergency room physician picks up a patient's chart, which shows the patient's physical measurements, medical history, any obvious trauma, current drug therapy, and past responses to classes of drugs. This is the patient's database. To continue diagnosis and recommend therapy, the physician must use her medical knowledge, including what she learned in medical school, during residence practice, from studying journals, and from the mistakes of others. These facts, relationships, and probabilities are the doctor's knowledge base.

Besides a knowledge base, some expert systems require access to vast amounts of data stored in remote databases, or to data generated in real time. For example, an expert system designed to advise and register college students about courses would need access to the school's course schedules, registration lists, and student transcripts. A patient monitoring system would need constant data on the patients' vital signs. The special data collection and management capabilities needed by these systems are not usually found in most development packages.

## The Inference Engine

An expert system also needs an **inference procedure**, or a method of reasoning, to understand and act on data and knowledge. Because this procedure or problem-solving method governs which question the user is asked next, and thus which tentative conclusions are confirmed first, it determines the system's efficiency. Any good inference procedure should first eliminate nonproductive lines of questioning. Research has shown that users do not trust expert systems that do not follow an efficient line of questioning.

One commonly used inference procedure is **backward chaining,** which is similar to deductive reasoning (the mental strategy of starting at the end goal and working back to the origin). For example, a maze might be solved by working backward from the ending position rather than forward from the starting position. Or in MARKET ANALYST, the inference procedure might start with a tentative conclusion, such as "Competitors in this market cluster are sending aggressive signals and threaten to react strongly." Working backward, the system would ask questions that might confirm the IF clauses associated with that conclusion. If the user's responses showed the tentative conclusion to be false, the inference procedure would select another tentative conclusion and begin questioning the user again.

Another common reasoning strategy is **forward chaining**—the opposite of backward chaining. In this inference procedure, the system begins with a specific original statement and searches for routes that lead to one or more conclusions. It does so by first selecting the question most likely to eliminate many rules. It continues to pose questions in this manner until all the conditions of a rule have been confirmed. Finally, it displays the THEN portion of the rule for the users.

In a system as simple as MARKET ANALYST, the method of reasoning used makes little difference. But in larger systems, choosing the wrong inference procedure usually results in an inefficient questioning strategy. Generally, backward chaining (see Figure 16.6) is more appropriate to use with many possible beginnings, whereas forward chaining is more appropriate with only a few.

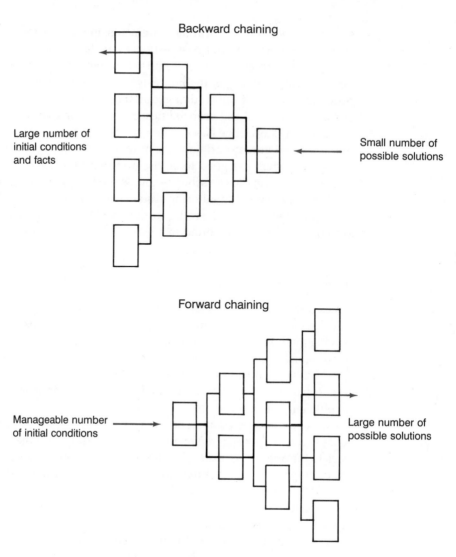

**Figure 16.6**
Uses of backward and forward chaining

Backward chaining

Large number of initial conditions and facts

Small number of possible solutions

Forward chaining

Manageable number of initial conditions

Large number of possible solutions

## Knowledge Acquisition Methods

As we have seen, many expert systems are now constructed using commercial development packages. These shell and tools kits began to appear on the mini and mainframe computer market in the late 1970s. They were followed in 1984 by micro-based tools and shells.

Until recently, most expert systems had to be constructed by knowledge engineers. But the availability of development packages now enables the end users to construct small expert systems by themselves. The movement of these powerful tools into the hands of the end users has speeded up the development of practical applications for artificial intelligence, causing widespread growth in the use of expert systems. Development packages cannot be used for all applications, however. Applications that require unusual kinds of reasoning or access to existing databases may have to be constructed from scratch with a programming language. Alternatively, they might be assembled from an assortment of standalone development tools, such as subroutine libraries, database management systems, and programming aids. Either of these methods would require the services of a skilled computer technician. (See Chapter 17 for information on programming languages.)

Recall that an expert system shell is made by stripping the knowledge base from an expert system, leaving the user interface and inferencing procedures intact. With the aid of an editing tool kit, a new knowledge base from a different problem area can be plugged in. MARKET ANALYST was developed with EXSYS, a micro-based development system that includes a complete knowledge-engineering tool kit, support for constructing user interfaces, question-and-answer facility, and powerful inference engine. General Electric has used EXSYS to develop a system for identifying metals and alloys. Pacific Bell has used it to develop a system for diagnosing Local Area Network (LAN) problems. Additionally, the Department of Agriculture has used the package to put together a system for controlling the design of experiments.

Most development packages have two parts: a **run-time module,** which includes an additional program necessary to run the completed system (top half of Figure 16.5), and a *knowledge engineering environment*, which contains the needed tools to build the system (bottom half of Figure 16.5). These tools include knowledge editors, user interface construction tools, testing modules, system monitoring routines, and debugging tools.

The more advanced commercial development packages include sophisticated support tools for entering and manipulating rules. These systems automatically check rules for consistency. They may also speed up development by testing new rules against a database of representative cases. If a rule isn't consistent with a case, the system will display the reasoning behind the case so that the knowledge engineer can refine the new rules.

# ADVANTAGES AND LIMITATIONS OF EXPERT SYSTEMS

For most problems, expert systems that are in use today are still not as good as human experts, but they are getting better. Current expert systems are confined to well-defined tasks. These systems cannot reason across disciplines or broad ranges of knowledge, nor from general or partial theories. In fact, no problem that requires large amounts of reasoning by analogy is suited to an expert system, especially if it is poorly defined and far ranging. Legal problems are characteristically poor subjects for a small expert system because they require all the capabilities just mentioned.

Human expertise is also clearly superior to the artificial kind in tasks requiring common sense. There is no easy way to build large quantities of common sense

**Table 16.3**
**Checklist for Determining Whether an Expert System Should Be Developed**

| Possible | Justified | Appropriate |
|---|---|---|
| 1. Do experts exist? | 1. Can human expertise be lost? | 1. Is the problem reasonably difficult? |
| 2. Do experts generally agree on solutions? | 2. Is human expertise scarce? | 2. Are heuristic solutions required? |
| 3. Does the task require more than common sense? | 3. Is the potential yield high? | 3. Is the task a manageable size? |
| 4. Are only cognitive skills required? | 4. Is expertise needed in many locations? | 4. Is the activity a valuable one? |
| 5. Can experts describe what they do? | 5. Is expertise is needed in a dangerous environment? | 5. Can symbols be manipulated? |
| | 6. Is the problem reasonably clear? | |

knowledge into a computer program or knowledge base. Humans easily recognize incompatible facts as nonsense—we know hot air balloons are not made of lead, for instance—but how much of that kind of learning can be included in a knowledge base? Common sense also includes what we know we don't know. For example, if you were asked for the phone number of Sherlock Holmes, you would instantly know there is no answer. Expert systems, however, do not give up when they can't solve a problem. They assume they need more information and persist in questioning the user in an attempt to secure the necessary facts.

Another area humans excel in is learning. Human experts can adapt to new conditions by adjusting their heuristics, but expert systems are not adept at learning new rules and concepts. In fact, knowledge acquisition has become the major bottleneck in developing expert systems. As we have seen, the process of extracting knowledge from an expert and translating it into rules is a tedious one. Thus current systems are limited to narrow domains. Designing tools that will automatically add and update rules is one of the most urgent research problems in artificial intelligence.

On the other hand, expert systems do offer some advantages over human experts. They do not display biased judgments, nor do they jump to conclusions in the face of contrary evidence. They always attend to details and never have a bad day. Best of all, they always consider all the possible alternatives systematically. As new techniques and concepts are applied to the design and development of knowledge-based systems, we can expect these systems to become even more flexible in their applications.

In general, tasks chosen for treatment by expert systems should be possible, justified, and appropriate.

• Possible. The most important requirement for creating an expert system is that experts exist and generally agree on solutions. If they do not agree, the system's performance cannot be verified. Experts must also be able to describe their methods; otherwise, an expert system cannot be created.

- Justified. Just because it is possible to develop an expert system that does not necessarily mean it is desirable to do so. We have seen that expert systems are not constructed quickly and easily. With today's technology, the average development time from conception through testing of the finished system is between five and ten person years for a moderately complex problem. PUFF, a system that diagnoses the presence and severity of lung disease, required five person years of development even though it was based on MYCIN's shell. Obviously, few problems are so pressing that they could justify as great an expense in both time and money. Only when human experts are scarce—and therefore expensive—and their expertise is needed at several locations is the expenditure likely to be worth it.

- Appropriate. Expert systems are appropriate only for problems of very narrow scope. Suppose a system to advise plastic surgeons on surgical procedures has been proposed. That problem is too broad in scope for an expert system. It would have to be limited to a particular type of case, such as cosmetic facial changes, limb reconstruction, or cyst removal. Even within one of these categories, the scope might have to be limited further. Cosmetic facial changes might have to be narrowed to changes in specific features—perhaps nose reconstruction, eyelid changes, or chin tucks.

Table 16.3 provides a checklist that summarizes the evaluation process for potential expert systems.

---

## Summary

One of the most important successes in artificial intelligence has been the development of expert systems, which reproduce human expertise in narrow subject areas. Though expert systems are limited in scope, they seem to be equally applicable to many fields from finance and medicine to strategic planning and chemistry. Tasks that require considerable expertise and relatively little common sense are good candidates for expert systems. Expert systems are currently being used in various diverse industries including communications, aerospace, oil drilling, and insurance.

Expert systems can be designed from scratch using a special programming language. But increasingly they are constructed with the help of expert system shells and knowledge-engineering tools. Frequently, the most difficult part of building an expert system is capturing the expert's knowledge and then testing the system's reliability and validity. The domain expert and the knowledge engineer work closely to identify facts and relationships used to understand problems and search for solutions. Expert systems usually require many revisions before they meet the expert's expectations.

Expert systems store facts and rules in a knowledge base. They use a component called an inference engine to draw conclusions from the facts and rules. The separation of the knowledge base and inference engine allows the knowledge engineer to revise the knowledge base without affecting the system's programming logic. Unlike conventional programs, the inference engine can reason from uncertain or incomplete data. A question-and-answer facility lets the expert system explain its line of reasoning in an understandable way.

## Key Terms

| | |
|---|---|
| artificial intelligence | inference procedure |
| backward chaining | knowledge base |
| domain expert | knowledge editor |
| expert system | knowledge engineer |
| expert system shell | natural-language facility |
| forward chaining | question-and-answer facility |
| inference engine | run-time module |

## Discussion Questions

*1.* Why would teaching a freshman how to "get around" the campus be a good subject for an expert system?

*2.* Are there differences between conventional programs and expert systems other than those listed in the chapter?

*3.* How would you go about building an expert system for the following situations:

One of the most famous bootmakers in the southwest is about to retire. People seek his handmade boots from other continents. The company is afraid it may not be able to train someone before his retirement.

General Electric is considering selling an electronic device to monitor and control temperature and humidity in every room of a house for $50. It has several delicate instruments that need to be checked and calibrated every six months. Their concern is the high cost of supporting the customers with advice.

The Internal Revenue Service has had its budget cut again. Its auditors are turning over more rapidly than ever before. Training a competent tax diagnostician takes five years.

A small Alaskan fishing village needs a sewer system. They have few funds to conduct an environmental impact study. Clearly, they don't have enough to hire an architect and sanitation engineering firm.

# Making the Pieces: From Silicon Crystals to Computers

*Computers are constructed from electrical parts—mainly transistors, capacitors, resistors, and wires. It takes millions of these parts to build even a small personal computer. Because of intense competition, successful firms must use low-cost methods to build and connect electrical components. The fruit of this competition has been a number of fascinating and exotic manufacturing techniques. As you study this photo essay, you will gain insight into how these techniques work.*

1. Large silicon crystals are the raw material from which most integrated circuit chips are manufactured. The crystals are grown in a furnace containing an exceptionally pure bath of molten silicon. Usually they are from 3 to 5 inches in diameter; often they are several feet long.

# PREPARING THE SILICON SURFACE

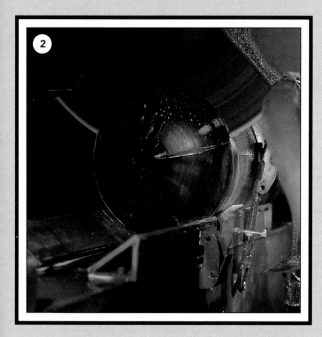

2. Each silicon crystal is sliced with a diamond-edged saw into round wafers that are less than one-half millimeter thick. Because silicon crystals are harder than most metals, cutting them is expensive and slow.

3. The first step in removing damage caused by cutting the crystals is called lapping. Wafers are placed in carriers between two rotating plates that remove a prescribed amount of damage. Later the wafers are polished to a mirror finish.

4. Wafers are inspected many times during the manufacturing process.

5. A finished wafer contains many integrated circuit chips organized like postage stamps on a piece of paper. These wafers range from 1 to 5 inches. The trend has been toward larger wafers.

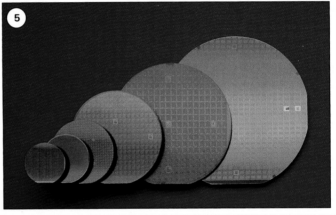

6. An IBM engineer inspects an experimental eight-inch silicon wafer that can accommodate more than 2,000 chips.

# MANUFACTURING THE CIRCUITS

*Photographic methods are used to transfer an image of circuit patterns into numerous copies on the silicon surface.*

7. This photomask contains one layer of circuitry. The mask is created by an electron-beam exposure system that etches tiny images on a metal-coated glass plate; the glass is transparent to ultraviolet rays, but the metal isn't. Before the mask can be used to create circuits, the wafers are dipped in a bath of ultraviolet-sensitive photoresist (a photographic-type emulsion). Then each wafer is exposed by shining ultraviolet light through the mask. Finally, the wafer is washed in a developing solution, leaving a pattern on the surface. This process deposits an image of one circuit layer on the surface of the chip. A completed chip may require from 5 to 18 circuit layers.

9. A rack of wafers enters the furnace.

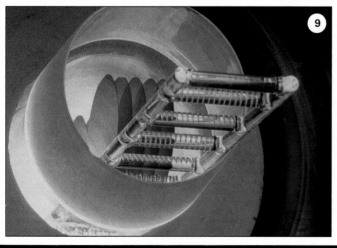

8. During some processing steps wafers are heated in ovens to produce an insulating layer of glass oxide on exposed silicon surfaces. Other steps use ovens to "dope" unoxidized surfaces with a thin layer of impurities, such as boron or phosphorus. The impurities create conductive and resistive regions in the silicon that form electronic circuits.

10. Peter Ferlita inserts a program card into an automatically controlled furnace at RCA's Solid State Division in Somerville, New Jersey. The card contains instructions for processing during a one-hour trip at temperatures of 1500° F. After more than 500 manufacturing operations, these wafers will be used in guidance control systems for missiles.

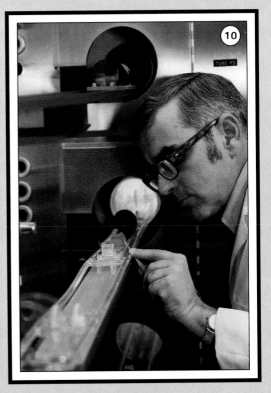

11. An Intel Corporation technician positions wafers to receive a thin coating of aluminum from an evaporator. Later most of the aluminum will be etched away, leaving trace lines that connect the circuits.

12. A wafer is washed after etching. This is a wafer of transducers to be used in read/write heads for hard disk drives.

*window 8*

# WAFER INSPECTION

13. Periodic inspections by microscope are necessary to ensure that the circuits are being constructed satisfactorily.

14. Microscopes are also necessary to align photomasks with the circuits on a partially completed wafer.

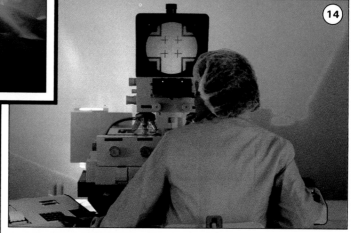

15. Even minute particles of dust in the air can land on the surface of the silicon and result in malfunctioning circuits. Manufacturing is done in highly controlled "clean rooms" where workers wear protective gloves and hats and the air is constantly filtered. This room is lit with yellow light to keep out extraneous ultraviolet rays.

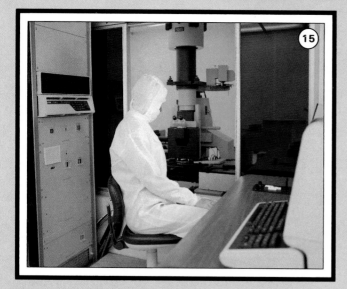

# TESTING AND CUTTING THE FINISHED WAFER

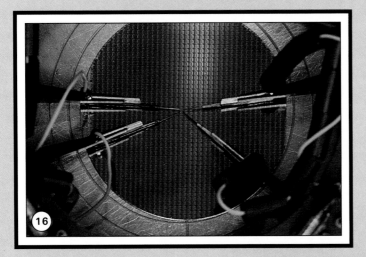

16. After the wafer is completed, each chip is tested to see if it functions correctly. The tests are conducted by placing probes on tiny electrical contact pads around the outside of the chip.

17. This testing machine at the National Semiconductor Corporation lowers 29 wires onto a chip and then runs it through a series of electrical tests. If the chip fails a test, a small ink spot is dropped on it to mark it as a reject.

18. Eventually the wafer is ready to be diced into separate chips. Here a diamond-edged tool scribes lines along the wafer's surface.

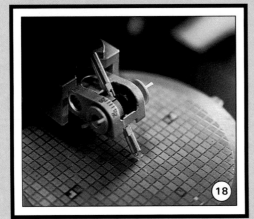

# PACKING MEMORY CHIPS

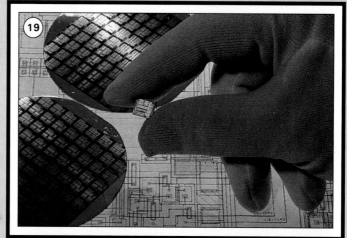

19. A composite drawing of circuit layers, two finished wafers, and a gloved hand holding an unmounted integrated circuit chip.

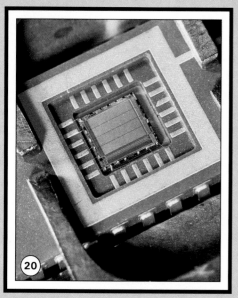

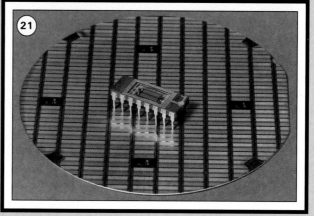

21. A packaged memory chip sits on top of a wafer of similar memory chips. Each chip can store 64K bits (65,536 bits) of digital data. Memory chips capable of storing more than one megabit are being developed in research labs.

20. Chips are mounted inside protective carrier packages to make them easier to handle and to help them dissipate heat. To mount the chip, tiny wires are soldered from pads on the chip's outside edges to contact areas on the carrier.

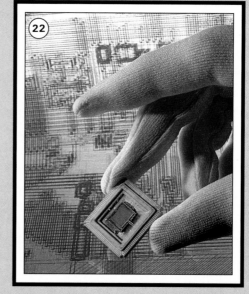

22. Very-large-scale-integrated (VLSI) chips require many input and output pins. Instead of having leads poked into holes in a circuit board, these chips have been mounted in leadless carriers that sit on the surface of a circuit board. This method produces smaller chips, which results in more densely populated circuit boards and, consequently, smaller and faster computers.

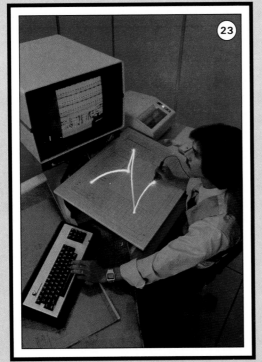

# DESIGNING THE CIRCUITS

*Chips can have well over 100,000 circuit elements. Creating and testing the circuit design require extensive use of computers.*

**23.** This computer-aided design system supports a wide range of design, drafting, and manufacturing operations on large-scale integrated (LSI) chips. The user enters data from either the keyboard or the graphics tablet.

**24.** Once a design is stored in memory, it receives thorough computerized testing. The circuit's functions are simulated by programs that check for problems with the speed, timing, logic, and voltage. Modifications to the chip's design can be entered from the keyboard.

**25.** Composite drawings of the various circuit layers are 400 times larger than actual size.

# DESIGNING CIRCUIT BOARDS

**The most common way of linking chips electrically is to mount them on printed circuit boards made of fiberglass.**

26. High-quality graphics terminals help lay out the design of circuit boards quickly and accurately.

27. After the position of chips has been entered, straight lines can be drawn on the screen to point out how the chips' pins are to be connected.

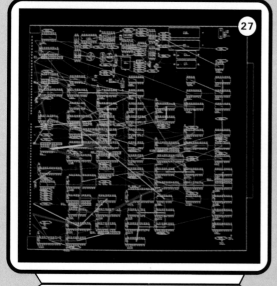

28. Once the connections among pins have been specified, computer programs help determine where the copper traces (wires) should run along the circuit board's surfaces.

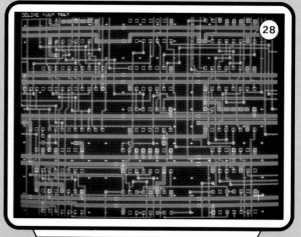

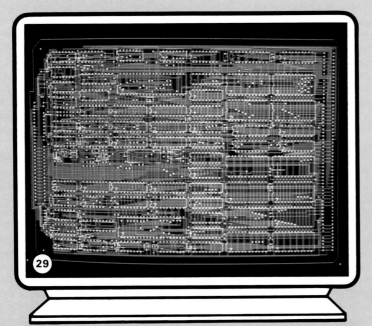

29. Even high-resolution terminals can be hard to read when they display an entire circuit board at once. Usually it is possible to zoom in to look at one portion more closely, or to scroll from one region of the board to another.

30. In minutes a color electrostatic plotter can produce a full-color plot of an entire circuit board so that designs can be previewed quickly.

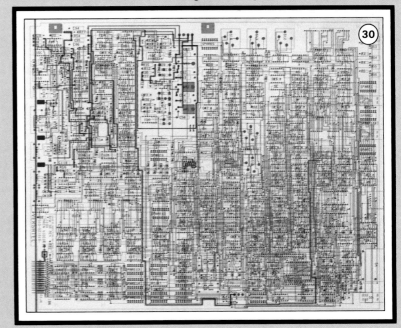

# COMPUTER-AIDED MANUFACTURING

31. Computers do more than speed up the design process; they produce the media needed to manufacture printed circuit boards. Among these media are artwork and silkscreen masters, component drawings, and tapes that direct drilling and insertion operations.

32. Artwork masters can be extracted directly from a computerized circuit board design aided by a computer-controlled photoplotter.

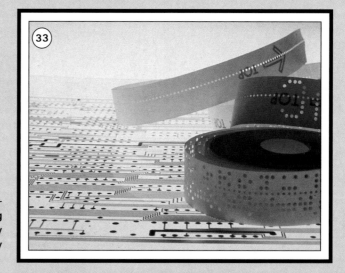

33. Punched tape is often used to load numerically controlled (N/C) manufacturing machines with control sequences. Many processes for manufacturing rely heavily on N/C machines.

# BUILDING THE BARE BOARD

34. An internal layer of a 16-layer printed circuit board is scanned by a programmable inspection machine to ensure high reliability. This circuit board will become part of an electronic system to protect military aircraft from radar-directed weapons.

35. A Cray Research technician coats a printed circuit board with copper. This step follows an operation that masks areas of the board so that only the unmasked areas are plated with copper.

36. Integrated circuit chips have been installed in this completed supercomputer circuit board manufactured by Cray Research.

# DRILLING, STUFFING, SOLDERING, AND INSPECTING THE BOARDS

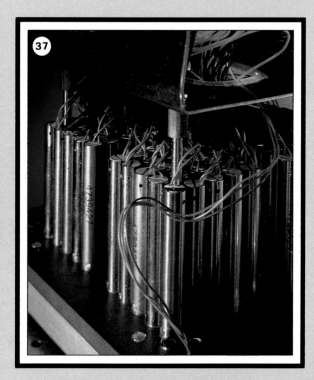

37. In one second this IBM-designed tool punches 1,440 precisely placed holes with the diameter of an eyelash; then it automatically inspects its own work. The holes are punched in ceramic substrates that serve as chip carriers in IBM's large-scale computers. As many as 40,000 holes in each of up to 33 sheets of ceramic substrate are punched with great accuracy in order to ensure the integrity of electrical connections.

38. An engineer completes the installation of a robotic system on an automated assembly line for IBM 3178 display terminals.

39. For low-volume manufacturing operations, electrical components are "stuffed" into a circuit board by hand. All of the components are mounted on one side of the board, leaving the back side bare. When the components have been added, the bare side of the board is passed over a flowing stream that solders all the pins in place in one operation.

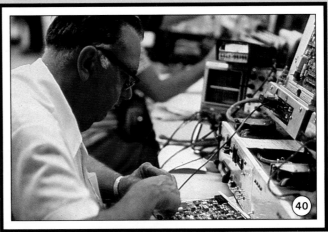

40. Paradyne has several manufacturing and assembly lines that produce printed circuit boards. They have a high ratio of inspectors to assemblers so that possible problems can be identified early in the manufacturing cycle.

41. At Tandem's circuit board assembly facility in Watsonville, California, computer-controlled production includes a variety of bar code readers.

# ASSEMBLING AND TESTING THE FINAL PRODUCT

**42.** As sales of personal computers climbed, the manufacturers required high-volume, assembly line production methods.

**43.** As many as one Macintosh every 27 seconds is built at Apple's highly automated factory in Fremont, California.

44. In Greenrock, Scotland, a technician monitors tests of the IBM PC/AT.

## Exercises

1. Find someone who uses judgment as a part of his or her job. Ask the person enough questions so that you can prepare a construction table (similar to the one in Table 16.2) for building rules.

2. One of the best ways to understand the problems of building an expert system is to use common, simple tasks that humans find easy. Try building a construction table for the task of tying a bow on your shoes. Although it seems simple and trivial, a complete set of rules will be a big challenge.

3. Using any microcomputer expert system shell you can find, prepare a report listing and explaining each of its parts and features. (There are several shells within the public domain; for example, the EXSYS Demo of EXSYS Version 3 is available from Exsys, Inc., P.O. Box 75158, Contr. Sta. 14, Albuquerque, NM 97194.)

4. Prepare a talk that explains other methods of representing ingknowledge. Read about semantic nets and frames.

# Programming

Near the end of World War II, a German soldier named Konrad Zuse escaped the oncoming Soviet army by secretly driving a truck through southern Germany into Switzerland. Zuse hoped to be captured by the U.S. Army, rather than the Soviets, because he had in his possession one of the first electronic digital computers ever constructed. Perhaps, he reasoned, the British or Americans would allow him to complete his work in peace. But more important than the computer was Zuse's fundamental work on a new mathematical notation for programming the machine. Zuse had already worked out the details of a notation for communicating ideas to a machine, details that would influence all of computing for the next forty years.

The basic concepts of modern programming are refinements of Zuse's programming language. These concepts are put to work every day by contemporary programmers, who convey ideas called algorithms to computers, in a notation

called a *programming language*. An **algorithm** is a step-by-step list of instructions for solving a problem. For example, an algorithm could be designed to do a calculation, move data, or control a monitor. Algorithms are expressed in a **programming language**, a formalized notation that allows algorithms to be represented in a rigorous and precise way. Because there is little room for an ambiguous or imprecise idea in an algorithm, most programming languages differ significantly from natural languages like English.

The word processing and spreadsheet software we discussed in previous chapters are elaborate algorithms written in a language that a computer can "understand." But occasionally a problem crops up that can't be solved efficiently with a prepackaged program. When this occurs, the only alternative is to write a new program that solves the problem. Even if you have someone else write the program, you should know something about programming in order to discuss the program.

In this chapter, you will see examples of programs written in several languages, and you will learn about different programming languages, the technique called *structured programming*, how to select a programming language, and very high-level languages.

## THE COMPUTER TOWER OF BABEL

### Machine Language versus Programming Languages

There is only one language a computer can run without modification: machine language. *Machine language programs* are nothing more than long sequences of binary numbers that have meaning for the computer. Programs written in other languages must be translated into machine language before they can be used to control a computer.

Machine language programs are the most elemental, or low-level, form of encoded algorithms. Seldom are they used to program computers directly. To understand why, consider the following example of low-level programming. Suppose you tell a friend how to go to a nearby store to get a quart of milk. Here is a list of the low-level instructions you might use.

*1.* Lean forward in your chair.

*2.* Push up with your hands and legs.

*3.* Raise up into a standing position.

*4.* Move your left foot forward.

*5.* Move your right foot forward.

    ...

*98.* Grasp the door knob with your right hand.

*99.* Turn the handle clockwise.

As you can see, these are extremely meticulous and tedious instructions. Although they accomplish the task, they are too detailed to repeat every time you want milk. To get around the need for such detailed instructions, you might compress the same meaning into fewer, more powerful words.

*1.* Stand up and walk out the door.

*2.* Get into your car and drive to the store.

*3.* Go into the store and get a quart of milk.

*4.* Pay for the milk and leave the store.

    ....

*12.* Get out of your car and come back into the house.

*13.* Give me the milk and sit down.

Similarly, if you use a programming language instead of machine language, you can express the same meaning with fewer instructions. For this reason, contemporary programmers use programming languages rather than machine language.

## Translation of Programs

People learn early in life how to translate the command "go to the store" into the numerous instructions to lean forward, stand up, walk, and so forth. A computer cannot learn a language by itself (at least not yet), so it must be programmed to translate all programs (except, of course, machine language programs) into machine language before they can be processed.

A **translator** is a program for converting other programs from one language to another. It is a powerful tool for increasing a programmer's productivity. Instead of giving detailed instructions in machine language, the programmer can give general directions at a higher level of abstraction, in a programming language, let a trans-

**Figure 17.1**
The difference between compilers and interpreters

To Compute, or not to . . .

French version → Translation → English version    Speaker

**(a) Translation by Compiling**

To Compute, or not to . . .

French version → Interpret → Speaker

**(b) Translation by Direct Interpretation**

lator fill in the machine-language details, and obtain the proper results in a shorter time.

A translator reads an input program, called the **source program**, and converts the lines in the source program one by one into another language. The converted program is the **target program.** Both the source and target programs do exactly the same thing, but they are encoded in different languages.

## Compilers and Interpreters

Translation can be done in two radically different ways. A **compiler** is a translator that translates and executes a program in separate stages, whereas an **interpreter** is a translator that translates and executes your program in only one stage.

To understand the difference between compiling a program and interpreting it, consider two ways for an American to translate a French document into an English speech. Using the *compiler* method, the American speaker would convert the French document into English *before* giving the speech. Using the *interpreter* method, the American would convert the French document into English, line by line, *while* giving the speech (see Figure 17.1). This removes the need for creating an intermediate English document, but the speaker would have to convert the French document into English each time it is presented.

*The Computer Tower of Babel*   **463**

A program can be either interpreted or compiled. If interpreted, no translated document is produced; each time the program is executed, it must be translated. If it is compiled, an output document is produced so that the translation need never be done again. The compiler program takes the following steps:

1. Translate the source program into an equivalent **object program**, an incomplete, intermediate program that must be linked with other programs before it is run.

2. Link the object program with other support programs, producing an equivalent target program written in machine language.

3. Execute the target program.

In the second step, the object program is read by a **linker program**, which converts the object program into machine language and combines it with operating system programs for writing lines of text on the screen, multiplying numbers, controlling the disks, and so on. This linking ties the program to a particular operating system, which is why application programs written for one operating system won't run on an identical computer that uses a different operating system.

Compilers produce fast, compact, and efficient machine language programs. They are the translators most frequently used by professional programmers. Compiled programs run much faster than interpreted programs because there is no translation; that is done before the program is run. However, the three steps (compile, link, and execute) interfere with programming productivity because they take extra time and attention.

Interpreters are good for novice programmers and professionals testing new programs. In fact, running a BASIC program via an interpreter is a good way to learn how to write simple programs, because the response is instantaneous: Your program's results are produced without inconvenient stages. Errors can be corrected and the program reinterpreted again and again until it is correct. However, because interpreters repeatedly translate and execute statements one at a time, they are slow. Moreover, the source program must coexist in memory with the interpreter while it is running. This usually means less memory is available for long programs.

BASIC, Lisp, APL, LOGO, and many other programming languages are usually interpreted. COBOL, FORTRAN, Pascal, C, and Ada are usually compiled. However, there are BASIC and Lisp compilers, and there are Pascal and C interpreters. So the choice is yours.

## High-Level Languages (HLL)

**Low-level programming languages**, such as various assembly languages, translate one for one into machine instructions. **Assembly language** is a symbolic machine language that uses mnemonic codes (ADD for addition, MUL for multiplication) in place of numbers and variable names instead of binary memory locations. Assembly language programs are compiled by an **assembler**, a translator that converts the mnemonic codes into machine language numbers. Low-level languages like assembly language are cryptic and require extra training and effort to comprehend.

**Figure 17.2**
A BASIC program to
compute PROFIT

```
NEW
10 INPUT "Enter number units sold:   ", UNITS
20 INPUT "Enter price per unit:   ", PRICE
30 INPUT "Enter cost per unit:   ", COST
40 PROFIT = UNITS * (PRICE - COST)
50 PRINT "Profit $", PROFIT
Ok
RUN
Enter number units sold:   300
Enter price per unit:  7
Enter cost per unit:  4.5
Profit $          750
```

In contrast, each "sentence" in a high-level language translates into two or more machine language instructions. A high-level programming language resembles a combination of English and mathematics. English keywords make the language readable, and a certain amount of mathematical formalism removes the ambiguity found in natural language. Indeed, a **high-level language (HLL)** is a restricted, formalized, and abbreviated version of a natural language. Its purpose is to express algorithms in a concise and unambiguous manner. Most programming languages are high-level languages.

### A Sample BASIC Program

Many computers come equipped with a BASIC interpreter as part of their system software. For this reason, we first use BASIC to illustrate a simple high-level language program. Suppose you want to compute the formula

$$E = U * (P - C)$$

where

$E$ = profit
$U$ = units sold
$P$ = price per unit
$C$ = cost per unit

Figure 17.2 shows a program written in BASIC, for doing so. You can type the program into your computer after first loading the BASIC interpreter. When you type NEW, the BASIC interpreter is told to begin a new program. It then allows you

**Figure 17.3**
A Pascal program to
compute PROFIT

```
PROGRAM PROFIT;

    VAR PROFIT      :   REAL;
        UNITS_SOLD  :   REAL;
        PRICE       :   REAL;
        COST        :   REAL;

    BEGIN
        WRITE ('Enter number units sold');
        READLN (UNITS_SOLD);
        WRITE  ('Enter price per unit');
        READLN (PRICE);
        WRITE  ('Enter cost per unit');
        READLN (COST);
        PROFIT := UNITS_SOLD * (PRICE - COST);
        WRITELN ('Profit $', PROFIT)
    END.
```

to enter commands as a list of numbered statements. After you have entered the program, typing RUN causes the interpreter to execute each statement one at a time.

When the program is executed, line 10 sends the prompt "Enter Number of Units Sold:" to the screen and waits for your response. Whatever number you type is stored in the memory location identified by the name UNITS_SOLD. Lines 20 and 30 do the same thing for PRICE and COST. PROFIT is calculated in line 40; the PRINT statement in line 50 tells the computer to display the answer on the screen.

*A Sample Pascal Program*

Pascal is a good language to illustrate the nature of normally compiled languages such as C, Ada, Modula-2, and PL/I. Pascal programs are divided into two sections: data definition and instruction processing. The *data definition section* is designated by the keyword VAR. All *variables* to be used in the program must be declared at the beginning of the program, inside the VAR section. A **variable** is a memory location that has been given a name. The *processing section* contains all actions to be carried out and the order to carry them out in. It begins with the keyword BEGIN and ends with the keyword END.

Figure 17.3 shows a simple Pascal program for computing profit. The VAR section tells the compiler to make PROFIT, UNITS_SOLD, PRICE, and COST variables. The VAR section also declares that these variables are real numbers (signed numbers with decimal points), so they can store dollars and cents. The processing section follows. As in BASIC, the first statement is done, then the next statement, and so on. Although the syntax for the Pascal processing section of Figure 17.3 is slightly more complicated than that for the BASIC statements in Figure 17.2, both programs accomplish the same task in the same general way.

Because Pascal programs are compiled rather than interpreted, you must compile, link, and execute this program before any answer can be obtained. First, the source program PROFIT is read by the Pascal compiler program and converted into an object program that can be thought of as halfway to machine language. Then the linker program converts the object program into a machine language file that can be run by typing its name.

## STRUCTURED PROGRAMMING

Knowledge of a programming language is only one of the skills required of a programmer. The most important skill is knowing when and how to apply the right techniques. In a sense, the language is a paintbrush; the computer, a canvas; and the programmer, an artist. Knowing how to mix colorful paints doesn't guarantee a work of art. Similarly, knowing about computers and a programming language is no assurance that you can produce a high-quality program.

### Steps in Programming

A programmer takes a written list of specifications and uses it to write a program that solves a specified problem. The programmer takes the first steps.

- Design an algorithm.
- Code it in a programming language.

The computer does the next steps.

- Translate the source program into the target program.
- Execute the target program.

The programmer takes the final steps.

- Debug the program. (Program errors are called *bugs*, and removing errors is called **debugging.**)
- Redesign, correcting for major errors, and recode.

This cycle is repeated until all errors have been removed and the program works as it should, meeting the original specifications. In some cases, the program is tested more than 100 times before all errors are removed.

Much of a programmer's time is spent debugging. This can to some extent be avoided by properly selecting a programming language. A high-level language is a good tool for minimizing bugs. But a high-level language isn't enough; a programming methodology is also needed. To minimize the time spent debugging and increase the availability of high-quality software, professional programmers have developed structured programming.

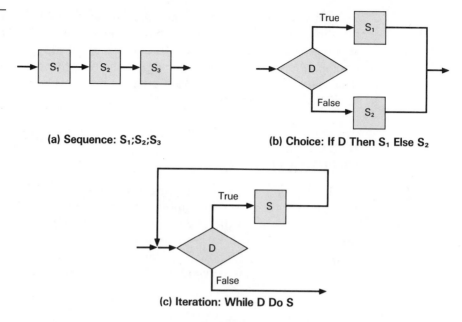

(a) Sequence: S₁;S₂;S₃

(b) Choice: If D Then S₁ Else S₂

(c) Iteration: While D Do S

## Structured Programs

In most disciplines, a "divide-and-conquer" approach is used; that is, a large, complex project is divided into several smaller, simpler projects. Large programs are difficult to write, so programmers have their own version of divide and conquer, called **structured programming** or *modular programming*, which is a programming methodology that involves the systematic design of software.

A fundamental principle of structured programming is *software reductionism*, which is the idea that complex programs can be reduced to a collection of logical parts or modules. Each **module** corresponds to a particular program function and can be treated as a separate entity. This simple idea is very effective for reducing errors in programs and lowering the cost of developing new software. When a programmer uses reductionism to design and write a program, the result is a *structured program*.

Structured programs can be reduced to elementary building blocks called **control structures,** which are statements that control the order other program statements are executed in. Every program can be constructed from the following three control structures:

1. *Sequence*. This control structure causes a program to execute statements placed one after the other in that sequence. Figure 17.4(a) shows the order of statement execution in a sequence of three statements (S₁, S₂, S₃).

2. *Choice*. When this control structure is used, statements in a program may or may not be executed, depending on a decision made during program execution. If the decision results in a true condition, one path is taken; otherwise, the other path is taken. Both paths finally merge at a single point, where program execution continues. Figure 17.4(b) shows an example. If D is true,

**Figure 17.5**
A structured BASIC
program that com-
putes an average of
*N* numbers

```
100 SUM  = 0                          'SEQUENCE OF 3 STATEMENTS...
110 COUNT= 0                          'COUNT HOW MANY INPUTS
120 INPUT "Enter # of NUMBERs "; N
125 WHILE N > COUNT 'ITERATION...
130     INPUT NUMBER                  'SEQUENCE INSIDE ITERATION...
140     SUM = SUM + NUMBER
150     COUNT = COUNT + 1
160 WEND                              'LOOP ENDS
170 AVG = SUM / COUNT
180 PRINT AVG
190 END
```

statement $S_1$ is executed; otherwise, statement $S_2$ is executed. IF designates the decision; THEN designates the path to be followed if the condition is true; and ELSE designates the path to be followed if the condition is false.

3. *Iteration.* Often called a *loop*, this control structure causes statements to be executed repeatedly until some termination condition is reached. Figure 17.4(c) shows a loop. As long as D remains true, the program repeatedly executes statement S. As soon as D becomes false, the loop terminates, and the program executes the next statement following the loop. WHILE designates the condition that is checked each time the loop is repeated; DO marks the statement to be repeated. The loop in Figure 17.4(c) reads, "While D is true, do statement S."

A typical program is composed of hundreds of these fundamental components put together like Lego blocks or Tinker Toys.

In a structured program, these three control structures are the only ones used. Another characteristic of a structured program is that each control structure and each program module should have only one entry point and one exit point. When completed, a structured program has two major advantages over a nonstructured program: It is more likely to work correctly because it is simple, and it can be easily modified, enhanced, and understood by someone else.

## A Sample Structured BASIC Program

Consider Figure 17.5, which shows a program that uses two of the three fundamental control structures—a loop and sequence statements. The loop begins with the keyword WHILE and ends with WEND. Indentations in the program indicate that

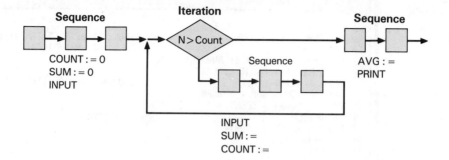

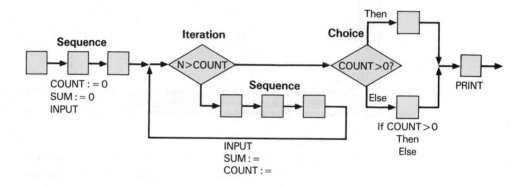

**Figure 17.6**
Two versions of a program to compute an average of *N* numbers. The first version **(a)** is the program given in Figure 17.5. In **(b)** a choice structure has been added.

---

the preceding statement contains the indented sequence of statements. Thus, within the loop, there is a sequence of three statements—those in lines 130, 140, and 150.

This program accepts a list of numbers from the keyboard, computes their average, and prints the average. But it contains a bug. If no input is entered at the keyboard, COUNT remains at zero, and the division by zero in line 170 causes the program to crash. We can fix this bug by using a choice structure to test for a zero value of COUNT. To do so, we change line 170 to read

170 IF COUNT 0 THEN AVG = SUM / COUNT ELSE AVG = 0

This is called an IF-THEN-ELSE statement. Figure 17.6 compares the two versions of the program.

We could have written the program in an unstructured manner. For example, instead of the IF statement we added to line 170, we could have used a GOTO statement—a command to go to a specified line, thereby skipping over other statements.

```
170 IF COUNT 0 GOTO 175
172  AVG = 0
173  GOTO 180
175 AVG = SUM / COUNT
```

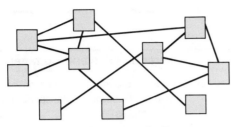 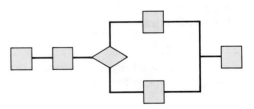

**(a) Typical Structure of a Program Containing GOTOs**

**(b) Typical Structure of a Program Without GOTOs**

**Figure 17.7**
Effect of GOTOs on program structure

But GOTO statements are forbidden in structured programming because they violate the restriction to use only sequence, choice, and iteration control structures. Figure 17.7 illustrates the effect of using many GOTO statements in a BASIC program. Programs without GOTO statements are easier to understand and, thus normally have fewer bugs.

## SELECTING A PROGRAM-MING LANGUAGE

Every programming language has its loyal followers, but no single programming language is best for all applications. The following list shows a small sample of the more than 400 programming languages that exist:

| *Problem or Application Area* | *Some Recommended Languages* |
|---|---|
| Numerical | BASIC, FORTRAN, APL, Pascal |
| Data files | COBOL, PL/I, dBASE II/dBASE III |
| Text processing | Lisp, SNOBOL |
| Simulation | Simscript, GASP, Simula, GPSS |
| Education | LOGO, Pascal |
| Factory control | Forth, machine language, APT |

Table 17.1 presents a more detailed view of some of the most popular programming languages. The choices can be overwhelming, but here are a few guidelines to help you choose which to use. First, decide what type of problem is to be solved. For instance, using a text-processing language to solve a numerical problem will end in disaster. Next, consider compatibility with your machine, operating system, other programs, and other files. This is called *system compatibility* and is important if you want the language to fit in with an existing system of hardware and software. Finally, consider technical features such as the readability and maintainability of programs written in the language and the language's input/output abilities, calculating abilities, text-processing features, control and data structures, processing efficiency, and portability. In the following sections, we take a closer look at these guidelines.

**Table 17.1**
**Popular Programming Languages**

| Name | Origin | Characteristics and Comments |
|------|--------|------------------------------|
| Ada (for Augusta Ada Byron, colleague of Charles Babbage) | From 1979 to 1982 by Honeywell for U.S. Dept. of Defense | Designed to control real-time processing problems. Resembles Pascal but has many more features |
| APL (A Programming Language) | In mid-1960s by Ken Iverson, a mathematician at IBM | Tremendously compact, powerful language. Highly interactive; interpreted |
| BASIC (Beginners All-Purpose Symbolic Instruction Code) | In mid-1960s by John Kemeny and Thomas Kurtz at Dartmouth | Easily learned language. Widely used on small computers. Many incompatible versions exist |
| C | In 1972 by Dennis Ritchie at Bell Laboratories | Originally designed to write system software. Very portable; generates fast compact code |
| COBOL (COmmon Business Oriented Language) | In 1960 by a group of users and manufacturers | By far the most popular language for commercial applications. Creates verbose, English-like, understandable code |
| FORTRAN (FORmula TRANslator) | In 1957 by IBM | Used for scientific and mathematical programming |
| Pascal (for Blaise Pascal, French mathematician) | From 1968 to 1971 by Professor Niklaus Wirth of Switzerland | Originally designed as a teaching vehicle to encourage structured programming. Small, efficient compilers. Limited I/O features |
| PL/I (Programming Language 1) | In 1966 by IBM | Designed to combine the best features of COBOL and FORTRAN. Used primarily on large computers |
| RPG (Report Program Generator) | In mid-1960s by IBM | Allows reports to be created quickly and easily. Uses specification forms rather than programming statements. Popular on business minicomputers |

## System Compatibility

An obvious first step in selecting a programming language is to make sure your computer has enough RAM to run the compiler or interpreter. Many compilers also require large amounts of disk space. They may occupy several floppy disks and can make several passes over the source program during conversion to machine language. If this is the case, it can be inconvenient or impossible to use floppy disk drives, and a hard disk may be needed.

You should choose the operating system you want to use before you choose a programming language. Most computers support more than one operating system; for example, an IBM PC can run programs for MS-DOS, OS/2, UNIX, CP/M, and several other operating systems. But a certain programming language may work under only one operating system. Although the language translator may work with the desired operating system, it may or may not be compatible with other programs that work under the same operating system. A FORTRAN program under MS-DOS, for example, may not be compatible with a Pascal program also under MS-DOS.

Lack of compatibility can happen at several other levels. For example, the data files created by a Pascal program may not be readable by a BASIC program. Similarly, a program written in Pascal and translated into machine language may not be usable by a BASIC program that has also been translated into machine language. However, if the two are compatible, considerable time might be saved by using the previously written Pascal program as part of the new BASIC program.

One major advantage of translation by compiling is the ability to combine programs from different languages into larger, more powerful programs through linking. When programs are written so that they can be used over again they are called **routines,** or *subroutines*; a routine is reused by *calling* it. The linker program combines previously written routines with operating system routines to complete the translation of your program into a machine-level program that will run on a particular computer. If you plan to use a variety of programming languages on one machine, it may be worthwhile to buy all the translators from one company to ensure compatibility among them.

## Readability and Maintainability

Readability and maintainability are important in the business world because some programs "live" for twenty years—far beyond the time the original programmers are likely to be around. Thus a readable and understandable program is a necessity for large banks, insurance companies, and corporations. If a million-dollar program cannot be maintained, it becomes worthless.

A programming language affects readability and maintainability in several ways.

- Syntax determines the grammar of the language. Familiarity refers to how similar the language is to natural languages.
- Modularity affects the degree to which the program can be divided into easily comprehended parts.
- Structuredness refers to whether the language provides good structured programming control constructs and encourages the use of well-structured programs.

### Syntax and Familiarity

The syntax of a language determines its parts of speech and keywords. For example, the syntax of a COBOL program is very verbose and English-like so that with a little practice anyone can understand it. COBOL uses familiar English keywords like SUBTRACT, MOVE, TO, FROM, and PERFORM. The following fragment from a program that prints a mailing list illustrates COBOL's syntax:

```
PROCEDURE DIVISION.
MAIN-ROUTINE.
    OPEN OUTPUT MAIL-LABELS-FILE
        INPUT ADDRESS-FILE.
    READ ADDRESS-FILE
        AT END
```

```
        MOVE "NO" TO MORE-INPUT.
    PERFORM PRINT-ADDRESS-LOOP
        UNTIL MORE-INPUT IS EQUAL TO "NO".
    CLOSE MAIL-LABELS-FILE
        ADDRESS-FILE.
    STOP RUN.
```

COBOL programs are self-documenting, portable, and very good at handling files and reports; but they are weak at processing mathematical data. COBOL is used more than any other language for developing large data processing programs.

FORTRAN, in contrast, uses a more mathematical syntax. For example,

```
DO 100 I=1,10
IF ( NUM-99 ) 2,3,3
X = SQRT( B**2 - 4.0 * A * C )
```

To a mathematician or engineer, FORTRAN's algebraic notation is familiar.

## Modularity

Modularity is important because it helps make large programs understandable. Each module can be understood as a "chunk" or box, and then larger modules can be composed of smaller modules. One feature of a modular language's syntax is the requirement to state explicitly where a module gets incoming data; this helps ensure the linkages among modules are well understood.

Modula-2 is an example of a highly modular programming language. The following is a simple Modula-2 module that imports Read, Write, Sqrt, Sin, and Cos functions from two other modules:

```
MODULE Main;
FROM InOut IMPORT Read, Write;
FROM Math IMPORT Sqrt, Sin, Cos;
BEGIN
    .
    .                    ← The module's processing statements belong here.
    .
END.
```

BASIC is a counterexample; most versions provide little support for cleanly separating a large program into independent modules.

Both Modula-2 and its predecessor, Pascal, were invented to be implemented efficiently on computers. Pascal was designed by Niklaus Wirth as a programming language that would teach students "the correct way" to program. It was one of the first languages to be designed with a familiar, consistent, and structured syntax. However, Pascal lacked the modularity of other languages, so Wirth went back to the drawing board to design Modula-2 to incorporate modularity, greater consistency, and extensive structuredness. Many other languages have been patterned after Pascal because of its clarity and elegance.

## Structuredness

Structuredness is the degree to which a language conforms to the structured programming concept that all modules and all program statements should have a single entry point and a single exit point. For example, there is only one entry point and one exit point for the statements in the following Pascal fragment:

```
IF A=0 THEN
     B:=100
ELSE
     B:=200;
WHILE B<200 DO
     BEGIN
     WriteLn( B );
     ReadLn( B )
END;
CASE B OF
10: A:= 0;
20: A:=10;
END;
```

Each of these statements has a single starting and ending point within the program. The IF-THEN-ELSE statement flows into the WHILE-DO statement; the BEGIN-END statement is nested within the WHILE-DO statement, and they both terminate in the same place; the CASE-OF-END statement executes either 10: or 20:, but not both, and then terminates at the END statement.

In contrast, BASIC and FORTRAN have no way to enforce structured programming. Here is an example using BASIC.

```
FOR I=1 TO 10
     IF I=J THEN GOTO 100
NEXT I
     [ ... ]
100 PRINT I
```

The IF-THEN-GOTO statement violates the requirement that there should be only one exit point because there are two paths out of the FOR-NEXT loop. One path leads out the bottom of the loop and would be taken after the loop has executed ten times; the other path jumps from the middle of the loop to line 100 if the value in variable I is the same as the value in J.

Because FORTRAN, BASIC, and COBOL were all invented before the idea of structured programming, they make it easy to write convoluted programs that lack structuredness. ALGOL (*ALGO*rithmic *L*anguage), the earliest language developed with good structure, was created in the early 1960s in Europe and used extensively there until Pascal replaced it. PL/I borrowed many of ALGOL's structured features. Pascal, C, Modula-2, and Ada are also derivatives of ALGOL.

*The number and quality of programming languages available for personal computers continues to proliferate.*

For several years the conventional wisdom held that if users wanted to program their personal computers, they would use MS-Basic or IBM PC Basic, since these are often supplied free with the machines. The average computer user, the thinking went, wasn't interested enough in programming to go out and buy a package.

That belief has been proven incorrect, largely through the phenomenal sales of one product, Borland International's Turbo Pascal. Turbo Pascal has sold more than half a million copies since it first appeared in 1983, and its sales show no sign of abating, according to a recent survey by market research firm Infocorp of Cupertino, California.

"Microcomputer users who formerly were not programming have now taken to it because of such products as Turbo Pascal and True Basic," says Martha Ash, assistant manager of microcomputer support for Northwestern University in Evanston, Illinois. The trend is toward menu-driven systems and documentation that is written for people who are not computer experts, she explains.

"There is a sense that people who have been using micros for several years and are familiar with spreadsheets, word processors, graphics programs, etc. are now asking what else they can do," Ash says. "Programming has become a natural alternative for people who several years ago would have taken one look at GW Basic and said, 'Forget this.'"

A brief examination indicates that several new languages are gaining popularity on microcomputers. Attributes common to this generation of microcomputer languages are emphasis on increased ease of use, modular approach, and low cost.

Borland International of Scotts Valley, California, led the way with its modular-systems approach to languages, first with the $69.95 Turbo Pascal, and more recently with the $99.95 Turbo Prolog. Both programs include interactive editors (similar to Wordstar), language compilers, windowing support, debuggers, and graphics support.

Like several other vendors, Borland offers add-ons to its entry-level language systems. For Turbo Pascal you can buy math coprocessor support (for floating-point arithmetic), binary-

## Input/Output Abilities

I/O processing is important because it determines how programs deal with printers, keyboards, screens, and other peripheral devices.

A good I/O-handling language must be able to read and write sequential, direct, and indexed files. Recall that a *direct file* is one in which each record of the file can be directly accessed; an *indexed file* can be accessed through a (sorted) index key. COBOL and PL/I incorporate these file types into the language, which makes it reasonably simple to store and retrieve data from large data files. Moreover, COBOL and PL/I are often extended to let them communicate with a database management system.

Most BASIC interpreters provide special verbs for creating graphics, but writing to the graphics screen from FORTRAN, Pascal, and C is difficult unless these languages are augmented with special graphics routines.

coded decimal support, a tutorial program, and other options.

A language development system that emphasizes ease of use is the Macscheme system for the Apple Macintosh. "Macscheme has gone through several revisions since its release last year," says Anne Hartheimer, president of Semantic Microsystems Inc. "With each release, we try to make it easier to use."

Macscheme is a $125 system that includes a Scheme interpreter, editor, and windowing system on the Macintosh and a toolbox to work with the Macintosh's graphics interface. Semantic Microsystems has also developed additional modules for Macscheme, including a complete programming development system that allows Macintosh applications to be designed, written, and used without any other programming aids, Hartheimer says.

The new entries in the market are still predominantly versions of languages that have been popular for years, such as Basic, Pascal, and C. But the Turbo Pascal success formula is

being applied by some vendors to more esoteric languages—such as Lisp and Prolog—developed for artificial intelligence programming.

According to Stuart Kurtz, associate professor of computer science at the University of Chicago, Turbo Prolog and Macscheme are "increasingly being used as development and exploratory languages for artificial intelligence software and expert systems. Lisp and Lisplike languages are beginning to dominate the undergraduate curricula of many computer science departments. Macscheme and Turbo Prolog are extending that dominance."

Language implementations geared toward novice programmers, as well as engineers and computer science professors, are filling the market. The biggest benefits for corporate users are better performance, lower prices, portable languages, improved ease of use, and products better geared to solving individual programming problems.

Source: Don Crabb, *Infoworld*, 4 August 1986, pp. 33–34.

Pascal, C, and most other languages can print a report on the printer, but COBOL and PL/I are especially good for formatting and printing reports. If your needs are limited to creating business reports, RPG might be an even better choice. It is a special-purpose report-generating programming language. RPG allows a programmer to write a report program by filling out several forms that describe the way the report will appear on the printed page. An RPG compiler takes this sample report and turns it into a program.

### Arithmetic Computation

COBOL and FORTRAN represent two extremes of ability to perform arithmetic calculations. FORTRAN was designed to do such mathematical calculations like exponentiation, logarithms, and transcendental functions. COBOL is limited to simple expressions. Compare this COBOL statement

```
COMPUTE INVENTORY = YEAR-TO-DATE-INVENTORY +
    ( ORDERED * PRICE ).
```

with the FORTRAN statement

```
HYPOT = SQRT ( A**2 + B**2 )
```

The differences may seem inconsequential until you try to do a calculation that doesn't exist in the language. For example, Pascal has no exponentiation operator, so our sample FORTRAN calculation can't be done directly in Pascal.

## Text Processing

Pascal, FORTRAN, COBOL, and most other widely used programming languages have difficulty processing characters and strings of text. Therefore, special-purpose symbol-processing languages like Lisp and SNOBOL were invented. Developed in the 1960s, these languages handle nonnumeric data.

Instead of adding, subtracting, and multiplying numbers, a text-processing language joins, separates, and inserts characters of text; searches for patterns of characters; and performs other related operations. For example, in Lisp, the CONS and CDR operators retrieve the first character and trailing characters of an alphanumeric list. These operators might be used, for example, to separate the first and last names of a full name.

Lisp has become the premier language of artificial intelligence because of its ability to handle lists and make associations and because of its familiarity to the artificial intelligence community. SNOBOL (invented by Griswald while at Bell Labs) is used to process and analyze text.

## Control Structures

Recall that a *control structure* is any statement in a programming language that controls the order other statements are to be executed in. We've given examples of several control statements, including IF-THEN-ELSE (for making two-way decisions), FOR (for repeating or looping), and CASE (for multiple-way decisions). In theory, every conceivable program can be written with only three control structures: sequence (one statement following another), iteration (loops), and choice (IF-THEN-ELSE). In practice, additional control statements are added to a language to make it more convenient for a programmer to use. For example, in Pascal derivatives, the CASE statement expands the IF-THEN-ELSE statement into a multiple-branching statement, and the CALL or PERFORM statements of FORTRAN and COBOL permit modules to be invoked from a main program, thus allowing modularity.

The control structures used in Ada are particularly interesting. Ada was created by the Department of Defense to reduce the huge expense of developing real-time systems—ones that could keep up with events happening in the real world. An Ada program can be divided into modules that run at the same time on multiple processors. Each module runs in parallel with the others. But when one module needs information computed by another parallel module, it exchanges this information through a **rendezvous statement,** a control structure that forces one module to wait while the other module catches up, thus synchronizing the two modules.

Other control structures include special statements for catching errors or unusual occurrences such as bad input data, a missing file, or an error in the program. These are called **exception statements** because they handle I/O errors. In PL/I, for example, the ON ERROR GOTO statement takes care of I/O exceptions, attempts to divide by zero, and handles any other unusual circumstances that might arise when the program is executed. Some versions of BASIC have ON ERROR GOTO control statements, as do many extended versions of Pascal.

## Data Structures

A **data structure** is a collection of values and associated information that provides a method of organizing and manipulating many values together as a unit. A simple example of a data structure is an **array,** an organized collection of data in a row-and-column format. The structure of an array makes it easy to update or retrieve any item in the array by referencing its position within the array. For example, in FORTRAN, a DIMENSION statement reserves an area of memory, as in

```
DIMENSION SCORES(100)
```

This DIMENSION statement establishes SCORES as the name of a one-dimensional numerical array with the ability to store one hundred values. You can think of this array as a single column of memory cells with one hundred rows; each row can store one number. This array might be used to store up to one hundred test scores in a way that lets you manipulate the scores easily, such as finding the highest test score in a list. To reference the number in the third row of SCORES, for example, the FORTRAN syntax says to enclose the index 3 inside parentheses, as in $X(3) = 3.14159$. This stores 3.14159 in the third memory cell of array X.

The following data structure in Pascal demonstrates how to express a list of names along with the street address and telephone number of each person:

```
VAR
    People : ARRAY[1..MAX] OF
            RECORD
                Name : string;
                Street: string;
                Tele: PhoneNumber
            END;
```

Data structures are also used to format external disk files. Again, in Pascal, the contents of a file can be clearly written as follows:

```
VAR
    DECK : FILE OF
            RECORD
                Name : PersonName;
                Age : 0..99;
                Bal : Dollars;
                Sex : ( Male, Female )
            END;
```

Here, the contents of the file are clearly designated and can be referenced later in the program by these same names.

FORTRAN and BASIC are especially deficient of data structures, whereas Pascal, Modula-2, Ada, Lisp, and most modern programming languages allow the programmer to define new types of data structures. The syntax data structure declarations in Pascal can be quite striking in their familiarity, consistency, and elegance.

## Processing Efficiency and Program Size

A program written in a high-level language trades speed for maintainability (ease of modification and improvement). It must be translated, and the translated program is larger and runs more slowly than if the program had been written initially in machine language. A program written in a high-level language is easier to understand and modify. If you expect to modify a program often, it is worthwhile to sacrifice speed and small size for maintainability and use a high-level language.

Most popular computer programs—such as Lotus 1-2-3, Symphony, Framework, and WordStar—are written in assembly language to achieve the greatest speed possible. However, unless you are an expert programmer and are going to sell a million copies of your program, using a high-level language is probably better.

The machine language version of a programming language may vary in size and speed, depending on how clever the compiler writers were. A "fast" compiler produces fast-running programs; a "compact" compiler produces small-sized programs. Depending on the compiler, the target programs compiled from typical Pascal or C programs may differ in size and speed by a factor of ten or more. One translator may produce very fast code but require twice the amount of memory as another translator to hold the running program.

**Benchmark programs** are usually used to measure the effectiveness of a compiler or an interpreter. One well-known benchmark program, the sieve of Eratosthenes, computes prime numbers; it is commonly used to compare the computational speed and memory requirements of programs.

## Portability

**Portability** refers to the ease with which a program can be moved from one machine to another—without modifications. The main method of achieving portability is to use a compiler for the other machine to recompile the source program. Suppose a Pascal program exists on an Apple computer, and you buy an IBM PC. If the source program is written in a portable version of Pascal, it can be copied onto an IBM PC disk (probably via communications), compiled by the IBM PC Pascal compiler, and then run on the IBM computer.

Few programs are 100 percent portable; instead, they must be modified before being recompiled for the new computer. If portability is important, plan for it in advance. Avoid machine-dependent features of programming languages, and consider buying compatible compilers for use on all the machines.

Another problem exists for programmers who aspire to sell programs: licensing. A software license is a contract between the programmer and the vendor of the compiler; it specifies limitations on the use of programs translated by the vendor's compiler. For example, a BASIC program may be compiled into machine language using a certain company's compiler. That company may prohibit the sale of the target program without its consent or payment for each copy sold. Some licensing agreements state that the target program produced from a compiler may be resold, run on more than one machine, or copied only after payment of a royalty to the compiler's vendor. (For more on these legal issues, see Chapter 19.)

COBOL is probably the most portable programming language because it has been standardized by the American National Standards Committee. FORTRAN 77 is a 1977 standardized dialect of FORTRAN; BASIC, Pascal, and many other languages have also been standardized. Manufacturers of programming language compilers often add features to standardized languages, thus creating nonstandard dialects.

Pascal is a classic example of a language that suffers from too many nonstandard dialects. Rarely can a Pascal program written on one machine be compiled and run on another machine without extensive modifications. This situation exists because Pascal was originally designed to teach programmers rather than to be a commercial programming language. Because of its elegance, Pascal was adapted to the real world of software through a variety of extensions. The most notable extension was done by the University of California at San Diego, and is called UCSD Pascal. This dialect became one of the most widely used languages in the world, but it reduced the portability of Pascal programs from one version of Pascal to another because it greatly extended the original language.

C has become almost a standard language because no dialects extend the language. The K & R standard (defined in a book by Kernighan and Richie[1]) is almost univesally accepted as the definition of C. Moreover, it is easy to write a C compiler because C is very close to machine language yet similar to Pascal and other ALGOL derivatives. Thus many software developers use C to write programs for all sizes and brands of computers. In contrast, COBOL compilers are difficult to write and often take years to develop for a new machine.

---

1. Brian Kernighan and Dennis Ritchie, *The C Programming Language* (New Jersey: Prentice-Hall, 1978).

# A Word About . . . Tomorrow's Programming Environment

*The next three to five years will bring enormous change to the working environment of programmer/analysts in both the skills they will need and the tools they will use. Examining the current trends in hardware and software should help predict and explain these changes and their impact on these computer industry professionals.*

The most obvious and significant hardware trend is the ever-expanding capacity and power of the personal computer. The current generation of PCs offers the processing speed and capacity of an IBM 370/168 at a fraction of the cost; the Model 168 costs $3.4 million while the IBM Personal System/2 Model 80 with similar million of instructions per second (MIPS) power is approximately $11,000.

The availability of desktop MIPS and the move to provide unlimited storage for the PC will make the intelligent workstation the preferred tool for use by knowledge workers. Programmers and end users will use similar tools to assist them in their daily tasks.

With the proliferation of desktop power and storage for each individual, the trend to connect the computers in a corporation will accelerate. The programmer of the future will have an Integrated Services Digital Network and will use equipment manufactured to the international connectivity standards.

Although hardware issues definitely will affect the work of the programmer/analyst, software advances will be much more significant. Computer-assisted software (or system) engineering (CASE) will find widespread use during the next few years. Tools for analysis and design—many of them PC based—will continue to improve in functionality, ease of use and power. Programmer/analysts will be working with application generation software. Working with users, the systems analysts will jointly develop system specifications, prototypes and data definitions under the control of system generation software. Once the system's specifications are built, they can generate error-free code.

Once constructed, the system will be highly flexible—allowing different life cycle methodologies, generating different languages or versions of languages for differing file access systems—and will be controlled by powerful dictionaries. These generators will also build bridges to all existing application software.

Reusable code techniques will be used under the control of software systems. Graphics and text processors will become a key part of the programmer/analyst's documentation tool kit.

Programmers will need to be familiar with the techniques of building expert systems and integrating them into standard software systems. Analysts will be using relational data base technology to create data repositories.

To address these changes in hardware and software, programmer/analysts need to develop new skills.

Using expert system shell languages and being able to build powerful expert systems from scratch will be a necessary skill. Traditional data base design must be updated to reflect the influence of relational systems. With a renewed emphasis on data, all programmer/analysts will require a strong background in data analysis and data-driven design techniques. Because data bases of the future will likely be accessible by IBM SQL, people will need to know and understand this language.

As software productivity aids become increasingly important, programmers must learn these complex packages to do their jobs. And the increased emphasis on the font-end skills of analysis and design demand that all programmer/analysts possess these essential skills. Knowing how to use CASE tools will be critical, as will the ability to interface with users.

Source: Dennis Farley and David Nickolich, *ComputerWorld Focus*, 4 November 1987, p. 7.

# BEYOND HIGH-LEVEL LANGUAGES

## Very High-Level Languages (VHLL)

Clearly the best way to tell your friend to go to the store to get milk is to use an abstract notation such as English. In English, the algorithm for getting a quart of milk might look like the following:

*1.* Go to the store and buy a quart of milk.

*2.* Bring the quart of milk to me.

This "program" tells your friend *what* you want done but not *how* to do it. The difference between a **very high-level language (VHLL)** and the programming languages we have discussed until now is the difference between saying *what* to do and giving detailed directions of *how* to do it. A very high-level language (sometimes called a *fourth-generation language*) is a **nonprocedural language** because it describes what processing is to be done without specifying the particular procedures to be used to complete the processing.

Database query languages and report generator languages (see Chapter 12) are examples of restricted VHLLs. Only a few VHLL translators exist because software designers are just beginning to solve the difficult problems associated with machine translation of nonprocedural programs. The few that do exist are limited to special purposes, such as creating a report, controlling the dialog in a learning module, or answering complex queries for information. But VHLLs are the computer languages of the future because they simplify programming, increase a programmer's productivity, are easy to modify and maintain, and can be understood by almost anyone. We discuss only two broad categories of VHLLs: application generators and program generators.

## Application Generators

An **application generator (AG)** gives a detailed explanation of what data is to be processed rather than how to process the data in an application. It is similar to a report generator, but it expresses processing steps in a notation similar to a high-level language. Hence programs written for an application generator appear to be slightly procedural, as Figure 17.8 shows. Typically (but not always), application generators are extensions to the query facility of a database management system. As such, they assume the DBMS model of data. The example shown in Figure 17.8 is closely related to the dBASE III model of data.

Most AG translators are interpreters, not compilers; hence the AG program is directly interpreted. To run the application, you enter its name after the command DO. It is read into the AG translator and executed one statement at a time. In Figure 17.8, the application finds all CUSTOMER_FILE records whose value stored in the field named YTD is greater than a value supplied by the user (YTD MIN). It prints these records according to the report format stored in F1.

**Figure 17.8**
Example of an
application gener-
ator program

```
BEGIN
      ERASE
      STORE '      ' TO MIN
      @ 10,5 SAY ' Enter minimum search condition'
      @ 10,35 GET MIN
      READ
      ? ' Printing in progress...'
      USE CUSTOMER_FILE
      INDEX ON YTD TO ORDERED_FILE
      REPORT FORM F1 FOR YTD > MIN TO PRINT
      RELEASE MIN
      RETURN
END.
```

The following list explains the meaning of each command word in Figure 17.8:

- *ERASE.* Erase the monitor screen.

- *STORE ' ' TO MIN.* Store a blank in MIN (no value).

- *@ 10,5 SAY.* Prompt the user with the message "Enter minimum search condition". The prompt begins in line 10, column 5 of the screen.

- *@ 10,35 GET MIN.* Wait for the user to enter a value for MIN.

- *READ.* This forces the AG to read the previous two @ commands and save them for use later.

- *?* Display the message "Printing in progress...".

- *USE.* Select the file named CUSTOMER_FILE.

- *INDEX ON YTD.* Build a separate index file in ORDERED_FILE that is in order by YTD field values. Use this index file to retrieve records from the OR-DERED_FILE in ascending order by YTD.

- *REPORT.* Use a previously defined report form stored in F1 to print a report. The report selects only those records from the database that satisfy the search conditions YTD > MIN.

- *RELEASE.* No longer use MIN as a storage variable; release the memory space used by MIN.

- *RETURN.* Return to whatever you were doing before you began this application.

**Figure 17.9**
Sample dialog with
a program generator

```
BEGIN
        What is the name of the input variable?  MIN
        What prompt is to be used? Enter minimum search condition
        What is the name of the input file?  CUSTOMER_FILE
        Is the input file sorted?  No
        Do you want to sort it?  No
        Is the input file indexed?  No
        Do you want to index it?  Yes
        Index what field?  YTD
        Index what field?
        Do you want to calculate?  No
        Do you want a report?  Yes
        What is the report format file?  F1
        Do you want to print in order?  Yes
        Enter index or sort key name:  YTD
        Do you want to limit retrieval?  Yes
        Enter limit or search condition:  YTD > MIN
        Enter limit or search condition:
        Do you want a disk copy of print?  No
        Are you done?  Yes
END.
```

The STORE, @, and RELEASE commands are procedural statements because they describe processing steps. In contrast, the USE, INDEX, and REPORT commands don't describe how their processing is to be done; they are nonprocedural. For the most part, this program tells the computer what to do, not how to do it.

## Program Generators

A **program generator (PG)** is a translator that converts nonprocedural information into a procedural program. Instead of using very high-level language statements, a PG usually uses a question-and-answer dialog to determine what processing is to be done. Then it takes this nonprocedural information and uses it to write a program in some programming language, often BASIC or COBOL, which must in turn be translated into machine language or directly interpreted. Most PGs let you display and modify the program they produce.

To use a PG, simply answer its questions. Figure 17.9 provides an example. The program generated from the dialog in Figure 17.9 does the same thing as the AG program in Figure 17.8.

Sophisticated PGs usually ask many questions. You might be asked for information concerning menus, file organization, printer configuration, the color and dimensions of the screen, and so forth. The questions asked by a PG are nonprocedural, as you can see in Figure 17.9. However, PGs are restricted in what they do. For applications requiring a lot of formulas, interaction with a user, or sophisticated data processing, you will probably need to use another method. But for uncomplicated tasks, program generators are excellent.

## A Word About . . . Application Generators

*Everyone agrees that application generators can speed up and simplify the application building process as compared with traditional programming. But there is less agreement on what features belong in an application generator and how they should work.*

In the computer industry, when users embrace a concept, that same concept—under a plethora of different names—is introduced by a number of vendors. Such is the case with application generation. These tools come under various names, including development workbenches, fourth-generation languages, program generators and programmer productivity tools. Some 300 vendors offer such tools for mainframes and another 150 do for micro-based systems.

As if the sheer number of available products was not enough, these tools also employ different approaches to the tasks of simplification of development, modification, and ongoing support.

One such tact is to make an application generator an integral part of a data base management system. When these two components work in tandem, programmers can generate software that allows application programs to be written faster and better.

What are some of the features that should be provided by a DBMS with application generation facilities?

- Procedural features.
- Interface to high-level procedural languages, for example, Cobol, PL/I, Fortran, and APL.
- Interface to a low-level procedural language such as assembler.
- Full set of structured constructs.
- Performance monitoring, tuning, and enhancement features.
- Third-generation language programmer usability feature.
- Nonprocedural features.
- Query language.
- Report generator.
- Graphics generator.
- Relational front-end feature.
- Two-dimensional menu interface feature.
- Easy-to-use editors.
- Integrated and active data dictionary/directory.
- Data base design techniques.
- Data definition, data manipulation, data control features.
- Decision support system features.
- Financial modeling language.
- Statistical analysis.
- Interface to standard statistical packages.
- Support of electronic spreadsheets.
- Mainframe-microcomputer connection features.
- Programming languages on mainframe and equivalent counterpart on microcomputer.

## Summary

Programming is a challenging intellectual activity that some people do exceptionally well and enjoy. For most of us, however, it is a chore requiring dedication and skill. Most people who use computers won't become programmers because of the specialized knowledge required to do so.

Machine language programs are the most elementary, or low-level, form of coded algorithms, and have immediate meaning for the computer. Most application programs that require fast responses are written in the symbolic form of machine

- Separate versions that run stand-alone on both microcomputer and mainframe.
- Mainframe-to-microcomputer communication link.
- Extraction capability on mainframe for down-loading.
- Multiuser environment support feature.

The chief advantage of using an application generator integrated with a DBMS is that these tools speed the application-building process. Equally important, applications are easily and quickly modified, thus minimizing debugging problems and thereby reducing maintenance costs. As is the case with most products, however, there are trade-offs. Computer resource usage with these tools is high, a significant drawback. An application generator uses up to 50 percent more computer resources than does a third-generation language performing an equivalent function. This is because application generators make the computer do most of the drudge work that third-generation languages make people do.

The difference comes primarily in the usage of I/O operations, rather than CPU processing. Poor data base design could balloon this figure much higher. Further, since most of today's application generators are targeted to IBM 370-compatible machines, program transportability is poor.

Moreover, these tools do not handle computation-intensive work well. The application generators target the same computer spectrum as does Cobol—I/O-intensive character- or byte-crunching operations rather than CPU-intensive number-crunching operations.

For this reason, a scientific third-generation language such as Fortran should still be used for computational work. If an application requires both character crunching and number crunching, I suggest writing the program with an application generator but calling the third-generation language routines for computational work.

The point is that applications must be selected carefully. A banking deposit and withdrawal system with high-speed real-time requirements would be a poor choice for an environment in which to use an application generator.

Material requirements planning, however, with its integration of inventory, purchasing, bill of materials, engineering planning and accounting data bases, would be ideal for application generator implementation.

Source: Shaku Atre, *Computerworld*, 4 August 1986, p. 42.

language called assembly language. However, machine language isn't the appropriate tool for the computer user who is simply trying to solve a problem.

High-level languages (HLLs) are by far the most frequently used tools in programming. They let you write any program with a reasonable amount of clarity and maintainability.

Knowing the syntax of a programming language is only a small part of knowing how to program. Good programmers have a storehouse of knowledge about control structures, algorithms, and techniques of design. Many of these techniques are based on the methodology known as structured programming. In computing, software reductionism states that every program can be broken down into fundamental control structures. Thus a program can be designed as a collection of fundamental control structures; sequence, choice, and iteration are the most basic of these.

Selecting the right language involves many decisions. Does it work with the other programs and the operating system on your computer? Is it readable and maintainable? Are its input/output abilities, calculating abilities, text-processing features, control and data structures, intrinsic functions, and processing efficiency adequate? Is it portable?

Very high-level languages (VHLLs) broaden the range of people who can program. The goal of VHLL design is to emphasize *what* to do, rather than *how* to do it. Most VHLLs fail to accomplish this 100 percent of the time, but they all use some sort of nonprocedural notation to avoid excess programming detail. A VHLL may be restrictive, but it can increase productivity, often a hundredfold. Report generators can be used by anyone with a modest amount of training. To use very high-level application or program generators, more practice is needed.

---

## Key Terms

| | |
|---|---|
| algorithm | module |
| application generator (AG) | nonprocedural language |
| array | object program |
| benchmark programs | portability |
| compiler | program generator |
| control structures | programming language |
| data structure | routine |
| exception statement | source program |
| high-level language (HLL) | target program |
| interpreter | translator |
| intrinsic function | variable |
| linker program | very high-level language (VHLL) |
| low-level language | |

---

## Discussion Questions

1. Why can't a computer "understand" English instead of only programming languages?
2. Compare a translator who works for the United Nations with a computer program that translates HLL programs. Is the human translator more like a program compiler or an interpreter?
3. List and describe the steps in programming. Why are there so many steps?
4. What is structured programming, and what does it accomplish?
5. If you were going to select and use a programming language, what would your criteria be?

**6.** What is the difference between an application generator and a program generator?

---

## Exercises

**1.** What is the purpose of a linker program? Describe the steps needed to run a new program using the compiling approach to translation.

**2.** Give both low-level and high-level instructions (in English) for brushing your teeth. How might you characterize the difference between the two algorithms?

**3.** What is a program bug? How are bugs typically removed from a program?

**4.** Modify the BASIC program in Figure 17.5 so that only values greater than or equal to zero are allowed for $N$. (Use only the basic building blocks of IF-THEN-ELSE, WHILE, and sequence.)

**5.** Use the three building blocks of structured programming and the notation in Figure 17.6 to describe an algorithm for computing the following two values:

$A = \text{PAY} / 10$
$B = \text{PAY} / (A - 5)$

Assume PAY is entered by the user and $A$ and $B$ are printed out. What happens if $(A - 5)$ is zero?

**6.** Go to the library and read about the history of the following languages, including who invented them. (You may not be able to find them all, but do the best you can.)

    *a.* FORTRAN
    *b.* COBOL
    *c.* Pascal
    *d.* Ada
    *e.* Modula-2
    *f.* SNOBOL
    *g.* BASIC

**7.** Is it possible for two programs written for the same computer to be incompatible? If so, how?

**8.** Compare the functions in a spreadsheet such as Lotus 1-2-3 with the functions in a programming language such as BASIC, FORTRAN, or Pascal.

**9.** Modify the application generator program in Figure 17.8 so that only YTD values equal to zero are printed in the report.

# The Evolution of Computing

The history of the computer field is not about people who have been dead for centuries or about events that only historians remember. Many of the key people are still alive and at work. Most of the significant technical developments have occurred so recently that our social systems are still adjusting to them.

Even if you assumed no new technical breakthroughs would occur, making accurate predictions about the ultimate effects of today's computer technology would be difficult. But new technical breakthroughs are inevitable; research advances are occurring at an ever-increasing rate. Businesses find it is difficult to make useful long-range plans for computing because in five years, the computing environment will be very different, and in ten years, it will likely be totally unrecognizable. All this makes studying the evolution of computers exciting and worthwhile.

In this chapter, we trace the 150-year process that led to the computer systems we use today. The major events we discuss are shown in the time line in Figure 18.1. In the first section, we describe a few pioneers who laid the foundation for practical electronic computers. Then we describe the four generations of mainframe

computers—from early vacuum tube systems to those of today. We next follow the development of personal computers. In the final section, we make some predictions about computer technology in our future.

## EARLY HISTORY OF COMPUTING

The computer was not invented by only one person. It was the product of many contributions by a host of people. We do not try to discuss each innovation or every person; instead, we highlight some critical milestones in the development of modern computer systems.

### Charles Babbage and Countess Ada Lovelace

**Charles Babbage** often is called the "father of computing" because he developed some of the essential concepts that underlie all modern computers. Ironically, he did not set out to build a computer, nor did he finish building one. A respected British mathematician, Babbage wanted to correct the errors in astronomical tables used for navigation by the British navy. Creating accurate tables was extremely important but difficult because hundreds of error-prone human computers performed the calculations. Babbage thought a mechanical engine could do the calculations without error, so he designed the *difference engine*, a steam-powered machine with thousands of gears, wheels, and barrels (see Figure 18.2). After spending some of his own funds on the initial design, Babbage persuaded the British government in 1822 to fund his difference engine. This was one of the earliest recorded instances of government-funded research.

Babbage never completed the difference engine—in part, because the technology of his day could not produce the gears and wheels with the precision required. But Babbage also abandoned the difference engine because he decided to build a different computer, which he called the *analytical engine*. The difference engine was

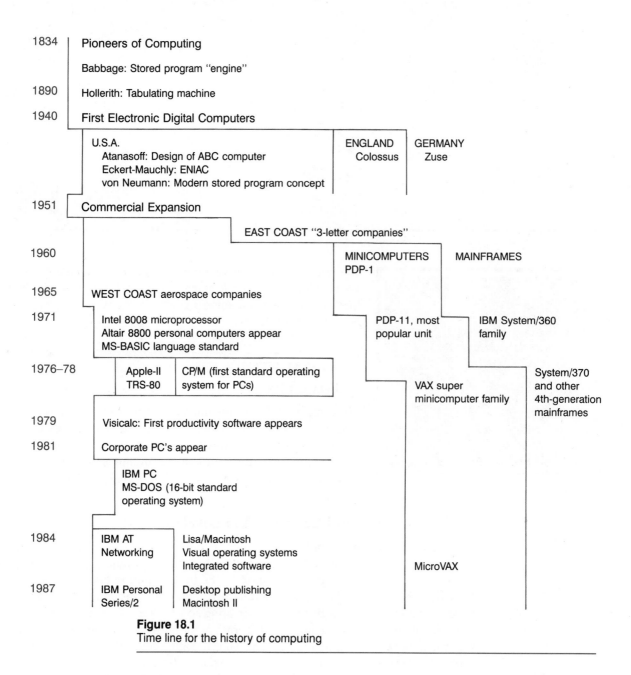

**Figure 18.1**
Time line for the history of computing

designed for specific computations, but the analytical engine was to be capable of performing *any* computation. In designing the machine, Babbage borrowed from **Joseph Jacquard**, who in 1801, had invented an automatic loom. The weaving sequences in Jacquard's loom were controlled by punched cards. Babbage struggled with the design of a general control mechanism:

This day I had a general but only indistinct conception of the possibility of making an engine work out *algebraic* developments. . . . I mean without *any* reference to the *value* of the letters. . . . My notion is that as the [instructions on] cards of the calculating engine direct a series of operations and then recommence with the first so it might perhaps be possible to cause some cards to punch others equivalent to any given number of repetitions.[1]

Thus Babbage came up with some key elements of the concept of a *stored program*.

**Countess Ada Lovelace**, fascinated by Babbage's genius, worked with him for several years. She wrote some punch code sequences and some important notes on their conceptions of how the machine should work. Because of these contributions, she is generally credited with being the first "programmer." And as the world's first programmer, an advanced programming language, Ada, was named after her.

## Herman Hollerith and the Tab Machine

**Herman Hollerith** is credited with providing the impetus for automated data processing. His invention came in response to a counting problem: By the late 1800s, the U.S. Census Bureau was still counting people by hand, and simply to count the responses from a census survey would take more than five years.

---

1. Anthony Hyman, *Charles Babbage: Pioneer of the Computer* (Princeton: Princeton University Press, 1982), p. 244.

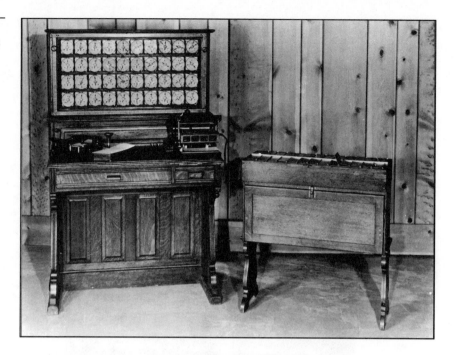

**Figure 18.3**
Hollerith's machines for sorting and tabulating

After working for the Census Bureau, Hollerith quit and devoted several years to inventing a machine system for tabulation. He also took a job at the U.S. Patent Office, so that he would be sure to understand patent policy. Hollerith built a *tab machine* (Figure 18.3) which tabulated (counted) data by sorting cards. The machine used eighty-column punched cards, often called Hollerith cards, about the size of a dollar bill. Using Hollerith's machines, the Census Bureau processed data for the 1890 census in less than two years.

Hollerith sold his company, which built punched-card tabulating equipment, to a company named Computing-Tabulating-Recording-Company. Later, this company changed its name to International Business Machines Corporation—IBM.

## First Electronic Computers

Unlike Babbage's engines, Hollerith's machines used electricity. But unlike modern computers, the tab machines were mostly mechanical, did not have a stored program, and were limited in their arithmetic. The complicated computations needed for scientific problems, especially those associated with World War II, led to the development of the electronic digital computer.

Controversy surrounds the question of who should receive credit for inventing the first electronic computer. **Konrad Zuse**, a German engineer recruited into the German army, is supposed to have had a program-controlled electronic computer working in 1941, but it was destroyed in an Allied bombing raid.

A British computer, Colossus, was used as early as 1943 to break German cipher codes. Its work is still classified as secret, and scant information about it is available. **John V. Atanasoff**, a physics professor at Iowa State College, designed—but

**Figure 18.4**
ENIAC computer

did not complete—the ABC electronic computer from 1939 to 1942. Atanasoff urged Iowa State to patent his computer, but they failed to act. From 1943 to 1946, **John W. Mauchly** and **J. Presper Eckert** of the University of Pennsylvania developed **ENIAC** (*Electronic Numerical Integrator and Calculator*) (see Figure 18.4). Its development was funded by the U.S. Army to compute ballistics tables for artillery shells. John Mauchly visited Atanasoff in 1940 and 1941 and based some of ENIAC on Atanasoff's work. In 1973, a U.S. federal court invalidated the Eckert and Mauchly patent for the electronic digital computer and declared Atanasoff the inventor.

Though Atanasoff had built a special-purpose electronic computer, the ENIAC was the first general-purpose electronic digital computer. Unlike Babbage's analytical engine or other early devices, it was totally electronic and had no mechanical counters. ENIAC contained 18,000 vacuum tubes, 70,000 resistors, and 500,000 hand-soldered connections. It weighed 30 tons, used 100 kilowatts of electricity, and occupied a 20-by-40 foot room. Supposedly, all the lights in a section of Philadelphia dimmed when ENIAC was turned on. It had a limited amount of storage and was unreliable because the vacuum tubes frequently burned out. These problems were tolerable because ENIAC could perform arithmetic at the unheard-of rate of five thousand additions or three hundred multiplications per second.

ENIAC was limited in another way. It was programmed by plugging wires into three walls of plug-boards containing more than six thousand switches. To change the program required resetting switches by replugging the plug-board (see Figure 18.5).

**Figure 18.5**
Plug board of the ENIAC

The last but most important step in the development of the electronic computer was the memory-stored program, an extension of Babbage's ideas of instruction cards to control the operation. In retrospect, the advantage of storing a program electronically in computer memory is obvious: The program can be changed simply by reading another program into memory.

**John von Neumann**, a famous mathematician at the Institute for Advanced Study at Princeton University, is credited with developing the modern concept of the stored program. Von Neumann developed the concept of the stored program in conjunction with the design of **EDVAC** (*Electronic Discrete Variable Automatic Computer*) at the University of Pennsylvania. EDVAC was the second computer developed by Mauchly and Eckert. When Mauchly and Eckert's computer company was in financial difficulty, Remington-Rand acquired it and produced the first commercial computer, the **UNIVAC I** (*Universal Automatic Computer*), in 1951. Significantly, the UNIVAC I was bought by the U.S. Census Bureau (see Figure 18.6).

Once it became possible to store a binary program in memory, the next major programming breakthroughs were assemblers and compilers, which produced loadable programs from symbolic expressions. **Grace Murray Hopper** (see Figure 18.7) developed the first compiler in 1952. As a gifted mathematician, she worked with Eckert and Mauchly for many years. She is credited with developing some of the first programming languages and had an enormous influence on the early evolution of procedure-oriented languages.

**Figure 18.6**
UNIVAC I, the first commercial computer

## MAINFRAME COMPUTER GENERATIONS

We can divide the second major stage of computing history into two paths followed by two groups: the East Coast companies and the West Coast companies. Generally, the East Coast companies have three-letter names—IBM, NCR, RCA, DEC, and so on. The West Coast companies tend to be associated with the aerospace industry and the military.

The East Coast companies pursued data processing in government and large financial, manufacturing, and retail businesses. Data processing in these organizations requires powerful mainframe computers with huge memories and a professional staff. Today, the financial community would collapse under tons of paper without large-scale, central mainframe computers. Never before have so many aspects of business depended on the infallibility of machines. The idea of a small personal computer would never have occurred to this group.

**Figure 18.7**
Commodore Grace Hopper, who recently retired from the U.S. Navy

The West Coast companies pursued the scientific and engineering uses of computers, in particular, for the military and the space program. Controlling a missile requires a small, lightweight computer that can rapidly calculate trajectories, adjust engines, and communicate with earth stations. The scientists and engineers who design these computers typically work alone or in small groups—an ideal combination for nurturing small, individualized personal computers.

Thus the history of computing takes two separate paths from 1951 to 1980. The East Coast companies evolved large data processing machines through four generations, as Table 18.1 shows. The West Coast companies developed microelectronic computer systems for the manned space program and ultimately turned space technology into down-to-earth products for commercial consumption—products such as pocket calculators, video games, and personal computers. To take a closer look at these two paths, we first discuss the development of mainframe computers by the East Coast companies.

## The First Generation: Vacuum Tube Systems (1951–1958)

First-generation computers used vacuum tubes to provide electronic circuits. For memory, these computers used a magnetic drum, a rotating cylinder whose outer surface could be magnetized. Punched cards were used for input of both data and programs, and program instructions were given in machine language. These computers were slow, unreliable, expensive, and tedious to program.

**Table 18.1**
**Generations of Mainframe Computers**

| | First Generation | Second Generation | Third Generation | Fourth Generation |
|---|---|---|---|---|
| **Technology** | Vacuum tubes | Transistors | Integrated circuits | Large-scale integration |
| **Speed** (instructions per second) | Up to 10,000 | Up to 1 million | Up to 10 million | Up to 1 billion |
| **Memory capacity** (in characters) | 1,000 to 8,000 | 4,000 to 64,000 | 32,000 to 4 million | 512,000 to 128 million |
| **Failure rate** (Mean time between failure) | Minutes | Days | Weeks | Months to years |
| **Relative cost** (per operation) | $10.00 | $1.00 | $0.10 | Less than $0.01 |
| **External storage** | Cards | Tape | Disk | Mass storage |
| **Operating system** | Single user Jobs scheduled manually | Single user Jobs scheduled automatically | Multiple user Timesharing | Multiple user Networks and distributed systems |

## The Second Generation: Transistor Systems (1958–1964)

The second generation of computers began when transistors replaced vacuum tubes. The transistors were 1/200th the size of a vacuum tube, generated less heat, were faster, and failed less often. The internal memory of these computers was composed of tiny, doughnut-shaped magnetic cores strung on thin intersecting wires. (This is the origin of the term *core memory*, which refers to internal memory.) Magnetic tape largely replaced punched cards for input and output, and printers with speeds up to six hundred lines per minute were developed.

The second generation also brought improvements in software. One important development was the invention of high-level programming languages in the mid-to-late 1950s, including FORTRAN for engineers and COBOL for business programmers. These languages represented a giant step forward because they are less detailed and easier to learn and use than machine language. Thus a person with little or no technical knowledge of the computer could write programs to solve problems. Meanwhile, the task of starting and scheduling the execution of programs had become too complex and time-sensitive to leave to a computer operator. The invention of the operating system solved this problem.

## The Third Generation: Integrated Circuits (1964–1971)

Integrated circuits replaced transistors in third-generation computers. An *integrated circuit* is a complex electronic circuit etched on a tiny chip of silicon about 1/4 inch square. It is smaller, faster, and more reliable than separate transistors wired together.

**Figure 18.8**
An IBM System/360 series computer system, complete with removable hard disk drives (foreground), workstation for the system operator (center), and line printer (background right).

Major improvements also occurred in the capabilities of peripheral devices. Magnetic disks replaced magnetic tapes for storing information when rapid access to data was required. Faster printers were developed; they could print nearly three thousand lines per minute. Cathode ray tubes (CRTs) were used to display input and output.

Operating systems capable of timesharing also began to appear during the third generation. This allowed many users to use a single computer simultaneously, thereby also permitting them to share the enormous cost of third-generation computers. The BASIC programming language was developed at Dartmouth under a grant from the National Science Foundation. It was designed to make programming as easy as possible.

In the early 1960s, IBM made a significant commitment to developing an entire family of computers that could run the same operating system and application programs. Five thousand people were assigned to develop the system software for this project on a two-year schedule. Then, on April 7, 1964, IBM announced the **System/360** family of computers (see Figure 18.8). The family consisted of six computers with memory sizes ranging from 16KB to more than 1MB. These computers were enormously successful because customers could upgrade from one member of the family to another without changing their application software. Most of the computers IBM has introduced since 1965 are upwardly compatible with the original System/360 computers. IBM captured and has held a 60 to 75 percent share of the mainframe computer market.

The success of its System/360 computers drove several major competitors from the computer business. General Electric quit the mainframe computer business in

1970, RCA in 1972, and Xerox in 1975. Other companies tried to survive by moving into defensible market niches.

One of these market niches was the small computer market. In 1960, the three-year-old Digital Equipment Corporation (DEC) brought out the first minicomputer, the PDP-1. It cost less than mainframe computers and had a much smaller instruction set. The PDP product line grew until the **PDP-11**, introduced in 1969, became the best selling general-purpose minicomputer ever.

### The Fourth Generation: Large-Scale Integration (1971–)

The beginning of the fourth computer generation coincided with the development of the **large-scale integrated (LSI)** circuit—a single chip that contains thousands of transistors. **Very large-scale integration (VLSI)** was introduced when chips began having tens of thousands of transistors. Today, VLSI chips can have millions of transistors. VLSI chips are made with lithographic methods and can be mass produced to spread their high research and development costs over many units.

The introduction of the IBM 370 series is generally considered to mark the beginning of the fourth computer generation. The computers in this series offered virtual memory so that they could run programs of enormous size.

By 1977, DEC was offering the VAX minicomputers with virtual memory. And in 1985, DEC announced the MicroVAX II, a complete minicomputer based on a set of three VLSI processor chips. DEC grew at a phenomenal rate to become the second-largest computer manufacturer in the United States.

Large fourth-generation computers can support extensive timesharing; up to several thousand users may use the computer at the same time. The computer allocates its resources so that each user feels he or she is the only one using it. Moreover, programs and peripheral devices such as disks and printers have grown by leaps and bounds in variety, capability, and sophistication.

## EVOLUTION OF PERSONAL COMPUTERS

While the East Coast companies continued to develop mainframe and minicomputers, the West Coast companies were busy applying LSI to products for the aerospace industry and the military. The main center for this work was in a string of small towns between San Jose and San Francisco—the famous Silicon Valley. It was here that two engineers working after hours in their bedrooms invented the first commercially successful personal computer.

Personal computers have gone through remarkable changes since they were introduced in the mid-1970s. The first personal computers were crude machines that could be used only by programmers. Today, the average person can learn to productively use a personal computer in a few hours. One way of viewing the evolution of personal computers is shown in Table 18.2, which divides the process into six three-year stages, four in the past and two predicted for the future. The first three stages are loosely based on a presentation given in 1983 by David House, vice-president of Intel, in which he correctly predicted that new generations of

**Table 18.2**
**Evolution of Personal Computers: Past, Present, and Future**

**Developmental Stage (1974–1977)**      **Example: the MITS Altair**
Sold in kits to hobbyists, mail-order distribution
Main memory from 4KB to 32KB; crude 8-bit processor
Computer and peripherals (keyboard, CRT, storage) bought separately
Cassette tape or paper tape storage
Programmed in machine language or BASIC

**Early Adopter Stage (1977–1981)**      **Examples: early Apple IIs, TRS-80**
Sold as a fully assembled computer through retail computer stores
Main memory from 16KB to 64KB; simple 8-bit processor
8-inch or small-capacity 5 1/4-inch floppy disk storage
Standardized, simple operating system; first end-user applications

**Corporate Stage (1981–1984)**      **Example: IBM PC**
Sold as a computer system by major corporations
Main memory from 64KB to 256KB; early 16-bit processor
Larger capacity 5 1/4-inch disk storage; expensive small hard disks
Enhanced operating systems; well-developed application packages

**Integrated Systems Stage (1984–1987)**      **Examples: Macintosh, IBM AT**
Sold as a personal productivity tool for knowledge workers
Main memory from 128KB to 1MB; early 32-bit processor
3 1/2-inch microfloppy, 5 1/4-inch minifloppy, and hard disk storage
Visual-based operating system; integrated application packages

**Networked Systems Stage (1987–1990)**      **Examples: Mac II, IBM PS/2**
Sold as compatible with integrated office systems
Main memory from 512KB to 8MB; advanced 32-bit processor
High-capacity microfloppy and hard disk storage; network access to huge hard disks
Multitasking operating system; standardized local area network interface

**Information Age Stage (1990–)**      **Examples: Compuphone, Stereoputer**
Sold as a commodity item for "reaching out to touch the world"
Main memory from 2MB to 16MB; several special-purpose 32-bit processors
Large hard disk; optical disk; network access to virtually any computer anywhere
Built-in digital phone; high-speed, built-in network interface
Voice/visual-based operating system

---

microprocessor systems will continue to be introduced on roughly a three-year cycle. We discuss each stage, but first it is appropriate to look at the development of the heart of every personal computer, the microprocessor.

## Microprocessors

On November 1, 1956, William Shockley, John Bardeen, and Walter Brattain received word that they had been awarded the Nobel Prize in Physics for inventing the transistor. A student of Shockley's, **Robert Noyce**, was to become the father of the integrated circuit—the basis of the microprocessor chip. (Recall that a *microprocessor* is a circuit built on a single silicon chip that can execute a program.) Noyce founded Intel Corporation, which in turn, developed the LSI circuits used in personal computers.

The first microprocessor, the Intel 4004, was announced in 1971 by the Intel Corporation. Designed by a small group of engineers led by Ted Hoff, the 4004 had the equivalent of 2,250 transistors, making it an exceedingly limited processor. It could process only 4 bits of information at a time.

A computer based on the 4004 contained two important chips: the 4004 microprocessor chip and a *fixed program chip*, which could permanently store the instructions for controlling an electrical device. Other chips could be added as needed. Millions of 4-bit microprocessors have been used in appliances, hand-held calculators, cars, toys, and digital watches. For these applications, the 4004 made a good special-purpose computer, but it was too slow and limited to be the processor for a personal computer.

Several 8-bit microprocessors were developed before 1974, but the 8-bit Intel 8008 (and its immediate successor, the 8080) was the first one with the speed and power needed for a personal computer. The 16-bit generation (1978–1981) began with the Intel 8086. The 32-bit generation began in 1981 with the Intel iAPX 432. Perhaps the most popular early 32-bit microprocessor is the Motorola 68000, which is used in hundreds of products including the Apple Macintosh and many laser printers.

In 1986, Intel began shipping production quantities of its 80386 microprocessor. This processor became an instant success because it is able to run existing software for IBM personal computers two to four times faster than previous microprocessors. The microprocessor also has several different *modes* or ways of operating. Its *protected mode* can manage up to 4 gigabytes of physical memory and offers the same sort of virtual memory features provided by mainframe computers. Its *virtual 86 mode* allows several application programs to run simultaneously as if you had separate microprocessors, a feature called *multitasking*.

A recently developed personal computer is likely to contain **coprocessor chips**, special-purpose microprocessors designed to handle specific functions such as graphics, spoken input and output, high-speed floating-point arithmetic, and interfaces for telecommunications and local area networks.

### Developmental Stage (1974–1977)

The first personal computer, the Micro Instrumentation and Telemetry Systems **(MITS) Altair 8800**, was based on the Intel 8008 microprocessor. In 1974, the company was facing bankruptcy and decided to try to sell an inexpensive computer in kit form. In a smart move, they sent one to *Popular Electronics* magazine, which published a feature article on it. Soon MITS was overwhelmed by orders. The Altair sold in kit form (unassembled) for $395 or fully assembled for $621. Most buyers were technically knowledgeable hobbyists. The Altair did not include a keyboard, CRT monitor, disk, or printer, these items were bought separately, much like the components of a stereo system.

Initially, the Altair was programmed by hobbyists in machine language, but this method was arduous and prone to error. **Bill Gates** (on the left in Figure 18.9)

**Figure 18.9**
**(left)** Bill Gates, chairman of the board and executive vice president of Microsoft.
**(right)** Gary Kildall, chairman of the board for Digital Research.

dropped out of Harvard to remedy the situation. Together with Paul Allen, Gates developed the first high-level language for a microprocessor. His version of BASIC on the MITS Altair soon became the standard programming language for personal computers. In 1974, Gates and Allen founded Microsoft Corporation.

In 1973, **Gary Kildall** (on the right in Figure 18.9) was working as a consultant for Intel. His job was to implement a programming language for the 8080 microprocessor. To make it easier for him to use the microprocessor, he developed *CP/M* (Control Program for Microcomputers), a program for controlling a keyboard, CRT, and disks. Kildall first offered the program to Intel, but Intel declined the offer, so Kildall sold CP/M by mail to hobbyists. In 1975, he set up Digital Research to sell CP/M. In no time at all, CP/M was being used on more than a million systems.

Kildall's CP/M had a dramatic effect on the development of personal computers. Computer manufacturers no longer had to develop an individual operating system for each different computer, and programmers could use the same commands for a variety of computers. CP/M remains the most widely used operating system for 8-bit computers.

The success of these early entrepreneurs led others to manufacture and sell personal computers and accessories. Within two years, many stores, clubs, and magazines were devoted entirely to the personal computer. By 1977, there were more than fifty brands of computers and by the end of 1978, more than seven hundred computer stores. Computer clubs provided members an opportunity to show off their computers, share experiences, and learn about new products. The Southern California Club had three thousand members in 1977. Computer magazines such as *BYTE*, *Creative Computing*, and *Dr. Dobbs' Journal of Computer Calisthenics and Orthodontics* publish advertisements and articles about personal computers, programs, and applications.

Together, CP/M and Microsoft BASIC constituted a powerful force in determining the direction of personal computer programs. They established both a standard language for programmers and a standard vehicle for disseminating programs. But the trouble was that you had to be a programmer to use them.

## Early Adopter Stage (1977–1981)

Steve Wozniak and Steve Jobs began business by selling the Apple I microcomputer in kit form out of a garage in California. Then, realizing the shortcomings of kits, they developed the **Apple II** personal computer. It was wildly successful because they sold it preassembled and included a disk drive and simple operating system. Consumers could buy a ready-to-use computer and a disk drive to store information in a form that could be quickly accessed. The Apple II soon set the standard for commercially successful personal computer manufacturers.

The Radio Shack division of Tandy Corporation introduced the first personal computer in their **TRS-80** line in 1977. The TRS-80 Model I was sold fully assembled and included a keyboard, cassette tape or disk, printer, and various sizes of memory. A true baby computer, the Model I was sold in Radio Shack's nationwide chain of retail stores for $500 to $1,500, depending on options. It also included the Microsoft BASIC language. The theory was that a person could write BASIC programs to solve his or her problems. Typical buyers were hobbyists, educators, and small businesses. Commodore Business Machines, a large adding machine company, introduced the **Commodore PET** in 1977. It was an assembled, complete computer with a keyboard, screen, and cassette tape drive that sold for $650.

A new idea in software soon expanded the usefulness of these machines. While taking a business course at Harvard University, **Dan Bricklin** got the idea for a program that anybody could use—VisiCalc. VisiCalc turned a personal computer like the Apple II into a familiar spreadsheet that would total numbers in rows and columns. It was important for many reasons: It made people realize that anybody could use a computer; it caused Apple II sales to soar; and it promoted the idea of a computer *paradigm*. That is, VisiCalc was more than a program; it was a metaphor, which many others soon copied. Even today, the best software emulates some familiar model such as a spreadsheet, desk top, file drawer, or library.

At about the same time, word processing software on personal computers became a popular alternative to expensive systems designed solely for word processing. Applewriter by Paul Lutus and Wordstar by Rob Barnaby were among the first best sellers. More than half a million copies of each program were sold during the late 1970s.

## Corporate Stage (1981–1984)

The large computer manufacturers such as IBM and DEC did not enter the personal computer field until the 1980s. This is quite surprising, especially since DEC specialized in minicomputers, which are only a step above microcomputers in size and power. Probably these companies delayed entering the personal computer market because they felt the marketplace was too volatile or did not realize its size and

**Figure 18.10**
The IBM Personal
Computer, an-
nounced in 1981

potential. When IBM and other large computer manufacturers did enter the market, they established a standard of excellence for personal computers and gave them legitimacy and credibility.

This corporate phase began with the introduction of the **IBM Personal Computer,** or PC, in 1981 (see Figure 18.10). It legitimized personal computing for Fortune 500 companies, began the era of the 16-bit personal computer, and established Microsoft's MS-DOS as the standard 16-bit operating system.

Corporations began to realize that the personal computer could increase office workers' productivity. So extensively were spreadsheet, word processing, and database management programs used that they became known as *productivity software.* Productivity software invaded noncomputer companies, bringing change at a rate rarely seen in the history of corporations.

### Integrated Systems Stage (1984–1987)

After the explosive growth of the corporate stage, personal computers went through a period of consolidation of hardware, software, and suppliers. Personal computers were integrated with other personal computers and mainframes to form computer networks. Programs were integrated with other programs to form integrated packages. And the industry went through a mid-life crisis that some of the smaller manufacturers were unable to survive. Some causes of this crisis were rapidly falling hardware prices, a downturn in the growth rate of personal computer sales, and an increased emphasis on hardware and software standards.

An interesting trend during this period was the rapid drop in the cost of personal computers designed specifically around a visual operating system. The Apple Lisa became the first member of this category of computers; it was introduced in early 1983 at $9,995. Then came the **Apple Macintosh** (introduced in early 1984 at $2,495)

## A Word About . . . *The Downward Migration of Computer Technology*

*When you look into the future, it is a good idea to use past trends as a guide. For the field of computing, the guideposts point to some remarkable possibilities.*

In predicting future developments in computer technology, David Nelson, chief technical officer at Apollo Computer, classifies computers into seven tiers, each separated from the other by a factor of 10 in cost (see chart). The aggregate improvement in performance across the tiers is about 35% a year, so a tenfold improvement (across one tier) occurs every seven years. Thus the virtual-memory capability of a $1 million IBM 370 mainframe computer, which first emerged in 1970, became available on the DEC VAX in 1977 (for approximately $100,000) and in the Apollo DN300 workstation in 1984 (for approximately $10,000). By extrapolation, claims Nelson, that same capability ought to be available in 1991 for close to $1,000.

At the higher end of the workstation market, he says, there will be increasing performance for constant cost. Thus a $50,000–$100,000 workstation, which approaches the performance of a mainframe today, should have the capabilities of a minisupercomputer by 1991.

Nelson also believes that a tenfold performance increase is matched by a weight decrease of the same order. "Computers seem to cost about $200 per pound, independent of their size," says Nelson, "a figure that has been valid for the last 30 years when adjusted for inflation." As computers become more of a "commodity," perhaps one day it will be possible to buy them by the pound.

Source: Jeffrey Bairstow, *High Technology*, March 1987, p. 20.

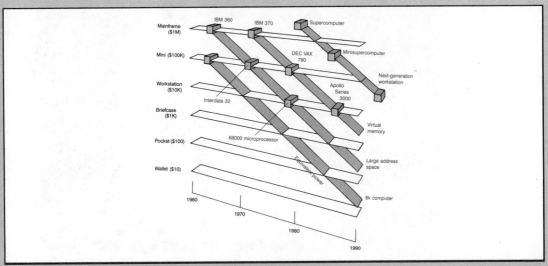

The multi-tier model is a good predictor of when concepts will appear, but a poor predictor of how the concepts will be used, says Apollo's David Nelson. "For example, although the model accurately predicts virtual-memory development, the importance of local-area networks for workstations would have been difficult to estimate."

**Figure 18.11**
The original Apple
Macintosh **(left)** in-
troduced in 1984,
and the Macintosh II
**(right)** introduced in
1987

(see Figure 18.11), the Commodore Amiga (introduced in mid-1985 at $1,295), and
finally, the Atari 520 ST (introduced in late 1985 at $799). All these machines use the
same processor (the Motorola 68000), but the latter two machines also have a sound
generation chip that can generate three or four simultaneous audio voices and a
graphics coprocessor that provides superior graphics manipulation capabilities.

In 1986, desktop publishing suddenly burst on the scene as the fastest growing segment of personal computing, and business began opening its doors to Macintosh computers. In March 1987, Apple announced its Macintosh II computer, which offered a color display, used a faster processor, and provided the option of an IBM-compatible microprocessor and easy conversion of files between IBM and Macintosh formats. In April 1987, IBM effectively replaced the entire Personal Computer family by announcing a new family of **IBM Personal System/2** computers, ranging in price from $1,695 to more than $7,000.

The new IBM and Apple systems have several features in common: They support high-quality color displays, have an open hardware architecture that offers expansion slots, and endorse the concept of a visual operating system.

### Future Personal Computer Stages

Table 18.2 predicts that personal computers will continue to evolve in three-year stages through 1990. The future characteristics listed in the table are informed guesses based on past trends and the predictions of industry analysts.

If Table 18.2 is correct, the networked systems stage (1987–1990) will bring an increased emphasis on linking personal computers with local area networks. Customers will no longer need to buy a network interface to attach a personal computer to a network; instead, the interface will be standard equipment, just as I/O ports are standard on most personal computers today. Larger memory capacities and an advanced 32-bit processor, such as the Motorola 60020 in the Macintosh II or the Intel 80386 in some of the IBM Personal System/2 computers, will allow several applications to be executed at the same time in different windows of a visual operating system. High-quality color displays will become common, while mass production and expanding markets will lower the cost of a complete working system.

## THE FUTURE OF COMPUTING

A major difficulty in predicting the future of computing is the rapidity with which research developments have moved from the laboratory to the marketplace. For example, Intel began planning the model 8088 microprocessor in 1976. Production of the chip began in 1979. By 1981, several operating systems, programming languages, and application programs had been written for the chip. In fourteen months, IBM designed a new personal computer that exploited the microprocessor's capabilities, announced the product in August 1981, and began selling it in quantity. By the end of 1983, the IBM PC had single-handedly given IBM the largest share of the personal computer market.

The speed of technological innovation in the electronics industry is not decreasing. Scientists report that fundamental physical limitations, such as the speed of light or properties of chemical reactions, will not preclude building cheaper, faster, smaller components and peripherals between now and the year 2000. And as automation in electronic manufacturing increases, the time between proving technical feasibility and widespread commercial use should continue to shorten.

*Nowhere is the continual improvement in electronics more visible than in the production of the semiconductor memory chip.*

Gary L. Tooker, vice-president and general manager of semiconductor products at Motorola, wrote in the August 1983 issue of *High Technology:*

> Every three to five years a new generation of RAMs has been unveiled, featuring four times the storage density of its predecessor. Each year, the cost per bit has fallen by 30 percent and semiconductor memory utilization has increased by 100 percent. Few, if any, other industries can claim a market where demand doubles annually. ... Obviously, the cycle cannot go on forever, but the end is not in sight.

So far, these predictions have been correct. Since 1983, the market for 64-kilobit memory chips has been decimated by shipments of 256-kilobit chips; 1-megabit chips have moved into production; and engineering prototypes of 4- and 16-megabit chips are being produced. To put this in perspective, a 16-megabit chip occupies no more space than your thumbnail but stores the equivalent of 700 typed pages of text. A single 16-megabit chip contains several times more memory than all the memory chips in a typical personal computer sold today.

Charles P. Lecht is a noted columnist for *Computerworld* magazine. In his February 2, 1987 column, he predicts we can expect "a 64-megabit chip followed shortly by one with a capacity of 256-megabits. After that, we won't be too surprised with the announcement of the first gigabit ... chip (125,000,000 characters). It's my bet that these chips will appear well before the end of the century."

What kinds of computers can we expect? Bill Joy, Sun Microsystems' co-founder and vice-president of research and development, predicts in the March 1987 issue of *High Technology,* that by the year 2001, $15,000 (in today's dollars) will buy a truly cognitive machine with such good voice and image input/output that a keyboard will no longer be needed. "Such a machine," he says, "would have at least 24 color planes and could show complex images at movie speed [24 frames per second], maybe with stereo sound and display."

In many ways, predicting technical developments is easier than predicting their economic and social effects. It is difficult to tell in advance how effectively a new technical ability will be exploited or how radically it will alter human behavior. According to Robert Noyce, Vice-Chairman of Intel,

> The usual futurist projections are too optimistic in the short term and too pessimistic in the long term. . . . Where we went wrong in our over-expectations [was the computer industry's inward focus and its inability to] project itself out to the plumber and what he does.[2]

2. Special section on Personal Computing, *The Wall Street Journal,* September 16, 1985.

## A Word About . . . *Computing in the 21st Century*

*John Sculley, president and CEO of Apple Computer, comments on the future in an interview.*

**What is your vision of Apple's 21st-century technology?**

All the major technologies to build revolutionary machines for the 21st century exist today or will be in motion by the end of the 1980s. The performance of the technologies will improve dramatically. Microprocessors of the 21st century will be 100 times faster, yet cost the same as today's. They will process software loaded with artificial intelligence, sophisticated 3-D image processing, high-resolution animation, speech recognition, and voice synthesis. Full-motion video—with image quality far better than current television sets—will be what computer users routinely expect.

The problem is the growth of information; the amount of information doubles every two years. So the ultimate aim of computers will not be to create more information. We need the ability to navigate in real time across vast expanses of information. So it is especially important that we develop a new perspective. Information is an interim step to the ultimate goal of knowledge. We have an opportunity in the early 21st century to create breakthrough products as important to people then as movable type was to people in the beginning of the Renaissance.

After Gutenberg developed movable type, it took more than a century of development before it had an impact on society. In 1360, 1 out of every 100 Europeans could read, but by 1500, 80 out of every 100 could read. Gutenberg's invention democratized knowledge in the process.

**What is your vision of the 21st-century personal computer?**

I developed a term, Knowledge Navigator, to describe it. While today's computers take users to the doorsteps of libraries and institutions, the Knowledge Navigator will drive us through them. By the 21st century, we will have the installed base to make the computer a mass personalized knowledge-based system. It will make incredible quantities of information understandable—and personalized. It will customize information automatically, because it will have the ability to "learn" about a user's habits and preferences. It will have the independent ability to search databases and perform content analysis on information. It will do a lot to transform information into personally tailored knowledge, thus improving the payback of companies' investments in computers.

The physical appearance of the 21st century personal computer would be more like a pilot's cockpit than today's machines. A large flat display screen might have navigational joysticks at both sides, allowing you to steer through menus, windows, and stacks. It will instantly accept or provide data in any mode you like: text, graphics, video, speech.

The key benefit of the Knowledge Navigator is that it will encourage learning and creativity. By the 21st century, intelligent information networks will make a world of knowledge much more accessible. Distributed databases will be widely installed. Brick-and-mortar libraries will give way to electronic ones. We will have super-highways of knowledge, and they will have as much impact on the American economy as the railroads did in the 1800s. The Knowledge Navigator will be the tool of choice for helping us understand better. It will be capable of helping us explore, connect concepts, and compare subjects.

Obviously, it will make learning experiences much more interesting for students. Not only that, but teachers will boost their own self-esteem because they will have more power to shape education. Students will be drawn into the educational experience, once it moves away from the mechanical, memorization-oriented path so many schools are on.

Source: MacWorld, November 1987, pp. 76–78.

## Summary

We can find the origins of the modern computer in Charles Babbage's designs and Herman Hollerith's tabulating machines. But the need to solve large scientific problems involving tedious calculations provided the motivation for developing the electronic computer. ENIAC, completed in 1946, was the first totally electronic general-purpose computer. UNIVAC I, produced by Remington-Rand Corporation in 1951, was the first commercial computer. It marked the start of the first generation of mainframe computers.

The second, third, and fourth generations of mainframe computers were marked by technological improvements—transistors, integrated circuits, and large-scale integrated circuits, respectively. These led to faster operation, decreased size, and increased memory. Because of their cost, large computers were timeshared among many users.

The development of the microprocessor in 1971 spawned a new breed of computers designed to be used by one person. Thus in 1975, the first personal computers appeared. A new stage in the development of personal computers has evolved every three years since 1975. Today, personal computers have the processing power of third-generation mainframe computers and are being integrated into computer networks.

The prospects for technical improvements in the computer field are so good that accurate predictions are likely to seem unbelievable to the average person. The fields of computing and communicating are merging, causing the development of larger and more complex distributed processing systems. Collectively, all these trends can be described as a shift from the Industrial Age to the Information Age—from physical tools to mental-support tools.

## Key Terms

| | |
|---|---|
| Apple II | large-scale integration (LSI) |
| Apple Macintosh | MITS Altair 8800 |
| Commodore PET | PDP-11 |
| coprocessor chip | System/360 |
| EDVAC | TRS-80 |
| ENIAC | UNIVAC I |
| IBM Personal Computer | very large-scale integration (VLSI) |
| IBM Personal System/2 | |

## Key People

| | |
|---|---|
| John Atanasoff | Bill Gates |
| Charles Babbage | Herman Hollerith |
| Dan Bricklin | Grace Hopper |
| J. Presper Eckert | Joseph Jacquard |

Gary Kildall                          John von Neumann

Countess Ada Lovelace                 Robert Noyce

John Mauchly                          Konrad Zuse

## Discussion Questions

1. Who do you think should be given credit for inventing the electronic computer?

2. The phenomenal development of the computer has occurred in a very short time—less than fifty years. Can you think of anything else with a similarly rapid development? Consider the automobile, airplane, and television. If they had developed as far and as fast as the computer, what would they be like?

3. If a fifth generation of computers is successfully developed, what do you think they will be like? How will they be used?

4. As the speed and capability of personal computers increase, do you think the distinction between mainframe and personal computers will disappear?

5. Which social institutions are likely to adapt quickly to the Information Age? Which are most likely to resist change? Will resistance be successful?

## Exercises

1. Match the persons in the left-hand column with the event in the right-hand column.

   ___ John Atanasoff        a. Developed CP/M
   ___ Charles Babbage       b. ENIAC computer
   ___ Dan Bricklin          c. Father of computing
   ___ Bill Gates            d. Developed VisiCalc
   ___ Herman Hollerith      e. Developed BASIC for personal computers
   ___ Gary Kildall          f. Data processing
   ___ J. Presper Eckert     g. Developed FORTRAN
   ___ John Mauchly          h. Apple II
   ___ John von Neumann      i. Developed COBOL
   ___ Robert Noyce          j. ABC computer
                             k. Stored program concept
                             l. MITS Altair 8800

2. Charles Babbage was quite a character with an unusual collection of friends. Read more about him and his inventions.

3. List some tasks that can be done on a large mainframe computer but not on a personal computer.

4. Choose an organization and write a report on how it is likely to be affected by changes in the computer field over the next five years.

# Software Piracy

| | |
|---|---|
| Basic Concepts | Software License Agreements |
| Legal Protection for Software | Thwarting Software Piracy |

Software piracy is a serious problem for software developers because software for personal computers is distributed on easy-to-copy floppy disks. How many backup copies are you allowed to make? May you use the same program on several computers? Certainly selling an unauthorized copy of a program is illegal, but is it also illegal to give a copy to a friend or relative for demonstration purposes?

These questions are unlikely to yield to simple answers. Guidelines, procedures, technical safeguards, regulations, and laws to address these issues are being discussed by lawyers, computer manufacturers, computer center directors, software publishers, and legislators. Their deliberations have been confused by continual and rapid technological developments. What actions they take will influence the future of computing.

## BASIC CONCEPTS

**Software piracy** is any unauthorized duplication of software. Illegal copying of software cuts into the potential market and thus tends to discourage developers from creating new and innovative software. When many potential consumers illegally duplicate software instead of buying it, all consumers suffer because there are fewer new products, and prices of existing software may remain high to compensate for the loss in revenue. Illegal duplication of software affects market economics; it also raises major legal and ethical issues.

Few instances of piracy involve software for mainframe computers. Typically, this software is specially tailored for a particular computer facility, and it is written by relatively few companies. A negotiated contract spells out what programs are to be developed, performance conditions they must satisfy, and maintenance respon-

sibilities. Vendors can easily monitor the use and distribution of this software. Moreover, business customers are accustomed to abiding by contracts. For the most part, they are honest and fair if only because unhappy employees serve as watchdogs. They may make a few more backup copies than their contracts allow, but they are not likely to engage in large-scale piracy.

The same cannot be said of the consumer and education markets. The personal computer completely changed the development and sale of software. Many companies and free-lance programmers write software for personal computers. Millions of these programs are sold by dealers, computer stores, and mail-order outlets. For example, more than a million copies of Lotus 1-2-3 have been sold. To monitor each program sold would be impractical if not impossible.

The prime targets of software pirates are games and popular application programs, such as word processing and spreadsheet programs. Games are easy to use and require no support from the seller, making them perfect targets for a pirate.

No one knows exactly how much piracy goes on or its cost to software companies. According to some, there may be as many as ten stolen copies for each legitimate copy of certain popular programs. If these estimates are accurate, most computer users may now be pirates. Perhaps most personal computer owners possess or have used illegal copies, but some of them may not be aware of the law and the implications of their actions.

How many people would have bought the software if they could not steal copies is not known. At least one recent survey found that many users buy software after trying an unauthorized version. Users said they had made costly mistakes in the past and did not want to risk money on a program without trying it first. This accounts for the recent popularity of *shareware* or *freeware* programs. Licensees of these programs can legally share or give away copies for others to evaluate and decide if they want to make a purchase. Popular shareware programs include PC-File, PC-Write, and PC-Calc, and ProComm. Some programs are placed in the *public domain*, which means the author or creator has authorized others to duplicate them at will.

## A Word About . . . Patents on Software

*Software development companies, which have long considered patents cumbersome and ineffective, are now turning them to protect their inventions.*

The change reflects the growing strength of the patent system. The Patent and Trademark Office now grants patents on many high-tech products, including software, which previously wouldn't have passed muster. And courts are levying stiff penalties on patent infringers—including triple damages and interest charges—and banning products that infringe on patents.

In a ruling that buoyed computer makers, Eastman Kodak Co. was recently forced out of the instant-photography market after it lost a patent-infringement case brought by Polaroid Corp. Now, Kodak faces potential damage judgments of more than $1 billion. Irving Rappaport, associate general counsel of Apple Computer Inc., says the ruling "shows that the patent system is alive, well and very vibrant for those who have inventions."

The number of computer companies applying for patents is increasing. Prime Computer Inc., which for 10 years didn't bother obtaining patents, now regularly files for patent protection on its hardware. International Business Machines Corp. and Apple, which previously patented computer hardware, now increasingly patent computer software technology too.

Smaller computer companies are also seeking patents. Quickview Systems Inc., a Los Altos, Calif., software company, patented a method for automatically abbreviating text. "If the big guys want to use it, they'll have to do business with us or take the chance of a costly patent battle," warns Paul Heckel, Quickview's president.

Patents give holders the exclusive right for 17 years to market inventions that are deemed "new, useful, and unobvious." That can be a powerful weapon. Using its patents, Apple obtained an International Trade Commission order banning imports to the U.S. of computers that violate Apple patents. As a result, says Mr. Rappaport, customs agents have seized "tens of thousands" of Apple imitations.

The patent system, however, also holds pitfalls for the computer industry. Samuel Miller, who teaches patent law at Georgetown University, says that the new appeals court may go too far in enforcing patents. "The patent system can create a monopoly in a technical area," he says. "If that monopoly is over broad, it's damaging to the competitive environment."

Filing for patents can also be a long and expensive process. Patenting a new computer system can require 10 patents at a cost of as much as $5,000 each, says Mr. Mirabito, the Boston patent attorney. The Patent and Trademark Office is so back logged that it sometimes takes three years to approve a filing.

Another disadvantage: Patent holders must disclose how their inventions work. While such

## LEGAL PROTECTION FOR SOFTWARE

There are three forms of legal protection for software: copyright, trade secret, and patent.

**Copyright** is the easiest and least expensive form of protection to obtain. In the United States, copyright protection is automatic once the work is published although to be safe (in case of legal action), the work should be registered with the Copyright Office. Copyrights were originally developed for literary works, but in 1980, the Federal Copyright Law was amended by the Software Protection Act to allow a user to make only archival copies of a software package. In the United States disclosure serves the lofty public goal of disseminating innovative ideas, "You can make an instant competitor," says Irving Kayton, a patent-law professor at George Washington University.

Because of these drawbacks, many computer companies use patents as only one of several ways to protect inventions. Prime Computer, for instance, won't patent its technology for wiring printed-circuit boards because it changes its methods every few years—making any patent obsolete. Instead, Prime keeps the wiring technology confidential and can sue under state trade-secret laws if a competitor somehow steals it.

Lotus Development Corp., a software company that now copyrights its programs, is investigating whether patents would give it additional protection. Copyrights let Lotus sue those who copy its programs; patents could protect Lotus's underlying technology. "Patents may allow us to protect certain features that aren't protected by copyright," say Lindsey Kiang, Lotus's general counsel.

Sometimes the value of a patent only becomes clear too late. In the late 1970s, Dan Bricklin invented VisiCalc, the first electronic spreadsheet for personal computers, but he didn't try to patent the technology. So even though spreadsheets have been incorporated into many top-selling programs, he hasn't received any royalties.

"I'll go down in history as the inventor of VisiCalc," Mr. Bricklin says. "With a patent, the only difference would have been several hundred million dollars."

Source: Bob David, *The Wall Street Journal*, 28 January 1986.

(and many other countries), a copyright gives a person exclusive use of the work for life plus fifty years. For corporations, a copyright is generally effective for seventy-five years. But a copyright protects only the tangible form an idea is expressed in, not the idea itself. Thus only the actual program code is protected, and writing a new program that does the same thing as a copyrighted program is generally permissible.

In contrast, if a program can be designated a **trade secret**, even the idea embodied in the program is protected. This is the most popular and successful form of software protection. A program can be protected as a trade secret if the program has some secret information or formula that gives it an advantage over its competitors. However, there are two shortcomings. First, once the secret is out, protection is lost. Thus a software developer must guard the secret by limiting access and enforcing nondisclosure agreements. Second, trade secrets are based on state rather than federal laws; the extent of protection varies from state to state.

**Patent** protection is the most difficult protection to obtain because of the paperwork, time the Patent Office takes to grant a patent (several years), and reluctance of the Patent Office to give patent protection to programs. A patent gives exclusive

## A Word About . . . *Copy Protection*

*Some of the biggest software companies—among them Microsoft Corp., Borland International Inc., and Ashton-Tate Inc.—have abandoned their efforts to protect their software packages from pirates after years of debate over copyright issues.*

The software giants cite customer resistance as a major factor in their decision to back off from increasingly more expensive copy protection plans. As Microsoft chairman William Gates put it, "The customer won."

Indeed, users will cheer at the prospect of software that is less cumbersome to use, and manufacturers will benefit from lower production costs. However, the decision not to inhibit software packages with copy protection schemes should by no means be interpreted as a general go-ahead for making illegal copies of software. Those programs are still copyrighted, and software manufacturers threaten to continue pursuing violators in court.

In the past, users who do not illegally copy software have complained that they as well as pirates are punished by copy protection devices. Such devices cause difficulty in making backup tapes of data, in using software and hardware in combination with other protected programs, and in installing hard disks. Now legitimate users will be able to purchase software that is uninhibited by protection schemes, and therefore less likely to cause them headaches.

Not all software manufacturers have leaped wholeheartedly into removal of copy protection devices. However, industry analysts estimate that by the end of 1986, at least fifty percent of all programs being shipped will be unprotected.

Source: Paul B. Carroll, *The Wall Street Journal*, 25 September 1986.

rights to the concepts embodied in the program for seventeen years, which is more than enough in view of recent computer developments. But a patent is granted by the Patent Office only if the applicant convincingly demonstrates that the concepts have not appeared in other programs, a mighty tall order for the applicant. Still, some software companies are turning to patents for the additional protection they provide.

## SOFTWARE LICENSE AGREEMENTS

Personal computer software usually comes in a shrink-wrapped box, or the disks are packaged in a sealed plastic bag. A notice warns the buyer not to open the package before reading and agreeing to the license agreement. For most programs, the license agreement is one-sided. It states that the software company is not liable for any losses resulting from use of the program, and it warns the buyers that they will be in big trouble if they make copies (other than backup copies, if allowed) or run the program on more than one machine at a time.

Many personal computer users are unsure of what is software piracy and what is legal. Copyright law includes some **fair-use provisions**, which designate limited copying of copyrighted material as acceptable and therefore fair and legal. But fair use is not always clear, and it may be redefined by the courts or national commissions, such as the Commission on National Technology Use (CONTU), which defined fair use guidelines for photocopying. Selling copies of the program is definitely not fair use. Making one backup copy certainly is fair use. But does fair use override an implied agreement to limit the number of backup copies? Many users would like a copy of their business software for use on their home machines. If your software's license does not allow its use on more than one machine at a time, it is not fair use to run copies simultaneously on more than one computer because then the copy is not a true backup copy.

For schools and companies that have many personal computers, preventing unauthorized copies is difficult. One solution is to negotiate a *site license agreement* with the vendor that allows the organization to make an unlimited number of copies as long as they are all used at designated locations.

## THWARTING SOFTWARE PIRACY

Software publishers have tried to combat software pirates by educational campaigns and a variety of technical schemes. Technical schemes use hardware, software, or a combination of the two, but they have not been completely successful. Ideally, the scheme should be transparent to the legitimate user or, at worst, a slight inconvenience.

The most common technical scheme is to **copy-protect** a disk by placing an error on the disk (such as an improperly formatted or improperly labeled sector) that does not interfere with the running of the program but does cause a standard disk-copy routine to report an error. This is not a permanent solution because for each new copy-protection scheme, a way will be found to defeat it.

Copy-protected disks are a nuisance, especially when used with a hard disk. One common copy-protection scheme requires that the copy-protected disk be inserted into the floppy disk drive each time the program is started. Programs that defeat this sort of copy-protection scheme usually cost between twenty-five and fifty dollars. Thus it is reasonably easy for a pirate to make an illegal copy of the floppy disk, but it is inconvenient for a legitimate user to use the software on a hard disk.

With copy-protected software, there is always the risk of damaging the original disk. So some copy-protected programs allow a specific number of backup copies to be made by encoding a count on the original disk that is decreased by one each time a copy is made. When the count reaches zero, no more copies can be made.

Two other protection schemes involve passwords and codes. In a password scheme, the user must remember a secret password to gain access to the program on the disk. In a code scheme, a different serial number is encoded in each personal computer's ROM by the manufacturer. The number is read by the program the first time it is run and is used thereafter to initialize the program. The program must read this number to run. As a result, it cannot be used on a different computer. Al-

## A Word About . . . *Lock-Busting Programs*

*A software-lock breaker becomes a hero to some, a villain to others.*

Attending a computer trade show takes a lot of courage for software developer Michael Brown. Other conventioneers sometimes mutter obscenities when they walk by his booth. Even some supporters shy away, afraid to be seen with him. Concedes Mr. Brown: "One of these days I'll probably get a pie in my face."

The personal computer industry usually treats its mavericks with tolerance, but it gives little quarter to Mr. Brown. That's because he's a professional lock picker of a sort," an expert at cracking open the intricate electronic padlocks affixed to software programs to keep people from making copies. His company, Central Point Software Inc. of Portland, Oregon, sells disks containing Mr. Brown's lock-busting schemes to computer owners, who use them to copy such popular programs as Lotus 1-2-3, which is used for business applications, and Flight Simulator, a game.

Copying such software is illegal except when people who purchase software make backup copies for their own use; giving away or selling copies to others is illegal. It is for fostering legal copying that Mr. Brown's lock-picking software is ostensibly sold. But nobody seems to doubt that some of his customers are software pirates. So Mr. Brown's skills have made him not only a lot of money—he says he's a multimillionaire at age 27—but also a lot of enemies.

"We're waging a war," says Ken Williams, the vice president for research and development of Softguard Systems Inc., a Santa Clara, California, company that devises many locks. Software companies "go ape" over the issue of copying, he says, to the point that some "want to get a gun" and shoot Mr. Brown.

That may be an exaggeration, but not much of one. Software publishers are outraged, partly because they believe that the pirates are costing them millions of dollars in lost revenue. According to market researchers, as many as nine bootleg copies of software are in use for each legitimate disk. And on top of the monetary losses is emotional pain. Says Vern L. Rabur, the president of a software publisher named Symantec Corp.: "People invest their lives in a product. When they find out someone has copied it, there's a phenomenal sense of personal violation . . . like being raped or having someone break into your home."

Mr. Brown concedes that some of his customers may be software pirates, but he says that most piracy is done by people "innocently confused" about the law. He adds: "I'm totally against piracy. And if I felt the incidence of it were high, I wouldn't do what I'm doing. People are basically honest." His company, which doesn't use locks itself, includes with its

though this scheme would probably be popular among software companies, few manufacturers have decided to take the first step by electronically numbering their personal computers. An exception is that Adobe Systems, which developed PostScript, requires manufacturers of PostScript printers to build unique identification numbers in each printer. These numbers are used to verify that copyrighted fonts are used only on designated printers.

No simple solution to the problem of software piracy exists. An ideal solution would make it impossible to copy a program illegally but would not inconvenience legitimate users. Thus far, copy protection has made it harder for casual users to copy a program at the cost of inconveniencing all users. Many software companies, giving in to pressure from users, have stopped using copy protection altogether.

programs a flier explaining that copying software is illegal except for backup copies.

To many computer owners, Mr. Brown is a hero. They argue that software locks gum up the workings of a computer and waste precious memory. Besides, they say, having one or two extra copies of a fragile software disk is perfectly legal—and important in case the original is damaged, by scratches or spilled coffee, for example. Declared one fan in a letter to a trade journal: "Mike Brown is the consumer's savior."

With raves such as that, Mr. Brown has little trouble selling his programs (brand name, Copy II), which bear retail prices of about $40. His programs are so popular that 15 telephone operators are hard-pressed to handle the orders.

Mr. Brown is a tall and stoop-shouldered man with a pudgy, innocent face and a sad smile. Bored with college, he dropped out in his junior year with a less-than-distinguished record; he had flunked calculus and barely scraped through physics. In 1980 he took a job at a computer store for $75 a week.

Before long, Mr. Brown found himself spending hours trying to placate angry software customers. "Computers were new and customers didn't know how to handle a floppy disk," he says. "How can you tell someone that a tiny scratch just cost him $150?" He adds: "The store was losing a lot of money giving away replacement software."

That prompted Mr. Brown to start fiddling with software locks. Working late into the night, he patiently unraveled tangled computer codes to determine how to crack his first lock. Today, after plenty of experience, he says he can pick a sophisticated lock in about 45 minutes.

Cracking the locks takes an intimate understanding of computer logic. One simple lock involves hiding a tiny fragment of scrambled code on a disk. When ordered to copy the program, the computer finds the fragment and, taking it for an error, corrects it. But without the telltale fragment, the copy won't work. Lock-busting programs such as Mr. Brown's interfere with the computer's error-correcting logic, foiling the lock.

Source: Patricia Bellew Gray, *The Wall Street Journal*, 28 February 1986.

Software publishers have not come up with a solution to stop software piracy. It is doubtful they will. Taking a combination of steps seems to be a reasonable approach. Some suggestions are

- Make it more difficult for pirates to copy programs and thereby discourage all but the most technically sophisticated of them.

- Develop protection schemes that minimally inconvenience legitimate users. Inconvenient schemes and the failure to provide a legitimate backup disk encourages piracy.

- Educate users about the rights of software distributors and the rights of buyers. Licensing agreements should be reasonable and clearly state the rights and responsibilities of each party.

## A Word About . . . *Software Copyrights*

*This is an abridged version of the* **1986 ICCE Policy Statement on Software Copyrights** *produced by the International Council for Computers in Education, University of Oregon, 1781 Agate St., Eugene, OR 97403. This policy statement was developed by a committee of educators, software developers, and industry representatives. A 1983 version of these guidelines was widely circulated and adopted by schools throughout the world.*

**Guidelines for Software Use.** The 1976 U.S. Copyright Act and its 1980 amendments remain vague in some areas of software and its application to education. Where the law itself is vague, software licenses tend to be much more specific. It is therefore imperative that educators understand the software's licensing restrictions. Users should look to the copyright page of software documentation to find information regarding their rights, obligations, and license restrictions regarding each piece of software. If these uses are not addressed by the license, the following Guidelines representing the collected opinion of a variety of experts in the software copyright field, are recommended.

**Back-up Copy:** The Copyright Act is clear in permitting the owner of software to make a back-up copy of the software to be held for use as an archival copy in the event the original disk fails to function. Such back-up copies are not to be used on a second computer at the same time the original is used.

**Multiple Loading:** The Copyright Act is most unclear as it applies to loading the contents of one disk into multiple computers for use at the same time. In the absence of a license expressly permitting the user to load the contents of one disk into many computers for use at the same time, it is suggested that you NOT allow this activity to take place. The fact that you physically can do so is irrelevant. In an effort to make it easier for schools to buy software for each computer station, many software publishers offer lab packs and other quantity buying incentives. Contact individual publishers for details.

**Local Area Network Software Use:** It is suggested that before placing a software program on a local area network or disk-sharing system for use by multiple users at the same time, you obtain a written license agreement from the copyright holder giving you permission to do so. The fact that you are able to physically load the program on the network is, again, irrelevant. You should obtain a license to do so before you act.

**Model Department Policy on Software Copyright**

1. The ethical and practical implications of software piracy will be taught to instructors and students.

2. Staff will be informed that they are expected to adhere to section 117 of the 1976 Copyright Act as amended in 1980, governing the use of software.

3. When permission is obtained from the copyright holder to use software on a disk-sharing system, efforts will be made to secure this software from copying.

4. Under no circumstances shall illegal copies of copyrighted software be made or used on school equipment.

- Reduce the cost of software to less than the cost of the user manual. This can work for programs with high volume sales but not software designed for thin markets.

Educators and educational publishers face these problems and have organized to develop guidelines for educational institutions. During the early 1980s, the International Council for Computers in Education (ICCE), a leading professional association for educational computing, developed guidelines for software copying. These guidelines will probably be updated every few years because new technology continues to raise new possibilities and problems.

## Summary

The personal computer has greatly magnified the problem of software piracy. No simple solution or policy has been developed that deals adequately with it. A first step in dealing with these abuses is to make the user of personal computers aware of what is legal and illegal. A second step is to institute safeguards against piracy. It is all but impossible to prevent a technically expert user from copying a program. But safeguards will discourage the casual user.

## Key Terms

| | |
|---|---|
| copy-protect | patent |
| copyright | software piracy |
| fair-use provisions | trade secret |

## Discussion Questions

1. Would lowering the price of software reduce piracy?

2. Is allowing computer software to be used on only one machine too restrictive? Can you suggest a more reasonable rule?

3. Some pirates justify their actions saying they are "helping their friends" or "making sure a good program doesn't go to waste." Are these valid arguments?

## Exercises

1. Read several software license agreements for personal computer software. What restrictions are included? If the programs come from different companies, list the differences.

2. Investigate the history of patents for computer programs.

3. Determine what laws, if any, your state has enacted concerning software piracy.

## About the Authors

**David Sullivan,** Associate Professor of Information Systems at Oregon State University, graduated from the University of Oregon in accounting. After joining Tektronix as a manufacturing accountant, he became the finance manager of the Information Display Systems Division—a division that produced graphical personal computers for scientists and engineers before the term *personal computing* became popular. His interest in the use of computers led him to graduate study at Carnegie Mellon University's Graduate School of Industrial Administration, from which he received a Ph.D. in system science.

**Curtis Cook,** Professor of Computer Science at Oregon State University, received his M.S. and Ph.D. in computer science from the University of Iowa. He received a B.A. in mathematics from Augustana College. His research interests are software complexity measures, minimal perfect hashing functions, and graph theory applications in computer science.

**T. G. Lewis,** Professor of Computer Science at Oregon State University, received his Ph.D. in computer science from Washington State University. He has been on the faculties of the Universities of Missouri and Southwestern Louisiana. He consults extensively for industry and is the author of twenty books and more than fifty articles on computing.

# Appendix
# How Computers Process Information

**Representing Information**
*Binary Versus Decimal*
*Characters and Strings of Text*
*Numeric Codes*

**Processing Information**
*How Electronic Circuits Compute*
*Numeric Precision*

T he basic building block of computers is the transistor. A **transistor** is an electronic device for controlling the flow of electrons in an electrical circuit. Think of a transistorized circuit as a switch like a light switch at home: the switch is either on or off and stays that way until it is flipped again. If electrons are allowed to flow, the circuit is on; if electrons are not allowed to flow, the circuit is off. The on-off flow of electrons in these small circuits is used to encode information as binary 1s and 0s.

A modern electronic computer is often called a *binary* computer because its most basic circuits can remember either one of the binary digits 0 and 1. These digits are called *bits*. Both the internal and external memory of a computer are nothing more than storehouses for bits. RAM (random-access memory), ROM (read-only memory), disk, and tape all store 1s and 0s. No other form of information is stored in a computer—not numbers, keyboard characters, programs, or word processing documents. How, then, does a computer store and process decimal numbers, business letters, and other forms of information? The binary number system and computer codes provide the answer.

# REPRESENTING INFORMATION

## Binary Versus Decimal

The key to understanding computers is the binary number system. Whereas the decimal number system has ten digits, 0 to 9; the binary number system has only two digits, 0 and 1. To understand how these digits are used, recall that decimal numbers represent powers of 10. For example, the decimal number 537 is really the sum of powers of 10.

$$537 \text{ decimal} = (5 \times 10^2) + (3 \times 10^1) + (7 \times 10^0)$$
$$= (5 \times 100) + (3 \times 10) + (7 \times 1)$$
$$= 500 + 30 + 7$$

Notice that the decimal number 1 is 10 raised to the 0 power; and 10, 100, 1,000, and so on are all 10 raised to some power.

Binary numbers are the sums of powers of 2 in the same way that decimal numbers are sums of powers of 10. The following list shows the decimal numbers that are represented by some powers of 2.

| | |
|---|---|
| $2^{-2} =$ | 0.25 |
| $2^{-1} =$ | 0.5 |
| $2^0 =$ | 1. |
| $2^1 =$ | 2. |
| $2^2 =$ | 4. |
| $2^3 =$ | 8. |
| $2^4 =$ | 16. |
| $2^8 =$ | 256. |
| $2^{16} =$ | 65,536. |
| $2^{20} =$ | 1,048,576. |
| $2^{24} =$ | 16,777,216. |
| $2^{32} =$ | 4,294,967,296. |

A binary number is a string of 1s and 0s, each indicating the presence or absence of a power of 2. For example, consider the binary number 101. This number is converted to its decimal equivalents as follows:

| Binary number | 0 | 0 | 0 | 0 | 0 | 1 | 0 | 1 |
|---|---|---|---|---|---|---|---|---|
| Power of two | 7 | 6 | 5 | 4 | 3 | 2 | 1 | 0 |
| Decimal number | 0 | 0 | 0 | 0 | 0 | 4 | 0 | 1 |

$$101 \text{ binary} = (1 \times 2^2) + (0 \times 2^1) + (1 \times 2^0)$$
$$= (1 \times 4) + (0 \times 2) + (1 \times 1)$$
$$= 4 + 0 + 1 = 5 \text{ decimal}$$

Thus 101 is the binary number representation of the decimal number 5.

The fractional part of a binary number such as 101.1 is a sum of *negative* powers of two. For example, 101.1 binary is converted to its decimal equivalent as follows:

$$101.1 \text{ binary} = (1 \times 2^2) + (0 \times 2^1) + (1 \times 2^0) + (1 \times 2^{-1})$$
$$= (1 \times 4) + (0 \times 2) + (1 \times 1) + (1 \times 1/2)$$
$$= 4 + 0 + 1 + 1/2 = 5.5 \text{ decimal}$$

Here are some other examples.

$$4 \text{ decimal} = 100 \text{ binary}$$
$$16 \text{ decimal} = 10000 \text{ binary}$$
$$31 \text{ decimal} = 111111 \text{ binary}$$
$$6.25 \text{ decimal} = 110.01 \text{ binary}$$
$$145.625 \text{ decimal} = 10010001.101 \text{ binary}$$

Keep in mind that computers work exclusively with binary numbers because they can store only a 1 or a 0. To do arithmetic and word processing they must convert from binary to decimal and back again. We see only the result of this conversion and not the binary numbers themselves. It is not necessary to know anything about binary arithmetic to use a computer. But if you want to know what happens inside a computer, then it is essential that you learn the "secret code" of binary numbers.

## Characters and Strings of Text

How does a binary computer process textual information? Individual keystrokes generate letters, numbers, and other symbols called *characters*. Groups of characters treated as a unit are called *strings*. Because characters and strings cannot be processed directly by a machine that "understands" only binary numbers, they must be encoded in some kind of binary code. One of these codes is ASCII (American Standard Code for Information Interchange), which associates a unique 7-bit binary number with each character.

In ASCII the letter *A* is associated with 1000001 binary. The numeral (not its value) 1 is associated with 0110001 binary. However, because binary numbers are tedious to remember, people usually convert binary codes to their decimal equivalents when they refer to them. Hence, *A* is represented by the decimal number 65, and the numeral 1 is represented by decimal number 49.

| Keyboard character | Binary code | Decimal code |
|---|---|---|
| A | 1000001 | 65 |
| a | 1100001 | 97 |
| Z | 1011010 | 90 |
| z | 1111010 | 122 |
| 0 (zero) | 0110000 | 48 |
| 9 | 0111001 | 57 |
| + | 0101011 | 43 |
| (carriage return) | 0001101 | 13 |

Suppose you want to store a line of text in the computer's memory. You enter the string of characters "Hello C3 PO" into the computer through the keyboard. The keyboard converts each keystroke (including the spaces) into ASCII binary code.

| Character (keyboard) | ASCII (decimal) |
|:---:|:---:|
| H | 72 |
| e | 101 |
| l | 108 |
| l | 108 |
| o | 111 |
| (space) | 32 |
| C | 67 |
| 3 | 51 |
| (space) | 32 |
| P | 80 |
| O | 79 |

When the computer displays this line of text on its screen, the reverse process occurs: circuits in the screen display convert the ASCII binary code in memory into visible characters.

A 7-bit coding system like ASCII can represent only a limited number of different characters. The largest decimal number we can express in a 7-bit binary number is the equivalent of the binary number 1111111, which is

$$1111111 \text{ binary} = 64 + 32 + 16 + 8 + 4 + 2 + 1 \text{ decimal}$$
$$= 255 \text{ decimal}$$

Everything is exactingly stored in the computer as binary numbers: letters of the alphabet, numerals, punctuation marks, and special characters ($, #, %, and so on). Each character has its own 7-bit code. Because the memory of a computer can record binary digits and nothing else, all kinds of information must be encoded. The power of a computer to manipulate symbols is hidden in the simplicity of a coding scheme.

## Numeric Codes

Values of numbers can be encoded in many ways; we will discuss the two most common ways. Natural or counting numbers are encoded as binary **integers** (whole numbers). Signed numbers with decimal points are called **real numbers** and must be encoded using **floating-point representation.** For example, a whole number like 35 is an integer, but a number with a decimal point in it—say, 35.0— is a real number and must be encoded in the floating-point format.

### Integers

A computer stores binary numbers in groups of bits called *bytes* (8 bits = 1 byte) and *words* (which may be 8, 16, 32, or more bits depending on the computer). An 8-bit byte can encode only 256 different integers—say, from $-128$ to $+127$ decimal value. A 16-bit word can encode binary integers from $-32,768$ to $+32,767$ decimal. The size in bits of a computer word affects the power of a computer because it limits the size of the numbers that a computer can represent conveniently. Our examples assume a 16-bit word length.

Computers perform addition, subtraction, multiplication, and division on the binary code, not on decimal integers. After the arithmetic is carried out in binary, a program converts the result from a binary number into a decimal number. Conversely, when a decimal integer is entered into a computer, it must be converted into a binary integer before any arithmetic can be performed.

The correspondence between decimal and binary integers is straightforward. The first bit of a binary integer is called a *sign bit*; it is a 0 if the number is positive and a 1 if the number is negative. All binary numbers from zero through 0111111111111111 (16 bits with a leading 0 bit) are equivalent to the decimal numbers 0 to 32,767. The binary numbers 1111111111111111 (16 bits, all set to 1) through 1000000000000000 (16 bits with a leading 1) are equivalent to decimal numbers $-1$ to $-32767$. Negative numbers count backward to make subtraction simple for electronic circuits.

Integer representation results in fast machine arithmetic, but it also has disadvantages. Only whole numbers can be manipulated, and the size of each number is restricted. To get around these limitations, computers also use floating-point representation.

## Floating-Point Numbers

Floating-point representation is based on scientific notation, which expresses each number as a magnitude times a power of 10. For example, in scientific notation 120 is written as $1.2 \times 10^2$. Similarly, floating-point representation separates a number into three parts.

1. The sign. This is either plus or minus.

2. The magnitude. This is expressed as a decimal fraction between 0 and 1.

3. The exponent. This is a power of 10 (or a power of 2). It reflects the location of the decimal point within the decimal (or binary) number.

In the computer field, floating-point numbers are often written in *scientific notation* as follows:

```
0.50 E + 01
↑   ↑    ↑
|   |    Exponent or power of 10
|   |
|   Separator
|
|   Fractional part
Sign of entire number (either + , − , or left blank for positive numbers)
```

To convert a decimal floating-point number to an ordinary decimal number you simply move the decimal point right or left (depending on the sign of the exponent) the number of digits specified by the exponent. For example, to obtain the value of 0.50 E + 01, move the decimal point one digit to the right of its original position, because the exponent is 1 and its sign is positive.

$$0.50 \text{ E} + 01 = 0.50 \times 10 = 5.0$$

The sign of the number is always the sign shown in front of the floating point representation. Here are several other examples.

| | | |
|---|---|---|
| 0.55  E −01 | is | 0.055 |
| 0.123 E +03 | is | 123.0 |
| −0.95  E +00 | is | −0.95 |
| −0.95  E +01 | is | −9.5 |
| −0.95  E +05 | is | −95,000.00 |

There is a limit to the size of number that can be encoded in this fashion. If two digits are allowed in the fraction and in the exponent, then the largest number that can be encoded is +0.99 E +99, and the smallest number is −0.99 E +99. The numbers nearest zero would be +0.01 E −99 and −0.01 E −99. Zero is a special case, usually represented by +0.00 E + 00.

## PROCESSING INFORMATION

### How Electronic Circuits Compute

The brain of a computer is its central processing unit, which contains the arithmetic logic unit (ALU). The brain of a personal computer is a microprocessor. Inside the ALU or microprocessor is a collection of circuits that add, multiply, transfer, compare, and so on. It is instructive to examine how these circuits work—for example, how an addition takes place.

Because all numbers, characters, and instructions are stored as binary numbers, addition of two numbers reduces to the addition of bits.

| | |
|---|---|
| 1010 | binary |
| + 1101 | binary |
| 10111 | binary |

The addition circuit must do just two things in order to perform this addition: add two bits together to get a sum, and produce a carry bit (0 or 1). The ability to perform these simple operations is wired into the computer by building circuits that obey two rules.

1.  If only one of the addend bits is a 1, then the resulting bit is a 1; otherwise the result is a 0. This is the rule for adding two bits.

2.  If one or both of the addend bits is a 0, then the resulting bit is a 0; otherwise the result is a 1 bit. This is the rule for obtaining the carry bit.

These rules are represented in the following **truth tables:**

SUM TABLE

First Addend

| | | 0 | 1 |
|---|---|---|---|
| Second Addend | 0 | 0 | 1 |
| | 1 | 1 | 0 |

CARRY TABLE

First Addend

| | | 0 | 1 |
|---|---|---|---|
| Second Addend | 0 | 0 | 0 |
| | 1 | 0 | 1 |

These two truth tables summarize how to perform binary addition one bit at a time. For instance, if a 0 is added (first addend) to a 1 (second addend), the result is 1, as shown in the corresponding entry of the sum table. Similarly, if a 1 is added to another 1, the result is 0 according to the sum table and a 1 according to the carry table.

If the sum and carry tables are used repeatedly, any binary numbers can be added. Suppose the computer is asked to add 1101 to 0111. The sum for each column is noted, and the carry bit is shifted one place to the left of the column just added and placed below the sum.

```
        1101 binary        (13 decimal)
      + 0111 binary        ( 7 decimal)
Sum =   1010 binary
Carry = 0101  (shifted left 1 place)
```

This sum and the carry bit are then added in the same way. These steps are repeated until there are no carry bits to be added (000), leaving the final answer. Thus

```
          1101 binary        (13 decimal)
        + 0111 binary        ( 7 decimal)
Sum   =   1010 binary
Carry =   0101  (shifted left one place)
Sum   =   0000
Carry =   1010  (shifted)
Sum   =   10100
Carry =   0000
Answer =  10100 binary       (20 decimal)
```

In short, the computer adds two numbers by performing sum, carry, and shift operations through repetitious steps. The operations are very simple; but when combined in just the right way, they can do powerful things.

We have just shown that computers work by simulating operations on binary numbers through electronic circuits that perform elementary functions. Addition, for example, is nothing more than a sequence of simple summation, carry, and shift operations. Higher-order operations are nothing more than lengthy sequences of elementary operations. This, combined with binary encoding of information, is the secret to how computers work.

Computers do not know how to think. They merely perform millions of simple truth table operations. To show how computers can blindly compute wrong answers, in the next section we consider the problems associated with arithmetic on real numbers.

## Numeric Precision

Sometimes the computer prints a value that is not quite what you expect. For instance, it might print 1.9999 instead of 2.0, or a calculation may be off by a few cents—yielding an answer of $12,235.20 instead of $12,235.24. Both of these results reflect the fact that the computer does not provide infinite precision. In particular, some information is lost during calculation because the encoding of floating-point numbers is approximate.

To understand this lack of precision, consider the following addition:

$$
\begin{array}{r}
3000.0001 \\
+\ 3000.0001 \\
\hline
6000.0002
\end{array}
$$

The computer must convert 3000.0001 to binary code; add the two binary-encoded numbers; convert the result back to 6000.0002 decimal; and display the result. When the floating-point number is stored in 32 bits, the encoded value of 3000.0001 is approximated as 0.3000000 E +01. Thus, when the computer adds these numbers, it comes up with a sum of 6000.0000 instead of 6000.0002.

Whenever computers calculate with floating-point numbers, they round off the numbers, which creates errors. For this reason, you should always ask yourself, To how many digits is this number reasonable and accurate? Typically, floating-point numbers are accurate to about the first six or seven digits. So unless the program uses double-precision arithmetic (which stores each number in twice as much storage space), you should use only the first six or seven digits in the answer even if the computer prints more than seven digits.

# Credits

*(Credits continued from p. iv)*

Chapter 3   Courtesy of Houston Instruments

Figure 3.1   Product of Key Tronic, Spokane, Washington

Figure 3.3   Courtesy of Hewlett-Packard Company

Figure 3.4   Photo courtesy of GTCO Corporation, Rockville, Maryland

Figure 3.5   Photo courtesy of Microsoft Corporation

Figure 3.7   Courtesy of Hewlett-Packard Company

Figure 3.8a   Courtesy of Qume Corporation, A subsidiary of ITT Corporation

Figure 3.12   Courtesy of Toshiba America, Inc. Information Systems Division

Figure 3.13   Courtesy of Hewlett-Packard Company

Chapter 4   Courtesy of Mentor Graphics

Figure 4.8   Photo courtesy of Xerox Corporation

Chapter 5   Courtesy of Apple Computer, Inc.

Part 2   Jerry Howard/Stock, Boston

Chapter 6   Courtesy of AST

Chapter 7   Courtesy of Hewlett-Packard Company

Chapter 8   Photo courtesy of Xerox Corporation

Figure 8.1   Ludwig Richter

Figure 8.3b   Graphic Arts Technical Foundation

Figure 8.4   Courtesy of MicroDisplay Systems, Inc.

Figure 8.5   Courtesy of Apple Computer, Inc.

Figure 8.6a,b   Courtesy of Hewlett-Packard Company

Figure 8.8   Linotronic

Figure 8.12   Courtesy of Hewlett-Packard Company

Box   Courtesy of Hewlett-Packard Company

Part 3   Courtesy of Industry News

Chapter 9   Courtesy of Candle

Chapter 10   Courtesy of Hewlett-Packard Company

Part 4   Charles Gupton/Stock, Boston

Chapter 11   Courtesy of Honeywell

Chapter 12   Courtesy of Apple Computer, Inc.

Figure 12.5   Courtesy of Microrim, Inc.

Part 5   Courtesy of AT&T Bell Laboratories

Chapter 13   Courtesy of Apple Computer, Inc.

Figure 13.22   Photo courtesy of Gerber Scientific, Inc.

Figure 13.23   Photo courtesy of Intergraph Corporation, Huntsville, Alabama

Figure 13.24   Courtesy of ARCAD

Chapter 14   Courtesy of AT&T Bell Laboratories

Figure 14.2a   Courtesy of Prentice Corporation

Figure 14.2b   Courtesy of Hayes Microcomputer Products

Chapter 15   Courtesy of AT&T Bell Laboratories

Figure 15.7   Courtesy of Apple Computer, Inc.

Figure 15.8   Courtesy of Corvus Systems, Inc.

Part 6   Courtesy of International Business Machines Corporation

Chapter 16   Photo Researchers, Inc.

Chapter 17   Courtesy of Aronson Photographics/Stock Boston

Figure 17.1   Copyright Will Eisner

Chapter 18   Courtesy of Los Alamos

Figure 18.2   Courtesy of International Business Machines Corporation

Figure 18.3   Courtesy of International Business Machines Corporation

Figure 18.4   Photograph courtesy of the Hagley Museum and Library

Figure 18.5   Courtesy of International Business Machines Corporation

Figure 18.6   Photograph courtesy of the Hagley Museum and Library

Figure 18.7   Photo courtesy of DAVA Still Media Depository/Info Edit

Figure 18.8   Courtesy of International Business Machines Corporation

Figure 18.9   (left) Photograph courtesy of Microsoft Corporation
(right) Photo reproduced with permission of Digital Research, Inc.

Figure 18.10   Courtesy of International Business Machines Corporation

Figure 18.11a,b   Courtesy of Apple Computer, Inc.

Box 18   Mark E. Alsop

Chapter 19   Courtesy of Honeywell

## Window 1

Figure 1   Courtesy of Commodore Electronics Ltd.

Figure 2   Courtesy of Management Science America, Inc. (MSA)

Figure 3   Courtesy of Apple Computer, Inc.

Figure 4   Courtesy of Hewlett-Packard Company

Figures 5, 6   Courtesy of Texas Instruments

Figure 7   Courtesy of Hewlett-Packard Company

Figures 8–10   Courtesy of Shared Medical System Corporation

Figures 11–13   Courtesy of Apple Computer, Inc.

Figure 14   Courtesy of Commodore Electronics Ltd.

Figures 15, 16   Courtesy of International Business Machines

Figure 17   Courtesy NCR Corporation

Figure 18   Courtesy of ROLM, an IBM Company

Figure 19   Courtesy of Hewlett-Packard Company

Figure 20   Courtesy of Compugraphic Corporation, Wilmington, Massachusetts

Figure 21   Courtesy of ROLM, an IBM Company

Figures 22–26   Photos courtesy of Atex, Inc., a Kodak Company, of Bedford, Massachusetts

Figures 27–30   Photos courtesy of Intergraph Corporation, Huntsville, Alabama

Figure 31   Courtesy of Monarch Marking Systems, a subsidiary of Pitney Bowes

Figure 32   Courtesy NCR Corporation

Figure 33   Photograph courtesy of Scope Incorporated, Reston, Virginia

Figures 34,35   Photos courtesy of Gerber Scientific, Inc.

Figures 36–42   Courtesy of International Business Machines Corporation

Figures 43–47   Photos courtesy of Gerber Scientific, Inc.

Figure 48   Photo: Loral Corporation

Figure 49   Courtesy of Sanders Associates

Figure 50   Photo: Loral Corporation

Figure 51   Courtesy of Sanders Associates

Figure 52   Courtesy of Hewlett-Packard Company

Figure 53   Courtesy of Compac Computer Corporation


## Window 2

Figure 1   Photo courtesy of Intergraph Corporation, Huntsville, Alabama

Figure 2   Courtesy of Apple Computer, Inc.

Figure 4   Courtesy of International Business Machines Corp.

Figure 5   Courtesy of Compac Computer Corp.

Figure 6   Courtesy of Apple Computer, Inc.

Figure 8, 10, 12, 13, 15, 16   Courtesy of International Business Machines Corporation

Figure 19   Courtesy of Memorex Corporation, a Burroughs subsidiary

Figure 20   Photo courtesy Seagate

Figure 21   Courtesy of Memorex Corporation, a Burroughs subsidiary

Figure 22   Courtesy of Storage Technology Corporation © 1984

Figure 23   Photo courtesy Seagate

Figure 24   Courtesy of International Business Machines Corporation

Figure 25   Courtesy of Comdisco, Inc.

Figure 26   Courtesy of Northern Telecom Inc.

Figure 27   Courtesy of Ampex Corporation, one of The Signal Companies, Inc.

Figure 28   Courtesy of Storage Technology Corporation © 1984

Figure 29   Courtesy of TRW Inc.

## Window 3

Figure 1   Photo courtesy of C. Itoh Electronics, Inc.

Figure 2   Courtesy of Apple Computer, Inc.

Figure 3   WordStar® is a trademark of MicroPro International Corporation®

Figure 4   Compugraphic Corporation, Wilmington, Massachusetts

Figure 5   Courtesy of International Business Machines Corporation

Figure 6   Courtesy of Hewlett-Packard Company

Figure 7   Courtesy of Toshiba America, Inc., Information Systems Division

Figure 8   Courtesy of Apple Computer, Inc.

Figure 9   Courtesy of Okidata

Figure 10   Courtesy of Qume Corporation, a subsidiary of ITT

Figure 11   Courtesy Martin Marietta Data Systems

Figures 12, 13   Courtesy of Apple Computer, Inc.

Figure 14   Sweet-P Plotters by Enter Computer, Inc., 6867 Nancy Ridge Drive, San Diego, California 92121. (619) 450-0601

Figure 15   Courtesy of Sanders Associates

Figure 16   Photograph courtesy of Gerber Scientific, Inc.

Figure 17   Courtesy of Versatec, a Xerox Company

Figures 18–20   Photos courtesy of Gerber Scientific, Inc.

Figure 21   Photo courtesy of GTCO Corporation, Rockville, Maryland

Figure 22   Courtesy of International Business Machines Corporation

Figure 23   Courtesy of Monarch Marking Systems, a subsidiary of Pitney Bowes

Figure 24   Courtesy of National Semiconductor Corporation

## Window 4

Figure 1   Courtesy of Caere Corporation

Figure 2   Courtesy of International Business Machines Corporation

Figure 3   Courtesy of Commodore Electronics Ltd.

Figure 4   Courtesy of Electronic Data Systems, Dallas, Texas

Figure 5   Courtesy of Apple Computer, Inc.

Figure 6   Courtesy of Radio Shack, a division of Tandy Corporation

Figure 7   Courtesy of International Business Machines Corporation

Figure 8   Courtesy Martin Marietta Data Systems

Figure 9   Compugraphic Corporation, Wilmington, Massachusetts

Figures 10, 11   Courtesy of Hewlett-Packard Company

Figures 12, 13   Courtesy of Apple Computer, Inc.

Figures 14, 15   Photos courtesy of Gerber Scientific, Inc.

Figure 16   Courtesy of TRW Inc.

Figure 17   Courtesy of Docutel/Olivette Corporation

Figure 18   Courtesy MSI Data Corporation

Figure 19   Photograph courtesy of Scope Incorporated, Reston, Virginia

Figure 20   Courtesy NCR Corporation

Figure 21   Courtesy of Caere Corporation

Figure 22   Courtesy NCR Corporation

Figure 23   Courtesy of Texas Instruments

Figure 24   Courtesy of Data Entry Systems

Figure 25   Courtesy of Sperry Corporation

## Window 5

Figure 1   Photo from Xerox Corporation

Figure 2   Courtesy of International Business Machines Corporation

Figure 3   SuperCalc is a registered trademark of Computer Associates International, Inc. Micro Products Division

Figure 4   Living Videotext, Inc.

Figures 5, 6, 7   Courtesy of Microsoft Corporation

Figure 12   Courtesy of International Business Machines Corporation

Figure 24   Courtesy of Hewlett-Packard Company

Figure 25–26   Ashton-Tate © 1987

Figure 27   Ashton-Tate

Figures 28–31   Living Videotext, Inc.

Figure 32   Courtesy of Hewlett-Packard Company

Figures 33–35, 37–39   Courtesy of Aldus Corporation

Figures 40–46   Courtesy of International Business Machines Corporation

Figure 47   Courtesy of © Lotus Development Corp. 1985. Used with permission. "Symphony" is a registered trademark of Lotus Development Corporation.

Figure 48   Computer Associates International, Inc.

Figures 49–52   Courtesy of Ansa Software

Figure 53   Courtesy of MicroPro. Reprinted with permission from "Machine Learning" by A.T. Kolokouris © McGraw Hill, Inc.

Figure 54   Courtesy of © Lotus Development Corp. 1985. Used with permission. "Symphony" is a registered trademark of Lotus Development Corporation.

## Window 6

Figure 1   Courtesy of Northern Telecom Inc.

Figures 2, 3   Courtesy of RCA

Figures 4, 5   Courtesy of Electronic Data Systems, Dallas, Texas

Figures 6, 7   Courtesy of Northern Telecom Inc.

Figure 8   Courtesy of TRW Inc.

Figure 9   Photograph provided by Tandem Computer Incorporated

Figure 10   Courtesy of General Electric Company

Figure 11   Courtesy of TRW Inc.

Figure 12   Photo courtesy of Telex Computer Products, Inc., Tulsa, Oklahoma

Figure 13   Courtesy of Electronic Data Systems, Dallas, Texas

Figure 14   Vitro Corporation, Silver Spring, Maryland

Figures 15, 16   Courtesy of Northern Telecom Inc.

Figures 17, 18   Courtesy of MICOM Systems, Inc.

Figure 19   Courtesy of Hewlett-Packard Company

Figures 20, 21   Courtesy of ROLM, an IBM Company

Figure 22   Photo courtesy of National Data Corporation

Figure 23   Courtesy of International Business Machines Corporation

Figure 24   Courtesy of MSI Data Corporation

Figure 25   Courtesy of General Electric Company

Figure 26   Courtesy of RCA

## Window 7

Figure 1   Photo courtesy of Intergraph Corporation, Huntsville, Alabama

Figures 2, 3   Courtesy of Apple Computer, Inc.

Figures 4, 5   Courtesy of International Business Machines Corporation

Figure 8   Courtesy of Graphic Communications, Inc.

Figures 11-13   Courtesy Design Resources, Inc.

Figure 15   Courtesy of Sanders Associates

Figures 16-25   Photos courtesy of Intergraph Corporation, Huntsville, Alabama

## Window 8

Figures 1–4   Photos courtesy of Monsanto

Figure 5   Courtesy of National Semiconductor Corporation

Figure 6   Courtesy of International Business Machines Corporation

Figure 7   Courtesy of National Semiconductor Corporation

Figure 8   Courtesy of Commodore Electronics Ltd.

Figure 9   Courtesy of TRW Inc.

Figure 10   Courtesy of RCA

Figure 11   Photograph courtesy of Intel Corporation

Figure 12   Courtesy of Memorex Corporation, a Burroughs subsidiary

Figure 13   Courtesy of National Semiconductor Corporation

Figure 14   Courtesy of Commodore Electronics Ltd.

Figure 15   Courtesy of Motorola, Inc.

Figure 16   Photo: Loral Corporation/Ovak Arslanian

Figure 17   Courtesy of National Semiconductor Corporation

Figure 18   Photograph courtesy of Intel Corporation

Figure 19   Courtesy of TRW Inc.

Figure 20   Courtesy Commodore Electronics Ltd.

Figure 21   Courtesy of Texas Instruments

Figure 22   Courtesy of TRW Inc.

Figure 23   Courtesy of Paradyne Corporation, Largo, Florida

Figures 24, 25   Courtesy of National Semiconductor Corporation

Figure 26   Courtesy of Gerber Scientific, Inc.

Figure 26   Photo courtesy of Gerber Scientific, Inc.

Figures 27, 28   Photos courtesy of Intergraph Corporation, Huntsville, Alabama

Figure 29   Photo courtesy of Gerber Scientific, Inc.

Figure 30   Courtesy of Versatec, Inc.

Figures 31-33   Photos courtesy of Gerber Scientific, Inc.

Figure 34   Courtesy of Sanders Associates

Figures 35, 36   Courtesy of Cray Research, Inc.

Figures 37, 38   Courtesy of International Business Machines Corporation

Figure 39   Courtesy of Hewlett-Packard Company

Figure 40   Courtesy of Paradyne Corporation, Largo, Florida

Figure 41   Photograph provided by Tandem Computer Incorporated

Figures 42, 43   Courtesy of Apple Computer, Inc.

Figure 44   Courtesy of International Business Machines Corporation

# Glossary

**Absolute cell reference** In spreadsheet processing, a reference to a cell location in the worksheet that is to remain unchanged if the formula that contains the reference is moved to a new location. Contrast with *Relative cell reference.*

**Access time** The time it takes to locate and begin transferring information from an external storage device.

**Acoustic coupler** A low-speed modem that is attached to the telephone system by jamming a telephone handset into two rubber cups on top of the coupler. Contrast with *Direct-connect modem.*

**Active cell** In spreadsheet processing, the worksheet cell currently available for use. It is pointed to by the cursor.

**Adapter card** A circuit board that can be inserted into a computer to provide optional functions, such as an interface for a hard disk or additional memory.

**Address** A number identifying a location in memory. Data in internal memory is organized into words, and each word is given its own numeric address.

**Algorithm** A step-by-step list of instructions for solving a problem.

**Alphanumeric** A set of characters that includes letters and digits and often includes punctuation characters as well.

**Analog** A way of representing data as a continuous, smoothly varying signal wave. Contrast with *Digital.*

**Analytic graphics** A type of presentation graphics built into a spreadsheet, database, or word processing program.

**Application generator** A very high-level language that allows the programmer to give a detailed explanation of what data is to be processed, rather than how to process the data.

**Application program** Programs written to perform specific tasks for computer users rather than computer programmers. Examples include accounting programs, word processing, and graphics programs. Contrast with *System software.*

**Archival copy** A back-up copy of information that is intended for long-term storage.

**Argument** See *Parameter.*

**Arithmetic/logic unit (ALU)** The part of the CPU that has circuits to perform arithmetic and logical operations such as adding, multiplying, comparing, jumping, and shifting.

**Array** An organized collection of data in a column or table format. An array associates many pieces of data with a single variable name. It is an important type of *data structure.*

**Artificial intelligence** A research area concerned with developing computer systems capable of simulating human reasoning and intelligence.

**ASCII** Short for the *American Standard Code for Information Interchange.* A code for representing ingingingletters, numerals, and special characters as a pattern of seven bits. ASCII is used in virtually all personal computers to store and manipulate textual information.

**Aspect ratio** The width to height ratio of an object. The aspect ratio of pixels on a CRT screen affects the screen's ability to represent circles and other images accurately.

**Assembler** A program to translate assembly language instructions into machine language.

**Assembly language** A programming language in which each instruction in the program corresponds to an instruction that the circuits of the computer can perform. Assembly language allows the programmer to write programs with words like MOVE, ADD, or JUMP instead of coding the binary numbers of machine language.

**Asynchronous protocol** A communications protocol that transmits data one character at a time without any prior arrangement as to how many characters are to be sent. Contrast with *Synchronous protocol.*

**Audit trail** The footprints left by a transaction as it is processed through an accounting or computer system.

**Auto-answer** A feature that allows a modem to answer a telephone and establish a connection with another computer without assistance from a computer operator.

**Auto-dialing** A feature that allows a modem to dial telephone numbers under software control.

**Auxiliary storage** See *External storage*

**Back-up copy** An extra copy of a file or disk, stored in case something happens to the original.

**Backward chaining** An inference procedure, similar to deductive reasoning, which begins with the end goal and works back to the origin.

**Bandwidth** The range of frequencies that a communications channel can carry. Bandwidth determines the channel's capacity for carrying information in the same way that a pipe's diameter determines its capacity for carrying water.

**Baseband** A type of transmission in which the entire communications spectrum is dedicated to one form of information. Because baseband signaling transmits digital signals without modulation, only one signal at a time can be present on a baseband channel. Contrast with *Broadband.*

**BASIC** *Beginner's All-purpose Symbolic Instruction Code.* A popular programming language that was originally developed for timesharing and interactive problem solving.

**Batch file** A file that contains a series of operating system commands.

**Batch processing** A processing technique that collects and processes data in groups.

**Baud rate** A measure of transmission speed. Technically the baud rate is the number of times the communication line changes state each second. Most people use baud rate and bits per second interchangeably.

**Benchmark program** A program that is used as a standard of comparison to test the relative capabilities of computer systems.

**Binary** The number system with two possible states for each digit: 0 or 1. This system is important to computers because their circuits have only two states: on or off.

**Bit** An abbreviation for *binary digit.* A bit is the smallest unit of computer memory.

**Bit-mapped display** A method of generating screen images by creating a one-for-one correspondence between bits in memory and pixels on the screen. In color graphics, three or more bits are required in the bit map to represent the red, green, and blue values of an individual pixel. Contrast with *Character-oriented display.*

**Boilerplate** Passages of text that are used over and over without modification.

**Boldface** An attribute of characters that are darker and slightly wider than normal.

**Boot** To start a computer by loading part of the operating system. Usually a computer is booted by inserting a system disk and turning on the computer or by pressing the computer's reset button. *Boot* is short for *bootstrap* as in "pulling yourself up by your bootstraps."

**Broadband** A type of transmission that uses frequency-division multiplexing to transmit text, data, and video or audio signals simultaneously. Contrast with *Baseband*.

**Buffer** A temporary storage area used to compensate for a difference in data transfer rates between two devices.

**Bug** An error in a program.

**Bulletin board system** A personal computer with an auto-answer modem that answers incoming telephone calls. Nearly all bulletin board systems allow the caller to read and leave messages; many allow the caller to send or receive programs as well.

**Bus** A cable or a set of electrical conductors that carry signals among the devices in a computer or network. Only one device at a time is allowed to send data on the bus, but each device continually listens to the bus for messages addressed to it. Because devices can be attached to any point along the bus, a computer network that uses a bus can be expanded easily.

**Byte** Eight adjacent bits of memory treated as a unit of information.

**Cache** A small high-speed memory that acts as a buffer between the CPU and the slower main memory.

**CAD** Short for either *computer-aided design* or *computer-aided drafting*—drawing with the aid of your computer.

**CAM** Short for *computer-aided manufacturing*—automated production.

**Cathode ray tube (CRT)** A display device that generates images by bombarding a phosphor-coated glass tube with a beam of electrons.

**CD-ROM** Short for *compact-disc read-only memory*. A small optical disk system.

**Cell** In spreadsheet processing, the intersection of a row and a column on a worksheet.

**Central processing unit (CPU)** The brain of a computer. The central processing unit contains circuits that execute instructions and control the other units.

**Character-oriented display** A method of generating screen images that breaks the screen into many boxes arranged in rows and columns. Each box can display one character. Contrast with *Bit-mapped display*.

**Characters per second (CPS)** A measure of the rate at which data is transferred.

**Clipboard** A temporary holding place for text, pictures, or graphics. Most electronic clipboards can hold only one item at a time. Thus, placing a new item on the clipboard throws the previous item away.

**Clock rate** The speed at which the central processing unit performs operations; usually measured in megahertz.

**Coaxial cable** A cable that consists of a wire that is encircled by a metallic tubular sleeve. Coaxial cable is used in cable television networks and in high-speed computer networks.

**COBOL** Short for *Common Business-Oriented Language*. COBOL is the most widely used high-level language and is best at creating application programs that manipulate large data files.

**Command** An instruction given to the computer to perform a specified task.

**Command-line operating system** A system of giving instructions to the computer by typing full-word keywords, which are often followed by arguments.

**Command processor** The part of an operating system that accept commands from the user for operating system tasks. Also called a *shell*.

**Compiler** A program that translates programs written in a high-level language into machine language. A compiler is dedicated to a single programming language, such as BASIC or Pascal, and translates the entire program before execution begins. Contrast with *Interpreter.*

**Composition**   The selection of type sizes and styles and the positioning of type on a page.

**Computed field**   A file field that is based on the values of other fields.

**Concentrator**   An "intelligent" multiplexer, which can perform preliminary operations on data before transmission.

**Context-sensitive help**   A system that displays information about the function currently being used when the [HELP] key is pressed.

**Control key**   A special key on the keyboard, usually labeled [CTRL]. Like a shift key, a control key is used in combination with other keys; unlike the shift key, it generates different character codes and is used to give commands.

**Control panel**   A portion of the screen reserved for status and help information.

**Control structure**   Any statement that determines the order in which other statements are executed. Common control structures include FOR statements (for repeating or looping), IF-THEN-ELSE statements (for making two-way decisions), and CASE statements (for multiple-way decisions).

**Control unit**   (1) The part of the CPU that interprets instructions and coordinates their execution. (2) A peripheral device that controls other peripheral devices. For example, a disk control unit might supervise the operation of several disk drives.

**Coprocessor chip**   A special-purpose microprocessor designed to handle specific functions such as floating-point arithmetic or high-speed graphics.

**Copyfitting**   To get text to fit within the available area.

**Copy-protect**   To prevent a disk from being copied by a standard disk-copying routine.

**Copyright**   The exclusive right to publish or sell a creative work. Copyrights are the most common

legal method of protecting computer programs from unauthorized distribution.

**CP/M**   Short for *Control Program for Microcomputers.* CP/M is a popular operating system for personal computers.

**CPU**   See *Central processing unit.*

**Crop**   To trim a graphics image for a better fit or to eliminate unwanted portions.

**CRT**   See *Cathode ray tube.*

**CSMA protocol**   A protocol that controls access to a network's bus. Short for *carrier-sensed multiple-access.*

**Cursor**   An indicator on the screen that shows where things will happen next. The cursor can be an underline (blinking or nonblinking), a rectangle, or even an arrow.

**Cursor-movement key**   A key that when pressed moves the cursor in a designated direction. Cursor-movement keys generally have directional arrows on their keytops, as in [←], [→], [↑], and [↓].

**Daisy wheel**   The print element of a letter-quality printer. Daisy wheels are made from metal or plastic and have spokes radiating from the center. Each spoke contains a letter, number, or symbol at the end.

**Data**   Information in code, text, or numerical form.

**Database**   A logically connected collection of data.

**Database management system (DBMS)**   A set of programs that provide for the input, retrieval, formatting, modification, output, transfer, and maintenance of information in a database.

**Data dictionary**   A list of all the files, fields, attributes, formats, and access rights in a database.

**Data independence**   The difference between the way *logical records* are perceived by application programs (or end users) and the way *physical records* are actually stored in a database management system.

**Data structure**  A method of organizing data. Some common data structures are arrays, lists, files, and stacks.

**Data transfer rate**  The rate at which data is transferred from external storage to computer memory or from computer memory to external storage.

**DBMS**  See *Database management system*.

**Debugger**  A program that aids a programmer in locating and removing the errors in a program.

**Decimal tab**  A tab stop that is used to align numbers in a column according to their decimal point.

**Default**  The standard value or setting that a program uses if the user does not specify a value.

**Delimiter**  A symbol that indicates the end of a command, argument, or parameter. In the command TYPE LETTER.JIM, a space is the delimiter between the command keyword TYPE and its argument, LETTER.JIM.

**Demodulate**  To convert an analog signal into a digital signal.

**Desk accessories**  Memory-resident utility programs that provide convenient services such as an electronic calendar, phone dialer, calculator, or note pad.

**Device driver**  Software that tells an operating system or application program how an add-on device functions.

**Device independence**  The ability to add an input, output, or storage device to a computer system by modifying only the I/O manager of the operating system, without altering other software.

**Dialing directory**  A file containing telephone numbers and communication parameters. In conjunction with smart modems, a dialing directory can be used to dial a telephone number and log onto a remote computer almost automatically.

**Dialog box**  A temporary window on the screen that contains a set of choices whenever the executing program needs to collect information from the user.

**Digital**  A way of processing information by storing it as binary numbers. A digital circuit is either on or off; a digital signal is either present or absent. Contrast with *Analog*.

**Digitize**  To register a visual image or real object in a format that can be processed by the computer. Digitized data is read into the system with graphics input devices, such as a puck or stylus.

**Direct-access**  A file organization in which records can be read directly, without reading all intervening records. As a result, the time required to retrieve a record is independent of its location.

**Direct-connect modem**  A modem that plugs directly into a telephone jack to make a direct electrical connection with the telephone system. Contrast with *Acoustic coupler*.

**Directory**  A system file that lists the names and locations of all other files on a disk.

**Disk pack**  See *Removable disk*

**Distributed computing**  The simultaneous use of independent computers that are linked in a network to work on a common problem. Contrasts with *centralized computing*, in which all jobs are fed into a central mainframe.

**Dither**  To approximate the levels of gray in a photograph with a pattern of white and black spots.

**Documentation**  Any written information that describes hardware or software, including tutorial lessons, reference manuals, pocket reference guides, and so forth.

**Document chaining**  The merging and sequential printing of information from several files.

**Domain expert**  A human expert who contributes to the development of an expert system.

**Dot matrix printer**  An impact printer that forms characters by printing a series of dots. Dot matrix printers are very popular and inexpensive, but unlike letter-quality printers, they do not create characters with smooth, fully formed edges.

**Double-clicking**  Quickly pressing a mouse button twice in order to make a selection or give a command.

**Downloading** To send information from a large computer to a smaller one.

**Drop shadow** A shaded or black repetition of an area. Drop shadows are usually shifted slightly below and to the right of a piece of graphic art to give the impression of depth.

**Dumb terminal** A terminal that has no processing capabilities of its own.

**Editor** A program used to write, enter, and edit programs. The major difference between an editor and a word processor is that word processors tend to have features for fancy printing.

**Electronic dictionary** A program that compares words in a document with its own list of correctly spelled words and displays the words that do not match. It is also called a *spelling checker*.

**Encryption** A method of protecting data by scrambling it.

**Endnotes** Footnotes that appear as a group at the end of a document.

**Expansion slot** A connector inside a microcomputer where a optional circuit board can be plugged in.

**Expert system** A computer program that simulates the reasoning process used by a human expert in a particular subject.

**Expert system shell** The portion of an expert system that remains after all the rules and user interfaces have been removed.

**External storage** Long-term nonvolatile storage that is not part of the central processing unit. Tapes and disks are the most common forms of external storage. It is also called *secondary storage* or *auxiliary storage*.

**Fax** *Fac*imile transmission, a method of sending documents through phone lines.

**Fiber optics cable** A cable made from strands of glass that carries data in the form of pulses of light.

**Field** The part of a record reserved for a particular item or type of data.

**File** (1) A collection of related records. (2) A named collection of bytes on a disk.

**File conversion program** A utility program that translates a file from one format to another.

**File manager** (1) The part of an operating system that is responsible for manipulating files. (2) A file management system.

**File server** A device in a computer network that controls the hard disk and connects it to the network.

**Fixed disk** A hard disk in which the disk platter is mounted permanently inside an airtight, factory-sealed unit.

**Fixed-width spacing** A form of printing that pads out short lines by inserting full-size spaces between words.

**Floating-point number** A number represented in scientific form. A floating-point number is broken into two parts: the fractional part and the exponent.

**Floppy disk** A flexible, flat, circular piece of magnetic material for storing information. It is the most common medium for external storage for personal computers.

**Font** A set of characters in a particular typeface and size.

**Footer** A line or lines of text printed in the bottom margin of a page.

**Form** A template that indicates both the items of data and where they are to be placed. Forms assist in the process of collecting and storing data.

**Format** (1) The arrangement of data. (2) To prepare a blank disk so that it can be used to store information. Also known as *initializing*.

**Forward chaining** A inference procedure in which an expert system begins with a specific original statement and searches for routes that lead to one or more conclusions.

**Frequency-division multiplexer** A multiplexer that divides a high-speed signal into frequency bands. Contrast with *Time-division multiplexer*.

**Frequency modulation** A method of analog signaling that encodes data as changes in the frequency of the signal. Frequency modulation is used in FM radio and in some low-speed methods of data transmission over telephone lines.

**Freeware** See *Shareware*

**Front end computer** A small computer that is located between a host computer and the terminals and other devices needing access to the host computer. The front end computer handles communications and error-checking tasks related to routing messages in and out of the host computer.

**Full-duplex** A method of transmitting data that allows the simultaneous sending and receiving of data. Contrast with *Half-duplex.*

**Function keys** Extra keyboard keys that are used for specific purposes, which depend on the program being executed. The keytops of function keys are frequently labeled with [F1], [F2], and so forth.

**Galley proof** A draft copy of a document used for proofreading or revision.

**Gantt chart** A visual representation of a project schedule; the columns are time intervals and the rows correspond to activities.

**Gateway** A device that allows devices on one network to communicate with another network.

**Gigabyte** A unit of storage—roughly one billion characters.

**Global search and replace** A search-and-replace operation that is performed repeatedly throughout an entire document.

**Graphics editor** A program for editing pictures. Typical operations include drawing, moving, rotating, and enlarging items on the screen.

**Graphics primitive** An elemental graphics object, such as a line segment, rectangle, or arc.

**Greeking** To represent text with shaded bars or dummy type having no meaning. Greeking is a processing trick that WYSIWYG programs use to repaint the screen quickly.

**Ground station** A station for sending and receiving information via satellite.

**Hacker** (1) A person who works alone and is obsessed with learning about programming and exploring the capabilities of computer systems. (2) A person who gains access to a system without authorization.

**Half-duplex** A method of transmitting data that does not allow data to travel in both directions at once. Contrast with *Full-duplex.*

**Halftone** An image composed of a pattern of dots.

**Handshaking** The exchange of signals that control the flow of information between two electrical devices.

**Hard characters** Formatting characters that the user types into a word processing system. For example, a *hard carriage return* is typically inserted by pressing the [Enter] key, and some systems allow a *hard page break* to be inserted by pressing Ctrl-[Enter]. Contrast with *Soft characters.*

**Hard disk** An external storage device that stores data on a quickly spinning rigid disk with a magnetic surface. Hard disks offer a much greater storage capacity and faster access time than floppy disks.

**Hardware** The physical equipment in a computer system.

**Hashing function** A procedure for transforming a record key into the position of the record in a random-access file.

**Head crash** A collision between a disk drive's read/write head and the surface of the disk.

**Header** A line or lines printed in the top margin of a page.

**Hierarchical database** A database that establishes a top-to-bottom relationship among the records, much like the members of a family on a family tree. Each item has a unique parent or owner but can have many items below it. Contrast with *Network database* and *Relational database.*

**High-level language (HLL)** A programming language with English-like constructs or mathematical notation that is used to describe a procedure for solving a problem. High-level languages require little or no knowledge of the computer being used.

**Home** The upper-left position on the screen.

**Horizontal software** Programs designed to serve a wide range of users who must tailor the programs to their own needs. Examples include word processors and database management systems.

**Hypertext** A document retrieval network having full-text files and dynamic indexes for links among documents.

**Icon** A picture that represents an object such as a printer, trash can, or pad of paper.

**Impact printer** A printer that forms images by bringing paper and ribbon into physical contact.

**Indexed file** A collection of two or more closely related files, one of which contains the data; each of the other files contains an index to the data file.

**Inference engine** A part of an expert system that generates inferences from the system's IF/THEN rules and the facts supplied by the user.

**Information utility** A timeshared computer that provides a wide range of processing and information retrieval services to customers who access the utility through telecommunications.

**Initializing** See *Format*

**Input device** A peripheral that converts information into signals that the CPU can process.

**Instruction set** The set of elemental operations that the circuits of a central processing unit are capable of performing directly.

**Integrated circuit** An electronic circuit etched on a tiny silicon chip. Integrated circuits replaced transistors in third-generation computers.

**Integrated program** A collection of related programs combined in a package that provides a means of transferring data between the programs.

**Interface** The connection between two data processing elements. For example, the central processing unit is connected to peripheral devices through hardware interfaces, and the control of an accounting program might be governed by a full-screen menu interface.

**Interpreter** A program that translates and executes a program written in a high-level language. An interpreter translates one line of the source program, then executes that line, then translates the next line, and so on. In contrast, a *compiler* translates the entire source program before execution begins.

**Inverse video** Reversing the colors on a CRT screen, for example, by displaying white characters on a black background when the screen normally displays black characters on a white background.

**I/O device** A peripheral that accepts input or provides output.

**I/O port** A standard interface between the computer and external devices.

**ISO layers** A standard for describing and categorizing network components.

**Justify** To align text. Text that is flush with both the left and right margins is often said to be *justified*.

**Kerning** Reducing the space between specific letter pairs based on their shape. For example, the pair *To* can be placed more closely together than the pair *Th* because the arm of the *T* fits over the top of the *o*. Kerning is especially important with large type sizes.

**Key** A piece of information that is used to identify a record in a data file.

**Keyboard macro** A series of keystrokes that is associated with a single key on the keyboard. Whenever the macro's key is pressed, the keystrokes in the macro are played back just as if they had all been typed.

**Keyword** A word with a special meaning or function in a command.

**Kilobit** A measure of storage capacity equal to 1,024 bits.

**Kilobyte**  A measure of storage equal to 1,024 bytes (or characters). Kilobyte is often abbreviated *K* or *KB*.

**Knowledge base**  The collection of facts and rules within an expert system's subject area.

**Knowledge engineer**  A computer professional who helps develop an expert system.

**Knowledge engineering environment**  The part of an expert system development package that contains the tools needed to build the system.

**LAN**  See *Local area network.*

**Landscape**  A short and wide page orientation. Contrast with *Portrait.*

**Large-scale integrated circuit (LSI)**  Semiconductor chip technology has progressed rapidly; the number of components per chip has grown by 50 percent annually since 1960. In the 1970s, most chips had between 1,000 and 100,000 components, known as *large-scale integration.* Today's technology produces chips with 100,000 to 10,000,000 components, known as *very large-scale integration.* Further refinements should produce *ultralarge-scale integration* (10 million to 1 billion components) and *gigascale integration* (over 1 billion components).

**Laser printer**  A page printer in which a laser beam traces the image to be printed.

**Leading**  The spacing between typeset lines.

**License agreement**  A document that spells out the legal and authorized uses of a program.

**Light pen**  A pencil-shaped, light-sensitive device used to select a location on the screen or to read bar codes on paper.

**Line printer**  A printer that prints an entire line of characters almost simultaneously rather than one character at a time.

**Linker program**  The part of the compiling process that converts the object program into machine language and combines it with operating system programs.

**Liquid crystal display (LCD)**  A display used in many portable computers because it is small, flat, and requires little power.

**Local area network (LAN)**  A system of interconnected data processing equipment in a limited physical area.

**Logging off**  The process of telling the computer you are through using it.

**Logging on**  The process of identifying yourself to a multiuser computer system—by typing an account number and a password97for billing and security purposes.

**Logical operator**  A word, such as *and, not,* or *or,* that is used to determine the truth or falsity of a statement.

**Logical schema**  The description of the files, records, fields, and relationships among the data in a database. Contrast with *Physical schema.*

**Low-level language**  A programming language that translates one for one into machine instructions.

**Machine independence**  The ability to move software from one type of computer system to another without reprogramming.

**Machine language**  The binary code that can be executed directly by the control unit of a CPU. All programs written in high-level languages are translated into machine language before they are executed.

**Macro**  A single instruction or command that invokes a previously stored sequence of commands.

**Mainframe**  A large multiuser computer. The term refers to the racks and cabinet used to house the central processing unit of a large computer.

**Mass storage unit**  A peripheral that functions as a jukebox for tape cartridges or optical disks. A mass storage unit can automatically load any tape or disk in its library to provide quick access to vast quantities of information.

**Megabyte**  A measure of storage roughly equal to one million characters, although technically a megabyte is equal to a kilobyte squared, or $2^{20} =$

1,045,576 bytes. Megabyte is often abbreviated *M*, *MB*, or in slang as *meg*.

**Megahertz** One million cycles per second. Megahertz is used to measure a CPU's clock rate.

**Memory** A portion of the computer where programs and data are stored while being used by the computer system. Memory is also called *main memory, primary memory, RAM,* or *internal memory.*

**Menu bar** A one- or two-line list of commands displayed on the screen. *Keyword menu bars* list the entire word for each available command. *One-letter menu bars* list only the first letter of each command.

**MFLOP** Short for *millions of floating-point operations per second.* Used as a rough measure of a computer's processing speed.

**Microcomputer** Any small computer based on a microprocessor.

**Microprocessor** A programmable processing circuit built on a single silicon chip.

**Microsecond** One-millionth of a second.

**Microspacing** A form of printing that inserts tiny spaces between letters and words to give text an even, professional appearance. Each character is assigned the same fixed-width field regardless of its shape; only the space between characters is adjusted. See *Proportional spacing.*

**Millisecond** One-thousandth of a second.

**Minicomputer** A medium-sized computer that is usually capable of timesharing. The distinctions among micro, mini, and mainframe computers are blurring, and there are no clear-cut dividing lines between them.

**Mode** A program state in which only a restricted set of operations can be performed. For example, in the entry mode of spreadsheet processing it is not possible to do anything other than enter or edit the contents of the active cell.

**Modem** A communications device that converts (modulates) the digital pulses generated by computer equipment into analog signals that can be sent over voice-grade telephone lines. When receiving data, it demodulates the incoming telephone signal to recreate the original digital signal.

**Modulate** To convert a digital signal into an analog signal.

**Module** An identifiable part of a program. Writing programs in modules enables programmers to focus attention on one part of the programming problem at a time. Many large programs are left in modules so that only part of the program needs to be in memory at once. See *Program overlay.*

**Monitor** A CRT-based visual display unit. Basically, a monitor is a high-resolution television set without a speaker, channel selector, or radio-frequency receiver. In a *monochrome monitor* each pixel can glow in only one color; in a *color monitor* each pixel is three dots: red, green, and blue.

**Mouse** A hand-operated pointing device that senses movements as it is dragged across a flat surface and conveys this information to the computer. Most mice also have buttons that can be clicked to signal to the computer.

**Multiplexer** A communications device that timeshares the communications line by merging data from many users into the same line. See also *Frequency-division multiplexer* and *Time-division multiplexer.*

**Multitasking** The ability of a computer to execute two or more programs simultaneously. For example, a multitasking computer might allow the user to edit a document with a word processing program while it uses a communications program to receive a file from another computer.

**Nanosecond** One-billionth of a second.

**Network** A system of machines that are connected electrically and can communicate with each other.

**Network database** A database that establishes a many-to-many relationship among records. Contrast with *Hierarchical model* and *Relational model.*

**Nonimpact printer** A printer which does not need to strike the paper to print an image. Examples include ink-jet, laser, and thermal printers.

**Nonprocedural language** A very high-level programming language in which the programmer describes *what* the desired results are, but does not need to be concerned about the details of *how* the work is done.

**Normalization** A step-by-step procedure for arranging data in tables so that the data in different tables can be used conveniently in a relational database management system.

**Object program** The machine language version of a source program that is created when the source program is compiled or assembled.

**OCR** Stands for *optical character recognition*. Optical character recognition devices allow computers to read printed information (usually in a special type face) more reliably and faster than it can be typed.

**Off-line** Not connected directly to the computer.

**On-line** Any device that is under the direct control of the computer.

**Operating system** The master set of programs that manage the computer. Among other things, an operating system controls input and output to and from the keyboard, screen, disks, and other peripheral devices; loads and begins the execution of other programs; and manages the storage of data on disks.

**Option switch** A parameter that can be included in a command to override a default value. For example, an option switch might be added to the command to execute a program in order to tell the program to send its output to a file rather than to the printer.

**Orphan** The first line of a paragraph if it is printed by itself at the bottom of a column or page.

**Outline processor** A program with special features for creating and manipulating outlines.

**Overlapping window** A method of presenting windows on the screen that allows them to overlap one another, like objects stacked on top of a desk. Contrast with *Tiled window*.

**Packet-switching network** A telecommunications network that sends information through the network in the form of units of data called *packets*.

**Page composition program** A program that controls page makeup, assembling elements on a printed page.

**Page description language (PDL)** A programming language with specialized instructions for describing how to print a whole page.

**Page design** The process of specifying the boundaries of text on a page. Includes choosing margins, headings, footings, and page length. Also called *page layout*.

**Page printer** A printer that prints an entire page at a time.

**Paging** Scrolling up or down screen-by-screen instead of line-by-line.

**Paragraph reforming** In word processing, to rearrange the text in a paragraph so that it fits neatly between the margins.

**Parameter** A piece of information that regulates the behavior of a program. For example, the command that tells the operating system how to communicate with a printer might include a parameter specifying the speed at which data is to be transferred.

**Parity bit** An extra bit that is added to a computer word to detect errors.

**Parsing** The process of breaking down a sentence or command into its basic units.

**Patent** The legal protection granted by the Patent Office for exclusive use of an original idea or invention. Patents are rarely granted for programs.

**PC-DOS** Short for *Personal Computer-Disk Operating System*. IBM's trade name for its version of MS-DOS, an operating system developed and licensed by Microsoft for computers that use Intel microprocessors.

**Peripheral** An external device connected to the computer, such as input and output devices and external storage units.

**Personal computer**  A small, inexpensive, single-user computer based on a microprocessor.

**PERT chart**  A chart that shows the dependencies among activities in a project.

**Physical schema**  The description of how data is physically stored on a disk. Contrast with *Logical schema*.

**Pipelining**  A processing technique in which several instructions can be moving through parts of the CPU in an assembly-line fashion.

**Pitch**  A type measure of how many characters fit within an inch.

**Pixel**  An acronym for *picture element*. A pixel is the smallest display element on the screen. See *Monitor*.

**Plotter**  An output device that produces a hard copy of pictures, drawings, or other graphical information.

**Point**  A measure of type size equal to 1/72 inch.

**Port**  A communications connector on a computer suitable for attaching peripherals, such as a printer or modem.

**Portability**  The ease with which a program can be moved from one machine to another.

**Portrait**  A tall and narrow page orientation. Contrast with *Landscape*.

**PostScript**  The most widely use page description language.

**Presentation graphics**  An easy-to-understand, high-quality display of numerical information, such as a bar chart, pie chart, or line graph.

**Primary memory**  The memory capacity of the CPU.

**Printer server**  A device in a local area network that shares a printer among all users connected to the network.

**Print spooling**  A procedure that enables a computer to print a file and execute another program at the same time.

**Program**  A set of instructions that directs a computer for solving a problem.

**Program generator**  A translator program that converts nonprocedural information into a procedural program. Program generators often use a question-and-answer dialog to determine what processing is to be done and are limited in type of application that they can produce.

**Programming language**  A formalized notation that allows algorithms to be represented in a rigorous way.

**Program overlay**  A program module that is moved from external storage into computer memory when it is needed for processing.

**Prompt**  A signal from the computer that it expects the user to enter information.

**Proportional spacing**  A form of printing that allocates room for characters based on their width. With proportional spacing an *M* is printed in a wider field than an *i*. Typeset documents are normally proportionally spaced, and an increasing portion of computer printers are capable of proportional spacing.

**Protocol**  A set of rules that controls the interchange of data between independent devices.

**Prototype**  A trial system that simulates the behavior of the real system in order to let users try the system before it is constructed.

**Puck**  A very precise hand-held pointing device with cross hairs and a magnifying glass; it is used to enter the coordinates of graphical data.

**Pull-down menu**  A list of commands that appears from the top of the screen when a command needs to be given and then disappears when the selection has been made.

**Query-By-Example (QBE)**  A relational database query language that allows the user to ask questions about information in the database by providing an example showing the answer's characteristics.

**Query language**  A programming language for giving commands that search or modify a database.

**Race condition** A condition where two concurrent processing activities interact to cause a processing error.

**RAM** An acronym for *random-access memory*. RAM is memory built from silicon chips that is used to store programs and data temporarily while they are being processed.

**RAM disk** An area of memory that mimics the operations of a very high-speed disk drive in order to speed up file processing.

**Random access** The ability to read or write each piece of information in a storage device in approximately the same length of time, regardless of its location. Internal memory and disks are random-access devices.

**Range of cells** In spreadsheet processing, a rectangular group of worksheet cells treated as one unit.

**Raster scan** A method of creating a CRT image in which an electron beam moves horizontally across each line of the screen fifteen or more times each second, turning pixels on and off.

**Read/write head** The part of the tape or disk drive that reads or writes information on magnetic media.

**Real-time processing** A type of on-line processing that acts on information quickly enough to keep up with events occurring in the outside world.

**Record** A collection of related data items treated as a unit. Often a line in a data file is thought of as a record.

**Register** A special high-speed memory location within the CPU where information is held temporarily and is manipulated according to program instructions.

**Relational database** A database designed in accordance with a set of principles called the *relational model*. A relational database is made up of *relations*, which are tables whose columns and rows correspond to fields and records, respectively.

**Relative cell reference** In spreadsheet processing, a reference to a location in the worksheet that is interpreted with respect to the formula's current cell location. Contrast with *Absolute cell reference*.

**Removable disk** A hard disk cartridge similar to a floppy disk. Also called *disk pack*.

**Repeating key** A keyboard key that generates a constant stream of characters when depressed. The keys on most computer keyboards will repeat after being held down for about a half second.

**Report break** A position in a report where one or more fields change value according to some rule. For example, in a sales report a report break might occur after the list of sales made by each salesperson.

**Report generator** A program that extracts information from one or more files, manipulates it, and then prints it in a formatted form.

**Resident routines** The parts of the operating system that are loaded into memory when the computer is turned on and remain there during processing. The opposite of a *Transient utility*.

**Resolution** A measure of the accuracy or fineness of detail in a picture or display device.

**RF modulator** A device that converts a video signal from a computer into the radio frequency of a television channel. RF modulators are used to attach television sets to home computers to serve as visual display units.

**Right-justified** Text aligned flush with the right margin.

**Ring network** A network consisting of a cluster of computers connected together by a ring.

**ROM** An abbreviation for *read-only memory*. ROM is a form of internal memory that stores information permanently. Thus, the information in ROM can be read but cannot be changed.

**Routine** Any program or set of instructions that has general or frequent use.

**RS-232** A standard that specifies the voltages and signals used to transmit data across a serial interface cable. The RS-232 standard is used to connect a wide range of peripheral devices to the I/O ports on computers.

**Run-time module** The part of an expert system development package or compiler that must be present to run the completed system.

**Scale** To increase or decrease the size of a picture or graphics image.

**Scanner** A light-sensitive device that converts drawings, printed text, or other images into digital form.

**Schema** See *Logical schema, Physical schema.*

**Screen** A pattern of tiny dots used as shading in a graphic.

**Script** A stored record of keystrokes or commands that can be played back to carry out a series of actions.

**Scrolling** The horizontal or vertical movement of information on a screen in order to display additional information.

**Secondary storage** See *External storage*

**Sector** A pie-shaped wedge of one track of a disk. On most computers a sector is the smallest unit of information sent between the disk drive and CPU.

**Sequential file** A file whose records can be accessed only sequentially.

**Sequential storage** The storage of information so that items must be read or written one after the other; thus, jumping from one item to another is not permitted. Tape is the most common type of sequential storage. Contrast with *Direct-access.*

**Shareware** Software that permits licensees to share or give away copies so that others can evaluate the program before purchasing. Also called *freeware.*

**Shell** See *Command processor.*

**Site license** An agreement with a software vendor that allows an unlimited or a specified number of copies at a designated site.

**Soft characters** Characters that are temporarily added by a word processing system to help format a document. For example, *soft spaces* may be added

by a word processor between the words in a line so that the line ends flush with the right margin. *Soft carriage returns* are added by word processors at the end of lines within a paragraph as part of the word-wrap process. Contrast with *Hard characters.*

**Software** The generic term for any program or programs.

**Software piracy** The illegal copying of a computer program.

**Software portability** The ability to move programs from one type of computer to another without reprogramming.

**Sort key** The field or fields on which a file is sorted. There are both *primary* and *secondary* sort keys. For example, a sales report might be sorted on the customer-name field, which becomes the primary sort key; and all the sales transactions with the same customer name might be sorted by the sales-amount field, which then is the secondary sort key.

**Source program** A program written in a high-level language. Source programs must be compiled or interpreted before they can be executed by the computer.

**Spelling checker** See *Electronic dictionary.*

**Spreadsheet program** An application program that manipulates numbers in an electronic worksheet containing a grid of cells.

**SQL** Short for *Structured Query Language,* a data manipulation and query language used by many full-featured relational database management systems.

**Star network** A network consisting of a central processor surrounded by one or more satellite computers.

**Status line** In spreadsheet processing, a line in the control panel that displays the coordinates and contents of the active cell.

**Streaming tape drive** A cartridge tape system designed to back up and restore information on hard disks.

**Structured programming** A disciplined approach to the design and coding of programs that leads to easily understood and maintainable program code. Structured programs use a restricted set of control structures and fit within a top-down design.

**Style sheet** A word processing file that contains formatting instructions but not text.

**Subdirectory** A directory that is contained within another directory.

**Subroutine** A set of instructions that has been taken out and made into a subprogram which can be executed from any point in a main program.

**Subschema** A description of the part of the logical schema that is relevant to a particular user or program. The subschema may also contain a description of how data should be formatted for presentation to the user.

**Supervisor** The part of the operating system that controls the execution of other programs.

**Synchronous protocol** A communications protocol that sends data in packets that do not contain timing signals. Contrast with *Asynchronous protocol.*

**System analyst** An information-processing specialist who studies systems in an organization. A system analyst defines the problem to be solved, analyzes the problem, and recommends solutions.

**System disk** A disk containing operating system programs.

**System software** Any program that controls the computer system or helps programmers develop new programs. System software includes the operating system, programming languages, utilities, debuggers, editors, and so forth.

**Telecommunications** Any transmission of information over long distances using electromagnetic signals.

**Template** In spreadsheet processing, a formatted worksheet that contains all the labels and formulas for an application but does not contain the user's data. For example, an income tax template might contain labels describing how to fill in the template and formulas for calculating the income tax due, but it would not contain the amount of income and expenses.

**Terminal** Any device that allows a person to communicate with a computer. A terminal usually includes a keyboard and either a video screen or a printing mechanism.

**Terminal emulator** A communications program that makes a personal computer act like a terminal for the purpose of interacting with a remote computer.

**Tiled window** A screen display divided into non-overlapping windows. The opposite of *Overlapping window.*

**Time-division multiplexer** A multiplexer that combines many low-speed channels into one high-speed transmission by interweaving them in time slots. Contrast with *Frequency-division multiplexer.*

**Timesharing** The simultaneous sharing of a computer's resources by many users.

**Toggle switch** A switch with two settings. Each time the switch is thrown, it maintains its new setting until it is thrown back again.

**Top-down design** A system analysis methodology in which the overall structure of the solution is developed first; each succeeding phase of the analysis is more detailed. Top-down design is one of the chief concepts underlying structured programming.

**Touch screen** A display unit that can sense where a finger or other object touches its screen.

**Touch-tablet** A touch-sensitive flat electrical device that transmits to the computer the location of a stylus or pen touching its surface.

**Track** A concentric circle of a disk on which information is stored.

**Trade secret** The legal protection of an idea, formula, or other valuable business information because it provides the basis for a competitive advantage in the marketplace.

**Transient utility** A program that is loaded from a disk into memory only when it is needed. The opposite of *Resident routines.*

**Transistor** An electronic device for controlling the flow of electrons in an electronic circuit.

**Transparency** Word used to describe a program action that occurs automatically and usually without the user's being aware of it. For example, the details of how a file is stored on tracks and sectors are transparent to the user.

**T-switch** An electrical switch that allows the user to change the connections between computing equipment just by turning a knob on the switch. T-switches are useful for sharing infrequently used peripheral devices such as a letter-quality printer.

**Tuple** A row of a relation (file) in a relational database.

**Turnkey system** A complete system of hardware and software purchased together.

**Typeface** A style of type, such as Palatino, Times Roman, or Helvetica.

**Typeset** The act of producing a document on a typesetting machine. The characters in typeset documents are precisely positioned and clearly defined.

**UNDO command** A command that reverses the effect of the previous command and thus is useful for correcting mistakes.

**Upload** To transfer a file from a small computer to a larger computer.

**Upward compatible** A piece of hardware is upward compatible if it can do everything the pervious model could. System software is upward compatible if it supports all of the application programs available for the previous release.

**User interface** A protocol for communicating between the computer and the user.

**Utility program** A system program that performs an operating system function or helps in the development or maintenance of programs.

**Variable** An area of memory that has been given a name. The term has the same meaning in programming as in mathematics.

**Vector graphics** A method of generating pictures by drawing numerous straight-line segments (vectors) on the screen.

**Vertical software** Specialized application software that is designed for a particular discipline or activity. Examples include software that tracks the stock market and medical billing systems.

**Very high-level language** See *Nonprocedural language.*

**Very large-scale integration (VLSI)** See *Large-scale integrated circuit.*

**Virtual** Synonymous with *logical.*

**Virtual circuit** A temporary connection that links two network devices during data transfer.

**Virtual memory** A method of simulating a very large main memory by automatically moving parts of a running program from internal to external memory as the program runs. Thus, if a program needs 10 megabytes of memory to execute, it might be run on a virtual memory computer that has only 2 megabytes of main memory and 100 megabytes of disk storage. Also called *virtual storage.*

**Visual display unit** Any televisionlike display unit, such as a CRT or a liquid crystal display.

**Visual operating system** An operating system that relies on icons and menus for giving commands to the computer.

**Volatile** Term used to describe memory devices that lose information if electrical power to the device is interrupted. The internal memory of almost all general-purpose computers is volatile, but special-purpose computers such as portable computers sometimes use nonvolatile memory. Memory devices relying on magnetic media (tapes and disks) are nonvolatile.

**Widow** (1) The last line of a paragraph if it is printed by itself at the top of a column or page. (2)

The last line of a paragraph if it contains only one word.

**Wild card character** A character used to specify a whole category of items.

**Window** A region of a screen through which part of a file or some data in memory can be viewed. Some programs allow windows to be split into several parts, called *window panes*.

**Word** A fixed-length packet of bits manipulated as a unit by the computer.

**Word processor** A program to help create written documents.

**Word size** The number of bits in each memory location or *word* of memory. Also called *word length*. Early personal computers had a word length of 8 bits, minicomputers typically have 16- or 32-bit words, and mainframe computers have 32 or more bits per word.

**Word wrap** A common and convenient word processing feature that automatically begins a new line of text whenever the word being entered does not fit within the margins of the current line.

**Worksheet** The grid of rows and columns used by a spreadsheet program.

**Write-protect** To prevent magnetic media from being written on by a program. Sometimes this is done physically by removing a tab from a tape case or by covering a notch on a floppy disk jacket. At other times various software methods are used to protect individual files.

**WYSIWYG** Short for *"what you see is what you get,"* a reference to programs that attempt to make the screen look just the way their output will look on paper.

# Index

Program size, and programming language, 480
Project management software, 374–376
Prompt, 20, 81
Proportional spacing, 175
PROSPECTOR, 443
PROTECT command, 277
Protected cell, 277
Protocols
    communications, 394, 400–402
    CSMA, 418
    token-passing, 417
Pseudocode, 180
Public access message system, 402–404
Publications, *see* Magazines, computer; Newsletters,
    computer
Public domain, 515
Publisher's Paintbrush, 361
Publishing
    and page design, 220
    history of, 198–202
Puck, 58
PUFF, 457
Pull-down menu, 92–93, 99, 101–103

QMS, 207
Quadram, 207
Query-by-example (QBE), 339, 342–344, 346
Query commands, 334–335
Query language, in DBMS, 335, 347–349
Question-and-answer facility, 449
Quitting, 22
    in spreadsheet, 270
    and transfer, 153
QWERTY keyboard, 53

Race condition, 353, 355
Radio Shack division of Tandy Corporation, 505
Ragged right margins, 174–175
RAM chips, 360
Random-access device, disks as, 40, 41
Random-access memory (RAM), 8, 35. *See also* Primary
    (main) memory
Range of cells, 246
Raster scan monitor, 362–363
Rate of return, internal, 296–297
R:BASE System V, 312, 326, 428
RCA, 501
Readability, of programs, 473–475, 480
Read-only memory (ROM), 18, 35–36
Ready (program), 178
ReadySetGo, 217
Real time, animation in, 388
Real-time systems, 478–479
Recalculation, 286–288
    automatic vs. manual, 249, 251

column-oriented vs. row-oriented, 286–287
    and current time, 300
Record, 47, 187, 314
Reductionism, software, 468
Redundant storage, 331
Reflex (file management system), 315, 318
Registers, 12
Regression analysis, 369
Relation, in DBMS, 333
Relational database, 333–335
Relational DBMS programs, 336–346
    vs. flat-file, 345
Relative cell references, 260
Remote echoing, 400
Removable disk cartridges, 43
Rendezvous statement, 479
Repeating keys, 54
Replacing, 148–150
Report break, 321–322
Report generator, 321–323, 350, 350(fig.), 352
Resident operating system, 78–79
Resolution
    for computer vs. fax scanner, 410
    of digitized image, 210, 210(fig.)
    of laser printers, 204, 206
    of monitors vs. printers, 133
    of screen, 67, 203, 203(fig.)
Restructure ability, in DBMS, 352
Return (Enter) key, 56
Revelation, 326
RIM (Relational Information Management System), 312
Ring network, 417, 418(fig.)
RMDIR (remove directory) command, 85
Root directory, 46, 77–78
Routines, 473
Row-oriented recalculation, 287
RPG, 472(tab.), 477
RS-232 serial port, 14
Ruler line, 171–173
Run-time module, 455

Saving
    in spreadsheet, 270
    of text, 131, 153
    *see also* Backup
Scaling, 229
Scan codes, 75
ScanJet, 211
ScanMaster, 409
Scanners, 209–215
Scanning Gallery, 211
Scatter charts, 369, 370(fig.)
Schema, 327–328
Scott, Greg, 428
Scrap area, 148. *See also* Buffer; Clipboard
Screen (in word processing), 131–133
Screen (in page composition), 225